POETRY
for Students

Advisors

Jayne M. Burton is a teacher of English, a member of the Delta Kappa Gamma International Society for Key Women Educators, and currently a master's degree candidate in the Interdisciplinary Study of Curriculum and Instruction and English at Angelo State University.

Tom Shilts is the youth librarian at the Okemos branch of Capital Area District Library in Okemos, Michigan. He holds an MSLS degree from Clarion University of Pennsylvania and an MA in U.S. History from the University of North Dakota.

Amy Spade Silverman has taught at independent schools in California, Texas, Michigan, and New York. She holds a bachelor of arts degree from the University of Michigan and a master of fine arts degree from the University of Houston. She is a member of the National Council of Teachers of English and Teachers and Writers. She is an exam reader for Advanced Placement Literature and Composition. She is also a poet, published in *North American Review*, *Nimrod*, and *Michigan Quarterly Review*, among others.

POETRY
for Students

Presenting Analysis, Context, and Criticism on Commonly Studied Poetry

VOLUME 45

Sara Constantakis, Project Editor

Foreword by David J. Kelly

GALE
CENGAGE Learning·

Detroit • New York • San Francisco • New Haven, Conn • Waterville, Maine • London

Poetry for Students, Volume 45

Project Editor: Sara Constantakis

Rights Acquisition and Management: Margaret Chamberlain-Gaston

Composition: Evi Abou-El-Seoud

Manufacturing: Rhonda Dover

Imaging: John Watkins

Product Design: Pamela A. E. Galbreath, Jennifer Wahi

Digital Content Production: Allie Semperger

Product Manager: Meggin Condino

For product information and technology assistance, contact us at
Gale Customer Support, 1-800-877-4253.
For permission to use material from this text or product,
submit all requests online at **www.cengage.com/permissions.**
Further permissions questions can be emailed to
permissionrequest@cengage.com

While every effort has been made to ensure the reliability of the information presented in this publication, Gale, a part of Cengage Learning, does not guarantee the accuracy of the data contained herein. Gale accepts no payment for listing; and inclusion in the publication of any organization, agency, institution, publication, service, or individual does not imply endorsement of the editors or publisher. Errors brought to the attention of the publisher and verified to the satisfaction of the publisher will be corrected in future editions.

Gale
27500 Drake Rd.
Farmington Hills, MI, 48331-3535

ISBN-13: 978-1-4144-9506-4
ISBN-10: 1-4144-9506-4
ISSN 1094-7019

This title is also available as an e-book.
ISBN-13: 978-1-4144-9279-7
ISBN-10: 1-4144-9279-0
Contact your Gale, a part of Cengage Learning sales representative for ordering information.

Printed in Mexico
1 2 3 4 5 6 7 18 17 16 15 14 13

Table of Contents

Just a Few Lines on a Page

I have often thought that poets have the easiest job in the world. A poem, after all, is just a few lines on a page, usually not even extending margin to margin—how long would that take to write, about five minutes? Maybe ten at the most, if you wanted it to rhyme or have a repeating meter. Why, I could start in the morning and produce a book of poetry by dinnertime. But we all know that it isn't that easy. Anyone can come up with enough words, but the poet's job is about writing the *right* ones. The right words will change lives, making people see the world somewhat differently than they saw it just a few minutes earlier. The right words can make a reader who relies on the dictionary for meanings take a greater responsibility for his or her own personal understanding. A poem that is put on the page correctly can bear any amount of analysis, probing, defining, explaining, and interrogating, and something about it will still feel new the next time you read it.

It would be fine with me if I could talk about poetry without using the word "magical," because that word is overused these days to imply "a really good time," often with a certain sweetness about it, and a lot of poetry is neither of these. But if you stop and think about magic—whether it brings to mind sorcery, witchcraft, or bunnies pulled from top hats—it always seems to involve stretching reality to produce a result greater than the sum of its parts and pulling unexpected results out of thin air. This book provides ample cases where a few simple words conjure up whole worlds. We do not actually travel to different times and different cultures, but the poems get into our minds, they find what little we know about the places they are talking about, and then they make that little bit blossom into a bouquet of someone else's life. Poets make us think we are following simple, specific events, but then they leave ideas in our heads that cannot be found on the printed page. Abracadabra.

Sometimes when you finish a poem it doesn't feel as if it has left any supernatural effect on you, like it did not have any more to say beyond the actual words that it used. This happens to everybody, but most often to inexperienced readers: regardless of what is often said about young people's infinite capacity to be amazed, you have to understand what usually does happen, and what could have happened instead, if you are going to be moved by what someone has accomplished. In those cases in which you finish a poem with a "So what?" attitude, the information provided in *Poetry for Students* comes in handy. Readers can feel assured that the poems included here actually are potent magic, not just because a few (or a hundred or ten thousand) professors of literature say they are: they're significant because they can withstand close inspection and still amaze the very same people who have just finished taking them apart and seeing how they work. Turn them inside out, and they will still be able to come alive, again and again. *Poetry for Students* gives readers of any age good practice in feeling the ways poems relate to both the reality of the time and place the poet lived in and the reality of our emotions. Practice is just another word for being a student. The information given here helps you understand the way to read poetry; what to look for, what to expect.

With all of this in mind, I really don't think I would actually like to have a poet's job at all. There are too many skills involved, including precision, honesty, taste, courage, linguistics, passion, compassion, and the ability to keep all sorts of people entertained at once. And that is

just what they do with one hand, while the other hand pulls some sort of trick that most of us will never fully understand. I can't even pack all that I need for a weekend into one suitcase, so what would be my chances of stuffing so much life into a few lines? With all that *Poetry for Students* tells us about each poem, I am impressed that any poet can finish three or four poems a year. Read the inside stories of these poems, and you won't be able to approach any poem in the same way you did before.

David J. Kelly
College of Lake County

Introduction

Purpose of the Book

The purpose of *Poetry for Students* (*PfS*) is to provide readers with a guide to understanding, enjoying, and studying poems by giving them easy access to information about the work. Part of Gale's "For Students" Literature line, *PfS* is specifically designed to meet the curricular needs of high school and undergraduate college students and their teachers, as well as the interests of general readers and researchers considering specific poems. While each volume contains entries on "classic" poems frequently studied in classrooms, there are also entries containing hard-to-find information on contemporary poems, including works by multicultural, international, and women poets.

The information covered in each entry includes an introduction to the poem and the poem's author; the actual poem text (if possible); a poem summary, to help readers unravel and understand the meaning of the poem; analysis of important themes in the poem; and an explanation of important literary techniques and movements as they are demonstrated in the poem.

In addition to this material, which helps the readers analyze the poem itself, students are also provided with important information on the literary and historical background informing each work. This includes a historical context essay, a box comparing the time or place the poem was written to modern Western culture, a critical overview essay, and excerpts from critical essays on the poem. A unique feature of *PfS* is a specially commissioned critical essay on each poem, targeted toward the student reader.

To further help today's student in studying and enjoying each poem, information on audio recordings and other media adaptations is provided (if available), as well as reading suggestions for works of fiction and nonfiction on similar themes and topics. Classroom aids include ideas for research papers and lists of critical and reference sources that provide additional material on the poem.

Selection Criteria

The titles for each volume of *PfS* are selected by surveying numerous sources on notable literary works and analyzing course curricula for various schools, school districts, and states. Some of the sources surveyed include: high school and undergraduate literature anthologies and textbooks; lists of award-winners, and recommended titles, including the Young Adult Library Services Association (YALSA) list of best books for young adults.

Input solicited from our expert advisory board—consisting of educators and librarians—guides us to maintain a mix of "classic" and contemporary literary works, a mix of challenging and engaging works (including genre titles that are commonly studied) appropriate for different age levels, and a mix of international, multicultural and women authors. These advisors also consult on each volume's entry list, advising on which titles are most studied, most appropriate, and meet the broadest interests across secondary (grades 7–12) curricula and undergraduate literature studies.

How Each Entry Is Organized

Each entry, or chapter, in *PfS* focuses on one poem. Each entry heading lists the full name of the poem, the author's name, and the date of the poem's publication. The following elements are contained in each entry:

Introduction: a brief overview of the poem which provides information about its first appearance, its literary standing, any controversies surrounding the work, and major conflicts or themes within the work.

Author Biography: this section includes basic facts about the poet's life, and focuses on events and times in the author's life that inspired the poem in question.

Poem Text: when permission has been granted, the poem is reprinted, allowing for quick reference when reading the explication of the following section.

Poem Summary: a description of the major events in the poem. Summaries are broken down with subheads that indicate the lines being discussed.

Themes: a thorough overview of how the major topics, themes, and issues are addressed within the poem. Each theme discussed appears in a separate subhead.

Style: this section addresses important style elements of the poem, such as form, meter, and rhyme scheme; important literary devices used, such as imagery, foreshadowing, and symbolism; and, if applicable, genres to which the work might have belonged, such as Gothicism or Romanticism. Literary terms are explained within the entry, but can also be found in the Glossary.

Historical Context: this section outlines the social, political, and cultural climate in which the author lived and the poem was created. This section may include descriptions of related historical events, pertinent aspects of daily life in the culture, and the artistic and literary sensibilities of the time in which the work was written. If the poem is

a historical work, information regarding the time in which the poem is set is also included. Each section is broken down with helpful subheads.

Critical Overview: this section provides background on the critical reputation of the poem, including bannings or any other public controversies surrounding the work. For older works, this section includes a history of how the poem was first received and how perceptions of it may have changed over the years; for more recent poems, direct quotes from early reviews may also be included.

Criticism: an essay commissioned by *PfS* which specifically deals with the poem and is written specifically for the student audience, as well as excerpts from previously published criticism on the work (if available).

Sources: an alphabetical list of critical material quoted in the entry, with full bibliographical information.

Further Reading: an alphabetical list of other critical sources which may prove useful for the student. Includes full bibliographical information and a brief annotation.

Suggested Search Terms: a list of search terms and phrases to jumpstart students' further information seeking. Terms include not just titles and author names but also terms and topics related to the historical and literary context of the works.

In addition, each entry contains the following highlighted sections, set apart from the main text as sidebars:

Media Adaptations: if available, a list of audio recordings as well as any film or television adaptations of the poem, including source information.

Topics for Further Study: a list of potential study questions or research topics dealing with the poem. This section includes questions related to other disciplines the student may be studying, such as American history, world history, science, math, government, business, geography, economics, psychology, etc.

Compare & Contrast: an "at-a-glance" comparison of the cultural and historical differences between the author's time and culture and late twentieth century or early twenty-first century Western culture. This box includes pertinent parallels between the major scientific, political, and cultural movements of the time or place the poem was written, the time or place the poem was set (if a historical work), and modern Western culture. Works written after 1990 may not have this box.

What Do I Read Next?: a list of works that might give a reader points of entry into a classic work (e.g., YA or multicultural titles) and/ or complement the featured poem or serve as a contrast to it. This includes works by the same author and others, works from various genres, YA works, and works from various cultures and eras.

Other Features

PfS includes "Just a Few Lines on a Page," a foreword by David J. Kelly, an adjunct professor of English, College of Lake County, Illinois. This essay provides a straightforward, unpretentious explanation of why poetry should be marveled at and how *PfS* can help teachers show students how to enrich their own reading experiences.

A Cumulative Author/Title Index lists the authors and titles covered in each volume of the *PfS* series.

A Cumulative Nationality/Ethnicity Index breaks down the authors and titles covered in each volume of the *PfS* series by nationality and ethnicity.

A Subject/Theme Index, specific to each volume, provides easy reference for users who may be studying a particular subject or theme rather than a single work. Significant subjects from events to broad themes are included.

A Cumulative Index of First Lines (beginning in Vol. 10) provides easy reference for users who may be familiar with the first line of a poem but may not remember the actual title.

A Cumulative Index of Last Lines (beginning in Vol. 10) provides easy reference for users who may be familiar with the last line of a poem but may not remember the actual title.

Each entry may include illustrations, including photo of the author and other graphics related to the poem.

Citing Poetry for Students

When writing papers, students who quote directly from any volume of *PfS* may use the following general forms. These examples are based on MLA style; teachers may request that students adhere to a different style, so the following examples may be adapted as needed.

When citing text from *PfS* that is not attributed to a particular author (i.e., the Themes, Style, Historical Context sections, etc.), the following format should be used in the bibliography section:

> "Grace." *Poetry for Students*. Ed. Sara Constantakis. Vol. 44. Detroit: Gale, Cengage Learning, 2013. 66–86. Print.

When quoting the specially commissioned essay from *PfS* (usually the first piece under the "Criticism" subhead), the following format should be used:

> Andersen, Susan. Critical Essay on "Grace." *Poetry for Students*. Ed. Sara Constantakis. Vol. 44. Detroit: Gale, Cengage Learning, 2013. 77–80. Print.

When quoting a journal or newspaper essay that is reprinted in a volume of *PfS*, the following form may be used:

> Molesworth, Charles. "Proving Irony by Compassion: The Poetry of Robert Pinsky." *Hollins Critic* 21.5 (1984): 1–18. Rpt. in *Poetry for Students*. Ed. Sara Constantakis. Vol. 44. Detroit: Gale, Cengage Learning, 2013. 189–92. Print.

When quoting material reprinted from a book that appears in a volume of *PfS*, the following form may be used:

> Flora, Joseph M. "W. E. Henley, Poet." *William Ernest Henley*. New York: Twayne, 1970. 119–41. Rpt. in *Poetry for Students*. Ed. Sara Constantakis. Vol. 43. Detroit: Gale, 213. 150–52. Print.

We Welcome Your Suggestions

The editorial staff of *Poetry for Students* welcomes your comments and ideas. Readers who wish to suggest poems to appear in future volumes, or who have other suggestions, are cordially invited to contact the editor. You may contact the editor via E-mail at: **ForStudentsEditors@cengage.com.** Or write to the editor at:

Editor, *Poetry for Students*

Gale

27500 Drake Road

Farmington Hills, MI 48331-3535

Literary Chronology

1656: Lady Mary Chudleigh is born in August in Devon, England.

1688: Alexander Pope is born on May 21 in London, England.

1703: Lady Mary Chudleigh's "To the Ladies" is published.

1710: Lady Mary Chudleigh dies of rheumatism on December 15 in Exeter, England.

1711: Alexander Pope's "Sound and Sense" is published in *An Essay on Criticism*.

1744: Alexander Pope dies of complications from asthma and tuberculosis on May 30 in Twickenham, England.

1812: Robert Browning is born on May 7 in London, England.

1828: Henrik Ibsen is born on March 20 in Skien, Norway.

1845: Robert Browning's "Meeting at Night" is published in *Dramatic Romances and Lyrics*.

1862: Henrik Ibsen's *Kjærlighedens Komedie* is published. It is translated into English by C. H. Herford as *Love's Comedy* in 1900.

1883: Henrik Ibsen's "In the Orchard," translated by Edmund W. Gosse, is published in *English Verse: Translations*.

1887: Rupert Chawner Brooke is born on August 3 in Rugby, England.

1889: Robert Browning dies of unspecified causes on December 12 in Venice, Italy.

1892: Edna St. Vincent Millay is born on February 22 in Rockland, Maine.

1902: Langston Hughes is born on February 1 in Joplin, Missouri.

1905: Phyllis McGinley is born on March 21 in Ontario, Oregon.

1906: Henrik Ibsen dies of natural causes on May 23 in Christiania (now Oslo), Norway.

1913: May Swenson is born on May 28 in Logan, Utah.

1913: Robert Hayden is born on August 4 in Detroit, Michigan.

1914: Rupert Chawner Brooke's "Peace" is published.

1915: Rupert Chawner Brooke dies of sepsis on April 23 in the Aegean Sea near the island of Skyros.

1923: Edna St. Vincent Millay's "What Lips My Lips Have Kissed" is published.

1923: Edna St.Vincent Millay is awarded the Pulitzer Prize in Poetry for *The Ballad of the Harp-Weaver*.

1935: Mary Oliver is born on September 10 in Maple Heights, Ohio.

1938: Langston Hughes's "Let America Be America Again" is published.

1939: Margaret Atwood is born on November 18 in Ottawa, Canada.

1944: Eavan Boland is born on September 24 in Dublin, Ireland.

1945: Kay Ryan is born on September 21 in San Jose, California.

1950: Edna St. Vincent Millay dies on October 19 from a heart attack in Steepletop, New York.

1953: Phyllis McGinley's "Midcentury Love Letter" is first published in the *New Yorker* on February 14.

1954: May Swenson's "Question" is published.

1957: Li-Young Lee is born on August 19 in Jakarta, Indonesia.

1961: Phyllis McGinley is awarded the Pulitzer Prize for Poetry for *Times Three*.

1962: Robert Hayden's "The Whipping" is published.

1966: Sherman Alexie is born on October 7 in Spokane, Washington.

1967: Langston Hughes dies of complications after abdominal surgery on May 22 in New York City, New York.

1978: Phyllis McGinley dies of unspecified causes on February 22 in New York City, New York.

1980: Robert Hayden dies on February 25 in Ann Arbor, Michigan.

1984: Mary Oliver is awarded the Pulitzer Prize for Poetry for *American Primitive*.

1989: May Swenson dies of a heart attack brought on by high blood pressure and severe asthma on December 4 in Bethany Beach, Delaware.

1990: Li-Young Lee's "A Story" is published in *The City in Which I Love You.*

1992: Mary Oliver's "The Esquimos Have No Word For 'War'" is published in *New and Selected Poems.*

1995: Margaret Atwood's "Half-hanged Mary" is published.

1996: Sherman Alexie's "Defending Walt Whitman" is published.

1997: Kay Ryan's "Blandeur" is published in the *New Yorker.*

2000: Margaret Atwood is awarded the Booker Prize for *The Blind Assassin.*

2001: Eavan Boland's "Against Love Poetry" is published in *Against Love Poetry: Poems.*

2011: Kay Ryan is awarded the Pulitzer Prize for Poetry for *The Best of It: New and Selected Poems.*

Acknowledgements

The editors wish to thank the copyright holders of the excerpted criticism included in this volume and the permissions managers of many book and magazine publishing companies for assisting us in securing reproduction rights. We are also grateful to the staffs of the Detroit Public Library, the Library of Congress, the University of Detroit Mercy Library, Wayne State University Purdy/Kresge Library Complex, and the University of Michigan Libraries for making their resources available to us. Following is a list of the copyright holders who have granted us permission to reproduce material in this volume of *PfS*. Every effort has been made to trace copyright, but if omissions have been made, please let us know.

COPYRIGHTED EXCERPTS IN *PfS*, VOLUME 45, WERE REPRODUCED FROM THE FOLLOWING PERIODICALS:

America, vol. 195, no. 10, October 9, 2006. Copyright © 2006 by America Press, Inc. All rights reserved. Reproduced by permission.— *American Scholar*, vol. 77, no. 3, Summer 2008. Copyright © 2008 by *The American Scholar*. All rights reserved. Reproduced by permission.— *Antioch Review*, vol. 54, no. 2, Spring 1996. Copyright © *Antioch Review*. All rights reserved. Reproduced by permission.— *Booklist*, vol. 92, no. 1, September 1, 1995. Copyright © 1995 by American Library Association. All rights reserved. Reproduced by permission.— *Hollins Critic*, vol. 16, no. 3, July 1979. Copyright © 1979 by *The Hollins Critic*. All rights reserved. Reproduced by permission.— *Journal of Literary Studies*, vol. 27, no. 2, July 2011. Copyright © 2011 by Taylor & Francis. All rights reserved. Reproduced by permission.—Brooke, Rupert, "Peace," *Poetry*, vol. 6, no. 1, 1915.— *Prairie Schooner*, vol. 80, no. 1, Spring 2006. Copyright © 2006 by *Prairie Schooner*. All rights reserved. Reproduced by permission.— *Publishers Weekly*, vol. 242, no. 35, August 28, 1995; vol. 243, no. 38, September 16, 1996; vol. 247, no. 30, July 24, 2000. Copyright © 1995, 1996, 2000 PYxyz, LLC. All rights reserved. Reproduced by permission.— *Queen's Quarterly*, vol. 103, no. 3, Fall 1996. Copyright © 1996 by *The Porcupine's Quill*. All rights reserved. Reproduced by permission.— *Rogoff, Jay*, "New Bottles," *Southern Review*, Winter 2011, vol. 47, no. 1. Copyright © 2011 by Jay Rogoff. All rights reserved. Reproduced by permission.— *World Literature Today*, vol. 80, no. 6, November-December 2006. Copyright © 2006 by *World Literature Today*. All rights reserved. Reproduced by permission.

COPYRIGHTED EXCERPTS IN *PfS*, VOLUME 45, WERE REPRODUCED FROM THE FOLLOWING BOOKS:

Alexie, Sherman. "Defending Walt Whitman," from *The Summer of Black Widows*, Hanging Loose Press. Copyright © Hanging

Loose Press. All rights reserved. Reproduced by permission.—Barchas, Janine. From *Eighteenth-Century Genre and Culture: Serious Reflections on Occasional Forms*, edited by Dennis Todd and Cynthia Wall, University of Delaware Press, 2001. Copyright © 2001 by The Associated University Presses. All rights reserved. Reproduced by permission.—Boland, Eavan. From *My Self, My Muse: Irish Women Poets Reflect on Life and Art*, edited by Patricia Boyle, Syracuse University Press, 2001. Copyright © 2001 by Syracuse University Press. All rights reserved. Reproduced by permission.—Brittin, Norman A. From *Edna St. Vincent Millay*, G.K. Hall, 1982. Copyright © 1983 Cengage Learning.—Browning, Robert. "Meeting at Night," from *The Poetical Works of Robert Browning: Bells and Pomegranates*, vol. 4, edited by Ian Jack, Rowena Fowler, and Margaret Smith, Clarendon Press, 1991.—Chudleigh, Mary. "To the Ladies," from *The Poems and Prose of Mary, Lady Chudleigh*, edited by Margaret J. M. Ezell, Oxford University Press, 1993.—Clark, Suzanne. From *Millay at 100: A Critical Reappraisal*, edited by Diane P. Freedman, Southern Illinois University Press, 1995. Copyright © 1995 by Southern Illinois University Press. All rights reserved. Reproduced by permission.—Foster, John Wilson. From *Critical Essays on Margaret Atwood*, edited by Judith McCombs, 1988. Copyright © 1988 by John Wilson Foster. All rights reserved. Reproduced by permission.—Fritzer, Penelope and Bartholomew Bland. From *Merry Wives and Others: A History of Domestic Humor Writing*, McFarland, 2002. Copyright © 2002 Penelope Fritzer and Bartholomew Bland by permission of McFarland & Company, Inc., Box 611, Jefferson NC 28640. www.mcfarlandpub.com.—Hatcher, John. From *From the Auroral Darkness: The Life and Poetry of Robert Hayden*, George Ronald, 1984. Copyright © 1984 by John Hatcher. All rights reserved. Reproduced by permission.—Hönnighausen, Lothar. From *Margaret Atwood: Works and Impact*, edited by Reingard M. Nischik, Boydell & Boydell, 2000. Copyright © 2000 by Boydell & Brewer. All rights reserved. Reproduced by permission.—Ibsen, Henrik. "In the Orchard," translated by Edmund William Gosse, from *English Verse*, edited by W. J. Linton and R. H. Stoddard, Charles Scribner's Sons, 1883.—Lee, Li-Young. "A Story," from *The City In Which I*

Love You, BOA Editions, 1990. Copyright © 1990 by Li-Young Lee. Reprinted with the permission of The Permissions Company, Inc. on behalf of BOA Editions Ltd., www.boaeditions.org.—Messenger, Ann. From *Pastoral Tradition and the Female Talent: Studies in Augustan Poetry*, AMS Press, 2001. Copyright © 2001 by AMS Press. All rights reserved. Reproduced by permission.—Meyer, Michael. From *Ibsen: A Biography*, Sutton Publishing Limited, 2004. Copyright © Michael Meyer. Reprinted with permission of David Higham Associates Limited. All rights reserved.—Miller, R. Baxter. From *The Art and Imagination of Langston Hughes*, University Press of Kentucky, 1989. Copyright © 1989 by the University of Kentucky. All rights reserved. Reproduced by permission.—O'Neill, Patricia. From *Robert Browning and Twentieth-Century Criticism*, Camden House, 1995. Copyright © 1995 by Boydell & Brewer. All rights reserved. Reproduced by permission.—Ostriker, Alicia. From *Shakespeare's Sisters: Feminist Essays on Women Poets*, edited by Sandra M. Gilbert and Susan Gubar, Indiana University Press, 1979. Copyright © 1979 by Indiana University Press. All rights reserved. Reproduced by permission.—Ostriker, Alicia. From *Body My House: May Swenson's Work and Life*, edited by Paul Crumbley and Patricia M. Gantt, Utah State University Press, 2006. Copyright © 2006 by the Utah State University Press. All rights reserved. Reproduced by permission.—Patey, Douglas Lane. From *Critical Essays on Alexander Pope*, G.K. Hall, 1993. Copyright © 1993 Cengage Learning.—Peterson, Nancy J. From *Sherman Alexie: A Collection of Critical Essays*, edited by Jeff Berglund and Jan Roush, University of Utah Press, 2010. Copyright © 2010 by the University of Utah Press. All rights reserved. Reproduced by permission.—Poper, Alexander. "Sound and Sense," from *The Poetical Works of Alexander Pope*, edited by William Pickering, 2nd edition, 1831.—Purdy, John. From *Conversations with Sherman Alexie*, edited by Nancy J. Peterson, University Press of Mississippi, 2009. Copyright © 2009 by John Purdy. All rights reserved. Reproduced by permission.—Quinn, Alice. From *Eavan Boland: A Critical Companion*, edited by Jody Allen Randolph, W.W. Norton, 2007. Copyright © Conde Nast. All rights reserved. Reproduced by permission.—Roberts, Adam. From *Robert Browning Revisited*, Twayne, 1996. Copyright © 1997

Cengage Learning.—Stanbrough, Jane. From *Shakespeare's Sisters: Feminist Essays on Women Poets*, edited by Sandra M. Gilbert and Susan Gubar, Indiana University Press, 1979. Copyright © 1979, Indiana University Press. Reprinted with permission of Indiana University Press.—Stout, Janis P. From *Coming out of War: Poetry, Grieving, and the Culture of the World Wars*, University of Alabama Press, 2005. Copyright © 2005 The University of Alabama Press. All rights reserved. Reproduced by permission.—St. Vincent Millay, Edna. "What Lips My Lips Have Kissed, and Where, and Why," from *Collected Poems: Edna St. Vincent Millay*, Harper and Brothers, 1956. Copyright © 1923, 1951 by Edna St. Vincent Millay and Norma Millay Ellis. Reprinted with permission of the Permissions Company, Inc., on behalf of Holly Peppe, Literary Executor, The Millay Society, www.millay.org.—Thomas, Claudia N. From *Alexander Pope and His Eighteenth-Century Women Readers*, Southern Illinois University Press, 1994. Copyright © 1994 by Southern Illinois University Press. All rights reserved. Reproduced by permission.—Tracy, Stephen T. From *Langston Hughes & the Blues*, University of Illinois Press, 1988. Copyright © 1988, 2001 by the Board of Trustees of the University of Illinois. Used with permission of the University of Illinois Press.—Villar-Argáiz, Pilar. From *The Poetry of Eavan Boland: A Postcolonial Reading*, Academica Press, 2008. Copyright © 2008 by Academica Press. All rights reserved. Reproduced by permission.—Wicksteed, Philip H. From *Henrik Ibsen: A Critical Anthology*, edited by James McFarlane, Penguin Books, 1970.—Williams, Pontheolla T. From *Robert Hayden: A Critical Analysis of His Poetry*, University of Illinois Press, 1987. Copyright © 1987 by the Board of Trustees of the University of Illinois. Used with permission of the University of Illinois Press.—Williamson, Marilyn L. From *Raising Their Voices: British Women Writers*, Wayne State University Press, 1990. Copyright © 1990 Wayne State University Press, with the permission of Wayne State University Press.—Wright, Richard. From *Critical Essays on Langston Hughes*, edited by Edward J. Mullen, G.K. Hall, 1986. Copyright © 1940 by *The New Republic*. All rights reserved. Reproduced by permission.—Yao, Steven G. From *Foreign Accents: Chinese American Verse from Exclusion to Postethnicity*, Oxford University Press, 2010. Copyright © 2010 by Oxford University Press. All rights reserved. Reproduced by permission.—Zhou, Xiaojing. From *The Ethics and Poetics of Alterity in Asian American Poetry*, University of Iowa Press, 2006. Copyright © 2006 by the University Press of Iowa. All rights reserved. Reproduced by permission.

Contributors

Susan K. Andersen: Andersen holds a PhD in literature. Entry on "Defending Walt Whitman." Original essay on "Defending Walt Whitman."

Bryan Aubrey: Aubrey holds a PhD in English. Entries on "Half-hanged Mary" and "The Whipping." Original essays on "Half-hanged Mary" and "The Whipping."

Andrea Betts: Betts is a freelance writer specializing in literature. Entry on "Blandeur." Original essay on "Blandeur."

Kristy Blackmon: Blackmon is a writer and critic from Dallas, Texas. Entry on "The Esquimos Have No Word for 'War.'" Original essay on "The Esquimos Have No Word for 'War.'"

Rita Brown: Brown is an English professor. Entry on "To the Ladies." Original essay on "To the Ladies."

Catherine Dominic: Dominic is a novelist and a freelance writer and editor. Entries on "Against Love Poetry" and "Sound and Sense." Original essays on "Against Love Poetry" and "Sound and Sense."

Kristen Sarlin Greenberg: Greenberg is a freelance writer specializing in literature. Entry on "Let America Be America Again." Original essay on "Let America be America Again."

Michael Allen Holmes: Holmes is a writer with existential interests. Entries on "In the Orchard" and "A Story." Original essays on "In the Orchard" and "A Story."

Sheri Karmiol: Karmiol teaches literature and drama at the University of New Mexico, where she is a term professor in the honors college. Entry on "What Lips My Lips Have Kissed." Original essay on "What Lips My Lips Have Kissed."

Dave Kelly: Kelly is an instructor of literature and creative writing. Entry on "Question." Original essay on "Question."

Michael J. O'Neal: O'Neal holds a PhD in English. Entries on "Meeting at Night" and "Midcentury Love Letter." Original essays on "Meeting at Night" and "Midcentury Love Letter."

Bradley A. Skeen: Skeen is a classicist. Entry on "Peace." Original essay on "Peace."

Against Love Poetry

EAVAN BOLAND

2001

Boland is an Irish poet, often described as a feminist, whose work is characterized by the exploration of the role of women in Irish culture and history. Her poem "Against Love Poetry" is part of a poetry collection by the same name. The first section of this volume of poetry deals with the theme of marriage. "Against Love Poetry" focuses largely on this theme as well. A prose poem, "Against Love Poetry" is written in paragraph form rather than as lines of verse. It does not include formal structures such as rhyme or meter. Yet through the use of such elements as repetition and imagery, Boland constructs a poem marked by the natural rhythm of the spoken word. Speaking out against the forms and themes of traditional love poetry, Boland focuses on the contradictions she observes in the notion of love, discussing the way freedom does not exist within the confines of marriage. The poem has a defiant tone, and in its very structure as a prose poem rather than a verse poem, it defies the conventions of traditional poetry.

"Against Love Poetry" first appeared in *Against Love Poetry: Poems* in 2001. The collection was published as *Code* that same year in the United Kingdom.

AUTHOR BIOGRAPHY

Born in Dublin, Ireland, on September 24, 1944, Boland is the youngest of the five children of

The poem's narrator mentions her wedding thirty years before. *(© Poprugin Aleksey | Shutterstock.com)*

Frederick and Frances Boland. Boland's father was a diplomat, serving as the Irish ambassador in London in the 1950s and to the United Nations during the late 1950s and early 1960s. Her mother, a painter, has works displayed in the Dublin Municipal Gallery. Boland grew up in London and New York but returned to Ireland when she entered secondary school, Holy Child Convent School, in Killiney, where she lived and studied from 1959 through 1962. She then attended Trinity College in Dublin from 1962 through 1966. She published her first collection of poetry, *23 Poems*, as a student in 1962. Boland worked as a lecturer following graduation from Trinity, first at her alma mater and later at the School of Irish Studies in Dublin. She married novelist Kevin Casey in 1969 and had two children. Boland published her first full-length poetry collection, *New Territory*, in 1967. She continued to write and publish poetry collections, garnering increasing respect for her work. Her 1994 collection, *In a Time of Violence*, for example, won a Lannan Award and was short-listed for the T. S. Eliot Prize, a highly coveted poetry award. In 2001, she published the collection known as *Against Love Poetry* in the United States and as *Code* in the United Kingdom. This collection contains the prose poem "Against Love Poetry." Recent collections include the 2007 *Domestic Violence* and the 2008 *New Collected Poems*. Boland has served as writer-in-residence at Trinity College and University College Dublin, and

has taught at Bowdoin College, in Brunswick, Maine, at the University of Utah, and at Washington University in St. Louis. She currently teaches at Stanford University and, in 2012, won the PEN award for creative nonfiction for her essay collection *A Journey with Two Maps: Becoming a Woman Poet*.

POEM SUMMARY

The text used for this summary from *Against Love Poetry: Poems*, W. W. Norton, 2001, p. 5.

As a prose poem, "Against Love Poetry" is not divided into lines of verse. It is composed simply as a paragraph. The poet opens the poem using the first-person plural pronoun "we," and she directs the poem to an unnamed "you," who is identified as the husband she married thirty years ago. The poet goes on to note the depth and duration of her love, but also comments that she has also loved other things, including the notion of freedom, specifically the freedom of women. Boland echoes the question that she assumes readers ask at this point when she rhetorically asks why she has linked the words "marriage" and "freedom" in this way. She answers that it is because she is a woman, and from her perspective as a woman, marriage is the antithesis of freedom.

Boland then insists that she has written each word "here," which one can take to mean the poem itself or possibly the collection that shares the poem's name, as an act of protest against the idea of love poetry. What is typically considered love poetry, she claims, cannot possibly address the idea she has just introduced, that freedom is inconsistent with the institution of marriage. Boland states that, since love poetry cannot adequately treat this concept, she offers instead a story from long ago. Boland does discuss here, or elsewhere in the poem where love poetry is specifically mentioned, what she understands the parameters of love poetry to be. The reader must infer, in this poem that declares itself in opposition to love poetry, what is meant by that term. Presumably, since Boland has already declared her love for the man she married, and also declared as fact the notion that marriage precludes freedom, the love poetry she is opposed to is poetry that views love and marriage in more harmonious terms. Yet Boland leaves much unsaid and, in doing so, provokes the reader to consider his or her own views on the compatibility of such concepts as love, marriage, and freedom.

The poet then goes on to relate the tale of a mighty king who, having lost a war, is marched through the streets of the enemy's city as a prisoner. The king is taunted by his enemies. When his wife and children are brought before him, he displays no emotion whatsoever. He has the same neutral, emotionless response when his courtiers are brought before him. When his enemies bring his former servant, however, he is reduced to tears.

After relating this tale, Boland returns to discussing her perspectives on marriage, freedom, and womanhood, stating that she did not discover her sense of self as a woman through adhering to the customs traditionally associated with marriage. She does assert, however, that she became aware of her own humanity through the customs of marriage. Boland then remarks that she is writing this poem in an effort to demonstrate the persistent contradictions that, on a daily basis, inform the notion of marital love. She closes the poem by repeating the words of the title, as if to emphasize that, in this poem, though she writes about love and marriage, she does so in a way that is markedly different from the conventions of love poetry.

THEMES

Marriage

Boland treats the theme of marriage in "Against Love Poetry" in a completely unvarnished manner. The poem opens with a declaration of love, with the poet asserting that, from the moment she and her husband were married thirty years ago to the present time, she has loved him intensely. Yet she goes on to assert the incompatibility of the notions of marriage and freedom. In relating a story about a captured king, she emphasizes that the king possesses a deep connection with his servant but not with his wife and children. Boland uses the story as a parable to discusses marriage and, in this manner uses the king to represent the figure of the husband. As the king's emotions are tied to his relationship with his servant rather than to that with his wife, Boland suggests that, in a marriage, the wife's service to her family is regarded as more important than an emotional

connection established between a husband and his wife. Boland further underscores the relationship between the ideas of service and marriage when she states that her understanding of her own womanhood is disconnected from her role as wife and servant in her family. She does concede, however, that her marriage and her place within it helped her to develop a sense of humanity. She uses the term "humanity" in a vague fashion here and is possibly referring to an understanding of human nature, or to her sense of connection to humanity, or to the world at large. In these ways, Boland explores the way marriage has both diminished her sense of freedom and enlarged her understanding of herself and/or her world. She goes on to characterize love—the everyday love in one's marriage—as an idea fraught with contradiction.

Marital love, then, is, in reality, more the subject of the poem than is the idea of love poetry that Boland speaks out against in the poem's title and at various points within the poem. She seeks to emphasize the conflicts and struggles that characterize a marriage; through the story of the captured king, Boland demonstrates the way marriage contributes to its participants' feeling constrained as well as disconnected from one another. The fact that she nevertheless returns to the love she feels for the man she married, when combined with her reflection on her understanding of her own humanity, suggests that, along with the tension and conflict, she has enjoyed positive experiences within the confining framework of marriage.

Female Identity

Boland returns repeatedly in "Against Love Poetry" to the notion of her identity as a woman. She uses the terms "woman" or "womanhood" three times in this short poem. Throughout the poem, womanhood is linked to the concepts of freedom, marriage, love, and humanity. Yet, repeatedly, she makes negative assertions rather than providing elaborations. Freedom is not a part of marriage, she states, and her sense of womanhood was not discovered within the confines of marriage. Yet Boland carefully intertwines ideas throughout the poem in such a way that the reader must carefully study the assertions and denials she makes. Boland connects the notion of "freedom" to that of "women" when she identifies the freedom of women as one of the ideas she has loved. In rhetorically questioning why she would follow

TOPICS FOR FURTHER STUDY

- "Against Love Poetry" is a prose poem. While it does not contain such formal elements as a metrical pattern or rhyme scheme, it utilizes repetition, metaphor, and careful word choice to create a poetic sensibility. Choose a topic that is meaningful to you and write your own prose poem. Use elements such as sound, word, or phrase repetition, vivid language and imagery, symbols, and metaphors to infuse your prose with poetry. Share your poem with the class by and create a multimedia presentation to accompany your poem.

- *I Wouldn't Thank You for a Valentine: Poems for Young Feminists* is a collection of poetry that is targeted at young-adult readers and imbued with feminist themes. The 1997 collection is edited by Carol Ann Duffy. With a small group, peruse the collection and select several of the poems to analyze. In what ways do the poems you have selected treat themes related to feminism, women's rights, or gender roles? How do the poems use their form, structure, language, and imagery to convey their message? What about the poems impacted your decision to study them in particular? In what ways do you relate to the subject matter in the poems? Create an online blog to use as a forum to discuss the poems, along with these and other issues.

- José Martí was a nineteenth-century Cuban poet who lived for a time in exile in the United States. Like Boland, Martí wrote about cultural identity, love, and family, among other topics. His *Versos Sencillos:*

Simple Verses, was published in 1997 as a dual-language work, featuring the original Spanish with English translations by Manuel A. Tellechea. Although Martí did not write specifically for young adults, the stylistically and thematically appropriate collection was published by Pinata Books for Young Adults. Read Martí's poetry and consider the types of themes he addresses. How does his simple four-line, rhymed stanza format complement his themes? Are his language and style complex and ornate, or simple and straightforward? Select one poem and provide a detailed analysis of its form, structure, language, imagery, rhyme pattern, and theme; alternatively, read the small collection as a whole and write a book review of the volume in which you offer an overview of the poet's themes and style.

- Prose poetry, though not a commonly used format today, has existed for over 150 years, according to Karen Volkman's "Mutable Boundaries: On Prose Poetry," on Poets.org (http://www.poets.org/viewmedia.php/prmMID/5910). Research the history of the prose poem, using Volkman's essay as a starting point, and write a research paper in which you trace it from its origins through its use in modern times. Be sure to give examples of prose poems from a variety of cultures, and discuss the way the prose poem has been employed and reinvented by poets over time. Cite all of your sources, both print and online.

---

a statement of marital love with one regarding her love of women's freedom, Boland suggests that these two things are not necessarily compatible, and, in the next two sentences, she affirms this idea emphatically. The poet answers her own question, asserting that she is a woman

and that marriage is an institution in which freedom does not exist, thereby decoupling the idea of marriage from the notions of womanhood and freedom. The poet expresses that contradictions and conflicts are inherent in the way she understands her identity as a woman, a woman

The poem suggests that traditional love poetry contains contradictions. *(© 4tolife | Shutterstock.com)*

who has experienced love and marriage. Boland characterizes her love for the man she married as significant, but falls short of insisting that this love informs her sense of self as a woman. Emphasizing that marital customs, or her adherence to them, did not aid her in her development of her female identity, Boland does not describe where, in fact, she *did* come to understand her identity as a woman. Just as she does not elaborate on what constitutes love poetry, she refuses to share with the reader those experiences that shaped her sense of self as a woman. However, when she looks back over the years of her marriage, she sees her own sense of humanity reflected. In this statement, it appears the poet is emphasizing that, through her marriage, with all its imbalances and imperfections, she has found a connection not to her female identity but to her human identity. Her identity as a woman, and the story of its discovery and development, Boland keeps hidden, a secret that exists outside of the walls of marriage as she has described them. What she refers to as her humanity, however, her identification with *people*, not women specifically, she discusses more

frankly, suggesting that this understanding of herself is less private. In keeping the secret of her sense of self as a woman hidden from the reader, and by describing it as separate from her marriage, Boland emphasizes a sense of ownership and independence. The secret is hers, and she seems to recognize a sense of personal power in keeping it. As a woman and as a poet, she reveals only what she chooses. In this way, she hints that, while she has not found her identity as a woman within marriage, she may have found it within her poetry.

STYLE

Prose Poetry

A prose poem is a poem that is written in paragraphs rather than verse and that does not contain such formal elements as metrical patterns (the pattern of unstressed and stressed syllables in lines of poetry) or rhyme schemes. Significantly, "Against Love Poetry" is a poem in which the poet speaks out against the idea of love poetry, and it is written in a way that opposes traditional poetry as well. Through its own content and title, it stands against the content of love poetry as well as the form of love poetry. While prose poetry is commonly described in terms of the features it lacks, it nevertheless contains some elements of poetic structure. In "Against Love Poetry," Boland incorporates the use of repetition as a means of supplying the prose poem with its own rhythm. Boland repeats individual words as well as phrases. This act of repetition establishes certain rhythms in parts of the poem—as when the poet describes the things she has loved, or when she tells the story of the vanquished king and, chorus-like, repeats a phrase about the people who were brought before the king. At the same time, these repetitions serve to link the disparate parts of the poem, providing it with an overall sense of unity. While incorporating these features of poetry, the prose poem is often similar to an essay in that it makes an argument, states an opinion, or proves a point. Boland wields her prose poem in this same manner. She uses the poem like an essay to describe her objection to love poetry and to make the point that love poetry is inadequate as a means of discussing marital love and the notion of self-identity. Boland further includes a parable-like story about a captured king to help prove her point and to make her case against love poetry.

Speaker and Structure

In "Against Love Poetry," Boland uses a first-person speaker, who is referred to as "I." This speaker in a first-person poem is often associated with the poet herself, or with a persona whose view is rooted in, but not exclusively representative of, that of the poet herself. The poet-speaker in "Against Love Poetry" addresses the man she married thirty years previously, speaking directly to him and referring to him as "you." Yet as the poem progresses, she seems to be speaking less to a specific reader—the husband—and more to a general audience of readers, for she does not call attention to the husband or use the pronoun "you" again throughout the remainder of the poem. The poem appears to reflect the thoughts of the speaker as they flow in a stream-of-consciousness manner. The poet moves quickly from one idea to the next, beginning with her own marriage and her deep love for

the man she married, to her love of other ideas and things, such as the notion of freedom as it applies to women. She then observes, emphatically, that marriage is not an idea that encompasses freedom. The rapid shifting of ideas continues, as the poet goes on to note that the words of this work have been written as an act of opposition to the notion of love poetry. Love poetry, she insists, cannot properly address the issues she has raised. She implies that love poetry is incapable of fully expressing such things, suggesting that in both traditional form and thematic approach to love, the idea of love poetry is somehow flawed or limited. The poet then recalls a story about a king, which she relates in some detail. The story emphasizes the king's emotional connection to his servant rather than to his family and, following the tale, the poet describes the way her own sense of womanhood is unrelated to her sense of duty to marital custom. After the poet's attention shifts once again to the idea of her humanity, and then to love and the contradictions inherent within that concept, she repeats the title of the poem. Throughout the work, the first-person speaker moves quickly from one thought to the next. The connections between the ideas are implied and at times reinforced through repeated words or phrases. Yet Boland opted to compose the prose poem as one paragraph, not several, and further chose to use a first-person speaker. In this way, the reader comes away with the sense that the poem reflects the unstructured nature of the poet's private thoughts as they are in the process of being organized to form an argument against the idea of love poetry. She returns to the same ideas repeatedly, but the rapid pace compels the reader to move swiftly through the poem, only to return to the beginning to study it again, seeking the embedded or suggested connections between the first-person speaker's thoughts and ideas.

HISTORICAL CONTEXT

Irish Poetry in the Twenty-First Century

Like twenty-first-century poetry in America, Irish poetry encompasses a variety of forms, themes, and styles. David Wheatley, writing for *The Cambridge Companion to Contemporary Irish Poetry*, focuses on the work of such modern Irish poets as Peter McDonald, Justin Quinn, and Vona Groarke, among others. In describing their work, Wheatley demonstrates the ways in which their poetry reflects trends in modern Irish poetry in general. Wheatley states,

> They are formalist or experimental as the mood takes them, writing small, exquisite lyrics, and long, loose free verse sequences, and offer in their variousness compelling examples of the range and scope of Irish poetry as it enters the twenty-first century.

Formalist poems are those that incorporate traditional structures such as meter and rhyme schemes, while experimental or free verse poetry eschews these structures. Wheatley goes on to claim that the popularity of poetry anthologies among readers has shaped perceptions of what modern Irish poetry is, based on what editors and scholars have chosen to include in such collections. Other trends in modern Irish poetry include a feminist focus and an examination of cultural identity. Guinn Batten, in *The Cambridge Companion to Contemporary Irish Poetry*, explores the work of three writers whose works center on these issues—Eavan Boland, Eilean Ni Chuilleanain, and Medbh McGuckian. Describing Boland as "Ireland's most influential feminist," Batten goes on to assess the way these writers have detailed the relationships between Irish nationalism, traditional Irish poetry, and the role of women in Irish culture. Justin Quinn, in *The Cambridge Introduction to Modern Irish Poetry, 1800–2000*, also investigates the influence of the feminist movement on modern Irish women writers, including Boland, McGuckian, and Ni Chuilleanain, along with Paula Meehan and Catherine Walsh. Quinn observes the way developments in Irish feminism, including debates about equal pay and contraception, have contributed to the fact that "greater attention is now paid to contemporary poetry by Irish women, and to the ways that these poets reflect the critical debates surrounding gender and nation."

Gender Roles and Feminism in Twenty-First-Century Ireland

The role of women in Irish society is intertwined with cultural views about gender and Roman Catholic notions about gender roles. As Quinn states, "Because certain ideas of gender are enshrined in nationalist ideology and Roman Catholicism, arguments about contraception and pay necessarily precipitated revaluations of the political and religious roles of women." These nationalist and Catholic conceptions of

Boland uses the image of the chained king to portray the restrictions of marriage. (© Pavels Rumme / Shutterstock.com)

gender roles often conflict with the modern aims of equality advanced by the European Union, an organization of nations of which Ireland is a member. The European Commission report on Ireland states that, despite a fifteen-percent pay gap between men and women, pay equality is gradually improving in Ireland, as are employment opportunities. The report also indicates that poverty poses a greater risk for women than for men. Other organizations have similarly examined the prevailing gender roles in Ireland and the problems associated with them. Writing for the World Student Christian Federation, John Delap discusses the way the family unit is perceived by Irish society, stating, "The prevailing view of the family is that the 'man of the house' is the chief breadwinner, while women and children stay at home." Delap goes on to observe that despite the recent trend of dual-income families—with both the husband and wife working full-time—"studies have shown that the women in each household end up contributing far more hours to cooking, cleaning, and child-rearing than their male counterparts." Stressing the private nature of family matters in Ireland, Delap suggests that cases of domestic violence are often unreported or overlooked due to this culture of privacy and cites a 2005 study conducted by the National Crime Council of Ireland in which it was estimated that about 213,000 women in Ireland have suffered severe abuse by a partner. Reproductive rights also remains a controversial issue in this predominantly Roman Catholic country. A 1979 Health Act allowed women to legally purchase contraceptives, while "fertility awareness methods of family planning" were advocated, explains Marian Engel in the *Encyclopedia of Birth Control*. Abortion remains illegal, except in the narrowly defined cases where the mother's life is at risk.

Feminist groups in Ireland have attempted to address these issues over the years. As a movement, feminism in Ireland is traced to the 1970 meeting of a group that came to label itself the Irish Women's Liberation Movement. Boland, along with other writers and activists, was a member. The group published a booklet, *Chains or Change*, in 1971, in which they demanded "equal pay, an end to the marriage bar, equal rights in law, justice for widows, deserted wives and unmarried mothers, equal educational opportunities and contraception," states Grainne Farren in the Irish *Independent*. Farren observes, "The Equal Pay Act, contraception, divorce and the right to work all came in eventually and are now taken for granted by the younger generation." An *Irish Times* article on current trends in feminism in Ireland addresses this perception, describing the reluctance of Irish women to call themselves feminist, despite their solidarity with feminist causes. The article, reporting on the 2012 conference of the Irish Feminist Network, describes the way young feminists, particularly students, have advocated for abortion law reform, among other issues.

CRITICAL OVERVIEW

Critical reception of Boland's collection *Against Love Poetry* has been largely favorable, although the form of the prose poem by the same name has been questioned. In a review for the *New York Times*, Melanie Rehak states that "Against

Love Poetry" is "the only prose poem in the collection, perhaps because it's meant as a statement of purpose and thus Boland wanted it to look weighty on the page—otherwise it seems a fairly arbitrary choice." In discussing "Against Love Poetry" in the *Georgia Review*, Judith Kitchen states,

> the title piece (the only prose work in the book) announces the tensions at its heart. But, the argumentative mind would ask, are the conditions of contemporary marriage any more free for a man? Although Boland's transparent style conveys honesty, in the end many of the poems feel more like arguments than evocations.

Kitchen finds that, as a whole, the collection of poetry is informed by Boland's feminism and insists that "the resulting poems raise the issue of limitation, the issue of gendered roles." Like Kitchen, Bruce F. Murphy, writing for *Poetry*, focuses on Boland's treatment of love and marriage in "Against Love Poetry." Murphy finds that the poem suggests "that marriage is an unfree relationship (particularly for women), and somehow opposed to that love born one summer thirty years ago—and also that traditional love poetry has failed to take this conflict into account." Murphy notes, however, the collection *Against Love Poetry* is less "combative" in tone than is the title poem.

CRITICISM

Catherine Dominic

Dominic is a novelist and freelance writer and editor. In the following essay, she studies the story of the captured king that Boland includes in "Against Love Poetry" and demonstrates the ways in which the tale serves to emphasize how marriage, in Boland's assessment, confines its participants and characterizes them as prisoners.

In "Against Love Poetry," Boland incorporates a story about a king who has lost a war. After his enemies have taken him prisoner, they proceed to taunt him by bringing forth others they have captured. Seeking to break the king's spirit, his enemies reveal they have taken prisoner the king's wife and children, his courtiers, and his servant. The king remains emotionless until he sees his servant; he then weeps. Boland includes this story directly after she insists that love poetry cannot truly do justice to her task of relating the complexities of marriage, love,

WHAT DO I READ NEXT?

- Boland's most recent—and acclaimed— poetry collection, *New Collected Poems*, was published in 2005. It treats themes of Irish identity, culture, and history; family and love; and gender roles.

- *A Journey with Two Maps: Becoming a Woman Poet*, published in 2011, is a collection of essays by Boland in which she explores her path to becoming the poet she is today. She assesses the way her gender influenced and shaped her journey as a poet.

- Eilean Ni Chuilleanain is, like Boland, an Irish poet concerned with womanhood, gender roles, and Irish culture and identity, themes she explores in the 2010 collection *The Sun-Fish*.

- Medbh McGuckian, another contemporary of Boland's, explores spirituality and Irish identity in the 2004 poetry collection *The Book of the Angel*, in which she experiments with traditional verse forms.

- Chinese poet Chun Yu, in the 2005 volume of young-adult poetry *Little Green: Growing Up during the Chinese Cultural Revolution*, writes about her childhood and adolescence in China, touching on themes of culture, identity, gender, and coming-of-age in China.

- *Irish Literature: Feminist Perspectives* is a 2008 collection of essays edited by Patricia Coughlan and Tina O'Toole. The essays in the volume explore the way Irish nationalism and feminism have informed works of Irish literature from the eighteenth century through today.

identity, and freedom (or lack of freedom). Instead, she informs the reader, she offers this tale. As the story of the king comprises almost half of the poem, its significance should not be overlooked.

"Against Love Poetry" is a poem about love and marriage and a woman's feeling of identity as it relates to her status as a lover and a wife.

> IF VIEWED WITHIN THE LARGER CONTEXT OF THE POEM, THE WAR IN THE STORY OF THE CAPTURED KING REPRESENTS MARRIAGE IN THE SAME WAY THAT THE KING REPRESENTS THE FIGURE OF THE HUSBAND."

The poem opens with an affirmation of love, a love that has lasted some thirty years. It is the poet's love for the man she married. But the poem, as the reader quickly ascertains, will not concern itself with why the speaker loves the man in question. She notes the existence and duration of that love and then asserts that she also loves things other than the man who is—or was—her husband. (It is worth noting that although the poet comments that she was married thirty years ago, and that she has continued to love that man from that day to the present time, she does not inform the reader whether or not the marriage has lasted as long as the love. It would be wrong to infer, therefore, that the "you" to whom she addresses the poem remains her husband.) The speaker then claims that one of these other things she has loved is an idea, the idea of freedom as it pertains to women. Aware that it might seem odd to the reader to have a comment about women's freedom follow that about love and marriage, the poet poses a question. She rhetorically wonders why such ideas have been linked in this fashion, why these notions of freedom and marriage have been thus paired. The poet answers simply and straightforwardly that it is because she is a woman and because marriage cannot be equated with freedom. Here the reader must consider what the poet is *not* saying. If marriage is *not* compatible with the notion of freedom, if these two things are mutually exclusive, than what *is* marriage? Does she consider it to be confinement? Is marriage a trap? A prison? She does not explicitly answer this implied question. What she does do is insist that love poetry is an inadequate means of exploring these issues. What she offers instead is the story, suggesting in doing so that this story offers a better way to understand the ideas of identity, love, and marriage.

Having thus set up the story, Boland relates the details of the captured king, the lost war. She describes the way his enemies seek to taunt, torture, and break him by bringing in front of him individuals they presume he cares about. The reader is forced to conclude that these individuals have likewise been captured in the war since they are in the enemy's clutches and are now being used as pawns against their own king. First, the king's wife and children are brought, then his courtiers, then his servant. When reading the story of the captured king, it becomes clear that in a poem in which the female speaker regards marriage as restrictive and confining, the king in the story can only be regarded as a symbol of a husband, maybe *the* husband (that is, the speaker's husband). Or perhaps the king is meant to be *every* husband. The reader must also consider the significance of the order in which the individuals are presented to the king, as well as the effect these individuals have on him.

The wife and children are brought before the king first. Presumably, the king's enemies assume that the thought of any harm coming to the king's wife or children would have the desired demoralizing effect on the king that they are clearly trying to achieve. After all, what could mean more to a king than his queen and his heirs? Yet the king shows no emotion at the appearance of his wife and children. Next, his courtiers are presented. These would be the king's friends, his confidantes, those who idolized him, loved him. But again, the king does not respond with any show of emotion. When the king's servant is brought before him, however, the king begins to weep. At the beginning of the story, the poet mentions the war, a war that has resulted in both the king and his wife being captured, along with his servant, his children, and his courtiers. If viewed within the larger context of the poem, the war in the story of the captured king represents marriage in the same way that the king represents the figure of the husband. Marriage, like the war in the story, results in its participants feeling captured, like the king and the wife in the story. Significantly, the king is as confined as his wife is; both participants in the marriage are held prisoner. Neither of them is free. Besides being captured, the wife suffers the additional humiliation of being less appreciated by her husband than his servant is. Further, the king's powerlessness is underscored. Because of him, and his enemies' desire to further destroy him, the king's family, friends,

and servant have also been taken prisoner. In depicting the king and his wife in the story in this manner, Boland emphasizes the feelings of degradation and impotence felt by the participants in a marriage. This view of marriage is grim indeed.

As the story concludes, the poet insists that she did not realize her own sense of womanhood while obeying the customs of marriage. In making this statement, she invokes the notion of service, and in doing so, she recalls the relationship of the king to the servant. Here the roles of wife and servant are conflated, and Boland seeks to distance herself from the notion of the servile spouse by claiming that, for her, a sense of self as a woman was found elsewhere, not within marriage. The poet's insistence that marriage cannot be regarded as freedom is now further informed by the repetition of this idea of servitude. As a wife, she has felt not free but oppressed, the way a servant—however beloved—might feel. If the king in the story has been rendered powerless, then his wife, who feels as though she is little more than a servant, must be regarded as even more impotent. In this section of the poem, Boland draws attention to the imbalance of power in the marital relationship by associating wives with servants. Boland then refers to her sense of humanity, realizing now, as she looks back on the thirty years of her marriage, that she is connected to her humanity and to her sense of herself as a person with experiences common among all people through the experience of her marriage. These experiences, however, appear to be rooted in suffering, in unhappiness, and in the sense of loss of power. Although Boland states that she has not developed a sense of her womanhood through her marriage, but through observing the relationship with all its flaws, she, in some ways, feels connected to humanity. The commingling of love and suffering—felt by both husband and wife who are trapped and imprisoned by marriage—inspires in the poet a sense of connection to others. As the poem concludes with a defiant repetition of the title, the reader is left to wonder if this generic connection to others who have suffered is enough to compensate for the loneliness that seems inseparable from the figure of the wife within the poem. In the penultimate sentence of this poem, Boland informs the reader that she has written it in an effort to delineate the inconsistencies she has observed in what passes for daily marital love. Although she has returned to the idea of love, she

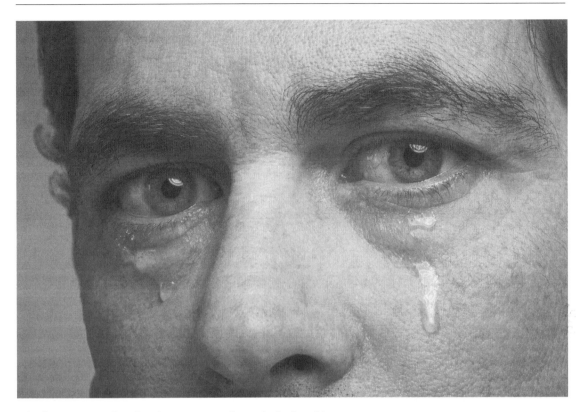

The king cries only when his servant is brought before him. *(© Andre Blais / Shutterstock.com)*

has colored this notion of love within the confines of marriage in bleak tones. Husbands and wives are depicted as trapped and powerless, and the disconnection and despair that attend the servitude of the wifely experience is palpable. When the poet asserts that she writes in opposition to the notion of love poetry, the reader, by the end of the poem, is better able to understand her stance.

Source: Catherine Dominic, Critical Essay on "Against Love Poetry," in *Poetry for Students*, Gale, Cengage Learning, 2014.

Pilar Villar-Argáiz

In the following excerpt, Villar-Argáiz looks at Boland's work as "minority" and "postcolonial" poetry in the context of the work of Irish women poets.

3.5.1. INTRODUCTION

Like the feminist literary critic Showalter (1999: 11), Eavan Boland has talked about her own work in terms of concepts such as 'minority' and 'subculture.' In an interview, she compares her own writing with Black American writing and dissident writing in Europe, because they all share powerful images which become "visible" in terms of their "invisibility" (Wilson 1990b: 88). In

this sense, Boland establishes an interesting parallelism between women's writing, in particular her own work, and that kind of writing which might be labeled (at least in the case of Black American literature) postcolonial. Furthermore, she argues in *Object Lessons* that women writers "are a minority within the expressive poetic tradition" because "[m]uch of their actual experience lacks even the most rudimentary poetic precedent" (Boland 1996a: 242). Although Boland defines women's writing as 'minority' discourse, and compares her own writing with dissident (postcolonial) productions, her stance on this matter is everything but simple. Boland remains skeptical toward those literary critics who tend to discuss Irish women's poetry as a "subculture" apart from mainstream poetry (147–148). She attacks these critics who marginalize women, on the grounds that women's project, in moving from being the objects to being the subjects of Irish poems, "is neither marginal nor specialist. It is a project which concerns all of poetry, all that leads into it in the past and everywhere it is going in the future" (235). In this sense, Boland makes a conscious distinction between women writers' 'minority' position and their 'subcultural' status, implying

"IN THIS SENSE, BOLAND'S POETRY RECORDS
A CONSTANT PROCESS OF SEARCHING FOR AN
APPROPRIATE LANGUAGE THAT ARTICULATES IN A
MORE TRUTHFUL WAY HER 'IRISHNESS' AND HER
'WOMANHOOD.'"

that occupying the very edges of the Irish literary tradition should not be a reason for 'marginalizing' women's writing under headings which might be dismissive.

In what follows, I intend to trace the different ways in which we can consider Boland's work a 'minor/ity' and 'postcolonial' poetry. As most of the features I am about to comment on here will be developed in more detail in subsequent chapters, I will only pay closer attention to some aspects.

3.5.2. MINORITY DISCOURSE ON THE MARGINS OF THE IRISH LITERARY CANON: COLLECTIVITY, LANGUAGE, AND POLITICS

As we have seen, Jan Mohamed and Lloyd (1999a: ix) have identified 'minority discourse' as that kind of literature which is written by a group which, despite their heterogeneous nature, share the same experiences of domination, marginalization, and exclusion by the majority groups. From this perspective, Boland's work could certainly be categorized as 'minor.' Eavan Boland shares with most women writers in the female literary tradition an exclusion from an overwhelmingly male-dominated literary canon. Her marginalized position as a female artist, her feelings of alienation from male predecessors, and her consequent ambivalent attitude toward the patriarchal authority of art link her struggle for artistic self-definition with the female literary tradition most successfully perceived in the nineteenth century. Furthermore, she is attached to contemporary women poets in Ireland, in her struggle within a potentially problematic culture in which literature, subjects, and symbols have already been predominantly defined by men. Boland herself is trying to subvert male aesthetic and poetic values, just like feminists and other contemporary women poets in Ireland, such as Eithne Strong, Eiléan Ní Chuilleanáin, Medbh McGuckian, and Nuala Ní Dhomhnaill (Haberstroh 1996: 16–27).

In the common personal and literary concerns that unite Boland with other Irish women poets, her poetry can also be categorized as 'literary subculture' and 'minor literature'. As we have seen, Showalter (1999: 11) argues that the members of all literary subcultures are united in their political interests and literary imagery. Similarly, Deleuze and Guattari (1986: 17) have argued that minor literature is identified by its "collective assemblage of enunciation." Precisely because of the difficulties Irish women have encountered in becoming poets, their work presents an incredible amalgam of common literary motives. A systematic approach to the most important differences between male poetry and women's poetry in Ireland gives us an insight into Boland's link with her female colleagues. These differences stem not from the sex of the authors (and therefore from biological features), but rather from the cultural circumstances that have affected both genders. In the context of (contemporary) Ireland, the woman poet must often make difficult choices in order to write. In an interview, Boland talks about her personal experience when conducting writing workshops, and notes the different sociological factors Irish male poets and women poets contemplate, when balancing their writing careers with other choices:

> I took away from those workshops two formative impressions. The first was the way Irish women poets were emerging. They came forward in a completely different way from men. The male poet often began publishing quite young, at a time when he didn't have a family and—if he wasn't economically independent—at least he didn't have dependants. [. . .] A woman was often a new poet rather than a young poet. Through the workshops I could see that it was quite common for an Irish woman poet to emerge in her thirties or even her forties. She might be publishing for the very first time in these years. By which time she had a job or a family, was less mobile and often economically dependent. [. . .] The second impression was more elusive. I was aware of certain resistances which amounted to subtle permissions and their consequent withholding. [. . .] Male poets frequently spoke to me—half joking and whole in earnest—about the bad writing [by women] these workshops were encouraging. (Allen-Randolph 1993b: 126)

Understanding these gender-related difficulties is essential when approaching the main distinctions between Irish male and female poetry. I will rely on Haberstroh's (1996: 19–27) identification of the most important characteristics observed in contemporary poetry by Irish women, for I think it sheds significant light on the contrast between both writings.

(1) Haberstroh (1996: 19) considers the theme of identity to be central in women's poetry. Whereas male poets take "gender as a given in assuming a poetic identity" (Foster 1999: 2), women poets find more difficulty in drawing together their femininity with their creative potential. Thus, at the core of Boland's poetry is the quest for autonomous self-definition, an attempt to attain her unique female identity. She admits that poetic self-definition is at the core of women's poetry, because "for a woman to explore and write her own poems in Ireland, sooner or later she will have to dismantle some pre-existing definitions" (interview with Allen-Randolph 1999b: 303). Her poems are reflections of her experiences as a woman. When asked about what the lyric "I" of the poems stands for, Boland replies:

> the voice is me. It isn't just the voice of an 'I.' It's me in the Yeatsian sense, in that it's the part of me that connects with something more durable and more permanent in my own experience. [. . .] I am a woman and write in terms of what defines me. (Interview with Wilson 1990b: 80–81)

This need to assert the speaking voice of the poem as female is a consequence of what Gilbert and Gubar (2000: 49) denominate "anxiety of authorship." Female writers' anxieties differ from those of male writers'. According to Harold Bloom (1973: 15), the male artist experiences an "anxiety of influence," that is, a fear that he is not the creator of his work of art, because he is excessively influenced by his literary predecessors. In contrast, the female writer cannot undergo this "anxiety of influence," as her predecessors are exclusively male (48). Fogarty (1999: 259) restates this point to include the specific case of Irish women poets:

> Unlike their male counterparts, it is not the anxiety of influence that serves as a goad for the individual creativity of the Irish woman writer but rather it is the entire absence of a female line of influence that acts both as a bogey and as a powerful impetus to question, refurbish, and invent poetic strategies of self-definition.

Rather than experiencing an "anxiety of influence," a woman writer is prone to feeling a deeper kind of anxiety: a conflict with her own autonomy, subjectivity, and creativity, as

traditional stereotypes have offered a distorted image of her own self. Thus, Gilbert and Gubar (2000: 48–49) assert:

> "the anxiety of influence" that a male poet experiences is felt by a female poet as an even more primary "anxiety of authorship"—a radical fear that she cannot create, that because she can never become a "precursor" the art of writing will isolate or destroy her.

Boland shows this fear of "authorship" in her highly feminist collection *In Her Own Image* (1980). The creative potential of the strong woman in this volume leads her to isolation and self-destruction. Writing is equated with an act of insanity by a woman shamefully exposing her naked body in public ("Exhibitionist"), or to the self-destructive activity of a witch burning her own body ("Witching"). Therefore, in contrast to male writers, Boland explores in her poetry all possible ways to come to terms with her own self, as a woman and a writer.

(2) Another characteristic which is generally identified as particular to Irish female poets is their interest in introducing new female images in literature. Celtic mythology and nationalist iconography have been inhospitable terrains for a woman writer. Thus, women poets feel the need to reconstruct old misconceived images of the feminine, in particular "[t]he static and sublimated images of mothers and motherhood that strew the pages of Irish patriarchal tradition" (Fogarty 1995: 5). Ostriker (1986: 211) considers this redefinition of cultural images a "revisionist mythmaking" technique, which is an important strategy in women's poetry. In her reconstruction of the myths of the past, Boland's poetry records a process of exploration of Irish women, from the everyday details of the housewife and the mother, to the emigrant and the sexually active whore.

(3) Haberstroh (1996: 21) identifies as characteristic in Irish women's poetry the recurrence of internal spaces, usually domestic interiors. In contrast, this critic explains, some of the better known Irish male poets are concerned with the land rather than with the people of the land, and they lay "less emphasis on the value of the self," which is a vital issue for women poets. In order to illustrate this point, Haberstroh mentions Heaney's *Field Work*, and other works by John Montague, Thomas Kinsella, Paul Muldoon, and Richard Murphy. Allen-Randolph (1999a: 207) believes that this tendency among male poets to focus on "public" landscapes may be due to the inherited

relationship of poet to history. Comparing American and Irish writers, this critic notes that Irish poets (consistently male poets) have been more obliged "to the history of their own country," and to a specifically national tradition which has often put public concerns before individual matters (ibid). On the other hand, Irish women poets tend to identify themselves with a different type of place. They frequently circumscribe a domestic world of kitchens and nursery rooms, "the world many women in Ireland inhabit" (Haberstroh 1996: 21). Their handling of the domestic may be understood as a way of subverting a tradition which exclusively revolved around the traditional subject matter of the heroic, dismissing the ordinary world as a trivial issue (Allen-Randolph 1999a: 207). Accordingly, Eavan Boland describes herself as an "indoor poet" interested in kitchen utensils, washing machines, bicycles, the baby's bottle, and patchwork (interview with Allen-Randolph 1993b: 124). As she says, "these were parts of my world. Not to write about them would have been artificial" (ibid). In a later prose work, she asserts:

> My children were born. I entered a world of routine out of which, slowly and mysteriously, a world of vision manifested itself. For all that, it was a commonsense and familiar world, a stretch of road with whitebeam trees and driveways where cars—the same, for all I knew, which had just moved down the hillside— returned at dusk and left first thing in the morning. (Boland 1996a: 192)

Thus, Boland starts writing poems about the invisible world of the suburbs, altering the "view of the elegy, the pastoral, and the nature poem," which did not account for this ordinary world (ibid). The legitimization as literary of what has been excluded from literature is a common characteristic of women writers in most cultures. Ostriker (1986: 89) explains that "it is immediately apparent that women who seek themselves will include the material of their daily lives and feelings in their poems." Thus, the roles of mothers, daughters and wives, and the routines of domesticity will be reclaimed by Irish women poets in an attempt to express their own womanhood and subvert feminine ideals, in contrast to Irish male poets, more supposedly concerned with Ireland's political history.

(4) Irish women poets are engaged nowadays in offering new representations of the female body (Haberstoh 1996: 22). They mention their anatomy both more frequently and far more intimately than male poets. Although they

have been discouraged from writing about their flesh, they assume control over their sexual and reproductive lives. Thus, when they start writing to praise their bodies, they take some kind of "liberating jump" and their "muted parts begin to explain themselves" (Ostriker 1986: 92). Haberstroh (1996: 22) identifies a wide movement in the 1980s among Irish women who began to "challenge sexual taboos [and to] express[. . .] a new view of female anatomy." Together with Eithne Strong's and Mary Dorcey's work, we come across *In Her Own Image*, wherein Eavan Boland (1980) examines the effects of traditional sexual representations of women.

(5) When women poets speak about their female experience, a recurrent subject matter appears in their work: the love between mother and child. As Haberstroh (1996: 23) points out, Irish women poets like Eavan Boland, Medbh McGuckian, Nuala Ní Dhomhnaill, and Eithne Strong have written extensively about "the value of motherhood" and "the difficulties of mothering." Whereas male poets are more concerned with father-son relationships (Gilbert & Gubar 2000: 46), the theme of maternity has proven extraordinarily intense in contemporary women's poetry. In volumes such as *Night Feed* (1982), Boland glorifies the close bond between mother and child, and laments the passing of time, as her child grows older and gradually moves away from her.

(6) Contemporary Irish women poets also tend to express a strong disapproval of literary idealizations of Irish battles (Haberstroh 1996: 24). As Boland (1996a: 183) explains, in the cultural nationalist tradition, poems were only limited to the public events and the communal interpretations of them. Mangan's "Dark Rosaleen," Patrick Pearse's "Mother Ireland," and Francis Ledwidge's "The Blackbirds" (Kennelly 1970: 149, 295, 305), are examples of this kind of political poem Boland talks about in which the poet-patriot invokes the land to incite rebellion. In her work, Boland tries to subvert this traditional nationalist poem by relying on her everyday and mundane experiences as mother and housewife. Her private world is used as a metaphor for public reality, for the national history of Ireland. She feels the need to see "the powerful public history of [her] own country joined by the private lives and solitary perspectives [. . .] which the Irish poetic tradition had not yet admitted to authorship" (Boland

1996a: 187). In order to do so, she relies on Yeats's example, for he managed to destabilize the conventional poem through the intensity of his private world (189). Therefore, some of Boland's poetry focuses on how important it is to rely on the bonds of love created in ordinary atmospheres, and laments the impact of war on home and family life.

All these six common motives Haberstroh (1996: 19–27) identifies in Irish women's poetry (its concern with poetic identity; its revision of conventional feminine images in literature; the predominance of internal spaces; its reliance on female bodily imagery and mother-child relationships; and its subversion of the traditional Irish political poem) are a sign of their collective value as a 'minor literature' or 'literary subculture.'

Furthermore, if we take into account other aspects of Deleuze and Guattari's (1986: 16–18) theories, Boland's work will be unquestionably considered as another instance of 'minor' literature. Together with its collective value, these theorists argue that two salient features of minor literature are the connection of the individual to politics and the "deterritorialization" of language. As I have attempted to demonstrate, these features have also been identified in some way or another by postcolonial theory and by feminist literary criticism. First of all, and as Deleuze and Guattari (1986: 17) would argue, Boland's can be considered a 'minor' literature in the sense that her poetry is deeply loaded with political content. Although Boland defines her own mature work as 'apolitical' and non-ideological, she has also acknowledged that just by "trying to record the life I lived in the poem," she becomes a political poet, because the "material" she uses is already "politicized" material in the Irish national tradition (Boland 1996a: 183). Secondly, Boland also experiences the "deterritorialization" of language of other 'minor' and 'postcolonial' writers. Her poetry, mostly her mature production, constantly draws us into the linguistic displacement she has experienced as a woman and an Irish citizen. Boland finds herself limited by the fact that she has never learned Irish, and therefore, she is distanced from much of her native literary tradition. In this sense, Boland becomes, as Deleuze and Guattari (1986: 26) argue in relation to Kafka, "a stranger *within* [her] own language," and she is bound to write in the only language she knows by birth, the 'major' English language (although,

as we will see, she finds "something wonderfully subversive about being an Irish writer in the English language," interview with Villar-Argáiz 2006: 55). Furthermore, as a woman, Boland notices that she has been forced to articulate her experiences in a nationalist (patriarchal) language that dictates how her feminine role is to be defined. In her semi-autobiographical book *Object Lessons*, Boland (1996a: 134–135) describes how the blurring of the feminine and the national in the Irish context has encouraged a distorted and simplified idea of womanhood:

> The majority of Irish male poets depended on women as motifs in their poetry. They moved easily, deftly, as if by right among images of women in which I did not believe and of which I could not approve. The women in their poems were often passive, decorative, raised to emblematic status. This was especially true where the woman and the idea of the nation were mixed: where a nation became a woman and the woman took on a national posture.

In this sense, Boland's poetry records a constant process of searching for an appropriate language that articulates in a more truthful way her 'Irishness' and her 'womanhood.' Her desire to create a new idiom that "reterritorializes" and subverts the authoritarian (imperialist and nationalist) languages is also a common feature of all 'minor' writers. Renza (1984: 37) maintains that every 'minor' writer manifests a "major" ambition, in his/her interest in "the possibility of producing one's own language," a language that will be "unique" and truthful to his/her own reality.

On the other hand, as Deleuze and Guattari (1986: 28) have argued, minor literature "begins by expressing itself and it doesn't conceptualize until afterwards." In her initial poetry, Boland elevates style over subject matter, something Yeats had also done (Kiberd 1996: 126). In volumes such as *New Territory* (1967), Boland shows her belief that linguistic expression and the poet's ability to use language effectively are more important than anything else. The "point of departure" in the journey of poets, Boland (2000b: xxix) argues, "remains clear. It is the form of the poem. That form which comes as a truth teller and intercessor from history itself, making structures of language, making music of feeling." In her mature work, Boland does not rely on conventional techniques and styles, but rather on experimental devices and "technical innovation" (xxix).

Source: Pilar Villar-Argáiz, "Boland's Work as Minority/
Postcolonial Poetry," in *The Poetry of Eavan Boland: A
Postcolonial Reading*, Academica Press, 2008, pp. 82–92.

Alice Quinn

*In the following interview, Quinn and Boland dis-
cuss poetry from a feminist perspective.*

The title of your new book, Against Love Poetry,
*is such a bold declaration. When did you begin to think
about these poems as having a thematic unity—as
poems written against a tradition of love poetry?*

Well, certainly not at the very beginning.
They were just individual poems. But it had
been, I suppose, something that I had thought
of, off and on, and not in a very conscious way.
So much of European love poetry is court
poetry, coming out of the glamorous traditions
of the court. Somebody used a gauntlet, somebody picked up a scarf, somebody was in a tour-
nament, somebody was in a joust. Love poetry,
from the troubadours on, is traditionally about
that romantic lyric moment. There's little about
the ordinariness of love, the dailyness of love, or
the steadfastness of love. John Donne is, to my
mind, the most beautiful poet of marriage and
the stoicisms of love. But he is rare.

*In your memoir, I was struck by your saying
that the exhilaration of language, particularly for
a young poet, is almost inseparable from its power,
but that, at a certain point, the suspect nature of
the power undermined the exhilaration you were
feeling, and you started to examine issues with
respect to women, and the passivity associated
with women and Irish poetry.*

When I was married with small children, I was
participating in a life that everyone else around me
was living. It was a life with a lot of dailyness, a lot
of durable and true feeling. But I didn't see a
reflection of it in the Irish poem—at least, I
couldn't find it there. I suppose in many ways
that poem had evolved from the nineteenth century. Yet, even in that century, you could go
through Irish poetry and not find any real references to the Irish famine, although it was the great,
defining event of that time. Instead, the poetry kept
up its heroism, its resistance to ordinariness, its
elevated stance. And, at some point in my life in
that suburb, I fell into some kind of disagreement
with that poem—or, at least, with its history.

*That summons up for me your reverence for the
antiauthoritarian romanticism of Wordsworth, your
advocacy of a poetry written in the voice of "a man
speaking to men."*

Yes, and against that place which accessor-
izes poetry to the ornamental. I have loved the
preface to the *Lyrical Ballads* since my twenties,
because I felt it was such a definite and brave
claiming of poetry for a much wider section of
life and experience than it could have been.

I think there's a great temptation coming
from the literary city that I first saw, and from
remembering it, to allow that essence to somehow
edit your own feeling of what your life is and what
your experience is. And, above all, to subtly imply
to you what is important in your experience and
what isn't. And I wanted to feel that the things
that I felt were important outside the poem could
be important inside the poem from my viewpoint.
And even though a lot of the poems began to be,
really, failures and had all the things people fear
they're going to have—sentimentality or bathos or
polemics—I still felt that they were trying to make
a clear line between what I felt was outside the
poem and what was inside it. And so I got confidence from that.

*In your memoir, you discuss the passivity of the
feminine within the traditional Irish poem, and your
feeling that the feminine imagery in the lore of Ireland
was at odds with your active determination to be a
poet and to belong to your country's version of history.
Was that a reflection of the shadow of Yeats?*

Well, I think Yeats comes into it but from the
end of that tradition. In the nineteenth century,
the poets—especially the poets who had come out
of a group clustered around the newspaper *The
Nation*, including some wonderful poets, like
James Clarence Mangan—were very patriotic.
They began, as a mode of protest, to represent
Ireland as a woman. She became the Shan Van
Vocht—the literal translation is poor old
woman—or she was a beautiful young girl.
Yeats ends his play *Cathleen Ní Houlihan* by referring to Ireland as a young girl with the walk of a
queen. So you had these very idealized ideas of the
national and the feminine fused together. And this
was at a time when, behind those images, women
were really living at the sharp end of history in
Ireland, especially in the years after the famine. I
remember going down to the famine museum in
Strokestown, where there is a framed letter on the
wall to a middleman from a woman who had left
her children in the workhouse and wanted to try
to get them back. And this was almost exactly in
the same year that James Clarence Mangan wrote
"Dark Rosaleen." And I just feel the gap is too
wide between the idealization and the reality. If

you're trying to be the contemporary woman, then I think your eye is going to turn to that letter. And you're going to say, What does that idealization mean? And what spaces does it leave? So it was something that kept coming across my mind, in both argumentative ways and thoughtful ways.

In one of the new poems, the beautiful one "Is It Still the Same," you portray a young woman at a desk, and you seem to imply a hope that you will have been able to give something to that young woman, to have altered the poetic tradition in your own country in a way that might be able to succor her or lift her up in her resolve.

Well, it's more a sense of my hope that I will witness that. You don't know that you've done anything in any space that you've made. But I do have a sense that when I was younger, writing those poems which turned out badly, I would have been glad to have had an Irish woman poet behind me. There were great and wonderful Irish male poets, all of whom I found inspiring in different ways. It meant an enormous amount to me in a very tribal way that William Yeats was Irish. And I would have liked, I suppose, to include in that tribalism a woman as well.

Source: Alice Quinn, "The Stoicisms of Love," in *Eavan Boland: A Critical Companion*, edited by Jody Allen Randolph, W. W. Norton, 2007, pp. 127–29.

Eavan Boland

In the following excerpt, Boland discusses the influence of Irish female poets on poetry as a whole.

THE IRISH WOMAN POET: HER PLACE IN IRISH LITERATURE

My subject is the woman poet and the national literature of Ireland. It may well seem—with such a subject—that my emphasis should be on finding a context for the Irish woman poet in that literature. But it is not. Even the words *finding a context* are, I feel, misleading. They imply permissions and allowances—a series of subtle adjustments made to fit a new arrival into an established order. I want to make it clear from the start that this is not my view. It seems to me critical to any accurate or useful interpretation of this subject—which remains a difficult and controversial one—to insist on this point. I want to make it very clear from the beginning that any relation between the Irish woman poet and the national literature is a two-way traffic. That in the process of finding a context in Irish literature through her work, the woman poet also redefines the part of that

> I BELIEVE THERE CANNOT BE A SOUND CRITIQUE WHICH DOES NOT RECOGNIZE THE POSSIBILITY OF THEIR DOING SO. NO POETIC TRADITION IS A STATIC OR CLOSED ENTITY; IT LIVES TO BE REFRESHED AND RESTATED, TO BE STRENGTHENED BY SUBVERSION."

literature which she enacts: namely, Irish poetry. She also redefines the relation between the national ethos and the Irish poem. I am not, in other words, talking about some grace-and-favor adjustment of Irish poetry to allow for the new energies of Irish women poets. I honestly think this is a doomed approach. I am talking about taking this chance—of new work and radical departures—to look again at Irish poetry and revise certain assumptions about it.

In his *Modern Poetry: A Broadcast*, Yeats makes a striking comment on T. S. Eliot. "In the third year of the War," he says, "came the most revolutionary man in poetry during my lifetime, though his revolution was stylistic alone—T. S. Eliot published his first book" ([1936] 1968). It is of course possible to read this assertion—that Eliot was a radical stylist but little more—as a conservative, not to say grudging, retrospect. I think a better way to read it reveals the opposite: that it is, essentially, the rebuke of one great modernist to another—a rebuke which suggested that Yeats felt Eliot had interpreted the letter of modernism, but may have imperfectly developed its rigorous and rewarding spirit. It also—and this is what concerns me here—contains the implicit warning that changes to poetic form need to happen at levels deeper than language, mannerism, or influence; that they must go well beyond those gestures of expression which seem to promise a temporary shift of fashion or response.

To sustain my view that women poets are influencing the form they enact, I want to propose a substantive argument for it—one that goes beyond changes in style or taste. Put as simply as possible, my argument is that both the Irish poem and the perception of it are radically changed by the fact that Irish women—within the space of a couple of decades—have gone from being the objects of the Irish poem to being the authors of it. This does not just mean that Irish women now write the Irish poem—although they do; it means they also claim it. Not as their own, I should quickly add: a claim of ownership should not and cannot be sustained in any art form. Claims of ownership are, in many ways, what women poets have implicitly contested by writing the Irish poem. Nevertheless, they do something exciting and unusual with that poem. Inasmuch as they are the old silent objects of it, now transformed into speaking parts and articulate visions, they make a momentous and instructive transformation in Irish poetry.

And, of course, a contentious one. By enacting their experience and expression within that poem, they have disturbed certain traditional balances in the Irish poem, between object and author, between poet and perspective. These balances were themselves an index and register of an old relation between the Irish poem and the national tradition. Perhaps, at this point, I should change the "they" here to "we." In disrupting such balances, Irish women poets such as myself and Nuala Ní Dhomhnaill and Medbh McGuckian and Paula Meehan have disordered an old, entrenched and even dangerous relation between Irish national assumptions and the Irish poem. Therefore, although I won't say that Irish poetry is at a crossroads, I will say that I believe it has changed. The landscape of it will never be politicized in exactly the same way again. The features of it will never be susceptible to the same definitions again. And the old critiques will not serve anymore in the new situation.

It is always tempting—to choose Yeats's word again—to claim a revolution for the work of any poetic generation. But it is rarely true. And in this case, also, I think there are precedents for the way Irish women poets and Irish poetry connect. I think the mode of connection—the relation of a disruptive energy to a national literature—goes back further than this moment in which poetry by Irish women has become a presence. I think of Irish women poets as refusing the passivity offered them by the inscriptions of a national literature. Their refusal makes a crucial difference and occurs in a crucial area; and I will return to be as precise as I can about it. But in my time, as a young poet in Dublin, I saw and was moved—and I think was also influenced—by the way in which other poets refused different but similar simplifications. I am especially thinking of Patrick Kavanagh. As a

poet—like so many of my generation—I continue to find him a liberating force and a poignant, living presence. I am still struck by the way he threw aside shibboleths and symmetries which it might have been thought he would live into, or at least write into. He resisted stereotypes, albeit with pain; he redefined his own power, albeit at cost. Whenever I want to measure that rare and elusive quality which is imaginative courage, I think first of him.

These are affinities and influences; however, they are not critical models. I think it is important to highlight that there is no preexisting critique for the particular conjunction I am speaking about: the emergence of a woman poet against a backdrop of a strong and entrenched national tradition. There are poets, such as Anna Akhmatova, in Russia who were luminously aware, largely through their own experience of it, of the encroachments of power. There are poets like Emily Dickinson, who defined, in her writing, an important puritan ethos, even while she was being eclipsed by it. There are writers like the African-American poet Gwendolyn Brooks who lived at the intersection of race and expression. She speaks for many of the others with her words: "I have heard in the voices of the wind my dim / killed children" (1963).

Nevertheless, the Irish situation is different. It requires a radical and thoughtful approach. It has been, in some senses, stressful for women poets such as myself to have to make the critique, at the same time as we are making the work for which the critique is fitted. I'm afraid it is a measure of the intermittent nature of scholarly discussion throughout the seventies and eighties—and what I feel has been a signal failure of the scholarly conferences in this regard—that there has been, until recently, no searching and eloquent critical literature to cover this subject, although there is almost an embarrassment of it in other areas of contemporary Irish poetry. This in turn reflects the assumptions—barely stated but easily sensed by a poet like myself—that, while women poets might contribute individual poems, they were unlikely to shift or radicalize the course of Irish poetry itself. I believe there cannot be a sound critique which does not recognize the possibility of their doing so. No poetic tradition is a static or closed entity; it lives to be refreshed and restated, to be strengthened by subversion. In the absence of such a critique, an analysis of the position of the woman poet in the national tradition and literature has only been brought forward through personal witness and private argument. I intend to continue this here. . . .

Source: Eavan Boland, "The Irish Woman Poet: Her Place in Literature," in *My Self, My Muse: Irish Women Poets Reflect on Life and Art*, edited by Patricia Boyle Haberstroh, Syracuse University Press, 2001, pp. 95–98.

SOURCES

Batten, Guinn, "Boland, McGuckian, Ni Chuilleanain and the Body of the Nation," in *The Cambridge Companion to Contemporary Irish Poetry*, edited by Matthew Campbell, Cambridge University Press, 2003, pp. 169–89.

Boland, Eavan, "Against Love Poetry," in *Against Love Poetry: Poems*, W. W. Norton, 2001, p. 5.

Browne, Joseph, "Eavan Boland," in *Dictionary of Literary Biography*, Vol. 40, *Poets of Great Britain and Ireland since 1960*, edited by Vincent B. Sherry Jr., Gale Research, 1985, pp. 36–41.

Delap, John, "Gender Roles and Domestic Violence in Ireland," in *World Student Christian Federation—Europe*, July 26, 2012, http://wscf-europe.org/mozaik-issues/mozaik-26-stop-being-silent/gender-roles-and-domestic-violence-in-ireland/ (accessed March 25, 2013).

"Eavan Boland," Poetry Foundation website, http://www.poetryfoundation.org/bio/eavan-boland (accessed March 25, 2013).

"The EU and Irish Women," European Commission website, http://ec.europa.eu/ireland/ireland_in_the_eu/impact_of_eu_on_irish_women/index_en.htm (accessed March 25, 2013).

Farren, Grainne, "The Essential Story of How Irish Women Cast Off Their Chains," Independent.ie website, May 21, 2006, http://www.independent.ie/entertainment/books-arts/the-essential-story-of-how-irish-women-cast-off-their-chains-26412042.html (accessed March 25, 2013).

"Feminism Now," in *Irish Times*, October 17, 2012, http://www.irishtimes.com/news/feminism-now-1.553554 (accessed March 25, 2013).

Kitchen, Judith, "Thinking About Love," in *Georgia Review*, Vol. 56, No. 2, Summer 2002, pp. 594–608.

Murphy, Bruce F., Review of *Against Love Poetry*, in *Poetry*, Vol. 181, No. 5, March 2003, pp. 347–49.

Newman, Cathy, "Ireland's Abortion Law is Virtually Meaningless," in *Telegraph*, http://www.telegraph.co.uk/women/womens-politics/9755082/Irelands-abortion-law-is-virtually-meaningless.html (accessed March 25, 2013).

"Prose Poem," Poets.org website, http://www.poets.org/viewmedia.php/prmMID/5787 (accessed March 25, 2013).

Quinn, Justin, "Feminism and Irish Poetry," in *The Cambridge Introduction to Modern Irish Poetry, 1800–2000*, Cambridge University Press, 2008, pp. 161–74.

Rehak, Melanie, "Map of Love," in *New York Times*, November 4, 2001, https://www.nytimes.com/2001/11/04/books/map-of-love.html?src=pm (accessed March 25, 2013).

Rengel, Marian, "Ireland," in *Encyclopedia of Birth Control*, Oryx Press, 2000, pp. 122–23.

Wheatley, David, "Irish Poetry into the Twenty-First Century," in *The Cambridge Companion to Contemporary Irish Poetry*, edited by Matthew Campbell, Cambridge University Press, 2003, pp. 250–67.

FURTHER READING

Davis, Wes, ed. *An Anthology of Modern Irish Poetry*, Belknap Press of Harvard University Press, 2010.
> Davis collects poetry from numerous poets from the twentieth and twenty-first centuries, and includes work by well-known poets, Nobel prize winners, and lesser-known poets.

McCarthy, John P., *Twenty-First Century Ireland: A View from America*, Academica Press, 2012.
> McCarthy explores modern-day Ireland's political, economic, social, and religious issues.

McDowell, Gary L., and F. Daniel Rzicznek, eds., *The Rose Metal Press Field Guide to Prose Poetry: Contemporary Poets in Discussion and Practice*, Rose Metal Press, 2010.
> McDowell and Rzicznek collect essays and poems by practitioners of the art of prose poetry. The poets discuss the definition and parameters of prose poetry, the reasons poets choose this form, and other elements of their craft. The collection also includes a selection of prose poems.

Pelan, Rebecca, *Two Irelands: Literary Feminisms North and South*, Syracuse University Press, 2005.
> Pelan offers an analysis of the way such factors as religion, regionalism, class, and cultural identity have shaped the development of feminism in Northern Ireland and the Irish Republic.

SUGGESTED SEARCH TERMS

Boland AND Against Love Poetry

Boland AND modern Irish poetry

Irish Women's Liberation Movement

Ireland AND feminism

modern prose poetry

Ireland AND Catholic views on marriage

Boland AND creative nonfiction

Ireland AND gender roles

Boland AND Eilean Ni Chuilleanain

Irish poetry AND nationalism

Blandeur

KAY RYAN

1997

In "Blandeur," Kay Ryan presents an unusual request: she asks God to make life less vivid. Suggesting numerous ways in which God might reshape the earth's landscape to lessen its grandeur, Ryan paints an evocative tableau of the upheaval required to achieve a neutral state. In one deft move at the end, Ryan shifts her attention from exterior landscapes to interior ones, asking God to relieve people's hearts.

Ryan is known for packing musicality, word-play, dense rhyme, wit, and melancholy into slender poems of ideas. Many critics have therefore characterized her poems as compressed—while their surface is accessible, her slim lines hide many layers of artistry and meaning. First published in the *New Yorker* in 1997, "Blandeur" is exemplary of Ryan's poetic technique and thematic palette, as well as her gift for surprising and intriguing readers. The poem appears in Ryan's fifth collection, *Say Uncle* (2000), and in her Pulitzer Prize–winning collection *The Best of It: New and Selected Poems* (2010).

AUTHOR BIOGRAPHY

Not unlike her deceptively simple poems, the career of poet Kay Ryan exemplifies quiet surprise. A remedial writing teacher at a community college, Ryan did not become a poet until age thirty and did not produce her first book until

Kay Ryan *(© John Lamparski | WireImage | Getty Images)*

she was nearly forty. She proceeded to produce poetry that diverges from that of many postmodern contemporaries, offering slender, plainlanguage yet highly musical poems that flirt with formal meter and make extensive use of rhyme. She labored for years in relative obscurity, but in 2008, despite a reputation for being a more withdrawn poet, Ryan was chosen to serve as US poet laureate. In 2011, Ryan won both the Pulitzer Prize for Poetry, for her collection *The Best of It: New and Selected Poems*, and a MacArthur Fellowship, better known as the "Genius Grant."

The daughter of an oil driller, Ryan was born Kay Pedersen on September 21, 1945, in San Jose, California. Ryan spent her youth in the more remote parts of Southern California—the San Joaquin Valley and the Mojave Desert. The influence of this terrain is evident in "Blandeur" and, more broadly, in her poetic style and themes. Ryan attended Antelope Valley College before transferring to the University of California at Los Angeles. She received both a BA (1967) and an MA (1968) in English literature. Since 1971, she has lived in Marin County, California, where she has taught remedial English at the College of Marin in Kentfield. In 1976, she took some time off from teaching to embark on a "bikecentennial," riding from Oregon to Virginia, in order to contemplate whether or not to become a poet. As she wrote in an essay published in *Zyzzyva* in 1998, a transcendent experience in the Colorado mountains reduced the previously loaded decision to one simple question: "*Do you like it?*" The answer was yes, and "that was all there was to it."

With the help of her partner Carol Adair and friends, she self-published her first volume of poetry, *Dragon Acts to Dragon Ends*, in 1983. Two years later, her first commercially published collection, *Strangely Marked Metal*, was released. Her third collection, *Flamingo Watching*, appeared in 1994, and it was with this volume that "she had fully assimilated her influences and fashioned her signature style," writes Paul Lake in the *Dictionary of Literary Biography*. "Blandeur" (1997) was published in the *New Yorker* before appearing in her fifth collection, *Say Uncle* (2000). The poem would appear again in her Pulitzer–winning collection *The Best of It*. Aside from that volume, one of Ryan's best-known collections is *The Niagara River* (2005).

Ryan has won numerous awards, including a 2001 National Endowment for the Arts fellowship, the 2004 Ruth Lilly Poetry Prize, and a 2004 Guggenheim Fellowship. Her work has been included in three Pushcart Prize anthologies and four volumes of *The Best American Poetry*. She has served as a chancellor of the Academy of American Poets since 1996, and she completed two terms as US poet laureate, from 2008 to 2010. In that capacity, her primary project was the revitalization of literature programs at community colleges.

As she told Barbara Chai in an interview for *Speakeasy*, a blog of the *Wall Street Journal*, Ryan began compiling *The Best of It* when Adair, her partner of thirty years, was diagnosed with terminal cancer. Adair did not survive to see its publication; she died in 2009.

POEM SUMMARY

The text used for this summary is from *Say Uncle*, Grove Press, 2000, p. 10. A version of the poem can be found on the following web page: http://www.poetryfoundation.org/poem/172276.

As Ryan says when she introduces the poem on the Poetry Foundation website, *blandeur* is a word she made up because there was no existing word to capture the sense of sensory deprivation that she longs for. As it is fashioned from the nearly opposite words *bland* and *grandeur*, the title has a sense of playfulness to it. It also encapsulates the primary paradox of the poem: Can the bland be grand? If God granted the poet's request, would that be desirable?

"Blandeur" consists of a single stanza of twenty lines comprising five sentences. The sentences are written in the imperative tense—the poet is making a request or plea that her primary audience, God, *do* something. Thus, "Blandeur" can be considered a prayer or appeal.

Though the poem does not adhere rigidly to a formal meter, much of it is written in dimeter; that is, many lines consist of two feet (the smallest rhythmic units within poetry) of two or three syllables each. Moreover, no line contains more than four words, and almost half of the lines contain only two words. The compactness of each line, and of the poem itself, reinforces its stated desire that less happen. This also produces a sense of understatement that contrasts with the enormity of what the poet is asking for.

The poem loosely employs "sprung rhythm," a rhythmic structure developed by Gerard Manley Hopkins (1844–1889). It is characterized by feet of a variable number of syllables with the emphasis always falling on the first syllable, as in the word urgent; this is a *trochee*, a stressed followed by an unstressed syllable. In "Blandeur," a sense of urgency is precisely what this rhythm contributes. Sprung rhythm characterizes most lines and nearly all of the verbs in the poem. This gives the poem and its commands a heft and weight, creating a latent power in each word that is heightened by Ryan's conciseness. The result is that a godlike authority is lent to Ryan's own voice.

The first two lines comprise a single sentence and state the poet's argument, which she elaborates on in the subsequent lines. The formality of

her address in the first line has an archaic ring to it. This style of supplication lends the poet an air of humility—which she later undermines through her commands—and a sense that the problem the poet is addressing is not particular to the present condition. It is an old problem, one that perhaps dates back to the earth's creation. This style of address also seems to place her in the company of a long-standing poetic tradition.

Line 2 presents the poet's unusual request, the irony of which will be borne out in the following lines. Beginning with line 3, which starts the second sentence, the poet suggests that God reshape the earth to remove its most extreme features, smoothing its round surface, using force to flatten Eiger, one of the peaks of the Swiss Alps, and making the Grand Canyon less beautiful. Marking a subtle shift in the author's tone, the gentle language of the first image gives way to the more visceral word *flatten* in the fourth line and the made-up word *blanden*, a variation on the title, in the fifth. With these words, Ryan also introduces one of the most prominent near rhymes of the poem.

With the third sentence, which begins on line 7, the poet's requests become a litany of imperatives. God really got things wrong, it seems. Valleys should be raised; rifts should be widened so that they can be farmed and lived on; glaciers should be sent back, their calving silenced. Notably, the word *calving* has a double meaning. While it refers to a mass of ice breaking off a larger mass, it can also mean to produce a calf or give birth. Though the first is the more literally appropriate definition, it is the latter image that comes to mind when Ryan orders silence.

In lines 15–17, Ryan gives a general instruction that could solve the whole problem: God should halve or double all of the earth's features in order to average them out, resulting, one can only infer, in a landscape fairly devoid of distinction. *Mean* in this context most explicitly refers to the average. Upon further inspection, the line blossoms with implications. *Mean* also brings to mind *harsh*, an adjective which might befit the poet's purportedly neutral landscape. It could also refer to *meaning* or *intention*. One wonders if, in Ryan's view, this averaging of the earth would distill it to its essence, its most essential state of being—in other words, to its meaning.

Line 18 is composed of a single sentence, the shortest one in the poem. In this line and the first part of line 19, Ryan shifts from trochaic to predominantly iambic rhythm, with feet of an unstressed followed by a stressed syllable, as in Ryan's newly coined imperative *unlean*. These departures of form accentuate line 18's uniqueness in the poem. While Ryan's propositions so far have been fairly extreme ones, this line packs the biggest punch, as it is here that Ryan reveals her motivation. The extreme features that she witnesses in the world, and which bear evidence of God's hand, she also feels in the heart. It is too much to bear, she implies. This revelation strikes the reader precisely because she gives only the briefest glimpse of it. She does not elaborate, and she even dampens a bit the intimacy it offers by referring to hearts collectively, using the plural pronoun *our*. In so doing, however, she suggests a universal desire to be relieved of intense feelings.

The shift to iambic rhythm makes lines 18 and 19 teem with a sudden emotion, as *unlean* and *withdraw* contrast in sound and sense with the visceral imperatives of force earlier in the poem. The reader may register an understated longing or pleading in the new rhythm.

With lines 19 and 20, which present the fifth and final sentence of the poem, Ryan concludes her prayer with a summation of her request for God to tame his intensity. However, in this sentence, she asks him not to reshape anything but to remove or retreat—to withdraw his grandeur.

With the final line, the poet suggests that both exterior and interior spaces need relief.

THEMES

Perception
In an interview with Josephine Reed for the National Endowment for the Arts radio program *ArtWorks*, Ryan explained the origin of "Blandeur":

> Blandeur is just the opposite of grandeur. And I found it on a yellow Post-It beside my bed in the morning. So I guess it was a little middle of the night inspiration. So I thought about what blandeur would be. And another one of my characteristic ambitions is to have less and to make, to make the world less sensational, to reduce the excess input. I remember once—this is a terribly sad story. Once a couple leapt from the Golden Gate Bridge and left in their car a note, which said, among other things, "Life was too vivid for us." And this is a poem for people who find life excessively vivid.

In another interview, appearing in *Publishers Weekly*, Ryan told Craig Morgan Teicher that her own home north of San Francisco was "almost unbearably picturesque." Ryan seems to long for the open spaces of the desert but without its harsh beauty. She envisions remolding the earth to remove its most visually arresting features. Interestingly, nature's way of averaging out its most extreme features—for instance, glaciers melting to the point that they begin to break apart—is still too much for Ryan. The glaciers must be sent away and silenced.

Ryan's desire for such sensory deprivation is unexpected because most people relish the sensory experience produced by the features she seeks to eliminate; most people find the earth's grandeur inspiring, and many poets have paid tribute to it. Blandness is generally an unwanted quality. But Ryan exalts it, and the privileged place she gives it is embodied in the new term she creates, *blandeur*.

Landscape
"I think that most writing is an effort to save one's life," Ryan told Reed in the *ArtWorks* interview. Interestingly, Ryan equates this task with an attempt to stake out a terrain:

> I think we are trying to find a place where we can live. You know, mark out a little territory for ourselves that is congenial to us. So that lots of times, my poems are trying to find a place where I can breathe.

TOPICS FOR FURTHER STUDY

- Write a poem in which you take a popular sentiment and express a desire for the opposite. Try to keep the poem mostly impersonal, but include one or two lines that hint at a deeper personal implication.

- Lead a class discussion in which you compare Gerard Manley Hopkins's poem "God's Grandeur" to Ryan's "Blandeur." What similarities and differences do you note between the two? Which poem do you find more compelling, and why? Be sure to address what you think are the most difficult aspects of each poem.

- "I've always been extremely enamored of cartoons and cartooning, in which you have essentially just the outline," Ryan told Andrea Seabrook in an interview for the National Public Radio program *All Things Considered.* She added, "I think if you leave something empty but charged in some way, not overly elaborated, you can have a surprising number of things come out of people when they read it." Browse through the book *Poetry Comics: An Animated Anthology* (2002), by Dave Morice, paying special attention to the poems by Emily Dickinson and Marianne Moore. Work with a small group to create a comic version of "Blandeur."

- Choose one of the geographic features that Ryan describes in "Blandeur," research its history, and create a website dedicated to that feature. Be sure to discuss its geologic origin, cultural significance, and whether or not that feature will continue to change over time. Include your sources and links to additional images and information, making sure that all sources are reliable.

Readers might wonder why, unless the poet suffers from migraine headaches, she would find nature's feasts of the senses so intrusive. The key to the question would seem to lie in line 18, when Ryan moves from discussing physical landscapes to metaphysical ones—the terrain of the heart.

Prior to this, the bulk of "Blandeur" is devoted to asking—or perhaps telling—God to rework his landscapes to make them more bland. Many of the landscapes that Ryan suggests need repair might be considered fairly static; one does not think of the Grand Canyon and Eiger, much less the earth's roundness, as being occurrences, as being things that have happened. And yet at the outset of her poem, Ryan asks for less to happen, and she then essentially lists such features as example offenders. The result is a logical jolt that alerts the reader to the notion that something else may be going on in the poem.

One possibility is that Ryan's sense of time in this poem is vast. While things like the Grand Canyon do not "happen" at a rate by which humans can witness them, they do in fact happen over long periods of time. Perhaps what Ryan seeks is a cosmic reversal of the circumstances in which humans find themselves. Whereas it seems that Ryan is asking the impossible, her proposal becomes somewhat more feasible when one considers the changes that may take place to a landscape and a planet over millions of years. This sense of expansive time is at once supported by the wide scope of Ryan's perspective—almost godlike, she surveys the earth in a few sweeping glances—and simultaneously undermined by her understated urgency.

The more immediately evident explanation for the sense of the poem is that the exterior landscape's extremes are reflective of interior ones. Ryan devotes her discussion of physical landscapes to cold heights, such as snowy Eiger and terrifying glaciers, and low points of all kinds—valleys, fissures, and the Grand Canyon. Line 18 connects these features to the heart, and the reader suspects that the highs and lows of emotional experience are actually what the poet longs to be freed of. In this context, the request of line 2 makes more sense, and the subsequent discussion of physical landscapes may be viewed more metaphorically. That is, the physical extremes are concrete representations of emotional extremes.

Lest readers become too comfortable with this interpretation, however, and attempt to reduce her poem to terms too simplistic, her last line offers ambiguity. What does the pronoun *these* refer to? People's hearts or the physical landscapes? The colloquial, or common-language, phrase *these parts* refers to a locality or region where the speaker lives. Given the

Ryan uses the image of the Grand Canyon as an example of the grandeur of nature. *(© Josemaria Toscano / Shutterstock.com)*

ambiguity, the poem's closing would seem to encompass both terrains. They are both evidence, Ryan seems to say, of a God too showy, too intense, too close—a sense reinforced by her final two verbs: *unlean* and *withdraw*.

STYLE

Wordplay

One of the signature elements of "Blandeur," and of Ryan's poetry in general, is wordplay. The title, a combination of the adjective *bland* and the noun *grandeur*, is the primary example in this case, and the poem is an exploration of the idea behind the word. By borrowing from *grandeur* the -*eur*, a honeyed French suffix that essentially serves the same function as -*ness*, bland becomes beautiful. Ryan also refashions bland into the verb *blanden*, which brings to mind *soften* or *lighten*.

In a sense, Ryan's play with language embodies the ideas she presents in the poem. Much as she asks God to reshape his landscape,

making high things lower and low things higher, Ryan reshapes words, raising the status of the lowly word *bland* and lowering that of the lofty word *grandeur*. At the same time, the wordplay gives the poem a lightness that belies a more serious message.

Rhyme

Contributing to the poem's deceptive playfulness is the extensive use of rhyme. Ryan commonly uses what she calls "recombinant rhyme." These recombinant rhymes repeat vowel sounds, a device known as assonance, as well as consonants, known as consonance. The result is the presence of "hidden rhymes" in which each word may appear at the beginning or in the middle of a line as well as at the end.

"Blandeur" is saturated with these recombinant rhymes. In fact, it is the rare word in the poem that does not employ some manner of rhyme. Most immediately evident are plays on *blandeur* or *blanden*. Words that present a syllable characterized by a short *a* sound—be it -*ap*, -*and*, -*at*, -*al*, or -*ar*—followed by an -*en* sound can be seen in lines 2, 4, 5, and 6, while variations using only one or the other of the sounds can be found in lines 3, 7, 10, 11, 13, 14, 15, 16, and 19. Ryan's play with these sounds produces a visceral sensibility. The verbs that use them acquire a slight air of *onomatopoeia*, producing a sound that almost seems to enact the word's meaning, as in *flatten, blanden, widen,* and *remand.*

Variations on the -er, -eur, -or, and -air sounds also recur, appearing in lines 3, 4, 5, 8, 9, 10, 11, 12, 14, 15, 16, 17, 18, and 19. Other notable recombinant rhymes employ the long *i* sound. Taken together, Ryan's vowels draw the mouth high and wide, creating a sonic expansiveness that mirrors her broad vision. The sounds echo across the poem, much as they might the Grand Canyon. Moreover, Ryan's shifting, slight altering, and recombining of vowel and consonant sounds mimics the reshaping of the landscape that she advocates. By contrast, the precise rhymes that link *mean* and *unlean, hearts* and *parts,* and *grandeur* and *blandeur* give the poem's closing a clarity and finality even as her final lines seem to lift from the page.

HISTORICAL CONTEXT

The Turn of the Millennium and Popular Culture

In 1997, when "Blandeur" was published, the world was anticipating the passage of two simultaneous historical milestones: the turn of the century and the turn of the millennium according to the Gregorian calendar, also known as the Western calendar. While not all cultures use the Gregorian calendar—a notable alternative is the Chinese calendar—most nations use it for business if not for traditional holidays. Some argued that the turn of the millennium should actually have been marked in 2001, as the Gregorian calendar has no year zero. Nevertheless, most people viewed the turn from 1999 to 2000 as the moment of cultural significance.

This historical moment was widely anticipated in popular culture for years prior to its arrival. Some of the earliest depictions of the year 2000 were utopian in vision, as was Edward Bellamy's 1888 science-fiction novel *Looking Backward: 2000–1887* and French artist Villemard's 1910 postcards depicting a whimsical, technology-driven Paris in the year 2000. Later

portrayals were frequently dystopian. Even in the early days of motion pictures, film artists projected fears about science and social evolution onto a twenty-first-century landscape. Set in the year 2000, German director Fritz Lang's classic silent film *Metropolis* (1927) features an evil scientist and a sinister robot in a socially controlled, classist, and racist society. Filmmaker Stanley Kubrick encapsulated fears about technology and the course of human evolution in his futuristic 1968 film *2001: A Space Odyssey.* Subsequent decades brought a slew of apocalyptic and post-apocalyptic films set in the near future, from James Cameron's *The Terminator* (1984) to Roland Emmerich's *Independence Day* (1996).

Music, too, evidenced a cultural fascination with the turn of the century. In 1980, the punk rock band the Ramones released their iconic album *End of the Century.* The title is taken from the song "Do You Remember Rock 'n' Roll Radio?," in which the Ramones envision the death of rock music. The title track of Prince's 1982 hit album *1999* is an apocalyptic party song that declares, "Two thousand zero zero party over, oops out of time / So tonight I'm gonna party like it's 1999." Not surprisingly, the song experienced a revival in 1999, as did rock band R.E.M.'s upbeat apocalyptic anthem "The End of the World as We Know It (and I Feel Fine)" (1987).

Pop culture's apocalyptic visions of the turn of the millennium took root in the popular psyche with the emergence of the Y2K phenomenon, which *Time* magazine dubbed one of the "Top 10 End-of-the-World Prophecies." In 1999, society had fairly recently become dependent on intricate computer networks for everything from power to financial management. However, computers had been designed with a fatal flaw: they used only the last two digits of the years instead of all four. Analysts thus speculated that the change from 1999 to 2000 would hijack the networks, spawning widespread fear of global insecurity. As *New York Times* op-ed contributor Denis Dutton wrote,

> Haywire navigation controls might cause aircraft to fall from the skies. Electricity grids, water systems and telephone networks would be knocked out, while nuclear power plants would be subject to meltdown. Savings and pension accounts would be wiped out in a general bank failure. A cascade of breakdowns in communication and commerce would create vast shortages of food and medicine, which would, in turn,

COMPARE
&
CONTRAST

- **1990s:** Nature tourism—travel to unspoiled places to enjoy nature and natural wonders—has long been a popular pastime. In the wake of concerns about environmental sustainability, ecotourism becomes the fastest-growing sector of the tourism industry, according to the Center for Responsible Travel. *Ecotourism* is defined as "travel to natural areas that conserves the environment and improves the welfare of local people."

  Today: Natural wonders continue to draw travelers. According to the National Park Service, US national parks draw approximately 280 million visitors every year. The Center for Responsible Travel reports that ecotourism is a $77-billion industry and is experiencing double-digit growth.

- **1990s:** Global climate change and the melting of the polar ice caps become major concerns to scientists but are politically controversial in the United States. In 1997, nations across the globe sign the Kyoto Protocol, an international agreement to lower emissions of greenhouse gases. The United States is the only country to sign the Kyoto Protocol but not ratify it, making its principles essentially null within the nation.

  Today: Global warming climate change is widely accepted as reality. In 2010, President Barack Obama introduces targets for reduced greenhouse-gas emissions from federal operations. Combating climate change is a primary component of the energy policy Obama advocates in his second term as president. In 2012, the University of Calgary reports that Arctic ice-cap melting has reached a record high.

- **1990s:** Ryan produces two volumes of poetry, *Flamingo Watching* and *Elephant Rocks*, and begins to see her work published in periodicals such as the *New Yorker*. Nevertheless, her work remains relatively unknown.

  Today: Ryan is one of the most celebrated poets of the day, having served two terms as US poet laureate. Given her newfound readership, she reintroduces earlier poems in the volume *The Best of It: New and Selected Poems*, which wins her the Pulitzer Prize in 2011.

---

produce riots, lawlessness and social collapse. Even worse, ICBMs [intercontinental ballistic missiles] might rise from their silos unbidden, spreading death across the globe.

Religious groups seized on Y2K as the fulfillment of prophecy, and as Dutton noted,

> The Y2K catastrophe was promoted with increasing shrillness toward century's end. . . . *Vanity Fair*'s January 1999 article "The Y2K Nightmare" caught the sensationalist tone, claiming that "folly, greed and denial" had "muffled two decades of warnings from technology experts."

Many individuals stockpiled food, water, batteries, and other emergency supplies in anticipation.

Programmers across the globe worked tirelessly to mitigate the impending disaster, and as Dutton reported, the United States spent upwards of $100 billion on fixes. Yet even in countries that had essentially ignored the issue, the event came and went with hardly a blip in normal functioning.

Seen within this context, "Blandeur" is interesting in that it presents its own version of the apocalyptic vision that so enthralled the culture of the time. In "Blandeur," Ryan envisions the earth being leveled, stripped, and made neutral. She invites this change, suggesting that the world as it is is too overwhelming.

The narrator wants the sound of glaciers splitting to be silenced. *(© Joshua Raif / Shutterstock.com)*

Most apocalyptic portrayals critique a world where science and technology have run amok, devastated nature, and nearly destroyed humanity. In "Blandeur," nature itself has run rampant; its grandeur has become overbearing and threatens internal peace. Thus, Ryan calls for a do-over.

Ryan's take is provocative in another historical sense: it anticipated a sense of overstimulation that became culturally significant in the wake of technologies such as the iPhone. First released in 2007, the iPhone brought constant access to media and the Internet to the fingertips of more than 100 million people within four years and spurred the development of a host of competing smartphones. The impact on lifestyle has been so significant that it has prompted scientists to study the effects of constant stimulation on the brain. For Ryan, writing a decade before the iPhone injected everyday experience with constant streams of information, this problem exceeds technology. Rather, it is built into our environment. Everywhere one looks, she suggests, there is too much.

CRITICAL OVERVIEW

Although she published her first book twenty-five years earlier, Ryan was relatively little-known until she won the poet laureate post in 2008. As Adam Kirsch notes in the *New Yorker*, "Kay Ryan has become a famous poet in much the same way Ernest Hemingway described a man going broke: 'gradually and then suddenly.'" In a review of *The Best of It* published in *Contemporary Poetry Review*, Rick Joines points out that "if we didn't know her it is because she was never much interested in knowing us." An intentional literary outsider, Ryan herself has often stated that she struggled with accepting the poetic calling; she told Reed, "It was very embarrassing to me.... If you write well, you are utterly exposed.... I wanted to be somebody with a pickup truck."

Nonetheless, Ryan's work eventually found a champion in poet and critic Dana Gioia, who offered the first serious review of her work in the *Dark Horse* in 1998. She writes,

Over the past five years no new poet has so deeply impressed me with her imaginative flair or originality as Kay Ryan.... Like Dickinson, Ryan has found a way of exploring ideas without losing either the musical impulse or imaginative intensity necessary to lyric poetry.

Ryan's slender yet charged poems, often characterized as compressed, have since drawn numerous comparisons to Dickinson as well as Robert Frost, Marianne Moore, Elizabeth Bishop, Amy Clampitt, and even piano composer Erik Satie, famous for his humorous miniatures.

Published in 2000, *Say Uncle* received a handful of serious reviews, all of them laudatory. In a review in *Poetry*, David Yezzi compares Ryan's poems to "*pastilles*, lemon drops hard enough to cut your lip on." Yezzi notes an "ineffable quality" in the poems arising from Ryan's

> concerted musicality, playful linguistic association, tonal range, and crisp imagery,... all taking her poems beyond the mere rational essaying of a subject, and leaving the reader elevated or changed or moved but at a loss to say precisely how this effect has been wrought.

In a piece for the *Alsop Review*, Jack Foley calls the poems of *Say Uncle* "something slightly to the left of Ogden Nash" and makes note of her verse's tension between light and darkness:

> We can find its rhyming "delightful"—as indeed it often is—and simply skip the "message" of the poems. That would of course be a considerable misreading—but it is a misreading which Ryan encourages in some respects. Her poems are in a constant state of subversiveness. The dark vision at their heart is an endless commentary on their apparently "light" form, yet their light form disguises the genuine horror which haunts them.

Critics later registered this tension in the highly acclaimed Pulitzer-winning selected volume *The Best of It*, in which "Blandeur" also appears. Referring specifically to this volume, Joines writes, "The greatest works by the greatest writers constantly remind us of our tragedies big and small.... But living well, and writing well, requires a little levity."

New Yorker critic Kirsch perhaps best understood this impulse in Ryan's work, stating,

> Melancholy lucidity is Ryan's greatest gift.... But her most startling discovery is that melancholy, with its tendency to brood and spread, is best contained in a form that is tight, witty, almost sprightly sounding. Her poems are often built on the logic of the pun, taking an ordinary word or dead cliché as a title and then jolting it to unexpected life.

In addition to puns and clichés, Ryan's poems often center around ideas, objects, and elements of nature, as does "Blandeur." "These subjects, though, always reflect back on the human," notes *Women's Review of Books* contributor Wendy Vardaman. She adds, "In what may be her overarching theme, Ryan asks us to consider our own smallness, our difficulty in conceptualizing this smallness and contextualizing ourselves, and the concept of scale itself."

Critics have also noted a tone of detachment in Ryan's poetry, a symptom perhaps of her impulse to avoid exposure. Ryan rarely uses the pronoun *I*, "the standard pronoun of contemporary poetry, and one Dickinson used without hesitation," as Jay Rogoff notes in the *Southern Review*. In "Blandeur," as in numerous other poems, Ryan prefers the first-person plural, using *our* instead of *my*. As Rogoff states,

> While Dickinson hid in her house, Ryan hides in her poems.... Her stances feel far more armored and impersonal.... The impression of personal feeling in Ryan's poetry results, paradoxically, not from her accounts of psychological experience, but from the eccentricities of her technique.... Her rhyming creates surprising, imaginary relationships among words and their referents that recall Gerard Manley Hopkins, and her sonic patterns can produce aural anagrams that rival his own "And wears man's smudge and shares man's smell" from "God's Grandeur."

Notably, a number of critics have suggested that "Blandeur" is in fact a response to Hopkins's "God's Grandeur," in which the poet characteristically hails nature as evidence of God's greatness.

In an overview of Ryan's style published in *American Scholar*, Langdon Hammer notes another quality that is characteristic of "Blandeur." Pointing out that Ryan's "language is plain but crowded with internal rhymes that create complex networks of sound, and the syntax is compressed, making those short lines extremely dense," Hammer concludes, "Ryan's poems reflect back on their own activity in ways that make the poem itself a model of the experience or idea it investigates."

CRITICISM

Andrea Betts

Betts is a freelance writer specializing in literature. In the following essay, she examines the layers of paradox in "Blandeur" to gain insight into Ryan's unusual perspective.

WHAT DO I READ NEXT?

- Ryan's Pulitzer Prize–winning collection *The Best of It: New and Selected Poems* (2010) offers readers a thorough survey of the first three decades of her poetic career.

- "Blandeur" is often said to be a response to Gerard Manley Hopkins's poem "God's Grandeur" (1918). The poem can be found online or in almost any collection of Hopkins's poetry, such as *Gerard Manley Hopkins: The Major Works*, published in 2002.

- Indian poet Maya Khosla explores the significance of nature's extremes in "Mount St. Helens," one of the poems in her acclaimed collection of nature poetry *Keel Bone* (2003).

- Interested in extremes of all kinds, Ryan often used the Ripley's Believe It or Not! series of books as inspiration for her poetry. *Ripley's Believe It or Not! In Celebration . . . A Special Reissue of the Original!* (2004) presents a facsimile of the original 1929 book.

- Designed for a young-adult readership, *Earth-Shattering Poems* (1998), edited by Liz Rosenberg, is a collection of poems spanning centuries and continents that express the emotional intensity of everyday experience.

- The National Geographic book *Visions of Earth: Beauty, Majesty, Wonder* (2011) presents stunning photographs highlighting the magnificence of the planet and its inhabitants.

Upon a first (or second, or third) reading, "Blandeur" seems an exercise in reverse psychology. Like an overconfident home remodeler, Ryan surveys her domain and blithely lays out plans to rectify all of earth's "defects." To which we want to respond: *Don't change a thing.* The neutral, featureless, place of "blandeur" hardly appeals. To the contrary, it borders on institutional. What would life be like without the

> PEELING AT THE CORNER OF A PARADOX IN 'BLANDEUR' REVEALS LAYER AFTER LAYER OF CONTRADICTIONS, DRAWING THE READER INTO A QUEST TO EXCAVATE THIS MOST EXQUISITE AND CURIOUS MIND."

immense beauty of the Grand Canyon, the imposing presence of Eiger? The curiosity of valleys and rifts and glaciers, and the way these landscapes quicken the pulse and slow the breath? Even when it is transposed onto the landscape of the heart, one feels that Ryan's proposition simply will not do. These highs and lows of experience, the leanings we feel on the heart, are what make life worth living.

We swiftly conclude that we shouldn't take Ryan at her word—that despite her understated tone, the grandeur of her vision for blandeur is intentionally, if succinctly, overstated, cleverly designed to elicit a contrarian response. Yet when Ryan discusses "Blandeur," she says it reflects a major (and earnest) impulse in her poetry—a desire for sensory deprivation, for less, quiet, emptiness. She told Josephine Reed in an interview for *ArtWorks*:

> So many times I'm calling for less, kind of the anti Oliver Twist, you know, "Less please." Wasn't it Oliver Twist, who holds up his bowl and says, "More please?" Yeah, I'm holding up my bowl and saying, "Take some out, please." [laughs]" Make life quieter." That's really the impulse in "Blandeur." It's saying: lessen the grandeur of life. Of course, the opposite is exposed. By the asking for less, you expose how much there is.

While Ryan acknowledges the paradox, the primary urge at work in the poem is her craving for minimalism. This desire, evident in numerous poems of Ryan's, is often projected onto landscapes or depicted as a tangible space or thing. In "Patience," Ryan portrays waiting—by definition, a state of stillness and inaction—as an expansive, sustainable land with rivers, harvests, and natives. Emptiness, according to Ryan in the poem of that title, is like the myth of the American West: while it seems endless, it is in fact an indefensible, finite territory that has been abused. In "Nothing Ventured," Ryan states that nothing is indivisible matter, a solid block.

Ryan's stance toward the notion of less is peculiar to say the least, particularly as revealed in "Blandeur." It causes readers to wonder: who is this Kay Ryan, and why does she seek such relief? And there is still this lingering sense that she is toying with us. She uses made-up, silly-sounding words. She makes them rhyme. Her most compelling image—that of a glacier giving birth to a calf—is at once terrifying and slightly absurd.

This may be what Jay Rogoff is getting at when he remarks in the *Southern Review* that "the impression of personal feeling in Ryan's poetry results, paradoxically, not from her accounts of psychological experience but from the eccentricities of her technique." Peeling at the corner of a paradox in "Blandeur" reveals layer after layer of contradictions, drawing the reader into a quest to excavate this most exquisite and curious mind.

Ryan is known to be a literary outsider, and in some ways, "Blandeur" seems to be a playful jab at the poetic institution. Ryan's treatment of landscape begs a comparison to the English romantic poetry of the late eighteenth and early nineteenth centuries. Romanticism valued intuition and emotion over reason and rejected the impersonal aesthetic of the classical arts. Most of all, the English romantic poets viewed nature as a gateway to the sublime—an elusive, ecstatic, and transcendent experience or state, one of connection with a divine spirit that animates nature and underlies all of human consciousness. As encounter with the sublime became the poetic ideal, English romantic poets like William Wordsworth, Samuel Taylor Coleridge, and William Blake devoted the bulk of their romantic attention to pastoral landscapes and nature's extremes. The grandeur of God and nature was their touchstone. Notably, many romantics found nature's extremes terrifying; for some, in fact, terror was the hallmark of the sublime. Yet it was in their presence that one found freedom from the weight of the world.

Wordsworth laments man's collective detachment from nature in his famous sonnet "The World Is Too Much with Us." Ryan would seem to stop him at the first line: the world is too much with us, period. Interestingly, both this poem and "Blandeur" refer to the status of our hearts. Wordsworth says that we have given our hearts away to materialism. To the contrary, Ryan seems to say, the weight of God is oppressing us. Whereas Wordsworth feels lighter in the presence of nature's extremes, Ryan feels heavier.

And yet, of course, Ryan's poem maintains a lightness—that sly humor achieved through her wordplay, rhyme, and sonic effects. Borrowing romanticism's most beloved term, Ryan told Reed, "I don't separate the funny from the serious. I absolutely don't. I don't see any distance between the ridiculous and the sublime. I think the sublime is ridiculous and the ridiculous is sublime."

Given its stylistic technique, "Blandeur" is likely speaking even more directly to a descendant of the romantics—and one of Ryan's forebears—Gerard Manley Hopkins. Hopkins, a Jesuit priest, was known for his poems exalting nature as evidence of God's greatness. Ryan may be responding specifically to his famous poem "God's Grandeur," first published in 1918. Much like Wordsworth's "The World Is Too Much with Us," "God's Grandeur" laments man's detachment from nature and God. As with most of Hopkins's work, this poem makes extensive use of alliteration (the repetition of initial consonants), assonance, and end/internal rhyme—devices near and dear to Ryan. It also makes use of Hopkins's "sprung rhythm," the sonic structure that Ryan employs in "Blandeur."

In Ryan's poem, such sonic devices both reinforce and undermine her message. On one hand, her shifting rhyme and wordplay enact the reshaping experiment she advocates. On the other, in addition to lightening her serious message, the density of her sonic effects contributes to a strong sense of activity in a poem that asks for less to happen. This paradox is also reflected in her imagery. While she asks for less to happen, she advocates a wholesale reworking of the earth.

The great irony of Ryan's response to Hopkins and the romantics is that their values are challenged in Ryan's specific language but affirmed by the reader's contrarian reaction. With this paradox, Ryan creates a triangular relationship between herself, her poetic predecessors, and her readers—a distance that heightens her intrigue. We are none of us quite on the same page. Seeking to close the gap, to know something more of Ryan, we dig deeper.

Of course, the most personal line of the poem is line 18, when Ryan admits to a pressure on the heart—a heartache, or perhaps even

In "Blandeur," the poet calls for valleys to be made higher. (© *Iakov Kalinin | Shutterstock.com*)

heartbreak. Ryan does not elaborate, but might the images that precede it shed additional light on this single moment of personal revelation? The first concrete image of the poem is a strange one, that of God evening out the earth's roundness. While we come to understand Ryan to mean smoothing out its surface, one cannot help but call to mind a time when the world was thought to be flat. Just in case we don't make the association, Ryan helps us along with her next word, *flatten*. Is she seeking a time when our knowledge was less complete? A state of willful ignorance?

Ryan next turns to Eiger, a snowy peak in the Bernese Alps of Switzerland. Eiger is notoriously difficult to scale, earning it the nickname "Murder Wall" in German. Disturbingly, some climbers who have reached the top have frozen there. The name *Eiger* is related to the German *eigen*, a term which has multiple meanings, including "own" (as in, my own) and "separate." This last definition becomes significant when one considers that most all of the subsequent images in the poem deal with rifts. The Grand Canyon, the most celebrated rift of its kind, should not be so glorified. Valleys and fissures

must be undone. Splintering glaciers should be sent away and silenced.

The image of the glaciers calving is particularly troubling. The suggestion of giving birth (a common metaphor for writing) and the demand that it be silenced conjures an agonized scream. Separation and pain hang in the air. By stating that God should remand and silence the glaciers, Ryan again seems to be saying, "I don't want to know about it."

The conclusion of the poem's longest sentence advocates halving or doubling all the earth's features. Notably, halving suggests separation, while doubling connotes coupling or pairing. Moreover, the joining of two parts is embodied in Ryan's use of dimeter and the predominance of lines containing exactly two words. Given her desire to lessen, mend, or silence previous rifts, it would seem that Ryan is seeking wholeness or reunion.

Thus all along, the poem bears traces, however fine, of heartbreak. Of what nature we cannot be sure; Ryan was in a committed relationship for more than thirty years. But separation and icy coldness are persistent if subtle themes of the work. Does Ryan mourn the isolation of the poet's task? The loss or estrangement of a loved one? A series of such losses? One can only speculate, but Ryan would seem to have distinct occurrences in mind, since her first supplication is for less to happen. And here at the end, one senses a great irony in that first appeal. According to the bulk of the poem, the achievement of her vision requires substantial tumult. We sense an emotional charge both in the separation and the upheaval required to repair it.

Even in this most personal glimpse, Ryan reflects back a paradox. If we accept the theme of separation, Ryan suggests its universality in referring collectively to *our* hearts. "I am not alone in loneliness," she implies. Who are we to argue?

Source: Andrea Betts, Critical Essay on "Blandeur," in *Poetry for Students*, Gale, Cengage Learning, 2014.

Jay Rogoff

In the following excerpt, Rogoff praises Ryan's unique, eccentric style.

Just as a good poem collapses immensities of feeling or experience into a small space, a devotion to reading and writing poetry condenses time. Poets you consider your contemporaries, whose first books you recall reading with varying combinations of admiration and envy, suddenly stare out from their dust jackets with weathered faces, their laurels now a wreath of white hair, and you realize with a shock that all of you have sixty or more winters on your heads. Suddenly you hold in your hands the poet's "new and selected," where work from that first book, some of it still vivid in your memory, no longer marks the adventurous uncertainty of setting forth, but a first firm step toward a destination the poet continues to pursue and continually redefines.

In recent decades the new and selected volume has evolved into a shape as rigid as a bottle's, into which the poet has decanted the best or most representative of a career's worth of work. The shoulders may slope or ride high, the punt may vary in its depth, but our method of tasting remains constant: We uncork it and first sample the new poems, whose familiarity might bring comfort, or whose novelty might strike our palates as strange, then, as the poetry breathes, we leap back in time to early pressings, proceeding chronologically, book by book, through the poems the poet has selected as those likeliest to

"AN INTENSIVELY AURAL, RHYME-DENSE STYLE LIKE RYAN'S CAN SPRING TRAPS FOR THE POET WHEN FLAMBOYANT TECHNIQUE DRIVES THE POEM INSTEAD OF PROVIDING THE VEHICLE FOR IMAGINATIVE EVENT AND FEELING."

age most gracefully and enduringly, from youthful fruitiness to mature complexity. The analogy ends, of course, when we finish the selection, since we can lay the volume back down in the rack for cellaring until we wish to sample it anew, curious how renewed acquaintance will color our enjoyment of the cru while we anticipate vintages still awaiting the press.

Recent months have yielded several notable new and selecteds, with volumes by Kay Ryan, Robert Dana, and Edward Hirsch following the typical model, opening with their newest work, then returning to the poet's beginnings to move forward chronologically. Only Michael Jennings—less well known than the other poets—has followed the sometimes frustrating lead of Randall Jarrell by grouping his poems thematically, heedless of autobiography. Either approach can result in a satisfying volume, though, and each of these volumes contains work that should continue to bring immediate pleasure to the nose and a long finish to the palate.

In both her poetic development and her poetry itself, Kay Ryan offers the headiest intensity of these four poets. Because her first full book, *Flamingo Watching*, only appeared in 1994, when her voice had already matured, even the early work in *The Best of It: New and Selected Poems* (2010) shows a poet fully formed, with a consistent, identifiable style that for two decades has characterized one of contemporary poetry's most indulgent, most musical ears. Her idiosyncratic method accumulates both end and internal rhymes and slant rhymes to propel her poems over a series of heavily enjambed short lines, creating, at her best, the impression that every word has found its perfect habitation and function. Her delightful sound, and her confident voice that bestows upon almost every poem the impression of wise insight about how to live our lives, chime simultaneously on the ear and in the mind, making her work appeal both to connoisseurs of the minutiae of technique and to folks who rarely read poetry. One of her new poems, "Bitter Pill," typifies these qualities:

> A bitter pill
> doesn't need
> to be swallowed
> to work. just
> reading your name
> on the bottle
> does the trick.
> As though there
> were some anti-
> placebo effect.
> As though the
> self were eager
> to be wrecked.

As we flip from new poems to early ones, we find these sonic, syntactic, and tonal strategies inexorably in place—for example, in "Is It Modest?" which complains about God's penchant for hiding in his creation, and punningly criticizes divine reticence as "un-becoming / on and on, leaving us like this":

> Is it modest or arrogant
> not to enter the scene;
> instead to push a parrot
> forward or make the air
> apparent in the spring . . .

Ryan's own reticence, combined with her stylistic eccentricities, has made it a critical commonplace to compare her with Emily Dickinson and Elizabeth Bishop. Yet while Dickinson hid in her house, Ryan hides in her poems. Though she alludes to Dickinson occasionally—when she discusses "the valves/of the attention" ("Attention") or "the pharaohs,/shutting their/cunning doors" ("The Pharaohs")—her stances feel far more armored and impersonal, less willing to admit any psychological upheaval in her speakers' minds. Without actually tallying them, I would guess that all the poems in *The Best of It* spoken by an 'I'—the standard pronoun of contemporary poetry, and one Dickinson used without hesitation—could be counted on the fingers of one hand. (One of those poems ferries us all the way back to "*After Zeno*," Ryan's 1965 elegy for her father, which begins, "When he was/I was./But I still am/and he is still," poignantly bandaging personal grief in layers of wordplay and rhyme.) She has also learned much from Bishop, whose dimeter "Sonnet" anticipates Ryan's syntax and compression, and whose last line in "The Bight,"

"awful but cheerful," stands both sonically and semantically as a model for Ryan's philosophy of slant rhyme. But even Bishop—famous, ironically, for her privacy—gives "One Art," her villanelle-elegy for Lota Soares, a jolt of personal intensity by having her speaker enumerate her own losses—a house, two cities, a continent, and, finally, "you"—in first person. Decades after "*After Zeno*," by contrast, we can only guess that Ryan might have intended one of her new poems, "Polish and Balm," as an elegy for her lover:

> No unguent
> can soothe
> the chap of
> abandonment.
> Who knew
> the polish
> and balm in
> a person's
> simple passage
> among her things.
> We knew she
> loved them
> but not what
> love means.

The impression of personal feeling in Ryan's poetry results, paradoxically, not from her accounts of psychological experience, but from the eccentricities of her technique. Following the mind of someone who writes with her precision of diction, her ambushes of rhyme, and her sudden, startling colloquialisms, as if the poem had tired of being a poem, gives us the illusion of understanding how she thinks and feels. Her rhyming creates surprising, imaginary relationships among words and their referents that recall Gerard Manley Hopkins, and her sonic patterns can produce aural anagrams that rival his own "And wears man's smudge and shares man's smell" from "God's Grandeur." In "The Silence Islands," Ryan speaks of "a refinement/so exquisite that,/for example, to rhyme/anything with *hibiscus*/is interdicted anytime/children or anyone weakened/by sickness is expected." Ryan's "Blandeur," in fact, takes on "God's Grandeur" directly, coining a Hopkinsian imperative in its concluding prayer: "Unlean against our hearts./Withdraw your grandeur/from these parts."

While the high-flown Jesuit also provides a possible antecedent for Ryan's virtuosic compression, she often ends her poems not with Hopkins's explosions into immanence, but with what seem throwaway lines, as if the poem were simply giving up. Not throwaways at all, their carefully casual diction resembles that of Stevie

Smith, another poet whose wit and eccentricity, like Ryan's, mask depths of feeling, and whose willful misunderstandings spark sudden recognitions in the reader of an intellectual and emotional crisis. In "Doubt," Ryan warns against welcoming Coleridge's "Person from Porlock," the hero of one of Smith's best-known poems, but she recalls Smith more particularly in the grumbling, world-weary, offhand style that sometimes dares to sound childish and often leaves her poems feeling a bit loopy—to cite just a few instances, in "Apology" ("how we have to leap in the morning/as early as high as possible,/ we are so fastened, we are so dutiful"); "Bestiary" ("*Best* is not to be confused with *good*—/a different creature altogether,/and treated of in the goodiary—"); and "Great Thoughts" ("Standing in a/grove of them/is hideous").

An intensively aural, rhyme-dense style like Ryan's can spring traps for the poet when flamboyant technique drives the poem instead of providing the vehicle for imaginative event and feeling. In "Osprey," Ryan describes the bird capturing its prey: "He fishes, riding four-pound salmon/home like rockets. They get/all the way there before they die,/so muscular and brilliant/swimming through the sky." This marvelous, ironic transformation of the helpless salmon into a creature whose capture has bestowed majesty upon it encounters a major problem, though: An osprey carries its fish transversely to the path of its flight, so depicting the salmon "like rockets . . . swimming through the sky" falsifies perceptual appearance for the sake of the poem's conceit, whereas such perceptions must register accurately for Ryan's playful visual puns to ring true. All poets bend the world to fit into their poems—casting phenomena and feeling into language marks the first step—but a willful misrepresentation like this one pulls the reader up short and turns Ryan's style into gimmickery. This puffing up of Ryan's fancy overinflates her most recent full-length book, *The Niagara River* (2005), where poems like "Felix Crow," "Hailstorm," "Rubbing Lamps," and "Tar Babies" feel forced, rather than the result of emotional or intellectual revelation that appears coincidentally, and miraculously, to chime with the revelations of language.

On the whole, though, Ryan's new poems show a return to form and truly merit inclusion among the best in *The Best of It*, a cleverly punning title that suggests dogged stoicism, making

the best of it, while also summing up the excellence of this poet whose ear, syntax, and wit place her among the best of today's best. . . .

Source: Jay Rogoff, "New Bottles," in *Southern Review*, Vol. 47, No. 1, Winter 2011, p. 156.

Langdon Hammer
In the following review, Hammer discusses Ryan's use of plain words and dense lines of poetry.

When she reads her poetry in public, Kay Ryan does something unusual: she reads poems, at least some poems, twice. Few poets write poems short enough to permit that repetition, or interesting enough to reward it, but Ryan's invite (and demand) rereading: they are that intricate and quick. They are built like jokes that create a pause after the punch line (wait, is that all there is?) before we start to laugh, ask to hear the joke again, and ask for another.

Critics compare her poems to those of Robert Frost and Emily Dickinson—Frost because of their moral seriousness and playful skepticism, and Dickinson because of their small-scale lyric intensity, the power the poems gain from compactness. They unfold as brief trials or "essays" (in the etymological sense of the word) in which the poet tests an idea, explores the implications of a pun or image, takes a figure of speech literally, or activates the figurative suggestions latent in a phrase we are used to taking literally, in order to see what knowledge that starting place—often declared in the title—might yield about the world and how we live in it.

Ryan's poems have a consistent look and feel. They tend to happen in the space of 20 lines or fewer, and those lines are very short, seldom more than three words per line, as if they had been composed in a tiny hand on the fortunes of Chinese fortune cookies or typed on strands of ribbon. Their language is plain but crowded with internal rhymes that create complex networks of sound, and the syntax is compressed, making those short lines extremely dense. This combination of simplicity and complexity is part of the poetry's off-center, idiosyncratic approach to the commonplace. The mind at work in them is both familiar and eccentric. There is no 'I' in them—Ryan is concerned with what "we" do and how "we" think and speak, or what "you" see and feel. If her perspective is impersonal, it is also quirky and individual.

Ryan is a Californian. She grew up in small towns in the Mojave Desert and San Joaquin

Valley, and she has taught basic English skills at the College of Marin since 1971. She makes a point, she says, of living "very quietly." Nonetheless, awards committees have sought her out (her body of work won the Poetry Foundation's Ruth Lilly Prize), and she is a chancellor of the American Academy of Poets. *The Niagara River*, her sixth and most recent book of poetry, was published in 2005.

Ryan's poems reflect back on their own activity in ways that make the poem itself a model of the experience or idea it investigates. Take "It Cannot Be Said for Certain." Here Ryan wonders whether the patterns we discover in experience are imposed ("self-flattering"). If not, then those patterns of meaningfulness are like a fork—an ordinary object, but a strange one to bring forward in a metaphysical argument like this one. How did she get there?

The poem's logic goes something like this. The frisson of recognition we feel when experience discloses a pattern gives us a "shiver." That word suggests to Ryan its neighbor "silver," which, put together with "shiver," neatly describes the kind of light spine tingle she means. These words together give concreteness to the feeling: it is almost something definite and objective. The feeling occurs periodically, regularly enough for the poet to hold it up as proof against the vacancy and randomness that she experiences when there is no "silver shiver" of coherence. Doing this mentally, she decides, is like holding up . . . a fork. What is a fork exactly? It consists of those tines and the spaces between them, those absences being "the necessary black." Even the random dark, Ryan reasons, is part of a necessary design.

Ryan develops this idea through a series of associations in which the sound of words is prominent. The key word "pattern" suggests "self-flattery" and "matter" (not true rhymes, but close); the "velvet dark" turns into the "silver shiver," and the "v" returns in "vacancies." As in other Ryan poems, sound seems essential to this poem's way of making meaning—while sound is also resistantly arbitrary here, not reducible to sense. But Ryan is redefining the random as necessary. Prepared by the end of the poem to trust not only the "silver shiver" of epiphany but also those gaps "between the tines," we can reread the poem, paying attention to the potential for meaning in seemingly random wordplay—and in everything else that happens between the lines.

Yes! We can bet that Ryan wants us to hear the cliche between (or behind) her final line, an old saw which she has ingenuously warped and sharpened, giving it back some bite. Every Ryan poem involves some pleasingly confounding confluence of sound and sense, thought and feeling, life and art. To get that silver feeling, we need to read between the tines.

Source: Langdon Hammer, "Confluences of Sound and Sense: Kay Ryan's Idiosyncratic Approach to the Commonplace," in *American Scholar*, Vol. 77, No. 3, Summer 2008, p. 58.

Fred Dings

In the following review, Dings criticizes the way Ryan sometimes attempts to transform a mundane poem with a grand final statement.

In *The Niagara River*, Kay Ryan delights with flashes of insight and recognition that emerge quickly and briefly from relatively mundane starting points. These poems are sometimes comprised of as little as one comparison of two things, the poems depending on the originality and freshness of the comparison. Here is a typically successful poem titled "Chop": "The bird / walks down / the beach along / the glazed edge / the last wave / reached. His / each step makes / a perfect stamp—/ smallish, but as / sharp as an / emperor's chop. / Stride, stride, / goes the emperor / down his wide / mirrored promenade / the sea bows / to repolish." This poem is exact, focused, lean, and effective; the image is memorable. Here's another example, "Chinese Foot Chart": "Every part of us / alerts another part. / Press a spot in / the tender arch and / feel the scalp / twitch. We are no / match for ourselves / but our own release. / Each touch / uncatches some / remote lock. Look, / boats of mercy / embark from / our heart at the / oddest knock." Of course, the final image in this poem is what's striking and memorable, but here we have occasion to observe some less satisfying things.

Ryan's poems often may have memorable and fresh tropes, but seldom if ever memorable lines; she has opted for the painful legacy of William Carlos Williams, the broken spine of the iambic pentameter line, the easy, chopped-up prose lineation of much contemporary free verse. While reading the poem "Chop," I could not help noticing its kinship with Elizabeth Bishop's poem "Sandpiper," with its up-close, focused eye and intimate detail, yet the kinship highlights the differences. Consider these lines from Bishop's poem: "The beach hisses like fat. On his left, a sheet / of interrupting water comes and goes / and glazes over his dark and brittle feet."

Ryan's poems are also often pedantic, which is not a fault, especially when they teach something worthy and delightful, as they often do. Nevertheless, too many, for my taste, seem to depend on some final observation or trope to save what is otherwise a pretty mundane poem, as in the poem "Chinese Foot Chart" quoted above. This tendency to hinge a poem's success on some final aphoristic click is common in Ryan's work, and while it is often exhilarating the first time through, the poems seldom invite me back. I think of the well-met first encounter of a person whose life is entirely on the surface—pleasant enough but no need for a second encounter. If Ryan ever takes an interest in some of the other things that poems and language can do, she will be unsurpassable.

In the meantime, we still have Kay Ryan's best moments to savor, as in the poem "Stardust": "Stardust is / the hardest thing / to hold out for. / You must / make of yourself / a perfect plane—/ something still / upon which / something settles—/ something like / sugar grains on / something like / metal, but with / none of the chill. / It's hard to explain."

Source: Fred Dings, "Review of *The Niagara River*," in *World Literature Today*, Vol. 80, No. 6, November–December 2006, p. 73.

Publishers Weekly

In the following review, a contributor explores the way Ryan's poems quietly make a point and considers her poetry "crafted, understated, funny and smart."

Witty, charming, serious and delightful, Ryan's fifth book of poems is also remarkably specialized. Beginning from single observations or sayings or from single facts of science or folklore, the poems seek compression, consonance, cute rhymes, and moral lessons; usually they stop short on single remarks. All are brief, irregularly rhymed, arranged in very tight acoustic patterns, and confined to very short lines (normally of no more than six syllables). Of "The Fabric of Life," Ryan begins, "It is very stretchy./ We know that, even if/ many details remain/ sketchy." "Agreement" (in a delectable set of off-rhymes) becomes "a syrup/ that lingers, shared/ not singular./ Many prefer it." Ryan, in contrast, prefers to disagree: her poems stand up, quietly, to the received ideas she takes up or inverts. These quick, clipped poems become

protests against complacency, laziness and self-pity (which can be prevented) and decay, death, entropy (which cannot). "The Old Cosmologists," Ryan explains, act "as if change were not/ something that just happens/ at certain stages/ but a private test failed/ moment by moment/ as age is." If that judgment is ambiguous, "The Pass" is not: "Things test you./ You are part of/ the Donners or/ part of the rescue." Ryan prefers to carve molehills from mountains, to garnish her ethical lessons with thinly sliced bitterness; she instructs and delights by refusing to raise her voice. Her casual manner and nods to the wisdom tradition might endear her to fans of A. R. Ammons or link her distantly to Emily Dickinson. But her tight structures, odd rhymes and ethical judgments place her more firmly in the tradition of Marianne Moore and, latterly, Amy Clampitt. Those poets, though, wrote many kinds of poems: Ryan, in this volume, writes just one kind. It is, however, a kind worth looking out for—well crafted, understated, funny and smart.

Source: Review of *Say Uncle*, in *Publishers Weekly*, Vol. 247, No. 30, July 24, 2000, p. 82.

SOURCES

Bogdanov, Vladimir, Chris Woodstra, and Stephen Thomas Erlewine, eds., *All Music Guide: The Definitive Guide to Popular Music*, Hal Leonard, 2001, pp. 318, 327, 334.

Buckwalter, Ian, "As Europe Watches, a 'Murder Wall' Awaits," NPR website, January 29, 2010, http://www.npr.org/templates/story/story.php?storyId = 1230241 12 (accessed March 25, 2013).

Chai, Barbara, "Pulitzer Winner Kay Ryan on Poetry, Rhyming, and Terminal Cancer," in *Speakeasy, Wall Street Journal* online, April 19, 2011, http://blogs.wsj.com/speakeasy/2011/04/19/pulitzer-winner-kay-ryan-on-poetry-rhyming-and-terminal-cancer/ (accessed March 19, 2013).

Dutton, Denis, "It's Always the End of the World as We Know It," in *New York Times*, January 1, 2010, p. A29, http://www.nytimes.com/2010/01/01/opinion/01dutton.html?pagewanted = all&_r = 0 (accessed March 20, 2013).

Ferber, Michael, *The Cambridge Introduction to British Romantic Poetry*, Cambridge University Press, 2012, pp. 1–13, 121.

Foley, Jack, Review of *Say Uncle*, in *Alsop Review*, October 19, 2006, http://web.archive.org/web/20061019191807/http:/www.alsopreview.com/columns/foley/jlkayryan.html (accessed March 21, 2013).

Gardner, Martin, "Looking Backward at Edward Bellamy's Utopia," in *New Criterion*, Vol. 19, No. 1, September 2000, p. 19.

Gioia, Dana, "Discovering Kay Ryan," in *Dark Horse*, No. 7, Winter 1998–1999, pp. 6–9.

Hammer, Langdon, "Confluences of Sound and Sense: Kay Ryan's Idiosyncratic Approach to the Commonplace," in *American Scholar*, Vol. 77, No. 3, Summer 2008, pp. 58–59.

Joines, Rick, "Rick Joines on the Gravity and Levity of Kay Ryan," in *Contemporary Poetry Review*, July 18, 2011, http://www.cprw.com/rick-joines-the-gravity-and-levity-of-kay-ryan/ (accessed March 18, 2013).

Kirsch, Adam, "Think Small," in *New Yorker*, Vol. 86, No. 8, April 12, 2010, p. 76.

Lake, Paul, "Kay Ryan," in *Dictionary of Literary Biography*, Vol. 282, *New Formalist Poets*, edited by Jonathan N. Barron and Bruce Meyer, Thomson Gale, 2003, pp. 258–64.

"Melting Arctic Ice Cap at Record," in *ScienceDaily*, September 24, 2012, http://www.sciencedaily.com/releases/2012/09/120924145143.htm (accessed March 21, 2013).

"NPS Stats," National Park Service website, https://irma.nps.gov/Stats/ (accessed March 21, 2013).

Patterson, R. Gary, *Take a Walk on the Dark Side: Rock and Roll Myths, Legends, and Curses*, Fireside, 2004, p. 178.

Reed, Josephine, "Transcript of an Interview with Kay Ryan," National Endowment for the Arts website, http://www.nea.gov/av/avCMS/Ryan-podcast-transcript.html (accessed March 18, 2013).

"Responsible Travel: Global Trends & Statistics," Center for Responsible Travel website, http://www.responsibletravel.org/news/Fact_sheets/Fact_Sheet_-_Global_Ecotourism.pdf (accessed March 21, 2013).

Review of *Say Uncle*, in *Atlantic Monthly*, Vol. 286, No. 4, October 2000, p. 137.

Roberts, Gerald, ed., *Gerard Manley Hopkins: The Critical Heritage*, Routledge, 1987, pp. 280–84.

Rogoff, Jay, "New Bottles," in *Southern Review*, Winter 2011, Vol. 47, No. 1, pp. 156–60.

Romero, Frances, "Top 10 End-of-the-World Prophecies: Y2K," in *Time*, May 20, 2011, http://www.time.com/time/specials/packages/article/0,28804,2072678_2072683_2072599,00.html (accessed March 21, 2013).

Ryan, Kay, "Blandeur," in *Say Uncle*, Grove Press, 2000, p. 10.

———, "Do You Like It?," in *Zyzzyva*, Winter 1998, http://www.zyzzyva.org/2012/10/24/do-you-like-it/ (accessed March 21, 2013).

Seabrook, Andrea, "Poet Kay Ryan on Words, Writing," *All Things Considered*, NPR website, July 20, 2008, http://www.npr.org/templates/story/story.php?storyId=92721707 (accessed March 18, 2013).

Shapiro, Jerome F., *Atomic Bomb Cinema: The Apocalyptic Imagination on Film*, Routledge, 2002, pp. 37, 158, 193, 223.

"Status of Ratification of the Kyoto Protocol," United Nations Framework Convention on Climate Change website, http://unfccc.int/kyoto_protocol/status_of_ratification/items/2613.php (accessed March 21, 2013).

Stromberg, Stephen, "In State of the Union, Obama Threatens Congress on Climate Change," in *PostPartisan, Washington Post* online, February 13, 2013, http://www.washingtonpost.com/blogs/post-partisan/wp/2013/02/13/obama-state-of-the-union-climate-change-sotu/ (accessed March 21, 2013).

Teicher, Craig Morgan, "Pedaling up Parnassus: Poet Kay Ryan and How She Got There," in *Publishers Weekly*, Vol. 253, No. 15, April 10, 2006, pp. 39–40.

Vardaman, Wendy, "Poets Laureate," in *Women's Review of Books*, Vol. 27, No. 5, September–October 2010, pp. 36–38.

Warren, Christina, "Apple: 100 Million iPhones Sold," Mashable website, March 2, 2011, http://mashable.com/2011/03/02/100-million-iphones/ (accessed March 21, 2013).

Yezzi, David, Review of *Say Uncle*, in *Poetry*, Vol. 178, No. 2, May 2001, pp. 103–105.

FURTHER READING

Fortey, Richard, *Earth: An Intimate History*, Knopf, 2004.
   British paleontologist and noted science writer Fortey uses Earth's natural wonders as windows into the planet's geologic past.

Ryan, Kay, *The Niagara River*, Grove Press, 2005.
   One of Ryan's most celebrated, this volume brings together previously unpublished poems and a number that had appeared in the *New Yorker* and elsewhere. The title poem, one of Ryan's most well known, uses one of nature's wonders to comment on the human condition.

Vendler, Helen, ed., *Dickinson: Selected Poems and Commentaries*, Belknap Press, 2010.
   Poetry critic Vendler brings together selections that shed light on Dickinson's poetic development with analysis by world-renowned poets and critics.

Vonnegut, Kurt, "Requiem," in *Man without a Country*, Seven Stories Press, 2005, p. 137.
   Famous American satirist Kurt Vonnegut considers humans' relationship to the earth in his poem "Requiem." The poem, which also features the Grand Canyon and provides an interesting contrast to "Blandeur," appeared in the last book Vonnegut would publish before he died.

SUGGESTED SEARCH TERMS

Kay Ryan

Blandeur

Kay Ryan AND recombinant rhyme

Kay Ryan AND Emily Dickinson

romantic poetry AND nature

Kay Ryan AND Pulitzer Prize

Kay Ryan AND Say Uncle

Kay Ryan AND Marianne Moore

Kay Ryan AND wordplay

Defending Walt Whitman

SHERMAN ALEXIE

1996

Sherman Alexie is of Spokane and Coeur d'Alene heritage. He prefers being called an American Indian rather than a Native American. His prolific literary career and instant fame as a writer in his early twenties were surprising, given his childhood in poverty on the Spokane Reservation. Alexie has been celebrated for his versatility in many genres: poetry, songwriting, short stories, novels, and screenplays. He has produced films and become a popular performer in poetry slams, on television guest appearances, and as a stand-up comedian. His themes have dealt with racism and the crippling legacy of American colonialism for Indians. Alexie is noted for his humor in pointing out the incongruities between white and native worlds.

His poem "Defending Walt Whitman" is a celebration of reservation basketball, one of Alexie's favorite topics. In this poem, he humorously imagines the nineteenth-century American poet, bearded and ecstatic, being defended on the basketball court by good-natured and muscular Indian boys as he tries to make a basket. Whitman does not know anything about the game but is infected with the same enthusiasm as the Indians. Whitman was a favorite poet of Alexie's, and the poem is written in the same style of free verse used in Whitman's *Leaves of Grass*. "Defending Walt Whitman" can be found in the collection *The Summer of Black Widows*, published in 1996.

Sherman Alexie *(© Ulf Andersen / Getty Images Entertainment / Getty Images)*

AUTHOR BIOGRAPHY

Sherman Joseph Alexie Jr. was born on October 7, 1966, in Spokane, Washington, to Lillian Agnes Cox (of the Spokane, Flathead, and Colville tribes) and Sherman Joseph Alexie (of the Coeur d'Alene tribe), one of six children. He was a hydrocephalic baby and underwent brain surgery at six months. The doctors said he would have mental retardation from this condition, but instead, he was very bright and an early learner, learning to read by the age of three. He grew up in poverty and with an alcoholic father on the Spokane Indian Reservation in Wellpinit, Washington, where he went to primary school. To prepare for college, Alexie transferred to Reardan High School, a primarily white school, in 1981. He excelled and flourished, becoming captain of the basketball team, class president, and a debater.

He attended Gonzaga University in Spokane from 1985 to 1987, intending to become a doctor, but overwhelmed, he began drinking to excess. In 1988, he transferred to Washington State University in Pullman, receiving a bachelor's degree in American Studies in 1994. There he took creative writing under Alex Kuo, his mentor. He began publishing his poems and stopped drinking to become serious about writing.

The Business of Fancydancing (a collection of poems and stories) and *I Would Steal Horses* were published in 1992, and Alexie's success was immediate. Two more books of poetry, *Old Shirts and New Skins* and *First Indian on the Moon*, came out in 1993, as well as a book of short stories, *The Lone Ranger and Tonto Fistfight in Heaven*.

In 1994, Alexie married Diane Tomhave (of the Hidatsa, Ho-Chunk, and Potawatomi tribes) and moved to Seattle. *Reservation Blues*, his first novel, came out in 1995, along with *Reservation Blues: The Soundtrack*, a musical collaboration between Alexie and Jim Boyd. The novel won the Before Columbus Foundation American Book Award and a Granta award. A second novel, *Indian Killer*, was published in 1996, as was the poetry chapbook *Water Flowing Home*. The same year, "Defending Walt Whitman" was published in the poetry collection *The Summer of Black Widows*. Alexie premiered his award-winning film *Smoke Signals* at the Sundance Film Festival in 1998. He began his career as a stand-up comedian, a poetry performer, and a TV guest at this time. His short story collection *The Toughest Indian in the World* and another volume of poetry, *One Stick Song*, both came out in 2000, the former book winning the PEN/Malamud Award for Short Fiction. A second film, *The Business of Fancydancing*, which he wrote and directed, was shown at the Sundance Film Festival in 2002. The short story collection *Ten Little Indians* was the *Publishers Weekly* Book of the Year in 2003. The story "What You Pawn I Will Redeem" from that book was included in *The Best American Short Stories 2004*.

In 2005, the poem "Avian Nights" from *Dangerous Astronomy*, a poetry chapbook, won the Pushcart Prize. Two novels, *Flight* and *The Absolutely True Diary of a Part-Time Indian*, came out in 2007. *True Diary* won a National Book Award for young-adult literature and an American Indian Youth Literature Award. *Face*, another poetry collection, was published in 2009. In 2010, *War Dances* (a story collection) won a PEN/Faulkner Award. The 2012 collection *Blasphemy:*

New and Selected Stories is Alexie's latest publication. As of 2011, Alexie and his wife live in Seattle with their two sons.

POEM TEXT

Basketball is like this for young Indian boys, all
    arms and legs
and serious stomach muscles. Every body is
    brown!
These are the twentieth-century warriors who
    will never kill,
although a few sat quietly in the deserts of
    Kuwait,
waiting for orders to do something, do something. 5

God, there is nothing as beautiful as a jump shot
on a reservation summer basketball court
where the ball is moist with sweat
and makes a sound when it swishes through
    the net
that causes Walt Whitman to weep because it is
    so perfect. 10

There are veterans of foreign wars here,
whose bodies are still dominated
by collarbones and knees, whose bodies still
    respond
in the ways that bodies are supposed to respond
    when we are young.
Every body is brown! Look there, that boy can run 15
up and down this court forever. He can leap for
    a rebound
with his back arched like a salmon, all meat and
    bone
synchronized, magnetic, as if the court were a
    river,
as if the rim were a dam, as if the air were a
    ladder
leading the Indian boy toward home. 20

Some of the Indian boys still wear their military
    haircuts
while a few have let their hair grow back.
It will never be the same as it was before!
One Indian boy has never cut his hair, not once,
    and he braids it
into wild patterns that do not measure anything. 25
He is just a boy with too much time on his
    hands.
Look at him. He wants to play this game in
    bare feet.

God, the sun is so bright! There is no place like this.
Walt Whitman stretches his calf muscles
on the sidelines. He has the next game. 30
His huge beard is ridiculous on the reservation.
Some body throws a crazy pass and Walt Whit-
    man catches it with quick hands.
He brings the ball close to his nose
and breathes in all of its smells: leather, brown
    skin, sweat, black hair,

burning oil, twisted ankle, long drink of warm
    water, 35
gunpowder, pine tree. Walt Whitman squeezes
    the ball tightly.
He wants to run. He hardly has the patience to
    wait for his turn.
"What's the score?" he asks. He asks, "What's
    the score?"

Basketball is like this for Walt Whitman. He
    watches these Indian boys
as if they were the last bodies on earth. Every body is
    brown! 40
Walt Whitman shakes because he believes in
    God.
Walt Whitman dreams of the Indian boy who
    will defend him,
trapping him in the corner, all flailing arms and
    legs
and legendary stomach muscles. Walt Whit-
    man shakes
because he believes in God. Walt Whitman dreams 45
of the first jump shot he will take, the ball
    arcing clumsily
from his fingers, striking the rim so hard that it
    sparks.
Walt Whitman shakes because he believes in
    God.
Walt Whitman closes his eyes. He is a small
    man and his beard
is ludicrous on the reservation, absolutely insane. 50
His beard makes the Indian boys laugh right-
    eously. His beard frightens
the smallest Indian boys. His beard tickles the
    skin
of the Indian boys who dribble past him. His
    beard, his beard!

God, there is beauty in every body. Walt Whitman
    stands
at center court while the Indian boys run from bas-
    ket to basket. 55
Walt Whitman cannot tell the difference
    between
offense and defense. He does not care if he
    touches the ball.
Half of the Indian boys wear T-shirts damp
    with sweat
and the other half are bareback, skin slick and
    shiny.
There is no place like this. Walt Whitman smiles. 60
Walt Whitman shakes. This game belongs to
    him

POEM SUMMARY

The text used for this summary is from *The Summer of Black Widows*, Hanging Loose Press, 1996, pp. 14–15. A version of the poem can be found on the following web page: http://www.bpj.org/poems/alexie_whitman.html.

MEDIA ADAPTATIONS

- *The Absolutely True Diary of a Part-time Indian*, an unabridged audiobook by Recorded Books (2009), is available as an MP3 download at Audio Book Store. The autobiographical young-adult novel about growing up on the reservation is read by Sherman Alexie in his funny and poetic style. It includes memories of playing basketball on the reservation and in high school.

Stanza 1

The first stanza of "Defending Walt Whitman" has five lines in free verse and describes a basketball game on an Indian reservation. The boys are young and athletic, all muscles, and their skin is brown. The narrator repeats several times in the poem that all the bodies on the basketball court are brown. This statement comes with an exclamation mark afterward, as if it is an amazing sight. This implies the audience is mostly white, probably never having seen brown bodies in such beautiful motion. The surprise about the brown bodies is especially for the guest of the basketball game, Walt Whitman, the nineteenth-century American poet. Whitman was known for celebrating the erotic and spiritual beauty of the body. He wrote poems admiring the strong bodies of men (the Calamus poems), assumed to be homosexual in nature. Here Alexie shows off the perfect bodies of the Indians and their perfect skill in basketball for the enthusiastic poet. This stanza also describes basketball as a game for twentieth-century warriors. These warriors excel but do not kill, even though some of the players have recently returned from military duty in Kuwait. The allusion to Kuwait hints that the Indian boys sent to the foreign war had to sit on the sidelines of the war in the desert, but in the basketball game, they are active stars. The war in Kuwait refers to the First Gulf War in 1991, with the name Operation Desert Storm, in which a United Nations coalition, led by the United States, liberated Kuwait after it had been illegally annexed by Saddam Hussein's Iraqi forces. The war was won after one hundred days, though peacekeeping forces were kept in the region for years. Alexie wants to contrast the peaceful competition on the court with the violence of war in the Middle East. The boys should be playing basketball, not killing in Kuwait.

Stanza 2

The second stanza, with five lines, describes a jump shot that goes through the hoop with a swishing noise. It is so perfect it makes Whitman cry. The narrator says that nothing is as beautiful as basketball in the summer on a reservation when the ball is sweaty. These are Alexie's own feelings about basketball, as he expresses in many other poems and books, such as "Why We Play Basketball" in *The Summer of Black Widows*. He imagines that Whitman is able to share his appreciation of this sight, because Whitman wrote of his joy in common things, people, and activities. Whitman looked on everything with wonder and innocence and acceptance. The sweaty ball is also a nod to Whitman's tendency to put such gross details about the body in poems such as the smell of his own armpits. Whitman wrote of things considered socially indelicate, like sweat and sex, considering them as much a part of life as anything else. Whereas the average onlooker might not feel ecstatic about this Indian basketball game, Alexie knows Whitman would see it as miraculous, a divine manifestation. The narrator uses God in the poem as an exclamation three times to show excitement, but he also mentions later that Whitman enjoys this game on the reservation because he believes in God. This is another nod to Whitman's mysticism; he declares that everything he sees is a sign from God.

Stanza 3

This longer stanza has ten free-verse lines. The narrator returns to the fact that the boys on the court are young, and yet many are veterans of foreign wars. He mentions again, with excitement, that their skin is brown. He points out one boy who can run up and down the court forever. He can leap up for a rebound like a leaping fish, as if the court were a river and the rim a dam. These metaphors of the court as a river and the boy as a salmon are references to the Spokane Reservation on the Spokane River in Washington, where the tribal people not only survived through salmon fishing but worshipped the salmon in their religion. The tragedy of the end of salmon fishing is hinted at with the damming of the rivers, so the salmon could not make their journey upstream to spawn. The boy is compared to the return of the magical salmon in the way he leaps in the air, as if the air were a ladder to take him home. The injustice done to the northwest tribes by destroying their fishing is thus transcended in the basketball game when the boy becomes the magical fish again. The tragedies of Indians (foreign wars and loss of fishing rights) are kept in the background of the glory of the basketball game.

Stanza 4

This seven-line stanza again begins with reference to foreign wars. Some of the boys still have military haircuts, but some have let their hair grow back. One of the boys has long hair, braided in elaborate patterns. He wants to play the game barefoot. In some cultures, warriors wear long braided hair because long hair is believed to have power in it. The image of the American soldier with short hair is thus an image of emasculation and loss of identity. The boys who come back to the reservation try to grow back their hair, but the narrator says it will never be the same as that of the wild boy who never cut his. Alexie thus replaces the image of a tough soldier with that of a wild Indian warrior. The Indian warrior is more masculine, beautiful, and worthy of playing basketball.

Stanza 5

Now, the narrator turns to the guest of honor, Walt Whitman, in this stanza of eleven lines. The narrator says the sun is bright and there is no place like a reservation basketball court. Whitman is on the sidelines stretching his muscles, waiting to play in the next game. His huge white beard looks funny in this setting, but when somebody throws a wild pass, Whitman deftly catches it. He sniffs the ball and smells brown skin, black hair, pine trees, and gunpowder. He is eager to join the game, though he does not know how to play, and wants to know the score. The accumulation of details shows Whitman appreciating sensory experience, as he had expressed in his famous poems "Song of Myself" and "I Sing the Body Electric." The poem points out that someone like Whitman would look silly and out of place on the reservation. As he does in other poems in *The Summer of Black Widows*, Alexie brings white people into the Indian world to show that they are as out of place in Indian culture as Indians are in white culture. In the "Visitors" series, he shows James Dean dancing clumsily at a pow-wow, for instance, and Marilyn Monroe in a sweat lodge. Indians do not generally have facial hair, and so a hairy Whitman would be a curiosity. He is also heavy and old while the boys are young, slim, and agile. Yet they accept him into their game.

Stanza 6

This is the longest stanza, fifteen lines. Here, Whitman is working himself into a frenzy to play. Alexie builds the excitement with rhythm, cutting some lines in two with a period (the pause is called a *caesura*), and others are longer than usual. Whitman sees the Indian bodies as if they were the last on earth, and again the poem remarks with excitement about their brown skin tones. Whitman dreams of the Indian boy who will defend him as he tries to make a basket. That boy will be all arms and legs and hard stomach muscles. This is an erotic image, exciting to the old poet. But the narrator says three times in this stanza that Walt Whitman is shaking because he believes in God. In his poetry, anything exciting to Whitman makes him believe in God. Here, the brown bodies, the game, the summer day, Alexie imagines, would also make Whitman believe in God. Alexie is sympathetic to this, as he expresses a similar sentiment in "Why We Play Basketball": it makes the boys believe in God; it is a kind of natural religious experience.

Whitman dreams of making a jump shot, though he knows it will be clumsy and hit the rim. Whitman closes his eyes. He is so small and his beard looks ridiculous, so the older boys laugh, but the small Indian boys are afraid. His beard tickles those who pass close to him. Even though the narrator seems to be making fun of Whitman's small clumsy body and white beard, he understands Whitman's excitement about the game, intense to the point of religious ecstasy. Alexie is using exaggeration for humorous effect, but he is serious in embracing Whitman as a fellow though inexperienced player. Whitman approaches the game in the right spirit. Thus, the title of the poem, "Defending Walt Whitman," can refer both to a defense of the poet as a poet and man and to defending him in the basketball game so he can make a basket.

TOPICS FOR FURTHER STUDY

- Read some Walt Whitman poems from *Leaves of Grass*. In a poem of your own, use Whitman's tone and form of free verse to celebrate someone, something, or someplace that makes you feel happy to be alive.

- Whitman set himself up as the model for future American poets. In the introduction to *Walt Whitman: The Centennial Essays* (University of Iowa, 1994), Ed Fulsom points out that almost every major twentieth-century American poet has talked back to Walt Whitman for this very reason. In poetic conversations with him or interactions like the one in Alexie's poem, they either agree with him or reject him. Construct a wiki with examples of Whitman's influence on other American poets, including poems like Alexie's that directly engage with him.

- Research the Spokane Indian tribe and the Spokane Reservation, using both Internet and library resources. Explain the history of this tribe, mention any famous leaders or events, and summarize their cultural values. Show how Alexie incorporates this history into one of his short stories or novels. Write this up as a research paper.

- Indian poets Joy Harjo and Alexie perform their poetry and use music and media in interesting ways. Give a talk (individual or group) on the similarities and differences of their poetry and style, finding examples of their performances on YouTube or elsewhere online, or show film clips of their work. They have both recorded music albums. Play selections from those as well. How do these authors take poetry off the page and make it relevant to audiences today?

- Watch the 1998 film *Smoke Signals* and give a group report on the movie's plot and production details. Examine how Alexie, who wrote the screenplay, uses humor to undermine stereotypes of Indians. Show relevant clips and discuss with a group.

- Read Gary Soto's young-adult short story "Baseball in April" (1990) about growing up Latino in California. How do American sports such as baseball and basketball give opportunities for equality, excellence, and friendship among people of different cultures and races? Set up a multicultural web page on sport as a peacemaking, humanizing activity, as it is used in "Defending Walt Whitman."

Whitman needs someone to defend him when he is in this strange setting, and he must look to the expertise and generosity of the Indian players.

Stanza 7

In this last, eight-line stanza, Whitman is actually in the game, standing at center court while the boys run up and down around him from basket to basket. The problem is that Whitman does not know offense from defense, and he decides now he does not care if he even touches the ball. He looks at all the beautiful bodies, some with damp T-shirts, some with sweaty bare backs. Alexie uses the image of sweat in almost every stanza, emphasizing the active physical bodies. There is

no place that compares to this, the poem repeats, and Whitman trembles in appreciation. He feels a sense of ownership of this game. There are different interpretations of this last line; probably it means that he feels at home, whether or not he can play. He does not find the Indians strange or foreign but wonderful, a gift to him.

THEMES

Native American Culture

Though "Defending Walt Whitman" is full of references to non-Indian culture such as the white American poet Walt Whitman, the game of basketball, and the war in Kuwait, it is essentially a celebration of the modern Indian warriors on the basketball court who play to perfection. The poet shows Indian culture today in the form of a basketball court on an Indian reservation in the summer; the brown bodies of muscular young people run and leap on the court, impressing the white audience of one, Whitman. The poem thus acknowledges the necessarily hybrid nature of postcolonial nations—that is, cultures that have been colonized and, to some degree, influenced by their colonizers—who have their own heritage plus that of the dominant culture. Alexie is known for putting Indian culture side by side with American popular culture, accepting both. He loves the universality of basketball and shows how the Indians have made it their own game. In fact, here the white man is the outsider and novice, while the Indians are the experts.

Some of the Indian boys have just come back from military duty in Kuwait, where, as soldiers, they were required to have short hair. On the reservation, they let their hair grow back, so they are once again Indian warriors. One boy with long braids is so wild he wants to play barefoot. Instead of seeing Indians as backward or drop-outs of society on the reservation, the poet praises their natural beauty and skill. Whitman is so excited, he wants to play and waits for the Indian boy who will defend him so he can make a basket. The speaker stresses that the players are true warriors, but they do not shed blood, implying a contrast to the American foreign war in Kuwait.

Alexie also says something about Indian culture in its humane embrace of Whitman. The boys are willing to play with him, though he is strange because of his beard. They accept him; Indians are not the belligerent stereotype shown in the movies.

Sports

Most Americans would not associate Indians and basketball, but for Alexie, it is a common topic in his poetry and novels, since he grew up with reservation and high school basketball. Alexie also celebrates basketball in "Why We Play Basketball," in which the narrator says Indians play basketball so they can know who is best, a friendly competition, and also because they know they can take the established game and make it into something new. When they play basketball, they believe in God, he says, implying that life is good and makes sense when they play. Playing also makes

Walt Whitman

them feel competence and self-respect. Basketball today is popular with many American Indians as a way to get together and as a way to encourage their youth to embrace education and success. Sports have always been a means of bridging cultural gaps and making friends with strangers. In this poem, the game unites young Indians and an older white man. Cultural differences, such as the beard, are put in the background as everyone has a good time. Alexie has also written a long prose meditation on his memory of reservation Little League baseball in *One Stick Song*. The poet has good childhood memories of baseball but says he does not like baseball as a sport, because he is mediocre in that game, whereas, in basketball, he was a star. Sports are shown as a peaceful way to compete and cultivate oneself, in body, mind, and values. They create tolerance.

Joy

Though Alexie is known as a poet of anger, with many ironic and satiric poems and images, in this poem, he celebrates the joy of a basketball game. The war in Kuwait is mentioned, but it is in the background. The Indian soldiers are home for the summer and enjoying their basketball game as their hair grows out and they become normal again. The boy who leaps like a salmon is described as magnetic and magical. Indians are denied their ancient salmon culture because of the dams on the Spokane and Columbia rivers but recreate it on the basketball court. The salmon leap again in the jump shot. The joy is so intense that their guest, Whitman, waits impatiently on the sidelines, wanting to get in the game. Alexie conveys the joy of the game with constant exclamations on its beauty, on the sensual brown Indian bodies, and Whitman's shaking excitement at the sight of it all.

STYLE

Free Verse

"Defending Walt Whitman" is written in free verse. Free verse is an open form of poetry that does not have a set pattern. It uses irregular meter (the grouping of stressed and unstressed syllables), rhythm, and line length, tending to sound more like speech than formal poetry. Most free verse looks like poetry with line breaks and stanzas, but these are created for effect where needed. It is often described as an organic form, where the form emerges naturally from the feeling, sound, and imagery. This practice became popular in the nineteenth century with many French poets and Victorian poets, such as Christina Rossetti, Robert Louis Stevenson, and Matthew Arnold. Some modern examples are "Fog" by Carl Sandburg; "The Far Field" by Theodore Roethke; "For the Union Dead" by Robert Lowell; and "Diving into the Wreck" by Denise Levertov. One of the pioneers of free verse was Walt Whitman, whose long lines of unrhymed verse were influenced by the King James Bible. Free verse is not like prose because it is rhythmical and uses imagery, repetition, line breaks, and poetic sound effects such as assonance and alliteration. Whitman likened his long lines to the rhythm of the sea with tides, going in and out.

In "Defending Walt Whitman," Alexie uses the free-verse form to reflect Whitman's own favorite verse form in such poems as "Song of Myself," where there are irregular length stanzas and long lines with sentences that can end and begin in the middle of a line. The lines are not the same length, and they do not rhyme. Like Whitman, Alexie uses repetition, long lines, sensual concrete imagery, and the building of rhythm to create an effect, in this case the excitement of the imaginary basketball game.

Native American Ceremony and Song

Native American ceremony is the basis of most modern Native American poetry, either directly or indirectly, because it embraces a certain perception of the world. Native American tribal ceremonies use incantation, song, dance, prayer, visual symbols, and gestures to restore wholeness to the land and community. These oral traditions had the purpose of integrating the community with the cosmic forces. "Defending Walt Whitman" partly suggests a healing ceremony between white and Indian cultures, with the basketball game like a powwow dance. As in tribal life, basketball works for Alexie like a powwow: it is a community activity that spreads joy and cements relationships. The oral tradition is felt in the narrator's embracing and confident voice, a voice of authority and wisdom and vision. Traditional tribal songs were chanted and used in a magical way to bring about change. Whitman's own poems suggest the Indian idea of language as healing. He called his poems chants. He used Indian names for places, such as Paumanok for Long Island. He believed his chants could heal the nation's wounds from the Civil War. Alexie admired Whitman as a poet and imitates his tone and style to place him in an Indian basketball game on the reservation.

Contemporary Native American or Indian Poetry

"Defending Walt Whitman" is a contemporary Indian poem that imaginatively integrates Indian tradition and point of view with modern culture. Most Indian poets writing in English experiment with ways to use both of their legacies, as all postcolonial authors must, using modern verse forms but with a native sensibility and references to Indian culture. Alexie frequently mentions the trickster Coyote, the Spokane salmon culture, and the Ghost Dance, for instance. He also refers to Spokane history. Here, Alexie confidently shows he can manage reservation basketball and the father of American poetry (Whitman) in one space. The poem is humorous because it shows Whitman a bit out of his usual place as the hallowed bearded prophet of the Civil War. Alexie's hallmark is the use of surreal scenes combining Indian life and pop culture to make his own point. Other Native American writers, such as the Muskogee poet Joy Harjo and the Acoma Pueblo poet Simon Ortiz, also blend incongruous details of city life today with a characteristic Native American point of view. Their poems picture the problems of contemporary Indian life and the survival of tribal people within American culture.

HISTORICAL CONTEXT

The Native Americans before Columbus
When the Europeans came to North America, they found hundreds of ethnic groups living there, each with its own nation, language, and culture. According to some theories, the indigenous people living in the Americas had migrated here some twelve thousand years ago from Europe and Asia on a land bridge across the Bering Strait in the far north. The indigenous people themselves have other, mythological versions of their origins. According to Alexie's tribe, the Spokane, Coyote, of the animal people, made the bodies of the Spokane out of the land, and then Amotkan, the Creator, gave them life. The Spokane call themselves Children of the Sun.

European Exploration and Colonization of America
Early Spanish and other European explorers in the fifteenth and sixteenth centuries, such as Christopher Columbus, Juan Ponce de Leon, and Hernando de Soto, brought back to Europe tales of the wealth of the Americas, prompting many European expeditions for plunder or settlement. At first, there seemed to be room for all. In North America, many early contacts between Europeans and natives were friendly, with Native Americans helping Europeans through the hard winters by giving food and showing them how to plant crops and survive. There is some evidence that the founders of American democracy borrowed political ideas from the tribal cultures where freedom was prized.

From the sixteenth century to the nineteenth century, more and more Europeans came to claim the land, and the natives were seen as a threat or a problem that had to be exterminated so white settlers could "civilize" the continent. The indigenous people were treated as foreigners and heathens who had no legal or moral right to the land. The Europeans not only made war on the Indians with superior weapons, they also took their lands by force or trickery (such as treaties that were not honored) and took advantage of the devastating effect of European

diseases such as smallpox, measles, and bubonic plague, for which the natives had no immunity.

The Europeans brought horses, guns, and alcohol, thus changing tribal life. Though there was some fruitful trade among indigenous Americans and Europeans, as with the Spokane and French fur traders, the influence of the whites was largely destructive to the Indians.

The Wild West
In the nineteenth century, as the settlers from Europe were pushing indigenous people from the east coast into the interior, the American Indians were romanticized by American writers as a noble but vanishing people. The Indians were now seen not so much as subhuman heathens but as noble savages, close to nature, a melancholy and disappearing race. This sentimental view of American Indians is a stereotype still believed today and satirized by Alexie in *The Lone Ranger and Tonto Fistfight in Heaven*. Although Whitman embraced Indians and their culture as part of American democracy, he did not go beyond this romantic, stereotyped view of them.

When white settlers wanted to move onto land that had been reserved for indigenous people, the Indians found themselves betrayed. Treaties between the US government's Bureau of Indian Affairs and various tribes were broken or falsely negotiated. Westward expansion, and the passage of the Indian Removal Act in 1830 relocating a hundred thousand Indians from eastern to western lands, led to Indian Resistance, or the Indian Wars. Indians were portrayed as warlike in the press, but many tribes sought peace. If they fought, it was for survival.

The Spokane in Washington, Idaho, and Montana originally accepted white settlers; they engaged in trade and accepted Christianity. The discovery of gold in Spokane country in the 1840s and 1850s, however, disrupted the delicate balance. The intrusion of the miners, settlers, and the railroad produced calls for the Indians to be removed to reservations. The last military defeat of the Spokane by United States Colonel George Wright in 1858 ended in his notorious slaughter of eight hundred Indian horses, shot and left to rot so the Indians could not use them. This cruel act is mentioned in many of Alexie's poems ("Sonnet: Tattoo Tears"), and Wright became a satirical character in *Reservation Blues*.

COMPARE
&
CONTRAST

- **1855:** The year Whitman first publishes *Leaves of Grass*, the Spokane and Coeur d'Alene Indians are being defeated by white soldiers and placed on reservations.

  1990s: When "Defending Walt Whitman" is published, approximately half the American Indian population lives on reservations.

  Today: Indians are becoming urbanized; sixty to seventy percent of American Indians live in cities.

- **1855:** Many Indians convert to Christianity, but they retain their tribal rituals and powwows.

  1990s: In "Defending Walt Whitman," Alexie shows basketball to be a new sort of communal and equalizing powwow where one can meet both friends and the former enemy.

Today: Basketball remains popular among American Indians. Organizations such as the Native American Basketball Invitational Foundation promote basketball and other sports for health and community building.

- **1855:** White settlers and trading begin to move Indians away from their once-rich fishing and hunting grounds, and they begin to experience poverty.

  1990s: Casino gaming becomes legally established on reservations as a way to take tribes out of poverty.

  Today: Indian casinos are popular with tourists, employing many Indians, but due to their competitive nature, they attract organized crime and violence to the reservation as well.

Assimilation

Reservations were not the sole answer to what was known as the Indian problem. Assimilation—encouraging or forcing Indians to adopt white American culture—was a policy meant to destroy native cultures. After the Civil War, boarding schools run by Christian missionaries were set up to convert and educate Indians. Children were taken from their parents and were not allowed to speak their native language or practice their religion. In 1894, all Indian religion was banned by the Bureau of Indian Affairs, even on the reservations, and Indians were prosecuted for singing or performing religious dances. Indians had few rights.

American Indians were granted US citizenship by the Indian Citizenship Act of 1924, though they were not allowed to vote in local elections. The final attempt to assimilate the native population came with the policy of Termination in the 1950s and 1960s. The policy tried to take all natives off the reservation and relocate them to cities, thus disbanding their tribal groups and taking their lands

for their natural resources. It meant the government no longer recognized tribal sovereignty. With the example of the African American civil rights movement of the 1960s, Native American activist groups were formed and fought Termination. In 1975, the Indian Self-Determination and Education Assistance Act allowed Native Americans to form their own governing bodies and to keep their reservations, and in 1978, the American Indian Freedom of Religion Act was passed. The United States still does not recognize Indian nations as sovereign nations, however, and manages their lands through the Bureau of Indian Affairs.

Today

Although they once constituted 100 percent of the population, today American Indians make up only 0.5 percent of the U.S. population; more than half of them live in cities. Individuals of mixed heritage may have difficulty establishing their legal identity as Indians to obtain tribal rights. The high rates of alcoholism, poverty, heart disease, and drug addiction among Indians and the low rate of college attendance testify to

Alexie compares the boys playing basketball to warriors. (© dotshock | Shutterstock.com)

their ongoing struggle to find a place in the modern world. Many tribes have sued the government for land compensation, as the Spokane have successfully sued over the flooding of their hunting grounds by the Grand Coulee Dam. Gambling casinos, such as the Two Rivers Casino run by the Spokane, are one economic strategy for tribes to survive. A Native American literary renaissance in the 1970s and 1980s, of which Alexie is the beneficiary and second-generation representative, proves the determined survival of American Indian cultures, transformed to meet contemporary challenges.

CRITICAL OVERVIEW

Sherman Alexie's prolific and successful literary career in poetry, fiction, and screenwriting, since his debut in 1992 has been met with consistent critical and popular praise. In his early years, readers noticed repetition of themes, characters, and motifs from one book to the next, as with

oral tradition. He deepened and reworked his material, all the while gaining technical skill and experimenting with form. Alexie won support from other Indian authors, such as Harjo and Leslie Marmon Silko. His work covers a familiar Indian landscape with stories of trauma and survival but adds an aggressive satire that is intentionally provoking.

The Summer of Black Widows (1996), which contains the poem "Defending Walt Whitman," is one of his best collections and secured his reputation as a sustained and serious poet. The reviews were uniformly favorable. *Publishers Weekly*, in September 1996, praises the book because it "opens to us the complexity and contradiction of a contemporary multicultural identity." The *Library Journal* says the poems give Indian people a sense of nobility in their continuing struggle. Robert L. Berner, writing for *World Literature Today*, mentions that the volume contains some of the most powerful contemporary statements about reservation life. He interprets "Defending Walt Whitman" as concerning "the complexity of literary influence," raising the idea that in this poem, Whitman is being to some degree defended *against* even as he is welcomed. Ray Gonzalez, writing in the *Bloomsbury Review*, welcomes Alexie's honesty and control of language. In a 1997 review for *Western American Literature*, David Cremean admires Alexie's ability to turn history into art and calls him one of the most significant Indian writers today, citing the book's humor as one of its strengths.

In 2001, Stephen F. Evans summarized the critical response to Alexie's poetry over the years in "Open Containers: Sherman Alexie's Drunken Indians." He praises Alexie's technical versatility in poetic genres and his improvisational comic cheek. Alexie has been criticized for his satire of reservation life by those who prefer romanticized Indians. Evans, however, considers Alexie to be a trickster figure, like Coyote, the unpredictable mythic god of some cultures, whom Alexie often mentions; he is the creator responsible for Indian survival. In later years, Alexie broadens his themes because he does not want to be seen as promoting fundamentalist tribalism after the terrorist attacks of September 11, 2001. An article in *World Literature Today* on Alexie as a humanitarian author mentions that he is "driven by a haunting lyricism and naked candor that go to the heart of the human experience."

CRITICISM

Susan K. Andersen

Andersen holds a PhD in literature. In the following essay, she looks at Sherman Alexie's "Defending Walt Whitman" as both an appreciation of Indian basketball and as an act that inserts Indian poetry into the tradition of American poetry that Whitman was trying to establish.

Sherman Alexie's famous formula, "Poetry = Anger x Imagination," has led most commentators to emphasize his anger, irony, and dark humor. He is seen as a postcolonial author embracing a hybrid white and Indian culture, simultaneously angry about the loss of Indian integrity and delighted with the freedom of modern popular culture, using both cultures to satirize each other. This makes it possible to interpret many poems in more than one way, depending on the tone of voice one hears behind the words. In "Defending Walt Whitman" from *The Summer of Black Widows*, a book with many angry images, the cartoonish basketball game with an old bearded Whitman among young agile Indian players transcends any simple classification. It is imaginative, it is serious, it is playful; its irony seems primarily humorous and affectionate rather than angry. In this poem, Alexie is not the angry young Indian man but, unexpectedly, Whitman's poetic son and heir, as Whitman had predicted in his poems about the future poets to come. Whitman was always preparing the way for future travelers, thinkers, and artists, imagining them reading his lines and taking inspiration. He felt they would understand and justify him, for his liberal vision was completely radical in nineteenth-century white America. Alexie shows that he completely understands Whitman and accepts him as he is, even allowing him to share the basketball floor with his people.

In an essay in the *American Indian Quarterly*, "'Another Kind of Violence': Sherman Alexie's Poems," Ron McFarland identifies two kinds of modern Indian writing. One mimics the traditional Indian culture to find wholeness from the oral tradition of ceremony and myth. This strategy is illustrated in the novel *Ceremony* by Leslie Marmon Silko. This kind of Indian writing tries to remember the Native American values and ways to positively assert the continuing identity of its people. McFarland sees Sherman Alexie following a different path, which he calls "polemic," an angry, argumentative stance toward the white dominant culture. This

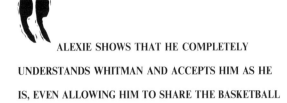

ALEXIE SHOWS THAT HE COMPLETELY UNDERSTANDS WHITMAN AND ACCEPTS HIM AS HE IS, EVEN ALLOWING HIM TO SHARE THE BASKETBALL FLOOR WITH HIS PEOPLE."

strategy uses all the tools for which Alexie is noted, such as allusions to pop culture and to Western literary culture, irony, satire, and dark humor. These are the province of Western writers, and Alexie has adopted them for his own purposes, using multicultural views. He scorns the romanticized, nostalgic view of Indians and instead feels free to put any image, form, phrase, or idea in his poems that make his point. Often, he puts pop culture figures such as John Wayne and Marilyn Monroe in the poem or story to highlight the fact that the life Indians live today is immersed in a foreign culture. Alexie tells interviewers that, if they go to a reservation, they will not see Indians with an ecological ethic communing with nature; they will see Indians watching TV and growing up on "The Brady Bunch," as Alexie himself did.

The ambiguity in Alexie's poetry comes from the fact that he is sometimes angry about the imposition of a foreign culture on Indian life, sometimes he is amused, and often he is exuberant about it, enjoying American culture on its own terms. The latter may be the case with "Defending Walt Whitman." It is true that one could read the poem as a mocking send-up of Whitman, the venerable father of American poetry, who looks ridiculous on the basketball court with Indians. In "Song of Ourself," in the same volume of poems, Alexie's title alludes to Whitman's poem "Song of Myself." He thus makes the critical point that Western culture is focused on individuality ("myself"), while Indian culture is about community ("ourself"). On the other hand, "Defending Walt Whitman" seems to lack the obvious anger of some of the poems in *The Summer of Black Widows*, such as "That Place Where Ghosts of Salmon Jump," mourning the loss of the Spokane salmon culture as it was ruined by the white man's cement dams.

In a later volume of poems, *One Stick Song* (2000), Alexie includes Walt Whitman in "An

WHAT DO I READ NEXT?

- *The Absolutely True Diary of a Part-time Indian* by Sherman Alexie (2007) is a young-adult book dealing with racism, poverty, and tradition, which won the National Book Award. This semi-autobiographical novel is about a young artist who decides to leave the reservation for a white high school.

- Alexie's own pick for the most important book on racial stereotyping in America is *The Invisible Man* by African American writer Ralph Ellison, published in 1952. This classic novel shows how prejudice makes a person invisible.

- *Native American Almanac: A Portrait of Native America Today* by Arlene Hirschfelder and Martha Kreipe de Montao (1998) presents an overview of past and present Native American life, including facts on reservations, laws, treaties, demographics, language, education, religion, sports, and media.

- Creek poet Joy Harjo's *Crazy Brave: A Memoir* (2012) is Harjo's spiritual coming-of-age memoir showing how she became a visionary Indian poet. Harjo has been one of Alexie's admirers and influences.

- Ken Mochizuki's *Baseball Saved Us*, published in 1995, is a young-adult novel about how the children in a Japanese American internment camp during World War II used the game of baseball to lift their spirits.

- Acoma Pueblo poet Simon Ortiz's *The People Shall Continue* (1977) is a history poetically told in an American Indian voice for young readers, from creation to the present day.

- William Saroyan's *My Name is Aram*, published in 1940, is a collection of short stories giving a picture of Armenian American heritage from the point of view of a boy growing up in Fresno, California. As a foreigner, Saroyan, like Alexie, found comfort in Whitman's ecstatic, embracing view of America.

- Walt Whitman's *Leaves of Grass* (1855), particularly "Starting from Paumanok," "Song of Myself," "Song of the Open Road," and "Poets to Come," gives a feel for the type of work that Alexie is imitating, in form and mood, in "Defending Walt Whitman."

Incomplete List of People I Wish Were Indian." He also includes Jesus Christ, Emily Dickinson, John Steinbeck, and Voltaire. Looking into Whitman's *Leaves of Grass* provides clues for why Alexie might admire Whitman and affectionately wish he could play basketball with him. "Defending Walt Whitman" is a poetic compliment written in free verse and in a style and tone like Whitman's. Whitman was not an ironic or angry poet. Even during the tragic Civil War, he sought to use his verse to heal wounds by accepting everyone with love. He wanted to be the poet of both the North and the South.

Whitman's stance is close to a traditional Indian point of view when it comes to language. Language is a sacred and magical gift to create change when spoken by someone like a medicine man (a traditional healer). Whitman believed himself to be a prophet of America, and said he was using his poems to prophesy and make things happen, as the prophets in the Bible did. He heard the magic in Indian names and uses them in his poems, which he called chants. In an openness that was not common at the time, he specifically includes African Americans, Indians, homosexuals, and women in his view of America. Surely, his democratic inclusiveness of marginal people in such poems as "Song of Myself" and "Starting from Paumanok" was admired by Alexie. In "Song of the Open Road," Whitman sets out on his life journey with the kind of excitement depicted in Alexie's poem, ready to like and embrace anyone he sees. This kind of tolerance of difference is reflected in Alexie's poem's lack of racial tension. Whitman is ludicrous to the Indians, but they accept him. Whitman is ecstatic about the brown bodies of the Indians, and he wants to be with them. There is no problem.

Whitman's views were radical and mystical. He says in "Song of Myself" and in "Song of the Open Road" that the universe is a road for traveling souls who meet on the road. They will all arrive at the goal, no matter who they are, the president or the slave. Alexie creates a similar image with the basketball court. Like the open road, the basketball court can accommodate anyone of any race or background. Whitman looks out of place with his big white beard, but he feels at home and claims that the game is for him. Some critics feel this shows Whitman's appropriation of the Indian game for himself, but read in the spirit of Whitman's poems, it shows his mystical belief that God makes everything for him to enjoy. It is possible that Alexie sees himself being able to offer the poet a beautiful sight he has never seen before. In "I Sing the Body Electric," Whitman praises the human body and sensory experience. He claims he is the poet of both body and soul. In "Defending Walt Whitman," Alexie makes the most out of the sensual brown bodies of the players, but he does not make it merely an erotic encounter. In "Why We Play Basketball," Alexie gives as reasons that Indian boys believe in their bodies when they play, and they also believe in God. Alexie includes the word God in "Defending Walt Whitman" several times; he makes basketball into a religious experience. As Nancy J. Peterson points out in "The Poetics of Tribalism in *The Summer of Black Widows*" (which is included in *Sherman Alexie: A Collection of Critical Essays*, edited by Jeff Berglund and Jan Roush): "Erotics, aesthetics, and spirituality come together in this charged encounter." This is partly humorous, and partly reflective of Alexie's enthusiasm for the sport. In his article for *Ethnic Studies Review*, "Sacred Hoop Dreams: Basketball in the Work of Sherman Alexie," David S. Goldstein points out that Alexie has frequently made jokes in his work to the effect that basketball is the new Indian religion, equal to a community powwow.

Many of Whitman's poems begin with the intention of celebrating something. Here, Alexie innocently celebrates Indian basketball with Whitman. Celebration in Whitman's work is spontaneous and democratic; he sees the good in everything. Whitman, unpretentious and curious, is just the sort of person who would be attracted to Indian basketball. He is also the sort of person who would not know or care if he looked strange on a basketball court on the reservation. Alexie provides a place where he can meet Whitman on equal footing, as both a man and a poet. He thus cleverly includes Indian poets in Whitman's address to future poets, making Indian poetry part of the American tradition Whitman was trying to create.

Alexie has named Whitman as an influence on his work. Whitman was fond of writing poems to his future audience, since his contemporary audience did not really understand him. He felt he was laying groundwork for writers of the future, as he references in the poem "Poets to Come." He sees those poets to come as native and athletic, writing something new—but surely he did not imagine a poetic son like Alexie! There is in Alexie's playfulness in "Defending Walt Whitman" the feeling that he is enjoying surprising Whitman. As Whitman seems to speak to future readers from the page, Alexie goes into the past and transports Whitman to the present. He amazes him with the Indian boys, basketball, and an Indian writer who takes up his call for a new kind of American poet.

In "By Blue Ontario's Shore," Whitman says the country needs a race of bards to hold the nation together. He gives a series of questions to test future poets. Do they know the land? Are they faithful? Are they merely from a sect or can they be universal? Whitman then gives his own qualifications for being an American poet: he has given charitable aid to those who asked and stood up for the marginal and socially unacceptable. He has rejected none. Alexie's own journey as a poet has also gone in this direction, especially after September 11, 2001, when he realized that the attack on the Twin Towers came from a kind of fundamentalist tribalism. In an interview with Duncan Campbell in 2002, quoted by John and Carl Bellante in *Conversations with Sherman Alexie*, Alexie says, "I am now desperately trying to let go of the idea of being right, the idea of making decisions based on imaginary tribes." Alexie's liberal humanism has embraced all races, cultures, and sexual orientations in his latest work. In an interview in 2010 with Joshua B. Nelson in *World Literature Today*, Alexie has said that humor is his "green card" that lets him enter any tribe.

Source: Susan K. Andersen, Critical Essay on "Defending Walt Whitman," in *Poetry for Students*, Gale, Cengage Learning, 2014.

Nancy J. Peterson

In the following excerpt, Peterson discusses the tension between Western and tribal traditions in "Defending Walt Whitman."

The transformation of tribal identity in contemporary society and culture is a concern that runs provocatively throughout the work of Spokane/Coeur d'Alene writer Sherman Alexie. Alexie, one of the most popular Indian authors working today, has had to reckon with the ambivalence of his own rise to success. He launched his career by voicing reservation realities often filtered through speakers who are young Indian men— poised on the verge of despair but longing for something more—who reveal themselves through eloquent "rez" talk. His later stories and poems, however, have experimented with diverse materials and forms, often borrowing from Anglo-American, African American, and Western cultures to depict Indians on the move, bringing tribal identities and Native worldviews into urban and mixed-blood environments. Alexie's penchant for fusing non-Native and Native traditions in unexpected ways lies at the heart of *The Summer of Black Widows*, his acclaimed volume of poetry published in 1996.

This volume significantly thematicizes and enacts at a formal level the tensions between Alexie's tribalist, reservation roots and the writer's engagement with non-Native and multicultural materials associated with the world beyond the reservation. The poems are grouped into seven sections under headings that echo the titles of individual poems and reiterate some of the major images and themes of the volume. The collection begins with a section titled "Why We Play Basketball"; its nine poems are set on the reservation, and several mention Spokane specifically. Taken together, they summon up images of rez ball, powwows and dancing, Coyote, the Ghost Dance, and poignant details of daily life on the reservation. The collection moves through subsequent sections focusing on family affiliations, powwows, tourists, and Sasquatch, culminating in a section titled "Bob's Coney Island," which includes nine poems set in urban and global locations, including Spain, Germany, Chicago, Los Angeles, New York City, and Coney Island. Through the shifting locations of these poems, *The Summer of Black Widows* explores the way that tribalism manifests itself in diverse modes and contemporary contexts.

> ALEXIE'S POEM LOCATES A LANGUAGE AND RHYTHM THAT INTONES A COMMITMENT TO THE INDIAN PLAYERS, THEIR TRIBAL CONNECTIONS, AND THEIR SENSE OF SOVEREIGNTY AT THE SAME TIME AS IT EMBRACES WHITMAN'S ANGLO POETIC AND AESTHETIC SENSIBILITY."

At a formal, technical level, the poems employ a dynamic, creative bricolage in blending Indian realities and traditional Western poetic forms. Alexie sometimes situates his work consciously within Western poetic traditions by labeling a poem a sonnet or villanelle, for instance, or referring to Anglo-American poetry icons such as Walt Whitman, Emily Dickinson, or Shakespeare. He includes Spokane and Coeur d'Alene traditions in his poems as well, using images from powwows and dancing, Sasquatch and salmon, and other markers of his specific tribal affiliations, along with allusions to tribal history and the Spokane Indian Reservation. Still other multicultural layers appear in his poems in references to African American music, mainstream pop-culture icons, and minority histories from other oppressed people. In the complex exchange of cultures, identities, and traditions that shapes *The Summer of Black Widows*, an interesting dynamic develops: as the poems move off the reservation to explore non-Native spaces, forms, and materials, they become ever so firmly rooted in tribalism. This essay explores the ways that tribalism as a worldview or critical consciousness permeates the aesthetics and ethics of the poems in *The Summer of Black Widows*.

TRIBALISM AND POETICS

In a 1997 interview with John Purdy, Alexie describes *The Summer of Black Widows* as "technically good"; "I thought it was probably my best book." He also critiques the volume—"but very few of the poems Indian people would relate to"—and comments that he wishes he could "go back to writing the kinds of poems I wrote in *Fancydancing*," his 1992 collection, which to him were more "Indian" and "accessible to Indian people." In contrast to Alexie's self-criticism, some of Alexie's most insightful readers have identified *The Summer of Black Widows* as an ambitious and accomplished volume: John Newton describes it as "more affirmative" and confident about "indigenous authority"; Ron McFarland echoes Alexie's evaluation of his technique by commending the volume for its ability to "demonstrate[e] his formal range"; Susan Brill de Ramírez describes the poems as "more hopeful" and invoking the "power of the sacred to overcome the horrors of the world." Alexie's comments about *The Summer of Black Widows*, however, reveal both approval and disavowal of his technical prowess and suggest that too much emphasis on poetic technique creates an uneasy detachment from Indian readers and reservation realities.

One way to navigate the relationship and tension between Native and Western poetics in Alexie's work is through the poem "Defending Walt Whitman," which stages a sometimes-comical, sometimes-inspiring encounter between young Indian men playing reservation basketball and Whitman, an iconic figure in Anglo-American poetry, who shows up at the game wanting more than anything to be a player. As Cyrus Patell observes, Alexie's poem simultaneously "pays homage to Whitman" and "shows us a Whitman who is out of place." On the one hand, the poem reveals a Whitman who "cannot tell the difference between / offense and defense" and who looks ridiculous with his long beard, which "frightens / the smallest Indian boys." On the other hand, Alexie's Whitman—observing the prowess of the Indian boys and young men playing basketball—is powerfully moved:

> God, there is nothing as beautiful as a jump shot
> on a reservation summer basketball court
> where the ball is moist with sweat
> and makes a sound when it swishes through the net
> that causes Walt Whitman to weep because it is so
>   perfect.
> (*SBW*)

Whitman's appreciation—even reverence—for the game emerges from a constellation of desires: for the game itself, for young men, for brown bodies, for beauty, and for God. Erotics, aesthetics, and spirituality come together in this charged encounter.

Alexie's Indian players have their own reasons for revering basketball. It is a game that provides an escape from the wars and military stints some have served (Kuwait and "foreign wars" are both cited in the first few stanzas of the poem). More importantly, basketball becomes a way for them to express their Indianness—to be "twentieth-century warriors who will never kill"; to leap "like a salmon" heading upriver "toward home" and run like ponies with their long hair swinging freely in the wind: "bareback, skin slick and shiny" (*SBW*). "Defending Walt Whitman" offers an eloquent depiction of reservation basketball that recurs throughout Alexie's poetry and fiction.

But it is not clear in the poem if Whitman ever glimpses the significance of basketball for the Indian players. In fact, the poem ends with a line that suggests Whitman's implicit egocentricity: "Walt Whitman shakes. This game belongs to him" (*SBW*). This arrogant claim brings us back to the title of the poem and its double (and dueling) implications—this is a poem that defends Walt Whitman (and what he symbolizes in terms of poetics and cultural encounters), but it also defends reservation life and Indian players from the prying eyes and imperialist assumptions of Whitman (himself and as a synecdoche for Anglo-Americans generally).

Rather than attempting to resolve this fundamental tension, I suggest that the power of the poem derives precisely and proportionally from the friction of this tension. Alexie's poem locates a language and rhythm that intones a commitment to the Indian players, their tribal connections, and their sense of sovereignty at the same time as it embraces Whitman's Anglo poetic and aesthetic sensibility. For it is Whitman, after all, who reveres the sensually rich details of the bright summer day, the sweat clinging to the basketball, and the swoosh of a ball that touches only net and who connects the game and the players profoundly to beauty and God. In other words, Alexie's poem—through its eloquent, poetic tribute to "rez" ball—suggests that it is possible to use Western traditions and aesthetics to strengthen tribal ties.

In his poetry, Alexie negotiates a desire for Indianness and sovereignty from within contemporary conditions in ways akin to Craig Womack's critical work on reading and interpreting Native American literature. In *Red on Red: Native American Literary Separatism* (1999), Womack demonstrates the way specific longtime tribal traditions continue to energize and preoccupy Creek writers—from oral storytellers living today to authors spanning the late-nineteenth through the twentieth centuries, including Alexander Posey, Alice Callahan, Louis Oliver, and Joy Harjo. Womack's insistent point is that, unless we read these writers in terms of tribal identity, we will make them vanish as Indians— we will fail to recognize them as Creek writers having something valuable to say about Creek traditions and sovereignty. In other words, Womack's method of reading Native writers in terms of tribal affiliations works counter to a Western model of the individual as Great Author and instead emphasizes the significant contributions Native literature can make to strengthen and sustain the political, aesthetic, intellectual, and spiritual traditions of Indian nations....

Source: Nancy J. Peterson, "The Poetics of Tribalism in Sherman Alexie's *The Summer of Black Widows*," in *Sherman Alexie: A Collection of Critical Essays*, edited by Jeff Berglund and Jan Roush, University of Utah Press, 2010, pp. 134–38.

John Purdy

In the following interview, Alexie explains to Purdy why he is a writer and for whom he is writing.

... JP: I was at a workshop once in Santa Fe and Vizenor was there, Owens, Anna Lee Walters was there, and some other people from the Navajo reservation. Someone asked her, "So who are you writing for, Anna?" She said, "Young Indian kids on the rez."

One thing I like about my classes is that sooner or later students are going to be asking that same question: "What is this Indian literature?" And then they wrestle through all those questions of audience, and definitions, by biology or whatever, and just when they start to feel comfortable, then we complicate it. Take the book for the book.

SA: But see, that doesn't work.

JP: What?

SA: Taking the book for a book.

JP: In what way?

SA: In an Indian definition, you can't separate the message from the messenger.

JP: That's not the same. I think "the book" can carry that. Your work carries it.

SA: Yeah. But I think you're referring to identity questions and such.

> AND INDIAN WRITERS, ALL WRITERS IN GENERAL, BUT INDIAN WRITERS, TOO, WERE THE WEIRD KIDS, THE BIZARRE KIDS. THE ONES WHO QUESTION INSTITUTIONS, THE ONES WHO WERE NOT ALL THAT POPULAR."

JP: Oh. That's how the issue shakes out, because that's what the students are interested in, but the question is how to take them back to the book, to the story itself.

SA: Most of our Indian literature is written by people whose lives are nothing like the Indians they're writing about. There's a lot of people pretending to be "traditional," all these academic professors living in university towns, who rarely spend any time on a reservation, writing all these "traditional" books. Momaday—he's not a traditional man. And there's nothing wrong with that, I'm not either, but this adherence to the expected idea, the bear and all this imagery. I think it is dangerous, and detrimental.

JP: It's the nineties, and now it's time to move on. So, we get back to the discussion of what "it" is.

SA: Well, I want to take it away. I want to take Indian lit *away* from that, and away from the people who own it now.

JP: I think you do, in your writing.

SA: That's what I mean. I'm starting to see it. A lot of younger writers are starting to write like me—writing like I do, in a way, not copying me, but writing about what happens to them, not about what they wish was happening. They aren't writing wish fulfillment books, they're writing books about reality. How they live, and who they are, and what they think about. Not about who they wish they were. The kind of Indian they wish they were. They are writing about the kind of Indian they are.

JP: Sure, and it makes sense. Whenever you have any group of individuals in any literature who start to define the center, then everybody has to ask whether or not that's sufficient over time.

SA: We've been stuck in place since *House Made of Dawn.*

JP: But there's some interesting work coming out. Have you read Carr's Eye Killers?

SA: I hate it.

JP: You did? Well, that's right, it does have that traditional thing going on, but to move into the genre of the vampire novel I thought was interesting.

SA: That's fun, but I thought that book was blasphemous as hell to Navajo culture, the way he used ceremonies and such. I have a real problem with that. I don't use any at all. And a white woman saved everybody.

JP: But she was *a teacher. (Laughter.)*

SA: But it read like a movie turned into a novel. I was supposed to review it, and I didn't.

JP: Tell me this. What do you see coming out right now that is doing what needs to be done?

SA: Irvin Morris. I like his book [*From the Glittering World: A Navajo Story*]. I think Tiffany Midge has a good future, once she stops copying me.

JP: She did a great reading that night in Bellingham High.

SA: The thing is she was so into my work then, she's not so much now. That night, ask the people who saw me read before that night, she read exactly like me. So even that night I had to change the way I read. I'd never heard her read in public before, and she got up and read and I thought, "O my god, that's me, that's my shtick." So I, literally, had to figure out a different way to read.

JP: Do you see anybody coming up through Wordcraft Circle?

SA: I'm in Wordcraft Circle; I'm a board member and all that. But I get worried. I think it's focusing too much on the idea of publication. The idea of writing as a career. It's becoming very careerist.

JP: So you either make it ... if you don't publish and not doing it for your whole life then you shouldn't be doing it? Is that the danger you see?

SA: Well, it's becoming less and less about art. The whole thing is full of publication opportunities, money to win, scholarships, news about Indian writers publishing. . . .

JP: "Done good."

SA: Done good, yeah. Which is all fine. We're having a meeting soon and I just want to share my concerns with them that I'm worried that the focus has gone wrong.

JP: That the joy of it is not there?

SA: Exactly. One percent of one percent of the people in Wordcraft are going to have a book published. I think it's setting up unrealistic expectations.

JP: There's a group that Liz Cook-Lynn is involved with, a storytellers' circle, and they publish what they come up with, themselves. The focus isn't on selling it, but on doing it.

SA: Yeah. The act is the thing. I know people who would rather be where I'm at now, but I'm jaded as hell. About publication, about the "art" of it. I sound like I'm complaining. I'm glad to be where I'm at; I worked hard to get where I am. But there's also a lot that's shady about it. Being a successful Indian writer, and being an Indian, a "good Indian" (in quotes) are often mutually exclusive things, and there's a lot of pressure. I spend a lot of time alone, working. Selfish. My friendships suffer, my relationships with my family suffer, my health suffers. To be where I'm at, to do what I do, you'd have to be an obsessive compulsive nut (much laughter) and I don't think we should be encouraging our children in that direction. (More laughter.) Or at least letting them know. I mean, Wordcraft should be talking about the ugliness, too. This is what happens. Hard truths about publishing.

JP: The reality rather than the ideal image of the author dashing about the world, vacationing on sunny beaches.

SA: Exactly.

JP: But there are other rewards, right? The joy?

SA: Money and attention.

JP: Besides that.

SA: Don't let any writer fool you.

JP: Now, a little bit ago you said the poetry was still there, that that's. . . .

SA: Yeah, but nobody buys that.

JP: Yeah, true. I almost said that. But they buy movies and they buy novels.

SA: First and foremost, writers like to get attention. Don't let any writer tell you different.

JP: Yeah, well, in my world it's tenure and promotion, so. . . .

SA: Which is attention. We want to be heard. We're standing on street corners shouting. If that's not a cry for attention, I don't know what is. And Indian writers, all writers in general, but Indian writers, too, were the weird kids, the bizarre kids. The ones who question institutions, the ones who were not all that popular. The ones who people looked at weird. There are big burdens involved in all of this, you know.

[Interruption]

JP: You were on the state governor's book award board, and one winner was Carolyn Kizer. She has a great poem, "Afternoon Happiness." It says the poet's job is to write about pain and suffering, all that is "grist for me," but all she wants to do is write a poem about being content, and this poem does it.

SA: Actually, I'm doing it, too. My next book is all happy rez poems.

JP: That ought to start a buzz.

SA: Yeah. All the joy I remember from growing up.

JP: Good. Think it will sell well in Europe?

SA: It's not corn pollen, eagle feathers, Mother Earth, Father Sky. It's everyday life. Remembering taking our bikes and setting up ramps to jump over the sewer pit. That kind of stuff.

JP: And making it!

SA: Yeah, yeah. Or *not.* (Laughter.) And some of it a little sad. I'm working on this poem; it's not very good right now, I just wrote it last night, but I remember, I remember, I dreamed it a couple of nights ago, but during the winter we would, in winter, we'd take our gloves and put them on the radiator in the old school whenever they'd get wet. But I remembered some kids didn't have gloves, because they couldn't afford it, they were too poor. And I didn't have gloves this one winter, and I remembered that. And so I had this dream where I was sitting in the classroom and there were twelve pair of gloves on the radiator and thirteen kids in the classroom, and so everybody's looking around trying to figure out who's the one who doesn't have gloves, so everybody's hiding their hands. So, I'm working on that poem, and that image of everyone hiding their hands so nobody will know who didn't have gloves. Kind of sad, kind of nostalgic....

JP: But positive in ways....

SA: And that is also funny, I mean. Another one's about...there's this series of lullaby poems, actually, that I've written, they're really rhymey lullaby poems. Pow-wow lullaby poems, I call 'em, 'cause where we live on the Spokane rez the pow-wow ground is a couple of miles away, and at night you can hear the drums and the stick game players playing all night long, and that would put me to sleep at night during pow-wows. I'm writing poems about that feeling, or walking in the dark back from the pow-wow grounds, hearing the drums or walking to the grounds at night, or falling asleep in teepees, or in Winnebagos, or when we were real little, at a pow-wow in Arlee or wherever, and you'd end up sleeping in cousins' teepees in just a big pile of Indian kids. Those are the kinds of poems I've been writing.

Like the last book, *The Summer of Black Widows,* I thought was technically good. My last book of poems, technically good. I thought it was probably my best book. But very few of the poems Indian people would relate to. Whereas a book like *Fancydancing* I think is incredibly Indian. I want to go back to writing the kind of poems I wrote in *Fancydancing.* I'm more happy now. I'm a happier person. When I wrote these books...I'm getting happier and getting healthier. Some people say I always write about drunks. Well, no I don't, but if you look at the books you can see a progression, actually. The alcohol is dropping out of the books, because the alcohol is dropping farther and farther out of my life, as I've been sober for more and more years....

Source: John Purdy, "Crossroads: A Conversation with Sherman Alexie," in *Conversations with Sherman Alexie,* edited by Nancy J. Peterson, University Press of Mississippi, 2009.

Doug Marx

In the following essay, Marx provides a biography, which offers insight into Alexie's portrayals of life on the reservation.

Six years ago, as a 24-year-old student at Washington State University, Sherman Alexie, a Spokane/Coeur d' Alene Indian, set down his career goals at the insistence of a friend: 1) to publish ten books by age 30; 2) to see a book on the silver screen by 35; and 3) to receive a major literary prize by 40.

With Indian Killer (Forecasts, July 29), his third prose work, a tragic thriller about the ravages of cultural dilution and dissolution, out this

THE PERCEPTION OF BEING AN OUTCAST AMONG OUTCASTS CONTRIBUTES TO ALEXIE'S COMPLEX PORTRAIT OF RESERVATION LIFE, A VIEW RIFE WITH IRONIES AND A SENSE OF COMPLICITY THAT HAS COME UNDER FIRE FROM INDIAN WRITERS FOR ITS APPARENT EMPHASIS ON HOPELESSNESS, ALCOHOLISM AND SUICIDE."

month from Grove/Atlantic, and *The Summer of Black Widows*, his seventh collection of poetry, out in October from Hanging Loose Press, the first goal will be achieved. Three of Alexie's books—his first shortstory collection, *The Lone Ranger and Tonto Fistfight in Heaven* (Atlantic Monthly, 1993); his novel *Reservation Blues* (Atlantic Monthly, 1994); and *Indian Killer*— are the subject of ongoing film negotiations. As for a major literary award, if review acclaim from such established masters as Reynolds Price, Leslie Marmon Silko and Frederick Bausch, not to mention inclusion in the recent "Best of Young American Novelists" issue of *Granta*, means anything, Alexie could well win his prize.

When asked how sudden success has affected him, Alexie flashes a quick smile and quips: "I like room service." The remark—even coming from a sometime stand-up comic—is revealing. Self-described as "mouthy, opinionated and arrogant," Alexie betrays no squeamishness about the mix of art and commerce. He loves the limelight, and his readings are known for their improvisational energy, costume changes and singing. Six years sober after a six-year binge that began the day he entered college, he explains: "Today, I get high, I get drunk off of public readings. I'm good at it. It comes from being a debater in high school, but also, crucially, it comes from the oral tradition of my own culture. It's in performance that the two cultures become one." Then he laughs, adding: "The most terrifying phrase in the world is when an Indian man grabs a microphone and says 'I have a few words to say.'"

Alexie has more than a few words to say. His memory runs deep. Whether cast in poetry or prose, his work offers a devastating and deeply human portrait of contemporary Indian life. Greeting *PW* in the modest Seattle apartment where he lives with his wife of two years, Diane, a beautiful, private woman of Hidatsa/Ho Chunk/Pottawatomi descent, Alexie proves to be affable and generous, ready to sit down around the kitchen table and talk about his life and art.

Tall, handsome, his long black hair tied in a ponytail, dressed casually in a beige knit shirt and khakis, Alexie, who played basketball in high school, has a shooting guard's easy movements and soft touch. One would never suspect that he was born hydrocephalic, endured a brain operation at six months that should have left him mentally retarded—if not dead—and for his first seven years was beset with seizures and medicated with regular doses of lithium, phenobarbital and other sedatives.

The son of Sherman Sr. and Lillian Alexie (his father is Coeur d' Alene, his mother Spokane), Alexie was born and reared in Wellpinit, the only town on the Spokane Indian Reservation—a place he describes as a landscape of "HUD shacks and abandoned cars"—which lies some 50 miles northwest of Spokane, Wash. Alcoholism, a central concern of Alexie's work, afflicted his family, but there was love in the house, along with a mix of traditional and contemporary culture. "I've come to realize my parents did a damn good job, considering the cards they were dealt," he says.

Then there was his maternal grandmother, Etta Adams, who died when Alexie was eight, and who appears as the eternal, wise and practical "Big Mom" in *Reservation Blues*. "She was one of the great spiritual leaders of the Spokane tribe," Alexie says, "one of the most powerful figures to visit the Northwest, and in her last days thousands came to pay their respects." The need for female strength and wisdom is a primary theme of Alexie's, sounded early on in "Indian Boy Love Songs," four poems collected in *The Business of Fancydancing* (Hanging Loose, 1992).

Alexie began reading in earnest at an early age. Because he was unable to participate in the wild athleticism of a young male Indian's rites of passage, books became his world. "I knew what a paragraph was before I could read the words," he says, claiming that at age six, he began working his way through *The Grapes of Wrath*. Steinbeck's final image of a starving man being breast-fed is fixed in his mind: "Ah, so that's the way a story's supposed to end," he recalls telling himself. "With that kind of huge moment, which is the way the stories we tell ourselves end." Through grade and high school, he devoured every book in the school libraries, reading and re-reading Steinbeck until the copies fell apart in his hands. "I was a total geek," Alexie recalls, "which automatically made me an outcast, so in order to succeed I had to be smarter than everybody else. My sense of competitiveness came out that way. I was fierce in the classroom, I humiliated everybody and had my nose broken five times after school for being the smart kid."

PLAYING THE GOOD WHITE INDIAN

Alexie's view of Indian life acquired more complexity when, in 1981, he enrolled at an all-white high school in Reardan, a reservation border town unfriendly to Indians. With his world turned upside-down, he became the "perfect Reardan kid": an honor student and class president and the only ponytail on the crewcut Reardan Indians basketball team. "I kept my mouth shut and became a good white Indian," he acknowledges. "All those qualities that made me unpopular on the reservation made me popular at Reardan. It got to the point where I don't think they saw me as Indian."

The hard work and conformity earned Alexie a scholarship to Gonzaga University in Spokane, where he enrolled with vague intentions of becoming a doctor or lawyer—"the usual options for a bright, brown kid"—and promptly fell apart. Feeling lost, lacking a life plan, he began drinking heavily. His misery found consolation in poetry, which he began to read avidly—Keats, Yeats, Dickinson, Whitman. "I didn't see myself in them," he says, "so I felt like I was doing anthropology, like I was studying white people. Obviously, something was drawing me in that I couldn't intellectualize or verbalize, and then I realized that the poems weren't just about white people. They were about everybody. I also realized that the poets were outcasts, too," he chuckles.

After two years, Alexie packed his bags and left Gonzaga for the University of Washington. Newly arrived in Seattle, he was robbed and soon found himself back in Wellpinit, on the verge of joining the long history of young Indians who come home to a slow death by alcohol. Waking one morning on the steps of the Assembly of God Church, hungover, his pants wet, he staggered home to mail off an application to WSU in Pullman. It was a poetry class at WSU taught by Alex Kuo that finally helped him to get his bearings as a writer, he recalls.

The boozing didn't stop, but the words poured out. Kuo, who became a father figure to Alexie, gave him a copy of the anthology *Songs of This Earth on Turtle's Back*. "In an instant I saw myself in literature," Alexie recalls. A line from an Adrian C. Louis poem called "Elegy for the Forgotten Oldsmobile" changed his life forever: "O Uncle Adrian! I'm in the reservation of my own mind." "I started crying. That was my whole life. Forget Steinbeck, forget Keats. I just kept saying that line over and over again. I sat down and started writing poems. And they came. It was scary."

Under Kuo's guidance, his first semester manuscript became his first book, *I Would Steal Horses*, which was published by Slipstream in 1992. With Native poets such as Louis and Simon Ortiz, Joy Harjo and Linda Hogan as models, he began to write his own story in his own voice. Lyrical, angry, poignant, socially engaged, the poems found their way into small literary magazines such as *Brooklyn's Hanging Loose*. Eventually, Hanging Loose Press brought out *The Business of Fancydancing*, which received a strong critical reception and has sold 11,000 copies, an astounding number for a book of poems from a small press. Serendipitously, the letter accepting the manuscript for publication arrived the day Alexie decided to quit drinking.

During his student days, and at Kuo's urging, Alexie began to experiment with prose—some of which appeared in *Fancydancing*. Other fictions were later collected in *The Lone Ranger and Tonto Fistfight in Heaven*, half of which was written in a four-month burst when agents, alert to his poetry, began calling with requests for fiction.

A friend introduced Alexie to Nancy Stauffer, who remains his agent to this day. "Nancy's really been good at helping me develop a career," he says. "We really have a plan. We're not just going book to book. First and foremost, I want to be a better writer, and I want a larger audience." In short order, Alexie found himself with a two-book, six-figure contract with Morgan Entrekin at the Atlantic Monthly Press at a time when, he says, he "didn't even have an idea for a novel."

The idea did come, in the guise of *Reservation Blues*, a novel that imagines legendary bluesman Robert Johnson arriving on a reservation seeking redemption from "a woman," in this case

Big Mom. Johnson's magic guitar carries four
young Indians off the reservation and into the
world of rock and roll. The book explores differences between reservation and urban Indians
and the effects of the church on traditional people, among other themes. It's also a bleak novel
that's leavened by Alexie's signature black
humor. "I'm not trying to be funny," he explains.
"I don't sit down to write something funny. In
my everyday life I'm funny, and when I write it
comes out. Laughter is a ceremony, it's the way
people cope."

There isn't much laughter in *Indian Killer*,
which depicts John Smith, an Indian without a
tribal affiliation. Adopted off the reservation
and reared by a white couple, he becomes a
suspect in a string of brutal scalpings that terrify
Seattle. Tangent to Smith are a host of characters, including a racist talk-show host, a white
professor of Native American studies and a defiant female Indian activist, all of whom are struggling with their senses of identity. The picture is
of a man divided by culture, a culture divided by
its tragic history, a city divided by race, and a
nation at war with itself. And it is a vision Alexie
paints with excruciating clarity.

The perception of being an outcast among
outcasts contributes to Alexie's complex portrait
of reservation life, a view rife with ironies and a
sense of complicity that has come under fire from
Indian writers for its apparent emphasis on hopelessness, alcoholism and suicide. "I write what I
know," he says, "and I don't try to mythologize
myself, which is what some seem to want, and
which some Indian women and men writers are
doing, this Earth Mother and Shaman Man thing,
trying to create these 'authentic, traditional' Indians. We don't live our lives that way."

Well aware that his poems and novels have
angered Indians and whites alike, Alexie enjoys
walking a kind of cultural highwire. "I use a
racial criterion in my literary critiques," he
says. "I have a very specific commitment to
Indian people, and I'm very tribal in that sense.
I want us to survive as Indians."

That said, Alexie's Indian characters are
never guileless victims. Echoing Big Mom, who
continually reminds her neighbors in *Reservation Blues* that their fate is in their own hands,
he explains: "It's a two-way street. The system
sets you up to fail, and then, somehow, you
choose it."

Source: Doug Marx, "Sherman Alexie: A Reservation
of the Mind," in *Publishers Weekly*, Vol. 243, No. 38,
September 16, 1996, p. 39.

SOURCES

Alexie, Sherman, "Defending Walt Whitman," in *The
Summer of Black Widows*, Hanging Loose Press, 1996,
pp. 14–15.

———, *One Stick Song*, Hanging Loose Press, 2000,
pp. 18, 20.

Bellante, John, and Carl Bellante, "Sherman Alexie:
Literary Rebel," in *Conversations with Sherman Alexie*,
edited by Nancy J. Peterson, University Press of Mississippi,
2009, pp. 8, 12; originally published in the *Bloomsbury
Review*, May–June 1994, p. 26.

Berglund, Jeff, "Introduction: 'Imagination Turns Every
Word into a Bottle Rocket,'" and "The Business of
Writing: Sherman Alexie's Meditations on Authorship,"
in *Sherman Alexie: A Collection of Critical Essays*, edited
by Jeff Berglund and Jan Roush, University of Utah
Press, 2010, pp. xxvi, 243, 245–46.

Berner, Robert L., Review of *The Summer of Black
Widows*, in *World Literature Today*, Vol. 71, No. 2,
Spring 1997, p. 430.

Brill de Ramírez, Susan, "The Distinctive Sonority of
Sherman Alexie's Indigenous Poetics," in *Sherman
Alexie: A Collection of Critical Essays*, edited by Jeff
Berglund and Jan Roush, University of Utah Press,
2010, pp. 107–109, 118, 125.

Cremean, David N., Review of *The Summer of Black
Widows*, in *Western American Literature*, Vol. 32,
Summer 1997, p. 182.

Evans, Stephen F., "'Open Containers': Sherman
Alexie's Drunken Indians," in *American Indian
Quarterly*, Vol. 25, No.1, Winter 2001, pp. 46–73.

Goldstein, David S., "Sacred Hoop Dreams: Basketball
in the Work of Sherman Alexie," in *Ethnic Studies
Review*, Vol. 32, No. 1, Summer 2009, pp. 77–89.

Gonzalez, Ray, Review of *The Summer of Black Widows*,
in *Bloomsbury Review*, January–February 1997, p. 7.

McFarland, Ron, "'Another Kind of Violence': Sherman
Alexie's Poems," in *American Indian Quarterly*, Vol. 21,
No. 2, 1997, pp. 251–263.

Nelson, Joshua B., "'Humor Is My Green Card': A
Conversation with Sherman Alexie," in *World Literature
Today*, Vol. 84, No. 4, July–August 2010, pp. 39–45.

Peterson, Nancy J., "The Poetics of Tribalism in Sherman
Alexie's *The Summer of Black Widows*," in *Sherman
Alexie: A Collection of Critical Essays*, edited by Jeff
Berglund and Jan Roush, University of Utah Press,
2010, pp. 134–37.

Review of *The Summer of Black Widows*, in *Library
Journal*, Vol. 121, No. 18, November 1, 1996, pp. 70–71.

Review of *The Summer of Black Widows*, in *Publishers Weekly*, Vol. 243, No. 40, September 30, 1996, p. 82.

"Sherman Alexie: The 2010 Puterbaugh Fellow," in *World Literature Today*, Vol. 84, No. 4, July–August 2010, p. 35.

Whitman, Walt, *Complete Poetry and Selected Prose*, edited by James E. Miller Jr., Houghton Mifflin, Boston, 1959, pp. 13, 15, 25, 70, 241.

FURTHER READING

Alexie, Sherman, *Reservation Blues*, Atlantic Monthly, 1995.

Alexie's satiric view of life on the reservation is a contrast to Silko's approach in *Ceremony* and makes a good parallel read.

Bernadin, Susan, "Alexie-Vision: Getting the Picture," in *World Literature Today*, Vol. 84, No. 4, July–August 2010, pp. 52–56.

Alexie's media success in television and film is changing the country's image of Indian identity.

Grassian, Daniel, *Understanding Sherman Alexie*, University of South Carolina Press, 2005.

This is an overview of Alexie's work with a chapter on each book that he has published, including one on *The Summer of Black Widows*.

Linda Hogan, *The Book of Medicines*, Coffee House Press, 1993.

Chickasaw poet Hogan uses the image of skin to invoke both pain and healing, reconciling Native American knowledge with contemporary life. Hogan's poetry is in the lyric vein of modern Indian poets, a contrast to Alexie's satiric and political style.

Ruby, Robert H., and John A. Brown, *The Spokane Indians: Children of the Sun*, University of Oklahoma Press, 1970.

This specific history of the Spokane tribe tells the background of some of Alexie's allusions in his poems, such as the relationship of the Spokane to the sacred salmon, the Christian and trading influence on the Spokane and Coeur d'Alene tribes, the war with United States soldiers, and the terrible horse slaughter by Colonel George Wright, a satiric figure in Alexie's work.

Silko, Leslie Marmon, *Ceremony*, Viking, 1977.

This novel is widely read and taught as an introduction to Native American culture today. It takes place on the Laguna Pueblo Reservation where the Indian of mixed heritage, Tayo, returns for healing in the ancestral way after being held a prisoner of war during World War II.

SUGGESTED SEARCH TERMS

Sherman Alexie

The Summer of Black Widows

Defending Walt Whitman

Walt Whitman

Sherman Alexie AND YouTube

Spokane Reservation

Spokane AND history

Native American AND poetry

Native American AND basketball

Indians AND salmon culture

The Esquimos Have No Word for "War"

MARY OLIVER

1992

"The Esquimos Have No Word for 'War'" is a free-verse lyric poem by Mary Oliver, perhaps the best-selling contemporary poet in America. Oliver is known for writing in the romantic tradition of poets such as Ralph Waldo Emerson, Walt Whitman, Emily Dickinson, and Robert Frost. She is widely known as a nature poet, and a large percentage of her poetry and prose revolves around humans' spiritual connection to nature.

The "Esquimos" referred to in the title are the Inuit, an aboriginal (native) people of the Arctic who mainly live in Canada, Greenland, and Alaska. Many Inuit consider *Eskimo* to be a pejorative term; in Inuktitut, the Inuit language, it translates to "eaters of raw meat." Much preferred is *Inuit*, which translates simply as "the people."

Published in Oliver's 1992 National Book Award–winning collection *New and Selected Poems*, "Esquimos" is typical of Oliver's poetry in its depiction of natural elements and elevation of a spiritual connection with the land over modernization. It deals with themes of language and examines the notion of cultural identity by contrasting the simple life of the Inuit with the warring, aggressive societies of other parts of the world. In its style, subject matter, and technical form, "The Esquimos Have No Word for 'War'" sits firmly in the romantic tradition passed down from the nature poets of the nineteenth century.

Mary Oliver (© Frederick M. Brown | Getty Images Entertainment | Getty Images)

AUTHOR BIOGRAPHY

Mary Oliver was born on September 10, 1935, in Maple Heights, Ohio, on the outskirts of Cleveland. As a teenager, she visited the home of deceased poet Edna St. Vincent Millay in upstate New York, eventually moving into the estate with Millay's sister, Norma, to help sort the work and correspondence that Millay had left behind. On a visit to the estate in the late 1950s, she met Molly Malone Cook, a young photographer who later served as Oliver's literary agent. Oliver and Cook began a romantic relationship that lasted until Cook's death in 2005.

In 1963, at the age of 28, Oliver published her first collection of poetry, *No Voyage, and Other Poems*. Since that time, Oliver has become one of the best-selling and most well-known poets in America. She has published more than twenty books of poetry and six books of prose, including books on the craft of poetry. She won the 1984 Pulitzer Prize for Poetry for her 1983 poetry collection *American Primitive*. *New and Selected Poems*, in which "The Esquimos Have No Word for 'War'" appears, won the 1992 National Book Award for Poetry and was a *New York Times* Notable Book of the Year for

1993. In 1998, she won the Christopher Award and the L. L. Winship/PEN New England Award for *House of Light*. Oliver was the recipient of a Guggenheim Fellowship and has received honorary doctorates from the Art Institute of Boston, Dartmouth College, and Tufts University. Oliver has taught workshops and held residencies at Case Western Reserve University, Bucknell University, Sweet Briar College, and Bennington College, where she held the Catharine Osgood Foster Chair for Distinguished Teaching from 1995 to 2001.

Oliver has granted very few interviews, preferring to reveal herself through her poetry and essays. She writes in the romantic tradition of Whitman and Henry David Thoreau, with nature as her primary subject and inspiration. Through her observations of the natural world and the human condition, Oliver's work examines the notion of identity and simplicity. As of 2013, she resides in Provincetown, Massachusetts, in the home she shared with Cook for several decades, and many of the observations of nature that she records in her poems are taken from this New England area.

POEM SUMMARY

The text used for this summary is from *New and Selected Poems*, Vol. 1, Beacon Press, 1992, p. 236.

"The Esquimos Have No Word for 'War'" is a free-verse poem divided into three stanzas of differing lengths and cadences. Though there is no set rhyme pattern or meter, Oliver uses other poetic techniques to give the poem a sense of form. The poetic elements that structure the poem are more subtle than the strict rhyme and meter of traditional poetic forms, and they are easier to identify if the poem is read aloud.

The title is an essential part of the poem, almost functioning as the first line (although line numbering in this summary starts with the first stanza and does not include the title). This is the only place where the word "war" appears. When Oliver refers to war in the body of the poem, she does so indirectly, using a pronoun in line 1 and naming some of its characteristics in lines 18 and 19. The only reason the reader knows the subject of the poem is that Oliver explicitly states it in the title. The title is also important because of Oliver's nontraditional spelling of the word *Eskimo*. Immediately, this catches the reader's attention and invites questions about cultural references and language.

The first stanza is written in an anonymous voice that seems slightly detached. In line 2, Oliver uses the pronoun "one," which establishes a certain point of view. If she had used "I," taking a first-person point of view, or "you," directly addressing the reader in the second person, she would have created a sense of intimacy and made the reader part of the poetic experience. The use of "he" or "she" would have meant that the poet was telling the story of a particular individual. By using "one," she makes the statements as general as possible. The speaker of the poem is not, at this point, recounting a personal experience; instead, she is making a broad statement. She is simply observing. This is supported by lines 3–6 in the first stanza in which the speaker uses imagery to describe the superficial aspects of Inuit life such as the landscape that surrounds the Inuit, natural phenomena that are unique to their environment (such as the long days and nights in lines 5–6), and the igloos in which they live.

Throughout this first stanza, Oliver's choice of imagery and metaphor establishes the speaker as an outsider in a foreign land that is unfamiliar and awesome in its timelessness. Consider line 4, in which she describes the Arctic tundra in positive terms of nature, giving what some would see as a barren, frozen wasteland the nobility of a constant, ageless persistence. Here, the ice never melts, and night and day each last for months on end. This is not merely a different environment, but almost a different world altogether. However, though the speaker may admire the Inuit people's perseverance and history, she does not envy them. Even though the outsider may feel crude and intrusive trying to explain Western culture to the Inuit, as the speaker says in line 2, certain words hint that she feels sorry for them in some way. In line 5, even as she is admiring their way of life, she implies that they are trapped in their world, held captive by something. The first stanza, with its detachment and sense of foreign observation, clearly separates the speaker from the people she is observing. The first stanza ends on a peaceful note, as the speaker tells the reader that the Inuit hear her explanation pleasantly enough, but in the end they leave to go back to their daily lives.

Line breaks are always significant in poetry, and perhaps especially in free-verse poetry with its lack of formal structure. When certain words or phrases are set apart at the beginning or end of a line, they are emphasized. This is even more true of stanza breaks. Oliver splits one sentence in half through the use of a stanza break between lines 7 and 8; by doing so, she changes the tone of the poem without interrupting the flow of the language. In one thought, she both notes the peaceful reaction of the Inuit to her lessons on war (line 7) and also portrays them as warriors themselves in line 8. With weapons at the ready, surrounded by frenzied hunting dogs, the Inuit have ceased to be the pleasant yet simple people the speaker describes in the first stanza. Now in the second stanza, the reader is brought into the rhythm of survival in the Inuit life. The men hunt, the women do their domestic chores, and the form of the poem begins to echo the steady structure of the Inuit way of life. Assonance (the repetition of vowel sounds) and consonance (the repetition of consonant sounds) are particularly evident in this short stanza; the repeated *s* and *w* sounds in lines 8–10 are one of the ways Oliver gives structure to this free-verse poem. This stanza is also written in a loose tetrameter, meaning that each line has four stressed syllables. Free verse is written in the cadence, or rhythm, of everyday language rather than the forced meter of traditional poetic forms such as sonnets or villanelles, but poets can still find ways to arrange their words in rhythmic patterns. Reading the second verse out loud clearly shows a steady, rolling meter in this stanza, which is symbolic of the steady and unchanging rhythm of life in the Arctic. The second stanza, then, drops the detached tone of superior observation evident in the first stanza and focuses on the people and their lifestyles. The speaker is clearly still an observer, but now she has turned her attention to the ways in which these people survive the landscape she described in the first stanza. This shift in the focus of the poem coincides with the shift in metrical structure.

Where the first stanza ends with an interrupted thought, breaking the line in two, the second stanza ends with finality. This signals to the reader that another shift is coming. The speaker's period of observation is over. In the third stanza, she sits among the Inuit she has, until now, just been watching. They eat together, and chores done, they give her their attention as she tries to describe more fully the Western way of life and a history that revolves around power struggles. This is reinforced especially when the speaker changes from the impersonal pronoun of the first stanza and begins referring directly to herself, in the first person, in line 14. Line 15 holds another clue that should show how vastly different the culture of the Inuit is from the speaker's culture when they do not identify her as a sister. Gender roles are an important facet of cultural identity, and the speaker emphasizes her otherness simply by showing the Inuit elimination of a male/female distinction in this line. The third stanza loses some of the lulling rhythm of the second stanza; however, when the speaker describes the Western pattern of war and technological advances in lines 18 and 19, the loose tetrameter reappears. It is as if she is recognizing that her world, too, operates in a repeating cycle. The poem ends with the speaker's observation that the Inuit people are unfazed by the information she has to share with them. They continue on with their traditions, smiling as she tries to define the concepts of war and power.

Throughout the poem, Oliver uses slant rhyme as another poetic technique to lend form to her free verse. In slant rhyme, the end words of lines often utilize assonance, meaning they have the same vowel sounds but do not fully rhyme. In many cases, a slant rhyme occurs between words that are spelled differently but have similar sounds when said aloud. This is one of the reasons that reading a poem out loud is so important if a reader wants to really catch the full technical intention of the poet. Some instances of slant rhyme occur in lines 6 and 7, lines 8 and 10, and lines 9 and 12.

THEMES

Nature

Society has always turned to nature to express the human experience. Nearly all ancient civilizations believed that the climate and terrain around them were governed by gods subject to human-like emotions such as anger and sadness, and thus, the humans saw nature as an extension of themselves. The seasonal cycle reflects our own life cycle: we are born and we grow as flowers do in spring, and we grow old and wither as leaves do in the fall. We personify weather as well when we associate sunshine with joy and storms with worry. This innate desire to turn to nature to express oneself has proven useful to poets, whose craft is defined by its use of imagery

to express the human experience. Oliver has stated that nature is almost the sole inspiration for her writing, and this is evident throughout her work. In "The Esquimos Have No Word for 'War,'" she uses a culture defined by nature to share her intended message. In the first stanza, for example, she describes a frozen landscape that is not subject to change with the seasons. Just as the Arctic tundra is unchanging, so too is the Inuit way of life as she portrays it.

Language

The language of the Inuit is called Inuktitut. Most Western languages, including English, communicate by stringing separate words together to form sentences. However, Inuktitut combines single words together to form long, complex words to communicate the same meaning as a sentence. Alexina Kublu and Mick Mallon, in their article "Our Language, Our Selves," use the English sentence "I am happy to be here" as an example. In Inuktitut, this expression is communicated as follows:

quviasuktunga tamaaniinnama (happy + I here + in + be + because I)

It is understandable, then, that there would be no Inuktitut word for "war," since the conflict being described would be much more precise and complex than the broader English word. Violent conflicts between tribes over territorial disputes were not uncommon to the Inuit, though due to the structure of their communities and cultures, the notion of huge warring nations was probably completely foreign to them. In the title of the poem, Oliver draws attention to language in two ways. First, she uses a variant spelling, *Esquimo*, rather than the usual modern English version, *Eskimo*. Second, she points out that there is no word for "war" in the Inuit language. Language, symbols, and grammatical structure—the way a culture expresses itself—are means of identifying with a certain culture. By placing such a focus on language, Oliver emphasizes the differences between her culture and that of the Inuit and reinforces the theme of cultural identity.

Inuit Culture

Eskimo is a term used primarily in the United States to describe the Inuit, who have lived in far northern Canada, Greenland, and Alaska for more than four thousand years. One would think that such an extensive history would be riddled with war and violence, but it is true that the Inuit do not have a word for "war." This does

TOPICS FOR FURTHER STUDY

- Watch the movie *Whale Rider*, paying special attention to the conflicts between the traditional way of life of the indigenous people in the movie and the modern, Western way of life to which they are trying to adjust. Pick one character and write a diary entry of a single day from his or her point of view. What might that day be like? What new concepts must the character confront? What traditions might he or she wish to leave behind? Do you think the character is impatient or angry, or longs to belong fully to one culture or the other?

- Every language contains words that do not translate to other languages. For example, *kayak*, *anorak*, and *husky* are all Inuktitut words that have been adopted into English because they had no English equivalent. The same is true for many other languages. German words such as *Schadenfreude*, French expressions such as *joie de vivre*, and Russian terms such as *toska* do not exist in English. Pick three words from three foreign languages and create a presentation that explains why you think these words, terms, or concepts have no English translation. Address cultural differences, historical developments, and geographical features of the word's home culture that may be different from your own. Online, find graphics, audio, and video that support your conclusions. Present your findings to the class.

- Choose a poem from Lee Francis's collection *When the Rain Sings: Poems by Young Native Americans*. Choose at least three phrases and key words that emphasize the native culture, identifying how each is especially applicable to the native culture of the poet. Using the Internet, find written, audio, visual, or interactive resources that support your claim. Working in groups, create a web page that contains the poem, the name of the poet, and a brief paragraph on the poet's relationship to his or her native culture. Link each of your three words or phrases to a separate page with your explanation and links to each of the examples you have found. Make sure to explain each link and the reasons why you have included it.

- Research a culture with which you are completely unfamiliar. Make a list of at least ten key words and phrases that especially resonate with and relate to the culture you have chosen. Group them according to the poetic techniques that are used in "The Esquimos Have No Word for 'War,'" such as assonance, consonance, or slant rhyme. Use these words to create a free-verse poem of your own. You should write the poem from your own point of view, making it clear that the culture is not your own, and emphasizing one or two differences between your own culture and the one you have chosen to research.

- Oliver's poetry centers on the natural world. She has said that she keeps a journal and records her thoughts on nature to use in her poetry. It can be difficult to notice the natural elements in our busy modern lives, which are centered on human technology. However, there are natural elements all around us: the sky, the wind, plants, and animals. For at least twenty minutes every day for one week, step away from all forms of technology—your phone, computer, television, or gaming systems—and study the natural world around you, recording your observations in a journal. At the end of the week, use your notes to compose an essay on the things you saw that you may not have noticed if you had not made an effort to concentrate on the natural world.

not mean that they have never had territory disputes or fights amongst different groups, but their culture and climate have prevented large-scale war in the traditional sense from breaking out; history has also shown that the farther north an Inuit settlement is, the less fighting has occurred in the area. It would appear that the harsher the climate, the more peaceful and unified the group. Without the modern technologies and warfare of Western culture, the Inuit were more defined by the nature surrounding them. Oliver spends the majority of the poem describing the harsh climate in which the Inuit live and their daily struggle to find food. The battle against nature for survival leaves little time or energy for the type of power struggles seen in many other cultures, eliminating the need for a word for "war" as we know it. Time spent fighting would be time lost in the quest for food and maintaining shelter in the difficult climate. Though hardly absolute, the Inuit also maintained a gender-based division of labor for most of their existence. Oliver references this when she mentions the women waiting for the hunters to return. Oliver makes explicit the Inuit connection to nature in the poem through her multiple references to the landscape and climate in which they live, elements that seem just as foreign to the speaker as the Inuit themselves do. This has the effect of portraying the Inuit more as elements of nature than as fellow people with whom the speaker can identify and emphasizes the spiritual connection that Inuit culture has to nature.

Noble Savage

The term *noble savage* is generally used to describe a stock character that is the idealization of a foreign person or someone from another culture; this concept may also be called romantic primitivism. Essentially, the concept is that Western civilization is so riddled with problems that aboriginal civilizations should be looked to for guidance. The idea is that a simpler life is a happier life. When people treat ancient proverbs as a higher form of wisdom, they are also playing into this notion of romantic primitivism. The implications behind Oliver's "The Esquimos Have No Word for 'War'" are a prime example of romantic primitivism in action. Lines 18 and 19 refer to the struggles of the modern world; the narrator discusses weapons, technology, and power with the Inuit, who just smile at one another in response. Oliver is suggesting that having no need for the word *war* is desirable. If there is no

The image of kettles over the fire creates a mood of warmth and welcome. (© Maria Bell | Shutterstock.com)

need for the word, the thing that that word identifies must not be a factor in their lifestyle, something she seems to admire. Her depiction of the Inuit as a steady, peaceful people is reflected in her portrayal of their landscape (in line 5) as not prone to rapid changes or melting down.

STYLE

Free Verse

Free verse is open-form poetry that does not have consistent rhyme, meter, or pattern. It tends to follow natural speech rhythm, though that is not a requirement. Some readers find free verse poetry easier to relate to than poetry with a rigid, formal structure because of its more natural flow. Open form does not necessary mean a lack of form, as a pattern in sound, figurative language, or layout may be used to give poetic structure. The use of free verse began in late 1800s France, and American authors Ezra Pound and T. S. Eliot contributed to its growing popularity in the early

1900s. "The Esquimos Have No Word for 'War'" lacks both formal rhyme and meter, though it utilizes poetic techniques such as alliteration, loose rhythm, and imagery to give it structure. The thematic divisions between stanzas are also effective in structuring the poem: the first stanza is detached observation of their landscape and climate, the second shows the Inuit in action, and the third focuses the speaker's efforts to communicate with them.

Romanticism

As a response to the reason-focused Enlightenment movement of the late 1700s and early 1800s, romanticism emerged as an intellectual movement centered on aesthetic (artistic) experience. This means it placed value on emotion and intuition, favored nature over industry, and considered both individual and universal human experience. It transformed artistic, political, and sociological thought, and it is still seen in works such as Oliver's today. A premise of romanticism is that human experience can be understood through the human relationship with nature, which is believed to be fundamental and preferable to human societal constructs. Oliver has said that nature is almost her sole inspiration, and her works are reflective of this. It is particularly evident in the first stanza of "The Esquimos Have No Word for 'War,'" where she describes their landscape. Romanticism rejects formal structure as it rejects reason; free verse, as seen here in this poem, is often used because of its more natural-sounding tone. Oliver's use of nature imagery and free verse and her focus on human experience have made many consider her a romantic poet.

Juxtaposition

Juxtaposition—placing things next to each other—is a literary tool an author uses to compare two people, things, themes, or ideas. Generally, the goal is to highlight the differences between the two, build suspense, or develop character. Oliver compares the Inuit in "The Esquimos Have No Word for 'War'" with her own culture in order to point out the differences. As an outsider in their world, the speaker is juxtaposed with the Inuit. Explaining the concept of war makes the speaker feel absurd and crude, which would not be the case in the speaker's own culture. Toward the end of the poem, the speaker talks about armaments, militaries, and unsteady alliances, and all the Inuit can do is smile; the concept is completely foreign and incomprehensible to them. Placing a character in juxtaposition with another culture highlights the differences between the two societies' values: the speaker's values industrialization and power, and theirs is focused on survival and living in harmony.

HISTORICAL CONTEXT

The Inuit

Oliver's portrayal of the Inuit in "The Esquimos Have No Word for 'War'" is more reflective of their history before European contact than at the actual time of publication in the early 1990s. The Inuit, descended from an ancient nomadic people called the Thule, have occupied the Arctic lands in what is today Canada, Alaska, and Greenland for more than four thousand years. Until European traders and missionaries arrived in the 1700s, their lifestyles remained largely unchanged. They lived in small communities and moved according to the seasons. When whalers, fur traders, and missionaries began to arrive in the eighteenth century, however, they brought permanent changes to the Inuit way of life. The whalers brought modern tools and trade to the Inuit in exchange for their help hunting the Arctic whale population to near extinction. The fur trade, driven largely by the Hudson's Bay Company, became an integral part of Inuit economic activity, and is still active today, though much less profitable since the animal rights advocacy movements gained traction in the second half of the twentieth century. With European trade came Christian missionaries, whose views often clashed with the traditions of the Inuit. The Europeans brought more than economic and cultural change, however; they brought diseases that the Inuit had no immunity to. The measles, tuberculosis, and other diseases had a devastating effect on Inuit populations.

In 1870, the Hudson's Bay Company sold the land that it had claimed from the Inuit to the Canadian government, which renamed it the Northwest Territories and divided governorship of the new territory among the existing provinces. By the mid-twentieth century, the Canadian government had expanded its reach into the Arctic region. Large, permanent settlements were built along prime trade routes, and the government began systematically forcing the Inuit to reside in these settlements, abandoning their traditionally nomadic way of life. Children were sent to Canadian schools, and the Inuit became increasingly dependent upon governmental social services.

COMPARE
&
CONTRAST

- **1990s:** The Inuit are just beginning to make real gains in the Canadian government with the start of land-claims negotiations, which designate the Inuit as having aboriginal rights to the Arctic lands.

  Today: With the land-claims agreements in place, there is new hope for the economic future of Inuit communities, as measurable and achievable goals are set to economically empower the Inuit so that they are no longer second-class citizens dependent on the federal government for their livelihoods.

- **1990s:** The Nunavut Land Claims Agreement, signed in 1993, becomes the largest land claims settlement in Canadian history.

  Today: Canada has four nationally recognized Inuit regions: Nunatsiavut, Nunavik, Nunavut, and the Inuvialuit Settlement Region. Each region operates under territorial agreements that give them separate responsibilities and rights from the provincial and federal governments.

- **1990s:** Though the Inuit culture is inextricably intertwined with nature, the main concerns about the future of the Inuit are related to economic and governmental autonomy.

  Today: Climate change is becoming a grave problem in the Arctic regions as global warming causes early breakup of ice, increased coastal erosion, shorter winters, and warmer summers. These changes cause alarming shifts in the migratory habits of Arctic animal life and threaten the Inuit's reliance on the natural world for survival.

- **1990s:** Critical approaches to nature poetry are taken from existing theoretical schools such as feminist theory, psychoanalytic theory, or postcolonial theory.

  Today: There are entire schools of thought that center around the relatively new field of ecopoetry. Ecocriticism is not solely restricted to nature poetry but seeks to apply environmental critical theories to other forms of literature.

In 1971, the Inuit of Canada formed their first political body, the Inuit Tapirisat of Canada (ITC), which lobbied for regulatory and legislative changes that would return some semblance of self-government back to the Inuit and worked to achieve aboriginal rights in the Canadian constitution. In 1975, groups such as the ITC won a huge victory for aboriginal rights with the James Bay and Northern Quebec Agreement, which halted a proposed massive hydroelectric construction project that would have had devastating effects on the Inuit way of life. It also gave significant territorial rights and administrative authority to the Inuit. This agreement paved the way for the comprehensive land-claims agreements that were negotiated over the next two and a half decades in the four Inuit regions in Canada of Nunavik, Inuvialuit, Nunavut, and Labrador, collectively known as the Inuit

Nunangat. In 2001, the group changed its name to Inuit Tapiriit Kanatami (ISK), and it remains an influential lobby in the Canadian government on behalf of Inuit rights.

Today, the Inuit are still working to find a balance between participating in the modern world and maintaining their grasp on traditional beliefs and culture. Though they enjoy the amenities of modern life such as television and film, the Internet, and contemporary shopping outlets, they still rely heavily on hunting and still place family and community at the top of their priority list. With only slightly more than 50,000 Canadian Inuit reporting on the 2006 census, spread over vast stretches of the Canadian Arctic, their communities are very small in comparison with the southern cities, in large part because of the high cost of getting building supplies, maintaining roads, and setting up communications in one of the

Oliver compares the shape of an igloo to a bowl. (© *Zastolskiy Victor | Shutterstock.com*)

harshest climates in the world. Many Inuit families leave their permanent settlements in the summer months and set up camp, where they teach their children the language and customs of their people to ensure that these traditions are not lost.

CRITICAL OVERVIEW

Perhaps Mary Oliver's greatest selling point is her accessibility. Her simple language and heartfelt explorations of the self, the spirit, and nature resonate with a wide audience, a rare feat for a poet in the contemporary age. A 2005 *Publishers Weekly* review classifies Oliver's poetry as "optimistic, clear and lyrical explorations of varying ecosystems...mingled with rapt self-questioning, consolation and spiritual claims some might call prayers."

Judith Barrington, writing in 1996 in the *Women's Review of Books*, calls attention to

Oliver's "fine, accessible lyrics, most of which celebrate the natural world in simple language filled with vibrant images," saying that "Oliver is that rare writer who has won acclaim in the upper echelons of the literary world while also inspiring widespread devotion from fans who pin her poems to refrigerators."

However, Barrington also criticizes Oliver's lofty take on the creative process. Regarding Oliver's assertion in her book of essays *Blue Pastures* that poets inhabit a world of their own and should not be held to the same social standards as non-poets, Barrington asks, "But what about sick friends? buying the dog-food? community and political involvement?...Surely it is this wide range of responsibilities that constitutes a truly adult life—and not necessarily one which is less productive of great writing." She rejects Oliver's insistence that the poet should not immerse herself too much in the material world, saying, "Great writing may, after all, encompass Adrienne Rich's political visions or Lucille Clifton's family stories, as well as Oliver's natural world."

Perhaps Oliver cannot win. When she expresses a desire to be apolitical, she draws criticism from many theoretical schools. When her poetry directly engages political issues, though, she does not meet with much critical success. Eli Lehrer, in a 2008 review for the *Weekly Standard*, criticizes Oliver's ability to eloquently comment on current events and advocacy, saying that "when Oliver takes on politics in a serious way, her verse becomes decidedly mediocre."

Political implications aside, few can argue with Oliver's poetic skills or her deservedly stellar reputation as one of the great nature poets of the modern age. Robert Hosmer, writing about *New and Selected Poems* for the *Southern Review* in 1994, says that "the panorama of Oliver's work exhibits an extraordinary and admirable consistency: simplicity, clarity, directness, sincerity . . . precision, discipline . . . [and] a skilled use of repetition." Her technical abilities remain largely undisputed, and her mastery of the language of romantic poetry is nearly universally recognized. However, her classification as a nature poet overshadows her technical skills amongst many critics and scholars. Linda Keegan, in a 1994 review of *New and Selected Poems*, says "the new poems immerse the reader in nature as the poet reaches deep into the pockets of the natural world for its treasures." Like many critics, Keegan focuses on Oliver's themes and style rather than her very successful employment of technical poetic elements.

Hosmer praises the poetic progression shown in *New and Selected Poems*, saying, "With the passing of years and one collection after another, Oliver's voice has developed a deeper music, and her imagery has become more richly dense as she has sharpened the metaphysical edge of her questions." Keegan takes a similar view, saying, "Oliver's new work suggests personal passage with insight. The terrain is familiar—nature as guidance—but it is not redundant; it is full of compassion and new spirit."

Hosmer concludes his review with a statement that surely would please Oliver, who has expressed the wish that her poetry should engage the reader by asking questions for which there

are no immediate answers. "The cumulative effect of Oliver's poems? Silence. The deep and embracing silence of amazed contemplation."

CRITICISM

Kristy Blackmon

Blackmon is a writer and critic from Dallas, Texas. In the following essay, she explores how Oliver attempts to erase the boundaries between nature and reason through a sophisticated use of poetic technique in "The Esquimos Have No Word for 'War.'"

Mary Oliver's poetry falls firmly within the tradition of the romantic poets of the mid-nineteenth to the early twentieth centuries. Poets such as Ralph Waldo Emerson, Henry David Thoreau, William Wordsworth, Emily Dickinson, and Robert Frost emphasized the preeminence of the natural state of being. The closer a person is to nature the better the understanding of life and the human condition. This was not merely a message they attempted to communicate through preexisting poetic forms; the philosophy extended to the technical elements of poetry. Forced metrical schemes, high poetic language, and formal line and stanza structures were seen as representative of the cold, reasoned, and difficult-to-understand poetry of the Enlightenment. Romantic poets favored the natural cadence of ordinary spoken language and experimented with techniques such as slant rhyme and free verse. Under the romantics, the lyric poem flourished and became the dominant poetic form of the modern age. However, romantic poetry is full of contradictions, especially in the contemporary age. Modern lyric poems in the romantic tradition are personal without being confessional, emotional without indulging in angst, and attempt to communicate some universal truth about life or the nature of humanity through the telling of a specific incident. In poems such as "The Esquimos Have No Word for 'War,'" Oliver masterfully navigates the tricky waters of the romantic paradox that results from the struggle to reconcile a philosophy based on nature, spirituality, and primitivism with the need to be relevant and meaningful.

In other words, romantic poets attempt to connect, as much as possible, to a natural state of being, rejecting an abundance of logic or reason;

WHAT
DO I READ
NEXT?

- In his 2010 book *Can Poetry Save the Earth? A Field Guide to Nature Poems*, John Felstiner uses nature poems to encourage participation in environmental activism. Using examples from sources as diverse as the Biblical Psalms to the traditional romantic poets, Felstiner encourages us to use poetry as a way to examine our connection with nature.

- The 2008 anthology *American Earth: Environmental Writing since Thoreau*, edited by Bill McKibben, is a collection of works from more than a hundred environmental poets, activists, and writers. Each entry has a short introduction from McKibben explaining its place in the larger scope of the environmental activist movement.

- Mary Oliver's 1994 book on the craft of poetry, *A Poetry Handbook*, addresses the technical side of poetry. Each chapter is dedicated to a different poetic technique, such as sound devices, form, and imagery.

- In 2011, author Duncan Heath and illustrator Judy Boreham published *Introducing Romanticism: A Graphic Guide*. In this unique volume appropriate for young-adults, Heath and Boreham present an overview of the philosophies that contributed to the rise of the romantic tradition in art, music, literature, and politics. In the style of a graphic novel, they explore how the movement transformed Western culture and led to the political movements of the twentieth century.

- Joy Harjo is one of the most celebrated Native American poets in history. In her 2004 collection *How We Became Human: New and Selected Poems 1975–2001*, Harjo presents work from a quarter century of her poetry, which focuses on Native American attempts to reconcile their traditional connection with nature and mythology with the harsh realities of modern life on the reservation. It is a collection that speaks volumes to the struggle of indigenous people who have had Western civilization thrust upon them, as well as the power of poetry to bring different cultures together.

- When the gray whale was removed from the endangered species list in 1994, the Makah tribe of northwest Washington State and the Nuu-chah-nulth nation of British Columbia began to exercise their legal right to engage in whaling for the first time in more than seventy years. The revival of this indigenous and ancient tradition sparked immense controversy from environmental and animal rights activists and started a global debate about the place of traditional aboriginal culture within the modern world. Charlotte Coté's 2010 book *Spirits of Our Whaling Ancestors* analyzes this culture clash, examining arguments from many sides. As a member of the Nuu-chah-nulth Nation, Cote provides valuable insight into what it means to be "native" in the context of contemporary Western civilization.

- *Gadi Mirrabooka: Australian Aboriginal Tales from the Dreaming* by Pauline E. McLeod, Francis Firebrace Jones, and June E. Barker is a collection of thirty-three traditional stories from Australian Aboriginal elders. The Dreamtime is how the Aboriginal people refer to the mythological birth of their people, and these stories reveal their customs, spirituality, view of nature, and ways of survival. Edited by Helen F. McKay and published in 2001, *Gadi Mirrabooka*, which means below the Southern Cross, gives an authentic look into the belief system of Australia's indigenous population.

- *Messengers of Rain: And Other Poems from Latin America*, edited by Claudia M. Lee and illustrated by Rafael Yockteng, is a 2002 anthology of poems from nineteen Latin American countries. The works range in time from the pre-Columbian era to the present, and include indigenous and well-known poets. This collection received a commendation in the Américas Book Award program.

> OLIVER MASTERFULLY NAVIGATES THE TRICKY WATERS OF THE ROMANTIC PARADOX THAT RESULTS FROM THE STRUGGLE TO RECONCILE A PHILOSOPHY BASED ON NATURE, SPIRITUALITY, AND PRIMITIVISM WITH THE NEED TO BE RELEVANT AND MEANINGFUL."

however, the act of creating poetry itself requires an engaged intellectualism. The poem is a first-person account of a specific experience, longer than a single moment but still isolated in its place in the speaker's life. Without crossing the line into sentimentality or melodrama, the poem does convey extreme and personal emotion, though the speaker never articulates it. It is in the speaker's recounting of her experience with the Inuit that the reader is able to understand her mood through the tone of the poem and the details she conveys. Like the romantic poets who came before her, Oliver must work to express the joy she takes in nature and her worry that it is slipping away. She must reach what Deborah Jurdjevic calls the "Romantic sublime" in a 2002 review in *Canadian Woman Studies*: "pure beauty, pure terror."

Emotion, for the romantics, is the original source of poetry. As opposed to the nature-based poems written prior to the Industrial Revolution and the Age of Enlightenment, romantic poetry is forced to work in order to prove the primacy of nature over industry, all the while knowing that it is an uphill battle. So while there is joy and sublimity evident in romantic poetry, there are also strong undercurrents of fear, dread, and awe. The natural world is no longer the Anglo-European native habitat, and even the most ardent of romantic poets in the nineteenth century knew they were products of cities, technology, and Western civilization. This disconnect results in a sort of resigned yearning that runs throughout much of Oliver's romantic poetry, a fierce admiration and longing for a return to nature mixed with the knowledge that it is never fully possible. In "Esquimos," the speaker relates seemingly benign and picturesque

details about the landscape and the Inuit culture, but there is a sadness there as well. As Oliver wrote in *Long Life: Essays and Other Writing*, "It is one of the perils of our so-called civilized age that we do not yet acknowledge enough, or cherish enough, this connection between soul and landscape."

Taking all that it means to be a "romantic poet" into account in a study of "Esquimos" reveals a fascinating underlying message. Secondary meanings are not uncommon in romantic poetry; Frost, for example, was famous for composing simple verse that seemed to verge on sentimentality while using specific word choices or poetic techniques to communicate a deeper, more intellectual message. Examination of a few key aspects will show that "Esquimos" is not *only* about language, the purity of nature, and the horrors that Anglo-European "civilization" brings native peoples during colonization.

"A strength of her poems," Jurdjevic writes, "and a mark of their stature is the readiness with which they call to mind the best of the past, only to remake it." Published in 1992, "Esquimos" does, in fact, remake history. The poem paints a picture of a native people completely untouched by the modern world. While the Inuit have managed to maintain strong ties to many of their traditions, Southern civilization (what we often refer to as Western civilization, a term that is not applicable to the Arctic aboriginal tribes) has been affecting their way of life since at least the mid-1800s. By the mid-twentieth century, at least forty years before the publication of "Esquimos," the Canadian government, in an effort to establish sovereign authority over the Arctic lands that were beginning to draw the attention of the Americans, Europeans, and Russians, had extended its reach above the tree line and into Inuit lands. Forced resettlements created a society that was dependent upon the government for everything from social services to economic growth. In the early 1970s, the Inuit began to organize politically and fight for aboriginal rights. By the time *New and Selected Poems* was published, these groups had scored major victories in the political fight for Inuit autonomy. In 1992, the year of publication, the residents of what would become the new, majority-Inuit Nunavut territory negotiated the landmark Nunavut Land Claims Agreement, the largest such settlement not only in Canadian history but arguably in the history of the world, according to James Merritt's findings for the *Canadian Parliamentary Review*. The Inuit way of life still differs from that of their Southern, Anglo neighbors, but by no means were they the primitive people Oliver portrays in "The Esquimos Have No Word for 'War.'"

The title of the poem is another misleading statement. While it is true that there is no equivalent word for "war" in Inuktitut, the Inuit language, it is not because violent conflict was unknown to them. Though the nature of the harsh Arctic climate did place more emphasis on survival than conquest, violent clashes between nomadic bands over territorial disputes, especially in the southern regions, were not uncommon. More than likely, the absence of an exact translation of "war" stems from the structure of Inuktitut itself, which combines words to communicate complex ideas, as opposed to European languages, which form sentences out of individual words for the same purpose. Nicole Gombay, a linguist and sociologist, writing in *Journal of Cultural Geography*, recounts a story about asking an Inuk for the Inuktitut translation of the word "economics." The woman consulted other members of the community. She referenced a government-issued translation guide. Finally, "she concluded that the word for the idea was *kiinaujatigut makittarasuarniq*, which literally translates as 'by money try to stand by itself.'" While Oliver's presentation of the fact that there is no Inuktitut word for "war" inspires the notion of a completely pacifist people, it is a romantic notion and a poetic device, used, in Jurdjevic's words, to "call to mind the best of the past, only to remake it."

Why is it necessary for Oliver and other romantic poets to "remake" the past? The answer goes back to the paradox discussed earlier, and a literary and philosophic notion known as binary opposition. Binary opposition means, at its most basic, that if a person identifies as one thing, it makes everything else an "other." It is a core tenet of contemporary Western identity studies. If Jane identifies as a female, she is not a male, male being the "other." If John identifies as an urbanite, then suburban and rural dwellers are "other." These dualities of course overlap constantly, complicating the modern search for identity. However, this is why the romantics and other nature poets writing after the Industrial Revolution struggle with portraying in a sincere and believable way nature

as superior to modern civilization. As a product of that civilization, there are limits to how well they will ever be able to understand or identify with nature. "Rooted in the binary oppositions that structure Western thinking," writes Vicki Graham in a 1994 article in *Papers on Language and Literature*, "Oliver can never fully escape the teaching of her culture that the mind is divided from the body and identity depends on keeping intact the boundaries between the self and others." Therefore, she must employ poetic devices in an attempt to erase those boundaries. We can never shed the knowledge we carry, and we bring it with us wherever we go. No matter how much the speaker in "Esquimos" may admire the Inuit, no matter how much she may wish to partake in their natural and primal way of life, she knows too much. She knows of war and governments and modern power struggles, and so she will always be partially blinded to the spiritual "truth" of the men and women of whom she is speaking.

Graham writes that in Oliver's poetry, "evoking and then becoming another depends on direct, sensuous contact with the other, on using the body rather than the mind to apprehend it." She emphasizes sensory details to elevate the natural world at least to the level of the human world, if not above it. Again and again, her poems speak to her belief that every living thing has a soul and is equal. In much of her poetry, she focuses on animals or elements of nature, which is perfectly consistent with the romantic tradition. In "Esquimos," however, her focus is on the people—people who do not talk or engage with the speaker other than to give her food and listen to her speak, people who are depicted more as elements of the natural world than as fellow humans. The surface meaning of the poem is concerned with themes of language and innocence, but underneath is another layer of meaning where the Inuit represent nature. This achieves a sort of reverse personification. It reduces people to elements of nature, to the equivalent of the flowers and bears that run through her other poems. But for Oliver, who has always elevated bears to the same level as people, this is no insult. Indeed, it is the highest of praise. As far as humans go, these people are as close to the natural as people can get. And for a romantic poet, this trick of "remaking" the history of the Inuit as Oliver did may be as close to erasing that binary boundary between humanity and nature that continues to pose a philosophical problem. Poetry is a way of experiencing the "other" that we can never become. Creating a symbolic representation of the

The barking of sled dogs adds to the atmosphere of the village. (© *Richard J Ashcroft | Shutterstock.com*)

and it emphasizes the need for a real attempt at understanding the "other" within each of us.

Charles Baudelaire wrote that "Romanticism is precisely situated neither in choice of subject nor exact truth, but in the way of feeling" (as quoted in the reference work *Christian Apologetics Past and Present: A Primary Source Reader*, edited by William Edgar and K. Scott Oliphint). Oliver's poem exemplifies this definition almost perfectly. The subject of this poem may seem to be the peaceful Inuit, but it is actually the experience of the speaker. There is no "exact truth" here, but that does not hinder the reader from sharing in the speaker's feelings of sadness, longing, and sense of not belonging.

Source: Kristy Blackmon, Critical Essay on "The Esquimos Have No Word for 'War,'" in *Poetry for Students*, Gale, Cengage Learning, 2014.

Gisela Ullyatt

In the following excerpt, Ullyatt explains the Buddhist concept of mindfulness and how it is reflected in Mary Oliver's poetry.

. . . Mindfulness has become a term used increasingly by both the scientific community and the self-help publishing industry. A plethora of scientific articles explore the effect of mindfulness, especially through sitting meditation, postulating outcomes such as a reduction in psychopathologies in research subjects by measuring neurological activity and the likes (Austin 1999; Kabat-Zinn 1996; Center for Mindfulness in Medicine, Health Care and Society). Although this type of research may be useful for the advancement of science, it is concerned mostly with outcomes rather than with explaining and teaching mindfulness. Furthermore, the environment in which subjects are tested is usually artificial, which is ironic because mindfulness is usually a practice that constitutes everyday life and activities. On the more popular side, authors such as Eckhard Tolle (2008, 2011) and Deepak Chopra (1989, 2010) do render mindfulness more accessible to readers but do not always explain its Eastern origins explicitly because their target market is mostly Western readers who, in many instances, are from religions that do not necessarily condone Eastern influences. In these cases, the original meaning of mindfulness is somewhat obscured because the emphasis falls rather on other positive psychology concepts. Mindfulness is not always called mindfulness either. Of course, one could

unattainable purely natural world out of the Inuit is a brilliant trick that puts Oliver on par with other romantic masters of poetic technique and secondary meaning such as Frost.

It is not enough just to bridge the binary disconnect, though. Oliver may give her readers a way of connecting to the natural world through her poetry, but to what end? "I want the poem to ask something and, at its best moments, I want the question to remain unanswered," Oliver wrote in her essay "The Swan" in *Winter Hours: Prose, Prose Poems, and Poems.* "I want it to be clear that answering the question is the reader's part in an implicit author-reader pact." In "The Esquimos Have No Word for 'War,'" Oliver pits a peaceful, natural world against a modern, warring one in order to get the reader to engage, to inspire a contemplation on what humankind has lost in the pursuit of power, and what we may still yet regain. It raises questions about the nature of spirituality and the excess of Western materialism. It inspires us to examine our own relationships with the earth,

> OLIVER'S POEMS ARE 'PEBBLES' TOSSED INTO THE MINDS OF HER READERS SO AS TO ENGAGE ALL THEIR SENSES."

argue that even an obscured understanding of mindfulness is better than none, and is a start in its understanding. Nonetheless, I undertake to lift the veil of obscuration that exists about mindfulness by placing it in its Eastern (in this case, Buddhist) context. Because of the constraints of an article, I will be unable to refer to, or discuss, mindfulness's pre-Buddhist Indian yogic origins.

In the Buddhist context, Right Mindfulness constitutes the seventh limb of the Noble Eightfold Path and is therefore one of Buddhism's central practices. (For the reader unfamiliar with this Path, consulting Naim (2002), and Brazier (2001) will be of great assistance.) David Brazier (2001: 164), founder of Western Pureland Buddhism, aptly summarises mindfulness when he writes: "To be mindful is to keep ill mind." Inherent in the terms mindfulness and to keep in mind is mind, which is the bedrock of Buddhist philosophy and practice. In the Dhammapada, which constitutes a central Buddhist scripture, the opening line of Verse 1 explains the central importance of mind most succinctly: "Everything proceeds from mind" (The Mother 2004: 3). This assertion comprises the underlying notion that Buddhist practice entails the conscious studying and observing of one's mind.

In the Eastern philosophical sense, mind is more inclusive than its usage and associations in a traditional Western sense; the East (traditionally referring to India, China, and Japan) does not regard the intellect as mind's only component, but rather more holistically; this is especially true of Zen Buddhism: "Zen has as its basic assumptions a world of wholeness that is obscured with illusion as a result of dualistic thinking" (Milstead 1998: 5–6). This particular non-dualistic premise is evident in the tack that mindfulness is not just an intellectual exercise when studying the mind but also entails mindfulness practice that the practitioner experiences. At the same time, mindfulness comprises more

than just a spiritual exercise and experience but becomes essential on the level of the practitioner's everyday life: "Practicing mindfulness in Buddhism means to perform consciously all activities, including everyday, automatic activities such as breathing, walking, etc., and to assume the attitude of 'pure observation', through which clear knowledge, i.e., clearly conscious thinking and acting, is attained" (Shambhala 1991:145).

. . . In order to awaken to the present moment, one has to cultivate a Beginner's Mind, which the Japanese refer to as shoshin. Shunryu Suzuki describes Beginner's Mind as being [t]he innocence of the first inquiry—just asking what you are is BEGINNER'S MIND. The mind of the beginner is needed throughout Zen practice. It is the open mind, the attitude that includes both doubt and possibility, the ability to see things fresh and new. It is needed in all aspects of life. Beginner's mind is the practice of Zen mind. (Suzuki 1971: 13–14)

It is this innocence of Beginner's Mind that Mary Oliver employs in her poetry but which may be read as naivete by the uninformed reader (of both Oliver's poetry and of Beginner's Mind): "Oliver's craft is deceptively simple—an emotional intensity that speaks clearly and directly to the reader. More appropriately, James Dickey characterises it as remarkable, creating richly complex poetry without throwing complexities in the way of the reader" (Alford 1988: 283). Beginner's Mind is further evident in the specific style Oliver utilises to engage readers in her poems by having a fresh perspective on the world she observes: "Oliver does not rely on an esoteric language or a private set of symbols. Her language is not arcane; her meanings are not hidden" (Thurston 1999: 30).

In addition, Oliver believes that the role of contemporary poetry, which naturally includes her own, differs a great deal from stylised, formalised metrical poetry which stresses formal tone and formal structures. According to Oliver, poetry has become more like conversational speech, which, when read, "would feel spontaneous, as true to the moment, as talk in the street, or talk between friends" (1994a: 70). This particular style dovetails with the idea of "[t]his [Zen], an ancient way of teaching, using the simplest language and situations of everyday life. This means the student should teach himself" (Suzuki 1971: 14). The language of Zen (and, by implication, Buddhism) is therefore vital to Oliver's stance about using simple language in order for readers to become participants in the poem. Moreover, the idea of participation further connects with one of Buddhism's key tenets: "The purpose of studying Buddhism is not to study Buddhism, but to study ourselves" (Suzuki 1971: 76).

In "When Death Comes", lines 20 to 27 articulate the spirit of Beginner's Mind.

> When it's over, I want to say: all my life
> I was a bride married to amazement.
> I was the bridegroom, taking the world into my arms.
> When it's over, I don't want to wonder
> If I have made of my life something particular, and real.
> I don't want to find myself sighing and frightened, or full of argument.
> I don't want to end up simply having visited this world.

> (Oliver 1992: 10)

First, the topos of amazement is directly stated in line 21, and is linked with the ability of Beginner's Mind to be that "kind of mind that's not already made up. The mind that's just investigating, open to whatever occurs, curious. Seeking, but not with expectation or grasping" (Hartman 2001). Furthermore, amazement is reinforced by the metaphor of the "bride married" to it. Significant here is the image of a bride. Supposedly, a bride is on the threshold of her marriage, a newly married woman for whom married life is in the "honeymoon phase." Therefore, she is essentially a beginner, a novice in the union of marriage. Who is this "bride" wedded to in this poem? Amazement. Therefore, the honeymoon phase for this bride is perpetual—lasting "all my life"—"just as Beginner's Mind always retains an element of that which is innocent of preconceptions and expectations, judgements and prejudices" (Hartman 2001). Linking here with the bride image is: "In the beginner's mind there are many possibilities, but in the expert's there are few" (Suzuki 1971: 21). A bride still perceives the marriage as having many possibilities whereas a married woman of a few years has usually become "an expert," probably realising that certain marital patterns and interpersonal relationships will not change or materialise.

Oliver takes the idea of marriage a step further in line 22: by linking line 21 with line 22, she in fact weds the female and male aspects of this union, bringing balance to this "marriage" by

giving both aspects equal resonance. The bridegroom is married to "the world" and here Oliver fulfils a prevalent theme in her poetry: "how to love this world." Examples of poems in which this theme predominates are "The Lover of Earth Cannot Help Herself" (2004b: 17) and "To Begin With, the Sweet Grass" in which the last line reads: "Love yourself. Then forget it. Then, love the world" (2009: 39), with the pinnacle reached in "October": "Look, I want to love this world / as though it's the last chance I'm ever going to get / to be alive / and know it" (1992: 61).

However, despite Oliver's explicit love of the world, the possibility exists for the Western reader to identify a certain paradoxical juxtapositioning of images in "bride, married to amazement" since "bride" seems to be a concrete image or metaphor where amazement is inclined more towards abstraction. To the Buddhist reader, these images would not be paradoxical since abstract and concrete are merely concepts or perceptions held by the individual and which, ultimately, may differ from person to person. Similarly, Oliver has the same propensity toward the interweaving of concrete and abstract images within her poetry, something that has been noted by Burton-Christie. He explains this predilection in terms of adequation and correspondence. The critic, Sherman Paul, whose terms these are, sees "adequation as describing carefully, letting things be in their concrete particularity, refraining from the temptation to symbolize. It is a literary equivalent that 'respects the thing and lets it stand forth . . . an activity in words that is literally comparable to the thing itself'" (Burton-Christie 1996: 79). Correspondence, on the other hand, amounts to "the search for symbolic meaning, the process of making imaginative connections between the ever-shifting and fathomless worlds of self and nature" (1996: 79).

Burton-Christie takes the position that Oliver has the ability to utilise both terms seamlessly in her poems: "These two apparently divergent impulses, one antisymbolic, the other symbolic, ebb back and forth in the poetry of Mary Oliver. Her ability to integrate them without confusing them yields an original vision of spirit and nature" (1996: 79). However, Oliver also marries two seemingly abstract ideas, death and amazement, in "When Death Comes", which emphasises the Buddhist undercurrent present in her work: impermanence (death) and

Beginner's Mind (amazement) which are two sides of one coin for the Buddhist practitioner.

Moreover, Beginner's Mind is taken a step further by describing the "suchness" or "thisness" which translates in the particular aspects of the poetic observer's "life," in the phrase "something particular and real." This "realness" is the "suchness" of something that is experienced through its emptiness, a term that may be misunderstood by the Western reader as nihilistic, akin to non-existence. However, simplistically put, emptiness is "openness, not negation. An object is Empty in that it has no self-identity beyond the sensory and phenomenal dimension" (Milstead 1998: 26). In addition, "When Emptiness is realized, the Zen concept of suchness is also uncovered. To perceive an object as empty is to see it in its suchness" (Milstead 1998: 26). In terms of Oliver's poem, the words "particular" and "real" get new meaning in terms of Buddhist thought because the suchness of life is implicit: "Suchness may also be described as 'as-it-isness'. The as-it-isness of the world is Zen reality" (Milstead 1998: 29). It is exactly this reality of the poetic observer's life that is imbued by amazement and which amounts to mindfulness: "Mindfulness is knowledge or wisdom that pulls the whole mind and heart of the knower toward a connection with the way things are in all their exciting particularity" (Goodenough & Woodruff 2001: 586).

The last line, "I don't want to end up simply having visited this world," resonates strongly with the poet's view of approaching every moment with Beginner's Mind. Looking at the preceding lines—"I don't want to find myself sighing and frightened, / or full of argument"— has a particular autobiographical element: "This I have always known—that if I did not live my life immersed in the one activity which suits me, and which also, to tell the truth, keeps me utterly happy and intrigued, I would come someday to bitter and mortal regret" (Oliver 1994a: 119). This activity is not just writing or being in nature—the two passions of her life, but life itself. This is corroborated by Judy Orloff (2004: 208): "I've watched my friend, poet Mary Oliver, treat going to the supermarket as a holy rite. Every Cape Cod morning, snowy or warm, she shows up at the A&P, just as it opens, ecstatic to get her food for the day. Mary approaches her poetry with the same inspiration" (Orloff 2004: 208).

This is the reason why Oliver does not only tell about being mindful but she shows it directly and, moreover, becomes mindfulness: "The mindful person, Buddhism tells us, assumes the attitude of pure observation, freed from all false views, and apprehends a reality that is not only objective but also becomes subjective. The mindful person really sees" (Goodenough & Woodruff 2001: 586).

2 AWAKENING THROUGH MINDFUL AWARENESS

How well do you look and see the things of this world?
(Mary Oliver 1994b: 121)

It is with the innocence of first inquiry of Beginner's Mind that Oliver approaches mindful awareness: In the poem "Sometimes" (2008: 37), Oliver offers what she calls "Instructions for living a life." Once again, her conviction is that life is to be lived intensely: we are not here merely to exist or survive.

Pay attention,
Be astonished.
Tell about it.

Once more, Oliver's accessible style may be misconstrued as functioning on a merely discursive level because these three lines seem like ordinary instructions to the reader. Syntactically, they may indeed be, but, semantically, they rest in intensity. However, Oliver's use of adequation breaks down the boundaries between the poet/reader that may sometimes exist because of symbols obscuring the essence of a poem, rendering it difficult for the reader to access through the use of correspondence. McEntyre claims that "it is the function of poets to restore to us the mystery of the ordinary" (1994: 7). As will be shown in the poem "Morning," later in the article, Oliver is a poet who deals mainly with the ordinary, but it is exactly through Buddhist simplicity that she invites readers to rethink their lives through the practice of mindfulness.

Oliver herself maintains that the role of the poet is to render "the poem clear and accessible" (1994a: 77). This view about accessibility and interaction between poet and reader, instead of creating distance through formal poetic devices, echoes Watt's stance about the haiku: "A good haiku is a pebble thrown into the pool of the listener's mind, evoking associations out of the richness of his own memory. It invites the listener to participate instead of leaving him dumb with admiration while the poet shows off" (1962: 202).

Oliver's poems are "pebbles" tossed into the minds of her readers so as to engage all their senses. Mann (2004: 54) reiterates the connection with the sensual experience in Oliver's poetry: "To recall a key theme—paying attention—one does not simply attend mentally to what one sees in nature; rather one must apprehend nature with all the senses". . . .

Source: Gisela Ullyatt, "'The Only Chance to Love This World': Buddhist Mindfulness in Mary Oliver's Poetry," in *Journal of Literary Studies*, Vol. 27, No. 2, July 2011, p. 115.

Angela O'Donnell

In the following review, O'Donnell discusses the reverence for nature reflected in Oliver's work.

To read *Thirst*, Mary Oliver's most recent book of poems, is to feel gratitude for the simple fact of being alive. This is not surprising, as it is the effect her best work has produced in readers for the past 43 years. Admirers of any one of the 15 previous collections by the Pulitzer Prize-winning poet will be pleased to find poems that celebrate the beauty and sacredness of the natural world. In "Messenger" and "When I Am Among the Trees," for instance, Oliver offers thanks and praise for creation and accords its creatures spiritual power that goes beyond the simple fact of their beauty: "I would almost say that they save me, and daily."

Indeed, the poet's regard for nature may seem to teeter occasionally on the brink of pantheism, yet attentiveness to the poems, especially within the context of this particular volume, soon dispels this misperception. Often the poet approaches God, uncharacteristically, through more conventionally religious means: through the language of prayer and meditation, through engagement of liturgical ritual and through participation in sacrament. The presence of these elements marks a movement away from the nonspecific spirituality implicit in Oliver's previous work and toward a frank acknowledgment of faith that is decidedly Christian.

Thirst is elegiac in genre and in spirit. A number of the poems mourn the death of Oliver's longtime companion and muse, Molly Malone Cook, who died in 2005. In the course of the collection, we witness the poet, who is ordinarily confident and hopeful in her disposition, struggle against doubt, grief and loneliness in her search for consolation. The short poem, "The Uses of Sorrow," states elegantly the central theme of the volume: "Someone I loved once gave me/ a box full of darkness./ It took me years to understand/ that this, too, was a gift."

The gifts the poet discovers as she endures this dark night of the soul are many, and chief among these is her faith. In a remarkable series of poems interspersed throughout the volume, she chronicles a process of awakening to God's loving presence through the reading of Scripture ("After Her Death"), through attending church and partaking of the Eucharist ("Coming to God: First Days," "The Vast Ocean Begins Just Outside Our Church: The Eucharist") and through imaginative engagement of Christ's words and events in his life ("Six Recognitions of the Lord," "The Poet Thinks About the Donkey" and "Gethsemane"). In these latter two poems, Oliver explores spiritual and aesthetic terrain that is traditional and yet does so in a way that is characteristically her own.

"The Poet Thinks About the Donkey" takes the form of an Ignatian meditation: the composition of place is evident in the first lines: "On the outskirts of Jerusalem/ the donkey waited." Then the speaker imagines the role played by this lowly creature in Christ's triumphal entry into the city—how he waits patiently, lets himself be led away, allows the stranger to mount and marvels at the loud crowds.

The conclusion, as well as the title, bears the stamp of Oliver's imagination, her sensitivity to every aspect of the creation and her conviction that all of it (including the donkey) is holy: "I hope, finally, he felt brave./ I hope, finally, he loved the man who rode so lightly upon him,/ as he lifted one dusty hoof and stepped, as he had to, forward." In "Gethsemane," the companion poem to this one, the poet's compassionate eye is directed toward the sleeping disciples who, unlike the grass, the lily and the cricket—all present in the garden—are human, and, therefore, weak: "Oh the dear bodies, slumped and eye-shut, that could not/ keep that vigil, how they must have wept,/ so utterly human, knowing this too/ must be a part of the story." Indeed, the disciples' story is our own, the poet obliquely reminds us, as we resemble them more closely than we do the faithful donkey or the attentive stars. To be human is to desire God and to lack the perfection he possesses. Many of these poems, echoing the urgency of the volume's title poem, articulate the speaker's relentless longing, this "thirst for the goodness I do not have."

The poet prepares the way for this extended exploration of her soul with a poem that occurs early in the collection, "Making the House Ready for the Lord." In a gesture reminiscent of the Roman centurion's declaration of faith and the prayer before Communion ("Lord, I am not worthy to receive you"), the speaker asks God's pardon for the disorganized jumble that constitutes her mind and heart. She apologizes for the "uproar of mice" under the sink, for the squirrels that have "gnawed their ragged entrances" into her home and her poems. Yet in her acknowledgment of faith, "still I believe you will/ come, Lord," and in her assurance to him that "when I speak to the fox,/ the sparrow, the lost dog, the shivering sea-goose, know/ that really I am speaking to you," the poet asserts that it is through the humble agency of these creatures that she has come to know God. Thus, as she has said to them these many years, the door of her poems flung wide open, she says to the reader and to the Lord: "Come in, come in." This fine poem, compelling in its lyric intensity and endearing in its honesty, serves as ars poetica, prayer of preparation, an open invitation that the lover of poetry and seeker of God would do well to accept.

Source: Angela O'Donnell, "God's Beautiful Lessons," in *America*, Vol. 195, No. 10, October 9, 2006, p. 23.

Dale E. Cottingham

In the following review, Cottingham points out Oliver's insistence that one must approach things with a sense of discovery.

It was the memorable French poet Paul Celan who perhaps best articulated what we've all felt about poets in the process of their making, and the poetry that results: "In this language I have sought, during those years and the years since then, to write poems: so as to speak to orient myself, to find out where I was and where I was meant to go, to sketch out reality for myself." Which, of course, most accurately, and acutely, applies to the poetry of Mary Oliver. For Oliver, who has already delivered such towering volumes of poems, including *American Primitive* and *White Pines*, is "that quiet person" continually in the world, in the sense of outdoors, walking, looking, seeing, listening, "fingering shells" pasted together, keenly observing the "ball of the foot and wide heel/and the naily, untrimmed/toes" of the bear track, and in doing so is not only taking the measure of what she finds, but more crucially the measure of her soul ("I am always trying to figure out/what the soul is"). And in this figuring out, although the project is never finished ("I believe I will never quite know./Though I play at the edges of knowing"), Oliver finds her bearings, not by looking at the self in the inherited egocentric sense of human

as the central character, but rather by seeking out an immaterialism that is immersed in the material, a reality without surrendering all that is or makes an individual, a counter-stipulation where the self is not overcome by the world,/but through the world finds renewal: "to keep us from ever-darkness,/to ease us with warm touching,/to hold us in the great hands of light. . ." Which is an antidote to human frailty, a strengthening, not a diminishing, of the human condition, and so after walking, after seeing, after listening, Oliver in her most recent volume, *Why I Wake Early*, gives us a book of praise.

For a case study, we need look no further than the title poem, "Why I Wake Early," where Oliver addresses the query posed in the title by turning to the morning sun:

> Hello, sun in my face.
> Hello, you who make the morning and spread it over
>   the fields . . . best preacher that ever was, dear
>   star that just happens
> to be where you are in the universe . . . Watch, now,
>   how I start the day
> in happiness, in kindness.

On this occasion Oliver is making the gestures of one invested to the point of faith; in the sense of having given herself over to this world, to her craft, the one so enthralled that she has no other means of expression except praise. And we should not let pass the sincerity of the utterance found in the book's epigraph ("Lord! who hath praise enough?"). Nor should we let pass Oliver's crisp choice of this literary gem, for its author, the English poet, George Herbert, is an important religious poet from seventeenth century, at a time before naturalism, before romanticism, even before the enlightenment, a poet who says "praise" and means it in its most genuine, and faithful, acceptation. Oliver's point is, thus, not to turn from death, or life, and not to insist on the individual, but to regard life in a sense of discovery, in the context where it resides.

This praise, this virtually religious experience, is not an ecstasy of isolation and it is not instantaneous combustion. Rather, it is derived from the careful, insightful looking at the world, by which Oliver means "not just standing around, but standing around/as though with your arms open." What follows then are poems describing her itinerate musings, including most notably "Have You Seen Blacksnake Swimming?," "Look and See," "This World," "Mindful," and "Spring at Blackwater: I Go Through the Lessons," and from her walking, her listening, her examination of the fecund record of the earth, love is spawned:

Oh, to love what is lovely, and will not last!
What a task to ask of anything, or anyone, yet
it is ours.

And this love, this agape, is not a self consuming love, but a love that inspires awe, veneration, even delight ("as if delight/were the most serious thing/you ever felt"). So that the poems offer not only a kind of wisdom, one that proceeds as if from the very soul, without a contrived form, from a reaching forward, inventing (listening to "a sound/ I do not know"; lying down among field grass so "that the little weightless pieces of gold/ may float over me"), but also with a voice from the deepest desire, and needs, of the heart, reaching the inexplicable ("not a vision,/not an answer, not a proof, but I put it/there, close against my heart, where the need is") giving the sense that the work on the page could not have been conceived or delivered in any way other than what we have received, making what Valery calls the Beautiful.

Suitably, and like true love, the love Oliver expresses is one that takes into account and commensurates those things that are seemingly incommensurable, such as appetite and prurient interests, demonstrating that love, in its most open sense, does not ignore need or desire, those things that can lead to ruin, but suggests that these too have a context. Consider "Yellowlegs" where a bird observed by the poet fishes in the surf along the beach, not over indulging, but taking "Two or three, enough to satisfy the appetite—all the/difference between/nothing and everything."

Oliver speaks as the one whose life is not only her body but "surely . . . something more," turning and confronting her life with an astonishing sense of purpose, as if finding her place; her language is, in the nature of her undertaking, without metrical norm, despite the typographical appearance of capitals and stanzas, yet in them is a harmony of meaning that grows into a richness unlimited by denotation (Northrop Frye's phrase), giving Oliver, and us, a place of respite, even grace:

Through the window
we could see

how far away it was to the gates of April.
Let the fire now
put on its red hat
and sing to us.

And when we are released to love in this crystal air where we actually see the world as our circumstance, we are likewise released from the shackles of our selves, those perennially carnal cores, giving us a poetry of openness, as if the poet has turned herself completely over to the earth, walking in reverence, offering us the image of one who is made manifest on the earth:

it is heaven to take what is given,
to see what is plain; what the sun
lights up willingly; for example—I think this
as I reach down, not to pick but merely to touch—
the suitability of the field for the daisies, and the
daisies for the field.

Oliver's poetry is a poetry of cognition, that says that a thing is itself, which is a poetry of statement. Yet it is also a poetry of reconciliation where the poems work out their symbolism as a mediating metaphor. And it is just here, in the reconciliation, that we find Oliver's purest genius, for she delivers a vision, a language with stilled resonance, a kind of verberation that resounds as if the very ground has found voice:

After rain after many days without rain,
it stays cool, private and cleansed, under the trees,
and the dampness there, married now to gravity,
falls branch to branch, leaf to leaf, down to the
ground . . .

and soon so many small stones, buried for a thousand years,
will feel themselves being touched.

Source: Dale E. Cottingham, Review of *Why I Wake Early*, in *Prairie Schooner*, Vol. 80, No. 1, Spring 2006, pp. 217–19.

SOURCES

"About Inuit," Inuit Tapiriit Kanatami website, https://www.itk.ca/about-inuit (accessed March 15, 2013).

Auger, Peter, "Juxtaposition," in *The Anthem Dictionary of Literary Terms and Theory*, Anthem Press, 2010, p. 160.

Barrington, Judith, Review of *Blue Pastures*, in *Women's Review of Books*, Vol. 13, No. 6, March 1996, p. 10.

Beckson, Karl, and Arthur Ganz, *Literary Terms: A Dictionary*, Farrar, Strauss and Giroux, 1989, pp. 94–95, 238–39.

Classen, Albrecht, "Other, The, European Views of," in *New Dictionary of the History of Ideas*, edited by Maryanne Cline Horowitz, Vol. 4, Charles Scribner's Sons, 2005, pp. 1691–92.

Davis, Todd, "The Earth as God's Body: Incarnation as Communion in the Poetry of Mary Oliver," in *Christianity and Literature*, Vol. 58, No. 4, Summer 2009, p. 605.

Edgar, William, and K. Scott Oliphint, eds., *Christian Apologetics Past and Present: A Primary Source Reader*, Crossway, 2011, p. 265.

Freeman, Minnie Aodla, "Inuit," in *The Canadian Encyclopedia* website, 2012, http://www.thecanadianencyclopedia.com/articles/inuit (accessed March 15, 2013).

Gombay, Nicole, "Placing Economies: Lessons from the Inuit about Economics, Time, and Existence," in *Journal of Cultural Geography*, Vol. 29, No. 1, February 2012, p. 19.

Graham, Vicki, "'Into the Body of Another': Mary Oliver and the Poetics of Becoming Other," in *Papers on Language & Literature*, Vol. 30, No. 4, Fall 1994, p. 352.

Hosmer, Robert, Review of *New and Selected Poems*, in *Southern Review*, Vol. 30, No. 3, Summer 1994, p. 631.

Jurdjevic, Deborah, Review of *What Do We Know*, in *Canadian Woman Studies*, Vol. 22, No. 2, Fall 2002, pp. 166–67.

Keegan, Linda, Review of *New and Selected Poems*, in *Belles Lettres: A Review of Books by Women*, Vol. 10, No. 1, Fall 1994, p. 92.

Kublu, Alexina, and Mick Mallon, "Our Language, Our Selves," Nunavut website, http://www.nunavut.com/nunavut99/english/our.html (accessed March 20, 2013).

Lehrer, Eli, "Natural Poet; Environmental Lyrics are More Appealing than Political Verse," in *Weekly Standard*, Vol. 14, No. 9, November 17, 2008.

Macfarlane, Jamie, "Canadian Inuit Realize Self-government," WorldFocus website, February 24, 2010, http://worldfocus.org/blog/2010/02/24/canadian-inuit-realize-self-government/ (accessed March 15, 2013).

Merritt, James, "Nunavut: Canada Turns a New Page in the Arctic," in *Canadian Parliamentary Review*, Summer 1993, pp. 2–6.

Micale, Mark S., "Romanticism," in *Europe 1789–1914: Encyclopedia of the Age of Industry and Empire*, edited by John Merriman and Jay Winter, Vol. 4, Charles Scribner's Sons, 2006, pp. 2026–33.

Oliver, Mary, "The Esquimos Have No Word for 'War,'" in *New and Selected Poems*, Beacon Press, 1992, p. 236.

———, *Long Life: Essays and Other Writings*, Da Capo Press, 2004, p. 91.

———, *Winter Hours: Prose, Prose Poems, and Poems*, First Mariner Books, 1999, p. 24.

Review of *New and Selected Poems, Volume Two*, in *Publishers Weekly*, Vol. 252, No. 42, October 24, 2005, p. 41.

Robinson, David M., "American Romanticism," in *Encyclopedia of American Cultural and Intellectual History*, edited by Mary Kupiec Cayton and Peter W. Williams, Charles Scribner's Sons, 2001.

Skipp, Frances E., "The Flowering of American Romanticism, 1820–1865," in *American Literature*, Barron's Educational Series, 1992, pp. 23–24.

Stern, Pamela R., "Inuit," in *International Encyclopedia of the Social Sciences*, edited by William A. Darity Jr., 2nd ed., Vol. 4, Macmillan Reference USA, 2008, pp. 124–26.

FURTHER READING

Andronik, Catherine M., *Wildly Romantic: The English Romantic Poets: The Mad, the Bad, and the Dangerous*, Henry Holt, 2007.

Andronik's book examines the personal lives of William Wordsworth, Samuel Taylor Coleridge, George Gordon Byron, Percy Bysshe Shelley, and John Keats, five of the major English romantic poets, to show the ways in which their new ways of thinking changed literature in permanent ways.

Armstrong, Jeannette, and Lally Grauer, *Native Poetry in Canada: A Contemporary Anthology*, Broadview Press, 2001.

This collection contains poetry from many unknown Native Canadian writers along with well-known, critically acclaimed poets, chronicling the evolution of the Canadian aboriginal cultural renaissance from the 1960s to the present.

Harjo, Joy, *Crazy Brave: A Memoir*, W. W. Norton, 2012.

Harjo has been one of the most celebrated Native American writers for the last quarter century. In this touching memoir, she details her journey from an abusive childhood on the reservation, through experiencing single motherhood, and finally to discovering poetry as a way to reconnect with her ancestral tribal roots and help her become a strong and independent Native American woman.

Holmes, Richard, *The Age of Wonder: How the Romantic Generation Discovered the Beauty and Terror of Science*, Pantheon, 2009.

Holmes focuses on the lives of three scientists during the end of the eighteenth century to explore the ways in which new scientific discoveries challenged all traditional notions of philosophy, spirituality, art, and poetry and gave birth to the romantic era.

Meeks, Arone Raymond, *Enora and the Black Crane: A Collection of Aboriginal Poetry*, Scholastic Australia, 1991.

Meeks, an Aboriginal filmmaker and writer, has collected the work of thirty-five Australian Aboriginal poets, such as Oodgeroo of the tribe Noonuccal, Jack Davis, Archie Weller, Bobbi Sykes, Eva Johnson, Kevin Gilbert, and Ruby Langford Ginibi. The poems are accompanied by illustrations by Meeks.

Oliver, Mary, and Molly Malone Cook, *Our World*, Beacon Press, 2009.

Oliver and Cook, romantic partners for more than forty years, were extremely private and rarely gave the public a glimpse into their personal lives. This volume, published four years after Cook's death, is a deeply moving testament to the world they built and shared together.

Rosen, Charles, *Romantic Poets, Critics, and Other Madmen*, Harvard University Press, 2000.
Music historian and critic Charles Rosen's collection of essays focuses on literary criticism of the romantic era as a way to understand the fundamental principles of romanticism itself. He examines the connection between romantic theories of aesthetic, music, art, literature, and criticism.

SUGGESTED SEARCH TERMS

Mary Oliver

The Esquimos Have No Word for War

nature poetry

Mary Oliver AND romantic poetry

Mary Oliver AND nature

Mary Oliver AND New and Selected Poems

romanticism

binary opposition AND literature

Half-hanged Mary

MARGARET ATWOOD

1995

"Half-hanged Mary" is a poem by Canadian poet and novelist Margaret Atwood. It was published in Atwood's poetry collection *Morning in the Burning House* in 1995. The poem is based on a real incident that took place in Hadley, Massachusetts, in 1684. The previous year, a local woman, Mary Webster, had been charged with being a witch. In June, she was tried in Boston and acquitted. Her neighbors, however, appear to have been unconvinced by the verdict, and about eighteen months later, Webster was again accused of witchcraft. Some of the men from Hadley hanged her from a tree, but she managed to survive the ordeal. When townspeople came in the morning to cut her down, she was still alive. (There are other versions of this incident in the historical records.) She lived another eleven years, until her death in 1696. Atwood believed that Webster was her ancestor, and she dedicated her 1985 novel *The Handmaid's Tale* to her. The poem "Half-hanged Mary" is a dramatic monologue in ten sections that correspond to specific times, from 7 p.m. when Mary was hanged, until 8 a.m. the following morning, with a concluding section about her life in the years following the hanging. The poem, which exhibits Atwood's typical wit, subtlety, and sharp images, shines a light on a dark period in American history when irrationalism and fear led to persecution of the innocent.

and American universities, including the University of Alberta, York University in Toronto, and New York University. Her works have been translated into more than forty languages, including Farsi, Japanese, Turkish, Finnish, Korean, Icelandic, and Estonian.

Atwood's many volumes of poetry include *The Animals in That Country* (1968), *The Journals of Susanna Moodie* (1970), *You Are Happy* (1974), *Two-Headed Poems* (1978), and *Interlunar* (1984). *Morning in the Burned House* (1995) includes the poem "Half-hanged Mary." This collection was a cowinner of the Trillium Award. Atwood's most recent collection, as of 2013, is *The Door* (2007).

Her fourteen novels include *The Edible Woman* (1969); *Surfacing* (1972); *Lady Oracle* (1976); *Life before Man* (1979); *Bodily Harm* (1981); *Encounters with the Element Man* (1982); *Unearthing Suite* (1983); *The Handmaid's Tale* (1985), which was a best seller and won the Governor General's Award, the *Los Angeles Times* Award, and the Arthur C. Clarke science fiction award; *Cat's Eye* (1988); *The Robber Bride* (1993), which won the Canadian Authors Association Novel of the Year Award; *Alias Grace* (1996), which won the Giller Prize; *The Blind Assassin* (2000), which won the Booker Prize; and the trilogy *Oryx and Crake* (2003), *The Year of the Flood* (2009), and *MaddAddam* (2013).

Atwood's nine short-story collections include *Dancing Girls and Other Stories* (1976), *Bluebeard's Egg and Other Stories* (1986), and *Moral Disorder and Other Stories* (2006); her nonfiction includes *Survival: A Thematic Guide to Canadian Literature* (1972) and *Payback: Debt and the Shadow Side of Wealth* (2008).

Atwood has worked and traveled extensively in Europe, and she has received honorary degrees from many institutions, including Trent University, Smith College, and the University of Toronto. She was president of the Writers Union of Canada from 1982 to 1983, and president of PEN International's Anglo-Canadian branch from 1984 to 1985. As of 2013, she is vice president of PEN International.

Atwood married James Polk, a novelist, in 1967. They divorced in 1973. Atwood lives in Toronto with Canadian writer Graeme Gibson. They have a daughter, Jess, who was born in 1977.

Margaret Atwood (© *Frances Guillot | AFP | Getty Images*)

AUTHOR BIOGRAPHY

Poet, novelist, short-story writer, essayist, and literary critic Margaret Eleanor Atwood was born on November 18, 1939, in Ottawa, Canada. Her father, Carl Edmund Atwood, was a forest entomologist; her mother, Margaret Dorothy (Killam), was a graduate in home economics from the University of Toronto. Atwood spent her earliest years in Ottawa during the winters and the rest of the year in northern Quebec and Ontario. In 1946, her father took up a position as professor at the University of Toronto, and the family moved to Toronto. In 1957, Atwood became a student of English at Victoria College, University of Toronto. In 1961, after graduation, she studied English at Radcliffe College, Harvard University, and was awarded a master's degree in 1962. She then went on to doctoral studies at Harvard until 1963. The following year, she taught English literature at the University of British Columbia. Her first collection of poetry, *The Circle Game* (1966), won the Governor General's Award. Since then, Atwood has published poetry, novels, short stories, children's literature, and nonfiction and has taught in many Canadian

POEM SUMMARY

The text used for this summary is from *Morning in the Burned House*, Houghton Mifflin, 1995, pp. 58–69.

The poem is divided into ten sections. Each section is headed by an exact time during which Mary, the woman who is being hanged, expresses her thoughts and feelings. The first section begins at seven o'clock in the evening. Mary recalls the circumstances in which she was seized. Rumors were flying around the town about witchcraft. She was milking a cow in the barn around sunset. The second stanza suggests that she was caught by surprise. She had no idea that she would be targeted as a witch. In the third stanza, she explains why she was picked on and hanged. First, she lived on her own; she was not married. (This is unlike the historical Mary Webster, on whom the poem is based, who was married.) Her appearance also helps to account for what happened to her, she thinks. She worked outside and got sunburned; her clothes were, it seems, not of the highest quality; and she owned the poorly kept farm where she lived. She also had knowledge of folk remedies for common ailments. In addition, as the last stanza of this section explains, she was a woman, and that made her a convenient target when people talked about demonic possession.

Section two starts one hour later, at eight o'clock. Mary describes how she was hanged. The men from the town grabbed a rope and she was hanged from a tree. Her hands were bound, and she was gagged. The men, thrilled by what they had done out of hatred, trudged back home. Mary thinks that they were projecting their own evil onto her.

Section three begins at nine o'clock. Mary relates how some women from the town come to stare at her. Mary looks down from her position high up and can see how fearful they are. In the second stanza she addresses two of the woman directly. It appears that they are both friends of hers. Mary cured the baby of one of the women from some unspecified ailment; she helped save the life of the other one, it seems, by performing an abortion on her.

Mary knows that the women lack the courage to bring her down from the tree. Were they to do so, they might be accused of being witches too. It is better not to bring attention to oneself in this kind of situation, Mary says in the fourth

stanza of this section. She understands that the women are unable to help her in any way at all.

At ten o'clock, which is the title of the next section, Mary addresses God directly. She wants to argue with him about free will. Was being hanged an act of free will on her part, a choice she made? She pours scorn on the concept of God's grace and suggests that the great Christian virtues of faith, hope, and charity are dead.

The next section begins at midnight. Mary describes the unpleasant physical sensations she is experiencing. She is being strangled; she clenches her teeth; she feels despair. She feels the approach of death, personifying it first as a bird of prey, then as a venomous judge pronouncing punishment, and then as an angel urging her to give in to death.

By two o'clock in the morning, when the next section begins, Mary hears herself uttering some kind of sound. It seems that it is both a struggle for air and a prayer, born of desperation, that she might survive, that mercy might be shown to her.

By three o'clock, the wind is raging and the birds are singing. Mary's strength is ebbing and it is hard for her to breathe. However, she affirms her innocence and is determined not to give up.

At six o'clock, the sun rises. Mary feels she has been up there a thousand years. She makes a sardonic joke about having grown taller (she means her body has been stretched by hanging).

At eight o'clock, the townspeople come to cut her down from the tree. She is still alive. She knows that, according to the law, they will not be allowed to hang her again for the same offense. She grins at them. She looks at them and scares them. They run away. Mary reflects that, if she was not a witch before, she has become one now.

In the final section of the poem, Mary discusses her life since the hanging. She says she goes around mumbling to herself, and the townspeople flee from her whenever they see her. She finds that she can now say anything she wants; having been hanged once, she cannot be hanged again. She also speaks of herself as having undergone two deaths. She eats a strange diet and commits blasphemies, she says. God understands her, she says, although no one else can. It seems that she has access to some secret knowledge or wisdom as a result of her ordeal, and she expresses it in words that only she and God can understand.

TOPICS FOR FURTHER STUDY

- Write a poem in the form of a dramatic monologue. Remember that a dramatic monologue features a first-person speaker who is not the poet offering his or her thoughts and feelings about a particular situation to one or more people who are not actually present and whose reactions can be guessed only by the speaker's words. The situation can be based on a real event or it can be fiction.

- Give a reading of "Half-hanged Mary" to your class, preceded by a two-minute introduction in which you discuss the poem's theme and structure. Have a classmate record your reading and upload it to YouTube.

- Watch *The Crucible*, the 1996 film based on Arthur Miller's 1953 play that was itself based on the Salem witch trials. Using Internet sources, write a review of the film in which you assess how accurately the film conveys not only the facts but the atmosphere of those times. How does the film fictionalize the events, and in what respects does it stay close to the facts? Post your review to the Amazon website.

- Read *Where to Park Your Broomstick: A Teen's Guide to Witchcraft* by Lauren Manoy and Yan Apostolides (2002), which explains the principles of Wicca. It also includes a history of paganism and witchcraft. Write an essay in which you outline the basic elements of Wicca and describe how they resemble or differ from those of Christianity, Judaism, or any other major world religion. Comment also on the fact that the authors make no mention of the persecution of witches in history, including the witch hunts that took place in seventeenth-century New England. What reasons might the authors have had for omitting this? What is the relationship between the traditional understanding of witchcraft and the modern version found in Wicca?

THEMES

Injustice

The speaker of the poem has suffered an injustice for which she was unprepared. The attack took her by surprise, and there has been no judicial process. The hanging she describes is an extra-judicial lynching. There is no evidence against her. Rumors have been flying around the town, she says in the first line of the poem, presumably about some unspecified act of so-called witchcraft, and Mary happens to be a convenient target for people who are looking for someone on whom to vent their anger and fear. Mary has done nothing to deserve it. In the section headed three o'clock in the morning, she affirms that she is innocent; she has committed no crime.

In the third stanza of the first section of the poem, Mary offers her own thoughts about why she was singled out. She was female, for a start, which made her more likely to be a target for the witch-hunters. She also lived alone and owned her own property. A woman owning property was not common in seventeenth-century New England and could have aroused resentment among men who felt it undermined their authority. The woman also practiced folk remedies; she says in this stanza that she knew a cure for warts. If someone in the town disliked her for some reason, the fact that she gave out remedies for common ailments and treated children (as she states in section three) might have been used against her if someone who took the remedy did not get better or even got worse. Such a situation might have led to an accusation that the woman had made a compact with the devil to do people harm. That such an accusation might have been made against the Mary of the poem is clear from the last stanza of the first section.

Atwood uses the image of the crow as a symbol of death. (© Hanka Steidle / Shutterstock.com)

The injustice the speaker has suffered is also a betrayal, as the third section reveals. At least two of the women who come to look at her as she hangs from a tree were her friends. But the women will not help her, and Mary realizes that they are too fearful to do so. In this kind of situation, when irrational thinking has taken hold, it is dangerous to speak out against a prevailing view. The hatred unleashed against one person could, in a flash, turn against another.

Mary continues the theme of injustice is continued by Mary as she addresses God in the fourth section. God's love is absent from the universe that Mary inhabits as she hangs from the tree, and God offers her no assistance, nor any response at all. In the absence of God's grace, all that remains is the human idea of justice, which in this case is based on irrational fear and hatred.

Transformation

In this extremely unusual, macabre experience, Mary undergoes not death, as everyone including herself might have expected, but transformation. Her survival may, in part, be due to her mental strength. She refuses to give up, even though she is tempted to do so at midnight (tempted, it would seem, by the same devil that she is, supposedly, as a witch, in league with). At three o'clock in the morning, she remains defiant, still with the will to live. The first signs of her transformation are apparent at eight o'clock in the morning, when the men come to cut her down. The fact that she is still alive and grins at the men terrifies them, and they run away. Now she really is a witch, she says, with some wit, at the end of that section.

The final section of the poem describes Mary's life after her hanging. Marked out by her unusual, perhaps even unique, experience, she speaks of having died once already. She becomes an eccentric figure, talking strangely to herself, eating berries and flowers from the fields, and experiencing a freedom to do and say exactly what she wants, not fearing any reprisals. The townspeople are scared of her. It is as if she has acquired some kind of secret knowledge that enables her to communicate with nature. She seems to live a paradox: while being close to the earth, she is somehow also in touch with the divine. She has acquired a new language for understanding the mysteries of life that take her beyond the normal range of human knowledge. Although she now calls herself, with some irony, a witch, her communication is not with the devil but, in a sense, with God.

STYLE

Dramatic Monologue

The poem is in the form of a dramatic monologue. The dramatic monologue was made famous by the nineteenth-century English poet Robert Browning in poems such as "My Last Duchess" and "Andrea del Sarto." According to M. H. Abrams in *A Glossary of Literary Terms*, the dramatic monologue, as exemplified by Browning, usually consists of three elements. First, it features a single, first-person speaker who is not the poet, who gives his or her account of a specific event in which he or she is involved at an important moment during that event. Second, the speaker of the poem addresses one or more people in the course of the poem. Their responses are not given directly but can be inferred from what the speaker says. Third, the speaker, in explaining the situation, reveals his or her character.

The dramatic monologue has been used by many poets, including Alfred, Lord Tennyson, in "Ulysses," and T. S. Eliot, in "The Love Song

of J. Alfred Prufrock." Atwood herself uses the form, with some variation, in "The Loneliness of the Military Historian," one of the poems in *Morning in the Burning House*. "Half-hanged Mary" meets all three elements identified by Abrams, with some variations. Mary, the speaker, is not the poet, and she relates a traumatic event that happened to her, extending the account to cover her life after the hanging. In addition to the reader, she addresses the women who come to stare at her in the evening (third section) and God (fourth section and part of the sixth section). She also shows herself to be a very spirited woman who possesses a sardonic sense of humor, as seen when she mocks her assailants and offers wry and witty observations about her own situation. She also reveals herself as a woman of great endurance and determination who is able to be defiant in the face of injustice and adversity to the extent that she is able to keep the flame of life alive within her.

Simile and Metaphor

The poem offers plentiful examples of simile and metaphor. Similes consist of a comparison between two unlike things in a way that brings out their underlying similarity. Similes are often recognizable by the words "as" or "like," and in this poem, the word "like" appears in this context no fewer than thirteen times. Each occurrence indicates the presence of a simile. For example, the accusation against her is compared to a bullet from a gun penetrating her. She compares herself as she is hoisted up onto the tree to a fallen apple being put back on the tree. In the section headed "midnight", the poet uses three similes, one after the other, for death. It is like a bird of prey, a prurient judge, or a persuasive, tempting angel. The poet even jokes about a simile that is not one. In the six o'clock section, the poet plays on the idea of the sun as a simile for God, which would be a common, scarcely original comparison, but the speaker gives it a twist: the sun is *not* a simile for God. Although it might have been in the past, the speaker implies, such a simile would no longer be appropriate for someone in her situation who is clinging to life in a universe in which God appears to be absent.

A metaphor occurs when two unlike things are linked not by a comparison between them but by identifying one as the other. In the eight o'clock section, Mary metaphorically becomes a flag, raised in the night. At the end of that section, the sky is a metaphor for the God who will not offer any solace or explanation for her fate.

HISTORICAL CONTEXT

Witches in Seventeenth-Century New England

Belief in witches was almost universal in the Puritan colonies of seventeenth-century New England. In a prescientific world, people believed in many things that modern people do not. Supernatural forces were thought to be at work in the day-to-day world, for example, and witches knew how to manipulate those forces for evil purposes. Witches, it was believed, had entered into a compact with the devil and were dedicated to inflicting harm on other people. If people were faced with a distressing event, such as illness, the death of a child, or the death of cattle, they might think that some evil force was at work and blame one of their neighbors whom they did not like or with whom they had recently quarreled or who was considered odd in some way.

David D. Hall, in his introduction to *Witch-Hunting in Seventeenth-Century New England: A Documentary History, 1638–1692*, notes that women, especially those over forty, were accused of being witches far more frequently than men were. The ratio was four to one. Men accused of witchcraft were also less likely to face trial, and their punishments were lighter than those meted out to women. Hall suggests that one reason for the discrepancy might have been because men held authority over women in all aspects of life and society. Witch-hunting might be seen as "a means of reaffirming this authority at a time when some women...were testing these constraints, and when others were experiencing a degree of independence, as when women without husbands or male siblings inherited property."

Legally, in New England in the seventeenth century, witchcraft was a felony punishable by death. The Puritans had scripture on their side in this respect, since the book of Exodus contains the statement, "Thou shalt not suffer a witch to live" (Exodus 22:18). The death penalty was carried out by hanging. Many alleged witches, however, were acquitted in trials, and people who made false charges against an alleged witch were subject to punishment themselves.

According to John Putnam Davos, in his introduction to *Entertaining Satan: Witchcraft*

and the Culture of Early New England, throughout the seventeenth century in New England, there were a total of 234 cases in which indictments were made or complaints filed against accused witches. There were thirty-six executions. Twenty of these took place as a result of the notorious witch trials in Salem, Massachusetts, in 1692—just eight years after Mary Webster was hanged a little more than one hundred miles away in Hadley.

The Case of Mary Webster

Mary Webster lived in Hadley, Massachusetts. She married William Webster in 1670. They were poor and depended on the town for assistance. She was accused of witchcraft by the county magistrates in Northampton in March 1683. It appears that there were many written testimonies against her, naming her as a witch. The county magistrates sent her to Boston for further examination at the Court of Assistants. The court ordered her to stand trial, accusing her, as quoted in David Hall's *Witch-Hunting in Seventeenth-Century New England: A Documentary History, 1638–1692*, of having "familiarity" with the devil in the "shape of a warraeage [an Indian word meaning "black cat"] and had her imps sucking her and teats or marks found in her secret parts." Webster pleaded not guilty, and on June 1, 1863, she was acquitted. At some point after the trial, Philip Smith, a church deacon who had been a member of the court that had considered Webster's case in Northampton, said he had tried to help her because she was poor, but she said something to him in reply that made him fear she might try to harm him. Smith then became ill. To the people who attended him, there were some strange things that happened during his sickness, as reported by Cotton Mather in *Memorable Providences*, a book published in Boston in 1689, excerpts from which are included in *Witch-Hunting in Seventeenth-Century New England*. There was a musk-like smell, the source of which could not be identified; there was a scratching sound near his feet, and sometimes fire was seen on the bed. Something as big as a cat was observed moving under the covers, but when the covers were lifted, nothing was found. These and other occurrences made people think that witchcraft was at work. Smith died of his illness. Mather was convinced that Smith had been murdered by witchcraft. While Smith was still alive, some local men, convinced of Webster's guilt, decided to take the law into their own hands. This is the

COMPARE
&
CONTRAST

- **Late 17th century:** The Salem witch trials begin in Salem, Massachusetts, in June 1692. Many people are denounced as witches as a wave of hysteria sweeps across the town. Within three months, nineteen men and women are convicted and hanged. Another man is pressed to death by large stones for refusing to submit to a trial.

  1990s: The Salem Witch Museum in Salem, Massachusetts, which opened in 1972, uses the three hundredth anniversary of the trials to bring a sense of reconciliation and an understanding of the lessons to be learned from them. In 1991, Pulitzer Prize-winning playwright Arthur Miller (author of the 1953 play *The Crucible* about the Salem witch trials) is the featured speaker at the opening press conference. In 1992, the museum helps to form the Salem Witch Trials Tercentenary Committee and oversees the building of the Salem Witch Trials Memorial, adjacent to Salem's seventeenth-century Charter Street Burying Point. Nobel Laureate and Holocaust survivor Elie Wiesel visits Salem to dedicate the Salem Witch Trials Memorial.

  Today: The Salem Award for Human Rights and Social Justice is given each year to keep alive the lessons to be learned from the witch trials of 1692. The award recognizes those who work to end discrimination and promote tolerance. In 2013, the Salem Award is given to Thomas Doyle, an ordained priest, who helped to expose sex abuse within the Catholic Church, and Horace Seldon, a former minister of the United Church of Christ, who has spent forty-five years teaching about racism and working to end it.

- **Late 17th century:** In Europe and North America, witchcraft is considered evil, a deviation from true religion, and witches are persecuted.

  1990s: Wicca, a pagan religion developed in the early twentieth century in England, com-

bines witchcraft with other beliefs and rituals. In 1990, Wicca has 8,000 adherents in the United States and is popularized in films and television programs, such as *Charmed*, a TV series aired on the WB beginning in 1998, about four witches who practice their art for good rather than evil. Popular books such as *The Truth about Witchcraft Today* (1998) by Scott Cunningham, disseminate knowledge about Wicca and witchcraft.

  Today: Wicca is a fast-growing religion, with 342,000 people identifying as Wiccans in a 2008 survey. Wiccans venerate nature and are forbidden to harm anyone. Many practice their beliefs alone, not connected to any organization. The status of Wicca as a religion has been upheld by US court rulings.

- **Late 17th century:** Estimates of the number of alleged witches killed between 1484 and 1700 in Europe range between 200,000 and 300,000.

  1990s: Witch hunts no longer take place in North America or Europe, but they continue in other parts of the world. The BBC reports that, in the Democratic Republic of Congo in the late 1990s, children are being labeled as witches. People in Congo society are superstitious, and when misfortunes occur, many blame them on sorcery committed by children. More than 14,000 accused children in the capital city, Kinshasa, have been thrown out of their homes onto the street. Others have been murdered by their own relatives. The BBC also reports on the murder of alleged witches in Tanzania.

  Today: Persecution of people accused of being witches still continues in Africa, India, and other parts of Asia. In February 2013, in Papua New Guinea, a twenty-year-old woman is accused of sorcery by relatives of a six-year-old boy who died in the hospital. The woman is tortured and burnt to death on a pile of tires and trash, watched by hundreds of people.

The narrator of "Half Hanged Mary" is killed because the townspeople fear she is a witch.
(© OlegDoroshin / Shutterstock.com)

description given by Sylvester Judd in *History of Hadley, Including the Early History of Hatfield, South Hadley, Amherst, and Granby*:

> A number of brisk lads tried an experiment upon the old woman. Having dragged her out of her house, they hung her up until she was near dead, let her down, rolled her sometime in the snow, and at last buried her in it, and there left her; but it happened that she survived.

Mary Webster died in 1696, at about the age of seventy.

CRITICAL OVERVIEW

Although Atwood's poetry has not attracted as much critical comment as her novels, "Half-hanged Mary" has received some attention from reviewers and literary critics. The reviewer for *Publishers Weekly* includes "Half-hanged Mary" as an example of "the most vivid poems" in *Morning in the Burning House*, which "forge an apprehensible human aspect from scholarly fields

of science, history and religion." In her review of *Morning in the Burning House* in the *Antioch Review*, Molly Bendall comments, "Atwood's savage, back-talking dramatic monologues have become her trademark," including "the tour de force 'Half-Hanged Mary,' a voice from the bleak theatre (Salem chapter) of our history." For Ray Olson, reviewing the same collection in *Booklist*, "if she [Atwood] is not consistently persuasive, she is always vital, powerful, magnetically readable." For Kathryn Van Spanckeren, in her essay "Humanizing the Fox: Atwood's Poetic Tricksters and *Morning in the Burned House*," "Half-hanged Mary" "recalls *The Journals of Susannah Moodie* [another poetry collection by Atwood] in its chronological construction and transformation from realistic woman protagonist to mythical figure (in this case a witch). It evokes a consciousness mysteriously continuing after death." However, Van Spanckeren adds that "after all her suffering Mary remains emotionally dead and cut off from others."

CRITICISM

Bryan Aubrey

Aubrey holds a PhD in English. In the following essay, he examines the historical context of "Half-hanged Mary" as well as its transcendence of that context.

"Half-hanged Mary" is a witty, sometimes harrowing poem based on a dramatic and shocking historical incident. Atwood wriggles inside the mind of the ill-fated Mary Webster, who, in 1684, was hanged as a witch in Hadley, Massachusetts, but improbably lived to tell the tale. The poem well conveys the feelings—physical, emotional, spiritual—of what it might be like to get strung up by your neighbors and hang all night from a tree being gradually strangled. Although the poem is rich with imagery, it is often conversational in tone as the stricken woman addresses her various auditors using colloquial expressions that, in context, acquire a sardonic humor. Mary emerges as a courageous soul, at once knowledgeable, questioning, defiant, and enduring. Atwood's free verse varies in line and stanza length, and she is adept at creating the effect she wants. The section in which Mary relates her ordeal from three o'clock in the morning is printed entirely in lower-case letters (with the exception of one word used to express her continuing refusal to give up), without a single punctuation

WHAT DO I READ NEXT?

- *The Handmaid's Tale* (1985) is one of Atwood's most famous novels. It takes place in a dystopia in the near future and explores the dangers of totalitarianism, religious fanaticism, and the devaluing of women. The United States has become the Republic of Gilead, a conservative Protestant theocracy in which women are strictly controlled in all areas of their lives. The novel is narrated by Offred, who serves as a Handmaid to the Commander, a powerful member of the government. Her only role is to produce his children.

- Atwood's *Selected Poems II: Poems Selected and New; 1976–1986* (2nd edition, 1987) contains seventy-three poems, including selections from four of her previous collections as well as seventeen previously unpublished poems.

- *The Door* (2007) is Atwood's first collection of poetry since *Morning in the Burned House* in 1995. These fifty poems explore topics such as writing and the role of the poet, time, aging, and mortality, as well as political and environmental themes, including war.

- Carol F. Karlsen's *The Devil in the Shape of a Woman: Witchcraft in Colonial New England* (1998) is a history of witchcraft in New England from 1620 to 1725. Karlsen examines gender relations during the period and argues that alleged witches were primarily older, sometimes financially independent women who were perceived as a threat to the dominance of men in society.

- *Teen Witch: Wicca for a New Generation* (1998) by Silver RavenWolf is an introduction to Wicca for young people. The author, at the time of writing, was the mother of two teenage children, and she understood the concerns of teens. She explains the basics of the Wiccan religion and takes a practical approach to spells and rituals. She emphasizes that magic does not mix well with alcohol or drugs and that Wiccans do not harm other people.

- Like Atwood, Alice Walker has major achievements in both novels and poetry. *Absolute Trust in the Goodness of the Earth: New Poems* (2003) is her sixth collection of poems. The title conveys one of the themes of the eighty-six poems in the collection. Walker employs simple diction and mostly very short lines as she writes in praise of the beauty of life in all its aspects and offers thoughtful reflection on a range of emotions.

---

mark, not even at the end. The chosen form captures the movement of Mary's mind as it races, trying to subdue panic as the wind whistles through the trees and she becomes increasingly desperate to cling to life even as her body weakens.

As for Mary's crime and punishment, a modern reader can only wonder at the sensibilities of those seventeenth-century folk, respectable citizens all, it would seem, who thought it was a capital idea—right and proper and just—to condemn as a witch, without judicial proceeding, a woman who was probably in her late fifties and then hang her from a tree. No doubt the twenty-first century has unspeakable cruelties

of its own, but to understand the hanging of alleged witches—for Mary Webster was not the only one—in New England only a little over three centuries ago requires a leap of the historical imagination. What, one has to ask, were these people thinking of?

The basic elements of their world view are not difficult to understand. The Puritans believed that supernatural forces were capable of penetrating the natural world and causing things to happen that would otherwise be impossible or inexplicable. The invisible, spiritual world was always acting upon the visible, physical world, either through what was referred to as God's providence

INDEED, PERHAPS THE MOST HAUNTING
PART OF THIS POEM ABOUT THE SUFFERING THAT
IGNORANCE AND MALICE CAN INFLICT ON ONE POOR
MIDDLE-AGED WOMAN IS NOT THE AGONY OF
TORTURED FLESH BUT WHAT HAPPENS TO THE
WOMAN AFTERWARD."

or through the power of evil as personified in Satan, or the devil. The Puritans knew from scripture that the devil was continually plotting evil against God and man. All Satan needed was a willing partner, and if people—witches—were to form a covenant with the devil, he and his agents would join with them in doing harm.

As for the historical Mary Webster, not a great deal is known about her except for the fact she was tried and acquitted of witchcraft in Boston in 1693 and that she later succeeded in greatly annoying a gentleman by the name of Philip Smith, whose suspicion that she was practicing witchcraft on him during his illness led directly to her hanging. According to the account of Smith's illness given by Cotton Mather in *Memorable Providences* (1689), strange events accompanied it.

At one point, Smith felt as if hundreds of pins were sticking into him, pricking him, but only one pin was ever found. Smith claimed that he could see Mary Webster and others standing in his room. No one else, it seems, could see them, but a core belief in the witchcraft trials was "spectral evidence," the idea that witches could leave their bodies and appear to someone they intended to harm in a spectral (i.e., ghostly) form. Further, when Smith was in great distress from his illness, his friends went to Mary's home and harassed her, and while they were doing so, Smith slept well (presumably because her unwelcome visitors had forced her into a lapse of concentration in her desire to do Smith harm). In other incidents, a pot of medicine for Smith that was nearly full and carefully watched over mysteriously became empty; fire was seen on the bed that would vanish when the people who saw it began talking about it; and after Smith died, an observer saw his bed move without cause.

To the modern mind, to interpret all this as evidence of witchcraft seems ridiculous, a tissue of nonsense, but it was not so for the people of Hadley in 1684. This was all it took for Mary Webster to feel the force of their cruel judgments. It must, of course, have been known that she had been tried in Boston for witchcraft a year prior, so perhaps belief in the old adage that there is no smoke without fire was also at work in her case.

In writing her poem, Atwood certainly did her research, not only into Mary Webster but into other cases of witchcraft from the period as well. The Mary of the poem, for example, is a healer. She makes this clear several times, and she believes her cures were effective, as she points out to the women who come at night to gawk at her. But perhaps doing her best to heal people was Mary's mistake, at least as far as her welfare was concerned, since being a healer and a woman in New England, at the time, could, on occasion, be a dangerous combination. According to John Putnam Demos in *Entertaining Satan: Witchcraft and the Culture of Early New England*, many of the women accused of witchcraft practiced informal methods of healing. Elizabeth Garlick of Easthampton, Long Island, who was tried and acquitted of witchcraft in 1658, prescribed herbal remedies. Katherine Harrison of Wethersfield, Connecticut, who was required to leave Connecticut in 1670 after the court failed to reach a verdict, was also a healer. Winifred Holman of Cambridge, Massachusetts, who was prosecuted in 1659 and acquitted, prescribed herbs for a sick woman. Margaret Jones of Charlestown, Massachusetts, executed in 1648, also practiced medicine on an informal basis. When combined with other factors, such as previous accusations of theft or slander, women healers could easily fall under suspicion.

However, in creating the character who delivers the dramatic monologue, Atwood makes her Mary, in other respects, somewhat atypical of the women who were accused of witchcraft and, indeed, unusual for a woman of her time and place. She lives alone on a farm she owns herself, and the bulk of her time is taken up with the daily chores of farm life. (Much of the imagery she uses is drawn from what would have been her day-to-day observations on the farm.) According to Demos, however, although women were sometimes assistants to farmers, they were not farmers in their own right; many, of course, lived and

The serene image of the barn at sunset is interrupted by the unexpected accusation. (© Cardens Design / Shutterstock.com)

worked on farms with their husbands and children. Mary of the poem, though, appears to have no children. Moreover, most accused witches, including the historical Mary Webster, were married. Perhaps Atwood's Mary is a widow who inherited the property. It is also possible that making her more of an isolated, independent figure than she was in actual life serves Atwood's dramatic intentions: it places Mary outside the traditional patriarchal order of things and therefore makes her an object of envy and fear. (Demos, however, does not consider that tension between patriarchal structures and women's aspirations played any role in the witch hunts. Men were dominant, of course, but Demos found no evidence of a conflict between the sexes that might explain why women were more often accused of being witches than men were.)

Of course, "Half-hanged Mary" is an imaginative creation and does not have to conform in every detail to historical fact, even if those facts could be known for sure. Indeed, perhaps the most haunting part of this poem about the suffering that ignorance and malice can inflict on one

poor middle-aged woman is not the agony of tortured flesh but what happens to the woman afterward. In the last section of the poem, Atwood departs from any historical facts or surmises (other than the fact that Mary Webster survived the hanging) and enters a world of pure imagination. Her Mary, shunned and ostracized by the locals who now fear her more than ever, lives in an isolated but imaginatively rich world of her own. It is as if she has gone beyond some invisible boundary and acquired a knowledge of life that only she can comprehend. Old categories of thinking have been transcended, and the notion of blasphemy no longer has any meaning. Instead, a new spirituality has emerged in her, one that seems to embrace the unity of all life and offers gratitude at every moment.

Source: Bryan Aubrey, Critical Essay on "Half-hanged Mary," in *Poetry for Students*, Gale, Cengage Learning, 2014.

Lothar Hönnighausen
In the following excerpt, Hönnighausen contrasts Atwood's poetry with her prose.

On the occasion of this essay on Margaret Atwood's poetry, I take my cue both from her painter Elaine Risley, favoring "a chronological approach" for this retrospective exhibition, and from her gallerist Charna, who "wants things to go together tonally and resonate" (*Cat's Eye*, 91). Atwood's work has been categorized and subdivided into so many styles and phases, in which she supposedly was a Canadian nationalist, literary lobbyist, liberal parodist, Amnesty International activist, or changed back and forth from poet to prose writer, from aggressive feminist harpy to soft-souled wife and mother, from progressive young woman to stone-faced sibyl, that the use of any traditional evolutionary scheme in approaching it is out of the question. Along the same lines, Atwood's poetic stance, which has been over-simplistically described as either *autobiographical* or *mythopoeic*, is probably neither or both, resulting, as with other writers, from the stylization, in changing forms, of a changing stream of experience. In any case, her sixtieth birthday seems to call not so much for yet more scholarly theorizing than for intense rereading, particularly of her poetry, which is not as well known as her fiction.

Although there are many affinities between Atwood's poetry and her fiction, her poems, in contrast to her novels, stories, or essays, seem to occur like entries into a kind of artistic logbook. Writing poetry for Atwood appears to be an irresistible, ongoing process of perception, reflection, and aesthetic organization. What makes this process of poetic exploration relevant to her readers is the radicality with which she puts things to the test, and the inventive craftsmanship with which she organizes her experiences as poems: "As for the ego—I wonder if it really exists?... One is simply a location where certain things occur, leaving trails & debris... something in one that organizes the random bits though" (Sullivan, 220).

Furthermore, there are some other continuous traits which endear Atwood the poet to her readers: her nimble intelligence and her comic sense, her precision and scientific curiosity, her inexhaustible productivity, and her insistence on shaping rather than shouting. If her literary personae hardly ever appear in a tragic predicament, they are often plagued by doubt and revulsion, but fortunately many convey a wry sense of humor. The fascinating experience for Atwood's readers is to share with her the wide range of her artistic moods and modes of expression, as the overview of the following volumes of poetry will show: *The Circle Game* (1966), *The Animals in That Country* (1968), *The Journals of Susanna Moodie* (1970), *Procedures for Underground* (1970), *Power Politics* (1971), *You Are Happy* (1974), *Two-Headed Poems* (1978), *True Stories* (1981), *Interlunar* (1984), *Morning in the Burned House* (1995).

In a retrospective of Atwood's poetry, the title poems of her various volumes obviously constitute nodes which can serve as points of departure and foci for the proposed rereadings. Atwood's debut as a fully fledged poet, *The Circle Game*, for which she received the Governor General's Award for 1966, was as convincing as her first novel, *The Edible Woman*, dating from 1965 and published in 1969. Both the volume of poetry and the novel fuse the narcissism of an antagonistic love affair with wider thematic concerns, such as the doubtful realities of the contemporary consumer and media culture, and both these apprentice works display the same amazing assurance of tone and performance. In fact, the basic poetic techniques that Atwood adopts in her first book of poetry undergo no substantial changes, notwithstanding many subtle modifications, from her first through her most recent volume. There are no fixed stanza forms, no rhyme, no regular meter, but a sure and continuous voice informs the poem through its remotest ramifications, and through the varying lengths of stanzas and lines. This medium proves flexible enough to accommodate widely varying topics, presenting, to somebody with the artistic ingenuity and shaping power of Atwood, every opportunity for formal precision....

Source: Lothar Hönnighausen, "Margaret Atwood's Poetry 1966–1995," in *Margaret Atwood: Works and Impact*, edited by Reingard M. Nischik, Camden House, 2000, pp. 97–99.

Molly Bendall

In the following review, Bendall reminds readers that Atwood is not only a "prolific novelist" but a "powerful poetic voice."

Let's not mistake Margaret Atwood's bare statements, bald-faced retorts, and declarative moments for banal plainspokenness. Atwood has made these, along with her clipped rhythms and bluntly sarcastic comeback lines, her own distinctive vehicles. She recognizes the complexity of a voice and constructs it with carefully modulated tones. Sure, one is reminded of Bette Davis or Katherine Hepburn when the speaker in "Manet's Olympia" says, "She reclines, more or less. / Try that posture, it's hardly languor." Or when Helen of Troy says, "There sure are a lot of dangerous birds around." However, it's more than a movie. Her process of remedying crises with light-hearted (sometimes) cynicism and of alchemizing sacredness into gossip is born of the fables and magic that she loves.

Atwood often dips into the rhetoric, and even the vocabulary, of folktales (using tools like anaphora); she gives her language the feel of a charm or vengeful spell, "You make a cut in yourself, / a little opening/for the pain to get in. / You set loose three drops of your blood." A reader might recognize occasional similarities with Sylvia Plath and the fact that Atwood has had an influence on many poets writing now (Louise Gluck, for instance). Atwood's savage, back-talking dramatic monologues have become her trademark. In this book stand-outs include "Ava Gardner Reincarnated as a Magnolia," "Helen of Troy does Counter Dancing," and the tour de force "Half-Hanged Mary," a voice from the bleak theatre (Salem chapter) of our history. Her range is darkened and deepened with a series of elegiac poems about her dying father, and she, the speaker, the daughter, faces the inevitable fall into the future from which her wit and magic can't save her. We know Atwood is a prolific novelist. Remember also her powerful poetic voice.

Source: Molly Bendall, Review of *Morning in the Burned House*, in *Antioch Review*, Vol. 54, No. 2, Spring 1996, p. 248.

Ray Olson

In the following review, Olson praises the collection and considers Atwood "adroit, imagistically rich," and "immediately accessible."

The blood of a sexually liberated generation ran cold at Atwood's lancing epigraph to *Power Politics* (1971): "You fit into me / like a hook into an eye//a fish-hook/an open eye." No poet better expressed the could-be-lethal frisson of deep love-lust, the tart, equivocal successes and failures of late-twentieth-century romance. In the first section in her new collection, she returns to the love dance, middle-aged and more experienced if not wiser, and gives us poems as right-sounding, memorable, and pithy as her best a quarter-century ago. In later sections, she turns to goddess myths, history, archaeology, family stories, and dreams—all subjects she has taken up before—and if she is not consistently persuasive, she is always vital,

powerful, magnetically readable. Political, too, although never propagandistic. Rather, she is a contemporary, female Whittier or Kipling—technically adroit, imagistically rich, immediately accessible. She is a popular poet of the very first [order]. Readers who know only her novels really owe it to themselves to read her poems.

Source: Ray Olson, Review of *Morning in the Burned House*, in *Booklist*, Vol. 92, No. 1, September 1, 1995, p. 32.

Publishers Weekly

In the following review, a contributor lauds Atwood's "swift, powerful energy" and her free-verse style, which makes these poems "intimate and immediate."

In her first poetry collection since 1987's *Selected Poems II*, Atwood brings a swift, powerful energy to meditative poems that often begin in domestic settings and then broaden into numinous dialogues. In "In the Secular Night," the speaker, who has wandered through her house talking to herself of the "sensed absences of God," realizes "Several hundred years ago / this could have been mysticism / or heresy. It isn't now." In five roughly thematic sections, Atwood often displays incisive humor ("Ava Gardner Reincarnated as a Magnolia"). The most vivid poems forge an apprehensible human aspect from scholarly fields of science, history and religion: in "Half-hanged Mary" a woman who was being hanged for witchery survives and tolls each hour until she is cut down. The final grouping seems compiled from the charred remains of a deeply examined life, where only "the power of what is not there" may transcend. Atwood's lean, free-verse style renders these apocryphal poems intimate and immediate.

Source: Review of *Morning in the Burned House*, in *Publishers Weekly*, Vol. 242, No. 35, August 28, 1995, pp. 107–108.

John Wilson Foster

In the following excerpt, Foster discusses how being Canadian has influenced Atwood's poetry.

Margaret Atwood's current popularity stems in part from the fact that her poetry explores certain fashionable minority psychologies. With its cultivation of barely controlled hysteria, for instance, her verse is that of a psychic individual at sea in a materialist society. This hysteria, however, assumes specifically feminine forms and lends Atwood's work certain affinities (of which current popularity is the least important) with that of Virginia Woolf and Sylvia Plath. For like these two predecessors, Atwood confronts her own sexuality and the contemporary roles laid down by men for her to play. A minority psychology similar to that which informs her identity as a woman informs her national identity, for Atwood is a contemporary Canadian aware of belonging to a minority culture on the North American continent and in reaction recollecting and re-enacting her pioneer ancestors' encounter with the wilderness and with the native people. Appropriately, the Canadian ancestral experience—repository of the spiritual identity of a people—happens to be best commemorated in the journals and memoirs of some remarkable women, including Catharine Parr Traill, Susanna Moodie and Anna Jameson.

Charges of opportunism could easily be levelled against a poet so deeply involved with the minority psyche. But they are answerable by our exhibiting, as I hope to do here, the essential coherence of Atwood's poetic themes. Her poetry succeeds not by masterly technique or style but by a peculiar force of content, by exciting transformations of experience that appear only to the superficial reader as mere opportunities. Among the experiences of being an individual, a woman and a Canadian, Atwood intuits an underlying connection deeper than minority membership. These experiences flesh out in multiple guise the root formula of her poetry. Like a mathematical expression, that formula sustains a wealth of individual existences—of image, motif, subject and dramatic situation. Stated briefly, Atwood's poetry in the six volumes to date concerns itself with the self's inhabitation of spaces and forms and the metamorphoses entailed therein. All that is thematically important derives from this: invasion, displacement, evolution and reversion, as well as those notions significant enough to warrant book titles—survival, ingestion (cf. *The Edible Woman*, a novel), and surfacing. The message of Atwood's poetry is that extinction and obsolescene are illusory, that life is a constant process of re-formation. The self is eternally divided in its attitude to the forms and spaces it inhabits, simultaneously needing, fearing, desiring and despising them.

. . . It is clear that Atwood has been profoundly influenced by Indian mythology, especially from British Columbia where she lived for a time. Many of the poems in *You Are Happy*, and certain poems elsewhere (for example, "The Totems"), resemble Indian tales of origination.

Moreover, Atwood's animal imagery is not naturalistic but heraldic and emblematic, and this heraldic stylism she shares with totem-carvers. Consider, for instance, the animals in "Buffalo in Compound: Alberta" which walk in profile "one by one, their / firelit outlines fixed as carvings" and enter "the shade of the gold-edged trees." Even more telling are the metamorphoses which operate within Atwood's sexual and pioneer contexts but which are also the transformations that inspire totemism and involve, as they do in Atwood, men, animals and the landscape. "A carver," wrote Viola E. Garfield, "may include a figure representing the dwelling place of a story character, a camp site or place of refuge, or any phenomenon he desires. He always depicts it as animate. Features of the landscape are usually illustrated as land animals, while those of the sea are given the anatomical characteristics of ocean dwelling creatures. Sometimes they are carved with human, rather than animal, attributes." The relationship between man and animal is paramount. "In the beginning people and animals were not distinct and separate, but animals were people, and many retain the ability to think and act as people in the present world . . . Down through the generations men have been known who assumed animal form. . . . " Anthropomorphism and zoomorphism animate *The Journals of Susanna Moodie* and indeed much of Atwood's poetry, and are aspects of the primordial unity to which her characters and personae revert. The section of poems in *You Are Happy* entitled "Songs of the Transformed" seems especially indebted to Indian cosmology, concerning as they do human spirits in animal shapes. It is no coincidence that "Owl Song," in which the owl is the heart of a murdered woman, bears a resemblance to the Tlingit and Haida tale of the unkind woman turned to an owl and depicted on totem poles (Garfield, pp. 26–27). We could even argue that the stylistic metamorphoses with which we are familiar in poetry—metaphor, simile and personification—are in Atwood's poetry derived as much from a totemic awareness as from poetic convention. . . .

Source: John Wilson Foster, "The Poetry of Margaret Atwood," in *Critical Essays on Margaret Atwood*, edited by Judith McCombs, G. K. Hall, 1988, pp. 153–54, 163–64.

Anne G. Jones

In the following excerpt, Jones examines how Atwood's poetry treats the issue of identity.

. . . One cannot separate Atwood's fascination with form, its sources, its extreme limits, from her exploration of identity. After all, it is form that permits identity: in "the lucidities of day/ . . . you are something I can/ trace a line around, with eyes/ cut shapes from air, the element/where we/must calculate according to/ solidities." Then growth or decay of an entity means a change in form, a transformation. And Atwood returns throughout her work to that theme. In a series of poems called "Songs of the Transformed," for instance, Atwood puts human voices into the bodies of animals. (The rat says, "All I want is love, you stupid humanist.") In "Eventual Proteus," Atwood describes the process of transformation:

. . . Form permits identity, then, but necessitates separation; lack of form, preventing clear identity, yet permits intimacy; the narrator holds Proteus, but only until he takes the form of man.

Transformations, shifts in identity, take place in nature without human control. But other transformations occur because people exert power and choice. The artist, the shaper, is the primary human transformer.

. . . If consciousness and nature are radically different, or if identity requires formal separateness, then one person is alienated from another, subject from object, even left hand from right. Margaret Atwood started publishing her work with a book of poems called *Double Persephone*; her latest (1978) volume of poems is called *Two-Headed Poems*. Much as her work finds these splits (even wars) in reality, Atwood suggested repeatedly that a profound similitude (even an identity) persists between human mind and nature, and can be revealed or created with the right tools. The pioneer, for instance, can let his straight lines be bent by nature, and not lose his mind. Nature and consciousness are joined ultimately and awesomely for Atwood in the mystical experience: in "Giving Birth," for instance, Jeannie actually sees the equivalence of mass and energy, and in *Surfacing* and *Susanna Moodie*, the protagonists become the spirit of place. Nature and consciousness, though, are also joined, in terror, by the insane.

And they are joined, with language, by the writer. The fact that metaphor exists at all suggests a continuity between mind and its objects. Morrison in "Polarities" says that "the only difference" between mad Louise and the other students is that "she's taken as real what the rest of us pretend is only metaphorical." Since the writer makes connections by making metaphor, it's no surprise that language should itself become a metaphor. In a love poem from *Power Politics*

> all of me
> breathes you in . . .
> the adjectives
> fall away from me, no
> threads left holding
> me, I flake apart
> layer by
> layer down
> quietly to the bone, my skull
> unfolds to an astounded flower
>
> regrowing the body, learning
> speech again takes
> days and longer
> each time / too much of
> this is fatal

Elsewhere, Atwood finds that nature and language were once more nearly one: the "earliest language/ was not our syntax of chained pebbles/ but liquid, made/ by the first tribes, the fish/ people."

The writer can do more than make single metaphors; she can make stories, for "a language is not words only,/ it is the stories/ that are told in it,/ the stories that are never told." And, ranging still further and deeper, she can create the extended metaphor of myth. Making "A Red Shirt" for her daughter, the poet remembers old myths, summed up in the warning that young girls should "keep silent and avoid/ red shoes, red stockings, dancing." "It may not be true," she concludes, still sewing, "that one myth cancels another./Nevertheless, in a corner/ of the hem, where it will not be seen,/ where you will inherit/ it, I make this tiny/ stitch, my private magic."

To use language, then, is to wield power, power to preserve, to create, to change, to understand. And power to lie. For "worn language clots our throats, making it difficult to say/ what we mean, making it/ difficult to see." Hence Atwood keeps weeding her word garden, pushing back "the coarse ones spreading themselves everywhere/ like thighs or starlings" and pulling off "inaccurate" versions of her lover: "the hinged bronze man, the fragile man/ built of glass pebbles,/ the ranged man with his opulent capes and boots/ peeling away from you in scales."

Finally, words have the power to heal or to harm. Because language has such power, it becomes, for Margaret Atwood, a question for ethics. In fact, her considerations of ethics have a great deal to do with power in general: the power of America, of men, of predators; the powerlessness of victims and prey. In *Survival: A Thematic Guide to Canadian Literature*, Atwood outlines four "victim" positions. In the first, the victim denies he or she is a victim. In the second, she admits that she is, but blames it on some "large powerful idea," like fate or biology. Position Three moves toward freedom: the victim no longer believes that victimhood is inevitable. And Position Four, that of "creative non-victim," moves beyond victimhood—but, presumably, not into the mirror role of victor. Atwood suggests there may be a fifth position, for mystics, yet she doesn't expect to find much literature written from that position.

Essential to the transformation of an individual from one position to the next is awareness of reality; positions one and two are notable for their denial or distortion of what is. And "a writer's job is to tell his society not how it ought to live, but how it does live," Atwood says baldly. "He is us." . . .

Source: Anne G. Jones, "Margaret Atwood: Songs of the Transformer, Songs of the Transformed," in *Hollins Critic*, Vol. 16, No. 3, June 1979, p. 1.

SOURCES

Abrams, M. H., *A Glossary of Literary Terms*, 4th ed., Holt, Rinehart and Winston, 1981, p. 45.

Atwood, Margaret, "Half-hanged Mary," in *Morning in the Burned House*, Houghton Mifflin, 1995, p. 58–69.

Bendall, Molly, Review of *Morning in the Burned House*, in *Antioch Review*, Vol. 54, No. 2, Spring 1996, p. 248.

Demos, John Putnam, *Entertaining Satan: Witchcraft and the Culture of Early New England*, Oxford University Press, 2004, pp. 3–15, 63, 81–82.

Evans, Ruth, "Eyewitness: Suspected Witches Murdered in Tanzania," BBC website, July 5, 1999, http://news.bbc.co.uk/2/hi/africa/386550.stm (accessed February 22, 2013).

Goldman, Russell, "Real Witches Practice Samhain: Wicca on the Rise in U.S.," ABC News website, October 30, 2009, http://abcnews.go.com/WN/real-witches-practice-samhain-wicca-rise-us/story?id=8957950 (accessed February 22, 2013).

Hall, David D., ed. *Witch-Hunting in Seventeenth-Century New England: A Documentary History, 1638–1692*, Northeastern University Press, 1991, pp. 7, 261.

Judd, Sylvester, *History of Hadley, Including the Early History of Hatfield, South Hadley, Amherst, and Granby, Massachusetts*, Metcalf, 1863, p. 239.

Linder, Douglas O., "The Witchcraft Trials in Salem: A Commentary," Salem Witchcraft Trials 1692 website, September 9, 2009, http://law2.umkc.edu/faculty/projects/ftrials/salem/SAL_ACCT.HTM (accessed February 22, 2013).

"Margaret Atwood: Biography," Margaret Atwood website, http://margaretatwood.ca/bio.php (accessed March 5, 2013).

"The Official King James Bible Online," King James Bible Online website, http://www.kingjamesbibleonline.org/Exodus-22-18/ (accessed March 5, 2013).

Olson, Ray, Review of *Morning in the Burned House*, in *Booklist*, Vol. 92, No. 1, September 1, 1995, p. 32.

Review of *Morning in the Burning [sic] House*, in *Publishers Weekly*, Vol. 242, No. 35, August 28, 1995, p. 107.

"The Salem Witch Museum – Past and Present," Salem, MA: Salem Witch Museum website, August 2010, http://www.salemwitchmuseum.com/media/SalemWitchMuseum_background.pdf (accessed February 22, 2013).

"The Salem Witch Museum – Timeline," Salem Witch Museum website, August 2010, http://www.salemwitchmuseum.com/media/timeline.pdf (accessed February 22, 2013).

Shumaker, Wayne, *The Occult Sciences in the Renaissance: A Study in Intellectual Passions*, University of California Press, 1972, p. 61.

"Spectral Evidence," Salem Witch Museum website, February 13, 2013, http://www.salemwitchmuseum.com/blog/ (accessed February 23, 2013).

Tatlow, Didi Kirsten, "Women Killed as 'Witches,' in Papua New Guinea, in 2013," in *International Herald Tribune*, February 19, 2013, http://rendezvous.blogs.nytimes.com/2013/02/19/women-tortured-killed-as-witches-in-papua-new-guinea-in-2013/ (accessed February 19, 2013).

"2013 Salem Award Winners Announced," Salem Awards Foundation website, 2013, http://www.salemaward.org/ (accessed February 22, 2013).

Van Spanckeren, Kathryn, "Humanizing the Fox: Atwood's Poetic Tricksters and *Morning in the Burned House*," in *Margaret Atwood's Textual Assassinations: Recent Poetry and Fiction*, edited by Sharon Rose Wilson, Ohio State University, 2003, pp. 107–108.

Vine, Jeremy, "Congo Witch-Hunt's Child Victims," BBC website, December 22, 1999, http://news.bbc.co.uk/2/hi/africa/575178.stm (accessed February 19, 2013).

FURTHER READING

Cooke, Nathalie, *Margaret Atwood: A Biography*, ECW Press, 1998.

> This is the first biography of Atwood. Cooke explores the ups and downs of Atwood's private life and her emergence as a major figure in Canadian literature and culture.

Howells, Coral Ann, *Margaret Atwood*, 2nd ed., Palgrave Macmillan, 2005.

>   This introduction to Atwood covers her work from the 1970s up through the novel *Oryx and Crake*, published in 2003. Howell explores all of Atwood's typical concerns, including Canadian identity and feminist issues.

Howells, Coral Ann, ed., *The Cambridge Companion to Margaret Atwood*, Cambridge University Press, 2006.

>   This is an examination of Atwood's work in all genres. The introduction traces trends in Atwood criticism since the 1970s, and the twelve essays by Atwood scholars analyze her work from a variety of critical standpoints.

Stein, Karen F., *Margaret Atwood Revisited*, Twayne Publishers, 1999.

>   This is an introduction to Atwood's major literary works that discusses theme and character, as well as her storytelling style and frequent use of paradoxes.

SUGGESTED SEARCH TERMS

Margaret Atwood

Half-hanged Mary

Mary Webster AND witch

witches

witchcraft

witchcraft AND New England

Salem witch trials

dramatic monologue

Wicca

In the Orchard

HENRIK IBSEN

1862

"In the Orchard" is a four-stanza poem by Henrik Ibsen in which the speaker extols living in the present and appreciating nature for its own sake. The strong and consistent rhyme and meter combine with active imagery to lushly convey the sense of being in a breezy apple orchard. Ibsen is a legendary playwright from Norway, with his most famous plays from his mid- to late career written in prose, as are *A Doll's House* (1879) and *An Enemy of the People* (1882), the latter of which was adapted in America by the famed dramatist Arthur Miller. But Ibsen wrote verse plays early in his career; he also published several collections of poems, and he considered himself foremost a poet.

"In the Orchard" came to the attention of the English-speaking public not through any collection of Ibsen's but through a translation of the stanzas that open his 1862 verse play *Kjærlighedens Komedie*, published in English in 1900 as *Love's Comedy*. The main character, Falk, an existential poet, delivers these thirty-two lines in heeding a request by the ladies at a garden party, piquing the staid bourgeois company in which he finds himself. The poem provokes much discussion and subtly introduces the major thematic realm of the play, the roles and realities of love and marriage. Edmund W. Gosse translated Falk's opening poem for a critical essay in the *Fortnightly Review* in 1873, and this version was included in the anthology *English Verse: Translations* in 1883, titled "In the Orchard." The poem has also been included as such in *An Anthology of World Poetry* (1936), edited by Mark Van Doren, and *A*

Henrik Ibsen *(© Nicku | Shutterstock.com)*

Junior Anthology of World Poetry (1929; also published as *The World's Best Poems*), edited by Van Doren and Garibaldi M. Lapolla. A different version, titled "The Poet's Song," can be found in *Lyrics and Poems from Ibsen* (1912), translated by Edmund Garret. The passage can also be approached directly in the context of the play (in which a chorus of gentlemen repeat the last two lines of each stanza as the poem is recited by Falk). In light of the creative effort needed to adapt the poem's Norwegian rhyme and meter to English, every translator's version is decidedly unique.

AUTHOR BIOGRAPHY

Henrik Johan Ibsen was born on March 20, 1828, in Skien, a market town in southeastern Norway near the sea. His father, Knud, was a merchant who had married the wealthy young Marichen Altenburg three years earlier. The father's business fortunes were rising, but before long, they collapsed; years of carefree enjoyment of upper society gave way by the mid-1830s to a small country house and private humiliation. The shy and introverted Henrik, who sometimes put on puppet shows for his family, was the oldest of five surviving children. At the age of fifteen, he was sent to become an apothecary's assistant in the town of Grimstad, where he stayed for six years.

Eventually running the shop, he studied meanwhile, hoping to attend university, and also wrote poetry and his first play, *Catilina* (1848–1849). He also fathered an illegitimate son with a maid in 1846, an experience conjectured to have fostered in him a fear of the consequences of carnal desire. Leaving for the capital, then called Christiania (but before and now called Oslo), in 1850, Ibsen visited his parents—whom he somewhat resented for their absorption in debt and bitterness—for what would be the final time.

Ibsen hoped to attend the university at Christiania, but he failed the entrance exams in Greek and mathematics. However, within months of his arrival in April 1850, the Christiania Theatre began mounting a production of his second play, *The Warrior's Barrow* (also translated as *The Burial Mound*), the national romanticism of which was well received. In 1851, having impressed virtuoso violinist Ole Bull with his verse and disposition, Ibsen was hired to run a new theater in the smaller city of Bergen. Writing as well as producing plays with limited resources, Ibsen toiled to little effect in terms of critical or popular reception. His prospects improved when, in 1857, he moved back to Christiania to become artistic director at the Christiania Norwegian Theatre, and in 1858, he married Suzannah Thoresen, who bore a son, Sigurd, in 1859. But his new position actually stifled his theatrical visions, and by the time the theater closed in 1862, he was dispirited and impoverished. For most of the rest of his life, he would stay away from the production side of stage drama. Leaving with his family for Rome in 1864, then Dresden in 1868, Ibsen would not return to live in Norway for twenty-seven years.

Love's Comedy, which includes the lines of "In the Orchard," was printed at the end of 1862, but critics balked at the content—in essence, a declaration that traditional marriage ruins love—and it would not be staged until 1873. Meanwhile, however, Ibsen solidified renown across Scandinavia through morally intriguing verse plays such as *Peer Gynt* (1867), about a dreamy man whose life is riddled with self-deception. His first of many awards was a medal bestowed by the king of Sweden and Norway, Charles XV. From this point onward, Ibsen favored prose over verse in his dramas, though he published a major verse collection, *Poems*, in 1871. Broader international recognition and fame came with his veritably feminist play *A Doll's House* (1879), about a woman in an oppressive marriage. Ibsen moved back to Rome in 1880, then back to Germany, to live in Munich, in 1885, and finally returned to Norway in 1891, publishing plays consistently all the while. After suffering a stroke that deprived him of the ability to write in 1900, followed by another in 1901, he died in Christiania on May 23, 1906.

POEM TEXT

In the sunny orchard closes,
While the warblers sing and swing,
Care not whether blustering Autumn
Break the promises of Spring!
Rose and white, the apple blossom   5
Hides you from the sultry sky,—
Let it flutter, blown and scatter'd,
On the meadows by-and-by!

Will you ask about the fruitage
In the season of the flowers?   10
Will you murmur, will you question,
Count the run of weary hours?
Will you let the scarecrow clapping
Drown all happy sounds and words?
Brothers! there is better music   15
In the singing of the birds.

From your heavy-laden garden
Will you hunt the mellow thrush?
He will pay you for protection
With his crown-song's liquid rush.   20
O but you will win the bargain,
Though your fruit be spare and late,
For remember Time is flying
And will shut your garden gate.

With my living, with my singing,   25
I will tear the hedges down.
Sweep the grass and heap the blossom!
Let it shrivel, pale and brown!
Swing the wicket! Sheep and cattle,
Let them graze among the best!   30
I broke off the flowers; what matter
Who may revel with the rest?

POEM SUMMARY

The text used for this summary, translated by Edmund W. Gosse, is from *English Verse: Translations*, edited by W. J. Linton and R. H. Stoddard, Charles Scribner's Sons, 1883, pp. 193–94. Versions of the poem can be found on the following web pages: http://www.gutenberg.org/ebooks/18657 (in *Love's Comedy*) and http:// www2.hn.psu.edu/faculty/jmanis/h-ibsen/loves-comedy.pdf (in *Love's Comedy*).

Stanza 1

The first stanza of "In the Orchard" sets the scene of a sunlit apple orchard, specifically the *closes*, which may refer both to the orchard's branching lanes, open at one end and closed at the other, and to the natural enclosures formed by the canopy of branches overhanging these lanes. Birds are singing and perhaps swooping from branch to branch in a way that looks like swinging. Line 3 implicitly addresses the listener or reader (the unspoken *you*), imploring that one not be concerned with whether spring's promises are broken by the fall, which *blusters* in terms of both increasing winds and a blunt assertiveness reflecting the personification of the seasons here.

Depicted by its colors is an apple blossom, which (representing all the blossoms) shelters the poem's addressee from an especially hot sky. With the addressee framed as such, the poem can be understood to either literally address a person within the orchard in question or figuratively deposit the reader within it. The poet invites the apple blossom(s) to be swept away by the wind and scattered over the meadows. This exhortation carries the sense of urging the listener/reader to be unconcerned with the blossoms' scattering.

Stanza 2

The questions of the second stanza establish a dichotomy between the expectation that the addressee will be concerned only with the size of the crop and the poet's suggestion that the addressee might instead derive aesthetic pleasure from the orchard. The question of lines 9–10 is relatively neutral, not quite judging the notion of thinking about the autumn's fruit amid the blossoms of the spring. The question of lines 11–12 begins to suggest that going about mumbling (say, about profits), worrying, and calculating the passage of time is perhaps not the best way to spend one's days. Furthermore, if the addressee employs a scarecrow in the orchard—which might clap as straw arms are buffeted by the wind, or perhaps sound-making devices are attached—the noise of the scarecrow will stifle the pleasant noises and words. Line 15 reveals a specific addressee, or rather group of addressees, who are in some sense the poets' brothers— perhaps actual relations, friends, peers, or simply fellow countrymen. This line specifically invokes the idea of music, which can refer back both to the scarecrow's sounds and to the daily rhythms suggested in lines 11–12. The singing of the birds is declared a superior sort of music.

Stanza 3

The poet now asks whether the addressee(s) will, in an orchard with an abundance of fruit, try to catch or kill the easygoing thrush, a bird with a highly regarded singing ability. Revising the notion of profiting from the orchard, the poet suggests in lines 19–20 that the bird will compensate the addressee for preserving its life with a musically smooth song, rendered by the wording equivalent to a crown (that is, five British shillings). The poet suggests that the addressee will be getting the better deal in such an exchange, even if the orchard gives less fruit, ripening late. This is because time is passing quickly, and inevitably the orchard—like the period of the addressee's life—will come to a close.

Stanza 4

The poet introduces himself into the poem only in the fourth stanza, with line 25 featuring the first use of first-person pronouns. The poet will, like the birds, live and sing, and his life and song will bring about the destruction of the hedges. As with earlier phrasings, this can be understood both literally and figuratively, as the poet's living actions may entail destroying the hedges, while his song, in traveling through and beyond the hedges, renders them irrelevant and metaphorically torn down.

The poet again addresses the poem's audience beginning in line 27, but throughout this stanza no *you* is mentioned, rendering the commands somewhat more universal—as if they are meant not just for any specific listeners or reader but for all people. The poet declares that the (cut) grass and (fallen) blossoms should be swept up, or swept away—as if by the wind—and left to dry up and decay in the sunshine. The *wicket* of line 29 is the gate, which should be left swinging open, so that sheep and cattle can come into the orchard (where they otherwise ought not be) and enjoy the choice greenery and fallen or even still-hanging fruits. The poet himself has plucked the blossoms—that is, some of the blossoms—from the trees, and he expresses total indifference toward whoever may happen to reap their own delight from what remains.

TOPICS FOR FURTHER STUDY

- Write a poem of twenty lines or more, on any topic, in which the favored metrical foot is the trochee, a stressed syllable followed by an unstressed syllable; this is the inverse of the often-favored iamb (found in most of Shakespeare). Give the poem a rhyme scheme of some sort, and if appropriate, employ such strategies for attaining the meter as demonstrated in Ibsen's "In the Orchard," including commands and questions.

- Create an illustration for each of the four stanzas of "In the Orchard," using a simple medium such as pencil, charcoal, watercolors, or pastels. Alternatively, use drawing or picture-editing software. The scene throughout is an orchard, so your illustrations should be at least subtly differentiated based on the precise content of each stanza.

- Read Robert Frost's poem "After Apple-Picking," which can be found in *Poetry for Young People: Robert Frost* (1994), edited by Gary D. Schmidt and illustrated by Henri Sorensen, or online at http://www.poetryfoundation.org/poem/173523. The poem presents a very different perspective on an orchard from the one provided in Ibsen's "In the Orchard." Write an essay comparing and especially contrasting the two poems, addressing for each the poet's occupation and personality, the current stage of his life, his understanding of the importance of the orchard, the role the orchard plays in the progress of the poem, and so forth.

- Using the Internet, research the practice of maintaining an orchard, including such aspects as how and where orchards can be started, how the trees and fruit are protected from blight, how methods differ in organic orchards, and what can be done to keep the birds away. Write a paper relating your findings.

THEMES

Nature

That Ibsen's poem revolves around nature is signaled by the title—which foregrounds not just an orchard but the state of being within an orchard—and by the opening lines, which present imagery of sunshine, birds, and the seasons. Indeed, the poem features constant references to aspects of nature, including the landscape, weather, and wildlife. Two aspects in particular are appreciated by the poet: the singing of the birds and the beauty of the apple blossoms. Notably, neither of these has any functional value beyond any lifting of mood they might provide; they are both strictly aesthetic concerns. In this respect, the poem is distinctly anticapitalist, valuing the experiences of natural sounds and sights within the orchard above any monetary value the orchard might have. This is somewhat ironic, since an orchard is specifically understood, like any farm, as a place where nature has been harnessed and structured to provide the best possible yield from the soil and vegetation. That is, for an orchard even to exist, presumably someone had to deliberately plant rows of trees that yield edible fruit, in this case apple trees, and it would seem unlikely that an orchard's owner would be inclined to let birds nest and forage there as they please. Thus, beyond suggesting an ordinary pastoral appreciation for nature, the poem has something of an anarchist feel to it, with a "tear down the walls" angle—or rather, a "tear down the hedges" one, as directly stated in line 26. The poet seemingly wants nature not just to be appreciated for what it is but to overrun human control and influence, to break free from the confines in which humans hold it hostage for the sake of its profit-turning products.

Music

The poet especially heralds the beautiful music provided by the birds who alight in the orchard. Through the first stanza, the tone of the poem is ambiguous. Precisely what is meant by spring's promises is not quite clear, nor is the import of letting the blossoms be scattered by the winds. But without blossoms there will not be fruit, so the owner must indeed value the blossoms. That is, the owner's possessive attitude toward the fruit would extend to the blossoms themselves; thus, for a person to "let go" of one's compulsion to value the fruit, one might also have to let the blossoms go, let them be ravaged by the birds and swept away by the winds. The three questions of stanza 2 are what make clear the poet's intent to advise his listeners away from any possessive attitude toward the orchard. His answer to all three of these questions is contained in the second stanza's final lines, which, being centrally placed within the poem, also amount to the motto or central theme: to appreciate the music of the birds and, more broadly, the music of life.

To appreciate music at all is to devote one's attention to something that cannot necessarily be assigned any functional value. In the modern day, of course, people do assign a functional value to music, as signified by the amounts they spend on portable listening devices, which can effectively reduce the tension of, say, a walk down a dozen automobile-choked city blocks or a long afternoon in an airport. But this poem was written in 1862, at a time when industry was altering the urban experience but had not yet despoiled rural environs as well. So on the one hand, non-urban nineteenth-century peoples perhaps needed music less, having far less civilization-inflicted tension to flush out of their systems through soothing or energizing patterns of vibrations. On the other hand, with music being far less accessible—musicians and their instruments being needed to produce it—such peoples surely appreciated music more. For any time period, the poet of "In the Orchard" demonstrates an uncommon affinity for music, at least natural music, considering birdsong so valuable that one should let birds do as they please, even consume the very fruits of one's labor, simply in order that one may hear it.

Time

The passage of time is accorded great thematic weight in this poem, as alluded to both directly and indirectly. By lines 3–4, the poet is setting up a sharp distinction between appreciation for the present and concern over the future, with the present aptly figured in the lush vibrancy of springtime, while the future is rendered bleak in its association with autumn. Although autumn is often positively associated with the bright colors of changing foliage, it is nonetheless the season marked by the annual death of the majority of visible flora, with leaves and grasses turning withered and brown; the life remains in roots and the skeletons of trees, but in terms of imagery, the dissonance with the living beauty of spring is unmistakable. The passage of time is alluded to again in the opening lines of stanza 2, which question the wisdom of ignoring the present to attend to the future. The person focused on the future is depicted as mumbling, uncertain, and burdened by the need to count the passing hours, which are rendered weary by the very act of endlessly counting them. Such a person does not seem to be happy. The end of stanza 3 brings to a head the thematic role assigned to time, as the poet indicates what a focus on the future ultimately leads to: death. Line 24 states only that the garden's gate will be closed by time, but implicit in this image—which must be understood symbolically, given the inherent insignificance of the simple closing of the gate—is the closure or termination not only of the orchard but of the person's life as well.

Life

What the poet of "In the Orchard" ultimately wishes to convey is a fierce appreciation for life and living. In lines 25–26, the poet even affirms that his living, in and of itself, will be what brings down the hedges, what will destroy the barriers between the orderly orchard and the chaos of the world beyond. Such an existential affirmation looks beyond the individual's specific acts to vest power in one's mode of being in the world. In a more ordinary locution, the poet might have declared that he would tear down the hedges with his hands, or a scythe, or even his passion—but here, this poet will tear them down merely with his living, as well as with singing, which cannot literally do what is claimed. An almost supernatural sense of power is thus attributed to the poet's mode of living and the power of his voice.

The remainder of stanza 4 is a triumphant paean to a life lived in the present. The poet's excitement about the shriveling grass can be understood as a command to move beyond the past; what is dead is dead, and rather than sinking into dismay over what is lost, one must enjoy what one has and what remains. Ideally, not just the human with authority over this orchard but the animals who wander the countryside—cattle and sheep—should be allowed freedom of passage; everyone should be able to enjoy what currently exists while it is still possible. The poet, for one, is emotionally sustained by natural beauty, as embodied in the flowers he is proud to have plucked—they would have died on the branch in time anyway, he might have said—and if one seizes life and lives fully in the present, one can have no regrets about who else seizes what they can and lives life to the fullest.

Ibsen portrays the personification of time, closing the orchard gate. (© *Chrislofotos | Shutterstock.com*)

STYLE

Meter and Rhyme

Translators of these four octets of Ibsen's verse have typically strived to retain the feel of the original by preserving the rhyme and meter. In the original Norwegian, the rhyme runs *abab* through each quatrain (group of four lines), and translators including C. H. Herford and Jens Arup have duly rendered that rhyme pattern in English. Edmund W. Gosse chose not to, regularly rhyming only the even-numbered lines, or the *b* lines of each quatrain as schemed above—his quatrains would be notated as *abcb* and so forth. There is occasional rhyme to be found in the odd-numbered lines, including lines 3 and 5; lines 17, 19, and 21; and, loosely, lines 29 and 31. Furthermore, similar sounds can be found at the ends of odd-numbered lines throughout the poem: lines 29 and 31 echo line 7; line 27 echoes lines 3 and 5; and several odd lines end in *-ing*. Overall, Gosse's reduced focus on rhyme would have allowed him more freedom to use the English words that most faithfully reproduce the meanings in Norwegian; yet, aptly, he retains a high degree of musicality even where regular rhyme is absent.

The meter of Gosse's translation, matching that of the original, is highly regular. The odd-numbered lines are in trochaic tetrameter—consisting of four trochees, each a stressed syllable followed by an unstressed one, for eight syllables altogether—while the even-numbered lines are one beat shorter, or seven syllables altogether. The trochee lends itself well to questions, commands, and first-person declarations, all of which are likely to start with a stressed syllable. In all, some fourteen lines in "In the Orchard" start with auxiliary or action verbs, lending a sense of activity to a poem that otherwise remains rooted in the orchard.

Poetic Address

Ibsen's poem is one in which the poet is speaking to a number of second-person listeners or readers, as made clear in the address to brothers of some kind in line 15. The reader might posit different occasions or circumstances suggesting who these listeners could be, but of course, the true circumstance is that established by Ibsen in his play *Love's Comedy*. There the four stanzas of "In the Orchard" (not titled as such) appear as an opening offering of verse by the central character, Falk, who is a poet. During his reading, several gentlemen repeat the last two lines of each octet as a chorus, while several ladies sit nearby. The setting is the grounds of a rural-esque villa outside Norway's capital city, described in the stage directions as an attractive garden with an irregular but tasteful layout. Visible in the background are a fjord and islands; the early summer sun is brightening the afternoon, while blossoms adorn the fruit trees.

As an address, the poem can only be considered a provocative one. The ladies and gentlemen in Falk's company skew to the conventional side of life, and before long, a few of them object to the poem's message. At first, the poem is readily dismissed as mere literature, with Miss Jay heeding only the quality of the verse in suggesting that the ending is less poetically satisfying than the rest. Several dozen lines on, the merchant (i.e., capitalist) Guldstad, who proves Falk's rival in both ideology and romance, finds the poem and its deplorable moral worthy of sarcastic ridicule. He affirms that, with fruitless trees and trampled grounds, the orchard of Falk's poem has been rendered a veritable wasteland, its natural treasures utterly squandered. Guldstad concludes by pitying the orchard owner's dim prospects for the next year.

But Falk, in accord with his focus on the present and his antipathy to concern for the future, proceeds to scorn the very word *next*, which ever directs a person's attention away from the current state of affairs. On this point,

two other characters, Anna and Lind—who are presently falling for each other—stand behind Falk. When Falk asks after Lind's distracted air, Lind affirms that the poem has left him perfectly absorbed in the present and almost drunkenly blissful. He neither craves nor worries about anything; the world around him seems a wonderland of riches. Lind heartily thanks Falk for the timely poem and, echoing the verse, concludes by applauding the fragrant apple blossoms and proclaiming indifference to the fruits of autumn. In his enamored state, Lind's take on the poem contributes to the play's burgeoning focus on the questions of love and marriage.

The reader who comes across "In the Orchard" outside the context of *Love's Comedy* will not have the benefit of the other characters' reflections on Falk's offering of verse. Such a reader is left to respond to its contents independently in a contemplative manner that the action of the ongoing play in fact would not quite allow. Thus, it is quite appropriate that the poem has been extracted, isolating its message and, ideally, making a stronger impact on readers' minds.

HISTORICAL CONTEXT

Mid-nineteenth-Century Norway

The time period of Ibsen's early career in Norway was one of substantial growth in society, in terms of both the economy and the culture. Far more than in most Western countries, owing to the precipitous landscapes, dark seas, and partly arctic climate, Norway's society rests on the foundation of nature itself. As stated in *A Short History of Norway* by T. K. Derry, "Norway strikes the most casual visitor as a land where nature still reigns supreme," a fact deemed "the secret of its history." Edmund W. Gosse, in *Studies in the Literature of Northern Europe*, states the case more dramatically:

> A land of dark forests, gloomy waters, barren peaks, inundated by cold sharp airs off Arctic icebergs, a land where Nature must be won with violence, not wooed by the siren-songs of dream-impulses; Norway is the home of vigorous, ruddy lads and modest maidens, a healthy population, unexhausted and unrestrained. Here a man can open his chest, stride onward upright and sturdy, say out his honest word and be unabashed; here, if anywhere, human nature may hope to find a just development.

COMPARE
&
CONTRAST

- **1860s:** Norway is ruled by King Charles XV in a union with Sweden in which Norway is the subjugated partner, with the topmost post of *statholder*, or governor-general, indicating the king's personal absence from the lesser nation.

  Today: Norway became a constitutional monarchy upon gaining independence from Sweden in 1905. The head of state is King Harald V, who succeeded his father, Olav V, in 1991 while the government is led by Prime Minister Jens Stoltenberg, an economist whose center-left coalition was reelected in 2009.

- **1860s:** Ever since Norway was ruled by Denmark from 1397 to 1814, Danish has been the dominant language. But Henrik Ibsen and Bjørnsterne Bjørnson lead a surge of nationalist sentiment and practice in the theater, with Norwegian replacing Danish as the language and culture of choice.

  Today: Danish was in use long enough for a hybrid of Danish and Norwegian, *bokmål*— "book language," created through the Norwegian inflection of Danish words read aloud—to remain the nation's primary language even after twentieth-century attempts to bring a composite of Norwegian dialects to common usage.

- **1860s:** The Norwegian economy is booming thanks to recent increases in free trade, industrial advances, and Norway's expanding merchant marine sector.

  Today: Ever since offshore oil and gas deposits were discovered in the 1960s, Norway has enjoyed one of the highest standards of living in the world. Largely unaffected by the 2008 financial crisis, the country had just a 3-percent unemployment rate as of 2009.

One can discern something of the naturalist poet of "In the Orchard" in Gosse's description.

It was precisely in Ibsen's time that the character of the nation was being modified by more southerly influences, especially in terms of industry. The first coal-fueled cotton factories were opened in Oslo (then Christiania) and Bergen in the late 1840s, with support from English technicians and coal ships. The early 1850s saw national communication revolutionized by the introduction of the telegraph and a seaborne postal service, and the first freight railway was laid by 1854. Owing to the opening of marine trade with the British Empire and others from 1849 onward, Norway saw a threefold rise in imports through the 1850s and 1860s, with corresponding rises in exports, especially of timber, cod, and herring. The Norwegian mercantile marine as a body would grow to surpass the French, German, and Dutch mercantile marines and become the third largest in the world. In domestic terms, Oslo was at last developing, in Derry's words, a capitalist infrastructure "on a European level." All in all, the period is considered a Norwegian golden age.

Within Norway, the increased exposure to overseas influences contributed to surges in nationalist sentiment and study. By 1860, schooling was made obligatory not just in towns but in country districts as well, from seven until the age of Christian confirmation. On the one hand this brought increased attention to the character of the peasantry, with the nation's first social economist, Eilert Sundt, finding in rural areas a variety of "dark and primitive survivals" (cited in Derry). On the other hand, wider promotion of education helped bring rural culture out into the mainstream, with peasant philologist Ivar Aasen advancing appreciation for rural dialects, which were favorably compared to Old Norse, and poet A. O. Vinje bringing peasant sensibilities, even if at times vulgar, into national literary light. Ibsen himself declined to incorporate such speech into his plays, but he did contribute to a nationalist movement in the theater, whereby Danish acting styles and the Danish language fell

The poem alludes to the flute-like, haunting song of the thrush. (© BogdanBoev / Shutterstock.com)

out of favor while Norwegian subject matter and dialect predominated. In terms of printed literature, Peter Christen Asbjörnsen and Jørgen Moe, inspired by Germany's Grimm brothers, traveled the nation collecting tales from the oral tradition for a decade, at last publishing *Norwegian Folk Tales* in 1851. Inspiring national pride and affection for rustic idioms and words of Norse origin, the tales also gave an aura of history to the figure of the peasant, who, in Derry's words, became viewed by the well-off as "an imaginative, poetic figure, attuned to nature and steeped in the thoughts of his country's past."

Ibsen's take on the societal and cultural activity that transpired during his twenties and early thirties can, to an extent, be gleaned from "In the Orchard." The speaker, the character of Falk, does not appear to be a peasant himself, but he is certainly far from allied with the capitalist interests of some of the ladies and gentlemen of the company. His poem envisioning an orchard overrun by nature provokes scorn and even ridicule from the merchant Guldstad. It is as if Falk would rather re-create a time of "dark and primitive survival" in which man lives off the

land in the purest sense, by his own fishing or farming perhaps, rather than living on the profit to be gained from an abundant crop of fruit to be sold on the market. Ibsen's Falk may not be a peasant, but he fairly aligns with Derry's formulation of society's conception of the noble peasant, steeped in the past but living in the present.

CRITICAL OVERVIEW

Owing to the gradual manner of its presentation to the English-speaking world, little if any specific critical response to "In the Orchard" ever appeared. Although it occupies a prominent place as the opening passage of *Love's Comedy*, the poem is not given a title there and bears only an indirect relation to the play's subject matter, and commentators treating *Love's Comedy* have rarely addressed the poem itself. Edmund W. Gosse, in *Studies in the Literature of Northern Europe*, does note that, in this opening passage, Falk "proclaims the *carpe diem* that is his ideal," but Gosse stops short of critically analyzing the poem itself.

WHAT DO I READ NEXT?

- The reader who is intrigued by "In the Orchard" might turn next to Ibsen's *Brand* (1866), the verse play that followed *Love's Comedy*. The main character of *Brand* is a strong-willed priest who alienates himself from human society through his unflinching idealism. In a fate reminiscent of Falk's in *Love's Comedy*, Brand ends up wandering over the snowy mountain peaks.

- A collection of Ibsen's verse is *Lyrical Poems* (1902), translated by R. A. Streatfeild, with "A Bird Song" bearing an interesting relation to "In the Orchard."

- Ibsen's countryman and fellow poet Bjørnsterne Bjørnson—whose daughter, Bergliot, married Ibsen's son, Sigurd—won the Nobel Prize for Literature in 1903. Bjørnson's verse can be explored in *Poems and Songs* (1915), translated by Arthur Hubbell Palmer; of note are "The Day of Sunshine" and "Over the Lofty Mountains."

- On the heels of Ibsen in the history of Norwegian literature was Alexander L. Kielland, who wrote novels, stories, plays, and essays. His collection *Norse Tales and Sketches* (1896), translated by R. L. Cassie, includes a rumination on birds, nature, and the like titled "Autumn."

- Alongside Ibsen, Bjørnson, and Kielland, Jonas Lie was one of Norway's "Four Greats" of literature. Lie's first novel, *Dem Fremsynte* (1870), translated by Jessie Muir as *The Visionary; or, Pictures from Nordland* (1894), is a tale that offers meditations on nature and life from a perspective grounded in one of the northernmost regions of Norway.

- A great many poems that meditate on nature, usually from an aesthetic and/or compassionate perspective, can be found in the Emily Dickinson collection *Final Harvest* (1961).

- Holly Thompson's award-winning young-adult verse novel *Orchards* (2011) tells the story of a half-Jewish, half–Japanese American teenage girl who spends a summer working in her grandparents' orange orchards after a classmate commits suicide.

- The possibility of a complete absence of birdsong in the world—seen as a legitimate possibility due to the murderous effects of now-banned pesticides—is central to the title and content of Rachel Carson's famous pioneering environmental nonfiction book *Silent Spring* (1962).

The critical response to *Love's Comedy* as a whole is relevant nevertheless, in that the unconventional impulses of Falk, so evident in "In the Orchard," were a point of wide contention among the earliest reviewers. In particular, critics like M. J. Monrad (cited in Meyer) found Falk's/Ibsen's devaluation of both love and marriage to be unpalatable, even "immoral." Monrad spoke to both the play as a whole and Falk's opening stanzas when he warned Ibsen against becoming "a mouthpiece for the loose thinking and debilitating nihilism that is now fashionable." In a word, Monrad considered the play "unpoetical, as any viewpoint must be which claims that idealism and reality are incompatible." Reviewers Ditmar Meidell and Botten Hansen (cited in Heiberg) echoed Monrad's distaste, with Meidell calling the play "an appalling product of literary amateurism," while Hansen suggested that the play's author "unfortunately was entirely lacking in ideals and convictions." A more accurate statement, perhaps, would be that the ideals and convictions embodied by the protagonist Falk ran counter to those of the majority of the Norwegian literary public. Despite all this, James Walter McFarlane, in his commentary on *Love's Comedy* in volume 2 of *The Oxford Ibsen*, assures readers that the 1873 premiere of the 1862 play was "a popular success."

Regardless of the uncertain reception accorded *Love's Comedy*, critics have more broadly taken admiring note of Ibsen's poetic sensibilities. Gosse, in an essay from 1873 included in his *Studies in the Literature of Northern Europe*, points out that the announcement that an Ibsen poem is to be published "causes more stir than, perhaps, any other can, among literary circles in Scandinavia." Considering *Love's Comedy* from a more objective standpoint than did the first Norwegian critics, Gosse affirms, "It is impossible to express in brief quotation the perfection of faultless verse, the epigrammatic lancet-thrusts of wit, the boundless riot of mirth that make a lyrical saturnalia in this astonishing drama."

The praise of aesthetic appreciation found in "In the Orchard" reflects James Hurt's comment, in *Catiline's Dream: An Essay on Ibsen's Plays*, that "the project of the will that appears most often in Ibsen is art." David Thomas, in *Henrik Ibsen*, observes that with his "quick facility for rhyming verse," Ibsen, in some of his poems, "manages to express precisely and succinctly crucial ideas that were to remain in the forefront of his consciousness as a creative writer." Michael Meyer, in *Ibsen: A Biography*, affirms that, in *Love's Comedy*, Ibsen presents exemplary "rhymed verse, of remarkable concentration and ingenuity," if marked by "an extreme formalism." Meyer concludes that the work may fall short as a "poetic play," but that "it remains a brilliant dramatic poem." M. C. Bradbrook, in *Ibsen the Norwegian: A Revaluation*, affirms of *Love's Comedy*, "Never again did Ibsen write so wittily, or . . . so exuberantly," and concludes that the play's "headlong and happy vitality carries the reader along." Bradbrook declares, "The world-famous artist was moulded and conditioned by the young poet from whom he had so spectacularly cut himself off."

CRITICISM

Michael Allen Holmes

Holmes is a writer with existential interests. In the following essay, he draws on the play in which "In the Orchard" appears to identify the poem's subtext as a call to solitude.

Beyond the simple pastoral title, Henrik Ibsen's poem "In the Orchard" is a somewhat challenging read, being filled with ambiguous imagery, rhetorical questions, and brusque proclamations. The

> APPARENTLY, THE POET HAS LITTLE INCLINATION TO PAY HEED TO WHAT THE ORCHARD REPRESENTS, THE ABILITY TO PROVIDE FOR ONESELF AS WELL AS FOR A FAMILY."

setting of a sunny orchard is clear. Less apparent are what the fluttering blossoms and clapping scarecrow might symbolize, how listening to birds could be the best way to spend one's time, and why one should be so dismissive of all that delicious fruit. Arguably, an obscure poem is an excellent way to start a play: presenting imagery that wakens the senses and perhaps intrigues, the poem sets the audience's minds churning while laying a foundation of ideas that can be slowly elaborated as the play progresses. Readers of English translations often approach the poem in isolation, but a deeper appreciation of the poem's connotations within the play not only makes the surface meaning clearer but also reveals a hidden subtext.

Only by analogy is "In the Orchard" connected to the guiding theme of *Love's Comedy*, the merits of love versus marriage. The setting is a villa where the owner, the widowed Mrs. Halm, is hoping to marry off her two daughters, Anna and Svanhild, who are courted by Lind and Falk, respectively. Anna and Lind will soon unite. But Falk expresses his antipathy to the idea of marriage, which he sees as inevitably squelching a man's ideals and visions for his life. An illustration of his contention is provided by the dull and conventional Pastor Strawman, whose youthful idealism disappeared with his acquisition of a plump wife and an eventual total of twelve children. Thus, Falk pleads with Svanhild to join him in love but forsake marriage, which he fears would spell the end of their passion for each other. Svanhild admires his philosophy but judges that she would only be a prop in his intently poetic life; he specifically likens her to the wind that would carry him to great heights; she demurs. But after Falk scandalizes the company by publicly denouncing marriage—saying that marriage is to love as a potted plant is to wildflowers—Svanhild's admiration increases, and she offers to run off with him. But after further exposition, the merchant Guldstad intercedes: he praises the love that blossoms within a happy marriage—different from but not inferior to the original passion—and argues that Svanhild should marry him and be happy till death rather than enjoy a fling with Falk that can only end in emptiness. When Falk cannot assure her that his love would last forever, Svanhild accepts Guldstad's offer of marriage, and Falk is left to pursue the life of a solitary poet in the mountains.

Given the controversial nature of what can be summed up as a dramatic disparagement of traditional marriage, early critics were inclined to wonder about the extent to which Falk is serving as the mouthpiece of Ibsen—that is, communicating what the author himself truly thought. Hans Heiberg, in *Ibsen: A Portrait of the Artist*, after observing the deteriorating conditions of Ibsen's life just before *Love's Comedy* was published, concludes, "In short Ibsen had written a farcical comedy about his own time and his own wretched life." This is not to say that, condemning marriage, Ibsen must have been unhappy in his own. C. H. Herford, introducing his translation of the play, assures that Ibsen was, at the time, "quite recently and beyond question happily, married." But Herford provides a description of Ibsen that easily evokes the character of Falk as well, saying he was "beyond question a poet, ardent, brilliant, and young." M. C. Bradbrook, in *Ibsen the Norwegian*, states that Ibsen, like Falk, "was first and foremost an artist." Ibsen himself, in an 1880 letter (cited in Thomas), declared,

> Everything I have written has the closest possible connection with what I have lived through, even if it has not been my actual experience; every piece of writing has for me served the function of acting as a means of finding spiritual release and purification.

Considering these words, one might reconsider Ibsen's marriage. However happy it may have originally been, it would become one that David Thomas, in *Henrik Ibsen*, could describe as "formal and respectful rather than warm and intimate." Thomas conceives that Ibsen must have lamented "the emotional sterility of his own respectable but loveless marriage and the emptiness of his formal, bourgeois life style." In sum, one would not appear to be overstepping life/work boundaries in suggesting that, in Falk, Ibsen created a purified, idealized form of himself, one who could foresee the fate of his own union as readily as any other.

As orated by Falk in *Love's Comedy*, "In the Orchard" effectively sets the stage for the love-marriage debate about to unfold. The poem says nothing directly about either love or marriage; there is not even a suggestion of a female presence to accompany the male orator and the brothers to whom he speaks. But as the play unfolds, it becomes clear that the seasons of spring and autumn stand not just for the vibrant present and the desolate future, respectively, but for the vigor of young romantic love and the desiccation of an old marriage. When Falk is feeling the first flush of love for Svanhild, he associates this stage of his life with the springtime, comparing his love and his earliest poems alike to blossoms; he also associates himself with the birds by referring to his own wings and flying. Svanhild intensifies the association of spring with romantic love when, later in the play, she gives herself to Falk and dramatically proclaims that the leaf is budding, her spring has just begun. When at the end of the play, she explains to Falk why their young love must end so soon, Svanhild remarks that the spring is their time, and they shall never know an autumn when the musical bird within Falk—perhaps his soul, his creative spirit, or his loving self—can no longer be heard. These lines especially hark back to the poem of Falk's that opened the play.

In light of Falk's reference to his wings and flying and Svanhild's reference to the bird of music within him, the bird imagery merits further attention. Falk's name is, in fact, the Norwegian word for *falcon*. (Edmund W. Gosse, translating the text for an essay in *Studies in the Literature of Northern Europe*, rendered Falk's name rather as Hawk in order to preserve the identity between his name and that of a bird.) When wooing Svanhild, Falk draws on his name in asserting that, like his avian namesake, he needs to be propelled by the wind—as by Svanhild's love—in order to scale the heights of the sky. All in all, Falk is strongly associated with the musical birds he so glorifies in the lines of "In the Orchard." And these birds represent the present, the springtime, and also romantic love. Altogether, then, Falk himself appears to be an embodiment of that romantic love.

Yet there is a significant moment in the play when Falk throws into question his own appreciation for birds, and thus for romantic love and even for his emotional self. In the middle of the first act, Falk mistakenly gets the impression

Images of nature are central to "In the Orchard." *(© Elena Elisseeva | Shutterstock.com)*

that Lind is in love not with Anna but with Svanhild. This upsets Falk greatly, and upon speaking with his beloved Svanhild, he jumps to the conclusion that she and Lind are engaged. Svanhild pauses to appreciate the singing of a bird, one that she imagines has been sent by God to soothe her soul, and remarks that the bird's warbling is so inspirational that it causes poetry to flow right into her mind. At this moment, the jealous Falk is disinclined to honor either her love or the idea of love generally. With the idea of love signified by the bird, Falk goes so far as to pick up a stone and, in the middle of Svanhild's ode to the bird, throw the stone and kill it. Svanhild is appalled, but Falk imagines he has wreaked proper vengeance on Svanhild: since she has slain the musical bird within him—his love for her—by supposedly loving Lind, Falk has slain the real songbird that sang for her. Now, this hardly seems like the same person who earlier recited a poem praising the unsurpassed beauty of the songs of the birds. He was carried away by his emotions, and his murder of the bird can be understood as a revolt not only against a love that excluded him but against his own loving self.

At this point, one can return to "In the Orchard" with an altered perspective. Falk appears to praise spring and despise autumn, and thus—in line with the seasonal symbolism advanced throughout the play—to praise romantic love and despise marriage. The image of the clapping scarecrow, defender of the abundant fruit, is readily linked to the aptly named Pastor Strawman, domestic defender of his abundant brood of children. The images of birds, in turn, are linked with the spring and with love. In the poem, Falk questions the wisdom of hunting these birds—of destroying young love—for the sake of the crop of fruit to come. Yet in the play, when it seems a bird sings not for him, Falk becomes the hunter, and the death of the bird is not something he can undo. Whether mistakenly or not, he has belied the sense of his opening poem and killed the idea of romantic love, not only for Svanhild but within himself as well. Sure enough, the two never consummate their love, and Svanhild resigns herself to a conventional marriage with a merchant.

It is only the last stanza of "In the Orchard," then, that Falk is left to fulfill. There, with no further mention of any birds, an abundance of first-person pronouns—all singular—emphasize the notion that the poet is in truth no lover but a fierce individualist, one who is content to pluck the flowers, tear down the hedges, let the gate swing open, and, in effect, leave the orchard in ruins. Apparently, the poet has little inclination to pay heed to what the orchard represents, the ability to provide for oneself as well as for a family. Clearly, such a destructive person is fit for neither love nor marriage. Ibsen remarked in an 1870 letter, cited by Bradbrook, that *Love's Comedy* represents his "full expression" of a "desire for emancipation." And in Bradbrook's wry estimation, the subject of *Love's Comedy* "is the artist's duty to renounce love, marriage and all ordinary ties for a life on the mountain peaks." Falk, indeed, is destined to climb up into the mountains, freed from the very idea of love, and this fate is most subtly prefigured in the passage of verse that opens the play.

Source: Michael Allen Holmes, Critical Essay on "In the Orchard," in *Poetry for Students*, Gale, Cengage Learning, 2014.

Michael Meyer

In the following excerpt, Meyer describes the reception of Ibsen's collection, Poems.

. . . Ibsen's *Poems* were published on 3 May 1871. The edition was a large one, 4,000 copies (the equivalent, counting Norway and Denmark as one, of something approaching 200,000 in modern America). The reviews were generally most favourable. An anonymous critic in *Bergens Tidende* complained that "he seems to look down at everything from a poetic iceberg," but found in the "Balloon Letter" hope that Ibsen, "in addition to his latest brilliant but ugly works, will also give us something brilliant and beautiful." The Danish poet Otto Borchsenius, writing in *Bergens-Posten*, praised Ibsen for omitting his early poems, wished he had omitted some others (including, surprisingly, the "Elegy to J. L. Heiberg"), regretted the absence of the Priest's sermon in *Peer Gynt*, and feared that the lines about the "well-pressed morning coat" (in the "Balloon Letter") might imply an intent to withdraw from the battle. He hoped Ibsen might "gradually mellow this half-ironical, half-melancholy view of life, people and their actions," but admitted that "the age needs a disciplinarian, and we should be sorry to see Herr Ibsen withdraw from the battle as long as he can still wield his sword."

Rudolf Schmidt, in *Fædrelandet*, compared the volume with Bjørnson's recent collection; he found Bjørnson's poems "certainly the richer and weightier," and complained that: "Behind all doubt there must lie a conviction which must be equally strong, so that doubt strikes out in scorn and indignation. But sometimes with Henrik Ibsen this expresses itself rather as hesitation, as though doubt had struck inwards and quenched the spark of inner wisdom." Bjørnson himself, predictably, disliked the book. "I have now read Ibsen's poems," he wrote to his wife Karoline on 14 May. "Except for the old ones and one to his wife and a few others, and apart from an almost too virtuoso style in some, such as the one to Fru Heiberg, I find nothing noteworthy about the collection. As with almost everything by Ibsen I am left so empty afterwards. His standing vis-à-vis his country is becoming almost comic, and his poem to the king, praising him for not daring to do anything in 1864, seems to me criminal."

The man about whose opinion Ibsen was most anxious had mixed reactions. "I was so uncontrollably delighted with Ibsen's book when it arrived," Brandes wrote to Hegel, "that the reading of the poems put me in a most violent state of nervous emotion. It went through me like a storm through an Aeolian harp. . . . But later my critical sense asserted itself, and my judgment on these poems is that only a few of them are good, and those the ones already known. Most of them are *obscure* to the point of incomprehensibility, many are clumsy, and the humour is nearly always unsuccessful. It's nearly all doggerel. But there are things in the book which carry me away, and despite everything I *was* greatly carried away." Writing to his family a month later, he declared: "I was tremendously moved by "Terje Vigen." It is a true masterpiece, a real classic. . . . The only pity is that there is so much rubbish in the book"—a not altogether unfair comment, for a number of the poems fall far below Ibsen's best standard. He was much more uneven as a poet than as a dramatist. Brandes did not review the book until the autumn, by which time he had met Ibsen, and his review was to reflect that meeting. . . .

Source: Michael Meyer, "The Farewell to Poetry (1871)," in *Ibsen: A Biography*, Doubleday, 1971, pp. 340–41.

Philip H. Wicksteed

In the following excerpt, Wicksteed praises the power and vitality of Ibsen's style.

But when all this is said something more specific remains to be reckoned with in Ibsen. The secret of his power alike of attraction and of repulsion is perhaps to be found in his indomitable sense of vitality, coupled with his growing incapacity to express it otherwise than in negations. He always seemed to be diving into the darkness, Bjørnson has said of him that he is like the lighthouses on the Norway coast. They show folk where *not* to sail, and they are the first things that any one sees when his eye is turned to Norway. Ibsen's searching analysis of how not to do it strikes those who have less inherent sense of the worth of life than he as amounting to a terrible fatalism, whereas to those who share his vital force . . . they are what they ought to be—a warning to enable a man to sail more safely, not a proclamation that he who sails on the sea of life sails to inevitable wreck.

But yet, for all his sense of the worth of life, that 'fight with trolls' of which he was so deeply conscious indicates some exceptional feeling in Ibsen's soul of a hostile power which cramped and conditioned his self-expression; and his most fervent admirers must often feel that he was a haunted man, that he was in some sense possessed, that he had paid a terrible price for his insight and his achievement, and that though he was always seeking to break through to the light, he was often beset by a doubt whether darkness might not after all be the natural abode of man. It is not only in his later work, but in poems of almost every date, that we feel this spirit. That mysterious and fascinating poem *Musicians* gives hints, which the reader may shape according to his fancy, to support or refute these contentions, but in the *Bird and Birdcatcher* Ibsen reveals himself clearly enough as scared and bruised by the grim powers that encompass him. In *The Daylight Coward*, which the reader will compare with a passage in *Brand*, he tries (at least dramatically) to find his reconciliation with life in the thought that man is born to darkness, and can only be happy when he renounces his insane desire to live in the sunshine. In *The Miner* we find him persistently working deeper into the darkness with an only half-retained conviction that it is the true path to light. But in that terrible poem *On the Fells* we have a conscious working out of this theory, together with a *reductio ad absurdum* of the belief that by hardening the heart and cultivating an artistic attitude of aloofness you can win emancipation.

Source: Philip H. Wicksteed, "Introduction to F. E. Garrett's translation of *Lyrics and Poems from Ibsen*," in *Henrik Ibsen: A Critical Anthology*, edited by James McFarlane, Penguin Books, 1970, pp. 216–17.

SOURCES

Bradbrook, M. C., *Ibsen the Norwegian: A Revaluation*, Chatto & Windus, 1948, pp. 26–42.

Derry, T. K., *A Short History of Norway*, George Allen & Unwin, 1957, pp. 9–13, 152–72.

Gosse, Edmund W., *Studies in the Literature of Northern Europe*, C. Kegan Paul, 1879, pp. 35–47.

Gray, Ronald, *Ibsen—a Dissenting View: A Study of the Last Twelve Plays*, Cambridge University Press, 1977, p. 72.

Heiberg, Hans, *Ibsen: A Portrait of the Artist*, translated by Joan Tate, University of Miami Press, 1969, pp. 107–109.

Heller, Otto, *Henrik Ibsen: Plays and Problems*, Houghton Mifflin, 1912, pp. 42–48.

Herford, C. H., Introduction to *Love's Comedy*, in *The Collected Works of Henrik Ibsen*, Vol. 1, Charles Scribner's Sons, 1910, pp. xxxix–xliv.

Hurt, James, *Catiline's Dream: An Essay on Ibsen's Plays*, University of Illinois Press, 1972, pp. 11–12.

Ibsen, Henrik, "In the Orchard," translated by Edmund W. Gosse, in *English Verse: Translations*, edited by W. J. Linton and R. H. Stoddard, Charles Scribner's Sons, 1883, pp. 193–94.

———, *Love's Comedy*, translated by C. H. Herford, in *The Collected Works of Henrik Ibsen*, Vol. 1, Charles Scribner's Sons, 1910, pp. 285–464.

———, "The Task of the Poet," in *Modern Critical Views: Henrik Ibsen*, edited by Harold Bloom, Chelsea House Publishers, 1999, pp. 5–6; originally published in *Masterpieces of the Modern Scandinavian Theatre*, edited by Robert W. Corrigan, translated by Evert Sprinchorn, Collier Books, 1967.

McFarlane, James Walter, "*Love's Comedy*: Commentary," in *The Oxford Ibsen*, Vol. 2, edited by James Walter McFarlane, Oxford University Press, 1962, pp. 351–65.

———, ed., *The Cambridge Companion to Ibsen*, Cambridge University Press, 1994, pp. xiv–xx.

Meyer, Michael, *Ibsen: A Biography*, Penguin Books, 1985, pp. 209–14.

"Norway Profile," BBC News website, August 29, 2012, http://www.bbc.co.uk/news/world-europe-17743896 (accessed March 31, 2013).

Taylor-Wilkie, Doreen, et al., *Norway*, 4th ed., Insight Guides, APA Publications, 2011, pp. 51–77.

Thomas, David, *Henrik Ibsen*, Grove Press, 1983, pp. 1–24.

Van Laan, Thomas F., "Generic Complexity in Ibsen's 'An Enemy of the People,'" in *Comparative Drama*, Vol. 20, No. 2, Summer 1986, pp. 95–114.

FURTHER READING

Campolo, Anthony, *Carpe Diem: Seize the Day*, Thomas Nelson Publishers, 2008.
Writing from a Christian perspective, Campolo provides an instructive text intended to inspire people to get the most out of their daily lives.

Hand, Carol, *Norway*, ABDO, 2013.
Aimed at a young-adult audience, Hand's up-to-date, photograph-laced study provides an excellent overview of Norway's geography, history, society, and status in the modern era.

Masset, Claire, *Orchards*, Shire Publications, 2012.
This popular treatment of the nature and history of orchards, with a focus on those in Britain, provides artful photographs and an abundance of information within its limited span of pages.

Rodnick, David, *The Norwegians: A Study in National Culture*, Public Affairs Press, 1955.
Published in the mid-twentieth century, Rodnick's cultural study gives an excellent sense of the Norwegian character in an era closer to Ibsen's, before the modern era of globalization took hold.

Rose, Henry, *Henrik Ibsen: Poet, Mystic and Moralist*, Dodd Mead, 1913.
Considering Ibsen's plays and verse from an uncommon angle, Rose's concise text focuses on Ibsen's status as a poet and discusses the spiritual and ethical strains in his works.

SUGGESTED SEARCH TERMS

Henrik Ibsen AND In the Orchard

Henrik Ibsen AND Love's Comedy

Love's Comedy AND Falk

Henrik Ibsen AND Norway AND literature

Henrik Ibsen AND poetry

Norway AND Four Greats

Norway AND agriculture

Norway AND independent

orchard AND poem

Let America Be America Again

LANGSTON HUGHES

1938

Langston Hughes's poem "Let America Be America Again," first published in 1938, is representative of much of the famous writer's work. Hughes first became known during the Harlem Renaissance. His poetry, plays, and essays speak to and portray the African American everyman and use the rhythms of blues, jazz, and black spirituals. His impact, however, did not end on the page, as he continued to be a popular and influential voice for decades: in 1966, the year before he died, he was appointed by President Lyndon B. Johnson to be the American representative to the First World Festival of Negro Arts in Dakar, Senegal. While Hughes was there, according to the *New York Times* (as quoted by Arnold Rampersad in a biography of Hughes), "young writers from all over Africa followed him about the city and haunted his hotel the way American youngsters dog favorite baseball players."

"Let America Be America Again" tackles the complicated issues of racial and social equality using simple language and clear images. Although the poem mentions many examples of hardship and unfairness, portraying the difficult economic situation in the United States in the 1930s, the final lines offer some hope for the future of the American dream. The poem first appeared in *Esquire* magazine as well as the pamphlet *The New Song* and can be found in the modern Hughes editions *The Collected Poems of Langston Hughes* (1994) and *Poems* (1999).

Langston Hughes *(© Fred Stein Archive | Archive Photos |*
Getty Images)

AUTHOR BIOGRAPHY

James Mercer Langston Hughes was born on
February 1, 1902, in Joplin, Missouri, to James
Hughes and Carrie Langston. His parents
divorced soon after he was born, and he was
raised by his grandmother until she died. The
thirteen-year-old Hughes then went to live with
his mother and stepfather. The family settled in
Cleveland, Ohio. A teacher introduced Hughes to
the poetry of Walt Whitman and Carl Sandburg,
and he began writing poetry himself. He contributed often to the school literary magazine but did
not have any luck in getting published elsewhere.

After graduating from high school in 1920,
Hughes spent a year in Mexico with his father and
then enrolled at Columbia University. In June 1921,
Hughes had his first poem published, "The Negro
Speaks of Rivers." After dropping out of college in
1922, he worked various jobs, including a stint as a
steward on a ship traveling to Africa and Europe.
He lived briefly in Paris, still writing poetry and
striving to get it published.

Upon his return to the United States,
Hughes again worked odd jobs. With the help

MEDIA ADAPTATIONS

- On the recording *Essential Langston
  Hughes*, Hughes reads some of his poems,
  relates personal experiences, and explains
  the inspiration behind some of his writing.
  The one-hour CD was released in 2007 by
  Harper Audio/Caedmon.
- Dominic Hoffman reads Hughes's autobiography *The Big Sea* in an audiobook
  released by Books on Tape on CD in 2000
  and by Random House Audio in 2011. The
  running time is ten hours and forty-one
  minutes.

and encouragement of poet Vachel Lindsay,
Hughes entered a poetry contest in *Opportunity*
magazine and won a scholarship to attend Lincoln University, in Pennsylvania, from which he
graduated in 1929. While Hughes was in college,
novelist and critic Carl Van Vechten helped
Hughes publish his first collection, *The Weary
Blues* (1926). A second volume, *Fine Clothes to
the Jew*, followed in 1927, and then the novel *Not
without Laughter* appeared in 1930, winning the
Harmon Gold Medal for Literature. The commercial success of this book gave Hughes hope
that he could make his living as a writer.

Hughes continued writing poetry, novels,
and short stories and also began to write a column for the *Chicago Defender* in which he
explored racial issues. Hughes created a huge
body of work throughout his career: he wrote
eleven plays, books of essays, and an autobiography; edited poetry anthologies; and translated
the work of other poets into English. He once
taught creative writing at Atlanta University.
Hughes was hugely influential in the literature
of the Harlem Renaissance.

Hughes's poem "Let America Be America
Again" first appeared in 1938 in *Esquire* and in a
pamphlet titled *A New Song*, which was published
by the International Workers Order, a fraternal
organization affiliated with the Communist Party
that provided low-cost health care and supported

educational and cultural activities. Hughes had traveled to the Soviet Union in the 1930s and had been impressed with some of the practices he saw there, such as medical care and schooling provided for everyone equally.

Hughes died of cancer on May 22, 1967. His home in Harlem was made a New York City Landmark in 1981 and added to the National Register of Historic Places in 1982.

POEM SUMMARY

The text used for this summary is from *Poems*, edited by David Roessel, Alfred A. Knopf, 1999, pp. 97–100. Versions of the poem can be found on the following web pages: http://www.poets. org/viewmedia.php/prmMID/15609 and http:// allpoetry.com/poem/8495513-Let_America_Be _America_Again-by-Langston_Hughes.

Lines 1–16
The first four lines of "Let America Be America Again" set up the premise of the poem: the speaker asks for America to fulfill its reputation as a place where people have freedom. Lines 2 and 6 allude to the American dream, which is supposed to be attainable by anyone willing to work hard, as with the example of a pioneer working to create a home on the prairies (lines 3–4). In lines 7–9, the speaker alludes to America's own fight for independence against England, pointing out that the United States has no monarch, and therefore everyone should be free and equal.

Lines 5 and 10 are set apart from the other lines by parentheses. The parentheses make these lines seem like quiet asides, separate from the main narrative of the poem. The larger stanzas relate the hope that America can live up to its promise, but lines 5 and 10 state simply that the speaker has not experienced the country's declared ideals.

Line 11 brings up the personification of the concept of liberty, and line 12 asks that she not be decorated with patriotism if that patriotism is not honest. The next two lines ask that freedom, equality, and opportunity be made real, for everyone in America. However, line 16, set apart like lines 5 and 10 in parentheses, clarifies the fact that the speaker does not feel that he has experienced equality and freedom in America. Line 16 echoes the final lines of the national anthem, but the words are enclosed within quotation marks to draw attention to the fact that they are not true for everyone.

Lines 17–50
The italics in lines 17–18 mark them as different from the others in the poem. The words might come from someone other than the speaker. These lines seem to challenge the speaker, asking why he is saying such negative things about his country.

The next three stanzas list all of the Americans who might respond to the lines in italics above. Hughes includes not only African Americans—former slaves and servants and poor workers—but also Native Americans, who have been forced to leave the territory their families lived on for generations; immigrants from all over the world who come to America full of optimism but find that they still cannot make a decent life for themselves; young people disillusioned by the greed, selfishness, and materialism they find in society; and tenant farmers, sharecroppers, and factory workers.

The following stanza, lines 39–50, explains that these poor and downtrodden people, the peasants from Europe and people taken from Africa and enslaved, are the ones who made America. Their labor built the cities and farmed the countryside. These people worked hard because they hoped for something better in the future.

Lines 51–61
Lines 51–55 are questions with which the speaker demands to know who has freedom in America. Lines 56–59 serve as a continuation of the question in line 55, which is restated in line 60. The speaker is clearly frustrated that, in spite of everything the common people have done to build America and make lives for themselves, they have little to show for it. Dreams and hope are all the people have now, and that hope is fading.

Lines 62–74
In this part of the poem, the mood changes from barely restrained anger and frustration to something more inspiring. The speaker asks again for America to live up to its reputation—to be better than it has ever been before. He demands that America be a place where everyone is free, regardless of wealth or race. Then the speaker calls on the workers of America to fill themselves with a sense of purpose and give new life to their hopes. In spite of what anyone might say, people must be strong and fight for the country they dream of.

TOPICS FOR FURTHER STUDY

- The Harlem Renaissance was a time of huge cultural growth in the African American community, not only for authors and poets but also for artists and musicians. Using online and print resources, research the artists who became prominent during this period. Collect images of their work, set the pictures to music from the period, and make a PowerPoint presentation to share with your class.

- Read another of Hughes's poems that, like "Let America Be America Again," has political themes (almost one hundred Hughes poems are available at PoemHunter.com). Compare the two. Are the messages of the poems similar? How do the poems create a certain mood or reaction in the reader? Write an essay explaining your answers to these questions and further thoughts on the poems.

- In 1929, Jessie Redmon Fauset published *Plum Bun: A Novel without a Moral*. It tells the story of Angela Murray, a young African American woman who moves to New York to "pass" for white. She hopes to escape racism, but she learns that her problems will not disappear. Read the novel, and then imagine a scene in which Angela meets some of the central writers of the Harlem Renaissance, like Hughes, who argued against sacrificing one's racial and cultural identity in order to integrate into mainstream society. What might these historical figures say to Angela? Write your imagined scene as a short story, or perform the scene with some of your classmates as dialogue from a play.

- Artist E. B. Lewis created illustrations for "The Negro Speaks of Rivers," which was the first poem Hughes ever published. The illustrations and poem were published together in a book in 2009. Sketch or paint pictures of images called to mind by "Let America Be America Again." Share your pictures with the class.

Lines 75–86

Lines 75–79 bring the two threads of the poem together. The negative feelings that were allowed to appear only in parentheses at the beginning of the poem are stated bravely in line 77, and the words of inspiration that the poet offered in lines 62–74 build up to a pledge by the speaker in lines 78–79 that America will be what he hopes it can be.

The last stanza summarizes the poem well. Lines 80–81 admit the problems society faces, but the rest of the stanza is more hopeful and patriotic. Line 82 calls to mind the first line of the preamble to the Constitution, and line 84 echoes the lyrics of "God Bless America." In this final stanza, Hughes offers hope that America can be remade into the country it should be.

THEMES

Injustice

The United States has set itself up as an ideal, a country founded on the principles of liberty and equality, where, with hard work, anyone can achieve their dreams. In actuality, however, many people face injustice rather than freedom and fairness, and in his poem "Let America Be America Again," Hughes identifies some of these people. He speaks for African Americans, of course, but he also mentions others who struggle, such as Native Americans, poor white farmers, people hurt when they go on strike to protest unfair working conditions, and immigrants who find disappointment after they arrive on American soil. Many people have not been given the opportunity to achieve the American dream, and

Hughes draws attention to this injustice in "Let America Be America Again" and much of his other work.

National Identity

At the time when Hughes began writing poetry in the first half of the twentieth century, the country was going through a lot of changes. One major change was a population shift known as the Great Migration, during which many African Americans moved from rural areas in the South to northern cities. In 1900, 90 percent of African Americans lived in the South. By 1930, that number had decreased to 70 percent, and by 1970, it had dropped further to 50 percent. Migrating African Americans left behind the economic and social oppression of the South for better opportunities.

In the 1930s, the Great Depression ruined the nation's economy, and many people were desperate to make a living and feed their families. Jobs were scarce everywhere, which cut down on the number of people moving north to find work. However, communities like New York City's Harlem—which was not inhabited by African Americans only but was perceived as a black community, as certainly African Americans rather than mainstream influences dominated the culture there—were beginning to forge a cultural identity. The people living in these communities wanted their voices to be heard on a broader, national level. They were no longer willing to be less than full citizens. It was the beginning of the civil rights movement.

In his poem "Let America Be America Again," Hughes gives voice to these collective feelings, calling for a change in the national identity of the United States. Although he saw the problems in society, where people had more power because of their race or because they were wealthy, he still believed America could be great. By including everyone, both politically and culturally, and allowing every voice to be heard, Americans could forge a new national identity that more closely reflected all of the country's population. The use of the opening words of the preamble to the Constitution in line 82 reinforces this theme: just as the Constitution is the plan for how to run the country, Hughes is proposing a new plan in his poem, a plan that offers true freedom and equality for all.

Hughes condemns people who take advantage of those less fortunate, comparing them to leeches.
(© clearviewstock / Shutterstock.com)

STYLE

Typography

Typography refers to how printed matter appears on the page. Poets sometimes use different kinds of typography to enhance the meanings of their poems. Sometimes this can be done dramatically, such as with using a lot of capital letters, drastically changing the size of the type, or having the poem printed in a certain shape. Hughes uses less obvious methods in "Let America Be America Again," but examining the simple typographic tools he employs to set certain lines apart illuminates the poem's meaning.

Lines 5, 10, and 15 of the poem are enclosed in parentheses. They are also very short stanzas—only one or two lines each—set apart from the longer stanzas that precede and follow them. The mention of a dream and the image of the pioneer seeking freedom in the first stanza might lead the reader to think at first that the poem is going to be unreservedly patriotic, but Hughes draws attention to the line that immediately follows with parentheses—setting it apart

COMPARE
&
CONTRAST

- **1930s:** The terrible economic conditions of the Great Depression make both employers and workers desperate. Unions organize labor strikes to protest unfair working conditions, but employers and government agencies often come down hard on those involved. Approximately ninety people are killed in the summer of 1937 alone in the United States because of violence resulting from strikes, and many more are injured, evicted, or jailed as a direct result of taking part in a strike. In spite of this discouragement, almost 35 percent of industrial workers in the country belong to a union by the middle of the twentieth century.

  Today: New trade agreements and increasing costs in the last third of the twentieth century and early twenty-first century have driven many employers to move their operations outside the United States. Fear of losing jobs in this manner forces many American union leaders to make concessions to business owners, and as a result, membership in unions decreases to about 8 percent by 2007. Organizations like the Change to Win Coalition work to increase participation in union activity and militant action, such as labor strikes, but have made little progress.

- **1930s:** Many farmers in the South are share-tenants or sharecroppers who do not own their own land—the bondsmen Hughes mentions in "Let America Be America Again." Share-tenants rent land but provide their own equipment and might have some cash for other supplies, keeping two-thirds to three-quarters of their profits while passing the rest on to their landlords. Sharecroppers, however, contribute only their labor and therefore might receive only half of their profit. They need to borrow equipment as well as credit for groceries to feed their families. Because the landlords charge very high interest rates for the loans, at the end of the year, when the profits are calculated, the sharecroppers are always left in debt.

  Today: Government agencies in the 1930s and 1940s struggled to correct the conditions of tenancy farming and sharecropping. As the farming of cotton became mechanized, a process that was sped along by the need for material during World War II, and as farmworkers began to look for jobs in cities, sharecropping declined. By the beginning of the twenty-first century, sharecropping and tenancy had become extremely rare.

- **1930s:** US unemployment rates during the Great Depression soar to above 25 percent. This figure may even be a low estimate, because many either become too discouraged to seek work or leave cities to try to feed their family in the countryside and therefore are not counted as unemployed. The unemployment rates for African Americans are estimated to be 30 to 50 percent higher than among whites.

  Today: An economic recession causes unemployment in the United States to increase from below 5 percent in 2006 to 10 percent in 2009. As of February 2013, the unemployment rate is 7.7 percent.

---

with typography—so that the reader quickly sees the importance of the thread of discontent that runs through the poem. The parenthetical lines are like rebellious, insistent voices in a crowd, standing out because they are different.

Lines 17 and 18 are in italics. Because they are the only lines in the entire poem set in italics, the reader knows immediately that they are different from the others. When compared with the surrounding lines, the italicized lines can be read as someone other than the speaker talking; they become a kind of challenge to the poet. The next several stanzas of the poem respond to the questions asked in the italicized lines.

Simple Language

Hughes was a poet who wanted his work to be read and appreciated by a variety of people. He was not only writing for fellow poets and professors. He thought that everyone could appreciate the beauty and music in a poem. Because of this, Hughes used relatively simple language in his poetry. In "Let America Be America Again," there are very few words that are more than three syllables, and the vast majority of the words chosen are of only one or two syllables. None of the words are likely to send a reader looking for a dictionary. When Hughes wrote his poems, he spoke for and to regular people, and he used clear and basic language and easily understood imagery to communicate his meanings. Hughes was sometimes criticized for the simplicity of his style, but what a poem such as "Let America Be America Again" lacks in complexity of language it makes up for in difficulty of subject matter, tackling issues like social and racial equality.

HISTORICAL CONTEXT

The Harlem Renaissance

The term *renaissance* means "rebirth." Therefore, the Harlem Renaissance is, in a sense, named incorrectly. It was not truly a rebirth because nothing like it had ever happened before. However, just as the Renaissance in Europe was a time when art, literature, and science made huge advances, the Harlem Renaissance encompassed an explosion of work by African American writers, poets, artists, and musicians. The effects were not only felt in New York—there were also cultural movements in Philadelphia, Boston, Washington, DC and elsewhere—but regardless of location, the motivation was virtually the same. African American writers, musicians, playwrights, and visual artists wanted to create a space for themselves that was separate from the stereotypes that were formed and reinforced by mainstream white culture.

The Harlem Renaissance as a movement had three general stages of development. In the first, white authors began to portray racial issues and realistic black characters. Although this was an improvement over the stereotyping that had been almost universal up to that point in mainstream culture, it was frustrating, if not insulting, to a community eager to find its own voice. Civil rights activist W. E. B Du Bois (cited in an essay by Arnold Rampersad) asserted in 1926 that "until the art of the black folk compels recognition they will not be rated as human." This view moved the Harlem Renaissance into its second stage, where African American artists, sometimes helped by white patrons, received more recognition for their work.

These artists and writers were encouraged but often manipulated by political leaders with an agenda of improving the mainstream image of African Americans and thereby improving race relations. Du Bois claimed in his essay "Criteria of Negro Art" that he did not care "a damn for any art that is not used for propaganda." Because the more politically motivated black leaders hoped that literature and the visual arts could be used as examples demonstrating the admirable qualities of their race, there was controversy over what was deemed "appropriate" to represent. For example, Hughes explains in his autobiography, *The Big Sea*, how he was criticized for his "parading of all our racial defects before the public" because he used dialect rather than "proper" English in some of his work.

The third stage of the Harlem Renaissance was a kind of rebellion against this political agenda, and this encompassed some artists, like Hughes, who had previously benefited from this agenda. Hughes wrote an essay in 1926 called "The Negro Artist and the Racial Mountain," in which he insists that African American artists and writers should express themselves with neither shame nor fear. He did not believe that African Americans should seek to integrate themselves into mainstream culture by giving up pride in themselves and their heritage. Hughes, and many others, wanted to portray realistic images, both good and bad, rather than obey an abstract political agenda.

In addition to Hughes, the Harlem Renaissance launched the careers of countless others: writers Jean Toomer, Jessie Redmon Fauset, Claude McKay, Zora Neale Hurston, James Weldon Johnson, and Alain Locke; musicians Fats Waller, Duke Ellington, and Jelly Roll Morton; and visual artists Palmer C. Hayden, Laura Wheeler Waring, Richmond Barthé, Sargent Johnson, Augusta Savage, and James Lesesne Wells, to name only a small sample. African American culture, and American culture as a whole, was indelibly changed.

Hughes regrets the fate of many African Americans but does not ignore the problems of other minorities. (© Laurin Rinder | Shutterstock.com)

CRITICAL OVERVIEW

Critical reception of Hughes's poetry has been generally positive. Milton Meltzer, in a *Cobblestone* article, mentions Hughes's first collection, *The Weary Blues*, which "critics hailed as powerful, warm, and lyrical." In a review of *The Collected Poems of Langston Hughes*, Donna Seaman calls Hughes's work "exceptional," praising the way he "stayed true to his muse, chronicling the black American experience and contrasting the beauty of the soul with the loathsomeness of circumstance." Seaman describes his poems as being "charged with the immediacy of life and the rhythm of speech and song." *Booklist*'s Hazel Rochman agrees, pronouncing Hughes's work to be "colloquial and direct yet mysterious and complex." A *Publishers Weekly* review of the collected poems

also praises "the clarity of his language, his wise humor and his insight into the human condition."

However, not everyone has had praise for Hughes. Some saw his plain language as lacking in style. Seaman admits in her review that Hughes was sometimes "castigated for being trite and simplistic" by critics of his era. Also, the tension surrounding racial issues that was prevalent during Hughes's lifetime affected the reception of his work. In his autobiography, *The Big Sea* (cited on the Poetry Foundation website), Hughes describes how his 1927 collection *Fine Clothes to the Jew* "was well received by the literary magazines and the white press, but the Negro critics did not like it at all." Hughes goes on to explain that because "Negro critics and many of the intellectuals were very sensitive about their race in books," some "called the

WHAT DO I READ NEXT?

- *Langston Hughes: The Harlem Renaissance* (2008), by Maurice Wallace, is a biography of Hughes appropriate for young-adults. The book covers Hughes's life and his role in the Harlem Renaissance and also offers detailed analysis of individual works.

- Like Hughes, Jean Toomer was an influential writer during the Harlem Renaissance. His groundbreaking book *Cane* (1923) is a collection of fiction, drama, and poetry that portrays life in the South for African Americans of the time.

- *Langston Hughes and the "Chicago Defender": Essays on Race, Politics, and Culture, 1942–62* (1995), edited by Christopher C. De Santis, collects the essays Hughes wrote for his weekly newspaper column. The essays discuss timely topics from World War I to the civil rights movement and the Cold War.

- John Steinbeck won the National Book Award and the Pulitzer Prize for his novel *The Grapes of Wrath* (1939). The book describes the trials of the Joad family, poor tenant farmers who leave the Oklahoma dust bowl for California.

- Published in 2002, volume 15 of *The Collected Works of Langston Hughes*, edited by R. Baxter Miller, includes all of Hughes's short stories.

- The action in Harper Lee's Pulitzer Prize–winning novel *To Kill a Mockingbird* (1960) takes place in the 1930s. Lee addresses issues of racial inequality with warmth and humor.

book a disgrace to the race, a return to the dialect tradition, and a parading of all our racial defects before the public." Hughes was criticized for his realistic portrayals of poor or uneducated African Americans and the way they spoke because these critics, "in anything that white people were likely to read, ... wanted to put their best foot forward, their politely polished and cultural foot—and only that foot."

A review in *American Heritage* perhaps summarizes the totality of Hughes's poetry best: it "begins in the Jazz Age, takes up the radical styles of the thirties, joins in the revival of patriotism of World War II, and ends in the triumph of the civil rights movement." Writing over several decades, Hughes was a lasting and influential voice in America.

CRITICISM

Kristen Sarlin Greenberg

Greenberg is a freelance writer and editor with a background in literature and philosophy. In the following essay, she examines how Hughes uses basic poetic tools to build a hopeful, inspirational tone in "Let America Be America Again."

Langston Hughes was a man of strong, sometimes controversial political opinions. For example, after traveling to the Soviet Union, he openly praised some of the central beliefs of Soviet Communism. He was widely criticized for this, although in its purest, most ideal form, communism has obvious attractions: everyone is considered equal, and everyone's needs are met in terms of food, health care, and education. Because political issues were important to him, Hughes often wrote poems that tackled difficult themes, such as racism and injustice.

However, Hughes did not write for a select, academic audience. Donald B. Gibson, in his introduction to *Modern Black Poets: A Collection of Critical Essays* (cited on the Poetry Foundation website), explains:

> During the twenties when most American poets were turning inward, writing obscure and esoteric poetry to an ever decreasing audience of readers, Hughes was turning outward, using language and themes, attitudes and ideas familiar to anyone who had the ability simply to read.

Hughes supported himself with a wide variety of odd jobs before making his name as a writer, and he was not a pretentious man. He identified with his audience. His attitude is illustrated in his creation of the character of Jesse B. Semple, a name later shortened to "Simple." Hughes wrote many columns for the *Chicago Defender* and the *New York Post* that featured the fictional Simple telling about his life. He was a poor African American man living in Harlem, and the stories he told highlighted a lot of the injustice he faced living in a racist world. Hughes

> HUGHES'S GREATEST TALENT LIES IN HIS
> SUBTLE USE OF BASIC POETIC TOOLS LIKE
> TYPOGRAPHY, WORD CHOICE, AND ALLUSION TO
> DIRECT THE READER'S ATTENTION AND AFFECT THE
> READER'S MOOD. IN THIS POEM, HUGHES USES
> THESE TOOLS TO SLOWLY BUILD THE TONE FROM
> WISHFUL THINKING TO AN INSPIRING, PATRIOTIC
> CONCLUSION."

wrote for and spoke for people like Simple, folks who might be caught up in the troubles of their daily lives, such as work, money, and love, but who could still understand the bigger issues.

"Let America Be America Again" is a good example of Hughes's trademark uncomplicated language and style. There are no confusing or obscure images—everything is straightforward. Hughes's greatest talent lies in his subtle use of basic poetic tools like typography, word choice, and allusion to direct the reader's attention and affect the reader's mood. In this poem, Hughes uses these tools to slowly build the tone from wishful thinking to an inspiring, patriotic conclusion.

The first stanza of the poem is composed of simple wishes for what the speaker wants America to be. Then there is a single line with which Hughes introduces the first bit of negativity and doubt. The speaker expresses his personal truth, that he does not feel America has fulfilled its promise of freedom and opportunity for him, but Hughes uses typography to complicate the meaning of the sentence. The fact that this line, as well as line 10 below, is closed off in parentheses makes it seem like the speaker is whispering. He seems afraid or uncertain and therefore is unable to speak bravely. The third time Hughes uses parentheses, that whisper seems to grow a little louder. The parentheses surround two lines rather than just one, and the quotation marks introduce a sense of irony.

Hughes also uses italics to alter the meaning of the text. Only two lines in the poem are italicized. They seem to be coming from another person who is confronting the main speaker

and criticizing him for being negative. This confrontation seems to goad the speaker into greater bravery. From that point on, the tone of the poem has more strength and certainty. The lofty wishes of the first few stanzas give way to declarations, representing the many Americans who have been treated unfairly.

Starting with line 51, Hughes asks a series of questions. Questions sometimes introduce a feeling of doubt or uncertainty, but here, the questions have an air of challenge. The speaker's frustration and anger with the unfairness he has experienced in his lifetime seem to swell up, and Hughes increases the strength and intensity of the words even more. The lines take on the feeling of a song, with repetition of certain phrases (lines 56–59). In the stanza there are numerous dashes, which make it seem like the speaker is growing excited, talking quickly and trying to catch his breath.

This section of the poem culminates with the word *ME* in line 65. The use of capital letters in this word communicates a vehemence on the part of the speaker. He is no longer willing to hide his dissatisfaction in parentheses. Instead, he is clearly asserting himself. There are no more question marks in the poem after this line. The speaker finishes the poem with confident and stirring statements. The words that Hughes employs are also strong: *steel, must, swear, oath*. The final three stanzas of the poem also end with exclamation points, which add to the feeling of excitement and confidence.

In addition to typography and careful word choice, Hughes introduces allusions to manipulate the mood of the poem. An *allusion* is a passing reference meant to remind the reader of something without directly and explicitly stating it. Twice in "Let America Be America Again," in lines 16 and 50, Hughes uses a phrase that recalls the final words of the national anthem: "the land of the free and the home of the brave." Rather than eliciting a feeling of patriotism in the reader, however, Hughes surrounds the phrase with quotation marks to highlight the fact that for many, America is not a true home, and there is no real and lasting freedom.

The first time Hughes uses this phrase (line 16), it is in parentheses. As explained above, this is still in the early part of the poem, where the speaker seems afraid to speak freely. In contrast, the second time the phrase appears (line 50), it is not in parentheses. The speaker's frustration is

Although Hughes points out many problems in America, the end of the poem seems to provide patriotic hope that the country can someday live up to its image. *(© sbko | Shutterstock.com)*

given more license in this section of the poem, and the quotation marks give the line an almost sarcastic tone. The speaker is angry and understandably resents empty patriotic slogans.

Then Hughes begins to channel the angry feelings into a kind of inspirational plea. As the speaker becomes more confident and urges the reader to take some kind of action, the tone of the poem shifts. In the final stanza of the poem, Hughes echoes the preamble to the Constitution, with its words "We the people." Also, line 84 brings to mind some of the lyrics of "God Bless America"—"From the mountains to the prairies"—and the reader cannot doubt that the patriotism has become genuine.

It is true that many negative aspects of American society are pointed out in Hughes's poem, so it can be difficult to think of it as communicating a positive message. However, when one examines another of Hughes's poems with a similar political message, one can see that "Let America Be America Again" is much more hopeful in comparison. In "Harlem" (available at http://www.poetryfoundation.org/poem/175

884), Hughes tackles many of the same issues as in "Let America Be America Again." Both poems mention dreams, referencing the ideal of the American dream. Both pose questions and point out that many Americans will never achieve their dreams. Also, both poems use italicized type to draw attention to certain lines. The italics in "Let America Be America Again" show a challenge to the speaker—another voice that demands to know why the speaker is saying such negative things about America. These lines appear fairly early in the poem and prompt a spirited response from the speaker. In "Harlem," however, the italics serve a very different purpose.

Where "Let America Be America Again" points out that America does not have true equality and that not everyone is free, "Harlem" seems to accept this as a given. "Harlem" begins with a question. If it is a fact that many Americans are oppressed, "Harlem" asks, what will be the result if that situation is allowed to continue? In a relatively short poem, most of the lines (nine of only eleven) offer possibilities of what might happen in the future if the current conditions persist. The images are all unpleasant—things drying out, crusting over, and rotting—but it is the final line that jars the reader. The last line of the poem, which is emphasized with italic type, suggests that there might be an explosion if nothing changes. It is this dramatic threat of violent consequences that makes "Harlem" so very different from "Let America Be America Again." The final words of "Let America Be America Again" are rousing and inspiring, ending in an exclamation point like a call to arms. However, Hughes is not calling for violence; he wants change, but he calls on the people to work hard to make change happen.

In "Let America Be America Again," Hughes is not afraid to examine the ugly side of American society, but with its words he tries not to threaten his readers or make them mourn for past mistakes. Instead, using simple, direct language and the basic tools of poetry, Hughes manages to inspire people to help make America truly great, with real freedom and opportunity for everyone.

Source: Kristen Sarlin Greenberg, Critical Essay on "Let America Be America Again," in *Poetry for Students*, Gale, Cengage Learning, 2014.

Langston Hughes

In the following essay, Hughes provides an example of the kind of treatment of African Americans that prompted him to write "Let America Be America Again."

September 29, 1962

I had thought that the custom on the part of whites of automatically equating Negroes with servants had died out in New York. Therefore, I was surprised to read recently in the public prints that the very charming Dr. Jane Wright of the cancer research staff at New York University Medical Center, when paying a social call, had been directed by the doorman of a fashionable apartment house to use the service elevator.

Dr. Wright is not only distinguished in her field, but beautiful as well and always handsomely gowned. Why any doorman would take her for a domestic is beyond me. But old customs die hard. She is brownskin. There was a time in Manhattan when many downtown apartment houses and hotels directed all Negroes to the service entrances.

ARE YOU DELIVERING SOMETHING?

I remember not too many years ago, togged in my best blue suit, I went to an ASCAP meeting at a big Times Square hotel. As a lyric writer, I have been a member of the American Society of Authors and Composers for many years. When I walked up to the elevators and asked the young woman starter where the ASCAP meeting was, she looked at me and inquired rather tartly, "Are you delivering something?" When I replied that I was not delivering anything, she told me where the meeting was and I went up without further incident.

But once upstairs, it occurred to me that since ASCAP has many members of color and some of them (like some of the white song writers) are of the rather tough and profane school of hard boiled old-time show business, such personalities might be inclined to make a scene were they asked brusquely, "Are you delivering something?"

For the sake of racial amity, I thought it wise to go back downstairs, find the manager's office, and report what had happened to me. I did. The manager was most courteous, but evasive, and offered no apology for his employee in charge of elevators. Instead, the manager informed me that they often had pimps, prostitutes, and other undesirable individuals to contend with, and that his staff could, if its members felt the need, inquire as to a person's business in the hotel.

I had already informed the manager that I was associated with ASCAP and by profession a writer. He proceeded to ask me if I had ever read Richard Wright's *Native Son*, and when I said, "Yes," he stated that he thought it a disgraceful book.

"You see the kind of people Richard Wright writes about," he said.

I replied that it seemed to me it was not the kind of people Wright wrote about, but how he wrote about them, that made his novel important. "But," I continued, "so far as I know, there are no Bigger Thomases in ASCAP. Even if there were, it would not be wise of your elevator starter to ask them on the afternoon of a meeting, 'Are you delivering something?'" I informed him that one of our Negro song writers once wrote a song called, "There'll Be Some Changes Made." With that I departed. I have since been in the same hotel many times. No such discourtesies occurred again.

CALL TO HOSTESS

Some years ago, before the Supreme Court decision affecting the public schools (I don't believe the court has as yet taken up the question of elevators) my aunt went to visit friends in a West End Avenue apartment house. The doorman informed her, "Servants use the service elevator." My aunt replied, "I don't doubt it," and walked into the lobby to enter the lift. The operator refused to take her up. She then asked him to get the manager. The manager came, but backed up his employee, again directing her (since she is colored) to the servant's car around the corner through the delivery entrance. My aunt had gone to the nearest telephone and called her hostess—who then came down to the lobby to meet her—before she could get upstairs. Her hostess was, of course, most apologetic for the ways of white folks.

At restaurants in New York and other cities about the country, I have noticed lately a subtle form of discrimination-with-a-smile that occurs too often to be coincidental. It is the custom on the part of polite and very gracious headwaiters or dining room hostesses to lead a Negro customer to the least desirable table.

I had occasion a few weeks ago to spend a couple of days in a charming New England inn. Each time I went into the dining room the same thing happened. A smiling young woman led me the first evening at dinner to a table right next to the bus boy's stand in an obscure corner.

In the Kansas City Union Station I was shown past dozens of empty tables to one hard by the kitchen. It even happened in Puerto Rico at a restaurant frequented by white vacationists. The table by the kitchen door. When I asked the headwaiter, who was as brown-skin as I am, if he could not do any better, he grinned and said, "I know what you are thinking. I used to live in New York."

I said, "Then you've had tables in the rear, too, when others are empty." He said, "Yes, I have. Come on, move up." This time he put me at the very front of the restaurant. After he took my order, he discussed the race problem. We decided it is hard to behave like Rev. Martin Luther King.

Source: Langston Hughes, "Old Customs Die Hard," in *Langston Hughes and the "Chicago Defender,"* edited by Christopher C. De Santis, University of Illinois Press, 1995, pp. 67–69.

R. Baxter Miller

In the following excerpt, Miller discusses Hughes as a lyric poet.

. . . Over nearly the last sixty years, during the need to reconsider his contribution to the genre, one has hardly dared think of Hughes in this way for both historical and social reasons. While the Greeks believed the lyric to be a communal performance in song, the shared epiphany between the singer and the audience, the form implied the aristocratic elitism at court during the Middle Ages and the Elizabethan period. In the romantic and Victorian eras, the genre suggested privacy and isolation from the masses. Today, with the genre somewhat diminished in favor of the dramatic monologue, as poetry has possibly ebbed into pedantry, those who prefer personal lyric often disclaim the social rhetoric of direct address. Indeed, one might almost take Langston Hughes at his word and accept the distinction between the forms. But while the margins between genres are convenient, they are yet flexible and partly illusory. Literary forms really mean only variations in degree.

Ironically, Black American history complicates the appreciation of Hughes as a lyricist. In a personal voice the poet revises the tradition he inherited. Where Phillis [*sic*] Wheatley praised George Washington, he honors the Black Everyman and, indeed, Everyperson. Though his contemporary Countee Cullen depended on sources in the poetry of John Keats, Hughes relied on allusions to the folk ballads of 1830–50, on the nature and prophetic poems of Walt Whitman, and on the more contemplative verse of Vachel Lindsay. Paul Laurence Dunbar had accommodated himself earlier to the Old South, but Hughes revised the pastoral for his times (though he was less naive about the folk integrity).

From *Weary Blues* in 1926 to his reprise of "Daybreak in Alabama" at the end of *The Panther and the Lash* in 1967, the lyric serves to open and close Hughes' literary life and work. Though other genres attract his attention, this one retains particular resilience. For him the lyric illuminates the graphic and timeless: "When I get to be a composer / I'm gonna write me some music about / Daybreak in Alabama" (*SP*, 157; *PL*; 101).

Against the backdrop of time, he invokes dynamic feeling in order to subordinate and control personal loneliness, but he never excludes the communal response to social history. In introspection, he plays down the narrative of miscegenation ("Cross," *Crisis*, 1925) and the allegorical tragedy ("Pierrot," *Weary Blues*, 1926) into precise understatement: "So I wept until the dawn / Dripped blood over the eastern hills" (*SP*, 66). Or, sometimes, he disguises the lyrics themselves as dramatic performances through the blues song and the jazz instrument:

> What can purge my heart
> Of the song
> And the sadness?
> What can purge my heart
> Of the sadness
> Of the song?
> ["Song for Billie Holiday," *SP*]

What one finds ultimately in the lyricist concerns the sensitive self who speaks to nature and the masses. In an epiphany the solo and the chorus face each other at the height of the performance, itself timeless through intensity and will. Eventually, we redescend from "The Negro Speaks of Rivers" (*Crisis*, 1921) or from "Oppression" (*Fields of Wonder*, 1947) to the fallen world. From the poetic re-creation of Black American history in particular and the American South in general, the narrator returns inevitably to certain death in Harlem, for sequential history is a fact.

For Langston Hughes the lyric highlights the human and social dream. Incarnated in the blues singer and player, it signifies the artistic performance in general:

> Beat the drums of tragedy for me,
> And let the white violins whir thin and slow,
> But blow one blaring trumpet note of sun
> To go with me
> to the darkness
> where I go.
> ["Fantasy in Purple," *SP*]

Lyric suggests the griot and the cultural priest, who recount the sacred story about experience and the past. From the history of 1855–65, the lyric records the poetic remembrance of the Civil War and of one poet, for instance, who wrote it down.

> Old Walt Whitman
> Went finding and seeking,
> Finding less than sought
> Seeking more than found,
> Every detail minding
> Of the seeking or the finding. [*SP*]

The speaker, almost indifferent to the historical context, neither mentions whom Whitman met or when, nor says why so. The narrator, excluding the death of Abraham Lincoln, overlooks the troubled circumstances. Still, what he manages involves a frozen moment in self- and human communion. . . .

Source: R. Baxter Miller, "'Deep like the Rivers': The Lyrical Imagination," in *The Art and Imagination of*

Langston Hughes, University Press of Kentucky, 1989, pp. 48–50.

Richard Wright

In the following essay, Wright explains that the title of his essay comes from Hughes's exemplary work both as an innovative poet and as a representative of the African American community.

The double role that Langston Hughes has played in the rise of a realistic literature among the Negro people resembles in one phase the role that Theodore Dreiser played in freeing American literary expression from the restrictions of Puritanism. Not that Negro literature was ever Puritanical, but it was timid and vaguely lyrical and folkish. Hughes's early poems, *The Weary Blues* and *Fine Clothes to the Jew*, full of irony and urban imagery, were greeted by a large section of the Negro reading public with suspicion and shock when they first appeared in the middle twenties. Since then the realistic position assumed by Hughes has become the dominant outlook of all those Negro writers who have something to say.

The other phase of Hughes's role has been, for the lack of a better term, that of a cultural ambassador. Performing his task quietly and almost casually, he has represented the Negros' case, in his poems, plays, short stories and novels, at the court of world opinion. On the other hand he has brought the experiences of other nations within the orbit of the Negro writer by his translations from the French, Russian and Spanish.

How Hughes became this forerunner and ambassador can best be understood in the cameo sequences of his own life that he gives us in his sixth and latest book, *The Big Sea*. Out of his experiences as a seaman, cook, laundry worker, farm helper, bus boy, doorman, unemployed worker, have come his writings dealing with black gals who wore red stockings and black men who sang the blues all night and slept like rocks all day.

Unlike the sons and daughters of Negro "society," Hughes was not ashamed of those of his race who had to scuffle for their bread. The jerky transitions of his own life did not admit of his remaining in one place long enough to become a slave of prevailing Negro middle-class prejudices. So beneficial does this ceaseless movement seem to Hughes that he has made it one of his life principles: six months in one place, he says, is long enough to make one's life complicated. The result has been a range of artistic interest and expression possessed by no other Negro writer of his time.

Born in Joplin, Missouri, in 1902, Hughes lived in half a dozen Mid-western towns until he entered high school in Cleveland, Ohio, where he began to write poetry. His father, succumbing to that fit of disgust which overtakes so many self-willed Negroes in the face of American restrictions, went off to Mexico to make money and proceeded to treat the Mexicans just as the whites in America had treated him. The father yearned to educate Hughes and establish him in business. His favorite phrase was "hurry up," and it irritated Hughes so much that he fled his father's home.

Later he entered Columbia University, only to find it dull. He got a job on a merchant ship, threw his books into the sea and sailed for Africa. But for all his work, he arrived home with only a monkey and a few dollars, much to his mother's bewilderment. Again he sailed, this time for Rotterdam, where he left the ship and made his way to Paris. After an interval of hunger he found a job as a doorman, then as second cook in a night club, which closed later because of bad business. He went to Italy to visit friends and had his passport stolen. Jobless in an alien land, he became a beachcomber until he found a ship on which he could work his way back to New York.

The poems he had written off and on had attracted the attention of some of his relatives in Washington and, at their invitation, he went to live with them. What Hughes has to say about Negro "society" in Washington, relatives and hunger are bitter poems in themselves. While living in Washington, he won his first poetry prize; shortly afterwards Carl Van Vechten submitted a batch of his poems to a publisher.

The rest of *The Big Sea* is literary history, most of it dealing with the Negro renaissance, that astonishing period of prolific productivity among Negro artists that coincided with America's "Golden age" of prosperity. Hughes writes of it with humor, urbanity and objectivity; one has the feeling that never for a moment was his sense of solidarity with those who had known hunger shaken by it. Even when a Park Avenue patron was having him driven about the streets of New York in her town car, he "felt bad because he could not share his new-found comfort with his mother and relatives." When the bubble burst in 1929, Hughes returned to the mood that seems to fit him best. He wrote of the opening of the Waldorf-Astoria: "Now,

won't that be charming when the last flop-house/has turned you down this winter?"

Hughes is tough; he bends but he never breaks, and he has carried on a manly tradition in literary expression when many of his fellow writers have gone to sleep at their posts.

Source: Richard Wright, "Forerunner and Ambassador," in *Critical Essays on Langston Hughes*, edited by Edward J. Mullen, G. K. Hall, 1986, pp. 67–68.

SOURCES

Canedo, Eduardo F., "Strikes," in *Encyclopedia of the Great Depression*, edited by Robert S. McElvaine, Vol. 2, Macmillan Reference USA, 2004, pp. 941–47.

Du Bois, W. E. B., "Criteria of Negro Art," in *The New Negro: Readings on Race, Representation, and African American Culture, 1892–1938*, edited by Henry Louis Gates Jr. and Gene Andrew Jarrett, Princeton University Press, 2007, p. 257.

"Great Migration," in *UXL Encyclopedia of U. S. History*, edited by Sonia Benson, Daniel E. Brannen Jr., and Rebecca Valentine, Vol. 3, Gale, Cengage Learning, 2009, pp. 658–59.

Hughes, Langston, "Let America Be America Again," in *Poems*, edited by David Roessel, Alfred A. Knopf, 1999, pp. 97–100.

"Labor Force Statistics from the Current Population Survey," Bureau of Labor Statistics website, http://www.bls.gov/cps/ (accessed March 22, 2013).

"Langston Hughes," Poets.org, http://www.poets.org/poet.php/prmPID/83 (accessed March 22, 2013).

"Langston Hughes," in *St. James Encyclopedia of Popular Culture*, edited by Tom Pendergast and Sara Pendergast, St. James Press, 2000.

"Langston Hughes: Biography," Biography.com, http://www.biography.com/people/langston-hughes-9346313?page=1 (accessed March 22, 2013).

"Langston Hughes: 1902–1967," Poetry Foundation website, http://www.poetryfoundation.org/bio/langston-hughes (accessed March 22, 2013).

Lewis, David Levering, "Harlem Renaissance," in *Encyclopedia of African-American Culture and History: The Black Experience in the Americas*, 2nd ed., edited by Colin A. Palmer, Vol. 3, Macmillan Reference USA, 2006, pp. 998–1018.

Meltzer, Milton, "Harlem Poet," in *Cobblestone*, Vol. 32, No. 6, July–August 2011, p. 29.

Mertz, Paul E., "Sharecroppers," in *Encyclopedia of the Great Depression*, edited by Robert S. McElvaine, Vol. 2, Macmillan Reference USA, 2004, pp. 877–80.

Powell, Richard J., "The Harlem Renaissance," in *Africana: The Encyclopedia of the African and African

American Experience, 2nd ed., edited by Kwame Anthony Appiah and Henry Louis Gates Jr., Oxford University Press, 2005.

Rampersad, Arnold, *The Life of Langston Hughes*, Vol. 2, *1914–1967: I Dream a World*, Oxford University Press, 1988, p. 400.

———, "W. E. B. Du Bois as a Man of Literature," in *W. E. B. Du Bois*, edited by Harold Bloom, Chelsea House, 2001, p. 75.

Review of *The Collected Poems of Langston Hughes*, in *American Heritage*, Vol. 46, No. 1, February–March 1995, p. 106.

Review of *The Collected Poems of Langston Hughes*, in *Publishers Weekly*, Vol. 241, No. 44, October 31, 1994, p. 54.

Rochman, Hazel, Review of *The Dream Keeper and Other Poems*, in *Booklist*, Vol. 90, No. 14, March 15, 1994, p. 1346.

Seaman, Donna, Review of *The Collected Poems of Langston Hughes*, in *Booklist*, Vol. 91, No. 3, October 1, 1994, p. 186.

Szostak, Rick, "Great Depression," in *Dictionary of American History*, 3rd ed., edited by Stanley I. Kutler, Vol. 4, Charles Scribner's Sons, 2003, pp. 44–49.

"Unions," in *International Encyclopedia of the Social Sciences*, 2nd ed., edited by William A. Darity Jr., Vol. 8, Macmillan Reference USA, 2008, pp. 513–17.

FURTHER READING

Bernard, Emily, ed., *Remember Me to Harlem: The Letters of Langston Hughes and Carl Van Vechten, 1925–1964*, Alfred A. Knopf, 2001.

> Van Vechten helped Hughes get his first poetry collection published in 1926. This volume collects their correspondence over four decades, creating an intimate, fascinating portrait of a lifelong friendship.

Feinstein, Stephen, *The 1920s: From Prohibition to Charles Lindbergh*, rev. ed., Enslow, 2006.

> This volume provides an overview of important social changes and historical events that led up to the Harlem Renaissance, with numerous photos and other illustrations included.

Hughes, Langston, *The Collected Poems of Langston Hughes*, edited by Arnold Rampersad and David Roessel,

Vintage Classics, 2008.

> This collection includes all of Hughes's poetry in one volume, showing the breadth and depth of his work and his development as a poet.

Hurston, Zora Neale, *The Complete Stories*, HarperCollins, 1995.

> This collection includes all of the short stories written by Hurston, a prominent figure in the Harlem Renaissance, over the course of more than thirty years. Hurston's stories address themes of social inequality for women and African Americans.

McKay, Claude, *Complete Poems*, edited by William J. Maxwell, University of Illinois Press, 2004.

> Born in Jamaica in 1889, McKay composed his early poems in Jamaican creole. He later moved to New York and became an influential figure in the Harlem Renaissance. This volume collects more than three hundred of McKay's poems, including almost a hundred never before published.

Powell, Richard J., and David A. Bailey, eds., *Rhapsodies in Black: Art of the Harlem Renaissance*, University of California Press, 1997.

> Rather than compiling an overview of the Harlem Renaissance, Powell and Bailey have gathered essays and illustrations into a controversial collection that investigates the nature of distinctly African American art. The work of actors and singers are represented in addition to the work of visual artists.

SUGGESTED SEARCH TERMS

Langston Hughes AND poetry

Langston Hughes AND Chicago Defender

Langston Hughes AND communism

Langston Hughes AND Carl Van Vechten

Harlem Renaissance AND history

Harlem Renaissance AND poetry

Harlem Renaissance AND white patronage

Great Depression

Meeting at Night

ROBERT BROWNING

1845

"Meeting at Night" is a brief lyric poem written by Victorian author Robert Browning. It is not known when the poem was written, but it was first published in 1845 in the author's collection *Dramatic Romances and Lyrics*. Originally, the poem was paired with a companion piece titled "Parting at Morning." The two poems originally appeared under the title "Night and Morning," with "Meeting at Night" subtitled "I.—Night." Later Browning separated the two poems and gave each a separate title.

Dramatic Romances and Lyrics was the seventh in a series of self-published collections Browning issued under the umbrella title *Bells and Pomegranates*. These volumes, however, were little more than pamphlets, a mode of publication Browning probably adopted so that they would be inexpensive and therefore perhaps reach a larger audience. As it happened, they did not sell very well; it was only after the 1849 publication of his *Collected Poems*, which includes *Bells and Pomegranates*, that Browning's reputation began to grow. Today, Browning is regarded as one of the three preeminent mainstream Victorian poets, alongside Alfred Lord Tennyson and Matthew Arnold, and many of his poems are regarded as classics of English literature.

"Meeting at Night" can be found in the fourth volume of *The Poetical Works of Robert Browning*, edited by Ian Jack, Rowena Fowler, and Margaret Smith and published by Oxford University Press in 1991.

Robert Browning

AUTHOR BIOGRAPHY

Robert Browning was born on May 7, 1812, in Camberwell, a suburb of London, England. He was the firstborn child of Robert Browning and Sarah Anna Wiedemann Browning, an accomplished pianist. The elder Robert angered the poet's grandfather by abandoning the West Indies sugar plantation he had been sent to oversee because he found the plantation's use of slaves abhorrent. He returned to England, took a job as a clerk with the Bank of England, raised his family, and, in time, amassed a personal library of six thousand volumes. In this way, he was able to provide the younger Robert with a broad, if unorganized, education at home. Browning was barred from the universities at Oxford and Cambridge because his parents, as staunch Evangelical Christians, did not adhere to the tenets of the Church of England, a requirement for admission to the universities. Accordingly, he enrolled at the newly formed University of London in 1828, but he soon withdrew, preferring to pursue his own course of studies in his father's library.

Browning's first published work, *Pauline: A Fragment of a Confession* (1833), was followed by *Paracelsus* (1835), which received some positive reviews, and *Sordello* (1840), which was a critical failure, largely because of its obscurity. In the 1830s and 1840s, Browning devoted much of his energy to verse drama, producing *Strafford* (1837), *Pippa Passes* (1841), and *King Victor and King Charles* (1842), among other plays. He discovered, however, that his real talent lay with the dramatic monologue, a type of poem that creates a speaker who reveals something about his character when he is caught unawares in a moment of time. Thus, in the third volume of *Bells and Pomegranates* (1842), titled *Dramatic Lyrics*, he published some of his most famous early dramatic monologues, including "My Last Duchess" and "Soliloquy of the Spanish Cloister." This volume also includes his retelling of a classic legend, "The Pied Piper of Hamelin."

More plays followed, including *The Blot on the 'Scutcheon* (1845), along with further volumes of verse, among them the seventh volume of *Bells and Pomegranates*, in which "Meeting a Night" appears (along with the highly regarded dramatic monologue "The Bishop Orders His Tomb at St. Praxed's Church"). Later collections of poetry include *Men and Women* (1855), which includes some of his most famous dramatic monologues (such as "Fra Lippo Lippi," "Childe Roland to the Dark Tower Came," "Andrea del Sarto," "Cleon," and "Bishop Blougram's Apology"), and *Dramatis Personae* (1864), which includes the well-known poems "Rabbi ben Ezra" and "Caliban upon Setebos." With this last collection, following hard on the heels of an 1863 collected edition of his poems, Browning began to win more widespread critical acclaim and to be mentioned in the same sentence as Tennyson as a major Victorian poet. He won further acclaim with what many scholars regard as his major work, *The Ring and the Book* (1868–69), a massive narrative poem that tells the story of a notorious trial that took place in Rome in 1698, after an impoverished nobleman was accused of murdering his young wife and her parents. Browning had an abiding interest in Italy, and a number of his poems are set in the Italian Renaissance. This interest spilled over into his personal life. In 1834, he visited Italy for the first time.

In 1844, the poet Elizabeth Barrett published a collection of poems; one poem contained an admiring reference to Browning, prompting him to write her a letter that launched a passionate two-year literary romance and courtship conducted primarily through letters. Elizabeth was an invalid who lived under the thumb of a domineering father, so in September 1846, she and Browning married in secret. A few days later, they departed for Italy, where they lived for the next fifteen years, briefly in Pisa and then in Florence. During her lifetime, Elizabeth was a more popular poet than her husband; she was even nominated for the post of Poet Laureate of England. Her reputation rested primarily on *Sonnets from the Portuguese* (1850), a collection of love poems dedicated to her husband. ("The Portuguese" was a nickname Browning gave her based on an earlier work of hers that depicted a Portuguese woman's love for a poet and on the fact that she had Creole blood in her heritage.) Elizabeth's death in 1861 won sympathy for her husband and in its own way helped boost his reputation.

After the publication of *The Ring and the Book*, Browning continued to write and publish for two decades, although many of his later volumes, including *Prince Hohenstiel-Schwangau* (1871), *Fifine at the Fair* (1872), *Dramatic Idylls* (1879), and others, lack the appeal of much of his earlier work. He traveled extensively, and he is reputed to have turned down an offer of marriage from one Louisa, Lady Ashburton, a wealthy heiress.

Browning's final collection, *Asolando*, was published on December 12, 1889, the day of the poet's death from unspecified causes. He died at Ca' Rezzonico, a palazzo on the Grand Canal in Venice, Italy, which, at that time, was the home of his only child, the painter Robert Barrett Browning. He is buried in Poets' Corner in London's Westminster Abbey, adjacent to the tomb of his contemporary, Tennyson.

POEM TEXT

I.

> The grey sea and the long black land;
> And the yellow half-moon large and low;
> And the startled little waves that leap
> In fiery ringlets from their sleep,
> As I gain the cove with pushing prow,   5
> And quench its speed i' the slushy sand.

II.

> Then a mile of warm sea-scented beach;
> Three fields to cross till a farm appears;
> A tap at the pane, the quick sharp scratch
> And blue spurt of a lighted match,   10
> And a voice less loud, thro' its joys and fears,
> Than the two hearts beating each to each!

MEDIA ADAPTATIONS

- A number of Browning poems, including "Meeting at Night," are read by Douglas Hodge, David Horovitch, Derek Jacobi, Jeremy Northam, Diana Quick, Prunella Scales, and other actors on *Robert Browning: Poems*, released as an audiobook by HighBridge Classics in 2006.

- Several YouTube renditions of "Meeting at Night" have been produced. A modern video version of the poem is available on YouTube at http://www.youtube.com/watch?v=zV87F2_EoBE. The video, uploaded in 2008, runs just over a minute.

POEM SUMMARY

The text used for this summary is from *The Poetical Works of Robert Browning*, Vol. 4, *Bells and Pomegranates*, edited by Ian Jack, Rowena Fowler, and Margaret Smith, Vol. 4, Oxford University Press, 1991, p. 149. A version of the poem can be found at the following web page: http://www.poetryfoundation.org/poem/173022.

"Meeting at Night" is divided into two six-line stanzas. In the first stanza, the speaker describes his surroundings, including the gray sea, the black land, and a large yellow half-moon that is low in the sky. He takes note of the small waves in the water that appear to be leaping in fiery circles from their sleep. It becomes apparent that the speaker is in a boat, for he notes that he arrives in a cove, slowing his progress by pushing the prow of his boat into the wet sand.

In the second stanza, the speaker makes his way over land. First he has to traverse a mile of warm beach that smells like the sea. He then crosses three fields to arrive at a farm. There, he taps on a windowpane and then hears the sharp sound of a match being scraped. He sees the blue flame of the lighted match. Finally, the

TOPICS FOR FURTHER STUDY

- Browning and one of the other major poets of the Victorian period, Tennyson, are interred adjacent to one another in Poets' Corner in London's Westminster Abbey. Imagine that one night the ghosts of the two authors materialize and have a conversation about love, poetry, literary fame, or any other topic that interests you. With a willing partner, recreate for your classmates the dialogue you imagine.

- Conduct Internet research to locate photos and other images of Florence, Italy, during the time the Brownings lived there; also search for photos and images from the time when Browning lived in Venice. Assemble a visual tour of Browning's life in Italy for your classmates using a tool such as Flickr or Jing.com.

- The romance between Browning and Elizabeth Barrett has spawned a number of media treatments. *The Barretts of Wimpole Street* is the title of a 1930 play by Rudolf Besier, which eventually became a Broadway production. In 1934, a film version of *The Barretts of Wimpole Street* was produced; a remake of the film was produced in 1957. In 1964, a musical, *Robert and Elizabeth*, opened in London, and in 1982, the BBC in England aired a television series titled *The Barretts of Wimpole Street*. Locate any one of these treatments in print or on film. Prepare an oral report for your classmates on how the relationship between the Brownings is depicted.

- The Browning Society is an organization that promotes the study of Robert and Elizabeth Barrett Browning. Conduct research on the history of the society and its various branches throughout the world. What sorts of activities does it sponsor? What are its goals? Prepare a time line on the Browning Society, and share it with your classmates.

- Locate a copy of Gary Soto's *Partly Cloudy: Poems about Love and Longing* (Houghton Mifflin, 2009). Select from this collection that explores first love one or more poems that you think capture the same emotions as those found in "Meeting at Night." Write a brief report in which you compare Browning's poem with the poem by Soto you have selected.

- If you have musical talent and interest in a love lyric from another cultural tradition, locate a copy of the sheet music for "By the Waters of Minnetonka: An Indian Love Song," written by Thurlow Lieurance and J. M. Cavanass and available from Occidental Graphics (2011). Perform the piece for your classmates, perhaps with another student, one of you playing the piano, the other singing the lyrics.

- Ai (which means "love" in Japanese) is the name of an African American poet who was born Florence Anthony. Ai's poems are typically written in the form of dramatic monologues that have been compared with the poems of Browning—although critics note that they have a raw twentieth-century American sensibility. Locate a collection of Ai's poetry. Perform an oral reading of one or more of the poems for your classmates and invite them to comment on any similarities or differences they see with Browning's poetry.

speaker hears a low voice, one marked with joy but also fear. The voice, he says, is less loud than the beating of his heart in conjunction with that of the woman he has met. The two characters embrace.

THEMES

Love

"Meeting at Night" is a love poem. The use of the word *meeting* in the title hints that

The narrator quietly beaches his boat before crossing farm fields in the darkness. (© *Rick S | Shutterstock.com*)

the poem is about a rendezvous between two people. The man has traveled to meet a woman at her farmhouse, perhaps to keep a prearranged appointment. She appears to have been expecting his arrival, for rather than being startled by his tap on the windowpane in the dark, she responds by lighting a match, which lends an air of secrecy to the meeting. The final line of the poem, which indicates that their hearts beat loudly in unison as they embrace, makes clear that the speaker has arrived at the home of the woman he loves. The poem does not make clear who the people are and why they are meeting at night, seemingly in secret. A reader could imagine them as husband and wife and conclude that the husband has arrived home when he could. It seems more likely, however, that Browning wants the reader to imagine two lovers meeting in secret, perhaps because they have to keep their relationship hidden for some reason. The poem does not resolve these uncertainties. Rather, it invites the reader to participate in the construction of the poem by imagining the circumstances surrounding the meeting.

Travel

One characteristic of much of Browning's poetry is that it captures characters at a moment in time. The reader is given little if any information about the character's past and is left to speculate about the character's future. In this poem, the character has arrived at the farmhouse of the woman he loves after a voyage by boat. The reader learns in the first stanza that the speaker is traveling by water, with help from the light of a half-moon. The speaker then arrives on the shore and pushes his boat into the wet sand before traveling on foot across the beach, then across three farm fields. His reference to a mile of beach suggests that the tide is very low so that the distance from the edge of the water to the far edge of the beach is great. The poem does not specify a location, but in some places along the coast of Great Britain, the difference in water level between high and low tide can as much as thirty-five to forty feet or more, meaning that a very wide expanse of beach can be exposed at low tide.

Further, the reader does not know anything about why the speaker has to travel by boat or whether the boat is one that he sails or has to row. The reader is invited to speculate that the speaker has traveled a great distance, perhaps from the European continent. Perhaps the speaker is a soldier coming home on leave. The poem raises the question of whether the man is brave in making such a perilous journey in a small boat at night, or whether he is foolish. Perhaps he and the woman he loves have to meet clandestinely because their relationship is opposed by family (much as Elizabeth Barrett Browning's father opposed any relationship in her life). The reader could speculate that one or both of the parties is married to someone else. None of these questions is answered by the poem, but the journey motif invites the reader to imagine the circumstances surrounding the meeting and to take part in the sheer physical difficulty of traveling under such circumstances, along with the determination the speaker exhibits in reaching his destination.

Nature

The poem sketches in a picture of the natural environment in which the action takes place. The reader is told that the sea is grey. The moon is half full, casting some light on the scene. The light from the moon glances off the tiny waves in the water, making the waves sparkle and seem to leap as if waking up from sleep. The speaker then makes landfall, having to push the prow of his boat into slushy sand. Now the speaker has to cross a vast open beach, seemingly at low tide. The reader is invited to imagine the speaker seeing foam, seaweed, driftwood, and other flotsam and jetsam, although the poem does not comment on this, other than to note that the beach is scented by the sea. The speaker then has to cross three farm fields; again, the poem invites the reader to imagine these low, flat fields, perhaps with soil that is sandy because of its proximity to the sea. Finally, the speaker arrives at the farmhouse where the woman he is meeting is waiting for him.

STYLE

Stanza

"Meeting at Night" is written in two six-line stanzas. Often the term *sestet* is used to refer to such a stanza, although traditionally this term has been reserved for the six-line division of a Petrarchan sonnet. (The first eight lines, the octave, of such a sonnet raise an issue, problem, or question, which the sestet answers or comments on.) For reasons unknown, Browning numbered each of the

stanzas, so they are numbered I and II. The numbering of the stanzas in such a short poem suggests that Browning might have seen the action of the poem in dramatic terms, almost as though the first stanza is "Act I" of a play and the second stanza is "Act II." During the 1840s, Browning devoted considerable effort to writing verse dramas, so perhaps, in his imagination, the "meeting at night" he depicts is a type of dramatic action. In "Act I," the speaker takes his journey over water and makes landfall. In "Act II," he arrives at the farmhouse where the woman he loves awaits him. Thus, the first "act" of the poem sets up a conflict between the speaker and the obstacles he faces, while the second "act" resolves the conflict by showing him attaining his goal.

Rhyme Scheme

Over the centuries, various poets have imposed an assortment of rhyme schemes on sestets, and numerous types of sestets have been specified: the Spanish (*aabccb*), the Wordsworth (*abbcac*), the Italian (*abcabc*), the English (*ababcc*), and others. The rhyme scheme of "Meeting at Night" is unique among poems written in the form of sestets, for the rhyme scheme in each stanza is *abccba*. The interesting feature of Browning's rhyme scheme is that it is imitative. Just as the reader can imagine the tide flowing and then ebbing, or imagine the water breaking and receding as waves flow, the rhyme scheme of this poem "flows" (*ab*), peaks at the center of the stanza (*cc*), and then reverses itself (*ba*). The rhyme scheme, then, seems appropriate to the movement of the poem.

This sense of ebbing and flowing, of movement, is reinforced by the meter of the poem. The first line consists of eight syllables, the second line of nine. The next two lines reverse the pattern; line 3 is nine syllables, line 4 is eight. The final two lines of the stanza each have nine syllables. This pattern is repeated in the second stanza. The varied line length again conveys a sense of ebb and flow, or motion forward and backward on the water.

Alliteration

"Meeting at Night" relies for its poetic effect on extensive use of alliteration, that is, the repetition of consonant sounds, usually at the beginnings of words. The first three lines of the poem rely on repeated *l* sounds: *long/land/large/low/little/leap*. These liquid *l* sounds have the effect of slowing the pace of the poem and mirroring

COMPARE
&
CONTRAST

- **1845:** A clandestine meeting at night between a man and a woman is considered shocking and is strongly discouraged by people concerned about respectability; a woman, in particular, might be socially ostracized for entertaining a man under these circumstances.

  Today: Meetings at night between men and women who have reached some level of maturity are not necessarily stigmatized as inappropriate, although they might still invite curiosity and comment.

- **1845:** Travel is slow and difficult. A man trying to meet with a girlfriend or wife from whom he is parted might have to struggle over water, beaches, farm fields, or similar obstacles in the landscape, or down unpaved roads, to meet her.

  Today: Travel is much more convenient; people in a long-distance relationship can meet after traveling by car, motorized public transportation, or plane, and they can stay in touch with each other by cell phone and texting.

- **1845:** Boats are not motorized; a boat manned by one person would be a rowboat or a small sailing boat.

  Today: While people continue to make use of nonmotorized watercraft such as rowboats, canoes, and small sailing vessels, many small boats manned by one person have motors.

- **1845:** Because people do not have electricity, light is provided primarily by oil lamps and candles lit by friction matches, at the time called "lucifers." These matches were made with white phosphorous, sulfur, and other substances that were smelly and potentially dangerous.

  Today: People meeting at night enjoy the convenience of modern electrical lighting, even if only with battery-powered flashlights, although candles are still often used to create a romantic or mysterious atmosphere.

the pace of the waves. The pace picks up as the speaker reaches shore, and the alliterative effects of *pushing/prow* and *sleep/speed/slushy/sand* convey the vigorous effect of the speaker's actions as he beaches the boat. That sense of vigor and masculine movement continues in the alliterative effects of the second stanza, particularly with the alliteration of *sharp/scratch/spurt*—which has the added effect of linking the second stanza with the first, where similar alliteration is used.

HISTORICAL CONTEXT

Courtship in Victorian Times
The scene depicted in "Meeting at Night" could have been considered shocking by Victorian readers for its implication that a man and a woman are having a clandestine meeting, unchaperoned, at night, although there is no reason to believe that the poem does not depict a husband coming home to his wife. This sense of shock would have been intensified by a reading of the companion poem, "Parting at Morning," which suggests that the man and woman had an overnight liaison, that the man left the next morning to return to the world of men, and that the woman, in the language of the time, was "ruined" or "fallen." Browning treated this theme in his play *A Blot on the 'Scutcheon*, which was published in the same year as "Meeting at Night." The play tells the story of a young woman of noble birth who is ostracized for receiving a lover in her chamber on multiple occasions. Browning denied that his intention in the pair of poems was to depict an illicit relationship; his intention, he said, was to show how fleeting the rapture of love can be. Love

can appear to be enduring and self-sufficient, but ultimately men are called back to the world.

During the Victorian era, relationships between men and women were tightly regulated, particularly among women and among the respectable middle class. In general, men and women did not date as the term is understood in the modern era. Meetings between potential partners were supervised, and a woman was generally not permitted to be alone with a man until the couple was engaged to be married. She would never be allowed to accompany a man anywhere unless she had the permission of a parent—and indeed, when a man called on a woman he wanted to court, the pretense was generally maintained that he was calling on the mother, who then might summon her marriageable daughter to appear if she thought the man had potential as a suitable husband. A young woman would never be caught out late with a man, and a man would violate standards of propriety by staying late at a woman's home. When a gentleman left a woman's home, she accompanied him only as far as the parlor door, allowing a servant or parent to show the man out. Kissing on the doorstep would be scandalous and entirely out of the question.

Men and women typically met at family gatherings, holiday dances and balls, or church socials. A woman would never speak to a man until she had been properly introduced to him, preferably by a relative or close friend. At a ball, a gentleman might dance with a woman to whom he had been introduced, but this did not grant him license to speak to her at another time or place. If the man wanted to pursue a relationship with her, he would offer hints to a friend or relative of the woman, who then would arrange for them to meet—always under the watchful eye of a chaperone, preferably a mother or close female relative.

In general, flirting was discouraged, and it would be considered immoral for a woman to encourage a man by flirting with him. However, certain types of flirting behaviors were accepted, particularly those carried out through the use of a fan, gloves, or parasol. A woman was able to send specific messages to a man using her fan, for example. In his novel *Contarini Fleming: A Psychological Romance* (1845), Benjamin Disraeli described this phenomenon. A woman could express interest, or lack of interest, simply by the way she handled her fan:

The fan is the most wonderful part of the whole scene.... Now she unfurls it with the slow pomp and conscious elegance of the bird of Juno; now she flutters it with all the languor of a listless beauty, now with all the liveliness of a vivacious one. Now, in the midst of a very tornado, she closes it with a whirr, which makes you start. In the midst of your confusion [she] taps you on your elbow; you turn round to listen.... Magical instrument! In this land it speaks a particular language, and gallantry requires no other mode to express its most subtle conceits or its most unreasonable demands than this delicate machine.

The use of calling cards was common. Once a couple was properly introduced, a man could offer his card to the woman as a first step in furthering the acquaintance. A woman could accept the man's offer, perhaps one of several such offers, by presenting him with her own calling card. If circumstances allowed the two to walk together, it was acceptable for the man to offer the woman his arm to help her over troublesome spots, but otherwise the two were not to touch. Once the relationship progressed and marriage was contemplated, it was commonplace for the man and woman to exchange love letters. Often, the woman kept a diary that chronicled the relationship. The couple would also exchange such objects as antique coins, lockets, poems, drawings, and locks of hair. These artifacts posed peril for the man, for they could be used as evidence at a trial for breach of promise should the man appear to have led the woman on only to back out of the relationship. A woman who backed out of an engagement was often stigmatized as a jilt unless it emerged that the man was unsuitable.

Women who violated these conventions ran the risk of ruining their reputations. Their chances of making a good marriage were severely reduced, and they faced the prospect of becoming "spinsters" or "old maids," living off the charity of relatives. Men, on the other hand, were regarded as more worldly and as less able to govern their sexual impulses. For this reason, a maddening double standard existed: a man could carry on an improper liaison with a woman and suffer few if any social consequences, but the woman would face social ruin. In this environment, a reader of "Meeting at Night" would likely find the poem almost risqué for its hints at conduct that was generally regarded as improper, if not immoral.

The half-moon provides some light by which the speaker can navigate. (© Boida Anatolii / Shutterstock.com)

CRITICAL OVERVIEW

Browning, in 1845, was not yet regarded as a major British poet, a fact acknowledged in an unsigned review of his work to that date ("The Problem of Obscurity") in *The English Review*:

> Mr. Browning unites within himself more of the elements of a true poet than perhaps any other of those whom we call "modern" amongst us; yet there are few writers so little read, so partially understood.

Browning's work, however, was already attracting some favorable notices from critics. In a review of *Dramatic Romances and Lyrics*, for example, a contributor to the *Examiner* writes that his work "has always the stamp and freshness of originality. It is in no respect imitative or commonplace. Whatever the verse may be, the man is in it: the music of it echoing to his mood." The reviewer continues:

> When he succeeds, there have been few so successful in the melodious transitions of his rhythm. In

all its most poetical and most musical varieties, he is a master; and to us it expresses, in a rare and exquisite degree, the delicacy and truth of his genius.

A contributor to the *Athenaeum*, in a review of the same volume, also calls attention to Browning's metrical skill:

> Mr. Browning is never ignoble: pushing versification to the extremity of all rational allowances, and sometimes beyond it, with a hardihood of rhythm and cadence.... he is rarely careless. His aims are truth and freedom.

Despite this praise, reviewers acknowledge what they regarded as faults. An anonymous article ("A Neglected Poet") in *Critic* opens in this way: "Robert Browning has faults—great and obvious faults, which obscure his many beauties to all eyes, not resolutely bent upon piercing the veil which he has himself thrown over his genius." Contradicting the *Athenaeum* reviewer cited earlier, the reviewer for *Critic* writes: "He is a singularly careless writer." Further, the contributor to the *English Review* makes reference to what he regarded as the poet's "occasional obscurity," calling his shorter poems "strenuous nervous work" that relies on "strange words." He adds that "ingenuity of rhymes is carried to an extreme."

In a later review of Browning's *Bells and Pomegranates*, author James Russell Lowell praised the author's work, writing that "these are works of art in the truest sense." Lowell compares them to "pure statues, in which every thing [sic] superfluous has been sternly chiseled away." Lowell also remarks that "his men and woman *are* men and women, and not Mr. Browning masquerading in different-colored dominos. We implied as much when we said that he was an artist." Finally, an anonymous reviewer for *Sharpe's London Magazine* lauds the author by writing: "We recognise in him a genius which soars above all the trammels of conventionalism."

CRITICISM

Michael J. O'Neal

O'Neal holds a PhD in English. In the following essay, he examines images of movement and energy in "Meeting at Night."

One of the first features the reader may notice about "Meeting at Night" is that the poem consists

WHAT DO I READ NEXT?

- "Parting at Morning" (1845) is a companion poem to "Meeting at Night." The two poems were originally published as a single piece, each with its own subtitle. Browning later severed them and gave each its own title. The poem is available in volume 4 of *The Poetical Works of Robert Browning*, edited by Ian Jack, Rowena Fowler, and Margaret Smith (Oxford University Press, 1991).

- One of Browning's most admired love poems is "Two in the Campagna," published in his 1855 collection *Men and Women*. A modern edition of *Men and Women* was published by the Orion Group in 1993.

- Another well-known love lyric by Browning is "Love among the Ruins," also published in his 1855 collection *Men and Women*. A modern edition of *Men and Women* was published by the Orion Group in 1993.

- Elizabeth Barrett Browning's sonnet 43 from *Sonnets from the Portuguese* contains the well-known line "How do I love thee? Let me count the ways." The sonnets are available in an edition published by St. Martin's Press in 2007.

- Christina Rossetti was a poet of some standing during the Victorian age. Her love poem "A Birthday," about a man who comes to her, was published in her 1862 collection *Goblin Market and Other Poems* and is available in *Christina Rossetti: The Complete Poems* (Penguin, 2001).

- Michael Mason's *The Making of Victorian Sexual Attitudes* (Oxford University Press, 1996) examines the cultural underpinnings of Victorian attitudes to relationships between the sexes.

- For another take on relationships between the sexes during the Victorian age, see Jennifer Phegley's *Courtship and Marriage in Victorian England* (Praeger, 2011). The book uses conduct books, letter-writing manuals, domestic guidebooks, periodical articles, letters, and novels to examine the age's dating and marriage conventions among the working, middle, and upper classes.

- As the title suggests, *Crush: Love Poems* (Word of Mouth Books, 2007) is a collection of love poetry. Assembled and written by NAACP Image Award nominee Kwame Alexander, the volume, for young adults, includes poems by Alexander and other poets, including the title poem, "Crush," by Naomi Shihab Nye.

- Although this book dates back many years, *American Indian Love Lyrics and Other Verse: From the Songs of the North American Indians*, edited by Nellie Barnes (Macmillan, 1925) remains a valuable source for love poems/ songs from the Native American tradition.

- In 1845, the year of the first publication of "Meeting at Night," American author Edgar Allan Poe first published his famous poem "The Raven" (*The Complete Poetry of Edgar Allan Poe*, Signet, 2008). The poem is about the speaker's loss of his lover, Lenore. The complicated meter and rhythm of the poem are borrowed from Elizabeth Barrett's 1844 poem "Lady Geraldine's Courtship."

- A love poem that bears similarities to "Meeting at Night" is "Night, Dim Night" by African American poet Paul Laurence Dunbar. It is available in *The Collected Poetry of Paul Laurence Dunbar*, published by University of Virginia Press in 1993 and edited by Joanne M. Braxton.

of two sentences, each one corresponding to one of the poem's two stanzas. Secondly, neither of these sentences has a main verb: Both are incomplete sentences that comprise a sequence of perceptions. A third characteristic is that the speaker records these perceptions in a rapid, brisk way. He does not linger over any of them. He notes, for instance, the color of the sea (grey), the land (black), and the moon (yellow). He records the fact that the half-moon is large and low. He moves on to the small waves in the sea that appear to be leaping in small circles. He arrives at the cove and the slushy sand before setting out across the beach and fields to arrive at the farmhouse where he keeps his appointment with the woman he meets.

The effect of this reliance on a sequence of images contained within noun phrases rather than on complete sentences is to reinforce the forward movement of the poem. The speaker is singularly intent on his goal. He moves toward it with buoyancy and assurance. His perceptions are vivid, but they are incidental to his purpose, so he takes them up in succession, then casts them aside as he impatiently covers the terrain that separates him from the woman he longs to meet.

Other features of the poem, including alliteration and imagery, contribute to this sense of forward movement and masculine energy. "Meeting at Night," in just twelve lines, is a highly alliterative poem. The repeated *l* sound in the first three lines creates something of a languorous atmosphere as the reader imagines the speaker struggling with the boat, trying to make his way across the water while fighting against the ebb tide. (The speaker has to cross a mile of beach, so the tide clearly has been going out.)

Beginning with line 3, however, the sounds of the poem take on a more assertive, energetic quality. The waves are said to be *startled*, a word that contrasts sharply with the languor that has preceded it, as does the word *leap*, a word that in turn works well with its rhyming word, *sleep*, emphasizing the stark contrast between the speaker's state of mind and the dim, placid nature of his surroundings. The ringlets of the waves are said to

be *fiery*, a word that echoes the striking of the match in the next stanza and that contrasts with the grey and the black of the first line. The speaker then is said to *gain* the cove—the verb suggesting the speaker's positive forward movement and the achievement of a goal—and can quench the speed of the boat only by pushing its prow into the slushy sand. The image suggested by *quench* is one of thirst; along with the image of fire, it becomes a projection of the speaker's ardor and single-mindedness as he surmounts all obstacles to achieve his goal.

The vibrant alliterative effects of these lines add to the atmosphere of movement, energy, and the attainment of a purpose. The stanza is not pensive, vague, or wistful. Despite its pictorial qualities, it is not a still-life. Nor does the first sestet of the poem set up an atmosphere of nocturnal forgetfulness, preoccupation, or dreaminess. The poem is set at night, but the imagery is purposeful, masculine, and forward moving.

The sense of movement and energy continues in the second stanza. Once again, the stanza does not contain any complete sentences but instead relies on a sequence of noun phrases. The speaker hurries the reader across a mile of beach, noting only that it is warm and scented like the sea. The speaker then hastens to adjacent farm fields and again merely notes that he crosses three of them until he arrives at a farm. Without lingering, he taps on a windowpane, perhaps giving a prearranged signal of his arrival. Clearly he knows where he is going and is not delayed by any uncertainty or hesitation. His tap is met with the energetic imagery of a match being lit.

The meter (the meter of a poem is the pattern of stressed and unstressed syllables) of line 9 reinforces the vigor of the image. The line begins with an iamb (da-DUM), gathers motion with an anapest (da-da-DUM), and then ends with another iamb followed by a spondee (DA-DUM). The line thus ends with three stressed syllables, an emphatic and forceful record of the speaker's perception. The flame of the match does not simply appear; rather it spurts, again lending energy and motion to the line. Reinforcing this energy is the alliteration of *sharp/scratch/spurt*. This is the poem's climactic line, its central dramatic moment, and Browning packs together imagery, rhythm, and alliteration to give the line the centrality it requires.

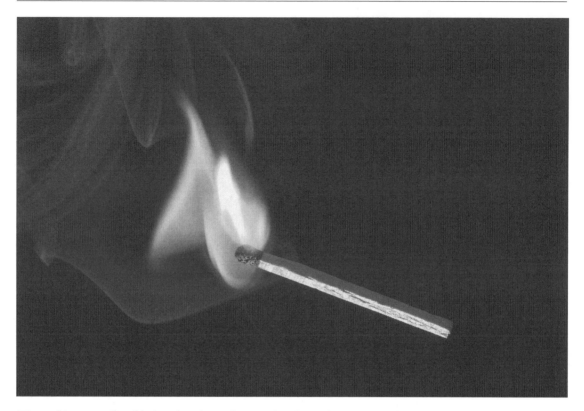

The sudden sound and light of striking the match echoes the passion of the lovers. (© Nikita Rogul / Shutterstock.com)

Having arrived at his goal, the speaker now shifts his attention to sound rather than to pictorial effects. He hears the voice of his lover. The voice is soft and quiet, so the poet returns to the languorous *l* sounds of the first three lines of the first stanza. While the language of the poem so far has been highly sensory and concrete, the poet introduces abstract emotional words by referring to the woman's joy and fear; the masculine energy of the speaker's journey is replaced by the more feminine language that records her response to their meeting. The aural imagery continues in the poem's final line, when the hearts of the two lovers are heard as beating in unison as they embrace. The image of the beating heart, with its regular rhythm, plays off against the rhythmic movement of the water and the tide from the first stanza. Motion, rhythm, and ebb and flow lie at the heart of the poem.

Although written by a Victorian poet, "Meeting at Night" in some respects defies many of the conventions of high Victorian poetry. It contains some of the lushness of the romantic poets of the early nineteenth century— Browning was a great admirer of the poetry of

Percy Bysshe Shelley—and in this manner resembles a good deal of early Victorian poetry, which continued to pay a debt to the romantics. However, the poem lacks any of the moral vision and seriousness of purpose that defines much of the age's literature, both in England and America (where Henry Wadsworth Longfellow was the most representative Victorian poet).

The emphasis on sound and on pictorial effects in "Meeting at Night" looks forward to much of the poetry of the late Victorian period, when more avant-garde artists were revolting against the sometimes dispassionate, rambling works typical of Victorianism. Among these artists were the pre-Raphaelites, including Dante Gabriel Rossetti, Christina Rossetti, George Meredith, William Morris, and Algernon Charles Swinburne. This school of poetry, whose members greatly admired Browning, placed emphasis on realistic depiction, sensuousness, visual imagery, and musicality in poetry. The poetry of the pre-Raphaelites then had a profound influence on such early modernist poets as Gerard Manley Hopkins and William

Butler Yeats, the poets of the end-of-century aesthetic and decadent movements (Oscar Wilde, Ernest Dowson, Lionel Johnson, Arthur Symons), and the imagists of the twentieth century—among them H. D. (Hilda Doolittle), Amy Lowell, Ezra Pound, William Carlos Williams, and numerous others.

The goal of the imagists was to create a poetry of clear, sharp images, without the sentimentality and occasional aimlessness that were often characteristic of the Victorians. Their poems were short, precise, and chiseled, composed with a directness and economy of language. They focused principally on a single image that conveyed an emotional reality in concrete, sensory terms, relying on what Ezra Pound called "luminous detail." "Meeting at Night," then, bears at least some resemblance to the work produced by the poets who emerged in the generations following the publication of *Dramatic Romances and Lyrics* and *Bells and Pomegranates*. Perhaps this ability to anticipate newer, more modern poetic sensibilities contributed to Browning's growing popularity as the nineteenth century progressed.

Source: Michael J. O'Neal, Critical Essay on "Meeting at Night," in *Poetry for Students*, Gale, Cengage Learning, 2014.

Adam Roberts

In the following excerpt, Roberts touches on Browning's view of women.

II. BROWNING AND WOMEN

Browning has a reputation as one of the great writers of heterosexual love poetry, yet an examination of Browning's representations of women reveals many difficulties. Most of these are contextual: the nineteenth century has a poor reputation when it comes to views of women. Victorian women had no vote, had limited rights to own property, had little access to education, and were in most important senses forced to depend upon men. The effective subordination of women was mirrored by an ideological figuring of them as superior moral beings, as pure and spiritual rather than rational entities (queens, angels in the house), that was in itself repressive.

We need to be careful here: no culture is so monolithic that it presents a single view on a subject so wide-ranging as "the rights of women." It is true, of course, that many prominent Victorian men regarded women as effectively children, and the burden of legislation was certainly straightforwardly repressive. John Ruskin, the widely respected writer and critic, gave voice in *Of Queen's Gardens* to a belief that women were simply inferior to men and that society ought to reflect that fact. Coventry Patmore's widely read poem of marriage, "The Angel in the House," articulated a vision of domestic happiness predicated on this view.

The phrase "the angel in the house" has been widely canvassed by critics as an encapsulation of this repressive ideology. The sense is that since woman is an angel, a madonna on a pedestal, it is simply inappropriate for her to partake in the messy real world. Thus, spared the opportunity of an education or earning a living for herself, she is to sit by the fire and darn while providing her husband with an emotional and moral center for his life. It should be pointed out, however, that Patmore's phrase has been equally widely misunderstood: "the angel in the house" is not a description of the wife in his marriage poem but an externalization of the love that exists between husband and wife. As soon as we posit a situation where women were repressed by a governing ideology, we start discovering important figures who contradict that very ideology. John Stuart Mill, the same man to have annotated Browning's *Pauline* so influentially, campaigned tirelessly for the emancipation of women, trying in the 1860s to pass legislation through Parliament giving them the vote. His *On the Subjection of Women* (1869) remains a very readable statement of basic feminism. In other words, Victorian England represents a transitional period in the movement toward modern-day feminism.

Browning displayed a distinct tendency to idealize women, and his literary representations of the female take shape from his own uxuriousness. He wrote to Elizabeth Barrett explaining that his love for her was rooted in a deeply felt sense of her superiority. There had been other women, but he had been unable to love them because

> there must be this disproportionateness in a beloved object—before I knew you, women seemed not much better than myself,—therefore, no love for them! There is no love but from beneath, far beneath. (August 10, 1846; qtd. in Kintner, 950)

Elizabeth was understandably alarmed by the implications of this statement. "But when you say," she replied, "that there can be no love except '*from beneath*'...is it right? Is it comforting to hear of? No, no—indeed" (August 10, 1846; qtd. in Kintner, 953). But Browning was adamant. "Do you not see how with this feeling," he wrote to her, "—how much my happiness would be disturbed by allying myself with a woman to whose intellect, as well as goodness, I could *not* look up?" He adds that it is not just a question of admiring intellect and goodness, but also of obeying—"in an obedience to whose desires, therefore, I should not be justified in indulging?" (August 13, 1846; qtd. in Kintner, 960).

This stance of the obedient devotee before the lofty female figure is often elaborated in the poetry. In a poem which was very much the product of the courtship years with Elizabeth Barrett, "The Flight of the Duchess," the narrator saddles a horse for the Duchess's escape and meditates on his own inferiority—"so far beneath her" that

> [I] would have been only too glad for her service
> To dance on hot ploughshares like a Turk dervise,
> But, unable to pay proper duty where owing it,
> Was reduced to that pitiful method of showing it.
> (750–753)

The flipside of this reiterated sense of veneration of women in the early work is darker and less defensible. The fate of many of the women in Browning's early work is grisly. The female protagonists in "Porphyria's Lover" and "My Last Duchess" are both violently murdered—by men who link female sexuality and violence against women directly in their minds. It is possible to trace a strand in Browning's work that leads up to Pompilia in *The Ring and the Book*—his most complete elaboration of female passivity and childishness, another heroine who is violently murdered.

It might be possible to construct a defence of the implied misogyny of having so many women violently murdered by suggesting that Browning is ironically commenting upon the tendency of men to dominate women. The Duke in "My Last Duchess," for instance, can be seen as a satire upon the male desire to completely dominate and possess womanhood. More realistically, I think, we must read Browning's early representations of woman as derived from literature rather than real life; the tendency to see woman as either excessively pure or excessively wicked is a long-standing literary tradition (however unfortunate). Browning's marriage and increasing maturity necessarily distanced him from this tradition, if only to certain degree....

Source: Adam Roberts, "Life with Elizabeth Barrett Browning, 1845–1861," in *Robert Browning Revisited*, Twayne, 1996, pp. 48–51.

Patricia O'Neill

In the following excerpt, O'Neill describes the enthusiastic following Browning's work inspired and his poetry's reflection of the values of American culture.

When Browning died in 1889, the whole machinery of his canonization was already in place. No miracles were necessary since the testimony of those who had met him and read his work confirmed his good influence. An official biographer and personal friend of the family, Alexandra Leighton Orr, had produced a reliable handbook explaining the poet's works, and a network of Browning clubs and societies created in the 1880s was well disposed to commemorate a poet so rich in ideas and obscure in style. It is fair to say that Browning was the first poet to require such a highly organized literary culture. In the first twenty years after his death, Browning's popularity sustained and was sustained by the broad and diverse relationships among a highly literate readership. Professional scholars connected to the universities, Browning's friends and critics, and an itinerant class of lecturers, performers and promoters of "culture" joined in discussions of Browning, his thought, and his poetry.

The interdependent nature of these relationships allowed the difficulty of reading Browning's poetry to appear, ironically, as an asset. For puzzling out the poet's meaning, hunting up the background to the enormous amount of historical allusion and subject matter in his works, and arguing over such professional literary critical concerns as the relative importance of his philosophy to his poetry and his value as a teacher or a poet created community wherever more than two people gathered in his name. The Browning societies' members were no frivolous or contemptible participants in the history of Browning's reception. They were the focal point for most of the important criticism and discussion of the poet's work at the turn of the century. Activities of the Browning societies and clubs were reported in the newspapers, and some of the most prominent figures of the day presented lectures at Browning society meetings.

In England, although the London Browning society folded soon after the poet's death, the setting up of memorial houses and publications of memoirs, letters, and biographical and critical monographs continued. In 1923 Emma J. Burt published essays originally written for a literary society, "in the hope that they may convey to a larger circle some helpful thoughts of the strength and comfort which are sometimes unperceived in the poems of England's great poet, Robert Browning." In the United States, Browning societies flourished well into the twentieth century. Louise Greer's *Browning and America* (1952) records the early history of Browning clubs in America, and the reasons for his popularity: "Browning's poetry, because of its intellectual challenge and its relation to nineteenth-century thought, was well-adapted" to the interests of a cross section of American society. What have been less well reviewed are the relations of Browning clubs and societies to the general developments of intellectual history in the United States. For the speakers at Browning society meetings were often prominent intellectuals and writers. Similarly, the history of these organizations provides insight into women's roles in American literary and intellectual life at a time when most women were excluded from universities and others were barred from taking degrees because of their sex. The country's increasing commitment to education as a method of social organization and progress made literary societies and magazines important sources of learning as well as social status. The difficulty of Browning's poetry and the "rage for elucidation" (Greer, 164) appealed especially to the aspiring middle-class reader. As Paul Elmer More notes in an 1905 article, "Why is Browning Popular?": "his roughness attracts a public which is sated with the too accessible" (rpt., Litzinger, 1965, 112).

The dramatic style of the works encouraged public recitations and promoted the reputations and purses of lecturers and performers like Mark Twain and Bliss Perry of Williams College. Another popular reciter of Browning, Hiram Corson, took time from his duties as professor of philosophy at Cornell to become personally acquainted with Browning. In 1877 he organized the first of several Browning clubs. Composed of faculty and their wives, Corson's Cornell Browning study group spent two years on *The Ring and the Book* alone (Greer, 167). Despite the condescension and hostility of some Browning critics, the activities of the members and visitors to Browning clubs were crucial to the poet's reputation and to the developing critical interest in his work. Moreover, they provided a forum for more general discussions of religion, art, and politics. For instance, in a 1881 undergraduate essay for

the *Andover Review*, John Dewey praises Browning for his "strenuous, abounding, triumphant optimism," which Dewey contrasts to Matthew Arnold's melancholia. Dewey recommends Browning's sense of a common purpose in nature and man. For the majority of Browning's readers at the turn of the century, the poet's thought was as important as his art. Perhaps that is why so many of Browning's early admirers were philosophy teachers and ministers.

Aside from university and intellectual circles, Browning's work filtered down to the most general forms of public appreciation. In 1909 a dramatization of "Pippa Passes" appeared through the New York City nickelodeons. According to Edward Guiliano and Richard C. Keenan, the success of D. W. Griffith's film "helped to elevate the cinema to a higher cultural level" and proved a turning point in Griffith's career as a filmmaker (1976, 126–30). A review of the production in the *Literary Digest* suggests that the demand for pictorial representations of "classics" coincided with the actions of the censorship boards against the more risque films from France. "Pippa"—without words—portrayed the heroine in a modern urban setting performing the miracle of her optimistic songs on a variety of recognizable social types: "the contrast between the 'tired businessman' at a roof-garden and the sweatshop worker applauding Pippa is certainly striking," wrote the reviewer (1909, 681–82). For both the educated and the uneducated, Browning's work provided meaningful entertainment, reflecting the values of American culture as a whole. . . .

Source: Patricia O'Neill, "The Browningites," in *Robert Browning and Twentieth-Century Criticism*, Camden House, 1995, pp. 1–3.

SOURCES

Browning, Robert, "Meeting at Night," in *The Poetical Works of Robert Browning*, Vol. 4, *Bells and Pomegranates*, edited by Ian Jack, Rowena Fowler, and Margaret Smith, Oxford University Press, 1991, p. 149.

"Browning, Robert," in *Merriam Webster's Encyclopedia of Literature*, Merriam-Webster, 1995, p. 180.

Disraeli, Benjamin, *Contarini Fleming: A Psychological Romance*, Peter Davies, 1927, pp. 295–96.

Everett, Glenn, "Robert Browning: Biography," in *Victorian Web*, http://www.victorianweb.org/authors/rb/rbbio.html (accessed February 13, 2013).

"How Matches Work," Discover.com website, http://dsc.discovery.com/tv-shows/mythbusters/about-this-show/how-matches-work.htm (accessed February 24, 2013).

Jack, Ian, Rowena Fowler, and Margaret Smith, Introduction to "Parting at Morning," in *The Poetical Works of Robert Browning*, Vol. 4, *Bells and Pomegranates*, Oxford University Press, 1991, p. 150.

Lowell, James Russell, Review of *Paracelsus, Sordello*, and *Bells and Pomegranates*, in *Robert Browning: The Critical Heritage*, edited by Boyd Litzinger and Donald Smalley, Barnes & Noble, 1970, p. 137; originally published in *North American Review*, April 1848, pp. 357–400.

"A Neglected Poet," in *Robert Browning: The Critical Heritage*, edited by Boyd Litzinger and Donald Smalley, Barnes & Noble, 1970, p. 121; originally published in *Critic*, December 27, 1845, pp. 701–702.

Perloff, Marjorie, "Poetics," in *The Ezra Pound Encyclopedia*, edited by Demetres P. Tryphonopoulos and Stephen J. Adams, Greenwood, 2005, p. 226.

"The Problem of Obscurity," in *Robert Browning: The Critical Heritage*, edited by Boyd Litzinger and Donald Smalley, Barnes & Nobel, 1970, p. 120; originally published in *English Review*, December 1845, pp. 273–77.

Review of *Dramatic Romances and Lyrics*, in *Robert Browning: The Critical Heritage*, edited by Boyd Litzinger and Donald Smalley, Barnes & Noble, 1970, p. 117; originally published in *Athenaeum*, January 17, 1846, pp. 58–59.

Review of *Dramatic Romances and Lyrics*, in *Robert Browning: The Critical Heritage*, edited by Boyd Litzinger and Donald Smalley, Barnes & Noble, 1970, p. 115; originally published in *Examiner*, November 15, 1845, pp. 723–24.

Review of *Dramatic Romances and Lyrics*, in *Robert Browning: The Critical Heritage*, edited by Boyd Litzinger and Donald Smalley, Barnes & Noble, 1970, p. 138; originally published in *Sharpe's London Magazine*, December 1848, pp. 122–27.

Sova, Dawn B., *Edgar Allan Poe: A to Z*, Checkmark Books, 2001, p. 208.

Wheeler, William Henry, *A Practical Manual of Tides and Waves*, Longmans, Green, 1906, p. 70.

FURTHER READING

Berdoe, Edward, *The Browning Cyclopèdia: A Guide to the Study of the Works of Robert Browning. With Copious Explanatory Notes and References on All Difficult Subjects*, Adamant Media Corporation, 2001.
> This volume's odd title is a product of its time: the book was originally published by George Allen in 1912. This edition is a facsimile reprint, and at 600 pages, it includes information on virtually every aspect of Browning's life and work as they would have been understood in the early twentieth century, just two decades or so after the poet's death.

Bloom, Harold, ed., *Robert Browning*, Chelsea House, 1990.
> Harold Bloom is a preeminent literary critic who edited a series of books for younger readers titled

Bloom's Modern Critical Views. This volume contains several essays on Browning by various critics, a biography of the author, and a time line.

Browning, Elizabeth Barrett, and Robert Browning, *The Love Letters of Elizabeth Barrett and Robert Browning*, Skyhorse Publishing, 2013.
> This volume reproduces the Brownings' 573 extant love letters to each other. The letters provide insight into their meeting, courtship, marriage, and removal to Italy, as well as Elizabeth's death.

Chesterton, G. K., *Robert Browning*, House of Stratus, 2001.
> A reader interested in a biography of the poet from an earlier era, along with commentary on his work without the trappings of modern literary criticism, will find this volume fascinating. Chesterton was one of England's most prominent, and most groundbreaking, men of letters in the early twentieth century.

Moran, Maureen, *Victorian Literature and Culture*, Continuum, 2007.
> This volume is a kind of handbook on the relationship between literature and culture in the Victorian era. It includes information not only about literature but also about the era's cultural, historical, economic, philosophical, and intellectual background.

Ryals, Clyde De L., *The Life of Robert Browning: A Critical Biography*, Blackwell, 1996.
> This is perhaps the standard biography of the poet. The book examines both the details of the author's life and the entire corpus of his work, from the early *Pauline* to *Asolando*, published on the day of the poet's death.

Warwick, Alexandra, and Martin Willis, *Victorian Literature Handbook*, Continuum, 2008.
> This volume is an alternative to Moran's *Victorian Literature and Culture*. It places greater emphasis on authors, literary texts, and critical approaches to Victorian literature, and it includes a time line of key literary and cultural events.

SUGGESTED SEARCH TERMS

Bells and Pomegranates

Browning AND Italy

Browning AND dramatic romances AND lyrics

Dramatic monologue

Elizabeth Barrett Browning

Robert Browning

Robert Browning AND Meeting at Night

Victorian courtship

Victorian poetry

Victorian sexuality

Midcentury Love Letter

PHYLLIS MCGINLEY

1953

"Midcentury Love Letter" is a love poem written by American author Phyllis McGinley. The poem, written in the form of a sonnet, was first published in the *New Yorker* magazine on February 14, 1953. It was then included in McGinley's 1954 poetry collection, *The Love Letters of Phyllis McGinley*. McGinley's poetry tends to be light and humorous, but "Midcentury Love Letter" runs counter to form in that it hints at the existence of a world of darkness, alienation, and loneliness in the cold war era following World War II.

McGinley achieved considerable popularity during the peak of her career in the 1950s and 1960s. She was a highly regarded author of books for children, and she remains perhaps best known in the twenty-first century as the author of "The Year without a Santa Claus" (originally published in *Good Housekeeping* magazine), on which an animated television classic is based. Her poetry was routinely published in the *New Yorker* and other prominent publications. Her 1960 poetry collection *Times Three* won the Pulitzer Prize for Poetry in 1961. McGinley was also an accomplished essayist, regularly publishing articles in *American Scholar* and in various women's magazines.

McGinley was a controversial figure, for much of her writing was a defense of domesticity and traditional feminine roles. It was thus out of step with a growing feminist movement that, for some readers, rendered her work irrelevant to

Phyllis McGinley (© Nina Leen | Time & Life Pictures | Getty Images)

the needs and concerns of modern women. Feminist author Betty Friedan would later dismiss her as one of a set of "housewife writers." In the context of this controversy, her image appeared on the cover of *Time* magazine on June 18, 1965. "Midcentury Love Letter" is available in *The Love Letters of Phyllis McGinley*, published by Viking in 1954.

AUTHOR BIOGRAPHY

Phyllis McGinley was born on March 21, 1905, in Ontario, Oregon; she was a descendant of an ancient Irish clan that included learned monks, bishops, military commanders, poets, political figures, and other distinguished individuals. Her father, a somewhat rootless and only partially successful land speculator, was Daniel McGinley; her mother, a pianist, was Julia Kiesel McGinley. During her childhood, the family moved often before finally settling on farmland in Colorado, where they lived until her father died when she was twelve years old. The family then lived with relatives in Ogden, Utah. McGinley graduated from Ogden High School before

enrolling at the University of Southern California, although she returned to Utah to take her degree from the University of Utah in 1927. During her college years, and even while she was still in high school, she began to write in earnest, often submitting her work to competitions that offered cash prizes.

After a brief stint as a teacher in Ogden, McGinley moved to New York to teach at a junior high school in New Rochelle. Meanwhile, she submitted her work to New York magazines, and her success prompted her to move to New York City in the 1930s, where she worked as a copywriter for an advertising agency and as a staff writer, later the poetry editor, for *Town and Country* magazine—and where she could focus on her career as a writer and poet. She published her first book of poetry, *On the Contrary*, in 1934, the same year she met Charles Hayden, a part-time jazz pianist who worked for the Bell Telephone Company. The two married in 1937. Later collections of poetry include *One More Manhattan* (1937), *A Pocketful of Wry* (1940), and *Stones from a Glass House* (1946). In 1944, she published *The Horse That Lived Upstairs* for younger readers, and in 1948, she wrote the lyrics for the musical review *Small Wonder*.

During the early years of her career, McGinley emphasized social issues and conditions that prevailed during the Great Depression and World War II. But then Katherine White, an editor at the *New Yorker*, famously wrote to her, "Dear Miss McGinley: We are buying your poem, but why do you sing the same sad songs all lady poets sing?" This remark prompted her to alter her style and emphasize lighter, more humorous verse. After the war, McGinley and her husband, along with their two daughters, settled in Larchmont, New York, an affluent Westchester County suburb of New York City. Later, she moved to Weston, Connecticut. It was in the suburbs that she began to write poetry that celebrated domestic suburban tranquility, although she would insist that much of her work continued to examine social concerns. "Midcentury Love Letter," published in 1953, was written during this period.

During the 1950s and beyond, McGinley published further collections of poetry, including *The Love Letters of Phyllis McGinley* (1954), the Pulitzer Prize–winning *Times Three: Selected Verse from Three Decades with Seventy New Poems* (1960), and *Confessions of a Reluctant Optimist* (1973). Juvenile books include, among numerous others, *The Most Wonderful Doll in the World* (1950), *Blunderbus* (1951), *The Make-Believe Twins* (1953), and *How Mrs. Santa Claus Saved Christmas* (1963). Prose collections include *The Province of the Heart* (1959), *Saint-Watching* (1969), and the 1964 best seller *Sixpence in Her Shoe*, a collection of pieces that served as a rejoinder to Betty Friedan's *The Feminine Mystique* (1963). Friedan had become a leading figure in the feminist movement by arguing that no intelligent women could possibly be happy confined in the home to the roles of wife and mother, but McGinley, in her poetry and prose, paid tribute to child-rearing, the home, and domestic life, becoming in the process what the *Larchmont Gazette* called the "poet laureate of the suburbs."

After her husband died in 1972, McGinley moved from the suburbs to a New York City apartment and virtually stopped writing. She died of unspecified causes on February 22, 1978.

POEM SUMMARY

The text used for this summary is from *The Love Letters of Phyllis McGinley*, Viking, 1954, p. 37.

"Midcentury Love Letter" is written in the form of a sonnet. It falls into two sections: an octave, or the first eight lines, and a sestet, or the concluding six lines.

Lines 1–8
The first words of the poem indicate that the speaker is addressing another person. She enjoins the person to stay by her and to speak her name. She pleads with the person not to wander away from her, even by the narrow span of a thought. It becomes clear that the poem is addressed to a person she loves, for the speaker indicates that the two of them, together, kindle a metaphorical fire that provides light and warmth in their lives. She calls the person her only defender in the darkness of the night and indicates that she is likewise his defender. She notes that the night is rapidly falling over the earth and will continue to do so, without benefit of starlight, until the world's landmarks change, that is, until the nature of the world fundamentally changes. In the process, the world is becoming bitterly cold. All that remains for the speaker and her beloved is for the two to provide warmth and shelter for each other by huddling and holding each other's hands.

MEDIA ADAPTATIONS

- Alec Wilder is the composer of the "Phyllis McGinley Song Cycle" for the bassoon, harp, and a mezzo-soprano voice. Included in the song cycle is "Midcentury Love Letter." The composition was released by Margun Music in 1980.
- "Midcentury Love Letter" is the title of a song by John Duke; the lyrics are Phyllis McGinley's poem by that title. This song is included in *Songs, Vol. 1, High Voice*, released by Southern Music in 1985.

Lines 9–14
In the sestet, the speaker draws a comparison between herself and her beloved and two mountain climbers who become lost in severe weather on a mountain slope. The two have been caught in a storm, and in the darkness, they are desperate. Yet they cling to each other and huddle under a cloak, where their breath keeps them warm. In the final two lines, the speaker again asks her beloved to stay by her, indicating that her spirit is as perishable as bone and that it cannot survive alone in the harsh winter.

THEMES

Romantic love
"Midcentury Love Letter" is clearly a love poem. Although the poem never specifies a particular person being addressed, readers familiar with McGinley's domestic concerns and her adherence to traditional religious values will likely conclude that the poem is to be thought of as addressed by a wife to her husband. The imperative sentences that begin the poem make clear that the speaker is addressing someone she loves. The speaker enjoins the lover to remain near her, to speak her name, and not to wander away from her. The speaker regards the one she loves as her sole defender in the night, just as she is the defender of her beloved. The two provide one another with warmth and light. They have each

TOPICS FOR FURTHER STUDY

- On a map of New York State, locate the Westchester County town of Larchmont, where McGinley lived much of her adult life. Where is the county in relation to New York City? Investigate why Westchester County has become virtually synonymous with East Coast affluence. Using a tool such as Flikr, prepare a visual display for your classmates showing some of the local sights McGinley might have been familiar with and that might have inspired her writing.

- Locate a copy of David Riesman's *Abundance for What?* (Doubleday, 1964; a newer edition was published in 1993 by Transaction Publishers). The book contains an essay titled "The Found Generation," which Riesman originally published in 1956 in *American Scholar*. Read the essay, which deals with the ambitions of college students in the 1950s, then write a brief report on the relevance of Riesman's findings to your understanding of McGinley as the female "poet laureate of the suburbs" and defender of suburban domesticity.

- Riesman's essay "The Found Generation" can also be found in *Antifeminism in America: A Reader: A Collection of Readings from the Literature of the Opponents to U. S. Feminism, 1848 to the Present* (Taylor & Francis, 2000). The volume is edited by Angela Howard and Sasha Ranaé Adams Tarrant. Peruse the volume and select one or two entries that you believe give the best picture of the social and political context in which McGinley wrote. Prepare an oral report for your classmates to discuss your findings.

- With a classmate, write a script in which you develop a debate between Betty Friedan, the feminist author who attacked McGinley and other "housewife writers" in *The Feminine Mystique*, and McGinley, who wrote *Sixpence in Her Shoe* as a rejoinder to Friedan in particular and to the feminist movement in general. Present your debate to your classmates and invite them to comment on the issues raised.

- *Crush: Love Poems*, a collection of poetry for young adults by NAACP Image Award nominee Kwame Alexander, explores love in all of its forms, including early romance. One section of the book also includes poems by Sherman Alexie, Pablo Neruda, and Nikki Giovanni, along with the title poem, "Crush," by Naomi Shihab Nye. Read one or more of the poems in the collection, then prepare a chart in which you specify similarities and differences between the poem(s) you selected and "Midcentury Love Letter."

- Women's magazines—*Ladies' Home Journal*, *Good Housekeeping*, *Woman's Home Companion*, *Better Homes and Gardens*, *Harper's Bazaar*, and *McCall's*, among others—can provide a window on the life of women who, like McGinley, lived in the 1940s and 1950s (and who in her case wrote articles for some of these magazines). Locate copies of past issues of one or more of these magazines in a library; they can also often be purchased in antique stores. Share with your classmates those portions of the magazines you believe would have reflected the life McGinley defended in her poetry and prose. Invite comment and discussion from your classmates. As an alternative, locate a copy of Nancy A. Walker's *Women's Magazines, 1940–1960: Gender Roles and the Popular Press* (Palgrave Macmillan, 1998) and rely for your presentation on excerpts from magazines that Walker presents.

- Among the world's most famous love poems are sonnet sequences by three writers: the fourteenth-century Italian writer Petrarch, William Shakespeare, and the Victorian poet Elizabeth Barrett Browning (author of *Sonnets from the Portuguese*, which contains the famous line "How do I love thee? Let me count the ways"). Select one of these writers. Examine one or more of the author's sonnets and prepare a written essay in which you explain how "Midcentury Love Letter" is part of a literary tradition established by the poet you have chosen.

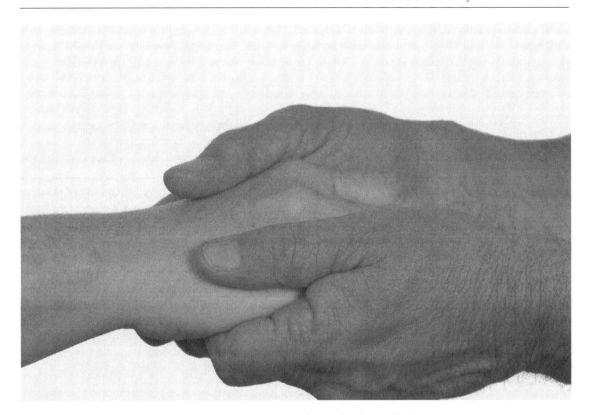

The speaker asking to hold her companion's hand reflects the desire for human connection. (© Cate Frost /
Shutterstock.com)

other for shelter, and they warm each other by
huddling together in the night and sharing the
warmth of their breath. Ultimately, the poem
asserts that a person's spirit is unable to survive
alone, making it more imperative that the
speaker and her partner sustain their romantic
love for each other in the face of the world's
potential for darkness, cold, and loneliness.

Loneliness

"Midcentury Love Letter" makes no reference
to people other than the speaker and the
partner she addresses. The poem, with its
images of darkness and cold, as well as the
comparison of the lovers to two climbers
caught on a mountain slope during a winter
storm, suggests that the speaker and her partner are isolated and alone. The sense of loneliness is enhanced by reference to the rapidly
falling night, the absence of starlight, and the
need for the speaker and the one she loves to
huddle together to provide each other with
warmth and light. The picture that emerges
is that of two people whose intense love enables them to join forces and provide each

other with support in a world that can isolate
and alienate them.

Allegory

"Midcentury Love Letter" makes no specific
reference to historical events or trends. It is perhaps telling, though, that the author uses the
word *midcentury* in the poem's title, thus calling
attention to a specific historical setting and context. Since the end of the Second World War, the
United States had been locked in an ideological
struggle with the Communist Soviet Union and
its satellite states, particularly those of Eastern
Europe. The development of nuclear weapons,
including the hydrogen bomb, was creating a
climate of anxiety and fear in the American public. There was a growing sense that an apocalyptic war could erupt at any moment, and the
escape of the nuclear genie would make such a
war unthinkable. At the time of the poem's first
publication in February 1953, the United States
was leading an international military coalition
opposing Communist North Korea in its effort
to subjugate democratic South Korea. In this
historical context, then, it is possible to read

"Midcentury Love Letter" as a kind of allegory in which the speaker and her beloved find in each other's arms refuge from the threats, storms, darkness, cold, and desperation of an uncertain world that surrounds them.

STYLE

Sonnet

"Midcentury Love Letter" is written in the form of a sonnet, a highly formal type of lyric poem that consists of fourteen lines that follow one of several possible rhyme schemes. Although many variations are possible, essentially two types of sonnets have historically been written. One is called the English sonnet, often called the Shakespearean sonnet after its most prominent practitioner. The English sonnet consists of four sections. The first three are quatrains, or four-line stanzas, each with its own rhyme scheme. A common rhyming pattern is *abab cdcd efef*. The final section is a couplet, that is, two rhymed lines (*gg*) that provide an epigrammatic comment on or resolution to the subject matter raised in the three quatrains.

"Midcentury Love Letter," however, is written in part using the conventions of the second broad type of sonnet, the Italian sonnet, often called the Petrarchan sonnet after the fourteen-century Italian poet Petrarch. The Italian sonnet consists of two main parts. The first is an octave, or eight lines that follow a rhyming pattern such as *abba abba*. The octave typically asks a question, raises a doubt, offers a reflection, expresses a desire, or presents a vision of the future. The final six lines, called the sestet, follow a rhyme scheme that can vary but that typically runs *cde cde, cdc cdc,* or *cde dce*. The sestet typically answers the question, resolves the doubt, comments on the reflection, satisfies the desire, or realizes the vision. It should be noted that a third type of sonnet, the Spenserian (named after Renaissance poet Edmund Spenser), is similar to the English sonnet but features a rhyme scheme— *abab bcbc cdcd ee*—that links the quatrains.

McGinley, however, does not adhere strictly to this classification, for "Midcentury Love Letter" combines elements of the two major forms. She follows the conventions of the Petrarchan sonnet by dividing her poem into an octave and a sestet. In the octave, she urges her beloved to remain by her side as her defender and as her source of warmth and light in a cold, dark world.

In the sestet, she comments on the relationship by comparing herself and her beloved to a pair of lost mountain climbers surviving in a storm. At the same time, she uses a rhyme scheme that somewhat resembles that of an English sonnet. The rhyme scheme of the octave is *abab acac*. The sestet is linked to the octave by repeating the *a* in the rhyme scheme *adadee*. Note, too, that the poem ends with a resolving rhymed couplet in the manner of the English sonnet.

It should be noted that some of the poem's rhymes are "near rhymes," that is, rhymes that are not true rhymes but approximate ones based on the similarity of vowels sounds. Thus, such words as *wander, defender,* and *alter* are not true rhymes (as are *light* and *night* or *cold* and *hold*), but the similarity of their sounds, including the *–er* ending, makes them near rhymes. In this regard, such pairs of words as *wander* and *defender* use what are called feminine rhymes, or rhymes achieved through unstressed rather than stressed syllables.

Alliteration

McGinley unifies "Midcentury Love Letter" in part by the use of alliteration, that is, repeated consonant sounds, usually at the beginnings of words. Thus, in the poem's first six words, the *s*, *m*, and *n* sounds are each repeated. Other alliterative words include *bitter/burning, huddle/ hand/hold, slope/storm, desperate/darkness, climbers/cling/cloak, breathe/bone, stay/spirit/ such/survive.* This reliance on alliteration adds to the musicality of the poem and serves to link its elements into a single whole. Overall, the poem relies less on formal rhythm and more on a pattern of sounds accentuated by alliteration.

Imagery

"Midcentury Love Letter" also relies heavily on the poetic device of imagery. An image in literature is a literal and concrete representation of a sensory experience. Imagery is the means by which a poet takes complex emotional or mental states and puts them into language that evokes similar states in readers who can share the physical experience of the poet; literary language therefore differs from the language of science, or even philosophy, by tapping into the rich sensory, mythical, and archetypal experience of readers and writers. The images of "Midcentury Love Letter" are in themselves fairly commonplace. They include references to fire and warmth, to cold and darkness, to the earth and the stars, to a storm and winter, to the

COMPARE
&
CONTRAST

- **1953:** It is not unusual for a woman to consider her male partner to be her sole defender against the threats of the world.

  Today: Women are more independent and are more likely to take an equal role with a man in their relationships.

- **1953:** Romantic partners communicate with each other through phone calls and written notes and letters. It is not uncommon for someone to address a love poem to his or her beloved.

Today: Romantic partners communicate in many different ways, including Skype, e-mail, Twitter, and through social networking sites such as Facebook.

- **1953:** Sexual relationships outside of marriage are frowned upon; women who have sexual relations outside of marriage are sometimes ostracized. Women are discouraged from expressing sexual desires.

  Today: Sexual relationships outside of marriage are much more widely accepted, and women feel much freer to express sexual longings.

---

breath and spirit. But the images provide the poem with a physical texture that it would otherwise lack.

HISTORICAL CONTEXT

McGinley first published "Midcentury Love Letter" at a time in history when American culture and society were undergoing profound and rapid changes, and the title, with the use of the word *midcentury*, calls attention to this period. World War II was still fresh in the minds of many Americans as the cold war between the United States and its Western allies and the Soviet Union and its Communist satellites was unfolding. The Cold War warmed up in 1948 when the Soviet Union blockaded West Berlin inside Communist East Germany, requiring the Western allies to execute the "Berlin Airlift" to ferry essential supplies to West Berliners. The Cold War threatened to turn hot in June 1950, when Communist North Korea, with the backing of its neighbor, the Communist People's Republic of China, invaded democratic South Korea, launching the Korean War. That year, too, German-born scientist Klaus Fuchs, who had played a major role in the development of the atomic bomb at Los Alamos, New Mexico, during World War II, confessed to being a Soviet spy. Fuchs had provided the Soviets with nuclear

secrets that enabled them to develop their own nuclear weapons.

In this context, many Americans were terrified when President Harry Truman announced in January 1953 that the United States had produced its first hydrogen bomb, popularly called the hell bomb, making the threat of thermonuclear war with the Soviets exponentially more frightening. In his play about the Salem Witch Trials, *The Crucible*, which opened in early 1953, Arthur Miller offered an oblique attack on the so-called Red Scares of the early 1950s—scares exemplified by the hearings conducted by Senator Joseph McCarthy that year to root out Communist infiltrators ("Reds") in the government. Those scares, however, seemed justified in June 1953, when Julius and Ethel Rosenberg, after a trial that had begun in March 1951, were executed for providing atomic secrets to the Soviets. These were some of the key midcentury geopolitical events that surrounded the composition of "Midcentury Love Letter" and that perhaps influenced the author's vision of a dark, cold, threatening world that could be redeemed only by love.

The midcentury witnessed a number of significant cultural developments as well. By early 1953, some twenty-five million American homes

The winter storm on a mountainside creates a bleak mood. *(© nodff / Shutterstock.com)*

had television sets, which they could tune to such shows as *I Love Lucy*—perhaps after checking their first issue of *TV Guide* published that year. Sexual mores were beginning to loosen ever so slightly. In *I Love Lucy*, Lucy Ricardo (played by Lucille Ball) was depicted as giving birth to little Ricky Ricardo on a live television broadcast (although the word *pregnancy* was censored out; the word *expecting* had to be used instead). In 1953, Hugh Hefner published the first issue of *Playboy* magazine. Alfred Kinsey published his landmark study of sexuality, *Sexual Behavior in the Human Female*. Burt Lancaster and Deborah Kerr filmed their steamy "beach kissing scene" in the movie *From Here to Eternity*. A crucial cultural event was the 1953 publication of the English translation of Simone de Beauvoir's *Le Deuxiéme Sexe*, or *The Second Sex*, a remarkably explicit examination of the facts and myths surrounding female sexuality and a book that is often thought of as having launched the modern feminist movement. These and numerous other events of the early 1950s hint at a post–World War II society that was rushing headlong into a new, more modern age, one, again, that was

potentially frightening and that perhaps spurred writers such as McGinley to defend traditional values, virtues, and gender roles.

Another set of important developments surrounded the growth and development of the suburbs—the world that McGinley celebrated in much of her writing. Beginning in 1950, the number of Americans living in the suburbs would double over the next fifty years, just as it had already doubled in the previous fifty years. The federal government encouraged suburban home ownership by insuring mortgage loans and making interest paid on home loans tax-deductible. Developers wanted to provide affordable housing for people away from urban centers, where the density of development from skyscrapers and high-rise buildings made land prohibitively expensive. The interstate highway system, along with the spread of commuter trains, made it easier for people living in suburbs (such as McGinley's Westchester County, New York) to commute to work, as well as to take advantage of the cultural opportunities afforded by cities. Along with new housing developments came retail outlets, giving rise to the shopping center and, eventually, the enclosed mall.

Many social observers decried the suburbanization of America, arguing that the suburbs tended to isolate people, in contrast to cities, which fostered community life. The suburbs, critics argued, induced bland conformity: People felt they had to have the same lush lawns, the same grills, the same household furnishings, the same country clubs, and the same automobiles. At the center of this critique was the suburban housewife, who was made to feel obligated to cook, clean, look after children, and provide a safe haven for her husband when he returned home from work, just as McGinley proposes to provide a safe haven for her beloved in "Midcentury Love Letter."

CRITICAL OVERVIEW

McGinley's poetry failed to elicit a great deal of critical response, partly because she was seen as a writer of children's books and light verse but, in large part because she was identified as a suburban housewife rather than as part of a sophisticated literary set. As Ginia Bellafante notes in a *New York Times* article "Suburban Rapture,"

> McGinley is almost entirely forgotten today, and while her anonymity is attributable in part to the disappearance of light verse, it seems equally a function of our refusal to believe that anyone living on the manicured fringes of a major American city in the middle of the 20th century might have been genuinely pleased to be there.

This focus on McGinley's suburban sensibilities is reflected in a review by Bette Richart in *Commonweal* magazine, where she writes, "Before McGinley, love and art were the proper (and almost only) subject of á la mode light verse. Mrs. McGinley is famous for adding suburbia to the list." Richart goes on, however, to find fault with the author's light verse, criticizing it for "coyness," for straining after irony in a way that "doesn't come off," for not recognizing that "light verse has a moral obligation not to make a point at the expense of truth," and for failing to "be chary of saying just anything for the sake of a clever rhyme."

Other critics, however, praised McGinley. The poet W. H. Auden opens his foreword to *Times Three* (which contains "Midcentury Love Letter") by writing:

Phyllis McGinley needs no puff. Her poems are known and loved by tens of thousands. They call for no learned exegesis. If a Ph.D. thesis is ever written about her work, it will be in an alien tongue and an alien alphabet.

David McCord, in a laudatory review published in the *Saturday Review* titled "The Envy of All," feels compelled to imitate McGinley's usual light verse style in remarking:

> And when the ink's in spate.
>
> And freshening a sonnet
>
> As on page 58,
>
> She can't be beat, doggone it!

In a later review in *Saturday Review*," She Speaks the Language of Delight," McCord comments more seriously on *Times Three*: "The variety is astonishing enough, but better than that is the quality." McCord goes on to specify what he admired about the author's poetry of the 1950s: "It is her eloquent moment, her compassion, her intuition, her ability to part the world's wormy apple with a razor blade, the new dimension that a word takes on in Miss McGinley's turn of phrase."

The only sustained, scholarly examination of McGinley's poetry was written by Linda Welshimer Wagner. In her book *Phyllis McGinley*, Wagner calls the author an "outstanding literary figure" and remarked,

> She writes with a technical proficiency equal to that of the best-known poets through history. She knows how to use the full range of poetic devices; and she writes with the freedom, the innovation, possible only after a person has thoroughly mastered the ground rules of an art.

Wagner goes on to note: "Her humanity infuses her technically adept poem; and her respect for workmanship keeps even her most emotional poems from being mawkish."

CRITICISM

Michael J. O'Neal

O'Neal holds a PhD in English. In the following essay, he examines the artistry of "Midcentury Love Letter."

From one point of view, "Midcentury Love Letter" does not say very much. A reader could distill the poem into a simple, almost mundane statement, such as "I love you. Let's stick together"—or perhaps more fully, "I love you. It's dark and cold and threatening out there, so let's the two of us stay together and keep each

WHAT DO I READ NEXT?

- "Melancholy Reflections after a Lost Argument," "The Seven Ages of a Newspaper Subscriber," and "Incident in the Afternoon" are three humorous poems McGinley published in the *New Yorker* magazine. They are available in *Fierce Pajamas: An Anthology of Humor Writing from the New Yorker* (2002), edited by David Remnick and Henry Finder.

- Another American author who celebrated the domestic life and her relationship with her husband was the seventeenth-century poet Anne Bradstreet. One of Bradstreet's most frequently anthologized poems is "To My Dear and Loving Husband," which can be found in a 2011 edition titled *To My Husband and Other Poems*.

- A prominent twentieth-century American writer known for her humor and biting wit was Dorothy Parker (who characteristically wanted her epitaph to read "Excuse my dust"). Her poem "Love Song" (1926), included in *The Portable Dorothy Parker* (2006), provides an example of her talents as a humorist in the context of a "love" poem.

- Another humorist who made her mark at the *New Yorker* was Veronica Geng, whose oftentimes bizarre short entries were send-ups of modern culture. A collection of her writings was published in 1988 under the title *Love Trouble Is My Business*.

- *The 1950s* (2004) by William H. Young and Nancy K. Young is part of Greenwood Press's American Popular Culture through History series and provides young-adult readers with a snapshot of political, cultural, and social life in the United States during the 1950s.

- Simon de Beauvoir's *The Second Sex*, like Friedan's *The Feminine Mystique*, is a core text in the history of modern feminism. It is available in a 2011 edition translated by Constance Borde and Sheila Malovany-Chevallier, an edition noteworthy in part for restoring passages from the original 1949 French edition that were cut in the 1953 English translation.

- At its title suggests, *Love's Witness: Five Centuries of Love Poetry by Women* (1993), edited by Jim Hollis, contains love poems written by women from a wide span of historical eras, including Stevie Smith, Emily Dickinson, Christina Rossetti, Emily Brontë, Elizabeth Barrett Browning, Edith Wharton, Katherine Mansfield, Amy Lowell, George Eliot, and even Queen Elizabeth I.

- Readers interested in love poetry by women from another cultural tradition might explore *Women Poets of China* (1982), edited and translated by Ling Chung and American poet Kenneth Rexroth.

- Love poetry from yet another cultural tradition is contained in *Songs of Love and War: Afghan Women's Poetry* (2010), written and edited by Sayd Majrouh and translated by Marjolijn de Jager. The book notes that the poetry is typically sung rather than simply read or recited, for the Afghani culture dissolves some of the distinction between text and song that is common in Western culture.

---

other safe." But these quotidian statements would not rise to the level of poetry. They get the thought across, but they do so without artistry.

Yet "Midcentury Love Letter" is manifestly poetic, for it engages the reader on an aesthetic and, more importantly, emotional level. It presents a stark contrast between the profound simplicity of the message and the profound richness and eloquence of the expression. It is this tension between message and medium that allows the poem to transcend mere statement to become a poignant appeal, an intensely emotional cry in the night. But while the poet has mastered the artistry that enables her magically to move the reader, the critic can only try to identify and remark upon the artistic techniques that transform the bare statement into poetry—that is, to look behind the curtain to find the source of the magic.

One of these techniques is form. McGinley could have written her poem in the form of free verse, allowing herself scope to express intense emotion without being bound by the strictures of a particular poetic form. Instead, she chose to write her poem in the form of a sonnet, one of the most demanding poetic forms because it requires the author to bind up the work in a set number of lines, a fixed rhyme scheme, and a structure that calls for a statement or problem, a turn, and some sort of resolution or commentary. Put simply, part 2 (the sestet) has to answer part 1 (the octave).

One way in which McGinley challenges the restrictions of the form is through frequent use of *enjambment*, referring to the completion in one poetic line of a thought (and grammatical unit) begun in the preceding line. Very often, poetry relies on the end-stopped line, that is, a line that contains a complete grammatical unit that does not spill over into the next line. End-stopped lines end with a pause signaled by a mark of punctuation, such as a period or a comma. Even without punctuation, the reader perceives a rhetorical pause at the end of the line. Enjambment, however, creates more of a sense that the thought, along with the grammatical unit, continues from one line to the next. Several of McGinley's lines are end-stopped, but several others (such as lines 1–2, 2–3, and 11–12) are enjambed. The poetic effect is that of a passionate utterance

trying to burst the seams of the form in which it is enclosed.

In a similar vein, McGinley avoids the use of a strict metrical pattern. Traditionally, the sonnet in English is written using the metrical pattern called iambic pentameter. In iambic pentameter verse, each line consists of five metrical units (pentameter), each one made up of an unstressed syllable followed by a stressed syllable (the iamb). Each line, then, totals ten syllables, although slight variations are common. McGinley alters this pattern by first making use of eleven-syllable lines, alternating them with ten-syllable lines in a regular pattern that looks like this in the octave:

11 – 10 – 11 – 11

11 – 10 – 11 – 11

and like this in the sestet:

11 – 10 – 11 – 10

11 – 11

Again, one way to respond to this alteration of the usual pattern is see it as the poetic utterance straining to escape from the confines of the traditional form. The intensity of the love and the passion of the poem's speaker are too intense to be held within the predictable limits of the form. Yet form is still imposed.

At the same time, the reader notices that McGinley does not rely on an iambic pattern, the "da-DUM da-DUM da-DUM . . ." pattern common to English poetry (common because the English language itself tends toward the iambic in its rhythms). The first line, consisting of eleven syllables, begins with ten stressed syllables, rendering the line remarkably emphatic; only the eleventh syllable is unstressed. The first three syllables constitute an imperative statement. So, too, do the next three. With the seventh syllable, the poet begins a third full sentence, again an imperative—and she is still in the first line of the poem. An examination of the remainder of the poem reveals that McGinley has employed each of the various kinds of metrical feet, including the trochee (DA-dum), the spondee (DA-DUM), the dactyl (DA-dum-dum), and the anapest (da-da-DUM). A scan of line eight, for example, would reveal a pattern that runs dactyl–trochee–trochee–trochee–iamb. It is impossible to say whether McGinley was conscious of these metrical variations as she composed the poem. It is highly likely that she heard the rhythm of the poem and strove for a rhythmical effect that pushed against the usual limits of the sonnet form without being explicitly conscious of accent marks and syllable counts.

"Midcentury Love Letter" relies heavily on sound and sound patterns in other ways as well. The poem is highly alliterative. In the first six words of the poem, the author repeats the *s*, *m*, and *n* sounds in two imperative statements that consist entirely of stressed syllables. The effect is to underline and highlight the urgency of the demand she is making on the person to whom the poem is addressed. The imperative that opens the poem is repeated at the beginning of line 13. As the poem proceeds, the alliterative effects gather and accumulate, serving to link the lines of the poem into a unified whole. The attentive reader will notice, for example, the repeated *w* sound to be found at the end of lines 1, 9, and 12, a sound that is also repeated at the start of lines 3, 5, and 7. Repeated *b* sounds (lines 2, 6, 7), *cl* sounds (9, 11, 12), and *d* sounds (11) serve a similar purpose. They link the lines of the poem aurally while adding a measure of insistence and intensity commensurate with the speaker's state of mind as she expresses her powerful love for the person she addresses.

A further element of the poem's artistry is its vocabulary. A common misconception is that poetic language is supposed to be "flowery" and "ornate," yet some of the most memorable lines in English poetry consist entirely of words of a single syllable; perhaps the most noteworthy example is "To be or not to be" from Shakespeare's *Hamlet*. "Midcentury Love Letter" consists largely of single-syllable words. Line 1 has one two-syllable word; so does line 2. Most of the two-syllable words are common words or words with an inflected ending (for example, *ing*). In this regard, perhaps the only word that stands out is *precipitous*, a four-syllable word, but one that works because of the image of the snowstorm (precipitation) that dominates the sestet. This reliance on a simple, unadorned vocabulary, buttressed by the poem's elemental images of heat, warmth, light, fire, cold, stars, darkness, and breath, adds to the emotional intensity of "Midcentury Love Letter." The speaker is not contemplating; the words of the poem do not emerge from a process of thought or reflection. Rather, they erupt from a sense of a strong emotion that fills the speaker with urgency and longing, almost as though they are a cry in response to an emergency.

"Midcentury Love Letter," then, is not an intellectual experience. While the poem appears on the printed page, and the reader's encounter with it is likely to be silent, its artistry reminds readers that poetry is an oral/aural art form: Poetry is meant to be read aloud. The artistic elements of the poem—its rhythms and metrics, its patterns of stress and relaxation, its repeated sounds, its relatively spare vocabulary—invite the reader to hear it by reciting it aloud. Only in this way can the reader fully and deeply appreciate the heart's intensity that gave rise to it.

Source: Michael J. O'Neal, Critical Essay on "Midcentury Love Letter," in *Poetry for Students*, Gale, Cengage Learning, 2014.

Penelope Fritzer and Bartholomew Bland
In the following essay, Fritzer and Bland criticize McGinley for expressing some anti-feminist and racially insensitive views.

Phyllis McGinley, a Pulitzer Prize-winning poet and popular magazine writer of the 1930s through the 1960s, often covered domestic life and issues, but in the warmth of her descriptions of family relationships, she ignores many of the negative aspects of housekeeping and domestic isolation in the postwar period. *Sixpence in Her Shoe*, about the "oldest honorable profession," was a long-term best seller, and McGinley was one of Bombeck's favorite writers, a writer that Bombeck cites as a seminal influence (*A Marriage Made in Heaven or Too Tired for an Affair* 84). However, McGinley's many books, articles, and poems show her as a writer with a very different style from that of Bombeck.

While *Sixpence in Her Shoe* (the title is based on an English legend that a good housewife would occasionally find the spirits leaving her a reward), an autobiographical ode to housewifery, was McGinley's best-known and longest selling book, it is one of her least humorous (McGinley herself was the wife of businessman Charles Hayden, and they lived in Larchmont, New York). A mild and pleasant ramble through her views of housewifery, homemaking (like Rawlings, with a special emphasis on cooking), and, family life, it is open-minded and commonsensical but never hilarious; rather, she saves much of her humor for her poetry and essays.

In such poems as "Apology for Husbands," McGinley acknowledges with humorous examples that husbands can be "more bother than they are worth," as a friend has written her, but

The climbers must cling together to stay warm during the storm. (© Pojoslaw | Shutterstock.com)

cheerfully maintains that "What gadget's useful as a spouse?/ Considering that a minute,/ Confess that every proper house/ Should have a husband in it" (*A Pocketful of Wry* 99–100). *Husbands Are Difficult or the Book of Oliver Ames* is something of a departure in the domestic humor genre, being an account of the foibles of married life with a generic husband written in the first person by his "wife." However, the humor is universal, and McGinley is clearly speaking from her own experiences.

The amusing "Comeuppance for a Progeny" discusses the discrepancy between the parents' affection for their child and the IRS contention that the child is only worth a small tax deduction (*Pocketful of Wry* 101). "Advice to a Tot About to Learn the Alphabet" contains the self-mocking observation "Unless you leap before you look,/ Your fate will be a trite one./ For first you'll learn to read a book/ And then you'll want to write one" (5). In "About Children" McGinley ruefully asks "Why's the resemblance, moral or mental,/ Of children to people so coincidental?" (*Times Three* 178).

McGinley has a huge body of work, and it is not limited to domestic life: much of her work is commentary on the passing scene. For example, *Stones from a Glass House*, published in 1946, contains a number of poems commenting on World War II as well as on various aspects of private and public life. It also contains "Occupation: Housewife," which ends with the phrase "She often says she might have been a painter/ Or maybe a writer, but she married young./ She diets. And with Contract [bridge] she delays/ The encroaching desolation of her days" (37). Remarkably, this is one of the very few negative remarks, even joking ones, that McGinley makes about being a housewife, an occupation she generally glorifies to the extent that nowadays it is difficult to read some of her commentary.

Because McGinley is less overtly funny than most housewife writers, her occasional complaints loom larger than they do for most writers in this genre. The poem "Primary Education," from *Pocketful of Wry*, has a sour flavor. It begins with a newspaper headline ("Pupils to Learn Tolerance Here Twice a Month") the premise of which McGinley goes on to ridicule in various witty and

"

AGAIN, MCGINLEY WRITES WITH WARMTH
AND DEEP FEELING ABOUT THE DUTIES AND JOYS OF
UPPER-MIDDLE-CLASS FAMILY LIFE, BUT HER HUMOR
IS SLIGHT, HER SELF-RIGHTEOUSNESS IS CLOYING,
AND THE CLASS GAP IS LARGE."

cutting phrases, perhaps refusing to believe that intolerance was a problem in the years before the civil rights movement (and still is for that matter). In the 1946 poem "Tiger, Tiger" from *Stones from a Glass House*, commenting on the Association for Childhood Education's calling *Little Black Sambo* inappropriate because of racial stereotyping, McGinley criticizes reform as "A striped thing with a public cry/ And a hot, fanatical tiger eye" (89). Further, she warns that "The peril stalks" even *Robinson Crusoe*'s Man Friday, Kipling's Mowgli, Uncle Tom, Uncle Remus, and even Othello (89). Her point that revisionism in literature is sometimes silly is well taken, but there is a lack of balance here and a lack of imagination in her refusal to see the world from any viewpoint but her own. Not once does she consider how the story might resonate with black people. (Interestingly, after being out of favor for some years, *Little Black Sambo* currently is enjoying a minor comeback with some groups as an example of an African-style tale.)

Additionally, McGinley is on the wrong side of history with some of her pronouncements on women's rights. Many housewife humorists are not overtly feminists and appeal to their varied audiences by presenting themselves as apolitical. Most do not go out of their way to comment on politics. *Sixpence in Her Shoe*, published about the same time as Betty Friedan's *The Feminine Mystique*, contains three earnest opening chapters in which McGinley, an upper-middle-class housewife/poet who works at home with a comfortable family income, household help, and two girls in boarding school, explains why the "average" housewife with cleaning help and a liberal arts degree (hardly average) should be happy with her lot, since men's jobs are not always fun, either.

Much of what McGinley says is sensible and practical, but much of it is oblivious to the reality of life for women before the women's movement:

job opportunities limited by ads classified by sex, no mortgages without a male co-signer, women whose economic situation gives them no choice but to work at low-paying jobs, and all the other daily indignities of life for women unprotected by a kindly, wealthy husband as McGinley is protected. Like Cornelia Otis Skinner, McGinley has a hard time putting herself in a more subservient position, so she sees little wrong with the status quo. But unlike most of Skinner's work, McGinley's has a yawning class gap that seems partly to be lack of imagination and empathy for those differently situated. This blindered approach to timely issues makes her work, so universal in its paean to the homemaker, seem in other ways limited and dated.

McGinley, however, clearly sees herself as a judicious moderator in the early "culture wars" by maintaining that women have the right to education even if they will be housewives, rebutting the idea "that education has no value unless it is brought to the marketplace" (*Sixpence* 17). Her reasons of support are valid but condescending: education "will not cripple a girl's talent for making chocolate brownies.... She will be able to ... talk over her husband's business problems with him more helpfully, and entertain her children more amusingly if her brain is tuned and humming with knowledge" (22). The reader is reassured that "Women with skills they love to employ, with training they mourn not to use, have every right to exert them; so long, that is, as the family is not essentially harmed," but nary a word appears about the responsibilities of similarly situated men or any sharing of the domestic work load (46).

McGinley just cannot let this subject alone. *The Province of the Heart* contains the essay "The Third Hand," which McGinley says is her response to an organization of college women who want her to write them an article on "How to Combine Marriage with a Career" (173). She disavows having a career (she just "writes for publication") and says that only a woman with a metaphorical "third hand" (one for wife, one for mother, one for career woman) can "both eat her cake and have it," since the world is full of "false promises" (174). Again, McGinley writes with warmth and deep feeling about the duties and joys of upper-middle-class family life, but her humor is slight, her self-righteousness is cloying, and the class gap is large. A little of her boring pontificating, correct though she may sometimes be, goes a long way and quickly becomes tiresome.

Source: Penelope Fritzer and Bartholomew Bland, "Midcentury Merry Wives: Phyllis McGinley," in *Merry Wives and Others: A History of Domestic Humor Writing*, McFarland, 2002, pp. 35–38.

SOURCES

Adler, Carlye, "Hugh Hefner Playboy Enterprises," CNN website, September 1, 2003, http://money.cnn.com/magazines/fsb/fsb_archive/2003/09/01/350793/index.htm (accessed February 18, 2013).

Auden, W. H., Foreword to *Times Three: Selected Verse from Three Decades with Seventy New Poems*, Viking, 1961, p. ix.

Bellafante, Ginia, "Suburban Rapture," in *New York Times*, December 28, 2008, http://www.nytimes.com/2008/12/28/books/review/Bellafante-t.html?_r=0 (accessed February 8, 2013).

"The Berlin Airlift," Truman Library website, http://www.trumanlibrary.org/teacher/berlin.htm (accessed February 8, 2013).

Bradshaw, Peter, "From Here to Eternity," in *Guardian*, September 23, 2010, http://www.guardian.co.uk/film/2010/sep/23/from-here-to-eternity-review (accessed February 18, 2013).

Ewbank, John, "Phyllis McGinley," Oregon Encyclopedia website, http://www.oregonencyclopedia.org/entry/view/mcginley_phyllis/ (accessed February 6, 2013).

"The Kinsey Report of 1953: Media Reaction to Sexual Behavior in the Human Female," Kinsey Institute website, http://kinseyinstitute.org/services/2003/media-reaction.html (accessed February 8, 2013).

"The Korean War and Its Origins, 1945–1953," Truman Library website, http://www.trumanlibrary.org/whistlestop/study_collections/koreanwar/index.php?action=sss (accessed February 8, 2013).

Linder, Douglas, "The Rosenberg Trial," Famous Trials website, http://law2.umkc.edu/faculty/projects/ftrials/rosenb/rosenb.htm (accessed February 8, 2013).

McCord, David, "The Envy of All," in *Saturday Review*, February 1, 1947, p. 31.

———, "She Speaks a Language of Delight," in *Saturday Review*, December 10, 1960, p. 32.

McGinley, Phyllis, "Midcentury Love Letter," in *The Love Letters of Phyllis McGinley*, Viking, 1954, p. 37.

"Phyllis McGinley," Poets.org website, http://www.poets.org/poet.php/prmPID/640 (accessed February 6, 2013).

"Phyllis McGinley," Utah History to Go website, http://historytogo.utah.gov/people/utahns_of_achievement/phyllismcginley.html (accessed February 11, 2013).

"Population: Urban, Rural, Suburban," PBS website, http://www.pbs.org/fmc/book/1population6.htm (accessed February 8, 2013).

"The Race for the Superbomb: Klaus Fuchs' Statement," PBS website, http://www.pbs.org/wgbh/amex/bomb/filmmore/reference/primary/fuchsstatement.html (accessed February 8, 2013).

Richart, Bette, "The Light Touch," in *Commonweal*, December 9, 1960, p. 278.

Roberts, Patti, "Poet Laureate of the Suburbs," in *Larchmont Gazette*, October 15, 2009, http://www.larchmontgazette.com/news/poet-laureate-of-the-suburbs-talkdinner-oct-22/ (accessed February 6, 2013).

Stein, Sadie, "Arthur Miller on *The Crucible*," in *Paris Review*, January 22, 2013, http://www.theparisreview.org/blog/2013/01/22/arthur-miller-on-the-crucible/ (accessed February 10, 2013).

"Television History: The First 75 Years," TV History website, http://www.tvhistory.tv/1953%20QF.htm (accessed February 8, 2013).

Wagner, Linda Welshimer, Preface to *Phyllis McGinley*, Twayne Publishers, 1971.

"Writing Ball's Pregnancy into the *I Love Lucy* Story Line, 1953," Library of Congress website, http://myloc.gov/Exhibitions/ilovelucy/castcrewset/ExhibitObjects/WritingInPregnancy.aspx (accessed February 18, 2013).

FURTHER READING

Friedan, Betty, *The Feminine Mystique*, Norton, 2001.
This landmark book was first published in 1963. With more than a million copies sold, it is essential reading in the history of second wave feminism, one of the crucial social and cultural developments of the 1960s and beyond.

Halliwell, Martin, *American Culture in the 1950s*, Edinburgh University Press, 2007.
This volume examines the major cultural outlets of the United States in the 1950s, including fiction and poetry, theater, film and television, music, radio, and the visual arts. It looks, for example, at Disneyland, the Seattle World's Fair, and *West Side Story* in an effort to show how the modernist movement and the cold war shaped post–World War II American culture.

Hamby, Barbara, and David Kirby, eds., *Seriously Funny: Poems about Love, Death, Religion, Art, Politics, Sex, and Everything Else*, University of Georgia Press, 2010.
This anthology includes 187 poems that address serious, timeless concerns but do so in a humorous way. Included are classic writers such as Chaucer and Shakespeare and more modern poets such as Frank O'Hara, the Beat poets, and John Ashbery and fellow members of the New York School of poetry.

Levin, Phillis, ed., *The Penguin Book of the Sonnet: 500 Years of Classic Tradition in English*, Penguin, 2001.

In this volume, Levin has assembled some six hundred examples of the sonnet by writers in English. Included are classic writers such as Chaucer, Shakespeare, Milton, and numerous writers from the Renaissance, as well as modern practitioners of the sonnet form such as Robert Frost, Edna St. Vincent Millay, E. E. Cummings, W. H. Auden, the poets of the Harlem Renaissance, and many others. The collection includes McGinley's sonnet "Evening Musicale."

Rattiner, Susan L., ed., *Great Poems by American Women: An Anthology*, Dover Publications, 1998.

As the title indicates, this volume is an anthology of poems written by American women. It includes more than two hundred entries, some dating to America's more distant past (Anne Bradstreet, Phillis Wheatley, Emily Dickinson, and Emma Lazarus), others written by more modern figures such as Marianne Moore, Sylvia Plath, Edna St. Vincent Millay, and Amy Lowell.

SUGGESTED SEARCH TERMS

American culture AND 1950s

Betty Friedan

humorous poetry

Love Letters of Phyllis McGinley

Phyllis McGinley

Phyllis McGinley AND Midcentury Love Letter

Second-wave feminism

Simone de Beauvoir AND Second Sex

suburbanization AND United States AND 1950s

Westchester County New York

Peace

RUPERT BROOKE
1914

Rupert Brooke's war sonnets, including "Peace," published at the end of 1914 during World War I, are among the best-known poems in the United Kingdom because of their resonance with British patriotism and history. They have been regularly studied in British schools for the last century. They caught exactly the expectant hope of their time that what was then called the Great War would somehow work toward the nation and the world's good and become a renewing baptism of fire. Because these poems so precisely caught the national mood, they became a runaway best seller, especially after Brooke's own death (of an infection, rather than in combat), which seemed to make him a martyr to the cause for which the war was being fought. But as the war dragged on through four years of increasingly senseless destruction, with more than a million Britons killed, and as the history of literature moved on to more modern forms, Brooke fell out of favor among critics. Yet even today, the illusory image of national renewal that he offers keeps him in the national consciousness.

AUTHOR BIOGRAPHY

Rupert Chawner Brooke was born on August 3, 1887, in the English town of Rugby. His father, William Brooke, was a schoolmaster (teacher) at Rugby school, where Rupert attended. Rugby is

Rupert Brooke (© Sherril Schell / Hulton Archive / Getty Images)

a public school (equivalent to a private school in the United States) patronized by the British aristocracy, and at that time, it was probably the finest secondary school in the world. Brooke never lost faith that he would someday be a noted poet, and he repeatedly boasted to his classmates that he would eventually have his portrait in the gallery at Rugby reserved for graduates who became great writers, as turned out to be the case. Brooke won a prize scholarship to Cambridge University, but he earned only a second-class honors degree in classics, which effectively barred him from any kind of graduate study or academic employment. However, at Cambridge, Brooke became the leader of a group that shared the rejection of Christianity and reaction against tradition that was then common among some intellectuals and artists. The group became known as the Neo-pagans; *pagan* in this case merely means "not Christian." They were devoted to finding new ways and new answers in every aspect of life, although they were under the wings of F. M. Cornford and Jane Harrison, Cambridge dons (professors) who were then among the leading experts in the world on Greek religion. Brooke's group was also connected to movements intent on

rethinking the structure of modern society, such as the Fabian Socialists and the literary circle known as the Bloomsbury group (which included noted author Virginia Woolf), to whom Brooke was introduced by his fellow student and lover Vita Sackville-West.

The Nobel Prize–winning poet William Butler Yeats (as quoted in *The Dictionary of Biographical Quotation*, edited by Justin Wintle and Richard Kenin) called Brooke "the handsomest man in England." This may seem trivial, but his good looks were a vital part of his persona, including his artistic image. Brooke's friend Walter de la Mare (writing in *Rupert Brooke and the Intellectual Imagination*) said of him: "We don't often meet people in this world who instantly recall the Golden Age and remind us that the Greek sculptors went to Life for their models." Brooke took advantage of his good looks, his great charm, and the new freedoms of modern society to have many romantic relationships, with both men and women, making more intellectual and professional connections. Brooke supported himself through publications in newspapers, which, in the early twentieth century, often printed literary material. Following a nervous breakdown in 1912, Brooke went on a world tour, paid for by publishing his travel diaries. He spent two months in Tahiti and probably had a child with a local woman named Taatamata. One of Brooke's lovers, Edward Marsh, who came to admire the poet through his performances in amateur theatricals at Cambridge, acted as Brooke's patron. A wealthy aristocrat, Marsh organized the Georgian group of poets (named after Marsh's journal, *Georgian Poetry*, but also known as the Dymock poets after the Gloucestershire town close to where many of them lived) that included Brooke, Robert Frost, and Robert Graves, and he supported the publication of their poetry. Marsh was also the private secretary of Winston Churchill (First Lord of the Admiralty during World War I), whom he interested in Brooke's career.

When war broke out in 1914 and Brooke volunteered, Churchill secured him a commission and employed him in his personal military projects, including the defense of Antwerp, Belgium, in 1914, and the invasion of Gallipoli in the Mediterranean in 1915. Brooke never experienced actual combat, however, and died of an infected mosquito bite (erroneously reported as sunstroke in the London *Times* obituary written by Churchill). He died on April 23, 1915, on a hospital ship just off the

Greek island of Skyros. Brooke's five war sonnets (which had recently been published by Marsh in his journal *New Numbers* in 1914), including "Peace," were reprinted in the *Times* and given public readings. They were quickly collected and reprinted, becoming a best seller and giving voice to the patriotism that was inspired by the ongoing war. These works and their reception secured Brooke's place as one of the most familiar poets of his generation.

POEM TEXT

> Now, God be thanked who has matched us
>   with his hour,
> And caught our youth, and wakened us from
>   sleeping!
> With hand made sure, clear eye, and sharpened
>   power,
> To turn, as swimmers into cleanness leaping,
> Glad from a world grown old and cold and weary; 5
> Leave the sick hearts that honor could not
>   move,
> And half-men, and their dirty songs and
>   dreary,
> And all the little emptiness of love!
> Oh! we, who have known shame, we have
>   found release there,
> Where there's no ill, no grief, but sleep
>   has mending,   10
> Naught broken save this body, lost but breath;
> Nothing to shake the laughing heart's long
>   peace there,
> But only agony, and that has ending;
> And the worst friend and enemy is but Death.

POEM SUMMARY

The text used for this summary is from *Poetry*, Vol 6, No. 1, April 1915, p. 18. A version of the poem can be found on the following web page: http://www.warpoetry.co.uk/brooke3.html.

"Peace" is spoken by a narrative character using the first-person plural, *we*. This is meant to refer to the whole generation of young men of military age in Britain. The poem had originally been titled "The Recruit," which would have implied a different audience, but the change of title that Brooke made before publication signals a wider audience, which, in this case, also includes the speaker himself.

"Peace" is a sonnet divided into two sections, an eight-line octave followed by a six-line sestet. The octave (which is a single sentence) takes the form of a prayer, in which the speaker invokes God and gives thanks for the various circumstances related to the Great War as detailed in the body of the poem. In general, the war is perceived as a blessing.

In the first line, the speaker gives thanks to God for sending the present generation the war. This idea has many possible meanings, but the most obvious is simply that the present crop of young men will have benefits attributed to the war's occurrence.

In the second line, the speaker notes that God has aroused the young generation from its sleep. This is the first time the poem indirectly references the New Testament; although Brooke never quotes from or mentions the New Testament, readers familiar with that work are intended to be reminded of key passages that Brooke has in mind by his echoing of their language and ideas. In the Bible, Christians are warned not to be caught sleeping when Jesus returns at the end of the world (Mark 13:36; 1 Thessalonians 5:6). Even more pointedly, sleep is often used as a metaphor for death in the New Testament, and the returning Jesus will rouse them too: "Awake thou that sleepest, and arise from the dead!" (Ephesians 5:15, King James Version). So Brooke is viewing the war in an apocalyptic light, as the fulfilling moment of history. When they are roused from their sleep, the nation's youth are changed beings, with greater faith, clearer vision, and keener powers.

The youth, in line 4, leap into action as a swimmer might leap into a pool of clean water. The image connects physical washing in a bath with washing away sin through the Christian ritual of baptism. Baptism is also an initiation, and in the next line, the youth have been initiated or reborn into a new life, leaving behind an old world that is tired and cold, like death. In other words, their old life, the common life that everyone on earth experiences and shares, is really death, and they will enter into a new life of spiritual existence.

The remaining three lines of the octave (lines 6–8) characterize the worst examples of the old life. These are people who are depraved and who are unmoved by honor. They are less than real men, they write dreadful obscene poetry, and what matters to them is the hollow experience of love (probably meaning the physical act of love). There is little doubt that this caricature refers to the Bloomsbury group, poets and novelists (such as Virginia Woolf) who experimented with new literary forms and who also opposed the war on grounds of pacifism. Brooke himself had love affairs with several members of the Bloomsbury group, both men and women. It is his own old life that Brooke is condemning; he recasts it as type of a death from which he is reborn into the new spiritual existence of the war.

In the sestet (beginning at line 9), the speaker of the poem condemns the youth of Britain (including himself) for the shame of their past lives. He rejoices in the release from sin that they have found in the new lives given to them by the war. They are convinced (line 10) that the only misfortunes they can now suffer will be repaired by the sleep they find in the war. It was made clear in the octave that Brooke is speaking in Biblical language, so sleep in this case is a euphemism for death. The ideal that the youth of Britain are here meant to be striving for is to find their own deaths in the war, an experience that will fix whatever was wrong with their lives. This too is an invocation of the Christian mythology of the Apostle Paul's letters, in which the dead will resurrected in new spiritual bodies and redeemed into a new life in heaven. The war, then, and death in combat, becomes a metaphor for Christian salvation.

The speaker goes on in line 11 to discount the importance of the destruction of their bodies and the loss of their lives. In line 12, death becomes a matter of no importance. The only virtuous desire is the peace that is to be found in dissolution. If one has to pay the price of physical suffering for that peace (line 13), that too is nothing because it is temporary, implying that the transformation that ends agony in death is eternal. Finally, in line 14, the young men may regard death as an enemy (in an echo of 1 Corinthians 15:26), but death is also a friend to be embraced, because it is to be celebrated as eternal life (1 Corinthians 15:29–32).

THEMES

Christianity

Since the Enlightenment and the romantic period of the eighteenth and nineteenth centuries, the relationship of European intellectualism to Christianity had changed remarkably. Naïve belief in doctrines that seemed to contradict everything known about the physical world and to support the unjust

medieval social order was, for some, no longer possible in the early twentieth century. Nevertheless, Christianity still maintained tremendous importance as a cultural artifact and could have tremendous artistic importance because of its resonance with history and its influence on literary and artistic traditions.

At the same time, a more popular level of British culture turned to Christianity as a source of spiritual renewal. The movement known as muscular Christianity looked to the athletics that were compulsory at English public schools such as Rugby as a new form of physical discipline that could purify the nation. Thomas Hughes' *Tom Brown's School Days* (set at Rugby), one of the most popular of all Victorian novels, was a great popularizer of this idea. In the sequel, *Tom Brown at Oxford*, he compares the virtue of the student athlete to the chivalrous virtues of the Christian knight: "The least of the muscular Christians has hold of the old chivalrous and Christian belief, that a man's body is given him to be trained and brought into subjection, and then used for the protection of the weak, the advancement of all righteous causes, and the subduing of the earth which God has given to the children of men." The movement looked to the teachings of St. Paul, who said, "What? know ye not that your body is the temple of the Holy Ghost which is in you, which ye have of God, and ye are not your own? For ye are bought with a price: therefore glorify God in your body, and in your spirit, which are God's" (1 Corinthians 6:19–20, King James Version). The body had to be washed clean through punishing exercise just as the soul was washed by baptism. This philosophy was forced onto Brooke at Rugby, but he felt a natural reaction against it. In his days at Rugby, Brooke had taken great pleasure in mocking religious people, shocking them by claiming that he had converted to the worship of Baal, or to Mormonism, or that he had left the Church of England for Christianity. In an unpublished memoir, Gwen Darwin (one of Brooke's closest friends among the Neo-pagans at Cambridge, as quoted by Paul Delany in *The Neo-pagans*) reported that Brooke could regularly be heard to laugh at "the ridiculous superstitions about God and Religion; the absurd prejudices of patriotism and decency." But Brooke could not get free of his religious training, and in "Peace" he tries to resolve his inner conflicts by embracing muscular Christianity. He presents the Great War as a

TOPICS FOR FURTHER STUDY

- Ernst Jünger's *Storm of Steel*, originally published in 1920, is a memoir of the author's experiences as a German soldier fighting in the trenches of the Western Front as a teenager. He describes the horrors of the war as well as the naïve patriotism that first led him to volunteer to fight. Read this memoir and the rest of Brooke's five war sonnets, and write a paper comparing the picture of the World War I presented by Jünger with that presented by Brooke.

- In the young-adult novel *Forgotten Fire*, Adam Bagdasarian tells the story (based on his own family's history) of a twelve-year-old boy who is suddenly made homeless and an orphan in 1915, when the Turkish government begins to carry out a genocide against the Armenian community to which he belongs. After reading the novel, try to encapsulate the boy's experience of World War I in a sonnet.

- Lina Granfield's 2005 *Where the Poppies Grow: A World War I Companion* is a sort of national British scrapbook of the Great War intended for young-adult readers. It collects letters home from soldiers at the front, together with anecdotes and memoirs of their families in Britain. In particular, the book is filled with images from postcards and collecting cards, which at the time were a way of expressing and recording popular consciousness, in much the same way as images that circulate on Facebook today. In a similar fashion, create a blog simulating the experience of a World War I family, using materials compiled from the Internet.

- The German artist Otto Dix made a definitive artistic representation of the war in his 1924 collection of etchings *The War* (*Der Krieg*), and in paintings such as *The Trench*, in which he rejected modernism and used the realistic style of German Renaissance painting to document his traumatic experience in the war. Another common subject of his paintings were the crippled and disfigured veterans whom the government's poverty and indifference left to live as beggars on the streets of German cities. Create and share with your class a PowerPoint presentation in which Dix's work, with its realistic depiction of World War I and its aftermath, is contrasted with the vision of the war as salvation offered by Brooke's "Peace."

grand athletic contest in which the soul of the nation will be purified by blood sacrifice, namely through destroying the bodies of its youth.

Peace

The peace of which Brooke speaks is, paradoxically, to be found only in the Great War. England will be transformed into a nation of virtue through the torture and death of its sons, who will find final peace only through death in battle. The purpose of the war in its early months, for the British public as mirrored by Brooke, was to regulate and restore the structure of English society. In "Peace," Brooke gives voice to ideas that would be more fully, and more critically,

expressed a generation after the Great War, by George Orwell in his novel *Nineteen Eighty-Four*. Orwell presents a vision of English society that is meant to seem like a fantasy but is really a shocking criticism of the real England as Orwell saw it. One of the core ideas of Ingsoc, a satirical restatement of English society's beliefs and values, is that war is peace. Ingsoc teaches that "the war is waged by each ruling group against its own subjects, and the object of the war is not to make or prevent conquests of territory, but to keep the structure of society intact." Although it is not outwardly acknowledged even in Orwell's nightmare vision, "this . . . is the inner meaning of the Party slogan: war is peace." The main

"Peace" was likely inspired by his experience figthing in World War I. *(© Olemac / Shutterstock.com)*

character of the novel is forced to accept this doctrine precisely through the breaking of his body and mind by torture, and finally by facing his own death. Orwell exposes the idea that war is actually peace as a destructive hypocrisy, but Brooke embraces this paradox.

STYLE

Sonnet

The sonnet (which means "little song") is one of the most prominent and traditional forms of verse in English literature, and indeed in Western European literature in general. It was developed in the Middle Ages by the troubadours, professional singers of love songs in northern Spain and southern France, who wrote in the local dialects, and it was made into a standard form by the Italian poets Petrarch and Dante. Shakespeare's collection of 154 sonnets perfected the form in English, and later poets such as John Donne and John Keats expanded the English

sonnet far beyond its origin in love poetry. Brooke's generation would be the last to write sonnets as a dominant form of serious work, as the revolution of modernism that washed over English literature after the war resulted in the discarding of such rigid and traditional forms.

Originally, a sonnet consisted of a problem established in the first eight lines (called the *octave*) followed by a resolution in the last six lines (*sestet*), and many English sonnets continued to use this format, known as a *Petrarchan sonnet*. But the typical English form of the sonnet was established by Edmund Spenser in the seventeenth century and is called the *Spenserian sonnet*. This consists of three groups of four lines (*quatrains*) whose meaning is self-contained, followed by a final couplet, or pair of rhymed lines. In any case, each line of a sonnet is an *iambic pentameter*, that is, it contains five iambs, metrical units made up of an unstressed syllable followed by a stressed syllable. A sonnet also follows a fixed and definite rhyme scheme. Rhyme is the property of poetry wherein the endings of different lines share the same stress and sound. For example, if the first and third lines of a poem ended in *hour* and *power*, while the second and fourth lines ended in *sleeping* and *leaping*, those lines would be said to follow the rhyme scheme *abab*. A Spenserian sonnet generally follows the rhyme scheme *abab bccb cdcd ee*. However, considerable substitution and variation in meter and rhyme scheme are allowed in sonnets.

Brooke's "Peace" is a Petrarchan sonnet and follows the rhyme scheme *ababcdcd ebfebf*. The octave establishes a prayer of thanks for God's use of the war to awaken the sleeping souls of English Christians, while the sestet moves to a contemplation of the Christian idea that the only real life is after death, in this case to be achieved through death in war, bringing peace to the fallen. As a traditional form, the sonnet was characteristic of the poetry of Brooke and the other Georgian poets (those Marsh patronized), the last literary movement to emerge in Britain before World War I. Ezra Pound and other imagist poets (who concentrated on simple images and avoided overt philosophy in their work) began to publish in 1911, beginning the rise of modern poetry and ending the reign of traditional forms.

Assonance

Assonance is the quality of poetic language achieved through the repeated use of similar

COMPARE
&
CONTRAST

- **1910s:** Europe is in the grip of World War I, a conflict that sees the first use of weapons of mass destruction (poison gas and strategic bombing) and an unprecedented loss of human life measured in the millions.

  Today: After the catastrophe of World War I and the even worse destruction of World War II, Western Europe has made arrangements for collective security (the North Atlantic Treaty Organization) that effectively make war in Western Europe impossible.

- **1910s:** Brooke's bisexuality and promiscuity, though common enough in his social and intellectual circles, are stigmatized by popular morality and punishable by law, creating an inner conflict in him over the moral character of his own actions.

  Today: Sexual orientation and sexual acts between consenting adults are no longer criminalized in British law, and increasingly progressive attitudes toward private sex lives make crippling guilt over sexual matters rarer.

- **1910s:** Traditional poetic forms such as the sonnet are still the standard, though experimentation by the imagists and others is increasing.

  Today: Artistic traditions, having been reexamined and generally rejected by the creative artists of the 1920s because they were associated with the civilization that had led to the calamity of World War I, are now rarely used in the era of modern art.

---

vowel sounds. Brooke was particularly a master of this kind of effect, building up a mood through the way his language sounds rather than what it means. A good example of this is line 5 of "Peace." In this line, the parade of long vowels evokes a depth that is wholly appropriate to the subject, but is not quite there in the meaning of the words considered objectively. The same line benefits from the marching rhythm suggested by its pattern of stressed and unstressed syllables.

Prayer

Brooke's "Peace" takes the form of a prayer. It is addressed as an offering of thanks to God, conventionally understood in England in his era (and because of the capitalization of the word) as the Christian God. Although "Peace" is far removed from the formal convention of any prayer in the Anglican *Book of Common Prayer*, it is intended to call to mind the most deeply rooted forms of religious faith in its hearers.

HISTORICAL CONTEXT

Brooke wrote "Peace" in 1914 in the midst of World War I, known then simply as the war and soon as the Great War. His purpose is to glorify the war as a socially transformative adventure, a view he could hold because he had never himself seen combat, and one for which he would quickly be sharply criticized by fellow poets Wilfred Owen, Siegfried Sassoon, and others who had fully experienced the horror of the conflict.

The war began over a political crisis that followed the assassination of the heir to the Austro-Hungarian monarchy by a Bosnian-Serb nationalist. Each of the great powers in Europe was a member of an international alliance, and they all had carefully determined plans for mobilization and deployment of their armed forces that they put into motion more or less automatically. Even today, there is no clearly understood cause that can be pointed to as the reason for the war, and certainly no moral or ideological reason that could justify the enormous loss it involved. Even the military and

The image of a swimmer diving into sparkling clean water symbolizes baptism and absolution. (© Kochneva
Tetyana / Shutterstock.com)

political leaders had not experienced a war in
Europe since 1870 and had little understanding
of what it would mean for themselves and the
people they ruled. Nor did anyone fully comprehend how advances in technology had transformed the nature of warfare and the
experience of battle. Many naively looked on
the war as a cleansing fire that would reforge
their nations into new, morally purified wholes.

The introduction of the relatively simple
devices of the machine gun and rapidly firing
artillery had made the defensive position in
warfare many times stronger than the offensive. After a period of maneuvering that
lasted only a few weeks, the war in Western
Europe settled into a line of trenches stretching from the Swiss border to the English
Channel on a line just west of the pre-war
French border. Thereafter, the normal
method of attack was to simply have masses
of soldiers to walk forward, just as in the
days of Napoleon or George Washington, to
cross the gap of a few hundred yards—called
"no man's land"—between the lines of
trenches. The defenders would respond to
such an advance with concentrated machine
gun and artillery fire into the unprotected
bodies of the massed soldiers with predictable

results. For instance, on July 1, 1916, more
than twenty thousand British soldiers died on
the first day (almost all in the first three
hours) of the failed Somme offensive. They
succeeded in taking the first line of German
trenches, but this merely pushed the enemy
back to an existing second trench line a few
hundred yards back. Repeating this process
over and over again cost the lives of almost
a million Englishmen between 1914 and 1918,
and millions more from the other countries
involved. Brooke himself died on the way to
an amphibious assault at Gallipoli on the
coast of Germany's ally Turkey, which
resulted in precisely the same tactical stale-
mate. Tens of thousands of soldiers died for
no purpose; the beachhead they had established had to be evacuated.

Other aspects of the war seemed to make it
more terrible and brutal than previous conflicts.
At about the same time as Brooke's death, a new
element was added to the battlefield, poison gas.
This weapon killed masses indiscriminately and
could mean a long, agonizing death. In addition,
civilians were targeted in some cases. Germany
was in a slightly worse strategic situation than
France and Britain and turned to unrestricted
submarine warfare—the sinking of civilian

merchant vessels at sea—and the strategic bombardment of Paris (with long-range artillery) and London (with bombs dropped from zeppelins), directly attacking civilian populations, until Germany finally collapsed, ending the war. The soldiers who suffered through it did not find any aspect of this industrial slaughter of human beings adventurous or cleansing, as the later war poets made clear. To put the matter in a more human perspective, about seven hundred graduates of Rugby school died in the four years of the war, the equivalent of a year's graduating class, or about one in ten of those the right age to serve.

CRITICAL OVERVIEW

The initial reaction to Brooke's war sonnets, including "Peace," was a rush not only to praise his work, as an expression of national will, but to appropriate it for wartime propaganda. In 1915, public figures such as Winston Churchill, in his *Times* obituary of Brookes, and William Inge, the Dean of St. Paul's Cathedral, in his Easter sermon, used Brooke's sonnets as a call to literal self-sacrifice to the young men of Britain. Their efforts succeeded, and the slim volume that collected the war sonnets sold hundreds of thousands of copies that year and entered public consciousness to such a degree that Brooke's sonnets, especially "The Soldier," are still memorized by British schoolchildren even today.

Brooke's reception with the artistic and critical community was not and is not so rapturous. The other war poets, who actually experienced combat in World War I, rejected Brooke's work as completely invalidated by what they perceived as his hypocrisy. John Gould Fletcher, writing in the imagist journal *Egoist* in December 1916, summed up the reaction to Brooke's war poetry among leading British poets: "We must go to prose to find out what the war is like, or else swallow the soothing syrups of . . . Brooke's *Sonnets*—charming soothing syrups, but not within a million miles of the stern crushing reality." Admitting as much through omission, Brooke's friend Walter de la Mare, in his 1919 lecture *Rupert Brooke and the Intellectual Imagination*, while addressing the audience most favorable to Brooke imaginable, the students and faculty of Rugby school, passes over Brooke's war sonnets in an embarrassed silence. These best known of Brooke's works were better left ignored after the

WHAT DO I READ NEXT?

- John Frayn Turner's 2004 *The Life and Selected Works of Rupert Brooke* offers a brief biography of the poet and a selection of his more important prose and verse in a single volume. Turner's perspective is military history and he takes a rather unapologetic view of Brooke's patriotic stance.

- *The Collected Poems of Rupert Brooke*, originally edited by his friend Edward Marsh in 1918 and revised for a third edition in 1960, is a standard edition of Brooke's complete poetical work.

- Shaun Tan's 2006 *The Arrival* is a graphic novel intended for a young-adult audience. Without using any dialogue or narration but only images, Tan, whose family immigrated from Malaysia to Australia, tells much of the history of the twentieth century in an allegorical form. The work includes the story of a young man recruited for war, led by optimism and patriotism to volunteer for service, who is emotionally devastated by his experience in combat as he sees his civilization destroyed.

- John Keegan's *The First World War* (1998) is a standard introduction to World War I by the twentieth century's greatest military historian.

- *Stolen Voices: Young People's War Diaries, from World War I to Iraq* (2006), edited by Zlata Filipovic and Melanie Challenger, is a collection of writings by young adults reflecting their firsthand experience of war all over the world throughout the twentieth century and into the twenty-first.

- Paul Fussell's 1975 *The Great War and Modern Memory* is the classic critical treatment of the war poets. The author is mainly interested in how World War I changed the poets and all of Western civilization, so deals only briefly with Brooke, who died before undergoing the kind of transformative experience common to some other figures, such as Siegfried Sassoon and Isaac Rosenberg.

war had proved to be of an entirely different character than Brooke had claimed.

Modern criticism of "Peace," well represented by Delany's comments in *The Neo-pagans*, has focused on the compromised nature of the poem. Delany observes that Brooke's "belief in the absolute purity of his mission could hardly have survived a month in the trenches." He looks instead to Brooke's personal life, even his inner life, as the true subject of the poem:

> The war let him feel that the whole nation had joined him in spurning homosexual and pacifist Bloomsbury. What the common reader could not know, however, was that Rupert hated Bloomsbury for its complicity with his own sexual guilt, and that *this* was what it would take a war to wash off.

Delany sees the Christian imagery in "Peace" as part of one many Brooke's carefully constructed masks. The poem's "fame was already ironic, since Rupert had long professed a Neo-pagan scorn for orthodox Christianity." Brooke concealed his inner conflict behind this Christian façade, expressing in his sonnets "the enticing myth that death purged away the sins of the flesh, so that war itself could seen as a long-awaited cleansing of national guilt." William E. Laskowski, in *Rupert Brooke*, also looks to Brooke's biography for the real meaning of the poem: "The reality is that the first line of 'Peace'"—the prayerful thanks to God for sending the war—"was true: Brooke's own personal sentiments had been precisely matched with the needs of his time." When the recruits of "Peace" "are washing away all the evils of modern life," this stands in for Brooke's desire to wash away what he perceives as his own sins.

CRITICISM

Bradley Skeen

Skeen is a classicist. In the following essay, he explains Brooke's "Peace" as an allegory, presenting a patriotic meaning but also revealing deeper layers of meaning relating to Brooke as a poet and as a human being.

Part of the brilliance of Brooke's "Peace" is that it can be read on many different levels. The poem offers an appeal to patriotism that proved useful for shaping popular reaction to the war. But other readings of the poem are subversive of the status of Brooke's poetry as a memorial to those who died in World War I and offer

> IT IS ALL THE MORE IRONIC THAT THE GOVERNMENTS THAT USED SUCH WEAPONS SHOULD TRY TO COVER OVER THE HORRIBLE REALITY OF THE WAR WITH BEAUTIFUL LANGUAGE LIKE BROOKE'S."

meanings relevant to Brooke's ambition as a poet and to his own inner struggles for what Brooke considered redemption. Brooke shows great skill, and greater daring, in letting these meanings stand side by side, almost as a challenge to the reader to see through the excessive, blind patriotism of the poem's surface.

On the simplest and most popular level, "Peace" can be read as an expression of patriotism. In this case, "Peace" is addressed to the British nation as a whole, or at least to Brooke's own generation of young men on whose shoulders fell the burden of fighting the war. The poem describes them as blessed by divine providence with the opportunity to find spiritual renewal through self-sacrifice in combat. The British public embraced this reading of the poem, because it seemed to give meaning to the otherwise unbearable suffering and loss caused by the war.

In 1914, Great Britain, at the head of an empire that covered about a quarter of the world's surface, was still the most powerful, most technologically advanced, and wealthiest nation in the world. Its imperial power was projected by a relatively small professional army and navy. The civilian population, benefiting from an unprecedented rise in the standard of living from a mature industrial economy, had no conception of what war was like. Even the commanders of the armed forces and politicians had no understanding of what modern war between industrial powers would mean. Amazingly, in retrospect, the view of war that prevailed in Great Britain was highly romantic. A widespread idea was that British society was becoming decadent because of its wealth and that the coming of war would strengthen the moral fiber of the nation. This view was put down on paper in the first weeks of the war by Edmund Gosse, a poet, influential critic and scholar, and librarian of the House of Lords. Gosse not only expressed commonly held ideas about war but somehow believed that had the ability to understand what war would mean for the nation without ever so much as having set foot on a battlefield. Gosse wrote,

> War is...the sovereign disinfectant, and its red stream of blood is the Condy's Fluid that cleans out the stagnant pools and clotted channels of the intellect. I suppose that hardly any Englishman who is capable of a renovation of the mind has failed to feel during the last few weeks a certain solemn refreshment of the spirit, a humble and mournful consciousness that his ideals, his aims, his hopes during our late past years of luxury and peace have been founded on a misconception of our aims as a nation.

Gosse actually seems anxious for Englishmen to die, viewing their deaths as a sacrifice that will redeem a spiritually corrupt nation.

These are exactly the same ideas that Brooke puts in poetic form in "Peace." God, Brooke says, has sent the war as a gift to the English people, who will be awakened and reborn from the sickness of personal pleasure to a new spiritual cleanness. All that Englishmen will have to pay for this great benefit is to have their bodies destroyed. But the death that brings spiritual cleansing, Brooke tells his reader, is a friend. Brooke had had no real experience of combat. Although he had been deployed in the defense of Antwerp in the fall of 1914, he had never come under enemy fire. He had no understanding of the physical agony that he advised his readers to accept with laughter when their bodies were broken, or what the loss of comrades means, or what it means to experience the immediacy of death.

Since Brooke was putting into a sophisticated poetic form ideas that were already widely held by British civilians, it was inevitable that the war sonnets would meet with tremendous popularity, and when they were published in late 1914, and particularly after Brooke's death in early 1915, they became best sellers. The British government was quick to realize that their message was useful, even necessary, to the war effort. In the absence of conscription (that is, a military draft), which was still more than a year in the future, young men had to be persuaded to volunteer to fight in the war. They might more easily be persuaded if they believed that war was a romantic, redemptive enterprise that, if they died, would give their deaths purpose and meaning. Brooke's patron, Winston Churchill, who was also First Lord of the Admiralty (that is, the political head of the navy), was quick to use his protégé's poetry and even his death to reinforce this essentially false popular conception of war held by the English public. Churchill himself wrote Brooke's obituary in the April 26, 1915, issue of the *Times*. He used the notice of Brooke's death to paint the by now familiar picture of the war as an adventure of medieval chivalry, saying of Brooke, "A voice had become audible, a note had been struck, more true, more thrilling, more able to do justice to the nobility of our youth in arms engaged in this present war than any other." In particular Churchill picked up the themes of "Peace" and reiterated them, calling a Brooke a representative of British youth who was "more able to express their thoughts of self-surrender, and with a power to carry comfort to those who watch them so intently from afar." Brooke's sacrifice, Churchill is asserting, and the sacrifices of any other young men reading, will morally sustain the whole of England. The sacrifice of war raised Brooke, and will raise other Englishmen, to a state of superhuman perfection and grace: "He expected to die: he was willing to die for the dear England whose beauty and majesty he knew: and he advanced towards the brink in perfect serenity, with absolute conviction of the rightness of his country's cause and a heart devoid of hate for fellow-men." Churchill specifically urges other young men reading the obituary to make the same sacrifice as Brooke, precisely because its redemptive force will be all the greater for the new difficulties and dangers of modern warfare: "The thoughts to which he gave expression... will be shared by many thousands of young men moving resolutely and blithely forward into this, the hardest, the cruelest, and the least-rewarded of all the wars that men have fought."

Brooke's "Peace" speaks to a fantasy that war is noble and redemptive. Churchill could not have used in this way a poet whose work reflected real experience of war. Wilfred Owen's 1916 "*Dulce et Decorum Est*" is such a poem that mockingly uses a line by the Roman poet Horace (*Dulce et decorum est pro patria mori*: "It is sweet and right to die for your country") to undercut any romantic ideas about the nobility of war. The glorification of war is the old lie that Owen denounces, almost certainly with "Peace" and Brooke in mind. In his poem, Owen describes in simple language a soldier's face being dissolved by exposure to mustard gas, one of the horrible new weapons that industrial technology had put at the disposal of the combatants. It is all the more ironic that the governments that used such weapons should try to cover over the horrible reality of the war with beautiful language like Brooke's.

However much the poem was read, and however much Brooke intended "Peace" to be read, as romantic praise of war and death, it reveals other meanings that are more personal and private to Brooke's own life, granting greater depth to the otherwise blindly patriotic work. The first and main idea of Brooke's "Peace" is that this war came at exactly the right moment when England was in need of the spiritual cleansing that he claims it will provide. But the same line (line 1), just as much, means that the war has provided Brooke with the opportunity to gain the reputation, at least, of being a great poet. The war has brought his own inner life and artistic purpose into line with the popular consciousness of England and will finally bring him the fame he had always craved. And indeed it did, making Brooke the most popular and beloved poet of his generation.

Read with knowledge of the author's biography, "Peace" seems to reveal a still more personal level of meaning. Brooke led a dual existence. His own personal life must have seemed depraved compared with the conventions of muscular Christianity that were drummed into his head at Rugby, leaving him with an unresolved inner conflict. The war must have seemed a chance to resolve that by washing away the decadent half of his own nature. Brooke expressed this same idea, in pretty nearly the same language as "Peace," in a letter to his fellow Georgian poet, John Drinkwater. Brooke says he "hopes that England'll get on her legs again, achieve youth and merriment and slough the things I loathe—capitalism and feminism and hermaphroditism and the rest." He is hoping to undergo, on a personal level, the same transformation as England. If his country will become clean by washing away capitalism and feminism (the suffragette movement, which sought to allow women to vote), Brooke hopes, he will in the same way be cleansed of his own bisexuality (which he calls "hermaphroditism," a term now widely considered offensive). The rest of the letter (like all of his last letters) was filled with the Christian machismo of Rugby, which he seems finally to have adopted as his own nature. For him, the Great War was a chance to go back to the camaraderie of the school athletic field and live his life over again in a different way: "But on service one has a great feeling of

The speaker is glad to leave the cold world. (© Rene Hartmann / Shutterstock.com)

fellowship, and a fine thrill, like nothing else in the world." As in the poem, the peace of his newly resolved identity will be found in death: "not a bad place and time to die, Belgium, 1915? I want to kill my Prussian first. Better than coughing out a civilian soul amid bedclothes and disinfectant and gulping medicines in 1950." But he died exactly three months later on a French hospital ship under those very circumstances he spoke against.

Brooke's acquaintance, the novelist D. H. Lawrence, saw that the re-creation of the self that Brooke boasts of in "Peace" was only another pose. In a letter to Lady Ottoline Morrell written a few days after Brooke's death (as quoted in *The Dictionary of Biographical Quotation*, edited by Justin Wintle and Richard Kenin), he sums up his growing dissatisfaction with the war by referencing Brooke: "The death of Rupert Brooke fills me more and more with the sense of the fatuity of it all." Brooke was incorrectly reported at the time to have died of sunstroke, which Lawrence mocks with a pompous reference to the plague that Apollo sends to the Greek camp at the beginning of the *Iliad*, "He was slain by bright Phoebus' shaft—it was in keeping with his general sunniness—it was the real climax of his pose." Lawrence viewed Brooke's whole life as a dramatic affectation, of which his newfound patriotism and enthusiasm for war were only the latest expression.

Source: Bradley Skeen, Critical Essay on "Peace," in *Poetry for Students*, Gale, Cengage Learning, 2014.

Janis P. Stout

In the following excerpt, Stout describes Brooke as a poet defined by World War I.

. . . Rupert Brooke was still in his twenties when the war broke out—indeed, he never lived to be thirty—but was already well established among the Georgian poets. He became a focal point of Britain's national sentiment about her soldiers abroad when he quickly enlisted. After serving briefly in Belgium, where he was present at the retreat from Antwerp, he was attached to the Royal Naval Division for the campaign in the Dardanelles but died on shipboard on the way, of blood poisoning apparently from an insect bite. Yet as David Perkins points out, despite the tragic quality of this story of untimely death, the war was for Brooke "a mode of redemption." Shifting his center of interest from his earlier aestheticism mixed with socialism and spasmodic bouts of emotional confusion, he took the war as his own "supreme cause" (Perkins 211–12), making it a vehicle for the expression of love of country.

It is difficult now to understand the elation with which Brooke and others like him greeted what was to be civilization's nightmare. Yet as scholars such as Samuel Hynes and Glen Wilkinson rightly remind us, Brooke was a member of a generation that for two decades had been reading newspaper and periodical discussions of the necessity and benefit of periodic wars as a cleansing or renewing agent for a moribund society. If such an attitude seems more than a little incredible from our perspective, the reason is that we cannot rid ourselves of our awareness of subsequent history. For Brooke and other Edwardians who "shouted and cheered for war" in 1914 (Wilkinson 34), there could be no such awareness. Casting the struggle as one between youth and all that would dash its hopes for nobility or cause it ennui—a different vision of enmity between the young and the old than would characterize writings of the later war—Brooke exulted in the opportunity for newness of life that he saw before him. It was the long-awaited chance to rid himself of the lingering fin de siècle sentiment of exhaustion and indifference. His feelings were only one conspicuous instance of what Eric Leed calls a widespread "euphoria of August" that extended beyond England to Germany and France as well.

Brooke is now best known for the "1914 Sonnets," a group of five sonnets published in a transitory literary journal in December 1914, four months after the beginning of the war. Probably the most famous of the group is number 5, "The Soldier," with its familiar opening "If I should die, think only this of me: / That there's some corner of a foreign field / That is for ever England" (Brooke 316). Brooke did die, of course, early in the war—as Gilbert and Gubar point out, "before disillusionment could set in" (*Sexchanges* 265). Beloved for its tone of reverent patriotism toward an idealized England and perhaps for its reassuring assumption that dead soldiers would find their deaths worthwhile, "The Soldier" was read in the pulpit by the dean of Saint Paul's on Easter Sunday, 1915 (Martin 32; Giddings 37, et al). This "plug," in Eby's words, made the "superciliously nationalistic" poem "an instant success" (230, 233). Gavin Ewart, writing not only after the Great War but after World War II as well, and therefore less intoxicated with glory than the good dean, says bluntly that Brooke "died in an imperialist war, and such a poem glorified it" (Ewart, Introduction 11). But glorifying it, along with glorifying England, was, after all, the point.

The language of Brooke's war sonnets is a distinctive and moving blend of martial convention with a gentle directness in expressing love of daily pleasures. A little more of the former and they would become bombast; a little more of the latter and they would scarcely be war poems at all. Yet the conventions that in lesser hands could become specious, indeed deceptive, are fully in evidence here. "Dawn was theirs, / And sunset"—the magical times of day that, with the entrenchment that came to define the Western Front in 1915, would become ironically the most dangerous times (because of the routine of "stand-to," a twice-daily ritual of mounting the firing step, weapon in hand, on alert for an assault). Here, these magical times are simply moving. But the prettiness of Brooke's syntactic inversion is the kind of poetic device that would soon be rejected by poets intent on stating a more brutal truth. Bugles and kings, capitalized abstractions such as Love and Pain, the assertion of certainty that the dying hero will carry on beyond death, substitutions such as "sweet wine of youth" for young men's blackened blood: these are the tropes of the "1914 Sonnets."

Perhaps most shocking to present readers and most poignant in its ignorance of what was to come (Ewart terms it "unthinking") is the opening of the first of the five sonnets:

Now, God be thanked Who has matched us with His
  hour,
And caught our youth, and wakened us from
  sleeping,
With hand made sure, clear eye, and sharpened
  power,
To turn, as swimmers into cleanness leaping,
Glad from a world grown old and cold and
  weary.... (Brooke 312)

God would be called on in many ways in the years of slaughter ahead, but seldom in thanks. Brooke was by no means the only British writer to employ a language of cleansing when speaking of the war; Hynes points out that such established spokespersons for the arts as Edmund Gosse and Selwyn Image also spoke of the newly launched war as a "sovereign disinfectant" or a "cleansing purge" (12–15). Since the war effort would soon become mired in the filth of the trenches, a rhetoric of cleansing appears in retrospect particularly ironic. Yet Brooke, who would not know any of that, announced confidently,

Honour has come back, as a king, to earth,
And paid his subjects with a royal wage;
And Nobleness walks in our ways again;
And we have come into our heritage. (314)

"It is this basic insincerity and lack of depth," one critic has complained, "that make his poetry ultimately disappointing" (Moeyes 467). But the charge of insincerity, if it means conscious dissembling, is questionable. Adrian Caesar is on sounder ground in calling Brooke's war sonnets "now infamous" for their "expression of a discredited, imperialist chauvinism" (1)....

Source: Janis P. Stout, "Aspirations to Heroism: The Old That Passed Away," in *Coming Out of War: Poetry, Grieving, and the Culture of the World Wars*, University of Alabama Press, 2005, pp. 13–16.

Kenneth Sherman

In the following excerpt, Sherman explains the effects of Brooke's personal image on the reaction to his poetry.

After the war, the simple white cross that marked Brooke's grave was replaced with a hideous bronze statue, modelled after the Apollo Belvedere. The memorial was English society's way of securing Brooke within the myth it had created for him. As Philip Larkin rightly observed, "People had ideas about Brooke." But this was partly Brooke's own doing, and the transformation of his grave to kitsch speaks not about Brooke's artistry, but about his aspirations and his relationship to the society he served.

> THOUGH RUPERT BROOKE'S LITERARY STOCK HAS BEEN PLUMMETING FOR THE LAST HALF CENTURY, IT IS INTERESTING TO NOTE THAT SUCH DISPARATE FIGURES AS D. H. LAWRENCE, T. S. ELIOT, AND HENRY JAMES TOOK HIS WORK SERIOUSLY."

What is apparent in the biographies and the letters is that Brooke was a young man working hard at promoting himself within the Edwardian literary establishment. He was charming and opportunistic. In the halcyon days before the First World War, he established a cosy life of comfort and connections. This comes across in the numerous photographs in Michael Hastings's biography, where the young poet and his circle are seen enjoying their hiking trips, horse rides, swim parties, and amateur theatrical ventures. It strikes us as a life of privilege and helps to convince us that Brooke, in contrast to some of his contemporaries, is historically irrelevant. The mannered literary world he inhabited was to be blown away by the haunting images we have been left of Owen, Rosenberg, post-war Graves and Sassoon, standing in grey and black contrast to the youth with blond waves and flashing blue eyes whom Yeats called "the handsomest man in England," and who would come to represent his countrymen's fallen Adonis.

Whether Brooke knew it or not, he played a dangerous game with his talent, one that would fossilize him for succeeding generations. In exchange for glamorization and applause, he was willing to serve English society. And be used by it. The Dean of St Paul's was quoting Brooke's famous sonnet "The Soldier" as part of his Sunday sermon to drum up patriotic support and encourage enlistment at the same time that its author was sailing with the Hood Battalion toward his death in the Dardanelles. The exploitation would intensify in the weeks that followed. On 23 April 1915, only three days after Brooke's death, Winston Churchill, in a widely published three-page generic obituary, would use the dead poet as follows:

> . . . he was willing to die for the dear England whose beauty and majesty he knew; and he advanced toward the brink in perfect serenity,

with absolute conviction of the rightness of his country's cause, and a heart devoid of hate for fellow-men.

This myth of the good and wholesome man would persist long after the war. In 1955, Sir Geoffrey Keynes' attempt to bring out *The Letters of Rupert Brooke* was blocked by his fellow trustees of Brooke's estate (Walter de la Mare, Dudley Ward, John Sheppard); they claimed the collection "seriously misrepresented" Brooke. When the book finally appeared in 1968, the letters were censored and the collection was far from complete. One reviewer counted 300 excisions from 600 letters. Why the omissions? To deny Brooke's anti-Semitism or downplay the extent of his sexual pursuits? To diminish his self-centredness and opportunism?

Christopher Hassall's detailed biography portrays a much more complex Brooke than the manufactured image suggests. He had a difficult relationship with his controlling mother (whom he referred to as "the Raj") and his tempestuous love affair with Ka Cox brought him to breakdown and near suicide. Those closest to him claim he often joked about his good looks and was sceptical about how people reacted to them. For instance, he reports after his meeting with Henry James: "I did the fresh boyish stunt, and it was a great success." Once, before a reading, he asks a friend: "Will you please disarrange my hair; I've got to read poetry to some old ladies." After a speech to the Arts and Letters Club in Toronto, he is approached by a young man who compliments him; his response: "Then I do my pet boyish-modesty-stunt and go pink all over, and everyone thinks it too delightful." If these comments reveal something distasteful and cynical about Brooke's personality, they also suggest he was aware of the image he was creating.

All of what I have written thus far is an attempt to disentangle the man from the myth because I want to comment on the poetry, which, by and large, is no longer regarded seriously. Since Brooke is perceived as a man who was on the "wrong side" in cultural and political matters, a retrospective irony haunts the reading of much of his work, especially his sonnet sequence "1914." None of his images has been picked upon more than the one in "Peace," in which he depicts new recruits as "swimmers into cleanness leaping," suggesting that enlistment is liberating these young men from "a world grown old and cold and weary." Paul Fussell, in his insightful study *The Great War And Modern Memory*,

points out how Brooke's "swimmers" of 1914, "metamorphose into the mud-flounderers of the Somme and Passchendaele sinking beneath the surface." And it is highly probable that Wilfred Owen had Brooke's line in mind when he described soldiers who "Leapt to swift unseen bullets," or when he depicted death by mustard gas as death by drowning in his searing indictment "Dulce et Decorum Est."

I myself have used Brooke. Some years ago I taught a humanities course whose intent was to deal with major events of the twentieth century through literature. I employed Brooke's famous sonnet "The Soldier" as a foil for Wilfred Owen's "Dulce et Decorum Est." Brooke's poem is a love sonnet, expressing love of nation, and for a liberal cosmopolitan, the values it espouses seem ludicrous, old-fashioned, class-conscious.

. . . Juxtaposed to such eye-witnessed horrors, Brooke's unconditional willingness to die for his country, his sense of cultural superiority, his notion of antiseptic wartime killing seem at least naive, at worst, sacrilegious. I was using the image we have inherited of Brooke, the quaint, establishment poet, against the image we have of Owen, the truthful, rebel poet; or to reduce things even further, I was setting Brooke's wavy golden locks against Owen's hair that had turned grey above the ears before the poet had turned twenty-five. My purpose was legitimate: to show students, through poetry, how radically sensibilities may change once they confront historical circumstance. Yet I was aware, even as I was engaging in this dialectic, that I was not being completely fair to Brooke.

For one thing, it is incorrect to call "The Soldier" a war poem since Brooke had seen no war when he wrote it. Its original, more honest title was "The Recruit." I also knew there was something unjust in my pedagogical set-up. Poetry resents being used in a didactic manner; it insists on its autonomy, its self-evolution, even in the case of a poem like Brooke's, where the poet is using his voice to express a popular, public emotion.

Something more happened over the years I continued to teach "The Soldier." I came to appreciate its technical mastery and musicality and to forgive its content and sentimentality. I also began to wonder what accounted for my shifting taste. Wilfred Owen's anger, his cutting irony and despair, have been a major influence on poetic sensibility in this century. His work has served as a touchstone for the darkness of Ted Hughes and the cynical resolve of Philip Larkin. (1) One hears echoes of the note he originally sounded behind the lines of Plath's "Daddy" and Ginsberg's "Howl." Perhaps Ginsberg's famous line, "I saw the best minds of my generation destroyed by madness, starving, hysterical, naked . . ." would more likely have been spoken by a survivor of the Somme than by a victim of corporate America. If there is any doubt about the connection in Ginsberg's imagination between the individual's struggle in America in the mid-fifties and the Great War, one need only look to the following passage in "Howl." Ginsberg is writing about those of his generation who

> were burned alive in their innocent flannel suits on Madison Avenue amid blasts of leaden verse and the tanked-up clatter of the iron regiments of fashion & nitroglycerine shrieks . . . & the mustard gas of sinister intelligent editors

It may well be that my growing acceptance of Brooke's poem was born of a growing disaffection for the eschatological darkness poetry has been stuck with since the Great War; it may indicate my wish to find something green and living beyond the wasteland.

Though Rupert Brooke's literary stock has been plummeting for the last half century, it is interesting to note that such disparate figures as D. H. Lawrence, T. S. Eliot, and Henry James took his work seriously. I remember that in high school, in the 1960s, in addition to "The Soldier," our class read Brooke's "The Great Lover" and "The Hill." But reading through Brooke's *Collected Poems*, one realizes that his best poems are those modelled after English Metaphysical poetry. It is not surprising to find among his essays a perceptive study of Andrew Marvell, and it is unfortunate that Brooke's more poignant, metaphysical poems, such as "Dust" or "The Call," are never anthologized. Still, one has to admit that much of Brooke's earlier poetry seems to be largely apprentice work—skilled, technically adept, but also derivative and uninformed by experience. . . .

Source: Kenneth Sherman, "Perishing Things and Strange Ghosts: Rupert Brooke's Last Poem," in *Queen's Quarterly*, Vol. 103, No. 3, Fall 1996, pp. 532–45.

SOURCES

Brooke, Rupert, *The Letters of Rupert Brooke*, edited by Geoffrey Keynes, Harcourt, Brace & World, 1968, p. 39.

———, "Peace," in *Poetry*, Vol. 6, No. 1, April 1915, p. 18.

C[hurchill], W[inston] S., "Death of Mr. Rupert Brooke," in *Times*, April 26, 1915, p. 5, col. F.

de la Mare, Walter, *Rupert Brooke and the Intellectual Imagination*, Sidgwick and Jackson, 1919, p. 31.

Delany, Paul, *The Neo-pagans: Rupert Brooke and the Ordeal of Youth*, The Free Press, 1987.

Fletcher, John Gould, "On Subject-Matter and War Poetry," in *Egoist*, Vol. 3, No. 12, December 1916, pp. 188–89.

Gosse, Edmund, "War and Literature," in *Living Age*, Vol. 273, October–December 1914, pp. 658–71.

Gregson, J., M., *Poetry of the First World War*, Edward Arnold, 1976, pp. 7–20.

Hughes, Thomas, *Tom Brown at Oxford*, Macmillan, 1888, p. 113.

Laskowski, William E., *Rupert Brooke*, Twayne, 1994, pp. 58–60.

Murray, Nicholas, *The Red Sweet Wine of Youth: British Poets of the First World War*, Little, Brown, 2010, pp. 11–38.

Orwell, George, *Nineteen Eighty-Four*, Harcourt, Brace, 1949, p. 200.

Owen, Wilfred, "Dulce et Decorum Est," in *The Collected Poems of Wilfred Owen*, edited by C. Day Lewis, New Directions, 1963, p. 55.

Parker, Rennie, *The Georgian Poets: Abercrombie, Brooke, Drinkwater, Gibson and Thomas*, Northcote House, 1999, pp. 75–76.

Wilkinson, Glenn R., "'The Blessings of War': The Depiction of Military Force in Edwardian Newspapers," in *Journal of Contemporary History*, Vol. 33, No. 1, 1998, pp. 97–115.

Wintle, Justin, and Richard Kenin, eds. "Brooke, Rupert," in *The Dictionary of Biographical Quotation of British and American Subjects*, Routledge and Keegan Paul, 1978, p. 99.

FURTHER READING

Caesar, Adrian, *Taking It Like a Man: Suffering, Sexuality and the War Poets: Brooke, Sassoon, Owen, Graves*, Manchester University Press, 1993.

> Caesar reads the work of the war poets against the background of their own inner suffering rather than the historical calamity of the war and argues that much of the popular reaction to the war poets is a voyeuristic misreading of their experience.

Keegan, John, *The Face of Battle*, Viking, 1976.

> *The Face of Battle* is a classic and transformative

work of military history. Keegan shifts the focus of his study away from the generals and politicians to common soldiers, focusing on their actual experience of battle. He looks at three conflicts spread over centuries but concentrated in a the small geographical area of Belgium and northwestern France: Agincourt, Waterloo, and the Somme. The last section will give readers insight into the experience of battle in World War I that Brooke never had and could only imagine as a romantic fantasy.

Ross, Robert H., *The Georgian Revolt: Rise and Fall of a Poetic Ideal, 1910–1922*, Southern Illinois University Press, 1973.

Concerned more with historical than literary analysis, Ross places the Georgians, including Brooke, Graves, Lawrence, and others, in the context of their time and their revolt against Edwardian verse. He bases his study on a close analysis of the unpublished correspondence between the various poets and Edward Marsh, the patron of the movement.

Stallworthy, Jon, *Anthem for Doomed Youth: Twelve Soldier Poets of the First World War*, Constable, 2005.

Stallworthy devotes a chapter to each of twelve poets, including Brooke, focusing on a few key poems related to World War I and exploring how the authors' biographies, especially their combat experience or lack thereof, shaped their work. He treats the poems themselves in great detail; for example, he includes photographs of the original manuscripts for each and analyzes the changes made for publication. His larger narrative focuses on the English public's growing revulsion through time at the mass slaughter of the first industrialized war.

SUGGESTED SEARCH TERMS

Rupert Brooke

Peace AND Brooke

Georgian poets

Dymock poets

war poets

Western Front

World War I

World War I AND poetry

Question

MAY SWENSON

1954

May Swenson was born into a large Mormon family in Utah but, soon after college, moved to New York City, where she became a fixture of the literary scene from the early 1950s to the late 1980s. Her poetry is not political in nature, but it has a powerful impact for the way that she questions the very nature of existence, appreciates the natural world with focused detail, and speaks openly about the poet's erotic experiences with other women at a time when such relationships were often hidden. Much of her influence in the world of literature came from the work that she did in addition to her own writing, such as editing the influential New Directions press at a time when it was the voice of the avant-garde and her chancellorship of the Academy of American Poets for the last decade of her long life.

"Question" is often included in poetry anthologies because it is a clear example of Swenson's work at its best. In this poem, the speaker wonders what life will be like after death separates her from her body. She speaks about the body in a sequence of easily recognizable metaphors: a house, a horse, a faithful dog. Talking about death this way allows readers to feel the looming sadness and the poet's sense of loss, an acknowledgment of the too-seldom-discussed emotional attachment between body and mind. After asking how she will cope with this separation, Swenson ends the poem with an even larger question, wondering what she will do when leaving her body exposes her to the world, leaving her with nowhere to hide.

May Swenson (© Oscar White | Corbis)

Swenson originally published "Question" in her 1954 collection *Another Animal*. It was reprinted in *Nature: Poems Old and New*, a collection published in 1994, five years after her death.

AUTHOR BIOGRAPHY

May Swenson was born on May 28, 1913, in Logan, Utah. Her parents both came from Sweden and ended up emigrating to Utah because they belonged to the Mormon religion, which was unpopular in their home country. She grew up in Logan along with nine brothers and sisters, becoming an avid reader and writer at an early age. She attended Utah State Agricultural College (which has been Utah State University since 1957). Even before enrolling, Swenson had been well familiar with the college, because her father had been a professor of mechanical engineering there since her childhood.

After graduating from college in 1934, Swenson lived in Salt Lake City for a year, working as a reporter on a newspaper there before moving to New York City. There, she held a number of jobs, including author's assistant, editor, secretary,

ghostwriter, reviewer, and teacher. Her first book of poetry, *Another Animal*, was published in 1954. In 1957, she became the editor of the acclaimed New Directions Press, where she worked until 1966.

As a poet, Swenson was recognized with numerous awards and accolades. She received a Guggenheim fellowship in 1959 and a grant from the National Endowment for the Arts and Letters in 1960, as well as a MacArthur Foundation fellowship in 1987. The Poetry Society of America awarded her their Shelley Memorial Award in 1969 and Yale University gave her their Bollingen Prize in 1981. She served as the Chancellor of the Academy of American Poets for nine years, from 1980 until 1989. Over the course of her life, she published eleven books of poetry. She also wrote translations of Swedish poets, including a much-praised translation of the poems of Nobel Prize–winning author Tomas Tranströmer.

From the late 1960s on, Swenson worked regularly in New York City and lived in rural Nassau County. She died of a heart attack on December 4, 1989, in Oceanview, Delaware.

POEM SUMMARY

The text used for this summary is from *Nature: Poems Old and New*, Houghton Mifflin, 1945, p. 45.

Lines 1–4

The first two lines of "Question" establish the problem posed by the poem: how death affects a person. They do this by metaphorically comparing the body of the poem's speaker to three different things. In the first line, the body is referred to as a home. This is a common comparison, and one that is not at all obscure: like a home, the body is where the spirit or soul dwells with a sense of ownership and comfort, the place from which a spirit looks out at the world at large.

In the second line, however, the comparisons become more tricky. The body is called both a horse and a hound. The horse image is somewhat related to the home image: if the home is seen as a stationary dwelling that one recedes into in order to be alone, the horse is a mode of transportation that can take one out, beyond one's narrowly defined world, to new encounters. The last element introduced in these lines, the hound, carries this thought forward. Swenson could have referred to a dog of any kind, but hound dogs are known for their drive and

MEDIA
ADAPTATIONS

- The May Swenson Society maintains a web page dedicated to all things related to this poet (copyright 2009) at http://www.mayswensonsociety.org/ with links to other interesting sites.

tenacity, chasing after experiences that capture their attention as if obsessed. Together, these three images of the body cover an entire range of inward and outward focus.

The last two lines of the first stanza are where the speaker steers the poem's focus toward mortality, wondering what will become of her soul after the body has died. Swenson is able to convey a larger scale of one person's death by linking the body to the other objects with the preceding metaphors, indicating that it would be more than just the death of one person; it would mean that such close, familiar things as a home, a horse, and a faithful dog would be lost upon death as well.

Lines 5–7
In the second stanza, the poet clarifies the significance of the three metaphors that have been brought up already. They are not merely the first three of many such images to be discussed but are, in fact, going to be the backbone of this poem. This stanza offers readers three actions, corresponding to the three objects that came earlier, giving hints at the three objects' significance without coming right out and explaining them explicitly. Readers can find here that the poem's speaker wants a home as a place to sleep, a horse to ride, and a hound to help her hunt, but it is left to the reader to determine why these activities might be viewed as the ones that cover the whole range of human existence.

This stanza is made of questions. Not only does this help the poem convey the speaker's fear and uneasiness about the future, but it also helps to establish a general mood of curiosity.

Lines 8–15
The poem's third stanza is by far its longest, twice the length of the longest of the others. It carries on the style of the previous stanza, with the poem's speaker wondering about what the future holds for her once her body has given out.

This stanza begins by raising a situation that is not commonly associated with the afterlife. The question of physical space is usually considered settled after death: if it is discussed at all, it is usually thought that the soul "goes to" heaven or some other version of a world that may or may not exist on the same plane of reality as this world. In "Question," however, Swenson's narrator worries about *where* her soul will go. In lines 9 and 10, she points out that her body has been her mount, her horse, which has taken her places. Without that physical method of travel, she does not know what movement will be like.

The middle of this stanza begins shifting the focus from the horse metaphor to the dog metaphor. Swenson uses the physical location of a thicket, or dense bush, that a horse could run over but that a hound would run into while following whatever scent it was after. Lines 13–15 carry on with the hound image, extending the metaphor. The poem imagines a hound that would be able to hunt down danger or treasure, and then the tone turns slightly sad at the thought of such a dog's death, with lines 14 and 15 giving the poem's most direct connection between the body and the dog, showing that the speaker will mourn the loss of her own body like she would mourn the loss of a beloved pet.

Lines 16–19
For the first time in this poem, the dog and horse metaphors are abandoned. The poem takes up a new image in the fourth stanza, that of the soul moving up into the sky, floating over the earth after death. Swenson continues to phrase the speaker's apprehension about future events as questions, but she also presents a concrete picture, as if she is certain about some of what is to come.

The metaphor of a body as a home, which was missing from the third stanza, is brought back in line 18, which mentions both roof and door. Overall, however, this stanza is focused on establishing the new image of the soul taking up residence in the sky. The stanza's final line states that the wind would then be the person's eye, as if the soul were not only in the sky but had actually become a part of it.

Lines 20 and 21

The brief couplet at the end of the poem raises the speaker's main concern, that of being exposed. The image of moving up into the sky in the previous stanza implies that the dead can look down upon those still walking the earth, but that perspective is reversed in this stanza. The house, horse, and hound images that begin the poem are used to imply specific attributes of each of these things, but in the end Swenson draws attention to the one thing they all have in common: each represents a cover that the soul can hide within.

After death, the soul has no such covering. The image of a soul drifting into the sky is extended to suppose that clouds can hide it, like a shift, or a lightweight dress. The speaker of the poem is not comfortable with this degree of exposure. The poem ends with no answers about what the future holds, only offering readers the fear of what it would be like if one's soul were openly available to the world

THEMES

Fear of Death

The main point made in this poem is the presentation of a person wondering what existence is going to be like after death. The fact that the entire poem is posed as one long question, with several smaller questions embedded within it, conveys the speaker's apprehension about what is going to come.

The fear expressed in this poem is slightly more specific than the usual fear of death. This speaker is not worried about her death marking the end of her existence. She believes that she will continue on after death, unlike some views of the subject, but she does not feel comfortable with the position she thinks death is going to leave her in. Rather than ending her existence, the poem's speaker thinks that death will strip her of just her physical covering. She will exist, but her existence will be exposed, and it is the thought of such openness that frightens her. Although the fear of death is usually associated with uncertainty, this speaker seems to think she knows what life after death is like: her fear is not about death itself but about the situation it will put her into.

TOPICS FOR FURTHER STUDY

- Read Amy Huntley's young-adult novel *The Everafter*, about a girl who wakes up to find herself dead and learns how the artifacts of her former life can be reminders of who she is. Compare Swenson's attitude toward death in "Question" to the evolving attitude of the novel's protagonist, Madison. Point out places where you think both authors' philosophies on the subject are the same and places where they differ. Present your opinions in an oral report to your class.

- Write a poem that copies Swenson's style, from the perspective of someone who can see the exposed spirit of a person floating over them in the sky. In a short essay, evaluate your poem, pointing out ways in which it is like Swenson's and ways in which you found her style hard to follow.

- Early in this poem, Swenson compares her body to a house, a horse, and a hound. Identify three new objects that you think could be useful for understanding the body's function, according to your view of the world, and explain the relevance of each. At least one must be a kind of animal. Post your explanations on a blog, and allow your classmates to comment.

- Swenson compares the body to a horse because it is a quick vehicle for transportation and to a hound because it can lead the hunt, whether that hunt takes it to trouble or to reward. Do these metaphors still apply to bodies that have limited or no ability for motion? Write an essay explaining the lessons people who have specific limitations can take from "Question."

Nature

After her death, the speaker of this poem expects to become one with nature. Her communion with nature is presented here with the image of a spirit of the deceased floating in the sky, hovering over the world.

Swenson uses the horse as a symbol of the soul or spirit. *(© Makarova Viktoria | Shutterstock.com)*

The fact that the soul will have a specific place in the sky, high enough to be blocked from view from the earth by a covering of clouds, indicates that this soul will still be a defined thing and will not have assimilated entirely into nature after death. It is expected to move on to another place and take on another form of being, but it will merge into nature enough to make the wind take up the function that the eye on its body once had.

Even so, the image of floating up into the sky, which is comparable to the traditional Christian image of a soul ascending to heaven after death, implies that this poem is drawing a distinction between life in the social world of humanity, which takes place on Earth, and the life that will be experienced after death, when one leaves people behind but is still in the natural world.

Loyalty

A main factor contributing to this poem's sorrowful mood is the speaker's loyalty to her body, which she knows she must part with upon dying. Her loyalty is most easily identified when she speaks of the body as a faithful dog, especially when she calls the body her good dog in lines 14

and 15. The reason for this emotional connection is obvious: loyalty is one characteristic that is frequently associated with dogs, and it is quite easy to imagine the speaker's loyalty to her body when she views it as having been loyal to her.

The other two main metaphors for the body used throughout the poem also imply that the speaker feels a sense of loyalty. She may have gotten more emotion out of using the word "home" rather than "house," but the word that she chose gives a stronger sense of an actual building, which helps strengthen the later references to structural elements such as the door and the roof, in line 18. The horse, too, is a creature that can elicit a strong emotional connection. In each of these cases, there is an implication that the speaker feels well-served by her body. This adds a sentimental aspect to the natural apprehension about death that is more common.

Self-Consciousness

Although there are many questions asked over the course of this poem, the final question, which is the only one punctuated with a question mark, concerns how the speaker will cope with exposure.

COMPARE
&
CONTRAST

- **1954:** In the United States, 36 percent of the population lives in rural areas. The imagery Swenson uses in this poem would include common everyday interactions to them.

  Today: As of the 2000 census, the US population living in rural areas has dropped substantially, to 20 percent.

- **1954:** Participation in organized religion soars in the postwar years, as the parents of the first Baby Boomers seek to solidify their family values.

  Today: Many young people identify with the sort of spirituality displayed in this poem rather than with the tenets of organized religion.

- **1954:** As this poem shows, privacy is assumed, and being out in open view is seen as being exposed.

  Today: With red light cameras, satellite cameras, and the cameras that most people carry with them on their phones, the sort of privacy that Swenson might have taken for granted is a thing of the past.

- **1954:** One of the biggest housing booms the country has known is in full swing, as a population traumatized by the insecurity from the start of the Great Depression in 1929 to the end of World War II in 1945 focuses on a sense of permanency.

  Today: A long streak of prosperity that lasted from the end of World War II up into the twenty-first century was broken with the onset of the Great Recession of 2008, creating a new sense of financial insecurity.

- **1954:** The use of hounds to hunt is a commonly recognizable image, as hunting is seen as a common sport without controversy.

  Today: Animal rights organizations around the world work to ban hunting for sport.

The last line, about hiding, clearly implies that the speaker feels that she have something that she wants to hide from the world, something that she feels will cause her shame if it were revealed.

Although this is the poem's ultimate, overriding question, the structure of the poem takes readers in several other directions before reaching it. The smaller questions in the initial stanzas indicate relatively small concerns about where the soul will go after death and what it will do, how it will understand the future, or what death will feel like. These diversions help to support the self-consciousness of the question asked in the final stanza: like any truly self-conscious person, the speaker tries to distract the reader and even herself from the issue that she feels is the most important concern. It is as if she is looking at the smaller issues in order to keep attention away from the big uncomfortable thought of what her existence will be like, and so she runs through a series of possible concerns that she knows in her heart are irrelevant by comparison.

STYLE

Metaphor

A *metaphor* is an implied comparison: it presents two things together, sometimes saying that one thing actually *is* another thing, and leaves the reader to think about what aspects of the two things link them. "Question" makes heavy use of metaphor. It says that the body is a house and then asks where the speaker will sleep, indicating that the soul is like the person who lives in the house, establishing a difference between soul and body that is like the difference between house and inhabitant. The poem compares the body to a hound that hunts, finding danger and treasure in a thicket, which reflects the way the mind or soul comes to know the world at large through the body's five senses. The body is also described as a horse, a mode of transportation for a soul just as a horse can be a person's means of traveling through the world. The poem also suggests that the soul will move up to the sky after death and be covered with clouds, which are like a shift, or a light, shapeless dress. All of these comparisons are implied, not acknowledged as comparisons: readers are responsible for deciding just how much of each comparison is valid and where the comparisons between body and object end.

Punctuation

This poem's title indicates that it is about just one question, though there are many questions asked throughout the course of the poem. It uses multiple interrogatives—question words—such as *what*, *where*, and *how*. Although it might seem that the title is inaccurate, given that the poem asks more than just one question, Swenson stays true to the title, taking liberties with the punctuation, leaving out the question marks that would be necessary in "proper" grammar. By including only one question mark, she affirms that the point of this poem is really only the one important question being asked here, the one about what existence will be like for the author's soul when there is no body to hide in.

Alliteration

Alliteration is the poetic technique of grouping together words that have similar beginning consonants. Swenson does not use this style throughout the poem, but she does use it in a crucial place, in naming the three metaphors that she is comparing the body to as *house, horse,* and *hound.* That this is a deliberate stylistic technique can be seen from the last one, which could easily and have legitimately been labeled *dog* if she were not trying to tie them all together with similar sounds. She makes them all equal to each other with alliteration, as well as by using words that have the letter *o* (although it is not pronounced the same in each word) and also by using words of equal length. This makes all three words look balanced on the page, so that no metaphor seems to be more important than the others.

HISTORICAL CONTEXT

1950s Poetry: Diversity of Styles

Swenson is generally considered to fall outside of the bounds of any literary movement. This raises the question of what literary movement was dominant when she published her first book in 1954. In fact, the 1950s were an extraordinarily diverse time in the world of literary poetry. It was a time of revolution against the standard and a time when the literary world exploded with the sort of creativity and originality that was to hit society as a whole during the 1960s.

Beat Poets

Around the time that Swenson published *Another Animal,* for instance, the famed Beat poetry movement hit its peak. 1954 was the year that poet Lawrence Ferlinghetti opened his influential book store, City Lights, in San Francisco. The store, along with the associated publisher, City Lights Press, gave a voice to the counterculture Beat poets who gravitated toward the Bay area during the 1950s. One of them, Allan Ginsberg, published his poem *Howl* through City Lights: the book-length, free-form discourse on modern civilization would become the most recognized example of Beat poetry and one of the most influential and recognized poems of the twentieth century. At the time, however, it was highly controversial. In 1957, Ferlinghetti and the City Lights manager were arrested for distributing obscene material, a charge that Ginsberg only avoided by being out of the country. This sort of battle against cultural standards was central to the counterculture ethos of the Beat poets, a group that includes Gregory Corso, Gary Snyder, Neal Cassady, and Anne Waldman.

In the influential anthology *The New American Poetry, 1945–1960,* editor Donald Allan grouped the Beats into a category that he called the "San Francisco Renaissance." Overall, he divided poetry covered in the book into geographical terms. His book had momentous impact on the literary world, so that the divisions that Allan gave them in 1960 have survived as the terms that are often used to categorize 1950s poetry today.

Black Mountain Poets

Another group identified in *The New American Poetry* was the Black Mountain Poets, centered around Black Mountain College, in Georgia. Black Mountain was a progressive liberal arts college that promoted creativity. The school itself opened in 1933, encouraging students to find their talents in a variety of arts, from painting to sculpting to music to writing. In 1950, Charles Olson, one of the school's professors, advanced theories of poetry that came to be recognized as the Black Mountain style in his famous essay "Projective Verse," which proposed that poetry should be built mainly on the

The speaker has no way to hide. *(© ilolab | Shutterstock.com)*

reader's immediate perception and only secondarily on reflection. The *Black Mountain Review* published the works of this school of poets, many of whom were influenced by the poetry of William Carlos Williams. Like Beat poetry, Black Mountain poetry arose out of a desire to create a new form of expression out of the poetic art.

The New York School of Poetry

If the Black Mountain school reflected its rural center, its opposite can be found in the group identified as the New York school, which was active at the same time. The poets associated with this "school" (which was actually just an informal grouping of writers who lived in or near New York for varying lengths of time) were generally associated with the visual arts, as exemplified by the two poets most frequently associated with this movement, Frank O'Hara and John Ashbury, both of whom worked as art critics while writing poetry. Influenced by innovative, modernist painting, the poetry of the New York school tended to be more light-hearted and self-mocking than the works of the other groups, although it was just as sincere in its attempt to broaden the idea of what poetry

could accomplish. Swenson, a New Yorker for most of her life, could be associated with this group because of her geographical proximity and the lightness of her style, but there are aspects of other poetic schools evident in her work as well, making it difficult to categorize her poetry at a time when poetry itself was bristling against definitions.

CRITICAL OVERVIEW

Swenson was a poet who was famous among other writers, in part because of her high-visibility work as an editor for the prestigious New Directions press in the late 1950s and early 1960s, as her writing career took off. She won a significant number of awards and fellowships within the focused world of poetry, but she never gained even the sort of minor recognition that other poets of her time, such as her friends Muriel Rukeyser or Elizabeth Bishop, were able to obtain. As Sue Russell wrote in the *Kenyon Review* after Swenson's death, her poems were riddles at heart and "seem more to have been constructed than composed," leading Russell to the conclusion

WHAT DO I READ NEXT?

- A very different look at Swenson's thoughts about death can be found in her poem "Deaths," which is almost a page long and written in a nearly prose style. This poem is available in the collection *New and Selected Things Taking Place*, published by Little, Brown, in 1978.

- Swenson's book *The Complete Poems to Solve* was published for a young-adult audience, with illustrations by Christie Hale. It contains all of the poems from her 1969 book *Poems to Solve* and the 1970 sequel *More Poems to Solve*, offering dozens of examples of poems (such as the often-anthologized "Southbound on the Freeway") that are purposely cryptic, offering young readers the chance to understand poetry in a fun and engaging way. The collection was published in 1993 by Simon and Schuster.

- Novelist Stephanie Meyer used this poem, appropriately, in her novel *The Host*, about a race of aliens who take over the bodies of humans when they invade. *The Host* was published in 2008 by Little, Brown.

- Swenson's poetry is often linked to the poetry of her longtime friend Elizabeth Bishop, although their styles are dramatically different. Bishop's "Song for the Rainy Season" shows how she implies just as much as Swenson does in her poetry, but in a more realistic, descriptive style. This

poem, along with Bishop's other most important writings, is available in the Library of America's *Elizabeth Bishop: Poems, Prose and Letters*, published in 2008.

- Poet Gary Soto wrote a powerful novel for young adults, *The Afterlife*, about Chuy, a boy growing up Fresno, California, who dies as soon as the book begins. The story shows what he learns from watching his neighborhood from the other side. Graphia published the book in 2005.

- Few poets have their lives laid open for their readers the way that Swenson did in the 1996 book *May Swenson: A Poet's Life in Photos*, with text by R. R. Knudson and Suzanne Bigelow and a forward by poet Richard Wilbur. The book mixes pictures and poems and quotes from Swenson with memories by other writers. It was published by the Utah State University Press.

- Readers can understand Swenson's impact on the world of poetry by reading the essays about her collected in *Body My House: May Swenson's Work and Life*, edited by Paul Crumbley and Patricia M. Gantt. This book, which takes its title from "Question," is one of the few scholarly companions to Swenson's writing. It was published by the Utah State University Press in 2006.

---

that "Swenson was clearly engaged in the experimental enterprise to a degree that would charm any scientist." Russell quotes noted critic Sven Birkerts as seeing in Swenson's first book, *Another Animal*, much in common with Bishop and Marianne Moore, but Birkerts felt that "Swenson seems to have grown beyond the influence of Moore and Bishop to establish an individual voice in her own later work." Still, her reputation outside of the world of poetry has been overshadowed by those better-known writers.

Critics almost universally praise Swenson's work: the introduction to her section in the 2006 edition of *The Oxford Book of American Poetry* notes that "Swenson's formal experiments...are undertaken in a bravura spirit that mingles the poet's self-delight with the belief that such displays of wit and craft may lead to sublime ends." At the same time, critics can see how general audiences might find her intellectual style daunting: not necessarily because it is too difficult, but on the contrary, because readers might believe it to be simple and think that they understand it after one quick reading. As Christian Wiman wrote in a review of the 2000 collection of Swenson's work *Nature: Poems Old and New* (in which the poem "Question" is reprinted):

> A lot of people are going to find a lot of Swenson merely decorative, and there's a truth to that accusation that I can't fully refute. It's disconcertingly easy to drift in and out of much of her poetry because there seems to be so little at stake, or because the real stakes of her romantic merging with nature are elided.

CRITICISM

David Kelly

Kelly is an instructor of creative writing and literature. In the following essay, he examines what the word question *means in the poem "Question" and how Swenson could apply this singular word to a poem that asks so many questions.*

Writing about May Swenson's poem "Question," Grace Schulman made this generalization about the poet's work overall: "Questions are the wellsprings of Swenson's art." That may be true, but, even so, how does it distinguish Swenson from any other artist? An artist, after all, has to know her or his subject—not thoroughly but in some significant way. To know it, he or she has to think about it, and thinking about it means raising questions. Even the most directly descriptive poems, those that seem to present no ideas, only snapshots of their subject, must have started with wondering.

The difference between Swenson's work and poetry focused on ideas is that Swenson admits, even though she does not say so, that a basic uncertainty is a part of the process that leads to any direct claim. In "Question," in particular, her line of inquiry about what existence after death would be like is frozen in its embryonic phase. Whether she truly is uncertain or is using her poem about the afterlife to make a separate point about uncertainty is beside the point. The final result is a narrative voice that is willing to play the role of the frightened inquisitor with no abstract theory to hide behind. This is someone who fears exposure, just as anyone would in the earliest stages of thought.

Swenson is a poet who works her words into puzzles and then sits back, leaving the reader and poem to work things out between themselves. In the case of "Question," the puzzle revolves around the title: it is written in the singular,

> OF THE EIGHT QUESTIONS THAT COMPRISE THE POEM 'QUESTION,' ONE CLEARLY STANDS OUT AS HAVING MORE SIGNIFICANCE. WHAT ARE THE OTHER SEVEN EVEN THERE FOR, THEN? AS IS APPROPRIATE FOR THIS POEM, AND SWENSON'S USUAL CRYPTIC STYLE, NO CLEAR ANSWER PRESENTS ITSELF, ONLY POSSIBLE OPTIONS."

even though the poem goes on to ask so much of its readers. Wondering, as every reader must at one time or another, why the title is not "Question*s*" can put one on the path to thinking about life and death without the fear of being preached at, giving us the sense that the poet is one of us and not speaking to us from above.

There are eight interrogatories in "Question," each identifiable because it starts with *what*, *where*, or *how*. The questions are generally spread out across two or three lines each, taking the time needed to develop the poet's thought in each case. This not always the case, however. There is one stanza, the poem's shortest one, that presents readers with a tight little package of questions; the second stanza asks three short questions in quick succession and can be considered the gravitational core of this poem, making it a good place to begin an inquiry into what "Question" is about.

In the first stanza, Swenson, with great economy, introduces two main aspects of the poem: the metaphoric sense that a person's body can be represented by a house, a horse, and a hound and the speaker's fear of death. Important as these are, however, they only set the stage for what is to come. The third line of the poem, in which the poet frets about what she will do, is a pretty common way of expressing the uneasiness one feels when facing an unfamiliar situation, and the anxiety it expresses is certainly understandable in one who is faced with an entirely new state of existence.

It is not until the second stanza that readers see Swenson's pattern developing. That one question in the first stanza is not a random thought, and it is not turning out to be the

The poem closes with the image of the sky, wind, and clouds. (© *majeczka | Shutterstock.com*)

singular question that was announced in the poem's title. Stanza 2 turns the metaphors already given into questions, and it drives the curiosity from the question in the first stanza deeper. This is not just a vague sense of uneasiness about what is to come: Swenson shows that she has put some serious thought into this and that a house's protection, a horse's mobility, and a hound's curiosity can well be thought of as the staples of worldly existence. Fusing the three questions of stanza two together, Swenson creates a character in this poem who goes beyond mere curiosity.

This aura of insecurity is important to the poem, and it helps explain why the title is "Question" and not "Questions." Yes, there are eight interrogative questions in the poem, but Swenson trims away the function of seven of them by leaving them without punctuation. Even though the fourth stanza steers the poem's situation away from the "house-horse-hound" metaphors that defined it most of the way through, it is still asking the same basic questions that the poem has asked all along: how will existence be after death?

It becomes clear that the last line of "Question" is unique, is *the one* question all of this has to raise. It is clear not only from its placement at the end or from the fact that it is decorated with a question mark but also from the fact that it asks a different quality of question than the other ones posed throughout the poem. The others worry about the future, while the question in the last line is concerned with the self.

Of the eight questions that comprise the poem "Question," one clearly stands out as having more significance. What are the other seven even there for, then? As is appropriate for this poem, and

Swenson's usual cryptic style, no clear answer presents itself, only possible options.

One could take it as a sign, for instance, that the first seven questions are left incomplete without their punctuation because they are all meant to meld together to build one Big Question that is greater than the sum of its parts. The evidence for this interpretation would be that it reflects the nature of all poetry and, in fact, all art: the parts are only relevant in the way they serve the whole.

What makes this interpretation unlikely, though, is that these parts do not all fit together to make one sentence: Swenson could have punctuated this as one question, with one final question mark, using internal punctuation such as dashes, commas, ellipses, and semicolons, to show that each smaller question exists to serve the final one. She chose not to. Instead, she establishes a pattern of seven questions that are independent and complete, except for their lack of question marks.

Another possible way to understand Swenson's method could be to wonder whether she intends for the first seven questions to be meaningless. This is poetry, however: everything on the page counts.

It seems best to view the relationship of the seven minor questions to the final question at the end in visual terms. By placing the question with the most weight at the end, Swenson invites readers to see the vagueness of the other questions, the ones supporting metaphors about the human body. The question with the question mark is in the foreground of the mind of a reader who has just finished reading, and the other questions provide background. They serve to establish a mood, one of curiosity and uncertainty, but it is the last line that resonates in the reader's mind hours after the poem is read.

Understanding this physically, putting the questions of the poem in back of the question at the end, helps put the pieces in perspective. It helps explain why some questions do not warrant a question mark, but one question does. It shows readers that, even if the earlier questions seem to be asked casually, mere musings of a worried person wondering about death, they are still important for understanding the poem's bottom line about the speaker's painful self-consciousness.

Swenson's poetry does not often give readers answers, and no reader picking up a poem titled "Question" should expect one. What readers can expect, however, is a question. Here, they are given eight questions, raising the question of how eight can be considered as one. The poem's early comparisons between the body and the things that symbolize it are clear and striking, and they do not need to be phrased as questions, but Swenson's style creates a questioning mood, putting readers in an environment of curiosity before the Big Question is unfolded for them. Creating a mood that prepares readers for her question, Swenson crafts a poem that cleverly and subtly melds thought and feeling.

Source: David Kelly, Critical Essay on "Question," in *Poetry for Students*, Gale, Cengage Learning, 2014.

Alicia Ostriker

In the following excerpt, Ostriker compares Swenson to poet Walt Whitman.

A great poet is a jewel of multiple faces or facets, and to see the poet from the angle of any one of those facets is to be freshly illuminated and elated. Two decades ago, elatedly writing my essay "May Swenson and the Shapes of Speculation" in the context of the post-1960s women's poetry movement, I felt I had made a wonderful discovery: Swenson wrote "like a woman"—a woman with the temperament of an experimental and speculative scientist (86–101). Today I relish the opportunity to look at Swenson not only as a woman poet (since no matter how proud one may be of the label, "women's poetry" is still ghettoized in the literary world) and not only as somebody in the line of Marianne Moore and Elizabeth Bishop, although she is that too—and charmingly so—but as the largest thing I can find to say: let us consider May Swenson as an *American* poet. Let us think about Swenson's Americanness in the sense that Tocqueville meant when he wrote, in *Democracy in America*, "It is not impossible to conceive the immense freedom enjoyed by the Americans, and one can also form an idea of their extreme equality.... " (242).

Freedom is absence of constraint. Equality is absence of hierarchy, absence of relations of domination and subordination. These principles can animate not only society but poetry. And what better way to demonstrate how exuberantly in the American grain May Swenson is than to see her romping in the leaves of grass, the free and equal leaves of grass Walt Whitman first made available to poetry? For in Swenson as in Whitman, we have a poet of democratic vision and vista, a poet of inclusiveness not exclusiveness, for whom all natural phenomena are equally eligible for celebration and all levels and layers of language are equally delectable, a poet who is always surprising, who is not *literary*, not *fashionable*, who belongs to no school (cf. Whitman's placing of "creeds and schools in abeyance," early in "Song of Myself") and doesn't need to show off how learned she is, or to condescend, or to be superior, or on the other hand to polemicize—a poet as fresh as fresh milk and as sound as an egg. A poet who looks around and enjoys herself. A poet who likes the idea of getting naked in poetry and is equally interested in speculating about death. A poet who admires her own body. And other people's bodies. And the material body of the world. And who has a sense of humor.

. . . I do not mean to say that Swenson "takes" from Whitman or that Whitman "influences" Swenson. Source studies are boring, and besides, how do I know Swenson even read Whitman? No, what I want to say is that Whitman is a door and Swenson walks through it. "Unscrew the locks from the doors! Unscrew the doors themselves from their jambs!" he cries (*CP* 41). That Whitman is "the meal equally set, the meat for natural hunger" (*CP* 37), and that Swenson partakes and is healthy. That Whitman, the most benign of father figures, gives poets—gives all of us—liberal permission to play, and Swenson plays liberally. That Whitman is America (Ezra Pound said of him, "His crudity is an exceeding great stench but it *is* America") and that Swenson inhabits this most generous of poetic landscapes.

Fresh air. Fresh language. Endlessly fresh observation. Whitman famously (and tirelessly) invokes "Poets to come!" and declares, "I spring from the pages into your arms" (*CP* 349). A rather lovely book called *The Continuing Presence of Walt Whitman* (Martin) includes essays pairing Whitman with Langston Hughes, Frank O'Hara, Allen Ginsberg, Thom Gunn, Hart Crane, and Fernando Pessoa. I myself have proposed that if it were not for the walker in the city of "Song of Myself," J. Alfred Prufrock would never have issued his famous invitation "Let us go then, you and I . . ." ("Loving Walt Whitman" 220). A plenitude of women poets have expressed their homage to Whitman—June Jordan and Sharon Olds among them (Middlebrook 14–27). Whitman "saw his poetry not as

meaning or a container of meaning but as the event at which or out of which meaning is made possible," claims the critic Ed Folsom (83), and I do think this is true of *American* meaning. Whitman inaugurates that breadth and openness that is America's peculiar contribution to world poetry. But Roy Harvey Pearce says "all American poetry [since *Leaves of Grass*] is, in essence if not in substance, a series of arguments with Whitman" (qtd. in Folsom 83), and here I am struck by the proto-Bloomian tone of "arguments." Do the poets want to kill the father? In fact, Whitman himself anticipates and supports that eventuality: "He most honors my style who learns under it to destroy the teacher" (*CP* 65).

So I imagine the process in Swenson as in many of us. Walk through the door; inhabit the landscape. Look and see. Speculate. The catalogs of phenomena in *Leaves of Grass* were endless and, one must confess, can be endlessly boring; now look, look, and look again at the specifics. Look at Swenson looking. How she looks, licks, touches, and tastes the details. The particularities. "Look Close," she titles one poem, and no poet does so with more inexhaustible attention. I feel an explosive amazement close to what I feel for Shakespeare when I read Swenson describing—for the *nth* time—water, for example. Or snow. Never the same metaphors twice, for Swenson is like the scientist who knows that any piece of reality may yield an infinite array of explanations. . . .

Source: Alicia Ostriker, "May Swenson: Whitman's Daughter," in *Body My House: May Swenson's Work and Life*, edited by Paul Crumbley and Patricia M. Gantt, Utah State University Press, 2006, pp. 40–41, 48–49.

Alicia Ostriker

In the following excerpt, Ostriker praises Swenson's nature poetry and her occasional use of feminist themes.

Most humanists show very little curiosity about the physical world outside the self, and usually a positive antipathy to the mental processes we call scientific. This was not always the case. Although Western literature has only one *De Rerum Naturam*, persons of letters were once expected to take all knowledge as their province, and to interpret scientific understanding as part of a unified vision of the world. Despite the expanding post-Renaissance hostility between science and art, even as late as the nineteenth century Blake was defining the implications of Newtonian mechanics for the human imagination, and apparently anticipating aspects of post-Newtonian physics, as he anticipated so much else. Shelley was thrilled by discoveries in electricity and magnetism. Tennyson registered the seismic shock of *The Origin of Species*. When William Carlos Williams in *Paterson* makes Madame Curie's discovery of radium a major metaphor for all artistic discovery, he bridges the supposed "two cultures" completely. Science will not go away because poets ignore it, and in fact we ignore any great human enterprise at our peril. Yet few poets presently venture beyond dread or annoyance toward the works and ways of physics, chemistry, biology, and fewer bring back more than a gimcrack souvenir or two. The Bomb and a fuzzy idea of Relativity were popular a while ago. Moon-landings and Ecology have recently cornered the market.

May Swenson, born in Utah in 1919, New Yorker by adoption since 1949, has written six well-received books of poems, beginning with *Another Animal* in 1954. She is known as a nature poet, "one of the few good poets who write good poems about nature . . . not just comparing it to states of mind or society," as Elizabeth Bishop has remarked. You can cull a bestiary from her work that would include geese, turtles, an owl and its prey, a bee and a rose, frogs, fireflies, cats and caterpillars, at least one lion, and many horses. She writes of sun, moon, clouds, landscapes and city-scapes, and always with a wondering, curious eye, an intense concern about the structure and texture of her subject, an extraordinary tactility. "The pines, aggressive as erect tails of cats," begins a poem called "Forest." Another called "Spring Uncovered" begins, "Gone the scab of ice that kept it snug, / The lake is naked," and ends where "a grackle, fat as burgundy, / gurgles on a limb" with "bottle-glossy feathers."

But beyond the naturalist's patient observation lies something else. What critics have called Swenson's "calculated naiveté" or her ability to become "a child, but a highly sophisticated child," is actually that childlike ability to envision something freshly, to ask incessant questions and always be prepared for unexpected answers, required of the creative scientist. "How things really are we should like to know," she murmurs, and what else is the motive of the speculative intellect? Swenson's poetry asks as many questions as a four-year-old, and she wants to know not only how things are made and what they resemble, but where they are going and how we fit in. The opening poem of *To*

Mix With Time unblushingly titles itself "The Universe." *Iconographs* includes poems on, for example, the response of a snail to tide, the rotation of a mobile, electronic sound, anti-matter, a telephoto of Earth taken from Orbiter 5, the history of astronomy, man as mammal and (maybe) anima, and the declaration that "THE DNA MOLECULE / is The Nude Descending a Staircase / a circular one." In "Let Us Prepare," the poet seriously considers the possibility of evolution "beyond the organic," although in a poem about flight—from the thistle seed to flying mammals to Lindbergh to John Glenn—she begins and concludes that "earth will not let go our foot"; thus demonstrating that she can, as a good scientist should, speculate on both sides of a given hypothesis.

. . . If this is not typical woman's poetry, Swenson is not a typical woman. All poetry by women just now is potentially interesting for the same reasons that all black poetry is potentially interesting: it may guide us where we've never been. As Carolyn Kizer has observed, women writers "are the custodians of the world's best-kept secret; / Merely the private lives of one-half of humanity." While Swenson does not write on feminist themes most of the time, she does so occasionally, with electrifying results. (I will look at one of those poems, "Bleeding," below.) Most often she blends, she balances. Science, technology, the mental life of observation, speculation: she has invaded these traditionally "masculine" territories. Yet her consistent intimacy with her world, which contains no trace of the archetypal "masculine" will to conquer or control it, seems archetypally "feminine." So does the way she lets herself be precise yet tentative and vulnerable about her observations, where a comparable male poet, perhaps driven by the need to overcome alienation, might be pretentious (Snyder?), pedantic (Olsen?), nervous (Ammons? James Wright?) or agonized (Kinnell?); and her affinity for the small-scale object, like Emily Dickinson's, also reads like a feminine characteristic.

Readers of contemporary American women's poetry will have noticed the extraordinary richness with which it dwells on the flesh, the body, to a degree unduplicated in most men's poetry. (Check your nearest anthology if you doubt this.) To Swenson, everything in the world speaks body-language: a tree has a toenail, spring grass grows "out of each pore . . . itching," a snowplow sucks "celestial clods into its turning neck." The same poet asks, "Body my house / my horse my hound / what will I do / when you are fallen," and concludes a poem on the senses, "in the legs' lair, / carnivora of Touch." If anatomy is destiny, Swenson is at home (and humorous) with that, knowing we share that fate, finding no discrepancy whatever between what some would call a woman's body and a man's mind.

But poetic originality shows itself most obviously through an original form, some shape of a poem that we have not seen, some refreshing play of syntax, a new way words have been thrown in the air and fallen together, been lain one next to the other. Exploratory poetry invites—demands—exploratory forms. When entering new territory, form can become quite palpably "an extension of content," a ship's prow, an arm reaching, a dog's nose sniffing the air.

Swenson has always had an individual style, though bearing traces here and there of Cummings, Marianne Moore, and especially Emily Dickinson. She has always been committed to formal experimentation, and she has often played with the shapes of poems....

Source: Alicia Ostriker, "May Swenson and the Shapes of Speculation," in *Shakespeare's Sisters: Feminist Essays on Women Poets*, edited by Sandra M. Gilbert and Susan Gubar, Indiana University Press, 1979, pp. 221–24.

SOURCES

"A Brief Guide to the Beat Poets," Poets.org website, The American Academy of Poets, 2013, http://www.poets.org/viewmedia.php/prmMID/5646 (accessed March 18, 2013).

"A Brief Guide to the Black Mountain School," Poets.org website, The American Academy of Poets, 2013, http://www.poets.org/viewmedia.php/prmMID/5648 (accessed March 18, 2013).

"Census 2000 Population Statistics: U. S. Population Living in Urban vs. Rural Areas," Federal Highway Administration, U.S. Department of Transportation website, http://www.fhwa.dot.gov/planning/census_issues/archives/metropolitan_planning/cps2k.cfm (accessed March 19, 2013).

Doty, Mark, "The 1950s," in *A Profile of Twentieth Century American Poetry*, edited by Jack Myers and David Wojahn, Southern Illinois University Press, 1991, pp. 145–46.

Knudson, R. R., and Suzzanne Bigelow, *May Swenson: A Poet's Life in Photos*, Utah State University Press, 1996.

"May Swenson," in *The Oxford Book of American Poetry*, edited by David Lehman, Oxford University Press, 2003, p. 599.

"May Swenson," Poets.org, American Academy of Poets, 2013 http://www.poets.org/poet.php/prmPID/168 (accessed March 14, 2013).

Russell, Sue, "A Mysterious and Lavish Power: How Things Continue to Take Place in the Work of May Swenson," in *Kenyon Review*, Vol. 16, No. 3, 1994, p. 128.

Schulman, Grace, "Life's Miracles: The Poetry of May Swenson," in *American Poetry Review*, Vol. 23, No. 5, September–October 1994, p. 9.

Swenson, May, "Question," in *Nature: Poems Old and New*, Houghton Mifflin, 1994, p. 45.

Tarmann, Allison, "Fifty Years of Demographic Change in Rural America," Population Reference Bureau website, 2013, http://www.prb.org/Articles/2003/FiftyYearsofDemographicChangeinRuralAmerica.aspx (accessed March 19, 2013).

Wiman, Christian, Review of *Nature*, in *Poetry*, Vol. 179, No. 2, 2001, pp. 97–99.

FURTHER READING

Arditi, Neil, "'In the Bodies of Words': The Swenson-Bishop Conversation," in *Parnassus: Poetry in Review*, Vol. 26, No. 2, January 2002, pp. 77–93.
This article chronicles the thirty-year friendship between Swenson and poet Elizabeth Bishop, as conducted through letters.

Felstiner, John, "'Why Is Your Mouth All Green?' Something Alive in May Swenson," in *American Poetry Review*, Vol. 36, No. 4, July/August 2007, pp. 19–21.
This article uses poetry and biography to discuss Swenson's relationship to the environment, chronicling her move from the wilds of Utah to the urban center of New York and how she always touched back to the land.

Howard, Richard, "May Swenson: 'Turned Back to the Wild by Love,'" in *Alone with America: Essays on the Art of Poetry in the United States since 1950*, Atheneum, 1969, 516–32.
Published at a time when Swenson was at the height of her literary fame, Howard's essay fits her into his understanding of the particularly American nature of his subjects. Although Swenson would live on for twenty years after this essay, it still captures the most relevant points about her themes and style.

Howe, Susan Elizabeth, "May Swenson's Spiritual Quest," in *Literature & Belief*, Vol. 26, No. 2, 2006, http://literatureandbelief.byu.edu/publications/landb_may_swenson.pdf.
This article, published online by the Center for the Study of Christian Values in Literature, is one of the few to take a comprehensive look at Swenson's ideas of God and the afterlife.

Zona, Kirstin Hotelling, *Marianne Moore, Elizabeth Bishop, and May Swenson: The Feminist Poetics of Self-Restraint*, University of Michigan Press, 2002.
This study of the three poets looks at how their political views were affected by the time in which they lived and wrote. It is a scholarly and abstract work, but a good view of the ideas that likely were major influences on Swenson's ideas and style.

SUGGESTED SEARCH TERMS

May Swenson

Swenson AND Question

Swenson AND nature

Swenson AND death

Swenson AND afterlife

Swenson AND religion

Swenson AND metaphor

poetry AND death

May Swenson AND Elizabeth Bishop

May Swenson AND self-consciousness

Sound and Sense

ALEXANDER POPE

1711

English poet and essayist Alexander Pope pub-lished the long poem *An Essay on Criticism* anonymously in 1711. The essay is a 744-line poem in which Pope discusses the principles of good poetic criticism and the flaws to which critics are prone. In the course of the poem, Pope also highlights the qualities of what he considers to be good poetry. All the while, the poetry itself typically, but not unfailingly, reflects the virtues he is describing. As he dis-cusses the importance of meter to the overall success of a poem, for example, he writes in perfectly metered verse. The poem that has become known as "Sound and Sense" is a four-teen-line excerpt from this much longer work. In this section, which consists of lines 362 through 375 of the larger work, Pope describes the way a poem's technical aspects, including meter and language, support the overall meaning of the poem. The sound of the poem, the rhythm, rhyme, and flow that are revealed when the poem is read, Pope insists, should mirror the sense, or meaning, of the poem. Throughout these fourteen lines, Pope emphasizes the way that mastery of technique results in a poem that reflects the writer's artistic aims.

An Essay on Criticism was included in later collections of Pope's work, appearing in such volumes as the 1831 *The Poetical Works of Alexander Pope*, Vol. II, published by William Pickering.

Alexander Pope (© *Hulton Archive | Getty Images*)

AUTHOR BIOGRAPHY

Born on May 21, 1688, in London, to Alexander Pope, a linen maker, and his second wife, Edith Pope suffered from physical disabilities. As a child, he contracted tuberculosis of the bone, also known as Potts' disease, which resulted in curvature of his spine and persistent headaches. Pope was raised in a Roman Catholic family in London and later in the countryside. At the time of Pope's childhood, England was ruled by the Protestants King William and Queen Mary, following the abdication of the Catholic King James II. In 1700, Pope's father moved the family to the village of Binfield. Despite a sporadic formal education, Pope was able to teach himself Latin, Greek, French, and Italian.

Pope published his first poems, *The Pastorals*, in 1709, in a volume collected by Jacob Tonson, *Miscellanies*. The poetic essay known as *An Essay on Criticism* was published anonymously in 1711; this lengthy work contains the lines that have come to be known separately as "Sound and Sense." A year later, Pope was published in another *Miscellany*, this one collected by Barnaby Bernard Lintot. This volume contained the first edition of one of Pope's best-known poems, *The Rape of the Lock*, a

lengthy poem written as a mock epic. It is concerned with a stolen lock of hair and the ensuing dispute between two Catholic families.

In 1716, Pope and his family moved from Binfield to Chiswick. He continued to write verse and prose, and his poems and essays were collected and published in the volume *Works* in 1717. The same year, Pope's father died. Pope and his mother moved to Twickenham in 1718, and Pope continued to write and publish essays and original and translated poetry. In 1725, he served as the editor of a six-volume collection of the works of English playwright William Shakespeare. Having completed translations of the Greek epic poems the *Iliad* and the *Odyssey*, Pope also focused on his essays and poems during the next several years, working closely with friend and fellow poet and essayist Jonathan Swift at this time as well. In 1733, Pope's mother died. Pope's late work included a lengthy mock-epic poem known as *The Dunciad*; it was published in 1743. Pope died not long after, on May 30, 1744.

POEM TEXT

True ease in writing comes from art, not chance,
As those move easiest who have learn'd to dance.
'Tis not enough no harshness gives offence;
The sound must seem an echo to the sense.
Soft is the strain when zephyr gently blows,   5
And the smooth stream in smoother numbers flows;
But when loud surges lash the sounding shore,
The hoarse rough verse should like the torrent roar.
When Ajax strives some rock's vast weight to throw,
The line too labours, and the words move slow;   10
Not so when swift Camilla scours the plain,
Flies o'er th' unbending corn, and skims along the main.
Hear how Timotheus' varied lays surprise,
And bid alternate passions fall and rise!

POEM SUMMARY

The text used for this summary is *An Essay on Criticism*, in *The Poetical Works of Alexander Pope*, Vol. 2, William Pickering, 1831, pp. 1–34. Versions of the poem can be found on the following web pages: http://www.poetryfoundation.org/poem/174163 and http://www.eng.fju.edu.tw/iacd_2000S/intro_lit/LitLab/AP1.htm.

MEDIA ADAPTATIONS

- Portions of Pope's *Essay on Criticism* have been published by Saland Publishing in 2011 as MP3 recordings read by George Rylands. The lines published include lines 215–232 and lines 337–357. (This recording does not include "Sound and Sense," which is lines 362–375.)

"Sound and Sense" consists of fourteen lines excerpted from *An Essay on Criticism*. It is written in *couplets*, or rhymed pairs of lines. *An Essay on Criticism* is divided into three parts, and "Sound and Sense" forms a portion of the second part of the longer poem. In the first couplet of "Sound and Sense," the poet insists there is little that is random when it comes to writing. Poetry that seems to have been written with ease has actually been constructed with great attention to artistic detail, Pope claims. Yet he points out that, when the craft of poetry is studied, the act of writing becomes increasingly natural, if not effortless. He compares the practiced art of writing to dancing: once a dancer has learned the steps, the dancer moves with ease.

The poet next observes that a poem must do more than avoid offending the reader with harsh or jarring tones; rather, it must display a unity between the meaning of the poem and its sound when read aloud. When the poem's subject or imagery is focused on such things as gently blowing wind or smoothly flowing streams, for example, Pope insists that the poem's rhythm and meter should emphasize the softness and smoothness of such images. Similarly, if a poem describes the waves pounding a beach, the poem should use language and meter that emphasize the roaring of the surf.

In the next couplet, Pope refers to a figure from ancient Greek mythology, Ajax, who fought in the Trojan War. Pope states that if a poet is describing the way Ajax lifts a heavy rock to throw, the lines of verse should slow and emphasize the labor involved in lifting the weight. Pope contrasts this with a reference to Roman mythology, the warrior

Camilla, who was given divine powers and who was swift enough to run through a field of corn without harming a stalk. Here Pope suggests that the verse should reflect Camilla's nimble movement.

In the final couplet, Pope refers to the Greek musician Timotheus. Just as the musician surprised the listener with the variety of his songs, so the poet should also be able to surprise the reader of the poem and inspire the ebb and flow of various emotions through mastery of meter and language.

THEMES

Structure

In the section of *An Essay on Criticism* that makes up the poem "Sound and Sense," Pope focuses on the importance of poetic form. Essentially, "Sound and Sense" is a poem about poetry—how to write it, how to read it, how it should sound when the poet seeks to express various ideas. Pope describes elements of the structure of the poem that, when attended to by a poet who has studied poetry as an art form, contribute to the poem's quality. He insists throughout the poem that elements of form, including sound, rhythm, and meter, must complement the meaning of the poem. Pope provides several examples of the way formal elements enhance the aesthetics of the poem and further complement the poem's meaning. Through word choice and the rhythm created by the poem's meter, Pope states, the poet can create a sense of gentleness that mirrors the image of the soft breath of wind, or the effortlessness of a stream flowing. Pope lists other examples of the way the sound of the verse—created by carefully constructed metrical patterns and rhythmic structures as well as word choice and rhyme pattern—should echo and support the meaning, or sense, that the lines of poetry are trying to convey. The pace, sound, and flow of the verse should grow harsh and rough when a poet describes waves crashing on a beach, for example, and should slow, as if to highlight a sense of struggle, when a poet is depicting an individual undergoing a trial or an arduous task. As Pope gives other examples of this cohesion—a unity that he values highly—between the poem's sound, structure, imagery, and meaning, poetic form becomes the prominent theme examined in this poem.

TOPICS FOR FURTHER STUDY

- "Sound and Sense" is written in heroic couplets, or rhymed pairs of lines in iambic pentameter. (An *iamb* is a set of two syllables, unstressed followed by stressed; in a *pentameter line*, there are five of these sets.) Select a topic that interests you and write a poem of ten lines or more in heroic couplets. In addition to counting the number of unaccented and accented syllables in your lines of poetry and making sure each pair of lines rhymes, consider the language you use and the imagery you incorporate in your poem. Share your poem with the class by reading it aloud, or by presenting it as a poster, embellished with your own artwork.

- In "Sound and Sense," Pope discusses the way poems should be written and, in doing so, suggests how they should be read. The young-adult collection *How to Eat a Poem: A Smorgasbord of Tasty and Delicious Poems for Young Readers*, edited by Andrew Carroll, Charles Flowers, and Douglas Korb and published in 2006, includes a section of poems about poetry and writing. Read these poems and consider the ways they are similar to or different from Pope's poem and his approach to writing poetry. Study in particular Eve Merriam's "How to Eat a Poem," Amy Lowell's "The Poem," and Archibald MacLeish's "Ars Poetica." Read these poems with a small group and discuss what they say about reading and writing poetry. How do their views compare to those of Pope? How do they structure their poems about poetry? Are they formal verses with rhyme schemes and meter, or are they free-verse poems? Create an online blog that serves as a forum for you to discuss these topics and your own views on writing poetry.

- Pope's work focused on Augustan English culture, politics, and society. Outside the borders of his homeland, however, writers of African descent living in nations colonized by English-speaking countries, including Africa and the West Indies, wrote about their experiences as slaves, or as native people whose own homelands became the property of other nations. Editor Vincent Carretta collects the work of these writers in the 1996 *Unchained Voices: An Anthology of Black Authors in the English-Speaking World of the Eighteenth Century*. Explore some of the poetry and writing in this collection. Select one of the authors and use the information in this volume, as well as additional research you gather, to write a biographical essay in which you discuss the author's life and works. Your essay should include some reference to the historical events that shaped the author's life.

- During Pope's lifetime, the English monarchy underwent a series of changes; the crown changed hands numerous times. Research the history of the English monarchy during the years in which Pope lived. Create a historical time line in which you chart the reigns of the monarchs, as well as major political events that occurred in England during that time period. Your time line may take the form of a poster, a PowerPoint presentation, or an online time line that you create on a web page. Share your time line with your class.

Neoclassicism

Pope was writing during what is called the neoclassical period of English literature. Neoclassical writers, including Pope, John Dryden, Jonathan Swift, and Joseph Addison, praised the works and ideals of the ancient classical literature of the Greeks and Romans, hence the term *neoclassicism*, which means "new classicism." Neoclassicism emphasized the rules of form and structure related to various types of literature; adherence to those rules indicated the skill of the poet and the worth of the poem.

Pope's poem is about the act of writing and the elements that make good poetry. (© Nejron Photo / Shutterstock.com)

Neoclassicism flourished as a literary school of thought from the mid- to late 1600s through the late 1700s. Evidence of the impact and guiding force of neoclassicism on Pope's work can be seen throughout *An Essay on Criticism*, as well as in the fourteen lines of it that have become known as "Sound and Sense." Not only does the poem focus on the importance of the elements of poetic form, but it also refers several times to figures from ancient Greek and Roman texts, such as Ajax, Camilla, and Timotheus. Ajax is associated with Greek mythology and appears in Homer's epic poem *The Iliad* and in Sophocles' play *Ajax*. Camilla is from Roman mythology and appears in Virgil's *Aeneid*. Timotheus was an ancient Greek musician from the time period of Greek dramatist Euripedes. Pope incorporates these references into his poem to show his own sense of the importance of neoclassical values. Additionally, he uses these classical references to them as examples of the types of references, allusions, or figures one might find—or *should* find—in the works of other poets. In exploring the elements of well-crafted

poetry, Pope incorporates classical references in order to emphasize that the honoring and emulating of classical texts is a praiseworthy and preferable method of writing poetry.

STYLE

Heroic Couplet and Mixed Meter

In poetry, *meter* is a term used to describe patterns of unstressed and stressed syllables in a line of verse. Lines are further divided into metrical feet, or groups of the unstressed and stressed of syllables. For example, an unstressed syllable followed by a stressed syllable is called an *iamb*. The number of times this pattern is repeated in a line of verse determines how it is described. If the unstressed-stressed pattern known as an *iamb* is repeated five times within a line of verse, the line has five iambic feet; it is therefore described as being written in iambic pentameter (where *penta-* is a prefix meaning "five"). In "Sound and Sense," Pope uses iambic pentameter frequently, but not exclusively.

COMPARE
&
CONTRAST

- **1711:** Queen Anne is the first ruler of what has become known as Great Britain, after England and Scotland unified their kingdoms and parliaments in 1707. Two political parties, the Whigs and the Tories, compete for political power in the unified Parliament.

  Today: The United Kingdom, or U. K.—formally the United Kingdom of Great Britain and Northern Ireland—includes England, Wales, Scotland, and Northern Ireland. It is presided over by Queen Elizabeth II and is governed by a Parliament headed by Prime Minister David Cameron.

- **1711:** Poetry is characterized by a revival of interest in the classical texts of ancient Greece and Rome. Neoclassical poets, including Alexander Pope, John Dryden, and Jonathan Swift, write highly structured verse and refer to Greek and Roman mythology and literature.

  Today: Twenty-first-century British poetry is characterized as much by traditional forms as by experimental and free-verse poetry. Popular and widely anthologized British poets include Andrew Motion, James Fenton, Glyn Maxwell, and Alice Oswald.

- **1711:** Literary magazines, concentrating on poetry and poetry criticism, become popular in Britain. Prominent literary magazines include the *Spectator* and *British Mercury*.

  Today: Twenty-first-century literary magazines abound and continue to publish poetry criticism, as well as the works of new and established poets alike. British literary magazines, including *Oxford Poetry*, *Acumen*, *Iota*, and the *Wolf*, may publish in print or online formats, or both.

One form of iambic pentameter is the *heroic couplet*. A couplet is a pair of rhymed lines; a heroic couplet is one written in iambic pentameter. Most of *An Essay on Criticism*, uses the heroic couplet form. (It is written entirely in couplets, but with some breaks in the iambic meter.) Pope uses the heroic couplet in a number of his other works as well, including his translations of Greek poetry.

Iambic pentameter is commonly regarded as a verse form that closely mirrors the natural speech patterns of the spoken English language. As poet and scholar Timothy Steele explains, "Because iambic rhythm suits English speech more naturally and flexibly than other rhythms, it has been the principal mode of English poetry [since] the time of Geoffrey Chaucer." The conversational tone that iambic pentameter lends Pope's verse exemplifies what Pope insists upon in "Sound and Sense," that the formal construction of a poem should complement its meaning.

In "Sound and Sense," Pope refers to a sense of ease that should be experienced by a poet when writing poetry, and claims that if a poet has properly studied this art form, the writing should not sound strained. In using the heroic couplet to write the poem, Pope demonstrates the partnership between form and meaning. The writing, in the way it flows smoothly and conversationally, is intended to have the appearance of having been an easy thing to accomplish.

Poetic Essay

"Sound and Sense" is an excerpt from the larger poem *An Essay on Criticism*, which has been described as a poetic essay. Although the work is clearly a poem, albeit a lengthy one, *An Essay on Criticism* takes up an argument in the way an essay would. The poetic essay stands apart from other poetic forms and conventions. Before writing *An Essay on Criticism*, Pope had written in the pastoral mode. Pastoral verse, often written in heroic couplets, focuses largely on idealized depictions of rural life, and includes shepherds and the objects of their romantic affections as subjects. In contrast to pastoral poetry, the poetic essay takes as its subject a contemporary issue about which the poet holds a strong opinion. In *An Essay on Criticism* Pope uses the heroic couplet to compose a poem about the nature and structure of poetry and about the appropriate way that critics should examine poetry. Pope uses this format to scold critics who do not recognize the qualities and craftsmanship of poetry, but he also cautions poets against overreaching and attempting poetic feats beyond their abilities. Pope's essay is as much targeted at poets as it is geared toward schooling critics of poetry in their task of review and analysis. By taking critics to task, Pope uses his poetic essay as a forum to guide poets in their composition of poems that exhibit technical expertise. Although the poetic essay was not a particularly common type of poetic expression, Pope revisited it in a later work, *An Essay on Man*. In that poetic essay, also written in heroic couplets, Pope explores such themes as philosophy and ethics.

HISTORICAL CONTEXT

Augustan Age in England

Pope was writing during a time period in which neoclassicism shaped the artistic output of essayists and poets. Neoclassical writers looked to the texts of ancient Greeks and Romans as sources of artistic values and forms, themes, and subject matter. The term *Augustan* refers specifically to the reign of the Roman emperor Augustus, roughly from 27 BCE through 14 CE, and signals the reverence with which eighteenth-century writers regarded ancient texts, Roman texts in particular. While neoclassicism informed English writing to some degree from the mid- to late seventeenth century through the late eighteenth century, the Augustan Age is often regarded as a shorter time span in which such neoclassical writers as Pope and Jonathan Swift flourished. Nicholas Hagger, in *A New Philosophy of Literature: The Fundamental Theme and Unity of World Literature*, explains, "The term 'Augustan Age' was used by [King] George I of himself, for he saw himself as an Augustus." Hagger describes the way the poets of England's Augustan Age "looked back to their Roman counterparts, the Roman Augustan poets, and aspired to emulate, and equal, their epistles, elegies and satires." Such

Roman Augustan poets included Virgil, Horace, and Ovid. English Augustan writers respected the forms and structures of their earlier Roman counterparts. Additionally, as Ian Ousby explains in *The Cambridge Paperback Guide to Literature in English*, "Common literary concerns, especially among the poets, included: the development of an elegant, well-turned style; the pursuit of fluency, precision of expression and a dislike of cant or slang; the observation of decorum; and the cultivation of good taste and the refinement of manner." In addition to Pope and Swift, Samuel Johnson, John Dryden, and Daniel Defoe are counted among England's most accomplished Augustan Age authors.

English Monarchy in the Early 1700s

The English monarchy underwent a number of changes during Pope's lifetime. In 1688, the year Pope was born, England was ruled by the Catholic King James II. James II reigned in the aftermath of the English Civil Wars, which were rooted not only in conflicts between Protestants and Catholics but also in the tensions between those individuals who supported the monarch as a divinely ordained ruler (that is, one chosen by God) and those who believed that the ruling powers of the monarchy should be balanced or limited by Parliament. Following the 1688 birth of James's son and heir, some Protestants feared the establishment of a Catholic dynasty. However, James also had a daughter, Mary, by his first wife, a Protestant. Mary had wed a Protestant husband, William, who invaded England in November of 1688. As the royal army and navy gave their loyalty to this Protestant rival for the throne, the Catholic King James II fled to France. William and Mary were subsequently offered the crown by Parliament. Mary died in 1694, and William continued to rule until his death in 1702. Under William and Mary, the balance of power between the monarchy and the Parliament became codified. Religion remained a source of conflict, however. Individuals described as dissenters against the Protestant faith as it was evolving in England were given the same religious freedoms as their non-dissenting Protestant counterparts. All other sects that were considered "nonconformist" in their opposition to the Church of England were also given similar freedoms—all except for Roman Catholics.

After William's death, James II's second daughter by his first wife (Mary's younger sister) became Queen Anne in 1702. Anne presided over a dispute between the Parliaments of England and Scotland. The disagreement over monarchial

Camilla was an ancient queen who was described by the poet Virgil as being so swift that she could run across the ocean without getting her feet wet.
(© Milana Tkachenko / Shutterstock.com)

succession resulted in the unification of the two kingdoms and the two governmental bodies. The disputes over who would succeed Anne ended with the agreement that James II's cousin Sophia of Hanover (a province of Germany) would become Queen of England and Scotland after Anne's death. However, Sophia died just months prior to Anne's own death. Following Anne's death in 1714, Sophia's eldest son, George, became King George I. During King George's rule, his claim to the throne was challenged by James's son, a Roman Catholic. George was also at a disadvantage as a ruler because he spoke little English, though he was fluent in German and French. Eventually, one of George's most powerful cabinet ministers, Robert Walpole, took on an increasing amount of responsibility in the power vacuum that resulted from George's weakness. Walpole would later become viewed as the first Prime Minister. George I died in 1727 and was succeeded by his son, George II.

CRITICAL OVERVIEW

Much of Pope's work was widely admired by his contemporaries. Although *An Essay on Criticism* was published anonymously, the work received much praise. John Barnard, in *Alexander Pope: The Critical Heritage*, observes that Pope's contemporary critics applauded his genius, as Joseph Addision did in the journal *Spectator*. The critic John Gay, Barnard notes, "described him in God-like terms." Barnard also cites critics who found fault with Pope's efforts. He points specifically to John Dennis, who attacked Pope repeatedly. In the nineteenth century, prominent essayist and critic Thomas De Quincey commented harshly on *An Essay on Criticism*. His remarks are quoted by Donald Greene in *The Enduring Legacy: Alexander Pope Tercentenary Essays*. Greene observes, "[De Quincey] goes on to tear the *Essay on Criticism* to Fpieces: 'It is a collection of independent maxims, tied together into a fasiculus by the printer, but having no natural order or logical dependency.'"

Modern assessments of *An Essay on Criticism* take varied approaches to the work. Philip Smallwood considers the "durability and aesthetic value of the *Essay on Criticism*," in his *Reconstructing Criticism: Pope's "Essay on Criticism" and the Logic of Definition*. Smallwood later notes, however, "Major studies of Pope give relatively scant attention to the *Essay [on Criticism]*, and the poem has inspired few theoretical 'rereadings.'" In providing his own assessment of *An Essay on Criticism*, Barnard comments that the poem's "episodic structure and conversational manner . . . admirably suited Pope's genius and his audience's taste."

CRITICISM

Catherine Dominic

Dominic is a novelist and a freelance writer and editor. In the following essay, she offers a detailed assessment of Pope's prosody in the fourteen lines of An Essay on Criticism *that has come to be known as "Sound and Sense."*

In the fourteen-line section of the second part of *An Essay on Criticism* that is referred to as "Sound and Sense," author Alexander Pope advocates a series of artistic principles. Yet throughout the course of the poem, he does not strictly adhere to the principles he outlines. Although poets often

WHAT DO I READ NEXT?

- Pope's *Essay on Man*, published between 1732 and 1734, is a lengthy philosophical poem written in heroic couplets. It is available in a modern edition, *Essay on Man and Other Poems*, through Empire Books, published in 2012.

- Pope's long mock-epic poem *The Rape of the Lock* was originally published in 1712, just a year after *Essay on Criticism*. It concerns a stolen lock of hair and the conflict between two Catholic families. It is available in a modern edition in the 2012 *Essay on Man and Other Poems*.

- Jonathan Swift was a contemporary and friend of Pope. Swift's *Gulliver's Travels*, originally published in 1726, is part travel adventure, part fantasy, and part satire. Gulliver travels to amazing places, and through his story, Swift offers satirical commentary on his own eighteenth-century English society.

- In *Yuan Mei: Eighteenth-Century Chinese Poet*, originally published in 1956, Arthur Waley provides translations of Yuan Mei's poetry. Students of Pope's work will be provided an opportunity to study the themes and styles of a contemporary poet from another country and culture. Waley also offers an overview of the life and work of the Chinese poet, who lived during roughly the same time period as Pope.

- The 2010 young-adult poetry anthology, *Modern British Poetry: The World Is Never the Same*, edited by Michelle M. Houle, includes the works of nineteenth- and twentieth-century British poets and provides biographical information on each of the poets included.

- Roger D. Lund's 2012 *Ridicule, Religion and the Politics of Wit in Augustan England* examines the use of wit as a rhetorical mode, used by writers such as Pope, Dryden, and Swift, to criticize contemporary religion and politics.

> POPE'S FOCUS APPEARS TO BE ON THE UNITY OF THE POEM'S STRUCTURE, THE SOUND THIS STRUCTURE CREATES, AND THE MEANING, OR SENSE, OF THE POEM. THROUGHOUT THESE FOURTEEN LINES, HOWEVER, THERE IS OFTEN DISUNITY."

intentionally deviate from the metrical patterns they have established in their work in order to create a particular aural effect or to signal to the reader the significance of a particular portion of the text, Pope's variations in meter in "Sound and Sense" are often not effective and therefore do not seem intentional. Pope's focus appears to be on the unity of the poem's structure, the sound this structure creates, and the meaning, or sense, of the poem. Throughout these fourteen lines, however, there is often disunity. In *The Enduring Legacy: Alexander Pope Tercentenary Essays*, Donald Greene quotes nineteenth-century essayist and critic Thomas De Quincey as stating, with regard to *An Essay on Criticism*, "Many of the rules are violated by no man so often as Pope." As De Quincey points out, Pope breaks the rules of artistic form that he outlines in *An Essay on Criticism*. In "Sound and Sense," these flaws are readily apparent. Pope's successful use of both meter and its intentional disruption is marginal in this excerpt of *An Essay on Criticism* and therefore hints at the flaws in the larger work that critics such as De Quincey have identified.

"Sound and Sense" begins well enough. In the first two couplets, Pope sticks to the iambic pentameter that characterizes the heroic couplet, which is the established form of *An Essay on Criticism*. The lines flow with the same ease that constitutes the subject of these lines. At the end of the first couplet, Pope incorporates the imagery of dancing and suggests that a poet who has studied the craft writes a poem as easily as a practiced dancer glides across the floor. The act—of writing or dancing—*appears* to be effortless because the writer or dancer has studied hard enough to put on such a performance. Here, the poet links effort, study, and practice with a resulting ease in exhibiting one's talents. In the next couplet, Pope goes on to discuss the way a poem sounds when it is read, emphasizing that harsh or jarring elements or tones should be absent, and further, that the sounds a poem produces should support the poem's meaning. In these first four lines, Pope does successfully exhibit a unity between sound and sense, between structure and meaning. Yet as his poem continues, this unity breaks down.

As the next couplet begins, Pope breaks form, interrupting his iambic pentameter by beginning the fifth line with a stressed syllable. A trochee (a stressed syllable followed by an unstressed syllable) opens the fifth line. This is surely something that many poets intentionally do in order to shift the tone of the poem or draw attention to a word, a line, or an image. Yet in this line, Pope is describing the gentle blowing of the west wind and is underscoring the softness in sound and rhythm that should accompany such imagery. The sixth line is even more disrupted. Rather than including five iambic feet in this line, Pope incorporates an anapestic foot (two unstressed syllables and a stressed syllable), followed by a monosyllabic foot (one stressed syllable), followed by three iambic feet. While the end result is still a line with five accented syllables, the pattern of unaccented and accented syllables is severely interrupted at the beginning of the line. The imagery of the line is that of a stream, smoothly flowing. Pope states that the image of a smoothly flowing stream is reinforced by a similarly smooth meter, but the line he composes to state this idea is anything but smoothly flowing.

In the next couplet, Pope describes the loud crashing of waves on a beach and states that, when such imagery is the focus of verse, the rhythm and sound should be correspondingly jarring. The first line of the couplet mirrors the one that precedes it, using an anapestic foot (two unstressed syllables and a stressed syllable) and a monosyllabic foot (one stressed syllable), and finishing with three iambic feet. This line, with two stressed syllables next to each other, does sound rough and jarring, successfully echoing the sense of the line. Similarly, the next line's pattern does not match the first line in the couplet but is likewise harsh sounding, as it incorporates a spondaic foot (two accented syllables) after the first iamb. Here, Pope uses interruptions and variations in meter effectively, to mirror the roughness of the imagery that forms the subject of the lines.

The ninth line of the poem once again returns to the smoothly flowing, conversational iambic pentameter of the heroic couplet. Yet what Pope describes is the figure from Greek mythology, Ajax, as he struggles to throw a heavy rock. There is no disruption of meter here to indicate Ajax's effort, despite the fact that, according to Pope's own advice, the meter of such a line should slow, or incorporate an interruption to the meter, in order to emphasize the struggle depicted in Ajax's efforts. In the tenth line, though, the second line of the couplet, Pope does use a spondee (two stressed syllables) after the first iambic foot. In this line, the poet remarks that a line describing the imagery he just mentioned, that of the struggling Ajax, should indicate this effort and should move with corresponding slowness. Pope's use of the spondee has this effect, as the disruption in meter forces the reader to emphasize syllables in a less fluid manner. This couplet, then, is only partially successful in demonstrating the effective manipulation of meter that the poet advocates.

In the eleventh and twelfth lines, Pope draws on imagery from Roman mythology, as he describes the swiftness of the warrior Camilla. Pope opens the line by contrasting the imagery of the quick Camilla with the slow and labored movements of Ajax. He indicates that a poet should not construct slow-moving lines when they concern Camilla, yet he opens this line with a metrical disruption that immediately slows the fluid nature of the surrounding iambic feet. The eleventh line opens with a spondee, two accented syllables, then continues on in iambic feet. The twelfth line features further disruptions, although if Pope wanted to convey the notion of swiftness and fluidity of motion, iambic pentameter would have more effectively achieved the goal. The line begins with an iambic foot, is followed by an anapestic foot, and then includes four more iambic feet. This results not only in the rhythmic disruption followed by the inclusion of an extra unaccented syllable in the iambic foot, but also in a further oddity caused by the addition of an extra accented syllable. Although Pope discusses the necessity of fluid motion in lines that concentrate on the swift-footed Camilla flying over a cornfield, the inclusion of extra syllables into an otherwise fluid pattern is counterproductive and slows the pace of the poem.

In the poem's final two lines, Pope is nearly consistent with the use of iambic pentameter. The thirteenth line, however, contains the problematic possessive form of the name Timotheus, which lends to a tricky reading of the line and

Ajax was a hero of ancient Greece, considered a great warrior. *(© Anastasios71 / Shutterstock.com)*

possibly an extra iambic foot. The final line is similarly *almost* smooth. Pope incorporates a trochee (a stressed syllable followed by an unstressed syllable, or a reversed iamb) for the second foot of the line. The content of these lines focuses on the songs of the Greek musician Timotheus, and how variations in the rhythms of his music suggest the alternating rising and falling of passionate emotions. Here, Pope underscores the necessity of metrical variation in poetry. He emphasizes that metrical variation can be effectively used to achieve a desired end. Yet his own success in these lines is limited. Although Pope, at times, uses meter and disruptions in meter to poetic effect, he does so in "Sound and Sense," somewhat inconsistently. As a result, the poem does not stand out as emblematic of a poet's successful cultivation of artistic skill but rather suggests a less polished piece of poetry, written, as it was, by a younger poet still practicing the steps of the dance he has not yet mastered.

Source: Catherine Dominic, Critical Essay on "Sound and Sense," in *Poetry for Students*, Gale, Cengage Learning, 2014.

Claudia N. Thomas

In the following excerpt, Thomas describes the effect of Pope's poetry on female readers and poets.

Pope's influence on women's poems extended far beyond their specific imitations of or replies to his poems. Pope's distinctive style was imitated by men and women throughout the century, but women were usually deprived of the Latin models and formal schooling in rhetoric from which Pope derived his effects. Their dependence on Pope and other accessible English writers was therefore pronounced.

. . . Like no writer before him, Pope moved eighteenth-century women readers to respond. Some used his poems as masks for their enactments of feminine passion. Others converted his poems into didactic texts. Still others emulated his persona or his prosody. Most women expressed or implied some ambivalence about writing, not to mention publishing, in what was traditionally an aristocratic men's genre. But whether angry or inspired, moved or amused, critical or emulative, women gradually followed Pope into the marketplace, where the rest is women's literary history.

As a group, Pope's eighteenth-century women readers suggest a model of fearless critical reading. Few of these women identified with Pope's constructions of femininity. Instead, women appropriated and revised Pope's images to suit their own contexts, whether more genteel, more devout, or more feminist. Current analyses implying that contemporary women were somehow victimized by Pope's gendered rhetoric should reconsider the critical acuity with which his female audience often read. Such a consideration necessarily extends the horizon of meanings we can assign to Pope's work at its earliest reception and the horizon of cultural perceptions we may assume available to eighteenth-century women readers.

As women eagerly sought to articulate their experiences in literary genres sanctioned by an exemplar of their male-dominated culture, their writings formed a subversive coda to Pope's canon. As Anne Ingram, Lady Irwin, commented in her "Epistle to Mr. Pope" (1736):

> By custom doom'd to folly, sloth and ease,
> No wonder, Pope such female triflers sees:
> But would the satyrist confess the truth,
> Nothing so like as male and female youth;
> Nothing so like as man and woman old;
> Their joys, their loves, their hates, if truly told.

Eighteenth-century women, trained to think of themselves as "the sex," nevertheless intuited the feminist principle that men and women are not essentially different. They read Pope as women but recognized the ease with which his "masculine" verse could often be altered to include, or articulate, the feminine point of view. Where his opinions seemed dangerous or inimical to women, they published their misgivings. Through their prose criticism and poetic revisions, Pope's women readers appropriated his texts' themes and images to express their own opinions, and versions, of experience: "Their joys, their loves, their hates... truly told."

Source: Claudia N. Thomas, "Conclusion: Pope's Influence on Eighteenth-Century Women's Poetry," in *Alexander Pope and His Eighteenth-Century Women Readers*, Southern Illinois University Press, 1994, pp. 227, 244–45.

Douglas Lane Patey

In the following excerpt, Patey explains the lack of division between professional and private life in Pope's time.

. . . Our most ordinary assumptions about life and art hide Pope's integrity from us. We have lost that vision of life's wholeness that motivated Solon's maxim, "Call no man happy

AS THIS ACCOUNT SUGGESTS, POPE'S VISION OF THE INTEGRITY OF MORAL AND POLITICAL LIFE, OF THE PUBLIC AND PRIVATE REALMS, AND INDEED OF ART AND LIFE, RESTS ON AN UNDERSTANDING OF THE SELF FUNDAMENTALLY AT ODDS WITH MORE MODERN NOTIONS OF HUMAN IDENTITY."

till he is dead"—of life as given shape by the effort to realize its proper shape, according to the hierarchy of ends that classical and Christian philosophy once provided. Alasdair MacIntyre writes in his great recent account of the passing of this vision, *After Virtue*:

> The social obstacles [to seeing life whole] derive from the way in which modernity partitions each human life into a variety of segments, each with its own norms and modes of behavior. So work is divided from leisure, private life from public, the corporate from the personal. So both childhood and old age have been wrenched away from the rest of human life and made over into distinct realms. And all these separations have been achieved so that it is the distinctiveness of each and not the unity of the life of the individual who passes through those parts in terms of which we are taught to think and to feel.

To MacIntyre's list must be added another fateful separation that originated in Pope's own age, the century that invented both the name and concept of "aesthetics": that between art and the rest of life. "Learn then what MORALS Criticks ought to show" exhorts the *Essay on Criticism*, but no longer can we accept Pope's effortless identification of literary—critical with moral skills—of critical acumen with "good nature," "good breeding," and "generosity," as against bad readers' "pride" and "faction"—nor, having separated off the realm of the aesthetic, can we any longer make intelligible his claim that in all the departments of life, "Nature's chief Masterpiece is writing well."

Pope's life, as much as his art, elides what we would sever. Sure of his vocation from the start, Pope seems to have reached maturity by a direct route, never detouring through ordinary childhood or adolescence (if we are to believe historians such as

J. H. Van den Berg, adolescence was only just being invented). The Victorians bequeathed to us a division between the private world of home and family (guided by a feminine moral intelligence) and the outer world of work, where different norms apply; but Pope and most of his closest friends were leisured bachelors, who conducted their work at home or in one another's houses. Of these very houses, practitioners of the new social history of architecture, such as Mark Girouard, report that only in the late seventeenth century were spaces commonly set aside for use solely as bedrooms—the result of a new concern for personal privacy—though for the often invalid Pope, sickroom, workroom, and drawing room could never fully be distinguished, either at Twickenham or at the many houses where he visited, wrote, and took physic. Pope wrote most of *An Essay on Man* during a long convalescence at Lord Bolingbroke's Dawley Farm; many of his house parties suggest a condition of permanent *levée*. As such reflections suggest, we do Pope a disservice in one-sidedly labelling him a "public poet": he did not understand the "public" and the "private" as do we. The same poet who condemned public men for their private lives—who found, even in a single, seemingly detached "private" vice a synecdoche for the whole moral and intellectual life of dunce, peer, or politician—made sure as had no poet before him that the public knew the details of his own life, so that Pope himself could stand surety to his poetic pronouncements. Thus the *Epistle to Arbuthnot*, Pope's defense of his career as a satirist, climaxes by referring his audience to the evidence—directly relevant from his point of view, dubiously so from ours—of his enduring friendships and exemplary filial piety.

For this poet who "thought a Lye in Verse or Prose the same," private and public life form an ethical continuity, while art and life conjoin to make a satire a mode of political action. Aristotle had taught that politics is the perfection of ethics; for Pope, during his last years chief poetic spokesman for the Opposition to Walpole, all political reform is finally not institutional but moral (in effect, doing one's duty). Isaac Kramnick and, more recently, Brean Hammond have shown us that it was more than anyone else his lifelong friend Henry St. John, Viscount Bolingbroke—through his periodical *The Craftsman*, the chief prose voice of Opposition—from whom Pope learned the terms in which to sing. Bolingbroke wrote in *The Idea of a Patriot King*: "Let not princes flatter themselves. They will be examined closely, in private as well as in public

life: and those, who cannot pierce further, will judge of them by the appearances they give in both. To obtain true popularity, that which is founded in esteem and affection, they must, therefore, maintain their characters in both; and to that end neglect appearances in neither, but observe the decorum necessary to preserve the esteem, whilst they win the affections, of mankind. Kings, they must never forget that they are men: men, they must never forget that they are kings." The evidence is overwhelming that it was Bolingbroke who taught Pope to understand the polity as the embodiment of an "ancient constitution," a Polybian balance of three estates (king, peers, and commons). As in any moral teleology, the ideal form of the state may be more or less completely realized: freedom and stability are the products of each member's actively fulfilling his role; tyranny and "corruption"—a word never far, at this period, from its Latin sense of division into parts—of failure to enact one's role. Thus, according to Bolingbroke, "Depravation of manners exposed the constitution to ruin; reformation [of manners] will secure it" (3:75). So much did Pope identify political with moral rectitude—doing one's duty—that he could write in *An Essay on Man* with a jab at Walpole's administration: "For Forms of Government let fools contest; / Whate'er is best administered is best" (3.303–4).

We should recognize in this political model a structure of thought that informs the whole universe of the *Essay on Man*, where, "reasoning but from what we know," Pope identifies all the levels in the chain of nature as "ranks," "callings," "stations," and "estates." (As the Marxists remind us, there is no better way to mask an ideology than to make it appear "natural.") The notion of a calling—what Martin Luther called *Berufung*—comes heavily freighted with religious overtones (it is a "vocation"), so we should not be surprised to discover that just as the natural universe is providentially ordered, so is the hierarchy of stations in society: Bolingbroke himself says that under the rule of a Patriot King, "the orders and forms of the constitution" will be "restored to their primitive integrity, and become what they were intended to be" (75). Right moral (and political) action, because it is action in accordance with the role given one by God, may therefore be understood in terms drawn from the arts, and in particular in the language of decorum: Pope writes in the *Essay on Man*, "Act well your part, there all the honor lies" (4.194), and Bolingbroke speaks of evildoing as "depravation of *manners*." Here, finally, we may find a clue to unlock one of the deepest paradoxes running through the *Essay on Man*: although Pope understands the virtuous life to be one of active pursuit, he persistently describes it in terms that suggest stasis: "rest" and "standing still." "The only point where human bliss stands still," he tells us, is virtue; "here we can rest." Right doing takes on the aspect of passivity (and immobility) because it consists finally in submission to role: thereby the self realizes its proper end, so that in virtuous *doing* the self is *being* what most truly it is.

As this account suggests, Pope's vision of the integrity of moral and political life, of the public and private realms, and indeed of art and life, rests on an understanding of the self fundamentally at odds with more modern notions of human identity. A number of recent writers have attempted to define a shift in concepts of the self that seems to have occurred in the later eighteenth century; we know that Pope and the Scriblerians spilled much ink to controvert Locke's doctrine of human identity (as continuity of consciousness, but not identity of substance), yet it remains to be explained what was their own understanding of what in the *Conjectures* Edward Young called "the stranger within thee." Because the eighteenth-century shift in concepts of self is at the heart of the modern impasse in ethical theory, MacIntyre's *After Virtue* is once again of help. Dryden's Almanzor, crying before he takes up the duties of kingship, "I am myself alone," might stand as a type of the modern self (better examples are villains such as Milton's Satan, whose protestations of his independence from God sound curiously like Sartre's account of the ego). This self exists antecedently to the roles in which it may happen to find itself and so is defined by none of them; constituted not from without but only from within, it is responsible only to itself, to the rules it itself makes (hence the predicament of modern ethics). The Popean self, on the other hand, is defined from without (by providence): it is essentially constituted by its roles, and so by the moral ends (in the broadest sense of "moral") that those roles embody. . . .

Source: Douglas Lane Patey, "Art and Integrity: Concepts of Self in Alexander Pope and Edward Young," in *Critical Essays on Alexander Pope*, edited by Wallace Jackson and R. Paul Yoder, G. K. Hall, 1993, pp. 176–79.

SOURCES

"Anne (1665–1714)," BBC website, http://www.bbc.co.uk/history/historic_figures/anne.shtml (accessed March 26, 2013).

Baldick, Chris, *Oxford Dictionary of Literary Terms*, Oxford University Press, 2001, pp. 28, 222–23.

Barnard, John, ed., Introduction to *Alexander Pope: The Critical Heritage*, Routledge, 1973, pp. 1–38.

Butt, John, ed., *The Poems of Alexander Pope: A Reduced Version of the Twickenham Text*, Sheridan Books, 1963, pp. xix–xxii.

"An Essay on Criticism (1711), by Alexander Pope," Poetry Foundation website, October 13, 2009, http://www.poetry foundation.org/learning/essay/237826 (accessed March 26, 2013).

Feder, Lillian, *The Handbook of Classical Literature*, Da Capo Press, 1998, pp. 23–25, 73, 142–43.

Greene, Donald, "An Anatomy of Pope Bashing," in *The Enduring Legacy: Alexander Pope Tercentenary Essays*, edited by G. S. Rousseau and Pat Rogers, Cambridge University Press, 1988, pp. 241–82.

Hagger, Nicholas, *A New Philosophy of Literature: The Fundamental Theme and Unity of the World*, O-Books, 2012, pp. 161–78.

Ousby, Ian, ed., *The Cambridge Paperback Guide to Literature in English*, Cambridge University Press, 1996, p. 20.

"Periodicals," in *Encyclopaedia Britannica*, Vol. 18, Henry G. Allen, 1890, pp. 535–44.

Piper, W. B., and S. Cushman, "Heroic Couplet," in *The Princeton Encyclopedia of Poetry and Poetics*, 4th ed., edited by Stephen Cushman, Clare Cavanagh, Jahen Ramazani, and Paul Rouzer, Princeton University Press, pp. 624–25.

"Pope, Alexander (1688–1744)," in *Representative Poetry Online*, University of Toronto Libraries, http://rpo.library.utoronto.ca/poets/pope-alexander (accessed March 26, 2013).

Pope, Alexander, *An Essay on Criticism*, in *The Poetical Works of Alexander Pope*, Vol. 2, William Pickering, 1831, pp. 1–34.

Smallwood, Phillip, *Reconstruction Criticism: Pope's "Essay on Criticism" and the Logic of Definition*, Rosemont Publishing, 2003, pp. 15–28, 183–205.

Steele, Timothy, "Introduction to Meter," CAL State LA website, 2001, http://instructional1.calstatela.edu/tsteele/TSpage5/meter.html (accessed March 26, 2013).

"United Kingdom Monarchs (1603–Present)," in *The Official Website of the British Monarchy*, http://www.royal.gov.uk/HistoryoftheMonarchy/KingsandQueensoftheUnitedKingdom/KingsandQueensoftheUnitedKingdom.aspx (accessed March 26, 2013).

FURTHER READING

Lonsdale, Roger, ed., *Eighteenth-Century Women Poets: An Oxford Anthology*, Oxford University Press, 1990.

> Lonsdale gathers examples of the poetry written by more than a hundred women in England in the Augustan Age, including the work of Octavia Walsh, Mary Locke, and Georgiana Cavendish.

Mack, Maynard, *Alexander Pope: A Life*, Yale University Press, 1988.

> Renowned scholar Maynard Mack offers a detailed assessment of Pope's life and literary career. He also discusses the English culture and politics that shaped the literature of this time period.

Parker, Blanford, *The Triumph of Augustan Poetics: English Literary Culture from Butler to Johnson*, Cambridge University Press, 1998.

> Parker's work explores the poetic principles of the Augustan Age in England and includes an analysis of the influence of religion and politics on these poetic developments. The work includes a chapter on Pope.

Richardson, John, *Slavery and Augustan Literature: Swift, Pope, Gay*, Routledge, 2004.

> In this work, Richardson assess the connections between Jonathan Swift, Pope, and John Gay, and a British Parliament that sought to increase the British share of global slave trade. Richardson examines the writings of these authors and claims that their work reveals ambiguous attitudes about slavery and freedom.

SUGGESTED SEARCH TERMS

Alexander Pope AND Essay on Criticism

Alexander Pope AND Sound and Sense

Neoclassicism AND England

Augustan Age AND England

Alexander Pope AND Jonathan Swift

George I AND Augustus

The Rape of the Lock

Essay on Man

eighteenth-century England AND monarchy

eighteenth-century England AND parliament

A Story

LI-YOUNG LEE

1990

"A Story," by Li-Young Lee, is a poem of twenty-three lines depicting a man who must confront his own bafflement when he is unable to think up a story to tell his young son. The poem suggests itself as highly autobiographical in nature, as do nearly all Lee's poems, but the reader will be hard-pressed to determine whether the poet should be identified with the father or with the son. Lee's poems on his experiences with, impressions of, and feelings for his father represent a major portion of his body of work, especially within his first and second collections. This is readily understood in light of his father's outsized role in his biography: Lee was born in Indonesia to Chinese parents who had been pushed into a kind of exile because of their controversial marriage. Over several years, the father led the family through a series of locales in East Asia, at last entering the United States when Lee was six. His father eventually became a Presbyterian minister in a small town in Pennsylvania, attaining a godlike status in the eyes of his son.

Given the difficulty Lee has had conceiving of a homeland for himself—he never lived in the China beloved by his parents and grandparents, and Indonesia, his country of birth, was never a true home for the family—it is perhaps unsurprising that he is disinclined to classify himself according to his heritage. Though many of his poems draw extensively upon his identity as Chinese American, he tends toward lyrical, universalized meditations treating themes of love, family, and home not for any one ethnicity but

The little boy wants his father to tell him a story.
(© robert_s | Shutterstock.com)

for all humanity. "A Story" is just such a broadly realized poem. It was published first in the *American Voice* and then in Lee's second collection, *The City in Which I Love You* (1990). The poem can also be found in the section on Lee in Bill Moyers's collection *The Language of Life: A Festival of Poets* (1995) and in *The American Voice: Anthology of Poetry* (1998).

AUTHOR BIOGRAPHY

Li-Young Lee was born on August 19, 1957, in Jakarta, Indonesia. Lee's mother's grandfather was China's first republican president, holding office from 1912 to 1916. Lee's father was a personal physician to China's Communist leader Mao Zedong, who took power after the revolution in 1949. Despite this connection to the ruling Communist Party, the parents' status was not entirely favorable: Lee's father was the son of an entrepreneur and reputed gangster, while his mother was in effect a daughter of royalty. In Lee's own words, as quoted by Moyers in *The Language of Life*, his "parents' marriage was very frowned upon in China."

The young couple fled to Indonesia, where Lee's father taught courses at Gamaliel University, covering the King James Bible, among other texts. Persecuted by the regime of President Sukarno for teaching Christian literature,

the father spent nineteen months in jail, and upon his escape with his family during a transfer to Macao, they lived in Hong Kong, where the father became an evangelical minister and head of a million-dollar business. They would later live in Japan, Singapore, and elsewhere. Finally, the father took the family to live in the United States, where they made stops in Seattle, Maryland, and New York City before settling in East Vandergrift, Pennsylvania.

Lee was highly influenced by his father's classical Chinese education, which entailed the memorization of some three hundred Tang dynasty poems, which the father then recited to his children, including Lee, two brothers, and a sister. Lee and his father alike considered the Bible one of the English language's best poetic works; perhaps because of his extensive travels in childhood, Lee is especially fond of the book of Exodus. Under these circumstances, Lee, as quoted by Moyers, came to view poetry as "some high and mighty thing of the angels and of the ancient dead in China"—until he attended the University of Pittsburgh and was exposed to the modern yet spiritually resonant verse of Gerald Stern, who would become his teacher and mentor. After double majoring in biochemistry and English—and marrying his wife, Donna, in 1978—Lee headed west to attend the University of Arizona. He left after a year and went back east to attend the State University of New York at Brockport for a year.

Lee's first book of poetry, *Rose*, came out in 1986, winning a poetry award from New York University. In the mid-1980s, Lee's two sons were born. His poem "A Story" was included in his second collection, *The City in Which I Love You* (1990), which was the Academy of American Poets' Lamont Poetry Selection, a national award given to the best second collection published that year. Lee has taught at the University of Iowa and at Northwestern University in Chicago, Illinois, where the family settled. Lee published a memoir, *The Winged Seed: A Remembrance*, in 1995 and two more books of poetry in the first decade of the twentieth century.

POEM TEXT

Sad is the man who is asked for a story
and can't come up with one.

His five-year-old son waits in his lap.

MEDIA ADAPTATIONS

- The episode of Bill Moyers's PBS series *The Power of the Word* of October 6, 1989, titled "Voices of Memory," featured Li-Young Lee. The episode can be viewed online at http://bill-moyers.com/content/voices-of-memory/, and Lee reads "A Story" to an audience at New Jersey's Glassboro State College beginning at 24:00. The poem can also be read within the transcript of the episode.

Not the same story, Baba. A new one.
The man rubs his chin, scratches his ear.   5

In a room full of books in a world
of stories, he can recall
not one, and soon, he thinks, the boy
will give up on his father.

Already the man lives far ahead, he sees   10
the day this boy will go. *Don't go!*
Hear the alligator story! The angel story once
*   more!*
You love the spider story. You laugh at the
*   spider.*
Let me tell it!

But the boy is packing his shirts,   15
he is looking for his keys. *Are you a god,*
the man screams, *that I sit mute before you?*
Am I a god that I should never disappoint?

But the boy is here. *Please, Baba, a story?*
It is an emotional rather than logical equation,   20
an earthly rather than heavenly one,
which posits that a boy's supplications
and a father's love add up to silence.

POEM SUMMARY

The text used for this summary is from *The City in Which I Love You*, BOA Editions, 1990, p. 65. Versions of the poem can be found on the following web pages: http://www.poets.org/viewmedia.php/prmMID/23343, http://www.indiana.edu/~primate/lee.html, and http://billmoyers.com/content/voices-of-memory/.

Stanzas 1–3

The opening word of "A Story" sets the tone for the poem, identifying the emotion of a man who is asked to tell a story but cannot come up with one at the moment. The phrasing suggests that the listener is specifically requesting that the man produce an original story on the spot. The fact that the poet mentions the emotion of sadness first lends a degree of permanence to it: with the statement "the man is sad," the *man* is established first in the reader's mind, and then the man is overlaid with the emotion, suggesting that the emotion could be altered or replaced with another. However, the poet reverses the sentence: the *sadness* is established first, and then the man is deposited within that emotion. The sadness is like a setting, such that it may be no easier to remove the man from the sadness than it would be to remove him from the setting of, say, a swamp or a desert.

After the first stanza provides, in effect, a close-up of a nondescript man who is sad for lack of a story to tell, the second stanza zooms out slightly to reveal that the listener is the man's son, a five-year-old sitting in his lap. The description of line 3 amounts to a moment of stillness in the scene. The son may suspect what the man is thinking—that a familiar story might be told—as line 4 indicates with italics the boy's speech: he wants not an old but a new story. The word *baba*, not commonly used by Anglo Americans to mean "father," suggests that the family is of non-Anglo origins (which, if the reader has seen the author's name, has already been suggested). The man responds with gestures indicating his perplexity.

The third stanza zooms out one step further to give an image of the room in which they sit, perhaps a library or at least one with several bookshelves. Beyond the physical setting, the wording greatly expands the conceptual setting in noting that there is, in fact, an abundance of stories in the world. However, because he is unable to think of a single one, the man seems to sink into despair. He imagines that, before long, the boy will simply give up on him—whether when seeking a story or with regard to any and all things a boy might expect from his father.

Stanzas 4 and 5

From the man's despair, a scene emerges in his mind, the scene in which the boy leaves the family home, having given up on the father for good. The italics now indicate the man's words to his son: he implores the boy not to leave and begs him to listen to one of the stories he knows and has loved so well. This imagined scene seems to combine the present and future: when the boy is old enough to be leaving home, he will likely no longer be the least bit interested in stories about alligators, angels, and spiders. This is not to say that the man's words are improbable; if the grown son were leaving after a falling out and the man were upset by the circumstances, he might indeed try to reestablish a connection with the son by harkening back to the years when the boy sat lovingly on the father's lap and listened to delightful stories about animals and angels.

In spite of the man's imploring words, the son continues the process of leaving, packing shirts and, at last, collecting his keys. More desperate than ever to keep the son from leaving, the man pleads for recognition of the injustice of the situation. The man asks first a rhetorical question as to whether the son is a god, that the man should sit silently before him. The sense of this question is perhaps twofold: it may suggest that the man feels as if he is mute because the son is not responding to his words; it may also suggest that the man feels that he is supposed to be mute because the god before him scorns the entreaties of a mere mortal. The man then asks a second, inverse rhetorical question, asking whether he himself is being held to expectations befitting an infallible god—one who loses the faith of a follower upon a single instance of failure to provide what the follower demands.

Stanza 6

Line 19, the first line of the final stanza, returns the poem from the father's daydream to the immediate circumstances: the boy sits before him and sweetly asks for a story. Line 20 proceeds with the opening clause of a broader conceptualization of the circumstances, where the contrasted notions of emotion and logic, along with the mathematical word *equation*, suggest a sudden withdrawal from the scene being narrated—as if the image of the boy pleading once more for a story is frozen in time, leaving the poem to close with a sort of voice-over narration. This closing four-line sentence suggests that the determining factor in the father's failure to produce a story is emotion, not logic—if all the situation required were the assembly of a story for the boy's consumption, logically, it should not be that difficult. The equation in question is one of earth, not of heaven—theirs is not a perfect, heavenly world, in which the father would ideally fulfill the son's wish,

TOPICS FOR FURTHER STUDY

- In the form of either a short story or a poem, write a fairy-tale version of an episode from your family's history.

- Read Walt Whitman's poem "A child said, What is the grass?," which is part of his "Song of Myself" and is available online (at http://www.poets.org/viewmedia.php/prmMID/15816) or in the 2008 volume *Walt Whitman*, edited by Jonathan Levin and illustrated by Jim Burke as part of the Poetry for Young People series.

- Record interviews with at least two people from your own family—whether siblings, parents or guardians, cousins, aunts, uncles, grandparents, etcetera—about the importance of stories in their lives. Ask about whether they remember being told stories as a child or telling their own children stories. Think of a variety of additional questions on what stories mean to them. Transcribe the interviews in order to produce an essay that summarizes what you learned from your family members, quoting where appropriate, and also includes personal reflections of your own on storytelling. If possible, make relevant clips from the interviews available on a website that also includes your essay.

- Identify passages in the Bible that address the responsibility of a parent toward one's children. (A helpful resource is the OpenBible.info page "Responsibility to Children," at http://www.openbible.info/topics/responsibility_to_children). Draw on and quote from these passages to write a paper elaborating on the type of parent-child relationship that is fostered by the Bible, and discuss the extent to which the Bible's parenting injunctions remain relevant in twenty-first-century America.

but an earthly one, marked by limitations and interactions fraught with human complexities. In this emotional, earthly framework, where the son pleads for a story, and the father loves the son, the sum of these two circumstances, on this particular occasion, is not a story but silence.

THEMES

Storytelling

First and foremost, as the title suggests, Lee's poem is about storytelling. Although only the man is mentioned in the first stanza, a family relationship is suggested by the fact that his inability to produce a story makes him sad. In professional or social circumstances, a man who fails to produce a requested story might be embarrassed or frustrated or self-deprecatory, but only if he is letting down a loved one, it seems, could he be sad. The man must appreciate the delight that he provides his child in telling stories and to see himself as a failure in this regard is a serious blow.

The intrinsic value of stories as a means of communication is thus highlighted. A story told is not simply a logical narrative that engages the listener's capacity for concentration and comprehension; it is a conduit of community and morality that passes through the voice of the speaker into the ear of the listener and unites them. Lee has spoken in interviews of the scientific framework in which the material world can be reduced to layers upon layers of vibrations—from the subatomic level to molecular bonds to heat transference to electromagnetic and sonic waves. While the live transmission of sound is devalued in an age when voices and songs are endlessly replicated and reproduced through cell phones, radios, televisions, films, loudspeakers, amplifiers, and so forth, Lee points toward the significance of the physical connection established when one person's voice reaches another's ear: the vibrations of the person's voice—as modulated by that person's muscular development, state of mind, and lifetime of emotional experience, producing a veritably unique voice print—literally enter the body of the listener and resonate within, contributing to the listener's intuitive comprehension of the personality and morality of the speaker. Whether a story told is invented or true to life, the physical connection between the individuals is there.

Father-Child Relationships

Lee's poem places great emphasis on the importance of storytelling within the relationship between parent and child, specifically between a father and his son. By the time a typical boy is five, he has developed enough to be capable of independently confronting the world by speaking and listening to others, but there remains a great deal about the world that he has yet to learn. The level of confidence a boy feels in putting his ego at risk by exposing himself to the interpersonal hazards of the world—unkindnesses, putdowns, threats, and so forth—will depend a great deal on his relationship with his parents; a boy who has a close bond with his parents will have that bond to fall back on and will be that much more able to confidently and successfully negotiate the difficulties of independent life. The mother and father, provided they are adequate caregivers, will be viewed with great filial love and perhaps even reverence; the well-raised child may hang on the wise parent's every word.

This relationship between young child and parent can be seen as embodied in the sharing of stories, because stories are such an effective way of teaching children about the world. Young children do not necessarily respond well to abstract ideas of what constitutes moral versus immoral behavior because they still fully inhabit the physical world; they have not yet gained the ability to retreat into a strictly conceptual one. Furthermore, a young child's capacity for compassion must be cultivated, since the relatively primitive world of children's interactions can actually encourage a lack of compassion. Without an authority figure present to reprimand him, a boy is, in reality, not punished but rewarded for, say, stealing a younger boy's snack, because he gets to eat the snack. Only if encouraged to focus on the younger boy's resulting sadness will the older boy begin to feel shame over such an unjust act. Stories, then, can present circumstances in which there is a clear good guy or bad guy, a clear obstacle to justice, and a clear resolution or conclusion, as in many of Aesop's animal fables and in folktales from around the world.

The story shared between father and son, then, has dual importance. On the one hand, it enhances the interpersonal connection between the father and son, with the familiar voice of the father instilling the son with comfort and reassurance. In addition, the story itself, no matter the content, in being told by one of the child's foremost authority figures, communicates to the child a moral worldview that the child will intuitively embrace and adopt. If a father really believes that slow and steady wins the race, his appreciation for the tortoise will be evident; if the father rather thinks the hare is superior but simply made a foolish mistake, then the child will take away a slightly different understanding. One way or another, the shared story is one of the most valuable verbal exchanges that can take place between a parent and child, and both parties intuitively understand this. It is for this reason that the father in "A Story" experiences such a dramatic response to his own inability to come up with a story to tell his son. The failure is seen as symbolic of the potential severing of the bond of dependence between father and son. The father even fears that the severing of this bond will signify the son's starting to feel indifferent toward the father's love.

Love

Only in the father's head is the pressing question of his son's love for him extrapolated from the circumstance at hand, the son's unfulfilled desire for a new story. The child really just wants to hear a story, and in truth, it is very unlikely that the father's failure to produce one will affect the degree of love felt for the father by the son. However, whether because of a long night of attending to a sick younger child or changing that younger child's diapers, or because of a long day at the office, or because of the momentary experience of an intense pressure—the pressure to perform in order to prove his love—the father has no story to tell, and this failure affects him profoundly. It provokes a great fear: that his son will view him as a failure and forsake him, will become intent on leaving home, indifferent to the father's pleas that he stay to hear another story, so to speak.

The man loves his son, and he knows it, and his son knows it. So on the one hand, the father believes in his own love for his son as well as his son's love for him, but on the other hand, his son's love for him feels like such a fragile thing that a single failure, it seems, might cause him to lose it. The son is, of course, his own person, and one day, he likely will move out of the house and make all his life decisions for himself. This does not mean that the son will cease to love the father, but it does mean that the son's love will one day be beyond the father's reach. Thus the father, able to envision so far into the future (an ability the son does not yet have), cannot help but grasp for his son's love with every chance he gets. He should not have to, he feels; the son ought to love his father unreservedly, and the father wants to believe this is possible.

If the father initially fails to think of a story simply because his mind is currently too empty, or too full, by the end of the poem he has undergone something of a transformation as a result of his

Though his son is still very young, the father already dreads the day when he will leave home.

(© Dragon Images / Shutterstock.com)

own anxieties. He now seems to willfully refuse to tell a story. He loves his son, and he knows his son loves him; he cannot bear to feel that his son's love is dependent on his fulfilling his son's every wish; thus rather than clinging to the love shared between them by desperately grasping around in his mind for a story, he elects to prove his *faith* in the love between them by telling no story at all. In this way, though it may seem illogical at first, the boy's entreaties and the love of the father add up on this occasion to silence.

STYLE

Free Verse

Lee's poem is written in free verse, meaning it features no consistent rhyme or meter, as well as, in this case, no fixed stanza structure. Free verse is heavily favored in modern-day poetry, with fixed meter (meter is the pattern of stressed and unstressed syllables in a line of poetry) and rhyme schemes often seen as limiting the poet's capacity for expression. From such a perspective, if a poetic impulse is subordinated to the demands of rhyme and meter, then the fullest possible unique expression of that impulse cannot be attained.

"A Story" demonstrates the merits of free verse, as the varying structure of the poem highlights the content in evolving ways. The opening couplet aptly presents in a focused manner the overarching circumstance of the poem. The second stanza is representative of an expansion of the field of perception, as now the son is included in the depiction of the man trying to scratch out a story, and this stanza is fittingly one line longer. The third stanza then incorporates the room, even the entire world, into the narrative, and again the stanza is one line longer than the last, further signifying the expanding field of perception. The fourth stanza, in turn, is also one line longer than the last, now delving deeper into the father's mind and emphasizing his appeals in concluding with the four-word plea of line 14, the shortest in the poem. With the stanzas increasing in length through stanza 4, the poem lends a mounting significance to the episode at hand, in accord with the father's intensifying worries.

The fifth stanza recedes back to four lines; it seems shorter because, after the catalog of favorite stories in stanza 4, the father's concerns have now been condensed and encapsulated in two dramatic rhetorical questions. In the sixth and final stanza, the opening line fixes an endpoint to the narrative at hand; the action of the poem ends here with the child's reiterated request for a story from his father. Joined to the narrative's close is a sort of lesson, like the moral in a fable. "A Story" proves that free-verse poetry, while not following a traditional, formal pattern, is not necessarily lacking in form. As a whole, the poem succeeds because of the free-verse form that Lee chose.

Enjambment

One poetic strategy facilitated by the use of free verse is *enjambment*, the ending of a line midthought or midsentence in such a way as to lend a particular emphasis to the words divided. In free verse, a poet can end a line whenever he chooses, with disregard for the demands of meter and rhyme, and also in the absence of rhyme the reader can assign more significance to the meanings of the poet's chosen words.

While one may speak of a poet's *choosing* to end lines in particular places, Lee has referred to his own choices in this regard as being physically founded and largely subconscious. In an interview with Matthew Fluharty, he described his process thus:

> What happens is when I am writing a poem—and I am not kidding—when I write a poem, writing from left to right, my elbow will only go so far before it is uncomfortable. That for me is a line break. The arc of my elbow determines as much as my ear, and as much as my eye or the ache in my foot or the kink in my back. All of that figures into writing.

One gathers, then, that Lee is not the sort of poet to deliberately craft line breaks to tweak the poem's impact on the reader, and accordingly, enjambment does not play a major role in "A Story." Nonetheless, his mind can subconsciously apply the technique, and here its effects can be discerned.

The break between lines 1 and 2 is curious in that the first line is so decidedly incomplete without the second—the break encourages the reader to use that moment to wonder why a man should be sad to be asked for a story. Line 6, ending with the word *world*, expands the sense of the poem even further than the words alone do, since the world, unqualified, can quite literally mean everything, the entire universe; specifically, it turns out, Lee is referring to the world *of stories.* In turn, line 7 begins to suggest that the man can indeed think of a story after all; the enjambment, however, highlights the baffling negation of that possibility in placing the word *not* at the beginning of the following line. Beyond this stanza, most of the remaining lines end with marks of punctuation, but the defiance of expectation embodied in the enjambment in the first and third stanzas carries on throughout the poem.

Lyrical Meditation

Lee's poems in general and especially "A Story" can be aptly characterized as presenting "lyrical meditation," a term offered by Rocío G. Davis in his literary profile of Lee. A *lyric* or *lyrical* poem is one that directly relates personal emotion, such as in many songs, while a *meditation*, in terms of writing, is something that ponders the significance of a topic in a philosophical or perhaps spiritual way. "A Story" begins with two basic narrative stanzas, then at the end of the third stanza begins to probe the father's thoughts and feelings. Stanzas 4 and 5 reveal the father's emotional state by sharing what he

COMPARE
&
CONTRAST

- **1990:** Following the mainstream literary success achieved by Maxine Hong Kingston with *The Woman Warrior* (1976) and later works, a number of American writers of Chinese descent gain national recognition, including Lee, David Henry Hwang for his Tony Award–winning play *M. Butterfly* (1988), and Amy Tan for *The Joy Luck Club* (1989).

  Today: Lee's latest book of poetry, *Behind My Eyes*, came out in 2008. Other recent publications by notable Chinese American authors include Gene Luen Yang's folktale-inspired graphic novel *American Born Chinese* (2006), Ha Jin's exile-focused story collection *A Good Fall* (2009), and Gish Jen's post-9/11 novel *World and Town* (2010).

- **1990:** Although cable channels and home video-game consoles like Nintendo and Sega Genesis have gained increasing shares of children's attention, these sources of entertainment remain attached to television screens, and bedtime, at least, remains an ideal time for family storytelling. The handheld Nintendo Game Boy, released in 1989, represents an even greater threat to family time.

Today: With the technological advances of cell phones, tablet computers (marketed to children as well as adults), and full-color handheld gaming systems, access to games has become ubiquitous for people of all ages. Parents are less likely than ever to wind down the day with their children by telling technology-free stories.

- **1990:** In congressional hearings, a fifteen-year-old Kuwaiti named Nayirah makes a dramatic impact in drumming up support for US military action to liberate Kuwait after the Iraqi invasion, telling a story about how Iraqi soldiers had removed hundreds of babies from incubators and left them to die. The story is later revealed to be fabricated.

Today: The fabricated story told to the American people by the George W. Bush administration about why Iraq needed to be invaded in 2003—because the country supposedly possessed weapons of mass destruction—lingers in the minds of Americans. Wary of any rationale for further deaths of American soldiers, the public offers dwindling support for the winding-down, if yet crucial, war effort in Afghanistan.

---

imagines himself saying in the situation he is anxiously envisioning, his son's leaving home. (Although the poem is written in the third person, because only the father's, not the son's, thoughts are shared, the narrator—and thus Lee himself—is most readily identified with the father.) Appended to the lyrical body of the poem is a final stanza that establishes a greater distance between the narration and the episode in question, using a pair of logical contrasts and several conceptual terms. In other words, the final four lines represent a meditation on the poem's narrative as well as the resolution of the father's plight, in the form of a meditative silence.

HISTORICAL CONTEXT

Three Generations in the Family of Li-Young Lee

It is difficult to assign any public historical context to Lee's poem "A Story." The poem itself is devoid of any societal circumstance and could be taking place anytime, anywhere (although the fact that it was originally written in English might be seen to narrow down the possible settings). The period of its composition and publication, circa 1990, might be examined as the poem's context, but Lee resists placement among his contemporaries because the sentimental and universal aspects of his verse link him more closely with past figures like Walt Whitman (1819–1892) and Germany's Rainer Maria Rilke (1875–1926) than with postmodern figures of the late twentieth century. The poem also resists a reading as a work of Asian American literature, because no Eastern influence is in evidence, and Lee himself is ambivalent to classification according to his ethnicity. As he told Fluharty, "I have good friends who...wish I would say I am fiercely Asian or fiercely American. I don't, and I refuse to. I want to be a global poet. I think it is the only chance we have."

Perhaps the most useful historical framework in which to consider the poem, then, is the one provided by Lee's family, including the generations before and after him. If the poem is considered to have autobiographical origins—even if it should not be read as factual autobiography—two possible time frames can be posited: one being around 1962, when Lee was five, the other being around 1990, when Lee's elder son was five. (Lee's family was not conversing in English when Lee was five, but this does not exclude the possibility of Lee envisioning a scene from that time period in English instead of in Japanese or Cantonese.) Lee has made a variety of comments in interviews that, addressing aspects of his and his father's lives and personalities, shed light on the narrative of "A Story."

With regard to his father, Kuo Yuan Lee (who took the first name Richard in America), Lee related to Moyers that the Presbyterian minister put forth a very self-assured persona, always seeming sure of himself and never brooking doubts about dogma or the worldly order of things. As quoted in *The Language of Life*, Lee thus gained the impression that his father, with a perfect understanding of everything, "was always right next to God." However, after his father's death in 1980, Lee inherited his books, and looking through the notes scrawled in the margins of his Bible, Lee realized his father had questions with regard to religious philosophy, biblical symbolism, and even his own belief. It was largely for his children that the father maintained a front of absolute certainty, because, as Lee told Moyers, "he wanted his children to have faith in him." Lee's father did tell his children stories, especially about the histories of his and his wife's families. In light of all this, one can readily imagine Lee conceiving "A Story" with his father in mind, presenting a man who experiences a creative lapse and is led to deeply question the love between himself and his son but

who lets the son perceive only a stoic silence that may be seen to represent not uncertainty but unreachability.

Lee has also revealed aspects of his own experience as father and storyteller suggesting that he had himself in mind when conceiving the father in "A Story." As quoted in *The Language of Life*, when asked about whether he tells his children stories, Lee replied,

> Yes, I tell them stories constantly, and they love to hear stories. I used to tell them the basic stories, and then I ran out of those, so I started making up stories in which the bad guy's name is Sukarno and the good guy's name is Yeh, which means grandfather in Chinese.

Lee went on to tell Moyers that the stories of his family's eventful history—such as those from their years under Sukarno in Indonesia, rendered as fairy tales for his children—are essentially the only ones he knows. By the year 2000, Lee could tell Fluharty that, with regard to stories, his sons, thirteen and fifteen years old at the time, "don't want to hear them as much as when they were little." More positively he noted, "I think it helps them somehow, gives them a feeling of an infinite background.... It helps them to look back at their father's past and see an infinite horizon." Lee clearly recognized the expansive value of the stories he shared with his children, and he also acknowledged how the children's maturation had affected their dependence on the bond forged through storytelling. Lee too, then, can be seen as the father in "A Story."

Critics have pointed toward the occasional impossibility of distinguishing Lee from his father in his poetry. In the words of Xiaojing Zhou in *The Heath Anthology of American Literature*, "For Lee, trying to understand his father is trying to understand himself." In the *Dictionary of Literary Biography*, Davis comments on how Lee's father's plays a substantial role in the poems of *The City in Which I Love You*: Lee "strongly identifies" with his father, and furthermore, "The idea of paternity recurs as Lee positions himself as both a son and a father." In another *Dictionary of Literary Biography* essay, Ruth Y. Hsu points out that Lee's portrayals "seem to merge the poet's life into his father's." Even Lee himself told Fluharty, "I have given up distinguishing between my voice and my father's."

As it happens, Moyers's PBS series *The Power of the Word* captured a moment when,

"A Story" describes the relationship between father and son. (© Alan Bailey / Shutterstock.com)

speaking to a crowd at Glassboro State College, Lee revealed the role he envisioned for himself when writing "A Story." After discussing how he drew on his family's life in Indonesia to fulfill his elder son's desire for stories, Lee acknowledged, "I run out of stories. And that's what this poem is about"—at which point he read "A Story." Regardless of Lee's actual inspiration, one might conclude that in defying identification as a poem treating the poet as father or the poet as son, "A Story" can indeed be about any father and any son and thus aligns with Lee's literary goal of approaching the universal.

CRITICAL OVERVIEW

Being the Lamont Poetry Selection of 1990—an American Academy of Poets award that brings the book to publication—*The City in Which I Love You* was widely reviewed, and the majority of reviews were highly favorable. (However, "A Story," in

particular, is rarely mentioned.) In his *World Literature Today* review, Edgar C. Knowlton Jr. notes, "The often simple verses evince depth of feeling." Hsu similarly observes that several of the collection's poems "evince a remarkable sense of peace and stillness." Carol Muske, in the *New York Times Book Review*, calls Lee's poems "explosive and earthy" and states,

> Like a pairing of Walt Whitman with the great Tang dynasty poet Tu Fu, Li-Young Lee emerges as an audacious and passionate poet-traveler.... He speaks colloquially but metaphysically; he meditates but always allows the noises of the world to enter.

Marilyn Nelson Waniek, in the *Kenyon Review*, calls Lee's second collection "more than interesting" and states that "one or two of its poems are, in my opinion, necessary. Elegant, delicate, and reticent, they achieve in graceful form the fulfillment of Lee's remarkable childhood history." David Baker, in *Poetry*, observes that "Lee writes with a loose, relaxed, open plainness." Less favorably, Baker

WHAT DO I READ NEXT?

- In the opinion of interviewer Amy Pence, the poems of Lee's third book of poetry, *Book of My Nights* (2001), "could only have been written from some deep contemplative silence." Lee explicitly expressed that, in these poems, he tried to connect with the greater consciousness of the universe.

- Among the classical Chinese authors Lee was exposed to through his father, he has cited the eighth-century poets Li Bai and Tu Fu as making a great impression on him. (He has a vision of them on a modern-day street in his "Furious Versions.") Poems by these two masters are presented in the bilingual publication *Facing the Moon: Poems of Li Bai and Du Fu* (2007), translated by Keith Holyoak.

- At a 1990 meeting of the Modern Language Association, Lee stood alongside Kyoko Mori and David Mura as writers featured by the Asian American Reading Group. Among Mori's publications are the book of essays *Polite Lies* (1997), addressing the dueling facets of her cultural identity as a Japanese American.

- The debut poetry collection by Mura, who is also Japanese American, was *After We Lost Our Way* (1989), a National Poetry Series winner.

- Lee's verse is often considered a modern echo of the poetic voice of the American patriarch of free verse, Walt Whitman. The most famous collection Whitman published during his lifetime was *Leaves of Grass* (1855).

- Lee also looked to Robert Frost as a poet who attained through his verse a dialogue not merely with culture or the canon but with his truest self, and thus with the universe. An excellent introduction to Frost's poetry is *The Road Not Taken: A Selection of Robert Frost's Poems* (2002).

- Lee's foremost poetic role model and mentor was Gerald Stern, who provided an introduction for Lee's debut collection, *Rose*. Lee reported carrying around a copy of Stern's collection *Lucky Life* (1977) for two years almost constantly.

- Poetry written by and for teens with focuses on family and also friendship can be found in *Teen Ink: Friends and Family* (2001), edited by Stephanie H. Meyer and John Meyer.

suggests that "Lee hasn't yet mastered his craft sufficiently to fully support his large embrace." Focusing on—and objecting to—the form of poems like "A Story," Baker comments,

> His poems are too loose and tend to dissipate. . . . Lee typically eschews a narrative stance in behalf of a lyric or meditative one, and therefore seldom provides a sufficient chronological or dramatic intensity to drive what instead tends to become reverie.

In these comments, Baker reveals a dislike of the postmodern aesthetic more generally, an aesthetic that often features fragmented and inconclusive narratives and intentional disruptions of ordinary dramatic flow. In these respects, although

Lee does not consider himself postmodernist, "A Story" is something of a postmodern poem.

In the *Georgia Review*, Judith Kitchen declares of *The City in Which I Love You*, "This is a work of remarkable scope—musically as well as thematically." Criticizing constructively, Kitchen states that Lee's poems

> challenge us with their heightened rhetoric, exhibiting the dangers (as well as the glories) of eloquence. Lee's very strengths are his potential weaknesses. The echo of Whitman may need to be muted; even Lee's own tremendous verbal resources may demand modulation in order to achieve their finest realization.

In *Publishers Weekly*, Penny Kaganoff asserts that, in his second collection, Lee "weaves a remarkable web of memory from the multi-farious fibers of his experience." Responding to the 1991 publication of *The City in Which I Love You* in the *American Poetry Review*, Sam Hamill affirms that Lee's "maturity as a poet is simply astonishing." Hamill goes on to declare,

> His humility is rare and refreshing. His voice and his people are particular, each unique, and he has none of the complacency—which is, after all, a form of cowardice—of so many of his contemporaries. His poems are made *from* his life *with* his life, his poems are earned. He dares to be simple. And he is surely among the finest young poets alive.

CRITICISM

Michael Allen Holmes

Holmes is a writer with existential interests. In the following essay, he reads "A Story" as culminating in a moment of transcendence.

Li-Young Lee's childhood was defined by the series of moves made by his family around East Asia from before his birth until he was six years old, before they at last landed in America. Therefore it seems apt that the poet is conversant in a variety of Eastern spiritual traditions. In interviews, he speaks with intimate knowledge about the Taoism of China, the Zen Buddhism of Japan, the Sufism of Islam—a majority religion of Indonesia—and even the Hinduism of India, not to mention the Christianity within which his minister father raised him. Lee's interest in these religious philosophies is not simply scholarly; he typically speaks of them when elaborating on his approach to writing poetry, his mode of existence in the world, or his own universalized spiritual leanings. An undercurrent of religiosity can be detected in his poem "A Story." As it happens, though the father in the poem appears to be stonewalled by a case of storyteller's block, left to falter in a morose silence by the end, the poem can instead be read as suggesting the father's momentary transcendence.

From the beginning, "A Story" presents a very human narrative. Foregrounded is a very human emotion, sadness, afflicting a man who has the simple difficulty of being unable to think of a story just then. This is hardly a situation of dire spiritual straits. Through the second stanza, the poem remains confined to the circumstance at hand, with the plaintive boy sitting atop his

> LEE'S YOUTHFUL SILENCE, IN WITHHOLDING HIM FROM THE MUNDANE ONE-TO-ONE CONNECTIONS ESTABLISHED BY CONVERSATION, ALLOWED HIM TO INSTEAD REMAIN CONNECTED BOTH TO HIS OWN DEEPEST SELF AND TO THE UNIVERSE AS A WHOLE OUTSIDE HIM."

father's lap. This ordinary circumstance, in and of itself, establishes a dialogue with Confucianism, an ethical tradition that, in its emphasis on rituals, approached the status of a religion in ancient China. Confucianism places strong emphasis on filial piety, the son's duty to be reverential toward his father. In book II of Arthur Waley's translation of *The Analects of Confucius*, a student

> asked about the treatment of parents. The Master said, Never disobey! ... While they are alive, serve them according to ritual. When they die, bury them according to ritual and sacrifice to them according to ritual.

Elsewhere, "The Master said, Behave in such a way that your father and mother have no anxiety about you, except concerning your health." Even after Confucianism fell out of official favor, Confucian attitudes persisted in the culture, which is attested to by Lee's descriptions of the reverence his Chinese father expected from his children. As cited in *The Language of Life*, Lee told Bill Moyers, "He would *always* be right, he would *always* be sure.... He was always right next to God."

In this light, it would seem unlikely that the father in the poem is meant to be Lee's father, because the poem's father is one who appears to practice devotion to his children, rather than expecting devotion from them. In other words, this is an inversion of the Confucian expectation for the father-son relationship, an inversion that accords with the identity of the father being not fundamentally Chinese but primarily American. Indeed, in an appearance at Glassboro State College filmed for *The Power of the Word*, Lee confirmed that he himself is the model for the father of "A Story." In the poem, the child appears to hold the dominant position. He speaks respectfully toward the father but also feels comfortable instructing him to provide a new story, not merely a familiar one. The father, in turn, seems to feel it his duty to honor the son's request. He tries to think of a story until, in the absence of any idea for one, his mind begins to wander toward the possible consequences of his failure; he even seems to fear an indirect punishment of sorts on the part of the son. By the end of the third stanza, when the father imagines the boy giving up on him, the poem's religious undercurrent begins rippling to the surface. The notion of the boy's loss of faith in the father is suggestive of not only filial abandonment but also an analogous religious situation, namely, a believer's loss of faith in God—but this suggestion only really becomes evident in retrospect.

The fourth stanza offers the merest hint of religious signification, as in between the two animal-centered stories, the alligator and spider ones, a story about an angel is mentioned. This mention of an angel is not expanded any further, but it nonetheless suggests a religious awareness on the part of the father; whether or not he "believes" in angels himself, he assigns enough value to them to see fit to regularly tell his son at least one story about an angel.

The fifth stanza is the one in which religious imagery brings the poem to its emotional zenith. By this time, the father, in his vision of the future, is not just pleading with his son to stay but is screaming out his rhetorical questions. The first question is perhaps the more curious, with the syntax allowing for ambiguity of meaning; the question is even paradoxical, because the man is supposedly screaming about being mute. His reference could thus be metaphorical, referring to the fact that his words are ignored by the godlike son, making him effectively mute. On the other hand, it is perhaps the screaming that is meant metaphorically, as if the man is only screaming in his mind—which, in the context of the narrative present, he is, and which, in the context of his vision or daydream, he could be.

The meaning of the first question becomes far clearer if one considers an aspect of Lee's past that he addresses in his memoir, *The Winged Seed*. He relates that, from birth onward, he was intermittently mute: "For the first three years of my life, I made not a sound. After that I was frequently plagued by long periods of dumbness, up until I was seven or eight." This can partly be understood as a reaction to the extremely trying circumstances endured by his family during his youngest years.

His father, Kuo Yuan Lee, was imprisoned for what the Indonesian government trumped up as suspicious activities the year after Lee's birth, and from then until the father escaped the nation along with his family nineteen months later, they lived in a state of constant anxiety over his fate. Aside from the difficulties of inconsistent visitations, social isolation, and the dread of execution, they even had to cope with freak hailstorms that pelted their house in particular and led the entire neighborhood to believe them cursed.

Regardless of the initial source of Lee's muteness, it came to be irrevocably associated with his father when, once they reached Hong Kong, the elder Lee made weekly, ritualized attempts to draw Lee's voice out of him, clasping one hand to the back of the boy's head and the other to his mouth while intoning prayers. This practice only seemed to solidify Lee's muteness, which amounted to a sort of spiritual experience. In *The Winged Seed*, he asks, "But why should I have spoken? . . . Why, when my silence was so present, so irreducible and true? Why, when my silence, like rock that's rock clear through, was silence so final?" Lee was almost repulsed by the use of language, which he condemns as "the traffic of talk, of indirection, the approximate, the almost." To him, "Talk was hovering, skirting, glancing. Talk was mere. And I wouldn't."

In effect, Lee's youthful silence, in withholding him from the mundane one-to-one connections established by conversation, allowed him to instead remain connected both to his own deepest self and to the universe as a whole outside him. He states in his memoir,

> I was opaque. Nothing passed through me. I only absorbed, contained, without emanation. . . . So, I grew in the core of my silent self, denser and denser with sound. For there was sound all around and I could hear it.

He thus gained an intensified appreciation for the sounds of the universe, and yet "it was all over there. *Here* was I, unto myself. And my silence was larger than myself. . . . I could hold everything without changing it into words, without violating it."

Lee relates his experience of muteness in terms that speak to his consciousness as a boy, but from his consciousness as a man, he has spoken in interviews more directly to the sort of mystical connection with the universe that he was establishing. In an interview with James

Kyung-Jin Lee, he described how his basic conception of the self is inherently a spiritual one:

> The whole enterprise of writing for me is spiritual. I'm at a point in my life where what's important is to discover a naked relationship between me and the greater self or the true self. In the Bhagavad Gita, they call it *the self*. They mean, of course, the godhead.

In an interview with Tod Marshall, Lee referred in greater depth to what he perceives as the ultimate unity of the self, God, and the universe, a conception that is especially prominent in Eastern religious traditions like Hinduism, Buddhism, and Taoism. Speaking of his most fundamental poetic impulse, Lee remarked, "For me, it's the realization of my identity . . . as the universe. I am perfectly convinced that that's what I am, the universe." He goes on to refer to "universe mind; that is, a mind I would describe as a 360-degree seeing," a notion that is readily linked with Ralph Waldo Emerson's famous transcendentalist conception of himself as "a transparent eyeball" in his essay *Nature*.

The identification of oneself with the universe is precisely the goal of Zen, with the permanent attainment of such identification amounting to enlightenment. Returning to "A Story," the father's concerns in the fourth and fifth stanzas, his profound anxieties about the future, represent a departure from the Zen worldview, which stresses the importance of being mindful of the present and implicitly counsels against excessive dwelling on the past or worrying about the future. Lee shows an awareness of his own liability to such dwelling or worrying in *The Winged Seed*, where he highlights words of wisdom shared with him by his mother: "*Elsewhere*, my mother says, *your head is always elsewhere, in the past or in the future. Why can't you be here?*"

The father in "A Story" seems to eventually heed just these words of wisdom. After he recalls the boy's favorite stories in the fourth stanza—even though the boy is ready to progress beyond these stories—and anxiously probes a possible future through the fifth stanza, the poem announces in the first line of the sixth stanza a sudden return to the present: the boy is not *there* in the past or in the future but *here*, in the present, and the boy summons the father back to the present with him. It is in this moment, after the son reiterates his plea for a story, that the narrative proper comes to an end. Through the moralization provided in the last four lines, only one more word, the poem's final word, offers any conclusion or closure to the situation at hand. As it happens, the scene does not conclude with a story—perhaps the feel-good ending many

readers would have hoped for—but with silence. This silence is posited by that moralization as being founded in emotion and the earth, not in the intellect or heaven. In light of Lee's comments on the personal meaning of silence for him—silence being something that provides him with access to the spiritual energy of the universe—the poem's moralization should perhaps in part be taken ironically. Lee claims that the equation that produces the father's silence is of earth, not of heaven, yet the silence itself, in being capable of leading him into a transcendent state, *is* of heaven.

Lee has forthrightly expressed that he is seeking to approach and even embody the divine in his poems. Speaking to James Kyung-Jin Lee, he remarked, "I'm trying to find a way to write sacred poetry, poetry that sends the reader to a sacred place or calls to a sacred place inside the reader." He told Amy Pence, "My poems, I hope, are nothing but idiosyncratic private individual expressions of God." As Lee said to Marshall,

> It's an exercise of the mind to think constantly that . . . my true self or identity is universe or God. There are certain assumptions that I secretly carry around, and I don't know if other poets share these. I assume that my true nature is God. I assume that I am God, in my true nature.

Reiterating this point, he declared,

> The poet is the one saying the best and brightest things to a reader: "You're God; you're cosmos; you're universe." The poet is walking around saying "We are the universe. You are the universe; I am the universe."

In "A Story," the father's urgent questions as to whether his son or perhaps he himself is a god seem best read rhetorically, as questions not meant to be answered; surely neither one is *a* god. Yet like many with universal or mystical sensibilities, Lee believes that each and every person is part of the universe, part of God, and thus, in a sense, each person *is* God. At first glance, the silence that closes "A Story" is a solemn one, even one of defeat. Upon closer inspection, it becomes evident that that very silence, in which the father and son commune not through words, not through demands and acquiescence, but through their presence alone, is the means by which the father and even the son accomplish their identification with the universe and with the divine; the silence is their transcendence.

The image of a book-filled room represents everything the father wants to teach his son, though he cannot find the words. (© jorisvo | Shutterstock.com)

Source: Michael Allen Holmes, Critical Essay on "A Story," in *Poetry for Students*, Gale, Cengage Learning, 2014.

Steven G. Yao

In the following excerpt, Yao addresses the tendency for critics to look at Lee's work only as that of an "ethnic writer."

Among writers of Asian descent in the contemporary United States who have gained recognition mainly for their efforts in verse, Li-Young Lee has earned arguably the most widespread reputation, garnering not only consistent acclaim from the American poetic establishment but also even a measure of mainstream popular attention. His first volume of poems, *Rose* (1986), won New York University's Delmore Schwartz Memorial Poetry award in 1987, and his second book of verse, *The City in Which I Love You*, became the Lamont Poetry Selection of the Academy of American Poets for 1990. In 1988, Lee won a Whiting Writer's Award from the Mrs. Giles Whiting Foundation, and in 1995 he received a Lannan Literary Award for poetry.

In addition, he has held fellowships from the National Endowment for the Arts, and the John Simon Guggenheim Memorial Foundation, as well grants from the Pennsylvania Council on the Arts, the Commonwealth of Pennsylvania, and the Illinois Arts Council. Furthermore, his initial foray into prose, a memoir titled *The Winged Seed: A Remembrance* (1995), was selected for an American Book Award from the Before Columbus Foundation. Even more telling of his broad notoriety as a poet, Lee has been featured in an interview with journalist Bill Moyers for the PBS broadcast series and companion volume *The Language of Life: A Festival of Poets* (1995). Most significant of all, perhaps, his poems have appeared in numerous anthologies. These have included ones dedicated specifically to different configurations of the category of "Asian American" literature, such as L. Ling-chi Wang and Henry Yiheng Zhao's *Chinese American Poetry: An Anthology* (1991) and Rajini Srikanth and Esther Iwanaga's *Bold Words: A Century of Asian America Writing* (2001), as well as those focusing more broadly

"
MOREOVER, STRUCTURED AS PERSONAL
RECOLLECTIONS OR MONOLOGUES IN FREE VERSE
THAT BUILD THROUGH ASSOCIATIVE CONNECTIONS
UP TO MOMENTS OF EMOTIONALLY CHARGED
REVELATION, HIS POETRY COLLECTIVELY AIMS TO
ENACT A RESOLUTION TO THE TWIN DILEMMAS
THAT CHARACTERIZE HIS CONCEPTION OF CHINESE
AMERICAN ETHNIC IDENTITY."

on the genre of poetry itself in English, like *The Norton Introduction to Poetry* (9th edition, 2006). Indeed, Lee has even taken the first, tentative steps in the uncertain journey toward canonization, having been for some time already included in influential texts that at once reflect and help to authorize the sanctioned canon of national "American" literature such as *The Norton Anthology of American Literature* (6th edition, volume E, 2002) and *The Harper American Literature* (3rd edition, 1999).

His considerable critical success and relatively broad popular appeal have together made Li-Young Lee one of a very small number of poets of Asian descent in the United States who, for better or worse, have come to represent the discursive field of "Asian American poetry" within the wider sphere of contemporary American culture. Significantly, though entirely not surprisingly, however, the ground of his acclaim has been decidedly split. On one side, during the early stages of his career, advocates like Gerald Stern viewed Lee in thinly veiled Orientalist terms, presenting and promoting his poetry as offering Western audiences an unmediated glimpse into the mysteries of Chinese culture. Thus Stern writes in his complimentary foreword to *Rose* that, among other purely personal qualities, a "pursuit of certain Chinese ideas, or Chinese memories, without any self-conscious ethnocentricity" characterizes Lee's verse. Similarly, in reviewing the same volume, B. Weigl figures Lee's achievement as intimately connected to and even stemming from a distinctive and timeless Chinese poetics, asserting that "Clearly Lee's Chinese heritage has contributed to these poems a kind

of cunning and wit seen in ancient Chinese poetry." For readers such as these, Lee merits his significance as an Asian American poet because he gives artfully transparent expression to his "foreign" cultural heritage.

On the other side, with the institutional solidification of Asian American studies as a formal academic field during the 1990s and the attendant increase in the critical sophistication of strategies for conceptualizing cultural production by people of Asian descent in the United States, a small but steadily growing number of critics have begun to argue expressly against the previously dominant tendency to read Lee, as well as, indeed, all Asian American poets, merely as conduits for the eternal wisdom of the East. So, for example, Juliana Chang has called attention to the essentialist assumptions and limitations implicit in "positioning 'Asian' or 'Chinese' as a monolithic cultural essence detached from historical change, unmarked by processes of migration and displacement, and unproblematically (mystically?) transmitted through and into anyone of Asian descent." Instead, they have sought to affirm and authorize a specifically "Asian American" (as opposed to simply an "Asian") cultural production by insisting upon the diversity of origin, background, and interest among Asian American writers themselves. Indeed, ever since Lisa Lowe introduced the notion of "cultural hybridity" as a model for Asian American cultural production, Asian Americanist critics have emphasized the generative importance to his poetry of Lee's experience as a refugee and immigrant, and his consequent "feeling of disconnection and displacement" from his Chinese heritage, together with the influence of such foundational Western texts as the Bible, especially the book of Exodus. Thus, emphasizing the poet's individual history of diaspora, Xiaojing Zhou argues that Lee's "position of straddling different cultures and histories" endows him with a genuinely "bi-cultural" sensibility, and his poems "enact and embody the processes of poetic innovation and identity invention beyond the boundaries of any single cultural heritage or ethnic identity." Similarly, more recent commentators have discussed Lee's treatment of themes such as sexual desire and food as sites through which he conveys and constructs his identity variously as an immigrant, ethnic, Asian diasporic American, and Chinese American poet.

Despite their important differences, however, critics and scholars on both sides of the debate have thus far shared a more basic set of assumptions, derived from the prevailing ideology of liberal multiculturalism, in using a range of methods to delineate the conceptual structure of Lee's "proper" identity as a writer, and thereupon tracing the ostensible political or ethical implications of his presentation in verse of that identity. For in persisting to read his work through a hermeneutic of authenticity, they have alike performed a de facto reification of the categories "ethnicity," "identity," and "experience," treating them as meaningful entities that enjoy an existence independent of or prior to their formal articulation, mediation, and even reception through different modes of discourse. So, for example, in her discussion of the frequently anthologized lyric, "Persimmons," Wenying Xu has asserted that "Lee seems to establish the speaker's ethnic authenticity via his relationship with persimmons," and that "this nondiscursive identification evinces how culture inscribes even our taste buds and metabolism." And in turn, such interpretative tendencies have at once reflected and facilitated the ongoing hegemony of predominantly thematic approaches to Lee's verse in particular, as well as to literary production by people of Asian descent in the United States more generally. Yet, as I discussed in the interchapter, the very notion of "ethnicity" itself inhabits its own distinctive historicity, having emerged only comparatively recently over the latter decades of the twentieth century. Furthermore, this emergence has constituted not so much the "discovery" of some hitherto unrecognized category of human difference, but rather the at once invested and contested "invention" of such a category by means of a broad range of discursive channels and procedures.

To be sure, such sweeping and basic textualism regarding the invention of "ethnicity" as a category of human difference hardly suffices as a warrant for disputing the demonstrably shaping effects that this discursively constituted relation of power has had and continues to have on the lives of individual members of both different minority and dominant groups in the United States and elsewhere. As Xu rightly notes, such effects have reached down even to the minutest details of everyday material and sensory existence, such as in the bodily inscription of gustatory taste. To this extent, I have no substantial

disagreement with the positions taken by her and others who have expended considerable effort on illuminating both the conditions and the dynamics of Lee's "ethnic" identity as part of the attempt to assess the significance of his literary production. Nevertheless, in affording the category of "identity," together with the related notions of "ethnicity" and "experience," privileged status as foundational hermeneutic assumptions, existing criticism has thus far consistently failed to advance very far beyond the stages of thematic explication and the isolated discussion of particular individual poems. Furthermore, such practices adhere to what Rey Chow has called a "coercive mimeticism" in the analysis of "ethnic" expression, therewith perpetuating the subdisciplinary segregation of literary and cultural production by people of Asian descent in the United States more generally by considering both their logic and their import virtually exclusively in relation to the concerns of ethnic "identity" and "experience" themselves. As a result, discussion of Lee's achievement has yet to begin evaluating in any sustained or systematic way the broader historical, cultural, political, and critical significance of the particular rhetorical and formal strategies that he employs in giving expressly poetic articulation to the terms of his identity as a writer in the United States who lays claim to a specifically Chinese descent at the levels of both personal history and cultural heritage.

Accordingly, then, in this chapter my discussion shall concentrate not simply on establishing the different parameters of Lee's identity as an "ethnic" writer, nor on explicating his treatment of themes such as discrimination, displacement, immigration, cultural loss, and so on. Rather, I focus on assessing and interrogating the formal logic and meaning, as well as the wider literary historical and politico-cultural significance, of the different poetic strategies by which he strives to represent in English specifically Chinese language and cultural practices and traditions in the process of setting forth a Chinese American subjectivity in verse. If such an approach departs from the established tendencies of existing criticism, it also at least implicitly challenges Lee's own conception of his goals and ambitions as a writer; for he has consistently rejected the label of "ethnic" or "Asian American" poet, oftentimes in starkly idealistic terms. Thus, in an interview conducted in 1996 and eventually appearing in the *Kenyon*

Review, he echoes a familiar sentiment that has been voiced by numerous American minority writers since at least the early decades of the twentieth century. Assuming a posture strikingly similar to the one taken by Countee Cullen during the Harlem Renaissance (at least as reported by Langston Hughes in the renowned essay, "The Negro Artist and the Racial Mountain"), Lee has declared:

> The fine print of that question—"Where do you stand as an Asian-American writer"—is a question about one's dialogue with cultural significance. I would say the answer is nil; I have no dialogue with cultural existence. Culture made that up—Asian-American, African-American, whatever. I have no interest in that. I have an interest in spiritual lineage connected to poetry—through Eliot, Donne, Lorca, Tu Fu, Neruda, David the Psalmist. But I've realized that that is still the culture. Somehow an artist has to discover a dialogue that is so essential to his being, to his self, that it is no longer cultural or canonical, but a dialogue with his truest self. His most naked spirit.

Notwithstanding such a spirited disavowal of any sort of identification with established categories of American ethnic identity, Lee nevertheless repeatedly and even reverently invokes throughout his writing a specifically Chinese familial and cultural affiliation or lineage as a fundamental part of his "dialogue with his truest self." In addition, premised on the basic conceit of an individual subjectivity giving voice to emblematic or representative experiences, his achievement affords a paradigmatic illustration of what I have been calling lyric testimony, the poetic mode that first emerged during the 1970s in the wake of the Asian American movement, and which has come to dominate the production, as well as the reception, of verse by people of Asian descent in the United States. Exemplifying this hegemonic mode, Lee relates in his poetry a varied array of both traumatic encounters with discrimination and compensatory perceptions and memories from a personalized history as an immigrant of Chinese parentage who arrived in America while still a child. By doing so, he thus in effect advances a version of Chinese American ethnic identity as a simultaneous condition of, on the one hand, problematic difference from the reigning norms of dominant (i.e., "white") American society, and on the other hand, generative but grievous separation from a cultural and linguistic tradition to which he formerly belonged in an

effortlessly organic way. And as both an expression and a result of this separation, his poetry displays, and indeed self-consciously plays upon, an incomplete knowledge of the cultural and linguistic traditions with which he affiliates himself in setting forth the terms of his identity. At the level of explicit theme, then, Lee offers a critique of various dominant stereotypical constructions of Asian Americans in general, and Chinese Americans in particular. Moreover, structured as personal recollections or monologues in free verse that build through associative connections up to moments of emotionally charged revelation, his poetry collectively aims to enact a resolution to the twin dilemmas that characterize his conception of Chinese American ethnic identity. Significantly, however, that attempted resolution finally comes to rest upon an appeal to a "deeper" knowledge of ethnic cultural heritage that finds its deepest grounding in the essentialist terrain of the body and the logic of biological descent. Consequently, his work ultimately reveals the limitations (under the current ideological regime of liberal multiculturalism) of a poetic, as well as a critical, practice built upon the conceptual foundation of a unified ethnic or minority subjectivity giving affective voice to individual experience....

Source: Steven G. Yao, "The Precision of Persimmons: Li-Young Lee, Ethnic Identity, and the Limits of Lyric Testimony," in *Foreign Accents: Chinese American Verse from Exclusion to Postethnicity*, Oxford University Press, 2010, pp. 143–48.

Xiaojing Zhou

In the following excerpt, Zhou examines how Lee's poems strive to define a sense of self separate from, rather than in reaction to, minority status.

At a 1993 symposium on Asian American literature sponsored by the Academy of American Poets, Li-Young Lee stated: "When I write, I'm trying to make that which is *visible*—this face, this body, this person—*invisible*, and at the same time, make what is *invisible*—that which exists at the level of pure *being*—completely visible" (qtd. in Hummer 5). While evoking his experience as a raced and ethnic other, Lee's statement articulates a poetics that resists social inscriptions of racial meanings on the bodily surfaces through exploration of interiority that is elusive, multifaceted, and protean. As Levinas states, "The inner life is the unique *way* for the real to exist as a plurality" (*TI* 58). Lyric poetry enables Lee to counter racial or ethnic

> IN HIS POEMS, LEE CHALLENGES THIS KIND
> OF ARROGANCE, WHILE OFFERING AN ALTERNATIVE
> WAY OF RESPONDING TO THE OTHER THROUGH AN
> EMBODIED, VULNERABLE SUBJECT WHO REFUSES TO
> CLAIM KNOWLEDGE OF OR ONENESS WITH THE
> OTHER."

stereotypes through articulation of the raced other's irreducible, ungraspable inner life erased in socially constructed uniform collective identities of race or ethnicity that are naturalized by discourses and representations which inscribe supposedly knowable essential differences on the body. Thus by rendering the racially marked body invisible, and making visible its interiority, Lee subverts precisely the logic that encodes the body with ideologies which privilege one particular type of body over others for humanity, citizenship, civil rights, and political responsibilities. At the same time, Lee rearticulates the raced and gendered body through a corporeal aesthetics that renders universal the body marked for exclusion, exploitation, and subjugation, redefining universal humanity monopolized by the white body and white male subject. His strategies and aesthetics for rendering the unseen visible and the racial markers invisible offer a unique and viable alternative to predominant modes of representing the body in Asian American literature.

Given its social and political valence, the body has been a contested site of competing ideologies in Asian American literature and criticism. Expanding on the well-established notion of the body as "*the* cultural product" (Grosz *Bodies* 23), Viet Thanh Nguyen in his incisive study, *Race and Resistance: Literature and Politics in Asian America*, emphasizes that the Asian American body is "a historical product" "invested with both symbolic and economic capital." In attempting to claim "the humanity of their individual bodies and . . . the legitimacy of their collective political body," Nguyen argues, Asian Americans "seek to turn the body from being negatively marked by a history of racist signification to being positively marked and marketable in the arena of multiethnic

identification and consumption." Moreover, he finds in Asian American prose writings "not a teleological development of the body but instead the development of multiple versions of bodily signification that exist simultaneously," including the Eurasian hybrid body, the wounded body, the remasculinized body, and the queer body produced in the contexts of resistance to racism and colonialism. Despite this diversity, however, Nguyen notes a problematic "internal division of Asian America . . . between the symbolic poles of black and nonblack, into bad subjects and model minority"—a division that can reinforce the imposition of Asian Americans' racial position by the dominant society. Nguyen's contention suggests, among other things, that Asian Americans' reinscription of the racially marked body within the existing binarized representational systems of racial identities allows problematic and limited strategies for political affiliations and critical intervention. Lee's corporeal aesthetic offers an alternative approach to the raced body and embodied subject through what Elizabeth Grosz calls "a certain resistance of the flesh, a residue of its materiality left untouched" by social inscriptions (*Bodies* 118).

Exploring the problems and contradictions of the visible and invisible aspects of Asian Canadian and Asian American identities, Eleanor Ty in her recent book, *The Politics of the Visible in Asian North American Narratives* (2004), offers further insights into Asian North American novelists' and filmmakers' reinscription of "their visibility" that is paradoxically bound up with their invisibility "in dominant culture and history." She argues that "in reinscribing the meaning of the visible markings on their bodies, the authors succeed in making visible to the public or to historical records the experiences and stories of those who have heretofore been invisible to majority culture" (12). One major strategy of these authors "is to recreate selves that have been effaced by the screen of the visible. For some, writing, producing a film, or telling a story becomes a struggle to avoid disappearing into oblivion; for others, it is a way to deal with the various selves that have been called into existence through spectacles of otherness" (12–13). While many of Lee's autobiographical poems accomplish similar tasks, they explore and make visible a different kind of invisibility—the interiority of the other who is reduced to transparent, inscrutable, and knowable spectacles.

An infinitely plural, various, and mysterious inner life of the supposedly homogenous, knowable other disrupts disciplinary, systematic productions of knowledge of otherness naturalized through bodily images represented as manifestations of essence. In a conversation with David Mura, Lee observes that racism can operate as "a type of arrogance, an unwarranted assumption of knowledge of the Other" (qtd. in Mura "Dim Sum Poetics" 98). To counter such assumptions, Lee insists on maintaining what Levinas calls "the ethical inviolability of the Other" (*TI* 195) through his lyric speaker, who is enthralled by the unknowable other whose alterity appeals, fascinates, and eludes. "Your otherness exhausts me, / like looking suddenly up from above here / to impossible stars fading," says Lee's persona to the loved other. In fact, Lee's persona makes no attempt to grasp the other's alterity as knowledge: "And your otherness is perfect as my death" (*City* 55). At the same time, Lee simultaneously debunks racial stereotypes and the disembodied lyric subject through his lyric speaker, who is a socially defined and violated other—"one of the drab population," who is a refugee, an immigrant, speaking English with an accent, and whose "blood motley... ways trespassed upon" (*City* 52). A particularized lyric I as such in Lee's poems renders his claim to universal humanity especially provocative and subversive.

Bearing visible features of the raced ethnic other, Lee and his family experienced painful racial discrimination in the United States. When Lee's father became the minister of a small town in Pennsylvania after completing his studies at the Pittsburgh Theological Seminary, his all-white Presbyterian congregation referred to him as "*Our heathen minister*" (Lee *Winged Seed* 130). The bodily and cultural differences of Asian Americans in the United States have been regarded as markers of their essential and completely knowable otherness that deviates from the norm of white America. In his prose-poem memoir, *The Winged Seed: A Remembrance* (1995), Lee recalls his childhood experience of being regarded and treated as an alien other. "Perceived as feeble-minded, I was, like my siblings, spoken to very loudly, as though the problem were deafness" (*Winged Seed* 78). And Lee was taunted by schoolmates with racist hearsay about his family: "*They say your house is always dark like no one lives there.... They say all you people have the same first and last names and your mother can't tell you apart.... They say you keep snakes and grasshoppers in a bush on your back porch and eat them. They say you don't have manners, you lift your plates to your mouths and*

push the food in with sticks.... They say you don't believe in God, but you worship the Devil" (*Winged Seed* 86). Underlying the circulation of such knowledge of the other is the kind of racism Lee speaks of—"a type of arrogance, an unwarranted assumption of knowledge of the Other." In his poems, Lee challenges this kind of arrogance, while offering an alternative way of responding to the other through an embodied, vulnerable subject who refuses to claim knowledge of or oneness with the other.

Given the social and cultural contexts of the United States and the poetic conventions of Western lyric, Lee's articulation of the corporeality of the lyric I in his poems has complex implications and functions. It breaks down the mind-versus-body dichotomy underlying Wordsworthian lyric poetry, in which the lyric I is a disembodied subject. Defined by an autonomous consciousness, the traditional lyric I is self-contained, self-enclosed, and self-centered, operating as the organizing principle of the poem. Its confidence in the sufficiency of its intentionality reduces the world and the other to the object of its knowledge. Rejecting these attributes and functions of the traditional lyric I, Lee insists on exploring the corporeality of his lyric persona. It is precisely because of its corporeality that Lee's lyric I is mortal, vulnerable, and resolutely implicated in the social, and inevitably bound to the world and others.

However, Lee refuses to assume sameness as or unity with the other. The other whom Lee's lyric I addresses maintains its irreducible otherness—an alterity that undermines the illusion of the autonomy of the self, pluralizing its world and rendering its intentionality insufficient for knowing the other. The self in Lee's poetry demonstrates a reconceptualized lyric I and its relations to the world and others through a corporeal aesthetics....

Source: Xiaojing Zhou, "Li-Young Lee: Your Otherness Is Perfect as My Death," in *The Ethics and Poetics of Alterity in Asian American Poetry*, University of Iowa Press, 2006, pp. 25–28.

SOURCES

Baker, David, "Culture, Inclusion, Craft," in *Poetry*, Vol. 158, No. 3, June 1991, pp. 158–75.

Confucius, *The Analects of Confucius*, translated and edited by Arthur Waley, Vintage Books, 1989, pp. 88–89.

Davis, Rocío G., "Li-Young Lee," in *Dictionary of Literary Biography*, Vol. 312, *Asian American Writers*, edited by Deborah L. Madsen, Gale, 2005, pp. 202–206.

Emerson, Ralph Waldo, *Selected Writings of Ralph Waldo Emerson*, edited by William H. Gilman, Signet Classic, 1983, p. 193.

Fluharty, Matthew, "An Interview with Li-Young Lee," in *Missouri Review*, Vol. 23, No. 1, 2000, pp. 81–100.

Greenbaum, Jessica, Review of *Rose* and *The City in Which I Love You*, in *Nation*, October 7, 1991, pp. 416–18.

Hamill, Sam, "A Fool's Paradise," in *American Poetry Review*, Vol. 20, No. 2, March–April 1991, pp. 33–40.

Hsu, Ruth, "Li-Young Lee," in *Dictionary of Literary Biography*, Vol. 165, *American Poets since World War II, Fourth Series*, edited by Joseph Conte, Gale Research, 1996, pp. 139–46.

Huntley, E. D., "Amy Tan and Asian American Literature," in *Asian-American Writers*, edited by Harold Bloom, Bloom's Literary Criticism, pp. 44–51.

Kaganoff, Penny, Review of *The City in Which I Love You*, in *Publishers Weekly*, Vol. 237, No. 30, July 27, 1990, p. 227.

Kitchen, Judith, "Auditory Imagination: The Sense of Sound," in *Georgia Review*, Vol. 45, No. 1, Spring 1991, pp. 154–69.

Knowlton, Edgar C., Jr., Review of *The City in Which I Love You*, in *World Literature Today*, Vol. 65, No. 4, Fall 1991, pp. 771–72.

Lee, James Kyung-Jin, "Li-Young Lee," in *Words Matter: Conversations with Asian American Writers*, edited by King-Kok Cheung, University of Hawai'i Press, 2000, pp. 270–82.

Lee, Li-Young, "A Story," in *The City in Which I Love You*, BOA Editions, 1990, p. 65.

———, *The Winged Seed: A Remembrance*, Simon & Schuster, 1995, pp. 24, 184–86.

Logan, Liz, "An Interview with Poet Li-Young Lee," Poets & Writers online, February 11, 2008, http://www.pw.org/content/interview_poet_liyoung_lee?cmnt_all=1 (accessed March 13, 2013).

Marshall, Tod, "To Witness the Invisible: A Talk with Li-Young Lee," in *Kenyon Review*, Vol. 22, No. 1, Winter 2000, pp. 129–47.

Moyers, Bill, "Li-Young Lee," in *The Language of Life: A Festival of Poets*, edited by James Haba, Doubleday, 1995, pp. 257–69.

Muske, Carol, "Sons, Lovers, Immigrant Souls," in *New York Times Book Review*, January 27, 1991, pp. 20–21.

Norris, Kathleen, "Poetry as Testimony," in *Christian Century*, Vol. 115, No. 28, October 21, 1998, pp. 968–70.

Pence, Amy, "Poems from God: A Conversation with Li-Young Lee," in *Poets & Writers*, November–December 2001, pp. 22–24.

"The Power of the Word (1989): Voices of Memory," October 6, 1989, http://billmoyers.com/content/voices-of-memory/ (accessed March 13, 2013).

Rowse, Ted, "Kuwaitgate—Killing of Kuwaiti Babies by Iraqi Soldiers Exaggerated," in *Washington Monthly*, September 1992, http://archive.is/oZMm (accessed March 13, 2013).

Waniek, Marilyn Nelson, "A Multitude of Dreams," in *Kenyon Review*, Vol. 13, No. 4, Fall 1991, pp. 214–26.

Xu, Wenying, "An Exile's Will to Canon and Its Tension with Ethnicity: Li-Young Lee," in *Multiethnic Literature and Canon Debates*, edited by Mary Jo Bona and Irma Maini, State University of New York Press, 2006, pp. 145–55.

Zhou, Xiaojing, "Inheritance and Invention in Li-Young Lee's Poetry," in *MELUS*, Vol. 21, No. 1, Spring 1996, pp. 113–32.

———, "Li-Young Lee," in *The Heath Anthology of American Literature*, edited by Paul Lauter, et al., 3rd ed., Vol. 2, Houghton Mifflin, 1998, pp. 3169–70.

FURTHER READING

Ingersoll, Earl G., *Breaking the Alabaster Jar: Conversations with Li-Young Lee*, BOA Editions, 2006.
    Lee's existential worldview is best appreciated through exposure to his interviews, in which he frequently delves into his mind-set with regard to writing poetry and his spiritual perspective on life.

Lew, Walter K., ed., *Premonitions: The Kaya Anthology of New North American Asian Poetry*, Kaya Productions, 1995.
    This volume includes work by poets who tend toward the experimental in their verse, including Li-Young Lee as well as Theresa Cha and John Yau.

Paley, Vivian Gussin, *The Boy Who Would Be a Helicopter: The Uses of Storytelling in the Classroom*, Harvard University Press, 1990.
    Longtime kindergarten teacher Paley has written many volumes on practical approaches to encouraging young children's cognitive development. This particular book explores the essential role that storytelling plays in helping children gain a capacity for compassion and an understanding of why people behave the way they do.

Zhao, Yanxia, *Father and Son in Confucianism and Christianity: A Comparative Study of Xunzi and Paul*, Sussex Academic Press, 2007.
    This scholarly volume provides a detailed exploration of how the roles of father and son compare in the contexts of Confucian and Christian thought, with a focus on the writings of a representative from each tradition.

SUGGESTED SEARCH TERMS

Li-Young Lee AND A Story

The City in Which I Love You

Li-Young Lee AND family

Li-Young Lee AND silence

Li-Young Lee AND Indonesia OR China

Chinese American literature

poetry AND storytelling

children AND storytelling

poetry AND children

To the Ladies

MARY CHUDLEIGH

1703

Mary, Lady Chudleigh's "To the Ladies," written more than three centuries ago, is one of the first stirrings of the feminist movement in Western culture. An aristocratic woman born into wealth and privilege, Chudleigh paints a picture of marriage as an institution no different from slavery for women. Chudleigh draws on the work of her friend and fellow feminist Mary Astell, a prominent philosopher of the period, and reshapes the ancient tradition of Stoic philosophy into a critical tool for exposing the unequal position of women in British culture. "To the Ladies" was published in 1703 in Chudleigh's collection *Poems on Several Occasions* and can also be found in the 1993 collection *The Poems and Prose of Mary, Lady Chudleigh.*

AUTHOR BIOGRAPHY

Mary Lee was baptized on August 19, 1656, in Devonshire, England. The date of her birth is not known but must have been not long before. The Lee family was well established in the British aristocracy. On March 25, 1674, Lee married George Chudleigh, a young man of her own class, and acquired the title Mary, Lady Chudleigh. She had six children, four of whom died before the age of eight. The first (also Mary, who lived only four months) was born in 1676, and the remainder came about every two years beginning in 1683. So much is known from parish records kept by the

Women in the eighteenth century had few freedoms, having to obey their husbands. (© Darja Vorontsova | Shutterstock.com)

Anglican Church. Not very much else is known about Chudleigh's life because there survive only five of her letters (which happen to be printed together with *The Poetical Works of Philip, Late Duke of Wharton*) and a very brief biography by George Ballard in his 1752 *Memoirs of Several Ladies of Great Britain*, based on his inquiries made to her family a generation after Chudleigh's death. Another scant source is the set of her introductions to her published works. As a result of her sketchy biography, scholars working on Chudleigh often rush to reconstruct the details of her life from her poetry, a very unsound procedure.

Chudleigh had a wide literary acquaintance. She knew Mary Astell, the leading female intellectual of her era, and was well versed in her writings, and she was on friendly terms with John Dryden, the greatest English poet of the eighteenth century. Dryden lived from time to time at the country estate of his patron, Lord Clifford, which was only a few miles from the Chudleigh estate in Devonshire.

Dryden let Chudleigh read and criticize his translation of Virgil's *Aeneid* prior to its publication and himself read and highly esteemed at least some of Chudleigh's poems in manuscript. More particularly, Chudleigh was part of a circle of literary-minded women, to many of whom she addressed poems and letters. Their identities are not generally known now though, since they referred to each other through pastoralist code names. Chudleigh herself, for example, was known as Marissa.

In 1699, a clergyman named John Sprint published *The Bride-Woman's Councellor*, a sermon in which he called on women nearly to submit themselves as voluntary slaves to their husbands. Chudleigh wrote a verse critique of it, *The Ladies Defence*, which she published in 1701. *The Female Advocate* was a prose attack on Sprint's work, penned anonymously by one of Chudleigh's circle, under the pastoralist name Eugenia. (Ballard mistakenly believed Chudleigh had written this essay also, a point uncritically accepted by some modern scholars; in fact, Chudleigh refers to it as the work of another in the introduction to *The Ladies Defence*.) Chudleigh's poem met with considerable success, which encouraged her to publish a collection of her verse in 1703, titled *Poems on Several Occasions*. This volume includes "To the Ladies," which more briefly revisits many of the themes of *The Ladies Defence*. In 1710 Chudleigh published *Essays upon Several Subjects*, which contains satires (meaning, in this case, texts that mix prose and poetry) on various virtues and vices. Ballard also lists several works of Chudleigh's (perhaps juvenilia) that were never published but which the Chudleigh family still held as manuscripts in 1752: two tragedies, two opera librettos, a masque, a verse version of some of Lucian's dialogues, *Satyrical Reflections on Saqualia* (a Lucian pastiche), and several brief poems. No trace of these remains.

Although Chudleigh met her difficulties with stoic resignation, she suffered from not only the death of four of her children but also, especially in the last years of her life, ill health. According to Ballard, "she had long laboured under the pains of a rheumatism, which had confined her to her chamber a considerable time before her death." She finally succumbed to her generally poor health on December 15, 1710. Ballard's summation of Chudleigh's life and achievement seems fitting: "Her own love of books, her great industry in the reading of them, and her great capacity to improve herself by them, enabled her to make a very considerable figure among the literati of her time."

POEM TEXT

> Wife and Servant are the same,
> But only differ in the Name:
> For when that fatal Knot is ty'd,
> Which nothing, nothing can divide:
> When she the word *obey* has said,   5
> And Man by Law supreme has made,
> Then all that's kind is laid aside,
> And nothing left but State and Pride:
> Fierce as an Eastern Prince he grows,
> And all his innate Rigor shows: 10
> Then but to look, to laugh, or speak,
> Will the Nuptial Contract break.
> Like Mutes she Signs alone must make,
> And never any Freedom take:
> But still be govern'd by a Nod,   15
> And fear her Husband as her God:
> Him still must serve, him still obey,
> And nothing act, and nothing say,
> But what her haughty Lord thinks fit,
> Who with the Pow'r, has all the Wit.   20
> Then shun, oh! shun that wretched State,
> And all the fawning Flatt'rers hate:
> Value your selves, and Men despise,
> You must be proud, if you'll be wise.

POEM SUMMARY

The text used for this summary is from *The Poems and Prose of Mary, Lady Chudleigh*, edited by Margaret J. M. Ezell, Oxford University Press, 1993, pp. 83–84. A version of the poem can be found on the following web page: http://www.poetryfoundation. org/poem/173199.

The twenty-four line text of "To the Ladies" is spoken by an impersonal narrator whose voice is not necessarily the same as Chudleigh's own. The poem is a lament over the condition of women once they enter marriage. It is broken into three sentences.

Lines 1–12
The narrator insists that a wife has a status no different from that of a domestic servant, only acquiring a more dignified title. In addition, in the time and class within which the poem was written, marriage could not be dissolved by divorce, so the wife's fate is recognized as forever after bound to the will of the husband. The narrator points out

that, during the marriage ceremony, the wife agrees to obey her husband, which, given the intertwining of church and state in eighteenth-century England, gives him legal authority over her. Chudleigh invokes the liturgical language of the Anglican marriage rite, which enjoins the wife alone to obedience. That document, in turn, is based on many biblical texts that place the husband in charge of his wife. The poem does not refer, however, to the accompanying instructions to Christian husbands to honor and protect their wives, perhaps suggesting the view that they are not followed in practice.

Once a woman enters into marriage she can expect none of the kindness with which her husband courted her. Instead, the husband will treat his wife as someone of inferior status and dominate her in accord with his own pride. The relationship of the husband to the wife is like the oppressive rule of an Oriental despot over one of his subjects. As the husband's power increases upon entering marriage, he becomes increasingly strict and controlling of his downtrodden wife. The husband alone dictates the terms of the marriage contract and does so with a growing and inhuman strictness. The wife is left unable even to complain about her situation because such a complaint would itself be an act of disobedience that would break the marriage vow of submission. Even a questioning look is forbidden to a wife, as is laughter, which might, after all, be at the expense of her husband.

Lines 13–20
The wife is left in the condition of a mute, who can indicate her desires only though gestures. Even the most basic human characteristic of language is stripped away from her. In this way, any hope of freedom within the marriage is lost, just as it is among the subjects of a despot, who also lack freedom of speech. By the same token, the slightest gesture of her husband, such as nodding his head, becomes a command the wife must obey. With respect to his wife, the husband has the position of a god ruling over mortals, another reference to biblical texts that compare the husband to Christ as the bridegroom of the church.

Within marriage, a wife is left with no choice but to indeed become her husband's servant. While an aristocratic household in the eighteenth century would have been full of maids, the *servant* to which Chudleigh repeatedly refers is a euphemism for a slave, as it often is in the King James Version of the

Bible. The wife's will and voice—her identity—is subsumed into obedience to her husband's commands. Chudleigh's use of the term *Lord* to describe the husband is highly pointed. It is at one and the same time the common biblical title for God, the term by which a slave might address her master, and also the title by which an aristocratic wife would address her husband. Chudleigh's husband, for example, would have been addressed as "Lord Chudleigh" by all but his most intimate associates, and in public, at least, even his wife would have called him by that title rather than his given name. She, in contrast, would be Lady Chudleigh, which, while ostensibly a term of respect, also erases any trace of her given name and hence her own identity. The point is that society was arranged to aggrandize male power by such associations and titles. The husband rules over his wife in marriage precisely because of his scheming and contrivance to subjugate her while courting her. The wife may not act or speak except as her husband wishes. While this leaves her free to think her own thoughts, it is precisely in the inability to express her will outwardly that the loss of freedom occurs.

Lines 21–24

Finally, Chudleigh advises women to avoid marriage altogether. In her social environment, this also means avoiding family and children altogether. Marriage is seen as a wretched condition, leaving the wife in the position of someone who has survived a disaster. While courting, the potential husband will use flattery and every other rhetorical contrivance to try to persuade her to voluntarily give up her freedom, and the conventions of society will support his arguments, as even her female friends and relatives urge her to marry. But prospective wives will be wiser to look after their own interests and have nothing to do with men and marriage. A woman's pride in refusing to submit to a husband will be criticized by the world, but an unmarried woman will instead enjoy a legitimate and not overweening pride in her freedom.

THEMES

Tyranny

One of the analogies that Chudleigh uses to characterize the position of the husband within marriage is that of an Oriental tyrant or despot. The idea of the Oriental despot is a central idea in Western ideology that has little association with any actual rulers of Near Eastern countries. In ancient Greece, the king of Persia was seen as a symbol of luxury and decadence, possessed of wealth far beyond any Western ruler's and also of the absolute power of life and death over his subjects—an image that already diverged from the reality. In the Enlightenment, the Oriental despot not only represented wealth and corrupt power but also became the foil, the reversed mirror image, of the Enlightenment political ideal. Enlightenment philosophy prized liberty and equality above all and favored democratic political institutions, ideas that are embodied in the Declaration of Independence and the US Constitution as well as the Declaration of the Rights of Man, produced during the French Revolution. The despot represented the negation of freedom and equality through the tyrannical rule of a single individual.

Although the despot continued to be presented, as it were, in Oriental fancy dress, as with the sultan of Turkey or the local rulers deposed by the British in India, for example, complete with inhuman excesses of luxury and sadistic cruelty, the idea became a way for Enlightenment philosophers to talk about the European monarchies, which could not be criticized without risking political persecution. In "To the Ladies," Chudleigh assigns all the fantastic powers and extremes of the despot to the husband within a marriage, creating a monster who not only has absolute rule over his wife but, further, whose authority and control virtually erase her identity, reducing her to a mute and entirely passive creature (recalling the trope of orientalist literature of the period in which the despot literally cuts out a rebellious subject's tongue).

Obedience

"To the Ladies" objects to the fact that, during the marriage ceremony, the wife must promise, in a legally binding fashion, to obey her husband. This refers to the language of the 1662 Book of Common Prayer (the official manual of the Church of England, giving the exact language to be used in religious ceremonies), in which the woman makes essentially the same pledge as the man, except that the promise to obey is added. In the text, the woman affirms that this obedience is in accord with divine law.

The Book of Common Prayer's language is derived from the teachings about marriage in the New Testament. Paul's Epistle to the Ephesians

TOPICS FOR FURTHER STUDY

- Read Betty Freidan's *The Feminine Mystique* (1963), the seminal work of second-wave feminism. Write a paper comparing the view of marriage given by Freidan with the picture of marriage given by Chudleigh in "To the Ladies."

- In "To the Ladies," Chudleigh compares the tyrannical husband to an Oriental despot. This hints at further associations, since the epitome of the Oriental despot was the Turkish sultan, famous for keeping a harem, in which his hundreds of wives were devalued to the level of mere sex objects. This idea is romanticized in Western culture, but the institution of the harem was somewhat different. Every aristocratic household in the Islamic world segregated its female members (which could include several wives) in an inner space in the house (technically called a *harem*), which included daughters and even young male children. Fatima Mernissi wrote a memoir of growing up in a harem in Morocco during the 1940s, published in the United States under the title *Dreams of Trespass: Tales of a Harem Girlhood* (1994). After reading this, write a paper evaluating the institution of the harem in terms of the limitations of the wife in "To the Ladies." Did harem women as Mernissi depicts them have more freedom than the wife in the poem, or less? Did they have the consciousness of oppression that permeates the poem?

- Search the Internet for blogs written by women about their marriages. Find a wide variety of cultural approaches to marriage: Islamic, Evangelical Christian, Jewish, feminist, secular, and so forth. How do the views of marriage expressed by these women compare to Chudleigh's? Present your conclusions to your class in a PowerPoint presentation.

- Read the misogynist sermon by John Sprint titled *The Bride-Woman's Councellor* (1699); its lengthy criticism by Chudleigh, *The Ladies Defence* (1701); and her ideological inspiration, Mary Astell's *Some Reflections upon Marriage* (1700). Write a paper explaining how these works relate to "To the Ladies."

- Dorothy A. Mays's *Women in Early America: Struggle, Survival, and Freedom in a New World* (2004) is an encyclopedic history for young adults of women's experiences in America from the beginning of colonization to 1812, frequently quoting and contextualizing narratives written by women themselves. Mays gives a wide treatment of marriage, which was somewhat less restrictive in the American colonies than in England, including marriage among slave women and even among the small number of Islamic immigrants in the colonial period. Write a paper critiquing the views on marriage that American women of that era themselves held in light of Chudleigh's views on marriage.

---

ordains, "Wives, submit yourselves unto your own husbands, as unto the Lord. For the husband is the head of the wife, even as Christ is the head of the church: and he is the saviour of the body. Therefore as the church is subject unto Christ, so let the wives be to their own husbands in every thing" (Ephesians 5:22–24; see also Colossians 3:18). Later in Chudleigh's poem, the wife is told that she must obey her husband as if he is God. This comes from 1 Peter. That epistle restates Paul's injunction, adding that

wives are to be subject "unto their own husbands, even as Sarah obeyed Abraham, calling him lord" (1 Peter 3:5–6). *Lord* is the most common biblical term for God. The marriage of Abraham and Sarah is held up as an ideal. In the bedouin culture that the book of Genesis places Abraham in, women are held as property no differently from slaves, which must be seen as part of the context for Chudleigh's attack on marriage; she objects to the diminishment of women's status by religion. It seems provocative

The speaker views marriage as "fatal" for women. (© Fedorova Alexandra / Shutterstock.com)

to hold the marriage of Abraham and Sarah as an ideal in a more enlightened modern society. Moreover, Abraham was, in addition to being her husband, Sarah's brother, and he evidently yields her to the pharaoh as a tribute, before God forces the Egyptian ruler to restore her by sending a plague on the nation, so their marriage makes a curious ideal.

"To the Ladies" further complains that wives are expected to remain silent, which is also a reference to biblical teaching. The apostle Paul gives the injunction "Let your women keep silence in the churches: for it is not permitted unto them to speak; but they are commanded to be under obedience, as also saith the law. And if they will learn any thing, let them ask their husbands at home: for it is a shame for women to speak in the church" (1 Corinthians 14:34–35). This ties women's silence to their obedience and dependence on their husbands. This command to women is restated in 1 Timothy 2:11–15, which adds that this silence is imposed on women as a punishment

for the transgression of Eve in the Garden of Eden. That passage also promises that obedient women will be kept safe in childbirth through God's miraculous protection. Chudleigh, who saw four of her own children die and probably had a number of miscarriages, might have considered this a particular affront.

STYLE

Meter

Chudleigh's "To the Ladies" is technically a Pindaric ode. The term originally referred to the form used by the ancient Greek poet Pindar, who wrote songs of praise for victors in the Olympic games and other athletic festivals. But the term *Pindaric* is used far more generally today to mean any substantial poem in lyric meter that expresses a substantially developed idea. The poem is written in trochaic quadrameter, meaning that each line consists of four metrical feet in the form of trochees. A *trochee* is a group of two syllables of which the first is stressed. The trochee is the opposite of the pattern of most metered English verse, such as the dialogue in Shakespeare's plays, which is iambic, that is, has an unstressed syllable followed by a stressed. While the overall verse structure is not very regular, the most striking lines, especially the poem's greatest metrical effect in the opening couplet, use this reversal, perhaps to symbolize the poem's reversal of the norm of gender relations in its time and place. Some lines of this poem, however, slip into the more common iambic rhythm. The trochaic rhythm was associated with dance in ancient Greek as much as in modern English, and it would not be difficult to set "To the Ladies" to music. The first line is marked by being trimeter only (i.e., one foot shorter than the rest). Chudleigh frequently ends lines by substituting an iamb or dactyl for a trochee in the last foot, shifting the stress to the last syllable of the line. This provides for so-called masculine rhyme, in which the rhymed syllable is also stressed. The rhyme scheme is organized into simple couplets, in which the first and second line rhyme, as do the third and fourth, and so on.

Figurative Language

Figurative language is a device where words are used as symbols to evoke something more than they actually say. It is a standard feature of poetry, and, indeed, of well-written prose and even of everyday speech. There are some clever and interesting examples of figurative language in "To the Ladies." Line 3 employs the phrase *tie the knot*, which is commonly used to describe marriage. This in any case is a metaphor, describing the joining of husband and wife through a literal description of tying two pieces of rope together. But Chudleigh gives the phrase a quite different nuance by combining it with the idea of a fatal knot, that is, the knot of the hangman's noose. In this way, she suggests that marriage is a death sentence for the wife's freedom.

Chudleigh develops the idea that the wife can give no outward sign of disobedience to her husband. This includes not speaking except at his leave, and saying only what he wants her to say. The wife is left, then, in the position of a deaf-mute who can only communicate through hand signs. This is an intriguing enough passage because of its historical obscurity. References to mutes communicating through gesture go back to Plato in classical antiquity, but for most of history, this merely meant a more concerted effort to use pointing, mimicry, and other such gestures to communicate in a more elaborate form—the way children do before they gain the power of speech, pointing to what they want and so forth. But a more useful form of gesture had been developed for the deaf in Spain and France beginning in the sixteenth century. This involved teaching them the letters of the alphabet and using a special code of hand gestures to represent the individual letters so that they could spell out words with their hands. Systems like this were just being introduced into Great Britain in books published in the 1680s and 1690s, so it is doubtful that Chudleigh could be referring so briefly to such a new and unusual thing in her poem. Certainly the natural languages expressed through hand gestures used by the deaf today did not exist in her time. So Chudleigh is most likely referring to the simple use of gesture for pointing and mimicry. The reader is left to make on one's own the obvious conclusion that poetry could not be expressed through such simple gestures. Thus the wife in Chudleigh's poem could not have produced poetry such as she herself is writing in "To the Ladies." This also opens up more questions than the poem can possibly answer, in this case about Chudleigh's personal life. Although "To the Ladies" is often taken as a complaint about her own unhappy marriage, the existence of the poem itself proves that this could not have been the case: Chudleigh was not silenced as a poet. To an extent, the very existence of the poem tends to undercut its message.

HISTORICAL CONTEXT

Mary Astell

Mary Astell (1666–1731) was a contemporary of Chudleigh's who produced several books and essays on philosophy. Her main enterprise was to establish an epistemological basis for the intellectual equality of men and women, working within the philosophical framework established by John Locke. She also published her correspondence with Locke's follower John Norris. In the seventeenth century, the perceived physical inferiority of women (in body size, strength, etcetera) was taken as an index of a corresponding intellectual inferiority. Astell argued, however, that since, as was then thought, the soul and the mind were independent of the body, this was no reasonable basis for claims of women's intellectual inferiority. She argued that any perceived

COMPARE
&
CONTRAST

- **1700s:** Marriage in England consists of a union between one man and one woman, as recognized by the Anglican Church (pointedly, Catholic marriages in Ireland are not recognized by the state).

  Today: Great Britain recognizes polygamous marriages performed in other countries, recognizes same-sex marriages as civil unions legally identical to marriages, and passed legislation in 2013 establishing same-sex marriage as well. While clergy of all recognized religions can perform marriages, marriage is a legal institution sanctioned by the state.

- **1700s:** Within English marriage, the husband's control of his wife's property and person is nearly absolute. Divorce, forbidden by biblical authority, is impossible, and concepts like marital rape have no legal existence.

- **Today:** British law has gradually recognized the equal rights of spouses within marriage, beginning with the legalization of divorce in 1857 and reaching completion in 1991 with the recognition that a woman's privacy rights allow her to refuse cohabitation with her husband.

- **1700s:** Poor women in England work in fields, shops, service, and, increasingly, industrial settings, but the lack of education afforded to aristocratic women debars them from the professions followed by their husbands and brothers.

  Today: British women of all classes have access to the most advanced education and are fully represented in the traditional professions such as law, medicine, academia, and politics.

intellectual inferiority could be accounted for by the denial of equal education to women, and that a separate but equal education system ought to be created for women. She worked toward the practical realization of this goal throughout the later part of her life, helping to found a charity school for girls in London. In her tract *Some Reflections upon Marriage*, originally published in 1700, she denounced marriage as an oppressive and inequitable institution because it assumed that women were inferior and that they were unfit because of their lack of education to properly make the decisions necessary to find a suitable husband. She highlighted the unequal position of women by asking, "If *all Men are born Free*, how is it that all Women are born Slaves?" Astell herself, from a middle-class background, never married. Chudleigh's *The Ladies Defence* and "To the Ladies" express many of Astell's ideas in poetical form. Astell and Chudleigh probably knew each other socially but would not have met until after Chudleigh's publication of *The Ladies Defence* in 1701. One or more of Chudleigh's unaddressed surviving letters may have been written to Astell.

Epictetus

Epictetus was a Stoic philosopher who lived in the late first and early second centuries. He is the only Stoic philosopher, apart from Seneca, for whom a substantial body of work survives from antiquity. While Stoicism was a systematic philosophy with its own logic, physics, and other disciplines, Epictetus was concerned exclusively with giving advice for practical living, especially for living in a compromised world. Epictetus had been born as a slave in Hierapolis, in modern Syria. Epictetus is not strictly speaking a name but rather a Greek word that means *bought*. He came to Rome as a slave of Epaphroditus, himself a freed slave of the emperor Nero who worked in the government bureaucracy in the capital. How or when Epictetus learned Stoicism is unknown. He was eventually freed and became a teacher of the philosophy, first in Rome and then, after Nero expelled all philosophers from the city, in Nicopolis, in modern Bulgaria.

Epictetus wrote nothing himself but attracted many aristocratic students, including

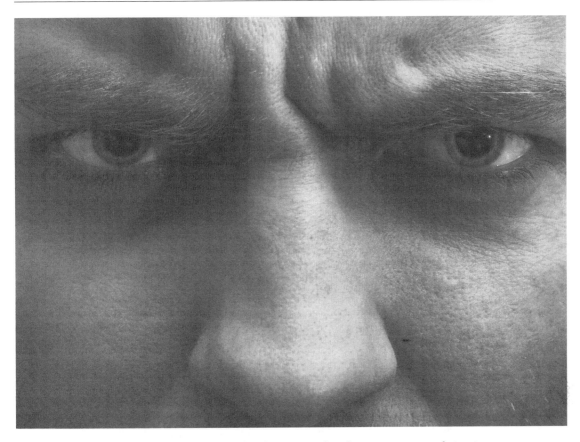

The narrator fears that all men lose their kindness once they have power over their wives. *(© Nomad_Soul /*
Shutterstock.com)

Arrian, who eventually became a provincial governor and also wrote an important surviving history of Alexander the Great. Arrian wrote up and
published his notes of Epictetus's lectures, filling
several books under the title *Discourses*, of which
the first four survive. Arrian also excerpted this
work into a brief handbook known simply as the
Enchiridion or *Manual*. These works today are
generally published under Epictetus's name. A
commentary on the *Manual* by the fifth-century
Greek Neoplatonic philosopher Simplicius also
survives, with a life of the philosopher included.
A. A. Long, in his *Epictetus: A Stoic and Socratic
Guide to Life*, notes that "translations of this
abridgement of Epictetus [i.e., the *Enchiridion*]
were so familiar during the seventeenth and eighteenth centuries that Epictetus became virtually a
household name for the European and early
American intelligentsia." A popular translation
of Epictetus in Chudleigh's time was George
Stanhope's *Epictetus His Morals, with Simplicius
His Comment* (1692).

Chudleigh herself is deeply indebted to Epictetus and mentions him frequently in her work.
In the introduction to *The Ladies Defence* she
praises him as

> that excellent Man, who in the worst of
> Times, and the most vicious Court in the
> World [i.e., in the time of Nero], kept his
> integrity inviolable, and was still true to his
> Principles, and constant to himself amidst
> all the Inconveniences, Discouragement and
> Disgraces that attended him.

She takes a special interest in his endurance
of circumstance: "Neither the Indisposition of
his Body, nor the Barbarity of a Savage Master,
nor that Poverty in which he spent his Life, cou'd
make him do or say any thing unworthy of himself, or unbecoming a Philosopher." The savag-
ery of Epictetus's master is a theme she
frequently turns to, alluding to an episode from
the life of Simplicius:

> While he was yet a Slave to *Epaphroditus*, this
> Brute of a Master one day took a Frolick to

wrench his Leg. *Epictetus* observing him delight with so barbarous a Pleasure, and that he continued it with greater Violence, said, with a smile, and free from any appearance of Passion, *If you go on, you will certainly break my Leg.* In short he did so, and then all the return he made was this, *Did I not tell you, Sir, that you would break my Leg?*

Epictetus's dignity and imperturbability in the face of a sadistic master whom he could not escape is the model of the wife's endurance of her brutish marriage in "To the Ladies."

CRITICAL OVERVIEW

Chudleigh has, through the turn of the twenty-first century, become the subject of an increasing body of scholarship as feminism has become an increasingly important ideology in literature studies. Chudleigh is typically seen today as a precursor of the feminist movement of the nineteenth and twentieth centuries. "To the Ladies" is one of the most frequently commented upon of her poems because it seems to encapsulate the main themes of her work. However, study of the poem is hampered by the lack of context, owing to the scant knowledge available about her life.

One of the main issues of contention is the degree to which the content of the poem reflects Chudleigh's marriage. The older tendency (especially in brief notices in reference works) is to read her poetry as a direct reflection of her own life and to imagine that Chudleigh was trapped in an oppressive, brutish marriage. Hilda L. Smith, for instance, in *Reason's Disciples*, uses the poet's verse about marriage to deduce that "Mary Chudleigh, who was married unhappily to a man she didn't love and whose children died young, had . . . personal experience . . . of what a prison marriage could be for women." There is no hint concerning the circumstances of Chudleigh's marriage in any source where she speaks about her life. Nevertheless, Smith unguardedly uses her inference to support her analysis of Chudleigh's other verse. Considering the highly idealized description of female friendship that Chudleigh gives in many poems, Smith comments, "The excessive quality of these pictures of the 'Sweets of Love' and eternal agreement was counteracted by the need Chudleigh felt to substitute for her unhappy real life an ideal poetic one."

More recently, Margaret J. M. Ezell, in her introduction to *The Poems and Prose of Mary, Lady Chudleigh*, dismisses scholarly discussion of Chudleigh's unhappy marriage as unsupportable speculation: "Since Mary Chudleigh herself wrote little about her own marriage and nothing specifically about her husband, this domestic discord is largely inferred from the subject matter of her" writings. Ann Messenger, in *Pastoral Tradition and the Female Talent*, introduces a new complication, pointing out that the poems against marriage do not purely represent Chudleigh's own ideas but derive from the writings of Mary Astell. Messenger remains cautious but, citing "To the Ladies" and *The Ladies Defence*, still concludes,

> Even if these and similar poems are not autobiography but expressions of agreement with the observations of the unmarried Astell, . . . the nature of her marriage remains a question. She certainly did not . . . call herself a happy wife.

One may yet ask, if Chudleigh's husband had been the oppressive brute of her poems, would he have allowed her to publish such scathing criticism of his character?

An important characteristic of Chudleigh's verse is the theme of retirement, flight from the world to a secluded refuge of safety and enjoyment. Marilyn L. Williamson, in *Raising Their Voices: British Women Writers, 1650–1750*, while noting the overwhelmingly Stoic cast of Chudleigh's poems, suggests that this impulse to retirement in her work derives from Epicurean philosophy, by which one seeks happiness in life by escaping the cares and temptations of the world in the simplicity of a place stereotypically called *the garden*. Messenger extends this discussion by seeing Chudleigh as longing for flight from the oppressive male world into the comfort of the friendship of her circle of intellectual women, and ultimately within herself. Thus even "To the Ladies," where a wife can find freedom from her husband's tyranny only in her own mind, and while giving no outward sign of lack of obedience, becomes a poem of retirement.

CRITICISM

Rita Brown

Brown is an English professor. In the following essay, she reads "To the Ladies" as a Stoic flight into the seclusion of the self where a wife may be free of the brutish circumstances of eighteenth-century marriage.

Chudleigh's work was regularly reprinted throughout the eighteenth and early nineteenth

WHAT DO I READ NEXT?

- Ruth Perry's 1986 biography *The Celebrated Mary Astell: An Early English Feminist* is the first modern major study of Astell. For purposes of comparison with Chudleigh, it is especially useful since it prints in an appendix a collection of Astell's poetic juvenalia (writings of a young adult) that Perry found unidentified in the Bodleian Library at Oxford.

- Mary, Lady Montagu, was a woman of Chudleigh's aristocratic class and the wife of the British ambassador to the Ottoman Empire in 1717–1718. A large body of her correspondence has been preserved, including letters she wrote from Constantinople during her husband's tenure there. They were the first widely popular reports of conditions in Turkey to the British reading public and have been frequently republished over the last three hundred years. Montagu took a special interest in the condition of women in the country, especially in the institution of the harem and polygamy. Her works, which are widely available on the Internet, played an important role in the formation of popular orientalist art and literature in Britain throughout the eighteenth century. One theme of Chudleigh's "To the Ladies" is the de facto identity of English marriage with the position of a wife in a harem in respect to the limitation of her freedom. Digital copies of these works can be viewed at http://archive.org/details/lettersworksofla01inmont and http://archive.org/details/lettersworksofla02inmont.

- The volume of Mary Astell's *Political Writings*, edited in 1996 by Patricia Springborg (perhaps the leading contemporary Astell researcher), offers a critique of John Locke's political philosophy and, surprisingly, defends the monarchy against the incipient democratic tendencies of early eighteenth-century Britain, grounding her proto-feminist thought in a staunch conservatism.

- The seven volumes of *The Works of Mary Wollstonecraft* (1989), edited by Janet Todd and Marilyn Butler, contain most of the writings of the chief eighteenth-century inheritor of Astell's and Chudleigh's proto-feminism, including *A Vindication of the Rights of Women* (1792), often considered the first truly feminist document.

- *Pamela; or, Virtue Rewarded*, a novel by Samuel Richardson, was phenomenally popular when it was first published in 1740. It tells the story of a maidservant who is literally kidnapped and held as a prisoner by her master after she refuses his amorous advances. She is eventually *rewarded* by being allowed to marry her captor. Through hyperbole, the novel illustrates the abusive nature of marriage that Chudleigh complains against in "To the Ladies."

- Bridget Hill has edited a collection of Mary Astell's writings, *The First English Feminist: Reflections upon Marriage and Other Writings* (1986), which offers a standard introduction to the proto-feminism of Astell and her circle among eighteenth-century female intellectuals.

- Chitra Banerjee Divakaruni's *Arranged Marriage* (1995) is a collection of short stories for young adults that deal with the practice of arranged marriages in both India and the Indian community in the United States.

---

centuries. In the late nineteenth century, however, the emergence of the study of English literature as an academic discipline tended to marginalize her work, and it fell into obscurity. Modern feminist critics, who are bringing Chudleigh back into a place of importance in English studies, tend to explain her eclipse as a sexist dismissal of a female poet. However, Chudleigh might have been dismissed for quite other reasons. Her basic worldview is taken from Stoic philosophy, and her greatest influence is the Roman Stoic Epictetus. Accordingly, her main

THE MARRIAGE IN CHUDLEIGH'S POEM STANDS AS A METAPHOR FOR THE WORLD AS IT IS CONCEIVED IN STOICISM."

concern is how human beings, in her case particularly women, can find happiness. Her solution to the problem is to retreat from the oppressive structures of the world into a place of repose that ultimately can only be found inside the self, since it is only there that the harsh constraints of the physical and societal worlds can be cast aside. This dovetails with the vibrant tradition of seventeenth-century pastoral poetry which sought refuge in the countryside from the insults of the modern city. Stoicism and the pastoral had little interest for the modern academy as it emerged at the end of the Victorian era, and the study of those trends and their ideas also waned. Modern man looked for a way to engage with the world in an era of progress and positivism. As Epictetus lost the central place he had held at the beginning of the Enlightenment, it is no wonder that his disciple Chudleigh was also forgotten.

Stoic ethics, Chudleigh and Epictetus's sphere of concern, grows out of the general principles of the philosophy. Stoicism is a system of philosophy devised in the years after 300 BCE by the Greek philosopher Zeno, who was born in Citium, on Cyprus. He came to Athens to study philosophy and live according to the same manner of life as the great philosopher Socrates. Zeno did not study at the Platonic Academy, however, or at the Aristotelian Lyceum, either of which might have been viewed as successors to the school of Socrates. Instead, Zeno followed the Cynic philosopher Crates of Thebes. He must have been impressed by Crates's teaching that humans should live strictly according to nature, meaning the obvious animal nature of human beings (from which derives the name Cynic, which means "canine"). After a decade of study, Zeno began to teach his own philosophy at the Stoa Poikile (the porch of the paintings), an Athenian public art gallery from which his school took its name—Stoicism. Zeno attracted many students, of whom the most important were Cleanthes and Chrysippus. Stoicism eventually became the dominant form of

philosophy in the early Roman Empire. Most ancient literature has been lost through the centuries, and the writings of these Old Stoics (as opposed to the Roman Stoic Epictetus) are preserved only in fragmentary quotations by later authors.

Stoicism differed from the philosophy of Plato and Aristotle in being entirely materialistic, teaching that nothing existed apart from physical matter. The Stoics rejected the idea that whatever human faculty is responsible for thoughts and feelings was some type of nonmaterial entity of a different character than the rest of the world, such as a soul, spirit, or divine spark. Thinking and feeling were seen as the results of a material process in the brain and body, just like everything else that can be observed. Stoics did not reject the idea of a God, but they held that "God" was simply the totality of the universe and, in particular, the cause of the universe existing in the best possible way. Just as human beings have reason, God is the reasoning power that arises from the body of the universe. Cleanthes praised this being in his poetic *Hymn to Zeus*, taking Zeus as only one of many names of this material divinity.

The Stoics insisted that the universe as a whole was perfect, and that if some condition or event, such as the death of a child, seemed imperfect to the human beings it affected, that was because their limited perspective was incapable of seeing the whole. Cleanthes expressed this idea in his hymn by saying that even what is hated by human beings is lovely in the eyes of God.

According to the Stoic view, it is impossible to change the state of the natural world, so it follows that human beings must live in accord with nature as it actually exists. A human being must learn to distinguish what one cannot control, external circumstances, from what one can control, one's reactions and feelings about external circumstances. Suffering is caused by wishing things to be different than they are and wishing to change what one is powerless to change. The Stoic sage who has perfected his ethical training wishes things to be just as they are and completely frees himself from suffering by perfecting his interior psychological composition. He is not emotionless, as is popularly conceived, but rejects those emotions (strong passions) that are not subordinate to reason as though they were a sort of mental illness. In this way, he becomes a god, since his reason becomes identical to the right reason that regulates the universe in the best possible way. Epictetus encapsulates this doctrine in a maxim in his *Manual*:

> The Things in our own Power, are in their own Nature free, not capable of being countermanded or hindered; but those that are not in our Power, are feeble, servile, liable to Opposition, and not ours, but another's. Remember then, that if you mistake those Things for free, which Nature hath made servile; and fancy that your own, which is indeed another's; you shall be sure to meet with many Hindrances and Disappointments, much Trouble, and great Distractions, and be continually finding fault both with God and Man. But if you take Things right, as they really are, looking upon no more to be your own, than indeed is so; and all that to be another's, which really belongs to him; no body shall ever be able to put any Constraint upon you, no body shall check or disappoint you: You shall accuse no body, shall complain of nothing, shall never do any thing unwillingly, shall receive harm from no body, shall have no Enemy; for no Man will be able to do you any Prejudice.

Epictetus's teaching speaks directly to the condition of marriage Chudleigh describes in "To the Ladies." Epictetus himself says nothing directly about marriage. In his text, women are mentioned only as temptations to the young men he teaches and as wives and daughters whose deaths may trouble husbands and fathers. Although there is no record of a female Stoic in antiquity, there is no inherent reason why women cannot embrace the philosophy, as Chudleigh certainly did (as have other female English intellectuals, such as the Brontë sisters). In the introduction to *Poems on Several Occasions* (the collection containing "To the Ladies"), Chudleigh claims that she is speaking entirely to a female audience. Moreover, she teaches them Stoicism, restating the lesson of Epictetus as a foundation for undertaking her verse. She instructs the reader to understand what is and is not within her power, and to care only about the former:

> to be pleas'd with nothing but what strictly and properly speaking, we may justly pretend a Right to; of which kind, such things can never be said to be, of which 'tis in the Power of Fortune to deprive us.

The marriage in Chudleigh's poem stands as a metaphor for the world as it is conceived in Stoicism. In marriage, Chudleigh claims, woman is a slave who must obey her husband as she would a god. In the world also, Epictetus claims that human beings are helpless and must obey the divine will, no matter how unpleasant it seems; they are, in a thought borrowed by Shakespeare, nothing but actors on a stage playing out a script they did not write and cannot change. In Chudleigh, too, the wife *acts* according to the will of her husband. For the wife in "To the Ladies," every action is constrained by the will of her husband, which constantly thwarts what she wants to do. These are the hindrances and disappointments, the trouble and great distractions that Epictetus mentions.

Epictetus offers a way out of the world's afflictions though. If one cannot change external evils, then the only thing to do is to not consider them evils. The only freedom that a human being who cannot change circumstance possesses is the freedom to understand what she can do something about, and what she cannot. If a wife's husband is brutal and oppressive, he is only playing the role that has been assigned to him by society. His wife cannot change his behavior, but can only recognize it and understand that it is unjust. If she realizes that that is the way things are, she will not be disappointed. She will, from Epictetus's perspective, experience unhappiness only if she wants to bring about change that is impossible.

In "To the Ladies," the only freedom the wife has left is within her own mind. Amid the long list of things that her husband controls, even her words and gestures, no mention is made of her thoughts, which must necessarily remain hers alone. But the wife is no different in this respect from anyone else. Since her brutish husband manifestly has not found freedom in Stoic terms (or else he would act justly), his life is equally prescribed and controlled, just by other forces than marriage. So the poem is really about a universal condition that is recognized in Stoicism, of which marriage is only a single specimen. Chudleigh writes about marriage only as a type of the limits placed on human actions by circumstances. Since she is a woman, it reflects her experience. But that does not mean she believes that other circumstances offer more freedom.

At the end of "To the Ladies," Chudleigh advises against marriage. Choice, after all, is the only freedom the Stoic has. But her advice instead is to cultivate the self as a means of gaining wisdom. And this ultimately is the only thing the Stoic can do. She must build up her powers of judgment until she understands what is in her control and what is not and becomes able to accept the unalterable aspects of reality.

"To the Ladies" uses the familiar metaphor of marriage as a knot, claiming that it ties a woman to the life of a servant. *(© Chepko Danil Vitalevich | Shutterstock.com)*

The attention of the Stoic must inevitably turn inward in a flight or retirement from the concerns of the world to find wisdom within oneself. If in the poem the retreat away from the world into the self is mostly implied, it is spelled out in the introduction to *Poems on Several Occasions*. Chudleigh tells her reader that as Stoics, the way for women "to have our Passions under a due Government, to be wholly our own, and not to have it in the Power of Accidents, of things foreign to us to ruffle and disturb our Thoughts, is to retire into our selves." Only within herself, within her own judgments, can the Stoic become a sage and be saved from all the difficulties of the world. Here, too, Chudleigh is following her friend Mary Astell, who in her *Serious Proposal to the Ladies* found in just such a retreat a refuge from the fallen state of women as an oppressed class in eighteenth-century England: "Happy Retreat! which will be the introducing you into such a *Paradise* as your Mother *Eve* forfeited.... Here are no Serpents to deceive you, whilst you entertain your selves in these delicious Gardens."

Source: Rita Brown, Critical Essay on "To the Ladies," in *Poetry for Students*, Gale, Cengage Learning, 2014.

Ann Messenger

In the following excerpt, Messenger examines why Chudleigh did not often incorporate pastoral themes into her poetry, though it was a popular subject of the time.

... Retirement is a major motif in the poetry of Mary, Lady Chudleigh, but the pastoral is not. A negative example, however, can be as revealing as a positive example, if not more so, and her rare uses of the mode illuminate the ambivalence that at least one woman poet felt about it. She does not just adapt it, as most women poets did. She does not discard it because it is untrue to real nature, as Lady Winchilsea came close to doing. Instead, fully informed of its conventions and its underlying assumptions, she uses pastoral, which is often "about" poetry in general and the power of art, actively to discredit the pastoral mode itself.

Her most sustained use of pastoral occurs in a lengthy Pindaric, "The Song of the Three

Children Paraphras'd" (155–233), which is a special case (see chapter 7, pp. 126–27). Otherwise, the pastoral element in her poetry rarely amounts to more than the form of a dialogue between women with pastoral names, while the imagery is limited to such bald phrases as "Dawn" and "refulgent Day" to characterize the poetic powers of Waller and Dryden (30), or simply "beauteous Nature" (27). On a few occasions, she was moved to describe the vicissitudes of human experience in nautical images—the deceptive calms and destructive storms of "the bois'trous Sea of Life" (75)—but that is all. And yet, habitually described as "learned" by her contemporaries, she knew the conventions of classical and English poetry—and she lived in the Devonshire countryside.

Unlike Lady Winchilsea, Lady Chudleigh apparently valued her country home not for its beauty but for its solitude, the peace and quiet that allowed her to read the many books to which she was devoted. In her retirement poems, she does not so much retire *to* the countryside as *into* her own mind. Again and again, she mentions the crowds and noise of the city and the joys of being alone, or with a single female companion, in her "lov'd Groves" (188). But she has little or no interest in what those groves looked like or in the rural life around her. Only once does she describe a pastoral scene which provides both delight and "Matter for Thought," and that is in the most general and clichéd terms: "lofty Hills, . . . winding Rivers, . . . murmuring   Brooks, . . . bleating Flocks, . . . melodious Birds," and so on. The contents of her books hold her attention; her surroundings do not.

. . . A close look at Lady Chudleigh's infrequent use of the pastoral mode may not throw much light on the vexed question of her marriage, but it helps in understanding her principles and her character. In almost all of her usages, she discredits pastoral, though not simply in the form of "The Nymph's Reply to the Shepherd" or other such anti-pastoral, which is itself part of the convention. As I have said before, the convention was conventionally subverted from its earliest days. Instead, she denies in several different ways the very basis of the convention, a convention that is rooted in the earth, most often by turning instead to the abstractions of reason, religion, and heaven.

The rusticated Lady Chudleigh gave traditional titles to two of her poems which lead the reader to expect the clichés of pastoral retirement poetry: "The Happy Man" and "The Choice." In the first, the clichés are flaunted; in the second, destroyed.

"The Happy Man" is the portrait of a stoic, "Who Fortune's Frowns without Concern can bear" because he is rich in intellectual acquirements (40–41). His reason governs his passions, he has no ambitions, and "a Grove, a Garden, or a Field" yields "sublimer Pleasures" than the "Charms of Pow'r." That is the only mention of the rural in the entire poem. Apparently, for this stoic, any private, non-urban place will do. He has books and friends, and, unafraid of death, will lie down "smiling" when his time comes. Røstvig says that this poem "paints a definitely Epicurean picture of the self-contained state of bliss" (I, 421). The bliss is slightly qualified, however: Fate and Fortune do frown on this man, and his rural pleasures are sublime essentially in contrast to the "splendid Ills" of the powerful and ambitious. Hoxie Neale Fairchild despairs of classifying Lady Chudleigh's thinking here and calls her "a stoical, epicurean, sentimental Platonist" (242). Lady Chudleigh herself would have described her happy man as someone like Socrates, to whom she refers elsewhere frequently and with admiration, or like Epictetus, whose principal ideas she explains at length in her essays (120–27). The basic stance of Epictetus is echoed in various formulations throughout Lady Chudleigh's verse and prose: that we should depend for happiness only on what cannot be taken away, which rules out material wealth, health, even life itself, leaving only a well-stocked mind and a devotion to virtue. For her, the happy person is an ascetic intellectual, who, except for friends and books, scorns the sources of pleasure listed in conventional retirement poems.

Although Lady Chudleigh shared these ascetic values, it is noteworthy that this picture of earthly happiness is about a man, not a woman. Her other retirement poems, and the retirement poems of other women, are personal, but here, describing happiness in this world, she must write about a man. The clichés of retirement poetry cannot be made to fit her own life.

. . . So Lady Chudleigh knew that poetry could not comfort where even Christian reason failed. Yet poetry was not worthless: she dedicates her poems to her admired Queen Anne, and offers the ideas they contain as advice to female readers. And if poetry could not relieve feelings, it could serve to express them: she describes her work as "a Picture of my Mind," struggling with its passions and striving for tranquillity (A4). Apparently, that mind contained particularly grave doubts about the power and value of pastoral.

Why? One can only guess, but I think there were several reasons. Apparently she cared little for the beauties of nature, but her antipathy to pastoral goes deeper than this. For her the life of the mind was of the first importance, and pastoral was seen as a lowly, unintellectual mode by her contemporaries, however copiously they read and wrote it—and Lady Chudleigh shared the literary judgments of her time. Furthermore, she apparently saw such a gap between edenic pastoral fictions and the sins and sorrows of real life in the fallen world that the mode was seriously invalidated; she did not have the kind of imagination that can use a false vision to express truth, and for her, poetry was a vehicle for truth. Perhaps even more important, pastoral fictions, however conventional, celebrate the things of this earth, all those "Dregs of Sense" for which she had such contempt. Central to its earthly concerns was heterosexual love, while her love was directed to her mother, daughter, and women friends. Pastoral did not transcend the flesh of which she was so weary.

To put all this another way, pastoral, a feminine mode, offered a kind of femininity which Lady Chudleigh rejected for herself—unintellectual, earth-bound. Other women poets could ignore or subvert or otherwise cope with the stereotype, but she could not. For her, pastoral was alien soil.

Source: Ann Messenger, "Mary, Lady Chudleigh (1656–1710)," in *Pastoral Tradition and the Female Talent: Studies in Augustan Poetry*, AMS Press, 2001, pp. 83–87, 95–96.

Janine Barchas

In the following excerpt, Barchas discusses Chudleigh's The Ladies Defense, *touching on many themes central to "To the Ladies."*

. . . *The Ladies Defence* is useful not least in confirming what we already know about the early development of print culture in eighteenth-century England. First, it evidences the existence of two known prerequisites for the transition into a print culture: female literacy and the assimilation of literary tradition through

> HER MEN ARE OF THE STRAW VARIETY AND SERVE (CRATYLICALLY) AS MOUTHPIECES FOR TWO-DIMENSIONAL POSITIONS MOTIVATED PRIMARILY BY THE DESIRE NOT TO LOSE THE CONVENIENCES OFFERED BY SILENT, STUPID WOMEN."

translation. Chudleigh's poem, which addresses an imagined audience of "Ladies" who spend "much of their Time in reading" offers additional evidence for the presence of a sizeable female reading public at the start of the eighteenth century, particularly among the landed gentry that served as the author's initial coterie audience (7). Similarly, the poem confirms a substantial market in translation. Chudleigh's works "display an impressive knowledge of classical philosophy, science, and history," which was enabled through her reliance upon the well-documented late-Restoration market in English translations of both classical and Continental literature. A woman with limited knowledge of Greek and Latin (a predicament shared, the poem implies, by many of her lady readers and, of course, later, by Pope), Chudleigh rejoices in her preface that the ancient poets "are now naturaliz'd, and wear an English Dress" (9–10). In these respects, Chudleigh's *The Ladies Defence* simply confirms what critics, including Hunter and Brewer, already surmised about the cultural conditions at the century's start, namely that female literacy and the creation of a literary lingua franca through accessible translations of the canon are interconnected phenomena.

Second, the fact that Chudleigh's poem is published anonymously gives evidence that in 1701 we have not yet attained the professionalization of the author associated with "high" print culture. Although we must not ignore the obvious—that as a previously unpublished author whose brand will not boost sales, Chudleigh operates within established print conventions and the titillating commercial traditions of aposiopesis and anonymity—her adherence to conventions of anonymity mitigates her professionalization. Chudleigh also does not take up her pen for financial reasons. When she becomes a published author "whom stangers read," she does not simultaneously transform into the professional author of high print culture. Although Aphra Behn might be "the first professional woman writer to be buried in Westminster Abbey," her fame and public recognition did not mark every woman who published subsequent to 1689 as a professional author. Well into the century, newspapers and booksellers offered works by writers who, like Chudleigh and Lady Mary Wortley Montagu after her, "looked askance at their own activities as authors." The examples of ambivalent authorship by writers such as Chudleigh suggest that at the century's start even participants in the publishing industry had not yet internalized the notion of authorship that would come to be, by century's end, irrevocably tied to the published, printed book.

At first blush, *The Ladies Defence, Or, the Bride-Woman's Counsellor Answer'd* is not about the advent of print culture, but about gender relations. This poem explicitly positions Chudleigh in the lonely proto-feminist pantheon with the likes of Margaret Cavendish, Duchess of Newcastle and Mary Astell. Although more consistent and expansionist than her enigmatic predecessor Cavendish. Chudleigh is perhaps less political as well as less hopeful than her contemporary, and possible friend, Astell. Chudleigh writes her *Defence* as a response to *The Bride-Woman Counseller* (1699), a misogynist screed by clergyman John Sprint. Originally a sermon preached at a spring wedding, Sprint's project does not—outside of the coincidental fact that its author has the popular technology embedded in his name—touch upon books or print. Sprint deploys religious authority in support of the subjugation of wives by their husbands. Taking as its opening theme Corinthians 7:34 (*"But she that is Married, careth for the things of the World, how she may please her Husband"*), Sprint's text depicts woman as an agent of male pleasure: "Woman was made for the Comfort and Benefit of Man [*Cor.* 11. 9]." Sprint's three-pronged outline of wifely duty ("*LOVE, HONOUR*, and *OBEY*") is predictable in its emphasis on female passivity and silence. He describes the ideal wife as "pliant and yielding," "submissive and obedient," and devoid of "*that Domestick Talk*" which breaks men's hearts and makes them prefer the "Thunder and Lightning and blustring Winds" of the outdoors to the "perpetual Scolding and Brawling within doors." In *The Ladies Defence*, Chudleigh both argues against this view, that women

should be silent, and attacks Sprint's fundamental assumption that "Women are of weaker Capacities to learn than Men."

Chudleigh's response to Sprint redirects his misogynist assessment of feminine inferiority into an examination of female education, and in so doing explicitly links her feminism to print (although in interesting and non-linear ways). Written in heroic couplets, her poem takes the form of a dialogue among four interlocutors, three men and one woman. The male speakers—Sir John Brute, the Parson, and Sir William Loveall—argue that women should speak little, if at all, and that any female access to books should be strictly controlled. Melissa, the female character through whom Chudleigh ventriloquises and to whom she gives the last word (as well as nearly 40 percent of the poem's lines), says that women should participate in an educated discourse specifically through access to printed books. The manner in which each of these characters triangulates the relationship between patriarchy and print illuminates the print-culture dimension of Chudleigh's feminist project. In fact, multiple alternative visions for the printed book are mapped out through Chudleigh's four characters, each of whom has a well-articulated, albeit uneasy, relationship to books, reading, and the nascent culture of print.

Before turning to Chudleigh's characters and her explicit participation in a debate about print, I wish to note that *The Ladies Defence* also participates in the advent of "bookishness" implicitly—through its use of language and metaphor borrowed from print. Perhaps these poetic features of Chudleigh's text allow us to measure the partial assimilation of the printed book at the century's start. Chudleigh's poem is shot through with minor bibliophilic references, both obvious and oblique. We will witness such language invading the speeches of even opponents of print, whose seemingly unconscious recourse to verbs of seeing and imprinting attests to the pervasiveness of the medium they resist. In this sense, *The Ladies Defence* is representative of a fundamental juxtaposition of the coterie (displaying oral and manuscript features) and print culture throughout Chudleigh's work. Remarkably, it is not just this one poem, but the whole of Chudleigh's published oeuvre (all appeared in print during the century's first decade), that is rife with the rhetoric of competing cultures—from quasi-technical terms borrowed from the printing trade to puns and double entendres that appear to refer to a historical moment in which oral display, manuscript, and print are jockeying for position in the culture. Even Chudleigh's many poems and essays about subjects which would appear wholly divorced from such matters (infant mortality, friendship, vanity, death) accommodate the language of the coterie alongside that of an emerging print culture, mentioning books and private reading with some frequency.

In shaping her characters in *The Ladies Defence*, Chudleigh is not subtle. Her men are of the straw variety and serve (cratylically) as mouthpieces for two-dimensional positions motivated primarily by the desire not to lose the conveniences offered by silent, stupid women. Yet, as Danielle Clarke notes in her review of Ezell's edition, "the rhetorical and logical force of polemical argument suits Chudleigh well, and she is adept at manipulating the dialogue form so that her male characters' cursory judgements of women become self-condemnatory." Sir John Brute is a prime example of this self-condemnatory transparency. Brute, whom the preface berates as having "all the extraordinary qualifications of an accomplished Husband," also offers the most Brute-ish perspective on print. A character borrowed from Sir John Vanbrugh's play *The Provoked Wife* (1697), Brute stands in Chudleigh's work for crude physicality; he is not just misogynistic, but anti-intellectual as well. In this respect, Melissa lumps Brute with "The formal Justice, and the jolly Knight," whom she describes as hostile to intellectual pursuits: "(Detesting Books) still Hunt, or Hawk, or Play, / And in laborious Trifles wast the Day" (ll. 766–67). Like Henry Fielding's Squire Western, Sir John Brute shuns books in favour of corporeal pleasures; he is one of those "Who Eat and Run, then Quarrel, Rail and Drink, / But never are at leisure once to Think" (ll. 762–63). Yet it is just these sorts of men, Melissa laments in political critique, who serve as "the Props, the Glory of the State" and on whom "depends the Nation's Fate" (ll. 770–71). Brute argues that books are bad: "Books are the Bane of States, the Plagues of Life" (l. 591). According to him, books "nourish Factions, and increase Debate, / Teach needless things, and causeless Fears create" (ll. 593–94). . . .

. . . Although the end result of this argument (women reading) would be liberating for women, the argument itself is hardly high feminism:

husbands will get more utility from educated wives than ignorant ones, promises Melissa, and therefore they should encourage wives to read since "our Discourses wou'd less tiresom be" (l. 704). Indeed, the poem's most wonderfully ironic "feminist" claim (where Chudleigh risks reinforcing Sprint) is that women should read Stoic philosophy so that they can better endure the hardship of married life—including, the text hints, subjugation, domestic violence, and infant mortality—and provide their husbands with greater obedience. Schooled in classical Stoicism, a wife will:

> Never dispute, when Duty leads the way,
> But its Commands without a Sigh Obey.
> To Reason, not to Humour, give the Reins,
> And be the same in Palaces and Chains.

Reading Epictetus and Seneca, implies Melissa, would make a woman a better life companion even for Sir John Brute.

Although with this argument Chudleigh (one hopes) has her tongue firmly in her cheek, she does blame women for wasting the power of their literacy on "Plays and Romances." Chudleigh does not advocate promiscuous reading; rather, she believes that print should be employed in the service of female education, urging the voluntary differentiation between "trifling Authors" and "useful'st Subjects" (ll. 697–98). In this, she is firmly engaged in a battle not over gender roles and rights, but over the shape of the nascent print culture at the turn of the eighteenth century. These genre claims complicate Chudleigh's relationship to a print-culture revolution. Chudleigh is capable of articulating a vision of "high" print culture, driven by pleasure rather than pedagogy and by economics rather than politics; yet she *rejects* this vision on feminist grounds. In other words, Chudleigh cautions *against* the unchecked evolution of print culture and *for* a more limited scope for print. She rejects the genre of romance as "trifling" because it compromises her political project, recommending instead ancient authors in "Moral Philosophy." The preface's lament that women are "spending so much of their Time in reading Plays and Romances" marks Chudleigh's imagined public audience as avid consumers of print. Chudleigh's argument implies that popular culture is shaping women's reading habits, just as the tastes and needs of readers will conversely shape the marketplace for print. She offers alternative reading material, "chiefly" recommending, "next to the Sacred Scripture, and Devotional Discourses," a large number of texts in classical philosophy and literature by, among others, Seneca, Plutarch, Epictetus, Socrates, Homer, Theocritus, Lucretius, Virgil, Horace, Ovid, Juvenal, and Persius. Although Chudleigh's unequivocal endorsement of traditional classical literature appears, in a twenty-first-century context, to be a recapitulation of the patriarchal canon, Chudleigh argues precisely the opposite. To Chudleigh, the prospect of an unanchored print culture appears dangerous, and her syllabus of ancient authors is intended as a compass for those women who intend to chart an independent course through the Scylla and Charybdis of print.

The Ladies Defence articulates its tentative view of print culture primarily from the perspective of the consumer of books. Yet, as an author, Chudleigh's experience with the process of getting the poem into print was similarly fraught with anxiety. Chudleigh found yielding to print problematic and, to at least some extent, disempowering....

Source: Janine Barchas, "Before Print Culture: Mary, Lady Chudleigh, and the Assimilation of the Book," in *Eighteenth-Century Genre and Culture: Serious Reflections on Occasional Forms*, edited by Dennis Todd and Cynthia Wall, University of Delaware Press, 2001, pp. 18–22, 28–29.

Marilyn L. Williamson

In the following excerpt, Williamson explains the significance that Queen Anne had for Chudleigh and many other women of the time.

... Lady Mary Chudleigh is an example of the meaning that Queen Anne's reign had for women writers. Although she was retiring, Chudleigh, we recall, shared with Mary Astell very strong convictions about improving women's lot in marriage and how they conducted their lives in order to have better control over them. Chudleigh's combination of rage and caution led her to look for a protector, one she found in Queen Anne, to whom she dedicated *Poems on Several Occasions* (1703). We note the characteristic undoing of the gesture: "The Address has too much Confidence; the Ambition is too aspiring; But to whom should a Woman unknown to the World, and who has not Merit enough to defend her from the Censure of Criticks, fly for Protection, but to Your Majesty? The Greatest, the Best, and the most Illustrious Person of Your Sex and Age."

In her later work, *Essays upon Several Subjects in Prose and Verse* (1710), where Chudleigh's whole purpose is to persuade women to improve control of their lives through knowledge and command of their passions, Queen Anne is an important example

for both women's capacity for learning and the ability to control anger. Chudleigh's argument about women's learning follows the practice of the defenses of women in accumulating many illustrious examples, and among the learned queens, Anne is the living instance. Later in the work, one of the most interesting essays is "Of Anger," which Chudleigh sees as an emotion particularly harmful to, and prevalent in, women because it comes from powerlessness. There Queen Anne is the only female example—among many males—of the capacity to control rage. (pp. 132–33) For Chudleigh, as for other women writers, Anne had as much significance in sexual politics as in matters of state....

Source: Marilyn L. Williamson, "Orinda and Daughters: Chudleigh, Egerton, Winchilsea, Rowe, Aubin, Barker, Masters, Barber," in *Raising Their Voices: British Women Writers, 1650–1750*, Wayne State University Press, 1990, pp. 267–68.

SOURCES

Astell, Mary, *A Serious Proposal to the Ladies, for the Advancement of Their True and Greatest Interest*, Richard Wilkin, 1697, pp. 44–45.

———, *Some Reflections upon Marriage*, 4th ed., William Parker, 1730, p. 150.

Ballard, George, *Memoirs of Several Ladies of Great Britain, Who Have Been Celebrated for Their Writings, or Skill in the Learned Languages, Arts and Sciences*, W. Jackson, 1752, pp. 409–13.

Chudleigh, Mary, Introduction to *The Ladies Defence*, Introduction to *Poems on Several Occasions*, and "To the Ladies," in *The Poems and Prose of Mary, Lady Chudleigh*, edited by Margaret J. M. Ezell, Oxford University Press, 1993, pp. 8, 45, 83–84.

Cleanthes, *Hymn to Zeus*, in *Greek and Roman Philosophy after Aristotle*, edited by Jason L. Saunders, Free Press, 1994, pp. 149–50.

Epictetus, *Epictetus His Morals, with Simplicius His Comment*, translated by George Stanhope, 5th ed., D. Midwinter, 1741, pp. x, 32–34.

Ezell, Margaret J. M., Introduction to *The Poems and Prose of Mary, Lady Chudleigh*, Oxford University Press, 1993, p. xxiv.

Long, A. A., *Epictetus: A Stoic and Socratic Guide to Life*, Oxford University Press, 2002, p. 2.

Messenger, Ann, *Pastoral Tradition and the Female Talent: Studies in Augustan Poetry*, AMS Press, 2001, pp. 83–96.

Smith, Hilda L., *Reason's Disciples: Seventeenth-Century English Feminists*, University of Illinois Press, 1982, pp. 163–69.

Wharton, Philip, *The Poetical Works of Philip, Late Duke of Wharton, and others of the Wharton Family, and of the Duke's Intimate Acquaintance*, William Warner, n.d. [1731?], pp. 107–15.

Williamson, Marilyn L., *Raising Their Voices: British Women Writers, 1650–1750*, Wayne State University Press, 1990, pp. 90–102.

FURTHER READING

Alpers, Paul, *What Is Pastoral?*, University of Chicago Press, 1996.

> Mary Chudleigh comes at the end of the Renaissance tradition of pastoral literature in English and other modern languages. A few of her lyrics are pastoral in character, and the genre shows other influences on her work, including the tendency to mix poetry and prose into a single work. In "To the Ladies," she transforms the idea of pastoral retirement into a vibrant psychological concept. Alpers's work is the standard introduction to this genre, largely ignored by modern critics.

Astell, Mary, and John Norris, *Letters Concerning the Love of God*, edited by E. Derek Taylor and Melvyn New, Ashgate, 2004.

> Largely because of the participation of Norris, an established male philosopher (and a friend of Chudleigh's), these letters helped to gain Astell recognition as a serious intellectual in her own lifetime. In the text, she makes several well-thought-out attacks against the ideas of John Locke which Norris must defend. The text has rarely gone out of print in the last three hundred years, and scans of older editions are widely available on the Internet.

Austen, Jane, *Pride and Prejudice*, T. Egerton, 1813.

> Although written a century after Chudleigh's death, Austen's masterpiece is set in the same aristocratic culture that the former inhabited. It demonstrates the anxieties that attended marriage for young women of that class and how their difficult choices in the finding of husbands represented the only power they had to control their lives.

Falco, Maria J., ed., *Feminist Interpretations of Mary Wollstonecraft*, Pennsylvania State University Press, 1996.

> The essays in this volume demonstrate feminist approaches to literature by eighteenth-century women. Wollstonecraft's works are read in light of various modern concerns that renew and liberate her texts from their historical circumstances.

SUGGESTED SEARCH TERMS

Mary, Lady Chudleigh

To the Ladies AND Chudleigh

feminism

Stoicism

Epictetus

Mary Astell

marriage AND history

Oriental despot

What Lips My Lips Have Kissed

EDNA ST. VINCENT MILLAY

1923

Edna St. Vincent Millay's sonnet "What Lips My Lips Have Kissed" was included in her 1923 collection of poems *The Harp-Weaver and Other Poems*. Most of the poems published in this collection were written between 1919 and 1920. "What Lips My Lips Have Kissed" is written in the same style as a Petrarchan love sonnet, with fourteen lines of rhymed poetry consisting of an octave and a sestet. The first eight lines of Millay's sonnet are one sentence that forms the octave. These lines suggest a remembrance of past love and romance and of a time that no longer exists. The final six lines are the sestet. This second complete sentence recognizes that there is no real resolution for the poet; instead, the sestet suggests a simple acceptance of a world that has changed.

Although on the surface "What Lips My Lips Have Kissed" might seem to be a simple love sonnet, the themes of loss and of a time that has now passed are also reminiscent of the sense of loss that was so common after World War I, which at that time was known as the Great War. *The Harp-Weaver and Other Poems* was reissued in 2004 by Kessinger. "What Lips My Lips Have Kissed" is also included in *Collected Poems of Edna St. Vincent Millay* (1956), the most recent edition of which was reissued in 2011.

Edna St. Vincent Millay (© *The Library of Congress*)

AUTHOR BIOGRAPHY

Millay was born February 22, 1892, in Rockland, Maine. She was the oldest of three daughters born to Henry Dolman Millay, a school teacher and school superintendent, and his wife, Cora Buzzelle Millay. The marriage ended in 1899 when Cora Millay could no longer tolerate her husband's gambling. Although she had been trained to be an opera singer, Mrs. Millay began working as a practical nurse to support her three daughters. While their mother worked, the three Millay girls were often left to their own devices to entertain and feed and care for themselves. Although her childhood might be considered unconventional and was sometimes difficult, Millay occupied herself with reading and music. She took piano lessons and began to write poetry at age five. She had several of her poems published in a children's magazine, *St. Nicholas*, between 1906 and 1910. When Millay was a teenager, her mother encouraged her to enter her poetry in a contest sponsored by

The Lyric Year, a literary anthology. Although her poems did not win a prize, one poem, "Renascence," received much praise. After a school director heard Millay read her poem and offered to help pay for her education, Millay entered Vassar College, from which she graduated in 1917.

Millay's first collection of poetry, *Renascence and Other Poems*, was published in 1917. This was followed by additional collections of poetry, *A Few Figs from Thistles: Poems and Four Sonnets* in 1920 and *Eight Sonnets in American Poetry, 1922: A Miscellany*. Millay received the Pulitzer Prize for Poetry in 1923 for these two earlier poetry collections plus *The Ballad of the Harp-Weaver*, which was initially published alone but was later included in *The Harp-Weaver and Other Poems*, published in 1923, which also included "What Lips My Lips Have Kissed." Millay was the first woman to receive a Pulitzer Prize for poetry and only the second poet to receive this prize. By 1923, Millay had already received several offers of marriage, which she rejected. However, in July of 1923, she married Eugen Jan Boissevain, a widowed businessman, who assumed the responsibility of managing her career and paying for her medical costs, since Millay was often in poor health. Although the Pulitzer Prize that she was awarded was for poetry, Millay was also busy during this period writing prose, drama, and even an opera libretto.

After her marriage, Millay and her husband purchased seven hundred acres and an old farm house in rural New York. For the next several years, Millay worked at the farm, which the couple referred to as Steepletop. In 1927, Millay was arrested for protesting the conviction and planned execution of Nicola Sacco and Bartolomeo Vanzetti, two Italian immigrants convicted as anarchists. She wrote about her disillusionment with mankind in her next volume of poems, *The Buck in the Snow, and Other Poems*, published in 1928. Although many of her poems after this period were focused on her involvement with political activism, many more were centered on love, the subject of her 1931 collection, *Fatal Interview, Sonnets. Wine from These Grapes* was published in 1934. The manuscript for Millay's next collection of poetry, *Conversation at Midnight*, was destroyed in a hotel fire, and Millay was forced to try and reconstruct the poems from memory. Shortly after the 1936 publication of *Conversation at Midnight*, Millay was seriously injured in an automobile accident. Repeated surgeries and an addiction to pain drugs continued to affect Millay's health for the rest of her life.

Although Millay had begun the 1930s as a pacifist, Hitler's march across Europe in the late 1930s and the Japanese attack on Pearl Harbor changed her views about war. During World War II, she wrote propaganda for the Writers' War Board. Millay continued to write poetry for the rest of her life, publishing several more collections of poems, including *Huntsman, What Quarry? Poems* (1939) and *Mine the Harvest*, published in 1954 after her death. Millay's husband died in 1949. On October 19, 1950, Millay's body was discovered by a handyman. Millay was lying at the foot of the stairs, at her home at Steepletop. Although some news reports cited her death as caused by a heart attack, other reports claimed that Millay died from a fall down the stairs. In a 2001 biography, *Savage Beauty: The Life of Edna St. Vincent Millay*, author Nancy Mitford includes a 1975 letter from Millay's doctor, in which he claims that Millay died from a fall down the stairs, breaking her neck.

POEM TEXT

> What lips my lips have kissed, and where, and
>   why,
> I have forgotten, and what arms have lain
> Under my head till morning; but the rain
> Is full of ghosts tonight, that tap and sigh
> Upon the glass and listen for reply,   5
> And in my heart there stirs a quiet pain
> For unremembered lads that not again
> Will turn to me at midnight with a cry.
> Thus in winter stands the lonely tree,
> Nor knows what birds have vanished one by one, 10
> Yet knows its boughs more silent than before:
> I cannot say what loves have come and gone,
> I only know that summer sang in me
> A little while, that in me sings no more.

POEM SUMMARY

The text used for this summary is from *Collected Poems*, Harper and Brothers, 1956, p. 602. A version of the poem can be found on the following web page: http://www.poemhunter.com/poem/what-lips-my-lips-have-kissed-and-where-and-why/.

MEDIA ADAPTATIONS

- *A Lovely Light* is an LP recording of the 1960 original Hudson Theatre performance of Dorothy Stickney reading several of Millay's poems. The recording is by Vanguard.

- *Edna St. Vincent Millay Reading Her Poetry* was released in 1961 and then rereleased in 1986 by Harper Audio. There is no information about when the original recording was created.

- *The Voice of the Poet: Five American Women: Gertrude Stein, Edna St. Vincent Millay, H.D., Louise Bogan, & Muriel Rukeyser* is a collection of audio cassettes of the poets reading some of their own work. Each of the audio cassettes also includes a matching book of poems. The actual dates of these recording are unknown, but Random House released the current edition in 2001.

- *Edna St. Vincent Millay: Journey through Life* is a 2001 video tribute by Monterey Video, in which several celebrities read Millay's poetry.

- *Millay at Steepletop* is a 2002 video tribute to Millay. This video, which was directed by Kevin Brownlow and filmed by Milestone Video, includes footage of Millay reading her poems, interviews with family and friends, and images of her home.

Lines 1 and 2

The first line of "What Lips My Lips Have Kissed" includes the title of the poem but also adds the interrogative words *where* and *why*. Although these words are most often used to ask direct questions, in this case, Millay appears to be asking a purely rhetorical question for which she offers no answer. Nor does she expect an answer to be forthcoming from the reader. Unlike a journalist who might use these interrogatives to probe for the complete story, the first line of Millay's poem appears to be more indicative of a reminiscence than a true desire to discover any answers. The poet's use of inter-rogative words makes clear that the kisses were all in the past, perhaps even the distant past. The implication is that there have been multiple lips that have kissed her, but because she does not recall names, there is no threat that the poet will divulge anyone's identity.

The first part of the second line of the poem is a continuation of the first line and completes the poet's thought process as she explains that she has forgotten the source of the kisses admitted to in the first line of the poem. The poet admits to having forgotten the details of when and under what circumstances she was kissed, and thus, it is not only the kisses that she no longer recalls but the details. The reader is left to wonder whether the number of lips are countless or whether the melancholy nature of the moment reflects disinter-est in the actual details. The second line continues with a structure identical to the first line. The poet now addresses arms instead of lips, but the thought process is the same. The use of *what* instead of *whose*, which is more commonly used to refer to something belonging to another person, suggests a distancing from the events. To use *whose* would suggest a fondness for the memory, but the use of *what* to describe the arms the poet has known makes the events further removed and less significant.

Lines 3 and 4
The first part of the third line of "What Lips My Lips Have Kissed" continues the memories begun in line 2. The arms the poet recalls have encircled her as she slept. Her head has rested on those arms, which suggests an intimacy and closeness, but those nights are in the past. Instead the tone shifts after the semicolon, with the inclusion of *but*, a conjunction that warns readers that there is an exception to what came before. The first two and a half lines have revealed the past, which the poet wants readers to believe is insignificant. As the third line con-tinues, the use of *but* serves to contradict the tone established in the earlier lines: the poet's mood has shifted from vague reminiscences to remem-bering a past that is not so easily shaken away. Rain suggests sadness and even despair at what has been lost.

Line 4 finally provides some of the answers that the first three lines of poem have only sug-gested. The gloom of the rain has resurrected the ghosts of the past. The lips and arms of the previous lines are not disembodied things; they are the lips and arms of past lovers, who fill the poet's thoughts with reminders of the past. Ghosts are spirits that only recall the reality that once was. They represent a fleeting memory, but the longing that they reflect for the past is their primary function in Millay's poem. The rain and the poet's loneliness have brought the ghosts forth. As the rain taps against the win-dows, perhaps the wind blows, seeming like a sigh of longing to the poet, who lingers in the memories of the past.

Lines 5 and 6
The fifth line continues the thought at the end of line 4. The ghosts of the past mingle with the rain to demand the poet's attention. As the poet lis-tens to the tapping of the rain on the glass, the insistence of the sound seems to require a response. There is a sadness or melancholy in the poet's words because the ghosts of the past are waiting for her to reply. Although the poet is sad that the ghosts are from the past, there is no shame or regret in her words. There is only sad-ness that she has no reply to their tapping.

It is in line 6 that the poet finally articulates what has been obvious in the first five lines of the poem. She feels some pain that love is in the past. The pain is in her heart, the repository for romantic love. She misses those loves from her past. The poet does not weep or express anguish or the pain of deep loss. Instead, the pain is a quiet one, the regret not that she loved but that love has now gone.

Lines 7 and 8
In line 7, the poet again reiterates the ideas expressed in lines 1 and 2. The lips, kisses, and arms are those of young men whom she no lon-ger recalls with clarity. She uses the word *lads*, which implies youth. She does not recall them individually but as a grouping of undetermined number. They are in the past, as the poet makes clear in the last two words of line 7. These young men will not return to her again.

In line 8, the poet notes a particular time that is now one of loneliness. It is midnight. In the past, she was not alone at this time, but now she remembers a time when young lads shared her life. Millay wrote "What Lips My Lips Have Kissed" only two years after the Great War, as World War I was called at that time. Many young men died in the war—many young lads who might have been a part of Millay's life before 1917, before the war called them all away. The death toll increased with the flu epidemic of 1918, when 43,000 troops died after the war ended. When Millay writes of the young lads, who are now ghosts of the past, she might also be referring to the many young lads who have died. These are also the ghosts of the past, who tap on the poet's window.

Line 8 concludes the octave of the poem. Traditionally in sonnets, the octave presents a query or problem that the poet is experiencing. The octave of "What Lips My Lips Have Kissed" looks to the past, when the poet was not alone, when young lads shared her life, when opportunities abounded for love, and when she need only reach out to find willing lips to kiss and arms to embrace her.

Lines 9 and 10

The shift in line 9 of "What Lips My Lips Have Kissed" is to the sestet, the final six lines of the poem. In these lines, the poet hopes to find resolution or acceptance for the longing of a past now finished that permeates the octave of the poem. This line begins an analogy, in which the poet writes of a tree that stands alone in the cold of winter. The poet is the tree. She is now lonely and misses the past when young lads circled around her. At one time, there were so many lads she did not need to recall their names or remember their faces. There was always another one to take the place of the one who had left. Now, as line 10 makes clear to readers, the young men are gone. If this winter in line 9 is the winter of her age, there will be no summer to follow and resurrect the poet's hope for the future.

Line 10 continues the analogy begun in line 9. The birds that have now abandoned the tree represent the young lads who are no longer in the poet's life. They have disappeared so slowly that as each slipped away, the poet did not notice, until, one day, all of them were gone. Her arms are now empty, and the loss of these loves has left an emptiness in her life.

Lines 11 and 12

In line 11, the symbolism of the lonely tree with its empty branches continues. The boughs are barren of leaves, because it is winter, but the branches are also empty of the birds, who, during summer, found solace and rest on its branches. As before, the poet is

the tree with arms now empty. Her life is similarly quiet in its emptiness. Where before there was gaiety and love in her life, there is now only silence, which is occasionally broken by the rain and the sighs of the ghosts from her past. Although there is regret in this remembrance of the past, there is no evidence that the poet is deeply unhappy or that the present silence of her life is not of her choice.

In line 12, the poet admits she no longer clearly remembers the loves who were once a part of her life and now are no longer in her life. Once again she refers to these loves as *what* and not *who*. This word choice allows her to maintain the distance that she requires to keep the memories in the past and to avert any loneliness. If she recalls these loves as individuals, as a *who* with a name and a face, the loss of love becomes more painful. In describing the loss of loves in the past, the use of *what* removes all reference to any individual or individuals.

Readers should not automatically assume that the poet's choice to use "loves" refers only to romantic love. The melancholy that pervades "What Lips My Lips Have Kissed" makes possible that the loneliness of the poet extends to all areas of her life and all those whom she loves and has loved. As the poem moves toward its conclusion, the emphasis shifts from lips that have kissed her, arms that have held her, and lads who have loved her. Now the love is more generic and without definition as romantic love. Love is missing—all love.

Lines 13 and 14

In the final two lines of "What Lips My Lips Have Kissed," the poet refers again to the seasons as representative of her life. In line 13, it was summer when she was loved and when she loved. This is when she heard the music of love, when her heart sang with the knowledge of love. As the poem moves into the final line, however, the poet makes clear that summer lasted only a brief time, as does youth. In the concluding line of the sonnet, line 14, summer and the love it represented no longer sing in her heart. All the love and song of her summer season is now memory.

These final two lines are also rich in analogy. Spring is youth, when love is new and tentative, but by summer, love reaches its maturity and is in full bloom. This is when the poet hears the strongest stirrings in her heart, when the music of love is at its loudest and cannot be ignored. As the summer season moves into fall, the lover's

TOPICS FOR FURTHER STUDY

- Millay's sonnet is written in the classic Petrarchan style, but when the Elizabethan poets adopted the sonnet form, they made changes to the sonnet to make it uniquely their own. Choose one of Shakespeare's love sonnets, perhaps sonnet 36 or 40, and write an analytical paper in which you compare Millay's sonnet to one of Shakespeare's. Discuss the sonnet form, the tone and word choice employed by each poet, and what each poet has to say about lost love. You should also consider if there are differences in the way that women and men discuss the loss of love.

- *Slow Dance Heart Break Blues*, by Arnold Adoff, is a collection of poetry for young adults. Adoff, who is African American, understands that love and heartbreak are not limited to adults or to any particular sex or race. Adoff's poem "Slow Dance Heart Break Blues" is about the effort to find love. Compare Adoff's poem on finding love with Millay's poem on losing love. After noting the similarities and differences, as well as any common elements in the two poems, prepare a multimedia presentation of the poems that you have chosen. Your presentation should include an oral component, in which you either download an audio of the poets reading their poems or, if that is not available, you or a classmate read the two poems aloud. Include several Power-Point slides in which you present what you have learned about these two poems and what you have learned about the kind of poetry these poets are writing.

- *In the Mood for Love* is a 2000 Chinese film with English subtitles. The film is about heartbreak and romantic longings. Watch this film and then compare the message in the film with what Millay is saying about the loss of love in "What Lips My Lips Have Kissed." Write an essay in which you compare these two messages and their respective formats—film and poem—and explain which format you think delivers the message more clearly and why.

- Spend some time looking through art books and select several illustrations that best represent Millay's poem. You might consider different images of love and heartbreak as topics. Compare the illustrations to "What Lips My Lips Have Kissed," noting both the similarities and the differences. Prepare an oral presentation that includes slides of the artwork that you have chosen, your comparisons, and what you think your classmates can learn by studying images that interpret lines of verse.

- Research the life of any one of the following twentieth century women poets who were contemporaries of Millay, such as H. D., Louise Bogan, Elinor Wylie, Vita Sackville-West, Stevie Smith, or Muriel Rukeyser. Write a research paper in which you discuss how this poet's life, her experiences, and her views are reflected in at least two of her poems.

- The best way to understand poetry is to read it aloud, and yet very few readers make an effort to read poetry aloud. Read Millay's poem aloud to yourself and then to an audience of friends or classmates. Ask one or two of your friends to read the poem aloud and listen to their voices, noting the inflections of tone. What do you discover about the poem in each of these readings? Consider whether the poem changes with these subsequent readings and what you learn about poetry, and prepare a reflection paper in which you discuss your observations.

movement away from the poet was so subtle that at first she did not notice. Like the birds of line 10, the young men began to leave, and her arms slowly emptied until no one was left to share her embrace. Finally it is winter, when her heart sings no more. When the sestet ends at line 14, it seems there is no satisfactory resolution. However, the poet ends the poem with an acknowledgment that love has ended. Winter brings stagnation and acceptance of what has been lost. Winter was inevitable, just as the loss of love was inevitable, when even a name or face cannot be recalled.

THEMES

Loss

"What Lips My Lips Have Kissed" is rich with themes of loss. The poet laments the loss of love. She no longer feels the lips that once kissed her or the arms that once held her. Now she sits alone, with only the rain tapping on the window to keep her company. Images of loss fill Millay's sonnet. She imagines the ghosts of line 4 sighing messages to her. Where once these lads were close enough to touch or to whisper a message of love, now there is only a suggestion of a sigh to fill the silence. Her heart is now empty of the love that once filled it, and now loss fills her heart with pain. Her heartbreak is real; the pain is quiet but still present. She need not screech or throw herself onto the floor to express the sense of loss. Her loss is bravely met, with only the quietest whisper of pain and not the loud laments of grief that might have been expected. Loss is suggested through images of rain on the window, bringing with it gloom and despair. Loss is imagined as a lonely tree in winter, abandoned by leaves and birds and barren of all that had previously made it feel glorious, beautiful, and strong. Now the tree is vulnerable in its loss, with nothing to protect it from the ravages of winter. This is what loss feels like and how it appears to the poet. Loss is images, sounds, and the passing of seasons. What remains is quiet pain and the sighs of those who are now lost.

Lost Generation

Although *Lost Generation* is a descriptive term often used to describe the literary writers of the World War I generation, such as Ernest Hemingway and F. Scott Fitzgerald, the term is also used to describe the young men and women who came of age during the decade of World War I. These young men and young women of the 1920s rejected the staidness and conformity of pre-war American life. Their ideas about sexual behavior, particularly for women, reflected the rejection of strict moral values that characterizes this generation. For Millay to admit in "What Lips My Lips Have Kissed" that she cannot count or remember the lips she has kissed or the arms that have embraced her is emblematic of the Lost Generation in the 1920s. In this sonnet, the poet rejects the values of the past, even though, in the poem's conclusion, she is alone. She recognizes a world that has changed and that continues to change. At its heart, the Lost Generation sought to reject the depression of war and of so many deaths with a frenzy of action, but as in Millay's sonnet, eventually the ghosts of what has been lost push their way back into the present.

Memory

The opening lines of "What Lips My Lips Have Kissed" recall the past. Millay's poem is rich in remembrance of a time that lives only in the past. Whether in the poet's youth or in a time before war when young lads were plentiful is never clearly established, but the poem relates a life no longer the same. In the poet's past, she loved many. There were many lips to kiss and many arms to hold her. There were so many that she cannot remember them, or perhaps she chooses not to remember them as individuals. What the poet does choose to remember is a feeling from a time when she was loved and not alone. The lips and arms are representative of a simpler time.

In 1920, when Millay was writing this poem, she was twenty-eight years old. She was not too old for love, and yet in this poem, the speaker remembers love as if looking back at it from a very great age, remembering a time when she was young, and lovers were plentiful, and there was no need to remember anyone's name. The poet writes of a time when the lads might be nameless or faceless because she was in great demand and they competed for her attention. That was a time before war, however. Now remembrances fill her heart with pain. At age twenty-eight, love may continue to be a part of her life for many years, and thus why the need to reminisce about times gone by? The world of her youth, before the war, is forever gone, and the innocence of the time has been lost. Thus in "What Lips My Lips Have Kissed," the poet chooses the remembrances of the past over the losses of the present.

The speaker tries to remember the passion of her past. (© ollyy | Shutterstock.com)

STYLE

Alliteration and Assonance

Alliteration is the repetition of consonant or vowel sounds in closely successive words. Assonance refers to a pattern of vowel sounds without any regard to consonants. While either alliteration or assonance might be connected to the end rhyme of a line, it often does not occur in that way, as in Millay's poem. In the first two lines of "What Lips My Lips Have Kissed," Millay provides examples of alliteration and assonance. In line 1, examples of alliteration include the *w* sound, which is repeated several times, as is the *l* sound. Line 2 includes multiple examples of repetition of *a* sounds. In many cases, the repetition of sounds creates a musical quality that is best appreciated when the poem is read aloud.

Imagery

In a very literal sense, imagery is the collection of images in a literary work. It is the representation of what the reader senses as he or she reads the poem. The pictures evoked when reading poetry are the images created through the poet's choice of words. To fully understand a poem, it is important to understand the images created by the poet, because imagery's function is to help the reader understand the meaning of a poem. Thus, imagery is not abstract but more concrete. The reader can easily imagine the rain tapping on the window because it is an experience that is familiar to readers. Millay uses imagery most effectively in line 10, when the image of the tree standing alone in winter recalls the isolation of winter. Trees are bereft of leaves during winter's chill. The imagery is one of loneliness, which fits the poet's remembrances of lost love.

Lyrical Poetry

Lyrical poetry describes poems that are strongly associated with emotion, imagination, and a song-like resonance, especially when associated with an individual speaker. Lyrical poetry emerged during the Archaic Age in ancient Greece. These poems were shorter than the previous narrative poetry of Homer or the didactic poetry of Hesiod. Because lyric poetry is so very individual and emotional in its content, it is, by its very nature, subjective. Lyrical poetry is also the most common form of poetry, especially because it encompasses many forms of poetry that share its attributes. Millay's poem combines many of the qualities of lyrical poetry, with its emphasis on love and loss and of a time now past.

Metaphor

A metaphor, which is also identified as an analogy, identifies objects or ideas within the poem with objects or ideas that are not mentioned within the poem. In a metaphor, one set of objects or ideas are presented in concrete form. For example, in "What Lips My Lips Have Kissed," the tree abandoned in the cold winter is meant to make the reader think of the poet, who is also alone. Winter can also be an analogy for advancing age and sometimes death, just as spring suggests new birth. In Millay's poem, winter is the time when romances have ended. She notes that, in summer, love was a song. It is common in poetry for the passing of seasons and references to seasons to be used as a metaphor or analogy for the passing of time.

Metaphor is also identified with symbolism. Symbolism is the use of one object to represent another. During the nineteenth century, American writers used symbolism as a way to infuse images of nature with ideas. In late–nineteenth-century France, writers used symbolism as a way to represent unique emotional responses, often in very complex ways. In Millay's poem, the birds of line 10 symbolize the people whom the poet once loved, whereas in line 11, the empty boughs symbolize the poet's arms, which are now empty.

Octave and Sestet

Technically, an octave refers to any eight-line stanza, but the term is most often applied to the Italian sonnet, with its division into two parts: the octave and the sestet. *Octave* is a synonym for *octet*, any grouping of eight. In the traditional sonnet, the octave states an issue or a problem that is then resolved in the sestet. The sestet is the final six lines of a sonnet. The sestet provides the solution or resolution to the problem that was set forth in the octave.

Petrarchan Sonnet

The Petrarchan sonnet originated in Italy during the fourteenth century and was later brought to England by Thomas Wyatt. Petrarchan sonnets were divided into an octave with a rhyme scheme of *abba abba* and a sestet with a rhyme scheme of *cdecde*. As originally created, sonnets were love poems that contained exaggerated descriptions of a woman's beauty, the lady's coldness, and the speaker's abject suffering. The writing of these sonnets was very popular in Elizabethan England. Poets wrote these exaggerated love poems in what was really a game to see who could be the most clever and witty. The poems themselves ridicule courtly love, with its exaggerated idealism and often stylized and artificial requirements. Poets like John Donne would later use the sonnet form to praise God through religious imagery, while John Milton, who was blind, used the sonnet to question why God had taken his sight. Millay uses the traditional Petrarchan sonnet form in "What Lips My Lips Have Kissed," with no alteration of rhyme scheme.

Tenor and Vehicle

Tenor and vehicle are terms used by I. A. Richards, a twentieth-century literary critic, to describe the two parts of a metaphor. The tenor is the subject, and the vehicle is the object used for comparison. It is necessary for a metaphor to have both a tenor and a vehicle. If both are not present, then no metaphor exists, and the sentence is just a sentence. A vehicle makes the tenor, an idea that might be obscure, clear to the reader. In "What Lips My Lips Have Kissed," the lonely tree of line 9 is the vehicle. Readers can visualize a tree standing alone. The tenor is the less visible idea—the poet, who is now alone.

HISTORICAL CONTEXT

Post–World War Society

In mid-1920, one of the first big social and cultural changes of the decade was printed on the fashion pages of the leading newspapers. The fashion news that was considered so scandalous was that women's skirts were now at least nine inches off the ground; for the first time, women were showing their ankles. Over the next few months, skirt lengths continued their rise. Soon women were wearing thin shapeless dresses that stopped well above the woman's shin-bone. Women were no longer strapped in by corsets. Suddenly the softness of a woman's body was available to be touched. Women were also wearing cosmetics and cutting their hair and letting it flow loosely. The new hairstyles and clothing were easier to maintain. Women were also dancing, and it was not the ladylike waltz that had been considered so proper for young ladies

COMPARE
&
CONTRAST

- **1920s:** In the United States, women finally have the right to vote. The Nineteenth Amendment to the Constitution was approved on the August 26, 1920. It took more than seventy years of hard work, beginning with a women's rights convention in 1848, for women to finally achieve this right.

  Today: The bitter and lengthy fight for the right to vote seems far removed for women today, many of whom never bother to vote. In many elections, women neglect the opportunity that voting offers and fail to recognize the fight that took place over securing this basic right. For instance, in the 2008 presidential race, only 65.7 percent of eligible female voters chose to vote.

- **1920s:** By 1922, the flapper girl has changed the image of women. A woman can smoke and drink in public, wear lipstick, and wear short skirts. She no longer has to cover her body from neck to toes. Sexual freedom for women is also a part of this movement, although the double standard that condemns women's sexuality remains in effect.

  Today: Women today show even more of their bodies in public, and there is no hesitancy about smoking and drinking or wearing cosmetics. Women feel free to express their individuality in whatever way they choose.

- **1920s:** T. S. Eliot publishes *The Waste Land* in October 1922. Eliot's long poem moves poetry in a new direction, incorporating a variety of poetic forms, languages, and references to older works. His poem also captures the despair of World War I and provides a counterpoint to the recklessness that otherwise grips the early 1920s.

  Today: Today, poetry is less regimented by formulas and is more individualistic. Eliot's poem, now largely relegated to classroom study, no longer seems so shocking in retrospect, unless it is studied within the context of its historical importance.

- **1920s:** US casualties during World War I are just over 116,500. An estimated 43,000 additional deaths of US soldiers are attributed to the Spanish flu epidemic of 1918.

  Today: US casualties during the Iraq and Afghanistan wars are just over 6,600. Access to daily casualty numbers via television and online media brings these numbers more vividly into our homes. As a result, support for the war in Afghanistan is steadily dropping.

---

in the past. In these dances, women were pressed close to their partners, and no stiff corset separated them. Moreover, young women were smoking in public and drinking, although the latter occurred somewhat more privately. Prohibition, after all, had outlawed drinking.

All of this youthful rebellion by young women did not go unnoticed. There were attempts to curtail women's freedom and return them to the old days of repression. Religious journals denounced the new kind of freer dancing as too carnal, and parents were lectured from religious pulpits to better control their children, especially their daughters. Still more opposition

to women's freedom came from leading society women, who proposed that a society be created to monitor women's clothing styles. Across the United States, local clergymen were asked to submit their ideas for the proper dress of women. In several states, bills were proposed that would make wearing skirts more than three inches above the ankle a crime; in one state even two inches above the ankle would be illegal. Bills were also introduced that would make the exposure of more than three inches of a woman's throat a crime.

The changes in women's clothing and behavior signaled huge changes in society.

Women were demanding more independence—not just from corsets but from antiquated rules that repressed and defined women as chaste and pure and as destined only for marriage and motherhood. Millay, who embraced this lifestyle during the 1920s, was well known for her bohemian lifestyle and for her willingness to embrace the changes in society that allowed women greater freedoms.

Cultural Changes

The early 1920s were a period of clashing ideals and traditions, of contradictions and sometimes frightening possibilities. The end of the terrible war, World War I, resulted in a *carpe diem* attitude, a view of the world that reflected a new awareness that life could end very quickly and therefore ought to be enjoyed in the moment. The loss of life from the war, followed by the flu epidemic of 1918, left many people frightened and unsure about the future. Many people just wanted to be happy and have fun after this terrible period in history.

At the same time, a series of social upheavals brought real change to American life. Women won the right to vote in 1920, after a fight of seventy-two years. Although some women voted as the men in their lives instructed, winning the vote allowed some women to believe that they were equal to men. In addition, there were other changes afoot that would set women free from the household duties that consumed their time. Apartments were being built; families were moving into these apartments, and the smaller apartments did not require as much work to keep clean. The sale of canned and convenience foods was growing, and as a result, much of the drudgery of cooking was eliminated. Bakeries opened, as did commercial laundries. There were washing machines and irons to aid with cleaning, and many houses had telephones and radios. It was easier to keep in touch with the outside world.

There were also other new technological advances that permeated people's lives. Many of these new inventions expanded people's lives far beyond the narrow surroundings that had been so familiar. Automobiles became more affordable, making independent transportation available to many people, who now used the car to journey beyond their towns. In the past, most people lived and died within only a few miles of their birthplace. The more widespread use of cars meant that people could begin to explore and experience different ways of life. The new

Feeling lifeless, the speaker compares herself to a bare winter tree. (© KR MEDIA Productions / Shutterstock.com)

and fledgling film industry brought images of this new world into towns across the United States and helped to spread the word that the world was changing.

CRITICAL OVERVIEW

By the time Millay's sonnet "What Lips My Lips Have Kissed" was published in 1923, the author was already a well-known and popular poet. The same year, she became the first woman to win a Pulitzer Prize for verse, for *The Harp-Weaver and Other Poems*. By then, Millay's books were selling well, and she was making money writing poetry and short stories. "What Lips My Lips Have Kissed" is rarely mentioned by name in reviews of Millay's work. Most reviewers of *The Harp-Weaver and Other Poems* focus on the "The Ballad of the Harp-Weaver," which is generally considered the centerpiece of the collection. In a review of this collection that appeared in the *New York Times*, critic Percy A. Hutchison claims that "Millay is a natural born lyricist," whose sonnets might best be compared to the great Elizabethan poets, whose "sonneteering was a graceful art." After comparing Millay to Shakespeare, Hutchison argues that Millay is the first woman poet to achieve success in the same way as the great Irish poets, whose poetry achieves a "detachment of the poet from his theme," which Hutchison believed was something only the great male poets had been able to achieve.

Millay's poetry continued to be recognized in the years following the publication of *The Harp-Weaver and Other Poems*. Ten years later, Philip Blair Rice's review of *Wine from These Grapes* for the *Nation* is typical. Rice begins by noting that this newest collection of poetry, the first in three years, shows evidence that Millay has matured as a poet. Rice notes that "there is evidence of a remarkable transformation, of a growth not only toward intellectual maturity but also toward poetic integrity." When Millay died in 1950, the *New York Times* announced her death and recalled her appeal during the three decades of her career, calling her "one of the greatest American poets of her time." Although Millay died at the end of those three decades of fame, there is no reason to think her less relevant today. Many of her poetry collections have been reissued in recent years, including two collections in 2010: *Millay: Poems* (Everyman's Library) and *Poetry for Young People: Edna St. Vincent Millay* (Sterling).

CRITICISM

Sheri Karmiol

Karmiol teaches literature and drama at the University of New Mexico, where she is a term professor in the honors college. In the following essay, she discusses "What Lips My Lips Have Kissed" as a modern feminist version of the male-dominated Petrarchan sonnet.

Petrarch's *Canzoniere*, a collection of love poems, was written over a period of forty years and, once published, quickly became popular outside of Italy. Traditionally, the Petrarchan sonnet was a male literary vehicle to express love, the fleeting nature of time, and a desire for love in the face of heartbreaking rejection. For six hundred years, the Petrarchan sonnet

WHAT DO I READ NEXT?

- *Collected Poems* (1956) is a selection of poems taken from each of Millay's published poetry collections and published together by her sister after Millay's death.

- Nancy Mitford's 2002 biography of Millay, *Savage Beauty: The Life of Edna St. Vincent Millay*, is a thoroughly researched biography of the poet.

- *Millay at 100: A Critical Reappraisal* (1995), by Diane Freedman, is a collection of twelve essays that reassess Millay's work and her legacy.

- *Selected Poems* (2006), edited by J. D. McClatchy, is the first book to be published in the Library of America's American Poets Project. The poems included in this book were selected as representative of Millay's use of different poetic forms and themes.

- *Poetry for Young People: Edna St. Vincent Millay* (1999), edited by Frances Schoonmaker and beautifully illustrated by Mike Bryce, is designed for children ages nine to twelve but is a good introduction to her work for any reader.

- *Unsettling America: An Anthology of Contemporary Multicultural Poetry* (1994), edited by Maria Gazette Gillan and Jennifer Gillan, is a collection of poetry that explores inequity, discrimination, and social injustice. This multicultural view of injustice pairs well with Millay's later poems, such as *Wine from These Grapes*, and her calls for social activism.

- To examine the work of a male poet from the same period, W. H. Auden's *Selected Poems* (2007), edited by Edward Mendelson, provides readers with works written by one of the most important poets of Millay's time.

belonged to the male sonneteers, who used it as a way to affirm their masculinity and to express their desire for the unattainable woman and

MILLAY ADOPTS A GENRE THAT IS
ESSENTIALLY MALE IN ITS ORIGIN AND APPLICATION,
REPLACES THE MALE SUBJECT WITH THE FEMALE,
AND USES THE PETRARCHAN SONNET TO REVEAL A
WOMAN'S EXPERIENCES IN LOVE."

their control over the sonnet form. That is not to
say there were no women who appropriated the
sonnet for their own use, but the few woman
who adopted that genre did so by adapting the
sonnet to discuss topics other than love and
desire, replacing those male subjects with religious fervor and death.

Only a few women ventured forth to use the
sonnet to discuss love and romance, and most
women writers were circumspect in avoiding any
topic that might violate the social or mannered
rules of their world. That careful approach to the
Petrarch sonnet changed in the early twentieth
century, when Edna St. Vincent Millay became
the first modern woman poet to turn to the classical Petrarchan form to discuss a very modern
view on love. She was not afraid to use the female
voice to talk about love and feminine desire.
Millay adopts a genre that is essentially male in
its origin and application, replaces the male subject with the female, and uses the Petrarchan sonnet to reveal a woman's experiences in love.

The Petrarchan sonnet is the perfect vehicle to
express the pain of lost love. When Petrarch
adopted the sonnet in fourteenth-century Italy, he
did so as a way to express feelings of unattainable
love and the pain of heartbreak. The formula was
initially rigid, with conventions of courtly love that
followed a formula, both in rhyme and in content.
The cold, unattainable woman, who easily rejects
her lover, causing him untold pain, was a staple of
this sonnet. When the Petrarchan sonnet made its
way to England in the early sixteenth century, the
rhyme scheme was altered and became less rigid,
and the content shifted to include a variety of
different topics, although love and heartbreak continued to be staples of the genre. In England, the
Petrarchan rhyme scheme of *abbaabba cdecde*
became the English rhyme scheme of *abab cdcd
efef gg*, although variations of both forms were,

and continue to be, very common. For the most
part, by the end of the sixteen century, the Petrarchan sonnet and the English sonnet had become
favored genres of poetry. One thing that did not
change, however, was that whether the sonnet was
Petrarchan or English, the form continued to be an
essentially male-dominated expression of love and
romantic desire.

In England, the Petrarchan sonnets became
the means by which the courier poets might
praise their unmarried Queen Elizabeth but
also adopt a seize-the-day kind of mentality
that might be useful in seducing women. The
object of the poet's desire needed to be chaste
or, if not, at least appear unavailable to justify
the effort made in creating the sonnet. She also
needed to be silent. The voice of the sonneteer
was the only voice that was present. In *Desire
and Gender in the Sonnet Tradition*, Natasha Distiller argues that the English adopters of the
Petrarchan sonnet used the sonnet as a kind of
performance. Sonnets were passed around the
English royal court, and the poets and speakers
made themselves visible in the court via the performance of their poems. Sonnet writing conveyed a kind of notoriety that male writers
enjoyed exclusively. Women did not use this
format to talk about love and desire, which was
strictly a male venue of discussion. The subject
of the poem, then, was the male poet's desire to
possess the woman he admired. This might have
been the rule for the Elizabethan poets, and not
much changed in the centuries that followed.
Although there were no rules that prevented
women poets from adopting this genre, few
women did so. This notion of Petrarchan desire
as a strictly male venue was not something that
inhibited Millay, who felt no such restriction in
writing her sonnets, as is clear in "What Lips My
Lips Have Kissed."

The octave in Millay's sonnet "What Lips
My Lips Have Kissed" is filled with undefined
images of those whom she has loved. Rather
than describing one unattainable lover as the
male Petrarchan writer might do, Millay's
speaker describes numbers too great to tally or
to remember. The focus of the octave is on the
poet herself. She uses the personal pronoun *I* to
make clear that the content of these opening
lines is about the speaker. The poet describes
disembodied lips that have kissed her and arms
that have embraced her. These loves from her
past are all ghostly memories now. They are

sighs transformed into memories, who, in tapping on her window, hope to be admitted. These sighs also nudge at her mind, stirring memories of a past when she chose not to be alone. These loves from her past are unremarkable in her mind. They have no names, nor do images of their faces stir memories in her.

As in the traditional Petrarchan sonnet, Millay's octave focuses on love that is out of reach. The lips and arms are gone, but there is no evidence in this sonnet that the speaker is a rejected lover. Was it the poet who initially rejected love? Readers cannot know and the poet divulges none of the history, except that she once experienced love and is now alone. The poet listens to the rain, a common symbol of despair and isolation, but her mind is filled with rich memories of when she was not alone. As Millay turns to the sestet, the tone also shifts. Rather than undefined images of lips, arms, and ghosts all mingling with the rain, the images become more concrete. The poet no longer uses *I* to describe what is happening. Instead, the poet describes herself using a metaphor. Although the metaphor creates distance from the speaker, there is no doubt that the speaker is the one standing alone. The lonely tree standing in winter, stripped of leaves and of the merry chirping of summer birds, captures the image of the Petrarchan lover, who ends his poem alone and unloved. The question to be pondered is: are these the thoughts and words of a rejected lover, or are they a play on convention?

Stacy Carson Hubbard examines Millay's love poetry in her essay "Love's 'Little Day,'" a phrase taken from one of Millay's sonnets "I Shall Forget You Presently, My Dear," in which Millay warns that she will soon reject and forget the man in her life. Hubbard points out that although Millay adopts the traditional form of the Petrarchan sonnet, she does so to undermine those same forms, as she does in this poem when she assures the man that she will soon forget all about him. Hubbard cites the "mannered literariness of Millay's poems" as a form of rebellion against the established male-dominated format. Rather than imitating the Petrarchan sonnet, Hubbard wonders if Millay is "rethinking poetic gender as an imitative practice and parody as one available response of the woman poet to a tradition predicated upon her silence." Millay rejects the Petrarchan role for women as the silent object of desire and instead writes as a woman of her own desire and romantic yearnings.

Thus in "What Lips My Lips Have Kissed," readers should not envision the poet as a lonely tree, abandoned and alone. Rather than "a prototype of abandoned womanhood, pathetic and powerless," Hubbard positions Millay as a strong woman who stands alone after she pushes away the many unnamed and unremembered lads. Although the birds who once rested on the boughs of the tree have moved away one by one, they have not fled because they rejected the woman. They are simply gone and little remembered except for their disembodied lips and arms, too numerous to recall. Hubbard concludes that "the speaker of Millay's sonnets attempts to outlive the seductive voices of those Renaissance lovers whose invitations were always to silence." Rather than remain the silent female object of the Petrarchan sonnet, Millay, instead, makes herself the speaker and the controlling subject of her own story.

Although Millay's sonnet ends with the loss of love and the poet alone, how she arrives at that place is vastly different than the experience of the Elizabethan Petrarchan poet, who ends up alone because he never achieves his desire. The Petrarchan poet is focused on seducing a woman, but the poem is always about the attempt—not his success. Distiller suggests that, although Lady Mary Wroth, in the early seventeenth century, and Elizabeth Barrett Browning, in the nineteenth century, used the Petrarchan sonnet to write about love, both were careful to remain within the proscribed rules of social convention. In contrast, Millay rejects the social and cultural pressures that confined those earlier women poets and is able to confront convention and rewrite the rules for the sonneteer. According to Distiller, Millay's "poetry suggests in more profound ways than Petrarchism previously had been able to suggest, that desire, once achieved, will always die, and that the subject of desire will die along with it." Whereas, in Petrarch, the woman dies and the male writer mourns, Millay's speaker lives, having succeeded in seducing the objects of her desire. In writing about Millay's sonnets, Distiller claims that "what makes her passionate and obstinate and ultimately revolutionary, is her commitment to remaining the speaking subject." The lonely tree may be intended to symbolize the speaker, but the memories she has accumulated suggest a past that was anything but lonely.

Although Millay found Petrarch useful as a model for her sonnet "What Lips My Lips Have

Though she no longer remembers the details, the speaker can still recall her feelings, like the warmth of summer inside her. (© Dudarev Mikhail / Shutterstock.com)

Kissed," she proves herself adept at challenging the traditional and making it her own. "What Lips My Lips Have Kissed" is a more intimate look at love than that provided by Petrarch and his fellow male poets. In Millay's sonnet, the admiring distance between lovers and the rote formula are replaced by the emotions of love lost and memories of love, as experienced through physical contact. It would be easy to ascribe the difference as simply reflective of six hundred years of change, but it is just as easy to point to Millay as a radical poet who takes Petrarch's example, remakes his sonnet, and then chooses to allow the reader to share the female poet's experience.

Source: Sheri Karmiol, Critical Essay on "What Lips My Lips Have Kissed," in *Poetry for Students*, Gale, Cengage Learning, 2014.

Suzanne Clark

In the following excerpt, Clark discusses how Millay used traditional poetic forms to make her own revolutionary statement.

Writing sonnets in the era of high modernism, popular though she was, Edna St. Vincent Millay courted oblivion. She has not, as it turns out, been forgotten. But as we remember her, I want to account for her endurance in terms that acknowledge, as she said: "Beauty is not enough" ("Spring"). I want to point out the difficult cultural work her poetry has done. The work of Millay impacts literary studies more unconsciously than most, if my experience is any marker. This is not because continuing interest exists only in the popular domain, outside the university. Academics across the country—male as well as female academics—can quote Millay for you when you walk past in the hall, at the drop of a hat, at the slightest mention that you might be working on her. What they quote probably depends on their generation, but the memorability of her lines persists. She is not forgotten; she is very much remembered, on the tip of so many tongues. But this is more like a memory of the body than of the mind, the repetition of a kind of unconscious evoked by her words, in the mnemonics of sound.

HER POEMS REQUIRE A DIFFERENT VIEW OF LITERATURE ALTOGETHER, AND OF LANGUAGE TOO, A VIEW OF LITERATURE THAT IS INTERESTED IN EXPLORING THE IMAGINATIVE POSSIBILITIES FOR DIFFERENT IDENTITIES OFFERED BY THE HETEROGENEITY OF LANGUAGE."

By speaking of the "uncanny," I mean to suggest the work of the unconscious, the ghostly reappearance analyzed by Freud, and the special functioning of women's fiction discussed by Hélène Cixous. Though the body of her work has made its ghostly reappearance, Millay was dismissed from the literary by a generation of critics. There were good reasons for keeping Millay's impact out of mind, because her work challenges the gendered identity assumed by the modernist aesthetic.

Millay criticized gender roles and sexuality explicitly, in defiant lines that made her notorious in 1923 and that once again delight feminist students today. "I, Being Born a Woman and Distressed" is a love sonnet that concludes: "I find this frenzy insufficient reason / For conversation when we meet again." The poem is made especially notable for this generation by being included in Sandra M. Gilbert and Susan Gubar's edition of the *Norton Anthology of Literature by Women* (1555–56). Millay also positioned herself firmly on the side of progressive politics, not only in her public life, but in poems like "Justice Denied in Massachusetts," on the Sacco-Vanzetti case. But such poems are not typical of her work; it cannot be said that most of her poetry thematizes a political feminism. I am interested, rather, in how she engages in a *poetic* politics as well. Within the modernist aesthetic, the speaker of a poem may be theatrical, figurative, and ironic without upsetting cultural assumptions about personal identity. The male poet (Wallace Stevens, for example) may write like a lady, but the rigorous separation of impersonal literary complexity from the reductiveness of ordinary life keeps the gender distinctions clear.

The modernist aesthetic separated literary language from ordinary language and, in particular, from the personal. Millay's poetry, however, does not acknowledge this separation of life from art. Modernist critics including Cleanth Brooks, Allan Tate, and John Crowe Ransom claimed that Millay's poetry was not only too susceptible to the conventional but also too easily overwhelmed by sensibility. Conversely, I wonder, doesn't Millay's poetry take the figurative, parodic—*conventional*—character of literary language and extend that rhetoricity to life, denaturalizing the personal? Her poems make visible through a theater of the personal how identity functions in culturally determined ways. If the social construction of male and female and the narrative of their sexual fates is produced by discourse, including literary discourse, this productivity is nevertheless hidden by the closure of identity. This cultural unconscious may therefore be exposed through doubling and parody—and, in Millay's case, in particular, masquerade. Literary techniques enable her to critique cultural ideology from inside its technology, at the level of producing subjects, that is, at the level of figuring through form certain possibilities for desire. In the displacement of the lyric subject from its singularity, Millay's poetry is "novelized," in Bakhtin's sense, moved away from the monologic.

Think about the performative context of Millay's work as America's best-known poetess. She would appear in a long gown for readings, her voice dramatic, her form girlish and attractive, more like a diva than like the gray-suited male poets. The self in her work is an actress performing, at once embodiment and interpretation. There is no separation of artist and person. She is neither inside nor outside the communal order because from inside she delineates the trying on of identities that might work a remedy to alienation at the same time that she denaturalizes this identity-making project and exposes its unconscious webbing as art. Masquerade functions as critique. Furthermore, allegorizing the forms of the imaginary, Millay tropes identity through personification, and the figures of personification define a specific poetics for her work. In other words, while the figure of masquerade may suggest a multiplicity of roles for a single person without really challenging the notion of a core identity, the figure of personification suggests that personhood itself is a trope. This is not to say that I see Millay in a new guise as a postmodern writer, because this play on the figures of identity takes place in the context of a historic body of language. The uncanny specters of a bardic tradition are evoked and embodied in this materiality of a voice. Or of a lyric *song*.

So Millay's poetry does not simply participate in the social construction of the personal, reinscribing love stories: her work troubles the process, sounding repetition in a new voice. Millay interrupts the closure of womanhood by her necessarily failed attempts to speak like a man, the equivalent on the level of sound of a cross-dressing. Without this kind of troublemaking, both the sounds of language and the familiarity of conventional stories and characters can work to reproduce and limit the possibilities for individual identity. Millay represents an unconscious that is at once of musicality and of cultural repetitions: a cultural unconscious. Millay's writing, even though it participates in the symbolic order, opens up a space for difference, for the uncanny return of the repressed, through disturbances of that order. She makes the traditional resources of a male literary tradition uncanny, strange. The resurrections of literary traditions inhering in forms like the sonnet, in figure and phrase, extend to influence the cultural politics that depend on their keeping their place.

A reader might assume that any repetition of traditional forms would serve a traditional or conservative purpose, at least at the level of the unconscious, but Millay mobilizes their power to her own ends. Literature, in Millay's work, is not kept separate from the political questions of gender. The ideology of the aesthetic, as Terry Eagleton argues, has provided for capitalism and the middle class a way to produce self-governing subjects. Millay's poetry reveals the way the ideology of the aesthetic works, through the imaginary, as a cultural unconscious that is exposed in the critical discomfort she provokes.

It is the masquerade of personal identity that distinguishes Millay from modernist poets. T. S. Eliot said, in "Tradition and the Individual Talent," that

> we shall often find that not only the best, but the most individual parts of [a poet's] work may be those in which the dead poets, his ancestors, assert their immortality most vigorously. And I do not mean the impressionable period of adolescence, but the period of full maturity.

Millay, too, writes with the sense of those poetic ancestors in her bones, and her style testifies to their influence. But Millay's poetry is not what Eliot had in mind. "The existing monuments form an ideal order among themselves, which is modified by the introduction of the new (the really new) work of art among them." Millay threatens to introduce something new

that unsettles the ideal order profoundly; she speaks among the poets as a woman.

Even though we encounter again and again in Millay the resurrected speech of dead poets, it is not with the effect of impersonality Eliot insisted upon. It is not in the form of an aesthetic influence, which leaves the person aside, intact. Rather, in Millay, the unassimilated speech of poetic history enters into an intertextuality that detaches the personal from its aura. Shortly, I will look closely at some examples of this—of appearances by Yeats and Ronsard in Millay's poems. Here what I want to make clear is how speaking as a woman while she speaks men's words might unsettle modernist impersonality. To retain the marker of gender is to resist that complete surrender of the ordinary embodied self that Eliot was advocating. Millay's poetry does not appear to practice "a continual self-sacrifice, a continual extinction of personality" ("Tradition and the Individual Talent" 7). The memorability of the poetic word involves effects of transference and identification that depend on personality. Poetry that mobilizes response like Millay's (the shared memories) discloses for us the uncanny powers that may account for the hold of ideology upon us and may offer a way to hold out *against* ideology.

Feminist criticism has often characterized its work as restoring the unconscious to consciousness, using writing to reorganize psychic space. In a related sense, Millay's poetry can be read as a restorative project that would propel the woman's uneasy figure into juxtaposition with the figure of the writer, shadowing the traditionally male-gendered creativity of the poet with another gender, another sexuality, another creativity. Millay's rhetoric of personification, her attentiveness to the question of Beauty, her violation of the modernist poem's autonomous objectivity raises a gendered poetic into view. When modernist critics such as John Crowe Ransom (of whom more later) called this a woman's poetic, however, they did not mean to be complimentary.

A ghostly body inhabits the poetry of Millay, a haunting image hovering between the fantasy and the impossible real, like poetry itself. It is the very figure of language and beauty, animated within the folded space of anamnesis or unforgetting where the past both is and is not recovered as the trace of embodied and sensuous experience. This figure invokes us as the subjects of the long book of literature, the realm where the apples are, Millay says, "half Baldwin, half Hesperides" ("To whom the house of Montagu was neighbor"). Readers, we are invited not to revere the poetic object but, as Millay writes in her sonnet to the feminist Inez Milholland, to "take up the song." The invitation to transference or identification makes a strong bond and opens literature out into the imaginary. The uncanny in Millay is the ghost of a cultural unconscious, the forgotten woman, but also the forgotten power of poetry. This imaginary power is forgotten by the most critical among us because it has seemed regressive, the mere slave of ideology—because identities have seemed to contemporary feminist and other critics either essentialist or fragmented and the politics of identity no question for poetry.

With the help of Millay, however, we can explore the role of literature in making identities and the difficult question of how the forgotten might use literary power. Because hers is not a narrowly aesthetic conception of literature, Millay dramatizes in both form and theme the way culture shapes individuals, what Teresa de Lauretis has characterized as the technology of subjects, beginning with herself. Does Millay know that she is problematizing the very idea of an identity by asserting the oxymoron of the woman poet? She seems to know that gender makes the cultural construction of selves as free, autonomous individuals questionable, that with gender we are plunged into the problem of the social, of empathy, of the love story, and of our entanglements with others, from mother to lover. What Millay may not know is that her challenge to the gendered identity of the poet might also problematize the very institution of literature as a separate aesthetic. As Cheryl Walker demonstrates, Millay cannot construct a space outside the commodification of culture, and indeed, by making the identity of the self the subject and the object of her poem, she enters that identity into the reifying forces of the culture around her.

The various appearances of a poetic avant-garde in the past two centuries have signaled a historical crisis in the personal and the literary alike. The school of Eliot, which led to the school of new criticism, tried to stabilize the crisis by insisting on separating the poem from the person. This formalist ideal of impersonal poetry had the virtue of calling attention to language, but at the cost of disavowing any connection between the situation of poems and of persons. The practice of an impersonal poetics kept the poetic/personal identity separate, away from the disruptive effects of an avant-garde discourse. Defamiliarization might call attention to literature without disrupting the family. The school of Eliot enlisted avant-garde poetics against a progressive politics, denying any rhetorical purpose for literature, denying especially that literature might have any connection with the way culture disciplines the body's emotions and desires.

Edna St. Vincent Millay's poems refuse to function within this aesthetic. Millay uses the traditional forms of poetry in a productive and radical challenge to the hierarchies of modernism. Millay's poems involve a different rhetorical situation for poetics, not based on self-contained symbols, but rather on figures—embodiments—that point outside themselves in an allegorical gesture. Millay's allegorical storytelling reproduces literature itself as a figure of reproduction. Her poems require a different view of literature altogether, and of language too, a view of literature that is interested in exploring the imaginative possibilities for different identities offered by the heterogeneity of language. There is an admitted doubleness to this productivity, an inevitable complicity with commodification and vulnerability to cultural definitions of self. Millay's work differs from the school of Eliot precisely because it does not deny the complicity of art with seduction or the way that beauty can betray. As Millay says: "Beauty is not enough."

If Millay was a public, contemporary figure who came to represent the new woman and who came to seem the voice of a rebellious generation, that image must be informed by how very seriously she took the historical and literary powers of language. This notion of literature as a public, not a private or separate art, contravened the dominant critical movement of her time. Are we, postmoderns, more receptive to such a sense of responsibility? Most especially, she challenged the critical agreements of the moderns not just by seeing herself as a public poet but by writing a poetry that moves the problem of female identity into the public domain. Though she used the leverage of all the history of literature, that very history carried with it the supposition of male authorship. Does Millay fully acknowledge the closure of poetry's high traditions against female authorship? . . .

Source: Suzanne Clark, "Uncanny Millay," in *Millay at 100: A Critical Reappraisal*, edited by Diane P. Freedman, Southern Illinois University Press, 1995, pp. 3–9.

Norman A. Brittin

In the following excerpt, Brittin describes Millay as a feminist.

. . . It is evident from her letters that Millay felt a sisterly solidarity with women. As Margaret Widdemer attested, "Edna Millay may have been temperamental, but she was never a woman who didn't want to bother with women's friendship. She had a great many women who were her devoted friends. . . . She was a loyal friend." In 1922 Millay wrote to Edmund Wilson that she had seen "a great deal of Anna Wickham" while in Paris during that spring, and had found her interesting, brilliant, and thrilling. "I like her tremendously." Millay knew Wickham's feminist poetry, which sprang from the tension between "modernity and maternity," for she was a "woman struggling between dreams and domesticity," as Louis Untermeyer wrote. It seems likely that Crystal Eastman, sister of Max Eastman, ardent feminist, militant suffragist, and leader of the Woman's Peace party in New York State, influenced Millay in the direction of feminism and pacifism during the Village years.

Millay was in the first generation of emancipated American women—"an embattled generation" which believed that "'advanced' women should complete their professional training and start careers before marrying at all." As for marriage, after Vassar and the success of her early poetry, she was determined to have a career as a poet; and so, in spite of the assiduous attentions of marriageable men in New York and the attraction that they held for her, she resisted marriage. It seems likely that the ending of Floyd Dell's story "The Kitten and the Masterpiece" is based on his relation with Millay; the heroine refuses the proposal of the hero although she is in love with him: ". . . I don't want to be your wife. I don't want to be anybody's wife. I want to write poetry. . . . That must come first always." On the other hand, various references in her letters, especially as she nears thirty, indicate that she would like to be married and is not reconciled to being an old maid.

Meanwhile, living in New York and in large European cities, Millay shared the urban anonymity that promoted women's freedom: having one's own apartment, smoking cigarettes, drinking cocktails, driving cars,

> IF SHE HAD BEEN BORN THIRTY-FIVE OR
> FORTY YEARS LATER, SHE WOULD CERTAINLY HAVE
> HELPED WOMEN OF THE PRESENT GENERATION IN
> THEIR FIGHT FOR WOMEN'S LIBERATION."

indulging in wild parties, jazz dancing, petting, and sexual freedom generally. All this individual independence she was able to take for granted, particularly after going to Greenwich Village. Floyd Dell, although he gradually became more traditional in his views, was an ardent believer in these new freedoms and in the comradeship of men and women. As a Socialist he favored the Woman Movement. The Village feminists favored socialism, reforms that would eliminate discrimination, allow all women to have labor-saving devices of the new technical society, and both "women and men to become whole human beings who might develop their full potential."

Dell wrote that Millay "was very much a revolutionary in all her sympathies, and a whole-hearted Feminist." He once gave her one of the bronze buttons awarded to women who were arrested for militant suffrage activities, and with tears in her eyes she said, "I would rather have the right to wear this than anything I can think of." Militant suffragists had been picketing the White House since 10 January 1917; but although Millay was a member of Alice Paul's National Woman's party, which pressed zealously for women's suffrage and, after the Nineteenth Amendment was passed, for an Equal Rights Amendment, Millay did not march or demonstrate. Having found her identity as a poet and being certain of her feminist values, she was more concerned to assert her individuality, her right to have a career, unfettered by husband or children, and to do whatever she pleased, unobstructed by outworn conventions and traditional taboos. In her writing and in her life she represented what is "generally spoken of as the revolution in morals of the 1920's" but "is more accurately a revolution in the position of women." Thus, *A Few Figs from Thistles* and other "daring" poems boldly voiced convictions about women and their equality with men that were close to the heart of Greenwich Village.

In Village fiction women scoffed at men for believing in "the mystery and beauty of love and the ethereal qualities of women"; in contrast to the male sentimentalists, the women "talked hardheadedly of the transitory features of life and love." This hardheaded attitude is expressed in such sonnets of Millay's as "I shall forget you presently, my dear," and "Only until this cigarette is ended" (*CP*, 571, 575) as well as in "Thursday" and "To the Not Impossible Him" from *Figs* (*CP*, 129–30), and is implied in "Passer Mortuus Est" (*CP*, 75). Her devotion to her poetic career, which she values more than "the puny fever and frail sweat / Of human love," is strongly asserted in the Pieria sonnet (*CP*, 583). The honesty of the feminist in love affairs, "free from guile," bringing "love in the open hand," and proud that she had not "played you slyly," is expressed in several sonnets of *Fatal Interview* (*CP*, 632, 640, 676). The speaker in that poem is a proudly independent new woman.

But poems in the *Harp-Weaver* volume particularly reveal the contemporary independent woman, for example, the dramatic monologue "The Concert": "No, I will go alone. / I will come back when it's over. / Yes, of course I love you. / No, it will not be long" (*CP*, 186). The speaker, who idealizes music, is explaining to her jealous, possessive lover her preference for attending a concert alone; she can be absorbed in the great art, with which the "you and I" would interfere; the impersonal beauty of music is something greater than the "filigree frame" of their love, and it will make her "a little taller" than before. Though the lover in Sonnet I (*CP*, 584) is "dearer than words on paper"—for a poet, the extreme admission—she anticipates the time when she will again possess the key of her heart. In the next sonnet, the woman, made to eat the "bitter crust" of unrequited love, declares: "But if I suffer, it is my own affair." The situation and the attitude of the intelligent woman who expects to be treated as an equal by men are illustrated by Sonnet 8: "Oh, oh, you will be sorry for that word! / Give back my book and take my kiss instead. / Was it my enemy or my friend I heard, / What a big book for such a little head!" (*CP*, 591). The superior woman's disappointment, her exasperation at being patronized, and her contempt for being thrust (automatically) back into her merely physical role are expressed in "Oh, I shall love you still, and all of that. / I never again shall tell you what I think." She can condescend to conceal herself in conventional femininity but at the sad expense of losing comradely frankness: "I shall be sweet and crafty, soft and sly; / You will not catch me reading any more...." But, finally, she anticipates "some sane day" when "I shall be gone, and you may whistle for me." As we have seen in Chapter 3, Millay's feminism is also manifested from time to time in her short stories.

Several incidents in Millay's life exhibit her adherence to feminist principles. She went to Washington with members of the National Woman's party for a ceremony honoring early suffragists, and on 18 November 1923—introduced by her friend Doris Stevens, whose book *Jailed for Freedom* (1920) had exposed the illegal and brutal imprisonment of the White House picketers—the "foremost woman poet of America, stirred the audience with a poem she had written for the occasion, and was called back to read it for a second time," *Equal Rights* reported, printing both her sonnet "The Pioneer" and her picture. In her *Collected Sonnets* she retitled the poem "To Inez Milholland"—a gracious tribute by Eugen Boissevain's second wife to his first: "I, that was proud and valiant, am no more;—/ Save as a dream that wanders wide and late . . ." (*CP*, 627). More significant in 1923 was the call to further action: "Only my standard on a taken hill / Can cheat the mildew...." Since Millay was listed (19 April 1924) as an associate editor of *Equal Rights*, she certainly approved of the drive for an Equal Rights Amendment, although many women, especially social workers, felt that the Woman's party was only for business and professional women because women workers on wages needed protective legislation.

Probably mixed feminism and Bohemianism caused Millay on 18 April 1927 to send Elinor Wylie an expostulation to be forwarded to the League of American Penwomen. She was protesting their "recent gross and shocking insolence to one of the most distinguished writers of our time":

> It is not in the power of an organization which has insulted Elinor Wylie, to honour me.
>
> And indeed I should find it unbecoming on my part, to sit as Guest of Honour in a gathering of writers, where honour is tendered not so much for the excellence of one's literary accomplishment as for the circumspection of one's personal life.
>
> Believe me, if the eminent object of your pusillanimous attack has not directed her movements in conformity with your timid philosophies, no more have I mine. I too am eligible for your disesteem. Strike me too from your lists....

Millay's devastatingly sharp letter was consistent with her scorn for respectability, more especially when it interfered with judgments of literary merit.

When the Boissevains visited the Fickes in New Mexico in the fall of 1926, and after the proofs of *The King's Henchman* had been read, Vincent and Gladys Brown Ficke went from Santa Fe to Zuni, expecting Eugen to join them two days later. Registering as Edna St. Vincent Millay, the poet took a hotel room with Gladys but asked the clerk to reserve a room for Mrs. Ficke, as Mr. Eugen Boissevain was coming to be with her. The clerk refused: hotel policy did not permit such an arrangement. Finally she told him Boissevain was her husband—"Don't you know famous women always use their own names?" Evidently her fame had not extended to the Zuni pueblo; evidently, too, Eugen was more likely to joke over being "Mr. Millay" than she was to change her name.

Millay was fortunate to marry a man who believed in women's rights and was, from the first, willing to subordinate himself to her career. Thus she never had to undergo the lacerating struggle that so many women have had to endure even during the last two decades in order to gain recognition from men of the authenticity and rightfulness of their aspirations to have careers, to achieve lives of their own, or even to emerge from thoughtlessly assumed domesticity.

But even a woman of her fame was not exempt from a slight which she felt as a humiliation because she was a woman. In a letter of 14 June 1937, her feminist principles flashed out as she protested to the Secretary of New York University over not being included among the male recipients of honorary degrees at a dinner given by Chancellor Harry Woodburn Chase.

> On an occasion, then, on which I shall be present solely for reasons of scholarship, I am, solely for reasons of sex, to be excluded from the company and the conversation of my fellow-doctors.

Mrs. Chase was including her at a dinner for ladies only.

> [But] Mrs. Chase should be the last, I think, to be offended by my attitude. I register this objection not for myself personally, but for all women....

> I beg of you, and of the eminent Council whose representative you are, that I may be the last woman so honoured, to be required to swallow from the very cup of this honour, the gall of this humiliation.

Chase had been a psychologist, but his specialty was obviously not the psychology of the new woman. Since for two decades women had not been excluded from clubs and meetings once for men only, Millay's exclusion from the chancellor's dinner—in cosmopolitan New York—must have seemed in 1937 like the action of moss-backed fuddy-duddies.

Millay was a person of great integrity; in any matter of principle she was willing to stand up and be counted. She did not make a career of promoting feminism; but throughout her life she adhered to feminist principles and repeatedly spoke out for the right of women to be judged on their merits as human beings and to be treated as human beings and not as members of an inferior group. If she had been born thirty-five or forty years later, she would certainly have helped women of the present generation in their fight for women's liberation. She long ago anticipated them in steadfast support of the feminist cause: "Take up the song; forget the epitaph" (*CP*, 627).

Source: Norman A. Brittin, "A Dream That Wanders Wide and Late," in *Edna St. Vincent Millay*, G. K. Hall, 1982, pp. 122–27.

Jane Stanbrough

In the following excerpt, Stanbrough contrasts Millay's confident and independent public image with the vulnerability seen in her poetry.

In 1917, when Edna St. Vincent Millay moved to Greenwich Village, her image as a woman of spirit and independence was already legendary. Previously, at Vassar, Millay had become a notorious public figure. She was a publishing poet, an impressive actress, and a dramatist of growing reputation. She had all along flaunted her independence impudently, smoking against the rules, cutting classes that were boring, earning a severe faculty reprimand which nearly deprived her of participation in her graduation ceremonies. This image of defiance was enhanced by her move to Greenwich Village, known as a hotbed of free-thinking radicals, and by her publication of five poems under the heading "Figs from Thistles" in *Poetry* in 1918, poems which vivified her inclination toward bohemianism and promiscuity. The famous first fig— "My candle burns at both ends; / It will not last the night; / But ah, my foes, and oh, my friends—/ It gives a lovely light!"—immortalized her public image of daring and unconventional behavior. It came as no real shock, then, when in 1920 she

> THE STRUCTURAL SIMPLICITY AND CHILDLIKE NARRATIVE VOICE ARE TECHNIQUES MILLAY USED FREQUENTLY IN HER EARLY WORK."

published an entire volume of poetry (including the first five figs) entitled *A Few Figs from Thistles*, dominated by a narrative voice that irreverently mocked public opinion and public morality, that scorned imposed values and prescribed behavior.

This image of liberation and self-assurance is the public image Millay deliberately cultivated, the self-projection that stole the show, demanded applause and attention, suited a loud and raucous jazz-age temper. For half a century it has captivated readers and critics and minimized or veiled entirely a private anxiety-ridden image of profound self-doubt and personal anguish with which Millay contended all her life. The braggadocio of the public image is, in fact, contradictory to experience as Millay inwardly felt it and is belied by both the language and the form through which she reflected her deepest sense of that experience. Although the poetry in *Figs* solidified that public image of defiance and independence, it did so in language and structural patterns that divulge a private image of submission and constriction. The dominant tone of the body of her work—the tone of heart-rending anguish—is apparent when she works at flippancy. Millay is unquestionably a woman who suffers, and the greatest source of her suffering seems to lie in an overwhelming sense of personal vulnerability—and ultimately of woman's vulnerability—to victimization by uncontrollable conditions in her environment.

This sense of vulnerability provides one of the richest linguistic patterns in her poetry, for in spite of her efforts to repress and protect a part of her emotional life, Millay is exposed and betrayed through a language pattern which calls attention to the emotional conflicts and tensions, the psychic realities of her existence. This pattern of self-revelation appears consistently throughout her work, though sometimes disguised by attitudes associated with the public image. "Grown-up," for example (from *Figs*),

seems to be merely a cute, little versified cliché about the disillusioning process of growing up.

> Was it for this I uttered prayers,
> And sobbed and cursed and kicked the stairs,
> That now, domestic as a plate,
> I should retire at half-past eight?

Notice the violence in the verbs; aptly, they do evoke an image of an unruly child, but they also suggest the strength of the frustration of the narrator for something absent from her life. The contrasting image, domestic as a plate, is perfectly appropriate to imply the flatness and brittleness and coldness that condition her existence. Growing into adult domesticity for this woman has been a process of subduing the will and shrinking the soul. The last line carries the shrinking image to its ultimate conclusion: oblivion, implied by the verb "retire." The woman is painfully aware of the disparity between her childhood hopes and the realities of her adult experience, a theme Millay treats at length in "Sonnets from an Ungrafted Tree." Here, the emptiness of the woman's life is made explicit by the fact that she retires at half-past eight, when for many the evening's activities have barely begun. This poem is a strong statement of protest against the processes that mitigate fulfilling and satisfying experience. Certainly, the poem might be read simply as a statement of the inadequacy of experience to measure up to the imaginative conception of it. But it is more. It is a specific statement about woman's experience. "Domestic as a plate" is an image that fits woman into her conventional place at rest on a shelf and out of the way. The poem reflects Millay's fears of her own fate and aids our understanding of the poet's excessive urge to proclaim herself a free and unconfined spirit.

Other poems in the *Figs* volume seem just as adolescently superficial as "Grown-up" but under closer analysis corroborate this deep sense of confinement and frustration. Both "The Unexplorer" and "To the Not Impossible Him" employ a central metaphor of limited travel to suggest the nature of the oppression and restriction felt by the narrators. In "The Unexplorer," the child-narrator is inspired to "explore" the road beyond the house, but on the basis of information provided by her mother—"It brought you to the milk-man's door"—she has resigned herself to confinement. She rather wistfully explains, "That's why I have not travelled more." The implications of familial repression in the socialization process of the female are rather grim. In "To the Not Impossible

Him," while the tone is light and the pose coyly provocative, the issue again is serious. The last stanza concludes:

> The fabric of my faithful love
> No power shall dim or ravel
> Whilst I stay here,—but oh, my dear,
> If I should ever travel!
> (130)

Confining the female, denying her experience, the narrator suggests, is the only sure way of forcing her into the social mold. Millay says a great deal more about this process in *Fatal Interview*, a collection of fifty-one sonnets published in 1931.

The structural simplicity and childlike narrative voice are techniques Millay used frequently in her early work. "Afternoon on a Hill," published in 1917, appears to be too simple a poem to give a serious reading. In imitation of childhood speech and thus childhood experience, its regular meter and rhymed quatrains, its childlike diction and sentence structure effectively convey the notion of woman as child. The stanzas, significantly without metrical variation, measure out their syllables as repetitiously as the child's days:

> I will be the gladdest thing
> Under the sun!
> I will touch a hundred flowers
> And not pick one.
>
> I will look at cliffs and clouds
> With quiet eyes,
> Watch the wind bow down the grass,
> And the grass rise.
>
> And when lights begin to show
> Up from the town,
> I will mark which must be mine,
> And then start down!
> (33)

Though appearing to lack subtlety and complexity, the poem does create a tension through an ironic disparity between the directness in tone and structure and the implications of the experience. The speaker seems to symbolize childhood's innocence and freedom. But the freedom, in fact, is artificial, for the child is regulated and restrained. She reaches out; she withdraws. "I will touch a hundred flowers," she decides, but then promises obediently: "And not pick one." The passivity outlined in this poem—looking, watching, obeying—again ends with the narrator's total retreat. It is, on the surface, an innocent-looking action. But it is a form of surrender. Throughout the poem one hears the promises of the "good little girl." She will do what is expected of her; she will watch quietly and disturb nothing.

Psychological experiences merely hinted at in this poem are verified directly and harshly in later poems. In "Above These Cares" Millay's narrator nearly screams out her recognition of her state:

> Painfully, under the pressure that obtains
> At the sea's bottom, crushing my lungs and my
>   brains
> (For the body makes shift to breathe and after a
>   fashion flourish
> Ten fathoms deep in care,
> Ten fathoms down in an element denser than air
> Wherein the soul must perish)
> I trap and harvest, stilling my stomach's needs;
> I crawl forever, hoping never to see
> Above my head the limbs of my spirit no longer free
> Kicking in frenzy, a swimmer enmeshed in weeds.
> (307)

The woman's vulnerability is absolute because she is so helplessly ensnared. Her feelings of oppression and spiritual suffocation are excruciatingly described, and she craves a numbing of her consciousness to dull the pain of her awareness....

Source: Jane Stanbrough, "Edna St. Vincent Millay and the Language of Vulnerability," in *Shakespeare's Sisters: Feminist Essays on Women Poets*, edited by Sandra M. Gilbert and Susan Gubar, Indiana University Press, 1979, pp. 183–86.

SOURCES

"American War and Military Operations Casualties: Lists and Statistics," the Navy Department Library website, http://www.history.navy.mil/library/online/american%20war%20casualty.htm (accessed March 11, 2013).

Billings, Molly, "The Influenza Pandemic of 1918," Stanford University website, http://virus.stanford.edu/uda/index.html (accessed March 11, 2013).

Distiller, Natasha, *Desire and Gender in the Sonnet Tradition*, Palgrave Macmillan, 2008, pp. 22, 29–35, 171–72.

Drowne, Kathleen Morgan, and Patrick Huber, *The 1920s*, Greenwood, 2004, pp. 29–31, 44–47, 186.

Dumenil, Lynn, *The Modern Temper: American Culture and Society in the 1920s*, Hill and Wang, 1995, pp. 111–43.

"Edna St. Vincent Millay Found Dead at 58," in *New York Times*, October 20, 1950, http://www.nytimes.com/learning/general/onthisday/bday/0222.html (accessed March 11, 2013).

"Faces of the Fallen," in *Washington Post*, http://apps.washingtonpost.com/national/fallen/ (accessed March 11, 2013).

Ferentinos, Susan, "Not for Old Fogies: The Flapper," Ultimate History Project website, http://ultimatehistoryproject.com/flapper.html (accessed March 12, 2013).

Harmon, William, *A Handbook to Literature*, 11th ed., Pearson Prentice Hall, 2009, pp. 14–15, 48, 300, 324–25, 340–41, 381, 507, 519–20, 547, 662.

Hollander, Anne, "The Costumer Is Always Right," in *New York Magazine*, Vol. 7, No. 2, January 14, 1974, p. 64.

———, *Seeing through Clothes*, University of California Press, 1993, pp. 152–53, 313–14.

Hubbard, Stacy Carson, "Love's 'Little Day,'" in *Millay at 100: A Critical Appraisal*, edited by Diane P. Freedman, Southern Illinois University Press, 1995, pp. 100–15.

Hutchison, Percy A., "Poets Who Sing at the Christmas-Shopping Season," Review of *The Harp-Weaver and Other Poems*, in *New York Times*, December 23, 1923, http://www.nytimes.com/1923/12/23/books/millay-warp.html?_r=0 (accessed March 8, 2013).

Millay, Edna St. Vincent, "What Lips My Lips Have Kissed," in *Collected Poems*, Harper and Brothers, 1956, p. 602.

Miller, Nathan, *New World Coming: The 1920s and the Making of Modern America*, Scribner, 2003, pp. 47–48, 253–64.

"19th Amendment to the U.S. Constitution: Women's Right to Vote," National Archives website, http://www.archives.gov/historical-docs/document.html?doc=13&title.raw=19th%20Amendment%20to%20the%20U.S.%20Constitution:%20Women's%20Right%20to%20Vote (accessed March 11, 2013)

"1920s–1930s Lost Generation," PBS website, http://www.pbs.org/wnet/americannovel/timeline/lostgeneration.html (accessed March 12, 2013).

Phelan, Julie, "Afghan War Support Hits a New Low," ABC News website, http://abcnews.go.com/blogs/politics/2012/04/new-low-in-support-for-afghanistan-war-and-a-call-for-mental-health-monitoring/ (accessed March 12, 2013).

Rice, Philip Blair, "Edna Millay's Maturity," Review of *Wine From These Grapes*, in *Nation*, Vol. 139, No. 3619, November 14, 1934, pp. 568, 570.

Schurer, Norbert, "Millay's What Lips My Lips Have Kissed, and Where, and Why," in *Explicator*, Vol. 63, No. 2, Winter 2005, p. 94–96.

"A Short History of the Sonnet," Folger Shakespeare Library, http://www.folger.edu/template.cfm?cid=3780 (accessed March 13, 2013).

Soland, Birgitte, *Becoming Modern: Young Women and the Reconstruction of Womanhood in the 1920s*, Princeton University Press, 2000, pp. 69–90.

Stark, Caitlin, "By the Numbers: Women Voters," CNN website, http://www.cnn.com/2012/10/25/politics/btn-women-voters (accessed March 11, 2013).

Tower, Samuel A., "She was the Most Popular Poet of Her Time," in *New York Times*, July 12, 1981, p. D33.

FURTHER READING

Allen, Frederick L., *Only Yesterday: An Informal History of the 1920s*, Harper Row, 1931.

Allen's book is a social history of the 1920s. First published more than eighty years ago, it is a very readable and entertaining history of a period of great social change.

Corrigan, Jim, *The 1920s Decade in Photos: The Roaring Twenties*, Enslow, 2010.

This book is filled with photos of the decade during which jazz and Prohibition competed for attention. This photo book is directed toward younger readers as a way to access the history of this period.

Fass, Paula S., *The Damned and the Beautiful: American Youth in the 1920s*, Oxford University Press, 1979.

This book is a comprehensive social history of the 1920s, with an emphasis on the youth who came of age between the two world wars. The author looks at childhood and peer conformity, as well as how people spent their time, either working or at play.

Fiell, Charlotte, and Emmanuelle Dirix, eds., *Fashion Sourcebook: 1920s*, Fiell, 2012.

This text is a reference book that provides detailed information, photographs, and illustrations depicting the kinds of fashions worn by women like Millay, who embraced the new flapper style. Every aspect of fashion, from hair and hats to shoes, is included.

Hatt, Christine, *World War I, 1914–18*, Franklin Watts, 2001.

This book is a history of World War I designed for middle-school readers and includes many photographs and maps.

Lamothe, Matt, Julia Rothman, and Jenny Volvovsku, *The Where, the Why, and the How: 75 Artists Illustrate Wondrous Mysteries of Science*, Chronicle, 2012.

This text asks seventy-five scientists to try to explain some of the mysteries of science. The answers to these mysteries, which are also well illustrated, focus on some of the most common interrogative words that are applied to science. Thus book nicely complements the where, who, and when of Millay's poem.

Ruiz, Vicki, and Ellen Carol DuBois, eds., *Unequal Sisters: A Multicultural Reader in U.S. Women's History*, 3rd ed., Routledge, 2000.

This book is a collection of thirty essays that provides a multicultural view of women's history. The selection of essays covers all of women's lives, including political, religious, social, racial, and sexual aspects.

Strachan, Hew, ed., *The Oxford Illustrated History of the First World War*, Oxford University Press, 2001.

This book is a collection of essays and photographs exploring several of the key issues that are important in understanding the events of World War I and their influence on the world after the war ended.

SUGGESTED SEARCH TERMS

Lost Generation AND poetry

Edna St. Vincent Millay AND What Lips My Lips Have Kissed

Edna St. Vincent Millay AND sonnet

What Lips My Lips Have Kissed AND lost love

Edna St. Vincent Millay AND The Harp-Weaver and Other Poems

Edna St. Vincent Millay AND biography

Edna St. Vincent Millay AND feminism

Edna St. Vincent Millay AND Pulitzer Prize

women's poetry AND heartbreak

The Whipping

ROBERT HAYDEN

1962

"The Whipping" is a poem by American poet Robert Hayden describing an incident in which a small boy is beaten with a stick by an old woman, who is presumably the boy's mother or grandmother. The incident is observed by the speaker in his own neighborhood, and the sight of the boy triggers his own difficult memories of having been subjected to corporal punishment by a parent when he was a child. The poem, which is in part autobiographical, is notable not only for the way it evokes the misery and fear associated with corporal punishment but also for its reflective conclusion about why such methods of punishment are employed generation after generation. "The Whipping" was first published in Hayden's poetry collection *A Ballad of Remembrance* in 1962 and was reprinted in his *Selected Poems* in 1966 and *Collected Poems* in 1985. The poem can also be found in the 1997 collections *I Am the Darker Brother: An Anthology of Modern Poems by African Americans*, edited by Arnold Adoff, and *Poetry after Lunch: Poems to Read Aloud*, edited by Joyce A. Carroll and Edward E. Wilson.

AUTHOR BIOGRAPHY

Hayden was born as Asa Bundy Sheffey on August 4, 1913, in Detroit, Michigan, to Ruth Finn and Asa Sheffey, an impoverished couple

Robert Hayden (© Pach Brothers / Corbis)

who soon separated and moved away. Their child was left with neighbors, William and Sue Ellen Hayden. The Haydens raised Asa as their own son, renaming him Robert Earl Hayden, although they never formally adopted him, a fact that Hayden did not discover until 1953, when he applied for a passport. Growing up with extreme nearsightedness meant that he did not participate in school sports; instead, he took to reading, and he began to write poetry at a young age. By the age of sixteen, when he was attending Northern High School in Detroit, his ambition was to become a poet. His first published poem appeared in 1931, shortly after he graduated from high school.

Hayden then attended Detroit City College (now Wayne State University), leaving in 1936 and not formally graduating until 1942. After college he began work as a writer and researcher for the Federal Writers' Project of the Works Project Administration. During this time, he studied black history, especially the Underground Railroad and the antislavery movement in Michigan. In the late 1930s, he wrote scripts for a radio station and news stories for the upcoming Negro Progress Exposition, which was held in Detroit in 1940. He also wrote

reviews of movies, plays, and music for the *Michigan Chronicle*, a weekly newspaper read by African Americans.

In 1940, Hayden published his first collection of poems, *Heart-Shape in the Dust*. In the same year, he married Erma Inez Morris, a schoolteacher, and studied under one of the major poets of the twentieth century, W. H. Auden, at the University of Michigan. He received an MA from that institution in 1944. In 1946, he became an assistant professor at Fisk University, in Nashville, Tennessee, and he remained there for twenty-three years, rising to the rank of professor. He became professor of English at the University of Michigan in 1969 and remained in that position until his death.

Hayden published many books of poetry, establishing himself as one of the leading African American poets of his time. From 1976 to 1978, he was the consultant in poetry at the Library of Congress, the first African American to hold this position (forerunner to the poet laureateship). His works include *Figure of Time* (1955); *A Ballad of Remembrance* (1962), in which "The Whipping" appears; *Selected Poems* (1966); *Words in the Mourning Time* (1970); *The Night-Blooming Cereus* (1972); *Angle of Ascent: New and Selected Poems* (1975); and *American Journal*, published in a limited edition in 1978 and posthumously in an enlarged edition in 1982. His *Collected Poems*, edited by Frederick Glaysher, was published in 1985. Hayden died of cancer on February 25, 1980, in Ann Arbor, Michigan, at the age of sixty-six.

POEM SUMMARY

The text used for this summary is from *Collected Poems*, Liveright, 1985, p. 40. Versions of the poem can be found on the following web pages: http://www.poemhunter.com/best-poems/robert-hayden/the-whipping/ and http://allpoetry.com/poem/8502015-The_Whipping-by-Robert_Hayden.

Stanzas 1–3

"The Whipping" consists of six unrhymed stanzas of four lines each. In the first stanza, the speaker, an unnamed adult, is observing an incident taking place across the street. It is possible that he is looking out of the window of his own home, although he does not explicitly say this. He sees an old woman beating a small boy.

Presumably, the woman is the boy's mother or grandmother, although, again, the poet does not specify this. Line 2 reveals that this is not the first time the speaker has witnessed an incident like this. As the woman administers the beating, she shouts about how the boy deserves to be whipped for his misdeeds. She also justifies the beating by saying that she is blameless and in the right; it is the boy's fault he is being beaten. The speaker gives the impression that the woman is shouting so loudly that the whole neighborhood can hear what is going on.

Stanza 2 elaborates on the picture presented in the first stanza. The boy is trying to escape the punishment by running across the yard. As he does so, he tramples the flower beds and begs for the woman to stop the beating. However, she shows him no mercy. In spite of the fact that she is very overweight, she chases after him and gets him in a corner.

In the third stanza, the woman repeatedly hits the boy with a stick while he screams and runs around in small circles. The beating finally ends only when the stick breaks. The boy is crying. As the speaker observes this, he is taken back to an incident from his own childhood, which he describes in the following stanza.

Stanzas 4–6

In stanza 4, the speaker describes his memories of being beaten as a child. He remembers having his head trapped between the knees of either his mother or father (he does not say which) and enduring a beating. He struggles to escape but cannot. He recalls the swats, but also says that the worst thing was not the beating itself but the fear of it. He also states in the last line of this stanza, the thought contained in which continues in the first line of the fifth stanza, that verbal abuse accompanied the beating.

In stanza 5, the speaker remembers that, while the beating was going on, he felt alienated from the parent who was administering it. He no longer recognized the person's face as that of someone he knew or loved. The memory ends in the middle of this stanza, and the speaker then describes how the boy has gone to his room and is crying. It is unlikely that the speaker actually witnessed this as part of the present-day incident he is observing, but he conflates the beating he has just watched with his own memory, so the boy he refers to in this stanza is both the boy

across the street and himself when he was young and had just suffered a beating.

In the last stanza, the speaker describes his observation of the old woman when the beating has finished. She props herself up against a tree, talking to herself. The speaker's interpretation of her feelings at that moment is that she has somehow cleansed herself of something through her act of beating the boy. The speaker thinks that she is in some sense taking revenge on someone else for beatings she herself has suffered in the past.

THEMES

Punishment

The theme of corporal punishment pervades Hayden's poem, involving not just the old woman and the boy but also the speaker and his memory of being beaten as a child, as well as his speculation about beatings the woman may have received as a child. Corporal punishment in this neighborhood may be a nearly universal experience, it seems, extending back several generations. This is simply the way children there are disciplined. The fact that the old woman administers the beating outside, in the yard, yelling as she does so, shows that such things are likely accepted in her neighborhood, since she clearly does not fear any outside intervention. Indeed, it seems as if she almost wants the neighborhood to know what is going on, as line 3 implies. Nor is this the first time the boy has suffered this kind of punishment, out in the open, for any neighbors or passersby to observe, as the first stanza makes clear.

However, it also seems likely that the old woman is in such a state of rage and righteous indignation that her judgment—about what her neighbors might think, about whether the punishment is appropriate in its level of severity—is impaired. Most probably, she is enraged by the boy's frantic efforts to escape the punishment. His disobedience in running away across the yard only ensures that she will hit him harder, it would seem. The way the speaker describes the incident makes it takes on a much darker tone than would a simple incident in which a mother or grandmother punishes her child. It appears to the speaker as an act of bullying. The old woman is stronger and will prevail. She has the instrument of punishment in her hand, and the boy is helpless before it. Because whatever offense the boy may have committed is not stated, the reader

TOPICS FOR FURTHER STUDY

- Write a poem in which you recall a difficult or painful experience with parents. Your poem could be based on personal experience or fictional. It does not have to be about corporal punishment but can be about any issue at all. Present the incident from whatever point of view works best for you. For inspiration, read some of the poems by teens in *Paint Me Like I Am: Teen Poems from WritersCorps* (2003).

- Initiate a debate in your class about the pros and cons of corporal punishment in schools. Speak for several minutes in support of the position you have chosen.

- Write an essay in which you discuss other forms of discipline that parents can use in the home while raising their children. Are these methods more or less effective than corporal punishment? Use research to back up your arguments, starting with the 2009 article by psychologist Carl E. Pickhardt for *Psychology Today* found at http://www.psychologytoday.com/blog/surviving-your-childs-adolescence/200911/effective-punishment-the-adolescent. Follow the links on that page for more perspectives on the topic. Search also on Google News or another outlet for any recent developments.

- Hayden's poem "Those Winter Sundays," like "The Whipping," is a reflective poem about the speaker's childhood. In a blog, write an entry in which you compare and contrast these two poems. Which poem do you prefer, and why? Share your blog with your classmates and invite their comments.

automatically, like the speaker, takes the boy's part. It is the woman, not the boy, who appears out of control and in need of restraint. The description in the second stanza of the chase across the flower bed until the boy is trapped in a corner resembles a hunt in which the boy is the prey. The impression that the punishment is too severe is confirmed when the stick she is using breaks. This is the only thing that stops the punishment.

In sum, the incident is presented more as a savage assault than as a justified act of punishment. Of course, the points of view of the participants differ. To the woman, she is merely administering a deserved punishment. She is certain she has right on her side. To the frightened boy, however, the incident must seem like a horrible injustice which he has no power to right. In this neighborhood, during this time period (the poem was written in the 1960s), it seems that parents are allowed to discipline their children in whatever way they see fit, whether their judgment is sound or not. No one appears ready to question this, except the speaker, who quietly observes the scene but makes no effort to intervene.

Alienation

In the second part of the poem, the poet brings a different perspective, his own, as he reflects on corporal punishment he received as a boy at home. In the first part of the poem, he was the detached observer, reporting what he saw. But now, triggered by the beating he has just witnessed, he delves into his own memories. What stanzas 4 and 5 reveal is the devastating effect the punishment has on the boy receiving it. The emphasis is not on the physical pain of the beating but how it affects his feelings for his mother or father. The combination of the beating and the harsh words uttered as it takes place results in a feeling of alienation in the boy. He no longer feels that he even knows the person who is beating him, and he does not love that person either. The punishment has the effect of poisoning his perception of his parent. How long that feeling lasts, the poet does not state. But the concluding lines of the poem make clear that, in the view of the poem's speaker, corporal punishment penetrates deeply into a person's psyche. It does not end when the blows end or even when the tears end.

The last two lines, which allude to corporal punishment that the old woman likely had to endure when she was young, show that the emotional and psychological effects of these beatings still remain, many decades after the bruises have subsided. The poet suggests that, in beating the child, the old woman is simply letting some of her old demons out of the closet of her wounded psyche. She is using the boy to avenge herself for

The boy runs through flowers and elephant ear plants when he is trying to escape the whipping. (© Steve
Cukrov / Shutterstock.com)

whippings she herself has suffered. The poet
carefully describes (in the penultimate line of
the poem) these beatings as occurring over a
lifetime, which suggests that the woman may
have suffered from them not only as a child but
also as an adult, perhaps from her husband, a
statement that raises but does not explore the
theme of domestic abuse. (The line might also
mean that she has spent a lifetime trying to cover
up or deal with the trauma inflicted on her
through corporal punishment as a child.) The
poet's insight into the woman's psychology further shapes the reader's attitude toward the punishment that she inflicts on the boy. The
punishment seems to be based as much on the
woman's need to inflict it as on anything the boy
may have done to deserve it. As such, it perhaps
shades over into what some might call abuse
rather than legitimate punishment, motivated
by some dark and uncontrollable impulse from
within a traumatized adult. The last lines also
reveal how corporal punishment is passed on
from generation to generation in a potentially
never-ending cycle of violence.

STYLE

Point of View

Point of view in a literary work refers to who is
telling the story. In this poem, the point of view
shifts suddenly in the middle of the poem. The
poem begins with a third-person speaker
describing in an objective way what he observes.
He sees the woman whipping the boy and
describes it as a reporter might, using strong
verbs and vivid adverbs to convey the reality of
the scene.

At the beginning of the third stanza, however, the point of view abruptly changes from
third person to first person. The first-person
speaker, using the pronouns *my* and *I*, describes
an incident from his own life, the memory of it
stimulated by what he has just witnessed. The
tone is no longer objective and impersonal. The
words rush out in short phrases as the speaker
brings the pain of the incident to mind. The
memory narrated in the first person also serves
as commentary on the incident the speaker has

observed in the first part of the poem, showing from an inside perspective what the beaten boy must be feeling and what the consequences of the punishment may be, beyond the pain itself.

Ellipsis

The ellipsis (marked by three periods with a space between each one) at the end of the second line of stanza 5 not only serves as a transition back to the earlier scene but also suggests that the speaker's thoughts are trailing off. It is as if there is so much more that could and should be said about the harmful effects the beatings had on the parent-child relationship, but perhaps there are no words for it, or the pain lies too deep for words.

HISTORICAL CONTEXT

Corporal Punishment up to the 1960s

"The Whipping" was published in 1962, but the personal incident recalled by the poet must have occurred much earlier than that. Since the poem is, to an extent, autobiographical, it is understood to refer to Hayden's childhood in Detroit in the 1910s and 1920s. Since the poem also states that the old woman had most likely experienced this kind of punishment herself, no doubt also as a child, the poem can be seen to span a time period from the late nineteenth century into the 1960s. As such, the poem reflects the fact that corporal punishment in the home throughout this period of time was extremely common in the United States, not to mention the fact that it was also frequently used in schools across the nation.

In *Family Life in 19th-Century America*, James M. Volo and Dorothy Denneen Volo note the lack of statistics about the frequency of corporal punishment in the home during the nineteenth century, but they do state that

> many men took a rod to their children at the first opportunity, thinking that it was the responsibility of a loving caregiver to do so. Others resorted to spankings, withheld food, or inflicted other corporal punishments even on toddlers.

The authors also point out the religious basis of such belief in corporal punishment. According to Christianity, children are born sinful and it is necessary for their self-will to be broken so that they can be raised in such a way that will ensure they choose the correct path in life, in accord with God's laws.

In the twentieth century, the first scientific research studies on corporal punishment were carried out. According to a study cited by Murray A. Straus in his book *Beating the Devil Out of Them*, 94 percent of parents in the United States believed in 1968 that a "good hard spanking is sometimes necessary" for children. Data gathered in 1968 by the National Commission on the Causes and Prevention of Violence, also cited by Straus, reported that 86 percent of parents approved of corporal punishment. Straus also mentions studies from the 1930s that produced similar statistics. In one study, for example, done in 1936, 79 percent of three-year-olds were spanked during the month preceding the research. Two decades later, in 1957, a study found that 99 percent of five-year-old children had been subjected to corporal punishment by their parents. Often, corporal punishment was employed even on infants of one to six months of age. A 1965 study in Los Angeles, Straus reports, showed that nearly one-half of infants of this age were being spanked. Corporal punishment was not limited to young children. In 1967, a study by Gerald Bachman, cited by Straus, showed that 61 percent of tenth-grade students had been slapped by their parents at least once that year.

One prominent advocate of spanking, at that time and since, was Dr. James Dobson. In his book *Dare to Discipline*, which was first published in 1970 and sold hundreds of thousands of copies, Dobson advocates spanking for children under ten whilst warning against excessive or unloving punishment: "It is not necessary to beat the child into submission; a little bit of pain goes a long way for a young child. However, the spanking should be of sufficient magnitude to cause the child to cry genuinely." Like many people who adhere to principles drawn from or endorsed by the Bible, Dobson points to biblical verses that advocate the use of corporal punishment in child rearing. He emphasizes, however, his concern "that some parents might apply the thrashings too frequently or too severely." This comment might certainly apply to the woman who beats the boy in "The Whipping," as might Dobson's further comment that, in severe cases, where corporal punishment is more properly called abuse, "Such abused children often grow up to become brutal parents themselves, inflicting similar pain on their own children."

COMPARE & CONTRAST

- **1960s:** Large numbers of young people rebel against traditional values and challenge authority. The 1960s is a violent decade full of social upheaval. Many parents and educators blame these unwelcome changes on permissive attitudes in the home and want to see a return to former days in which children were obedient and accepted parental authority. They point to what they see as a decline in corporal punishment and support a return to more frequent use of this method of punishment in schools and the home. However, while the severity and frequency of corporal punishment may be waning, 94 percent of adults still support the use of corporal punishment in the home and at school.

  Today: A 2010 ABC poll finds that about half of US parents say they sometimes spank their children, and two-thirds of parents support the practice in principle. The highest rates of spanking of children is found in the South, where 62 percent of parents spank their children. However, only 26 percent of parents believe that grade-school teachers should be allowed to spank students. Another poll shows that most parents in the United States support the right of parents to spank their very young children. A study of kindergarten children and their parents shows that more than three out of four parents have spanked their children. There are differences in ethnic groups. The group with the highest rate of spankings of children by kindergarten is African Americans (89 percent), followed by Hispanics (80 percent), whites (79 percent), and Asian Americans (73 percent).

- **1960s:** There is little discussion or research about the possible long-term damage caused to children by corporal punishment. Such punishment is widely accepted as necessary and beneficial in the process of child rearing.

  Today: A 2012 report in the *Canadian Medical Association Journal*, cited in *ScienceDaily*, indicates that over the long term, children may be harmed by corporal punishment. Those who have been punished in this way may show more aggressive and antisocial behavior than those who have not. Mental health problems such as depression, anxiety, and use of drugs and alcohol may also be higher in those who have received physical punishment.

- **1960s:** All US states permit corporal punishment in schools, with the exception of New Jersey. In 1971, Massachusetts will become the second state to ban corporal punishment.

  Today: Twenty-nine US states permit some form of corporal punishment in schools. This includes all the states in the South. Twenty-one states, including California, Illinois, Minnesota, New York, Pennsylvania, Virginia, and Wisconsin, have banned the practice. According to US Department of Education statistics, more than 220,000 students each year receive corporal punishment in public schools. Minority students are more likely to be punished in this way. For example, African American students make up 17 percent of the total student population but receive 36 percent of the corporal punishment. This is more than twice the rate for white students.

CRITICAL OVERVIEW

"The Whipping" has attracted some comment from literary critics over the years. Edward Hirsch, in his review essay "Mean to Be Free," counts "The Whipping" as one of his favorites among Hayden's "personal lyrics." He comments that these poems

> rely on childhood experiences in a Detroit slum ironically known as Paradise Valley. Hayden

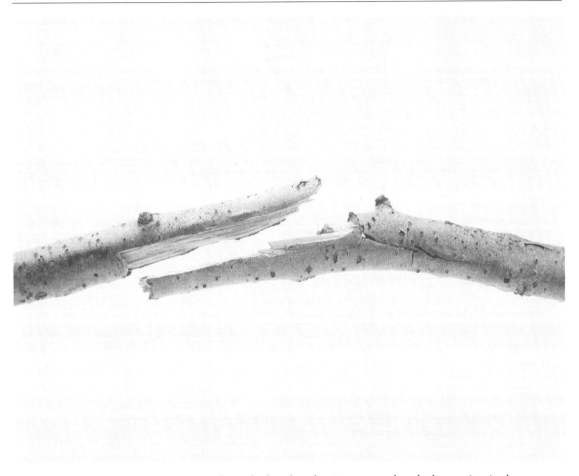

When the stick the woman is using to beat the boy breaks, it seems to break the tension in the poem as well. *(© optimarc | Shutterstock.com)*

refused to sentimentalize his past—as a child growing up his primary desire was to escape the world that surrounded him, and he also determined to remember it accurately.

In "Meditative, Ironic, Richly Human: The Poetry of Robert Hayden," Michael Paul Novak counts "The Whipping," along with "Those Winter Sundays," as two of Hayden's "finest poems," which "apparently recreate scenes from his childhood." Novak notes that, although the poet records the distress of the boy being beaten, along with his own painful memories of similar beatings, "in the final lines of the poem he also identifies with the woman and acknowledges the never ending circle of whippings." In "Minority Reporting and Psychic Distancing in the Poetry of Robert Hayden," Fred M. Fetrow comments that the poem

> recalls the stress of psychic punishment associated with ordinary discipline, and while the poet distances the actual experience (if indeed

the poem does grow out of a real event) with careful combinations of point of view, tone, and symbol, the final appeal of the poem is its universality. Hayden thus reminds us all of the love-hate dynamic which both bonds and repels parent and child, as he recalls such emotional trauma.

John Hatcher, in *From the Auroral Darkness: The Life and Poetry of Robert Hayden*, approaches the poem from a biographical point of view, since Hayden himself acknowledged that the origins of the poem lay in his own experience as a child. As quoted by Hatcher, Hayden specifically remarked, with respect to this poem and "Those Winter Sundays," that his poetic motivation was his "need to recall my past and to rid myself of the pain of so much of it." Hatcher writes that the poem is "an attempt to understand the deep frustration which drove his foster mother to vent her rage on her adopted child."

WHAT DO I READ NEXT?

- Hayden's poem "Those Winter Sundays," first published in 1962 in the same volume as "The Whipping," is often grouped with that poem, since it is also based on the poet's recollections of his childhood. "Those Winter Sundays" is not as harsh a poem as "The Whipping," although it does suggest that the poet's relationship with his father was a distant one and that his parents were frequently quarreling. The poem is available in Hayden's *Collected Poems* in a 1997 edition with an introduction by Arnold Rampersad.

- William Matthews (1942–1997) was a noted American poet of the second half of the twentieth century. His poem "A Happy Childhood" first appeared in the collection of that name in 1984. The title well describes the poem, which stands in contrast to Hayden's more conflicted poems about his childhood. The poem is also available in Matthews's *Selected Poems and Translations, 1969–1991* (1992).

- "In the Waiting Room," by Elizabeth Bishop, is another poem written from the perspective of childhood. In this case, it is written from the mind of the poet as a six-year-old girl who is accompanying her aunt to the dentist. As she waits while her aunt is treated, she gains her first awareness of her own identity and how mysterious and inexplicable it is. The poem can be found in Bishop's *The Complete Poems, 1927–1979* (1984).

- James Merrill was a prominent twentieth-century American poet who wrote a number of poems about his memories of childhood. The reflective poem "The World and the Child," in the form of a villanelle, shows a child's longing for affection from his father, which he does not receive. The poem was first published in the *New Yorker* in 1960 and was reprinted in Merrill's collection *Water Street* in 1962. It can also be found in his *Collected Poems* (2001).

- African American poet Gwendolyn Brooks (1917–2000) was a contemporary of Hayden's. Brooks won the Pulitzer Prize for Poetry in 1950. Her *Selected Poems* (1999) contains her best verse gathered from over a half century of publication, including the well-known poem "We Real Cool."

- *The Vintage Book of African American Poetry* (2000), edited by Michael S. Harper and Anthony Walton, is an anthology of the work of fifty-two African American poets. The book covers a period of more than two hundred years, ranging from eighteenth-century slaves to poets born after World War II. In addition to Hayden, poets represented include Phillis Wheatley, Paul Laurence Dunbar, Claude McKay, Langston Hughes, Countee Cullen, Gwendolyn Brooks, Amiri Baraka, Rita Dove, and many lesser-known figures.

- *Mother Poems* (2009) is a collection of poetry for young readers by African American poet Hope Anita Smith. The poems describe the happy relationship between an African American girl and her mother, which is ended by the mother's unexpected death. The girl struggles to deal with the ensuing pain of loss. The book, which contains illustrations by the author, has been favorably reviewed by publications such as the *New York Times Book Review* and *School Library Journal*.

- *Spare the Child: The Religious Roots of Punishment and the Psychological Impact of Physical Abuse* (1992), by Philip J. Greven, is a well-researched study of the history of corporal punishment in the United States and the religious arguments that have been made in support of it. Greven also details the harmful effects of such punishment and describes nonviolent alternatives.

CRITICISM

Bryan Aubrey

Aubrey holds a PhD in English. In the following essay, he discusses the autobiographical roots of "The Whipping" as well as how recent research on corporal punishment supports the poem's insights into the effects of such punishment.

Robert Hayden's "The Whipping" vividly re-creates from several different perspectives the corporal punishment inflicted on a boy by his mother. The roots of the poem lie in Hayden's own childhood. Hayden lived with foster parents, and he commented in an interview with Dennis Gendron that there was a lot of tension in the family home. His foster parents, Sue Ellen Hayden and William "Pa" Hayden, were unhappily married, and there were frequent fights and angry confrontations. It was Sue Ellen's second marriage, and according to the poet, she never got over the loss of her first husband, a man named Jim Barlow, with whom she had three children and who died young. Robert Hayden confirmed in this interview that he suffered beatings such as he describes in "The Whipping":

> Older people did that to children then, and I got a few hidings like that. But my aunt objected strenuously, and I didn't get whipped that way too much. But I was often abused and often hurt physically because they were ignorant people.

(The aunt he refers to was in fact his foster mother's daughter, who also lived with them. Hayden called her Aunt Roxie. She and Hayden's foster father did not get along well, which added to the lack of harmony in the home.)

Hayden also commented that his foster mother was "neurotic" and was frequently in physical pain that was diagnosed as being caused by neuralgia. Hayden came to believe that the pain was psychosomatic in origin; that is, it was caused or complicated by mental or emotional issues. The pain had real consequences for the child, however: "Very often it would be brought on by some great angry outburst or something that upset her, and then she would blame me. It was terrible." Hayden said that he did not want to describe this in further detail because it was still painful for him (over fifty years later): "It really hurts me to even think of it." His parents were "often cruel" to him, he recalled: "I really did get abused and hurt and so on. I saw dreadful things."

> THE POET EXTENDS HIS COMPASSION AND UNDERSTANDING TO THE MOTHER WHO BEAT THE BOY. HE REALIZES THE POWERFUL FORCES INSIDE HER THAT COMPELLED HER TO DO IT. THE ALIENATION HE FELT DURING THE WHIPPING APPEARS NOT TO HAVE BEEN PERMANENT."

Painful memories, of dreadful things seen and heard, are difficult for anyone to deal with. Poets and writers often turn to writing about such things as a way to come to terms with what happened to them. Childhood is a potent source of memories, both good and bad, and Hayden elected in "The Whipping" to write about one of the most distressing aspects of his childhood, when he was subjected to what sounds like unreasonable and quite savage physical punishment from his mother. The poem well conveys the terror of the young boy as he tries to escape the punishment but is forced to endure it.

Seen in this biographical light, the boy in the first half of the poem can be understood to be the poet's younger self, desperately fleeing from his angry foster mother as she beats him with a stick. The poet has chosen to present the incident in the third person, in the form of an adult observing the whipping from across the street. In other words, he has imagined what the scene might have looked like to another person, and that person acts like a reporter, taking note of what he sees. There is an emotional detachment in the description because the blows are falling not on the observer but on the boy. Although the terror of the boy as he pleads for mercy is vividly conveyed, the observer is not himself involved in the incident, and neither the boy nor the mother are aware that he is watching. It is possible to hear in the first stanza a certain exasperation in his tone, as he notes that this is not the first time he has witnessed such a scene, but overall, he constitutes a calm, neutral presence. His description does not get to the wrenching heart of the experience. It is one thing to watch someone getting whipped, it is quite another to feel it oneself. Perhaps beginning in this more distant way, as if he was observing himself from afar, was an easier way for the poet to confront this particular, painful experience. But this perspective does not last. In the second part of the poem, the poet, so to speak, changes the camera angle. He zooms up close, abandoning the stance of objectivity, and shows the beating very much from the child's point of view, as the switch to first-person narration shows. It is as if he is now feeling the blows as they land, with all the associated pain and psychological confusion they produce.

In the two stanzas that follow, several things are discernible. First, as he is being beaten, any positive feelings of love that the boy might have had toward the parent vanish. It is as if he no longer even knows the mother who is beating him. Interestingly, this is in line with what recent research on the effects of corporal punishment suggests. According to data gathered by Murray A. Straus and published in *Beating the Devil Out of Them: Corporal Punishment in American Families and Its Effects on Children*, corporal punishment has a negative effect on the relationship between parent and child. Straus conducted a study in which 270 students were asked how they reacted to being hit by one of their parents. The students were given a checklist of thirty-three items, one of which was "hated him or her." A total of 42 percent of the students checked this phrase with regard to the first instance of corporal punishment they recalled and also the most recent incident. Straus comments, "The large percentage who hated their parents for hitting them is important because it is evidence that corporal punishment does chip away at the bond between child and parent." So it is in "The Whipping."

Modern research into corporal punishment has reached some other conclusions that can also be inferred from the last stanza of the poem. First, those who experience corporal punishment most frequently at home are more likely to punish their own children in this manner. For example, in the Straus study, the mothers who used corporal punishment on their sixteen-year-old children were more likely to have experienced such punishments themselves when they were children. Also, Straus notes that corporal punishment that occurs in adolescence "seems to be almost indelibly burned in the minds of many people." Straus, an opponent of corporal punishment, acknowledges that some may regard this as evidence that corporal punishment is effective, since it makes such a lasting

The sight of the boy's tears reminds the narrator of beatings received as a child. (© Zurijeta / Shutterstock.com)

impression, but he suggests (and his research confirms) that instead it shows "the lasting damage that results when parents hit teenagers because the painful memories are still there decades later to evoke anger, humiliation, alienation, and depression." Readers of "The Whipping" will recognize this pattern from the last stanza of the poem. The old woman who whips the boy suffered beatings herself. She is therefore predisposed to treat her own child in this manner. The humiliation of the whippings she suffered live on inside her, and her whipping of the boy is somehow necessary for her because it purges her of these painful and disturbing memories.

However, if modern research confirms what a reader of the poem might also conclude, "The Whipping" still has one surprise left. The poet extends his compassion and understanding to the mother who beat the boy. He realizes the powerful forces inside her that compelled her to do it. The alienation he felt during the whipping appears not to have been permanent. He understands that people can be caught in a cycle of events over which they have little control. Those who have been beaten may feel the need to beat others. In seeking understanding of the woman's motivation, the poet offers hope that the cycle of violence may be broken. He affirms that the quest for understanding is better than unthinking condemnation, and that compassion for those who are driven helplessly by their inner demons lessens the possibility that one will hit out blindly when one's own turn comes.

Source: Bryan Aubrey, Critical Essay on "The Whipping," in *Poetry for Students*, Gale, Cengage Learning, 2014.

Pontheolla T. Williams

In the following excerpt, Williams describes critical reaction to Hayden's work.

Twenty-six years after the American publication of *Heart-Shape in the Dust*, Hayden found an American publisher for *Selected Poems*, a compilation of forty-one pieces. Reviews of the volume were, with few exceptions, favorable. David Galler, however, criticized Hayden for being "saddled with both sentimentality [and] super erudition." Hayden, he said, "oscillat[ed] from semi-dialect and corrupted ballads to Poundian notation." He also accused him of "high eclecticism on the theological plane" and with not being satisfied with the example of Jesus as a white man would be. Galler's most cutting criticism, however, was in the form of an ambiguous compliment: although Hayden is as gifted a poet as we have, his problem is not one of talent but of frame of reference. Citing what he felt to be the finest verse in the book, the ironic speech in "Middle Passage" spoken by the Spanish sailor who witnessed the *Amistad* mutiny, he criticized Hayden's use of his "best" irony to depict the Spanish cause. He concluded his review by stating that Hayden had "not chosen his *forte*; it had chosen him."

On the other hand, Robert Moore Allen wrote in the *Tennessean* that Hayden's "poetic talent is of the first order, and his poems reveal the hands of a skilled craftsman." He added that Hayden "had reached a profound understanding of his experience first as a human being and then as a human being involved in a particular situation...that of the Negro in the United States today." Whereas Galler stated, rather obscurely, that Hayden was mistakenly at his best when he portrayed the Spanish cause, Allen lauded Hayden's ability to portray the Mexican peon's oppression and suffering, especially in "Market." He joined other critics in pointing to

"Those Winter Sundays" and "The Whipping" as the superior poems in the volume.

Gwendolyn Brooks, writing before her conversion in 1967 to the black nationalist position, distinguished Hayden from the poet who, "gasping in the field, writes right then, his wounds like faucets above his page." She saw Hayden, rather, as one who "finds life always interesting, sometimes appalling, but consistently amenable to a clarifying enchantment via the power of Art." She cited "The Whipping" as an example of "life not lost in the refining process" and "Middle Passage" as being powerful.

Others who praised Hayden included book editor Herbert A. Kinney, Cynthia Sinderis, and Allen Tate. Kinney proclaimed Hayden to be the "foremost Negro poet in the United States today," and Cynthia Sinderis, unlike Galler, found Hayden's blues poetry and ballads impressive. Both she and Kinney were impressed with Hayden's use of his talent for artistic rather than propagandistic purposes. Allen Tate wrote that he "greatly admired" *Selected Poems* as a book done in Hayden's maturity when he would not, therefore, have to live down his youthful poetic mistakes. "There are," he said, "many fine short, or shorter poems" in the volume, and he cited "Middle Passage" as the piece that moved him most.

Selected Poems demonstrates the maturation of Hayden's craftsmanship. In a sense, as Hayden stated, it is the volume that marks the beginning of his career as a poet. Presenting as it does so much revised material from *A Ballad of Remembrance*, the *Selected Poems* necessarily repeats the themes of the earlier volume. The measure of Hayden's philosophic growth and thematic range during the 1960s, therefore, rests significantly on *A Ballad of Remembrance*, from which twenty-seven of the pieces in *Selected Poems* are revised reprints. Of the remaining poems, five were published previously while nine are new. His habit of constant revision, however, demonstrates the growth and perfecting of his craftsmanship....

Source: Pontheolla T. Williams, "*Selected Poems* (1966)," in *Robert Hayden: A Critical Analysis of His Poetry*, University of Illinois Press, 1987, pp. 97–98.

John Hatcher

In the following excerpt, Hatcher traces Hayden's development of a persona in some of his poems, including "The Whipping."

. . . In much of Hayden's poetry we are aware of the evolving persona who guides us through his world of thought and experience. In his dramatic monologues we forget the persona and concentrate on the fictive voice of a dramatic character who always reveals much more than he is aware. But unlike many poets who when they find an amenable narrative technique, hold fast to it, Hayden employed numerous voices and narrative devices. To begin with he employed the first-person point of view with a number of variations. As I have noted, in the 1982 *American Journal* he has a group of poems that seem clearly personal, almost confessional in tone. In 'Names' he describes directly his anguish over discovering he was not legally Robert Hayden. In 'As my blood was drawn' he seems to give vent to his fear and sadness at discovering the ominous progress of his disease. In one sense these poems are little different from his earlier personal poems like 'The Whipping' and 'Those Winter Sundays,' 'Electrical Storm' or 'The Night-Blooming Cereus,' all of which are mostly first-person narratives about the poet's life. But in the later poems, in 'Elegies for Paradise Valley' for example, the subject seems to be biographical insight into Robert Hayden, whereas 'The Whipping' concerns Sue Hayden, 'Those Winter Sundays' concerns Pa Hayden as a symbol of parental love, 'Electrical Storm' focuses on Divine intervention and 'The Night-Blooming Cereus' on the flower.

It could be well argued that even in these later first-person poems our interest goes beyond Hayden the individual to Hayden the Bahá'í viewing his own death as evidence of the world's painful transition, and I think this is true. With virtually no poem I am aware of is the poet's primary goal to present himself as an individual. As Wilburn Williams, Jr., noted in his study of *Angle of Ascent*, Hayden had the capacity to 'objectivize his own subjectivity. His private anguish never locks him into the sterile dead end of solipsism; it impels him outward into the world.'

Hayden's most frequent use of the first-person viewpoint involves his consistent use of the persona. It is sometimes a thinly guised mask, a fact which has led many critics to view his work as amplifications of biographical fact rather than to consider them as tropes for larger concerns. The continuity of Hayden's poetry demonstrates that one can trace the progress of the persona as he struggles for identity and his own

> THE EFFECT, OSTENSIBLY A VIOLATION OF NARRATIVE LOGIC, IS INCREDIBLY EFFECTIVE, IMPLYING AMONG OTHER THINGS THAT THE POET CAN BE OBJECTIVE IN RECOUNTING HIS PAST UNTIL THE SCENE RECALLS 'WOUNDLIKE MEMORIES' AND HE INSTANTLY LOSES THAT ANALYTICAL PERSPECTIVE."

voice in poems like 'A Ballad of Remembrance,' as he flees from his furies in 'The Broken Dark' or from the world's turmoil in "From the Corpse Woodpiles . . .", as he becomes dispirited in 'Words in the Mourning Time' or reconciled in 'October.' These poems also focus on the first-person poet/persona, his experiences and feelings, but more obviously as a character, as a representative of a particular historical perspective, a Bahá'í struggling in a period of wrenching transformation.

Another use of this same persona involves the speaker's recollection of himself in relation to something else—another character, an experience, a work of art, a powerfully evocative setting. All of the Mexico poems have this perspective—the speaker is involved, is affected by what he sees. But while we key on his reaction, our primary concern is with the symbolic materials he encounters—the ritualistic celebrations, the marketplace, the bull-fight. Likewise in 'The Night-Blooming Cereus' or 'Monet's "Waterlilies"' or 'The Peacock Room' we are interested in the speaker's personal reaction to these external objects; we learn about him from the relationship, but our primary attention is on the objects themselves as he reflects them to us.

A substantial part of this effect is Hayden's use of tenses. 'The Peacock Room' and 'Monet's "Waterlilies"' are narrated in the present tense and have immediacy, a feeling of emotional action taking place, whereas 'The Night-Blooming Cereus,' narrated in the past tense, displays before us the speaker and his wife in relation to the flower, but also the speaker remembering himself—we infer that he has learned something by remembering his reaction. 'The Moose

Wallow' and 'Electrical Storm' are also in the past tense as the narrator recalls himself as a character in the remembered anecdotes, whereas 'A Plague of Starlings' and 'Full Moon,' which are in the present tense, have a more uncertain tone, since the persona is in the midst of experience, not reflection.

One of Hayden's most celebrated usages of the first-person persona point of view is in his childhood recollections. 'Those Winter Sundays,' which Karl Shapiro called 'a fine example of the "pure lyric,"' is perhaps the best example, though most of the recollections of Paradise Valley are similar in mode and narrative construction. 'Elegies for Paradise Valley,' 'Free Fantasia: Tiger Flowers,' the middle portion of 'The Whipping,' 'The Rabbi' and 'Double Feature' all have more or less the same intent. The persona is not overwhelmed with nostalgia—these scenes do not flow naturally or easily before him. The persona dredges up some with pain, guilt, anguish; others he recalls with a sense of loss, but all of these scenes imply a persona willfully attempting a panoramic review of his beginnings in order to understand the mechanisms of the present—his lost identity, his guilt, his need for love, his appreciation of colorful characters.

In yet another use of the first-person narrative technique Hayden wrote a number of poems where the speaker focuses on something not so pointedly related to his own life or emotional response. In 'The Prisoners,' for example, the poet/speaker is certainly involved with the inmate, reads to him and ultimately is moved by the prisoner's reaction to the heartfelt attempt at communication, but the reader's attention is primarily on the prisoner himself as a symbol for our own condition, not on the speaker or the speaker's response. Likewise in 'The Performers,' 'Homage to Paul Robeson' and 'The Rag Man' the 'I' is important, if only because we view the exterior world through his biased perspective. The resulting impressionistic portraits do indeed give us added information about this artist/companion who guides us through his life, but here too our primary focus is on the external world, the window washers, Paul Robeson's career, the philosophical implications of the street scene in 'The Rag Man.'

Certainly the most dramatic distance between the poet and the poem with first-person narratives occurs when Hayden creates complete and complex characters who tell their stories. One of the most powerful of these is 'The Ballad of Nat Turner,' in which Turner himself recounts his vision for his 'brethren.' This remarkable use of the dramatic monologue portrays Turner's mystic vision and, more importantly, Turner's interpretation of that experience:

In scary night I wandered, praying,
Lord God my harshener,
speak to me now or let me die;
speak, Lord, to this mourner.

And came at length to livid trees
where Ibo warriors
hung shadowless, turning in wind
that moaned like Africa . . .
(*AA*, p. 125)

Hayden similarly creates the character of Daedalus who recalls how his 'gran' 'flew back to Africa,' and who chants his longing to escape his slavery. Likewise a good portion of 'John Brown' is in the form of a dramatic monologue, though the narrator's voice takes us in and out of that first-person narrative, in the same way that he does with the figure of Aunt Jemima. But in both poems, the heart of the narrative is the first-person recounting of lives by the characters themselves.

There are other minor examples of the dramatic monologue in earlier poems—Perseus, the speaker in 'The Wheel,' the bereft Medea figure in '"Incense of the Lucky Virgin."' But in his last volume Hayden created some of his most powerful examples of this effective narrative device. 'A Letter from Phillis Wheatley' is an epistolary dramatic monologue, and the last section of 'from *The Snow Lamp*' is also presented as the written log entry of Henson's experience. Hayden's most powerful uses of this narrative technique in *American Journal*, and perhaps in his career, are the monologue of the speaker in 'The Tattooed Man' and the journal of the alien visitor in '[American Journal]'. In fact, the emphatic use of the dramatic monologue in this last volume caused Fred Fetrow in his review of the work to observe that Hayden's 'narrative versatility' is one of his most distinguishing qualities as a poet:

In retrospect, Hayden's final poems appropriately exhibit his deft talent for creating diversified voices. Indeed, as partially indicated in *American Journal*, a significant element of his unique voice derives from his narrative versatility, a range in modality perhaps unmatched among contemporary poets.

Hayden's uses of the third-person narrative point of view are no less varied or innovative. Most of the poems which focus on anecdotes and elliptically told stories in the ballad tradition are presented in the third-person point of view. Among these are 'The Ballad of Sue Ellen Westerfield,' 'The Ballad of the True Beast,' 'Unidentified Flying Object,' the more elaborate 'For a Young Artist' and 'El-Hajj Malik El-Shabazz.' Likewise most of the character pieces are presented in the third person, though in various forms. There is the formal sonnet 'Frederick Douglass,' the richly ornate portrait in 'Witch Doctor,' the tightly imagistic sketch of the drug addict in 'Soledad', the surreal impression of the distraught boy in '"Mystery Boy" Looks for Kin in Nashville.' In some of these the third-person narrator is faceless, a dispassionate reporter, a clear mirror, as in 'Kid' or '"The Burly Fading One,"' whereas in 'Frederick Douglass' or 'Bahá'u'lláh in the Garden of Ridwan' the narrator makes no pretense at objectivity.

This same distinction holds true for Hayden's use of the third-person point of view in presenting settings. Sometimes the narrative voice objectively presents a place, from which we infer symbolic implications. There may be some tonal qualities in presentation as clues to thematic intent, but the narration itself does not imply that the setting is being filtered through a personality. 'Mountains,' 'Stars' and 'Locus,' for example, are presented through a keen-eyed but essentially objective point of view, even though we have some sense of that narrator. In pieces like 'Magnolias in Snow', 'Figures' or 'Market' the narrator, though unidentified, charges the portrait with his personal emotions, whereas in the highly compressed imagistic pieces, Hayden uses a dispassionate third-person narration. In such poems as '"Dance the Orange,"' 'Smelt Fishing' or 'Snow' we are not only unaware of the narrator; we are also left largely without tonal clues to guide us to the poet's meaning.

A variation on the third-person presentation occurs in several poems which are, strictly speaking, first-person narrations—there is a reference to an 'I' or 'we,' but the focus is so importantly on the subject that we are really oblivious to the narrative point of view. In 'Kodachromes of the Island,' for example, we are until the end of the poem concentrating on the photographic images of the setting. Likewise, in 'Theory of Evil' the only hint of the first-person speaker is in the lines 'We think of that/ as we follow the Trace' (*AJ*, p. 11). The rest of the poem focuses on the legend of the trail and the story of 'Them Harpes.' The most weighty use of this narrative approach

occurs in 'Homage to the Empress of the Blues.' In this poem Hayden presents a third-person portrait of the singer Billie Holiday on stage before an assemblage of entranced onlookers. Our view of this, like the camera's perspective in cinematography, is objective; we watch this interplay between performer and audience until the final line when the poet inserts a simple personal pronoun to suddenly place him there in the audience, and us there with him: 'She came out on the stage in ostrich feathers, beaded satin,/ and shone that smile on us and sang' (*AA*, p. 104).

The analogy of narrative point of view to cinematography is a useful one, for just as we see only what the camera can see so in poetry we view the literal imagery from a certain narrative perspective, and it is often crucial to discern the nature of that point of view, whether the lens is clear and whether the camera angle is distorting reality. Likewise, the camera sometimes presents the world as the character sees it, and sometimes it stands apart, above or beyond the character to show his relationship to the world. But always there is the artist controlling what that camera sees; therefore we must always be aware of what that camera eye represents.

Nowhere is this component of style more apparent than in variation of the third-person point of view in 'The Whipping.' The poem begins in the third person with the narrator viewing objectively the 'old woman across the way' who is 'whipping the boy again.' Then, after three stanzas of describing the boy who is vainly trying to flee, the poem suddenly shifts in the fourth stanza to the first-person perspective as the narrator becomes the boy: 'My head gripped in bony vise' (*AA*, p. 112). Halfway through the fifth stanza, when the whipping is over, the poem shifts back to the third-person point of view. The effect, ostensibly a violation of narrative logic, is incredibly effective, implying among other things that the poet can be objective in recounting his past until the scene recalls 'woundlike memories' and he instantly loses that analytical perspective....

Source: John Hatcher, "Shaping the Poem," in *From the Auroral Darkness: The Life and Poetry of Robert Hayden*, George Ronald, 1984, pp. 256–60.

SOURCES

"Corporal Punishment," National Association of Secondary School Principals website, February 2009, http://www.nassp.org/Content.aspx?topic=47093 (accessed February 7, 2013).

Crandall, Julie, "Poll: Most Approve of Spanking Kids," ABC News website, November 8, 2007, http://abcnews.go.com/US/story?id=90406&page=1 (accessed February 8, 2013).

Dobson, James, *Dare to Discipline*, Tyndale House Publishers, 1976, pp. 35, 60.

Fetrow, Fred M., "Minority Reporting and Psychic Distancing in the Poetry of Robert Hayden," in *CLA Journal*, Vol. 33, No. 2, December 1989, pp. 117–29.

Hatcher, John, *From the Auroral Darkness: The Life and Poetry of Robert Hayden*, George Ronald, 1984, p. 26.

Hayden, Robert, "An Interview with Dennis Gendron," in *Robert Hayden: Essays on the Poetry*, edited by Laurence Goldstein and Robert Chrisman, University of Michigan Press, 2001, p. 27.

———, "The Whipping," in *Collected Poems*, edited by Frederick Glaysher, Liveright, 1985, p. 40.

Hirsch, Edward, "Mean to Be Free," in *Nation*, Vol. 241, No. 21, December 21, 1985, pp. 685–86.

Novak, Michael Paul, "Meditative, Ironic, Richly Human: The Poetry of Robert Hayden," in *Midwest Quarterly*, Vol. 15, No. 3, Spring 1974, pp. 276–85.

"Physical Punishment of Children Potentially Harmful to Their Long-Term Development," in *ScienceDaily*, February 6, 2012, http://www.sciencedaily.com/releases/2012/02/120206122447.htm (accessed February 7, 2013).

Piele, Philip K., "Neither Corporal Punishment Cruel nor Due Process Due: The United States Supreme Court's Decision in *Ingraham v. Wright*," in *Corporal Punishment in American Education: Readings in History, Practice, and Alternatives*, edited by Irwin A. Hyman and James H. Wise, Temple University Press, 1979, p. 103.

Siek, Stephanie, "Researchers: African-Americans Most Likely to Use Physical Punishment," CNN website, November 10, 2011, http://inamerica.blogs.cnn.com/2011/11/10/researchers-african-americans-most-likely-to-use-physical-punishment/ (accessed February 8, 2013).

Straus, Murray A., and Denise A. Donnelly, *Beating the Devil Out of Them: Corporal Punishment in American Families and Its Effects on Children*, Transaction Publishers, 2001, pp. 38, 154–55, 206.

Volo, James M., and Dorothy Denneen Volo, *Family Life in 19th-Century America*, Greenwood Press, 2007, p. 133.

Wyman, Linda, "Hidings and Revelations: Robert Hayden's 'The Whipping,'" in *English Journal*, Vol. 77, No. 3, March 1988, pp. 82–84.

FURTHER READING

Bloom, Harold, ed., *Robert Hayden*, Chelsea House Publishers, 2005.
This volume in the Bloom's Modern Critical Views series is a collection of essays on Hayden's work.

Fetrow, Fred M., *Robert Hayden*, Twayne Publishers, 1984.
This is an introductory survey of Hayden's entire poetic output.

Haugen, David, and Susan Musser, eds., *Discipline and Punishment*, Greenhaven Press, 2013.
This book, part of the Teen Rights and Freedoms series, is an analysis of the rights of teenagers concerning discipline and punishment, including a discussion of the legality of corporal punishment in schools and the home. The authors also discuss rights issues relating to school suspension and expulsion hearings.

Pate, Matthew, and Laurie A. Gould, *Corporal Punishment around the World*, Praeger, 2012.
Corporal punishment in a variety of contexts is still practiced extensively around the world, and this book is a scholarly overview of such practices. The authors examine corporal punishment in both historical and contemporary contexts, as used in schools, homes, penal systems, and religious settings. Case studies are drawn from countries including the Bahamas, Bolivia, Nigeria, Saudi Arabia, and Singapore.

Williams, Pontheolla T., *Robert Hayden: A Critical Analysis of His Poetry*, University of Illinois Press, 1987.
Williams traces Hayden's development as a poet over the entire course of his career. She includes a biographical sketch, a chronology of Hayden's life, a chronological listing of all Hayden's poetry, and a list of his readings.

SUGGESTED SEARCH TERMS

corporal punishment AND schools

corporal punishment AND home

corporal punishment AND children

parental discipline

Robert Hayden

Hayden AND The Whipping

Hayden AND A Ballad of Remembrance

Hayden AND poetry

Glossary of Literary Terms

A

Abstract: Used as a noun, the term refers to a short summary or outline of a longer work. As an adjective applied to writing or literary works, abstract refers to words or phrases that name things not knowable through the five senses.

Accent: The emphasis or stress placed on a syllable in poetry. Traditional poetry commonly uses patterns of accented and unaccented syllables (known as feet) that create distinct rhythms. Much modern poetry uses less formal arrangements that create a sense of freedom and spontaneity.

Aestheticism: A literary and artistic movement of the nineteenth century. Followers of the movement believed that art should not be mixed with social, political, or moral teaching. The statement "art for art's sake" is a good summary of aestheticism. The movement had its roots in France, but it gained widespread importance in England in the last half of the nineteenth century, where it helped change the Victorian practice of including moral lessons in literature.

Affective Fallacy: An error in judging the merits or faults of a work of literature. The "error" results from stressing the importance of the work's effect upon the reader—that is, how it makes a reader "feel" emotionally, what it does as a literary work—instead of stressing its inner qualities as a created object, or what it "is."

Age of Johnson: The period in English literature between 1750 and 1798, named after the most prominent literary figure of the age, Samuel Johnson. Works written during this time are noted for their emphasis on "sensibility," or emotional quality. These works formed a transition between the rational works of the Age of Reason, or Neoclassical period, and the emphasis on individual feelings and responses of the Romantic period.

Age of Reason: See *Neoclassicism*

Age of Sensibility: See *Age of Johnson*

Agrarians: A group of Southern American writers of the 1930s and 1940s who fostered an economic and cultural program for the South based on agriculture, in opposition to the industrial society of the North. The term can refer to any group that promotes the value of farm life and agricultural society.

Alexandrine Meter: See *Meter*

Allegory: A narrative technique in which characters representing things or abstract ideas are used to convey a message or teach a lesson. Allegory is typically used to teach moral, ethical, or religious lessons but is sometimes used for satiric or political purposes.

Alliteration: A poetic device where the first consonant sounds or any vowel sounds in words or syllables are repeated.

Allusion: A reference to a familiar literary or historical person or event, used to make an idea more easily understood.

Amerind Literature: The writing and oral traditions of Native Americans. Native American literature was originally passed on by word of mouth, so it consisted largely of stories and events that were easily memorized. Amerind prose is often rhythmic like poetry because it was recited to the beat of a ceremonial drum.

Analogy: A comparison of two things made to explain something unfamiliar through its similarities to something familiar, or to prove one point based on the acceptedness of another. Similes and metaphors are types of analogies.

Anapest: See *Foot*

Angry Young Men: A group of British writers of the 1950s whose work expressed bitterness and disillusionment with society. Common to their work is an anti-hero who rebels against a corrupt social order and strives for personal integrity.

Anthropomorphism: The presentation of animals or objects in human shape or with human characteristics. The term is derived from the Greek word for "human form."

Antimasque: See *Masque*

Antithesis: The antithesis of something is its direct opposite. In literature, the use of antithesis as a figure of speech results in two statements that show a contrast through the balancing of two opposite ideas. Technically, it is the second portion of the statement that is defined as the "antithesis"; the first portion is the "thesis."

Apocrypha: Writings tentatively attributed to an author but not proven or universally accepted to be their works. The term was originally applied to certain books of the Bible that were not considered inspired and so were not included in the "sacred canon."

Apollonian and Dionysian: The two impulses believed to guide authors of dramatic tragedy. The Apollonian impulse is named after Apollo, the Greek god of light and beauty and the symbol of intellectual order. The Dionysian impulse is named after Dionysus, the Greek god of wine and the symbol of the unrestrained forces of nature. The Apollonian impulse is to create a rational, harmonious world, while the Dionysian is to express the irrational forces of personality.

Apostrophe: A statement, question, or request addressed to an inanimate object or concept or to a nonexistent or absent person.

Archetype: The word archetype is commonly used to describe an original pattern or model from which all other things of the same kind are made. This term was introduced to literary criticism from the psychology of Carl Jung. It expresses Jung's theory that behind every person's "unconscious," or repressed memories of the past, lies the "collective unconscious" of the human race: memories of the countless typical experiences of our ancestors. These memories are said to prompt illogical associations that trigger powerful emotions in the reader. Often, the emotional process is primitive, even primordial. Archetypes are the literary images that grow out of the "collective unconscious." They appear in literature as incidents and plots that repeat basic patterns of life. They may also appear as stereotyped characters.

Argument: The argument of a work is the author's subject matter or principal idea.

Art for Art's Sake: See *Aestheticism*

Assonance: The repetition of similar vowel sounds in poetry.

Audience: The people for whom a piece of literature is written. Authors usually write with a certain audience in mind, for example, children, members of a religious or ethnic group, or colleagues in a professional field. The term "audience" also applies to the people who gather to see or hear any performance, including plays, poetry readings, speeches, and concerts.

Automatic Writing: Writing carried out without a preconceived plan in an effort to capture every random thought. Authors who engage in automatic writing typically do not revise their work, preferring instead to preserve the revealed truth and beauty of spontaneous expression.

Avant-garde: A French term meaning "vanguard." It is used in literary criticism to describe new writing that rejects traditional approaches to literature in favor of innovations in style or content.

B

Ballad: A short poem that tells a simple story and has a repeated refrain. Ballads were originally intended to be sung. Early ballads, known as folk ballads, were passed down through generations, so their authors are often unknown. Later ballads composed by known authors are called literary ballads.

Baroque: A term used in literary criticism to describe literature that is complex or ornate in style or diction. Baroque works typically express tension, anxiety, and violent emotion. The term "Baroque Age" designates a period in Western European literature beginning in the late sixteenth century and ending about one hundred years later. Works of this period often mirror the qualities of works more generally associated with the label "baroque" and sometimes feature elaborate conceits.

Baroque Age: See *Baroque*

Baroque Period: See *Baroque*

Beat Generation: See *Beat Movement*

Beat Movement: A period featuring a group of American poets and novelists of the 1950s and 1960s—including Jack Kerouac, Allen Ginsberg, Gregory Corso, William S. Burroughs, and Lawrence Ferlinghetti—who rejected established social and literary values. Using such techniques as stream of consciousness writing and jazz-influenced free verse and focusing on unusual or abnormal states of mind—generated by religious ecstasy or the use of drugs—the Beat writers aimed to create works that were unconventional in both form and subject matter.

Beat Poets: See *Beat Movement*

Beats, The: See *Beat Movement*

Belles-lettres: A French term meaning "fine letters" or "beautiful writing." It is often used as a synonym for literature, typically referring to imaginative and artistic rather than scientific or expository writing. Current usage sometimes restricts the meaning to light or humorous writing and appreciative essays about literature.

Black Aesthetic Movement: A period of artistic and literary development among African Americans in the 1960s and early 1970s. This was the first major African-American artistic movement since the Harlem Renaissance and was closely paralleled by the civil rights and black power movements. The black aesthetic writers attempted to produce works of art that would be meaningful to the black masses. Key figures in black aesthetics included one of its founders, poet and playwright Amiri Baraka, formerly known as LeRoi Jones; poet and essayist Haki R. Madhubuti, formerly Don L. Lee; poet and playwright Sonia Sanchez; and dramatist Ed Bullins.

Black Arts Movement: See *Black Aesthetic Movement*

Black Comedy: See *Black Humor*

Black Humor: Writing that places grotesque elements side by side with humorous ones in an attempt to shock the reader, forcing him or her to laugh at the horrifying reality of a disordered world.

Black Mountain School: Black Mountain College and three of its instructors—Robert Creeley, Robert Duncan, and Charles Olson—were all influential in projective verse, so poets working in projective verse are now referred as members of the Black Mountain school.

Blank Verse: Loosely, any unrhymed poetry, but more generally, unrhymed iambic pentameter verse (composed of lines of five two-syllable feet with the first syllable accented, the second unaccented). Blank verse has been used by poets since the Renaissance for its flexibility and its graceful, dignified tone.

Bloomsbury Group: A group of English writers, artists, and intellectuals who held informal artistic and philosophical discussions in Bloomsbury, a district of London, from around 1907 to the early 1930s. The Bloomsbury Group held no uniform philosophical beliefs but did commonly express an aversion to moral prudery and a desire for greater social tolerance.

Bon Mot: A French term meaning "good word." A *bon mot* is a witty remark or clever observation.

Breath Verse: See *Projective Verse*

Burlesque: Any literary work that uses exaggeration to make its subject appear ridiculous, either by treating a trivial subject with profound seriousness or by treating a dignified subject frivolously. The word "burlesque" may also be used as an adjective, as in "burlesque show," to mean "striptease act."

C

Cadence: The natural rhythm of language caused by the alternation of accented and unaccented syllables. Much modern poetry—notably free verse—deliberately manipulates cadence to create complex rhythmic effects.

Caesura: A pause in a line of poetry, usually occurring near the middle. It typically corresponds to a break in the natural rhythm or sense of the line but is sometimes shifted to create special meanings or rhythmic effects.

Canzone: A short Italian or Provencal lyric poem, commonly about love and often set to music. The *canzone* has no set form but typically contains five or six stanzas made up of seven to twenty lines of eleven syllables each. A shorter, five- to ten-line "envoy," or concluding stanza, completes the poem.

Carpe Diem: A Latin term meaning "seize the day." This is a traditional theme of poetry, especially lyrics. A *carpe diem* poem advises the reader or the person it addresses to live for today and enjoy the pleasures of the moment.

Catharsis: The release or purging of unwanted emotions—specifically fear and pity—brought about by exposure to art. The term was first used by the Greek philosopher Aristotle in his *Poetics* to refer to the desired effect of tragedy on spectators.

Celtic Renaissance: A period of Irish literary and cultural history at the end of the nineteenth century. Followers of the movement aimed to create a romantic vision of Celtic myth and legend. The most significant works of the Celtic Renaissance typically present a dreamy, unreal world, usually in reaction against the reality of contemporary problems.

Celtic Twilight: See *Celtic Renaissance*

Character: Broadly speaking, a person in a literary work. The actions of characters are what constitute the plot of a story, novel, or poem. There are numerous types of characters, ranging from simple, stereotypical figures to intricate, multifaceted ones. In the techniques of anthropomorphism and personification, animals—and even places or things—can assume aspects of character. "Characterization" is the process by which an author creates vivid, believable characters in a work of art. This may be done in a variety of ways, including (1) direct description of the character by the narrator; (2) the direct presentation of the speech, thoughts, or actions of the character; and (3) the responses of other characters to the character. The term "character" also refers to a form originated by the ancient Greek writer Theophrastus that later became popular in the seventeenth and eighteenth centuries. It is a short essay or sketch of a person who prominently displays a specific attribute or quality, such as miserliness or ambition.

Characterization: See *Character*

Classical: In its strictest definition in literary criticism, classicism refers to works of ancient Greek or Roman literature. The term may also be used to describe a literary work of recognized importance (a "classic") from any time period or literature that exhibits the traits of classicism.

Classicism: A term used in literary criticism to describe critical doctrines that have their roots in ancient Greek and Roman literature, philosophy, and art. Works associated with classicism typically exhibit restraint on the part of the author, unity of design and purpose, clarity, simplicity, logical organization, and respect for tradition.

Colloquialism: A word, phrase, or form of pronunciation that is acceptable in casual conversation but not in formal, written communication. It is considered more acceptable than slang.

Complaint: A lyric poem, popular in the Renaissance, in which the speaker expresses sorrow about his or her condition. Typically, the speaker's sadness is caused by an unresponsive lover, but some complaints cite other sources of unhappiness, such as poverty or fate.

Conceit: A clever and fanciful metaphor, usually expressed through elaborate and extended comparison, that presents a striking parallel between two seemingly dissimilar things—for example, elaborately comparing a beautiful woman to an object like a garden or the sun. The conceit was a popular device throughout the Elizabethan Age and Baroque Age and was the principal technique of the seventeenth-century English metaphysical poets. This usage of the word conceit is unrelated to the best-known definition of conceit as an arrogant attitude or behavior.

Concrete: Concrete is the opposite of abstract, and refers to a thing that actually exists or a description that allows the reader to experience an object or concept with the senses.

Concrete Poetry: Poetry in which visual elements play a large part in the poetic effect. Punctuation marks, letters, or words are arranged on a page to form a visual design: a cross, for example, or a bumblebee.

Confessional Poetry: A form of poetry in which the poet reveals very personal, intimate, sometimes shocking information about himself or herself.

Connotation: The impression that a word gives beyond its defined meaning. Connotations may be universally understood or may be significant only to a certain group.

Consonance: Consonance occurs in poetry when words appearing at the ends of two or more verses have similar final consonant sounds but have final vowel sounds that differ, as with "stuff" and "off."

Convention: Any widely accepted literary device, style, or form.

Corrido: A Mexican ballad.

Couplet: Two lines of poetry with the same rhyme and meter, often expressing a complete and self-contained thought.

Criticism: The systematic study and evaluation of literary works, usually based on a specific method or set of principles. An important part of literary studies since ancient times, the practice of criticism has given rise to numerous theories, methods, and "schools," sometimes producing conflicting, even contradictory, interpretations of literature in general as well as of individual works. Even such basic issues as what constitutes a poem or a novel have been the subject of much criticism over the centuries.

D

Dactyl: See *Foot*

Dadaism: A protest movement in art and literature founded by Tristan Tzara in 1916. Followers of the movement expressed their outrage at the destruction brought about by World War I by revolting against numerous forms of social convention. The Dadaists presented works marked by calculated madness and flamboyant nonsense. They stressed total freedom of expression, commonly through primitive displays of emotion and illogical, often senseless, poetry. The movement ended shortly after the war, when it was replaced by surrealism.

Decadent: See *Decadents*

Decadents: The followers of a nineteenth-century literary movement that had its beginnings in French aestheticism. Decadent literature displays a fascination with perverse and morbid states; a search for novelty and sensation—the "new thrill"; a preoccupation with mysticism; and a belief in the senselessness of human existence. The movement is closely associated with the doctrine Art for Art's Sake. The term "decadence" is sometimes used to denote a decline in the quality of art or literature following a period of greatness.

Deconstruction: A method of literary criticism developed by Jacques Derrida and characterized by multiple conflicting interpretations of a given work. Deconstructionists consider the impact of the language of a work and suggest that the true meaning of the work is not necessarily the meaning that the author intended.

Deduction: The process of reaching a conclusion through reasoning from general premises to a specific premise.

Denotation: The definition of a word, apart from the impressions or feelings it creates in the reader.

Diction: The selection and arrangement of words in a literary work. Either or both may vary depending on the desired effect. There are four general types of diction: "formal," used in scholarly or lofty writing; "informal," used in relaxed but educated conversation; "colloquial," used in everyday speech; and "slang," containing newly coined words and other terms not accepted in formal usage.

Didactic: A term used to describe works of literature that aim to teach some moral, religious, political, or practical lesson. Although didactic elements are often found in artistically pleasing works, the term "didactic" usually refers to literature in which the message is more important than the form. The term may also be used to criticize a work that the critic finds "overly didactic," that is, heavy-handed in its delivery of a lesson.

Dimeter: See *Meter*

Dionysian: See *Apollonian and Dionysian*

Discordia concours: A Latin phrase meaning "discord in harmony." The term was coined by the eighteenth-century English writer Samuel Johnson to describe "a combination of dissimilar images or discovery of occult resemblances in things apparently unlike." Johnson created the expression by reversing a phrase by the Latin poet Horace.

Dissonance: A combination of harsh or jarring sounds, especially in poetry. Although such combinations may be accidental, poets sometimes intentionally make them to achieve particular effects. Dissonance is also sometimes used to refer to close but not identical rhymes. When this is the case, the word functions as a synonym for consonance.

Double Entendre: A corruption of a French phrase meaning "double meaning." The term is used to indicate a word or phrase that is deliberately ambiguous, especially when one of the meanings is risque or improper.

Draft: Any preliminary version of a written work. An author may write dozens of drafts which are revised to form the final work, or he or she may write only one, with few or no revisions.

Dramatic Monologue: See *Monologue*

Dramatic Poetry: Any lyric work that employs elements of drama such as dialogue, conflict, or characterization, but excluding works that are intended for stage presentation.

Dream Allegory: See *Dream Vision*

Dream Vision: A literary convention, chiefly of the Middle Ages. In a dream vision a story is presented as a literal dream of the narrator. This device was commonly used to teach moral and religious lessons.

E

Eclogue: In classical literature, a poem featuring rural themes and structured as a dialogue among shepherds. Eclogues often took specific poetic forms, such as elegies or love poems. Some were written as the soliloquy of a shepherd. In later centuries, "eclogue" came to refer to any poem that was in the pastoral tradition or that had a dialogue or monologue structure.

Edwardian: Describes cultural conventions identified with the period of the reign of Edward VII of England (1901-1910). Writers of the Edwardian Age typically displayed a strong reaction against the propriety and conservatism of the Victorian Age. Their work often exhibits distrust of authority in religion, politics, and art and expresses strong doubts about the soundness of conventional values.

Edwardian Age: See *Edwardian*

Electra Complex: A daughter's amorous obsession with her father.

Elegy: A lyric poem that laments the death of a person or the eventual death of all people. In a conventional elegy, set in a classical world, the poet and subject are spoken of as shepherds. In modern criticism, the word elegy is often used to refer to a poem that is melancholy or mournfully contemplative.

Elizabethan Age: A period of great economic growth, religious controversy, and nationalism closely associated with the reign of Elizabeth I of England (1558-1603). The Elizabethan Age is considered a part of the general renaissance—that is, the flowering of arts and literature—that took place in Europe during the fourteenth through sixteenth centuries. The era is considered the golden age of English literature. The most important dramas in English and a great deal of lyric poetry were produced during this period, and modern English criticism began around this time.

Empathy: A sense of shared experience, including emotional and physical feelings, with someone or something other than oneself. Empathy is often used to describe the response of a reader to a literary character.

English Sonnet: See *Sonnet*

Enjambment: The running over of the sense and structure of a line of verse or a couplet into the following verse or couplet.

Enlightenment, The: An eighteenth-century philosophical movement. It began in France but had a wide impact throughout Europe and America. Thinkers of the Enlightenment valued reason and believed that both the individual and society could achieve a state of perfection. Corresponding to this essentially humanist vision was a resistance to religious authority.

Epic: A long narrative poem about the adventures of a hero of great historic or legendary importance. The setting is vast and the action is often given cosmic significance through the intervention of supernatural forces such as gods, angels, or demons. Epics are typically written in a classical style of grand simplicity with elaborate metaphors and allusions that enhance the symbolic importance of a hero's adventures.

Epic Simile: See *Homeric Simile*

Epigram: A saying that makes the speaker's point quickly and concisely.

Epilogue: A concluding statement or section of a literary work. In dramas, particularly those of the seventeenth and eighteenth centuries, the epilogue is a closing speech, often in verse, delivered by an actor at the end of a play and spoken directly to the audience.

Epiphany: A sudden revelation of truth inspired by a seemingly trivial incident.

Epitaph: An inscription on a tomb or tombstone, or a verse written on the occasion of a person's death. Epitaphs may be serious or humorous.

Epithalamion: A song or poem written to honor and commemorate a marriage ceremony.

Epithalamium: See *Epithalamion*

Epithet: A word or phrase, often disparaging or abusive, that expresses a character trait of someone or something.

Erziehungsroman: See *Bildungsroman*

Essay: A prose composition with a focused subject of discussion. The term was coined by Michel de Montaigne to describe his 1580 collection of brief, informal reflections on himself and on various topics relating to human nature. An essay can also be a long, systematic discourse.

Existentialism: A predominantly twentieth-century philosophy concerned with the nature and perception of human existence. There are two major strains of existentialist thought: atheistic and Christian. Followers of atheistic existentialism believe that the individual is alone in a godless universe and that the basic human condition is one of suffering and loneliness. Nevertheless, because there are no fixed values, individuals can create their own characters—indeed, they can shape themselves—through the exercise of free will. The atheistic strain culminates in and is popularly associated with the works of Jean-Paul Sartre. The Christian existentialists, on the other hand, believe that only in God may people find freedom from life's anguish. The two strains hold certain beliefs in common: that existence cannot be fully understood or described through empirical effort; that anguish is a universal element of life; that individuals must bear responsibility for their actions; and that there is no common standard of behavior or perception for religious and ethical matters.

Expatriates: See *Expatriatism*

Expatriatism: The practice of leaving one's country to live for an extended period in another country.

Exposition: Writing intended to explain the nature of an idea, thing, or theme. Expository writing is often combined with description, narration, or argument. In dramatic writing, the exposition is the introductory material which presents the characters, setting, and tone of the play.

Expressionism: An indistinct literary term, originally used to describe an early twentieth-century school of German painting. The term applies to almost any mode of unconventional, highly subjective writing that distorts reality in some way.

Extended Monologue: See *Monologue*

F

Feet: See *Foot*

Feminine Rhyme: See *Rhyme*

Fiction: Any story that is the product of imagination rather than a documentation of fact. Characters and events in such narratives may be based in real life but their ultimate form and configuration is a creation of the author.

Figurative Language: A technique in writing in which the author temporarily interrupts the order, construction, or meaning of the writing for a particular effect. This interruption takes the form of one or more figures of speech such as hyperbole, irony, or simile. Figurative language is the opposite of literal language, in which every word is truthful, accurate, and free of exaggeration or embellishment.

Figures of Speech: Writing that differs from customary conventions for construction, meaning, order, or significance for the purpose of a special meaning or effect. There are two major types of figures of speech: rhetorical figures, which do not make changes in the meaning of the words, and tropes, which do.

Fin de siecle: A French term meaning "end of the century." The term is used to denote the last decade of the nineteenth century, a transition period when writers and other artists abandoned old conventions and looked for new techniques and objectives.

First Person: See *Point of View*

Folk Ballad: See *Ballad*

Folklore: Traditions and myths preserved in a culture or group of people. Typically, these are passed on by word of mouth in various forms—such as legends, songs, and proverbs—or preserved in customs and ceremonies. This term was first used by W. J. Thoms in 1846.

Folktale: A story originating in oral tradition. Folktales fall into a variety of categories, including legends, ghost stories, fairy tales, fables, and anecdotes based on historical figures and events.

Foot: The smallest unit of rhythm in a line of poetry. In English-language poetry, a foot is typically one accented syllable combined with one or two unaccented syllables.

Form: The pattern or construction of a work which identifies its genre and distinguishes it from other genres.

Formalism: In literary criticism, the belief that literature should follow prescribed rules of construction, such as those that govern the sonnet form.

Fourteener Meter: See *Meter*

Free Verse: Poetry that lacks regular metrical and rhyme patterns but that tries to capture the cadences of everyday speech. The form allows a poet to exploit a variety of rhythmical effects within a single poem.

Futurism: A flamboyant literary and artistic movement that developed in France, Italy, and Russia from 1908 through the 1920s. Futurist theater and poetry abandoned traditional literary forms. In their place, followers of the movement attempted to achieve total freedom of expression through bizarre imagery and deformed or newly invented words. The Futurists were self-consciously modern artists who attempted to incorporate the appearances and sounds of modern life into their work.

G

Genre: A category of literary work. In critical theory, genre may refer to both the content of a given work—tragedy, comedy, pastoral—and to its form, such as poetry, novel, or drama.

Genteel Tradition: A term coined by critic George Santayana to describe the literary practice of certain late nineteenth-century American writers, especially New Englanders. Followers of the Genteel Tradition emphasized conventionality in social, religious, moral, and literary standards.

Georgian Age: See *Georgian Poets*

Georgian Period: See *Georgian Poets*

Georgian Poets: A loose grouping of English poets during the years 1912-1922. The Georgians reacted against certain literary schools and practices, especially Victorian wordiness, turn-of-the-century aestheticism, and contemporary urban realism. In their place, the Georgians embraced the nineteenth-century poetic practices of William Wordsworth and the other Lake Poets.

Georgic: A poem about farming and the farmer's way of life, named from Virgil's *Georgics*.

Gilded Age: A period in American history during the 1870s characterized by political corruption and materialism. A number of important novels of social and political criticism were written during this time.

Gothic: See *Gothicism*

Gothicism: In literary criticism, works characterized by a taste for the medieval or morbidly attractive. A gothic novel prominently features elements of horror, the supernatural, gloom, and violence: clanking chains, terror, charnel houses, ghosts, medieval castles, and mysteriously slamming doors. The term "gothic novel" is also applied to novels that lack elements of the traditional Gothic setting but that create a similar atmosphere of terror or dread.

Graveyard School: A group of eighteenth-century English poets who wrote long, picturesque meditations on death. Their works were designed to cause the reader to ponder immortality.

Great Chain of Being: The belief that all things and creatures in nature are organized in a hierarchy from inanimate objects at the bottom to God at the top. This system of belief was popular in the seventeenth and eighteenth centuries.

Grotesque: In literary criticism, the subject matter of a work or a style of expression characterized by exaggeration, deformity, freakishness, and disorder. The grotesque often includes an element of comic absurdity.

H

Haiku: The shortest form of Japanese poetry, constructed in three lines of five, seven, and five syllables respectively. The message of a *haiku* poem usually centers on some aspect of spirituality and provokes an emotional response in the reader.

Half Rhyme: See *Consonance*

Harlem Renaissance: The Harlem Renaissance of the 1920s is generally considered the first significant movement of black writers and artists in the United States. During this period, new and established black writers published more fiction and poetry than ever before, the first influential black literary journals were established, and black authors and artists received their first widespread recognition and serious critical appraisal. Among the major writers associated with this period are Claude McKay, Jean Toomer, Countee Cullen, Langston Hughes, Arna Bontemps, Nella Larsen, and Zora Neale Hurston.

Hellenism: Imitation of ancient Greek thought or styles. Also, an approach to life that focuses on the growth and development of the intellect. "Hellenism" is sometimes used to refer to the belief that reason can be applied to examine all human experience.

Heptameter: See *Meter*

Hero/Heroine: The principal sympathetic character (male or female) in a literary work. Heroes and heroines typically exhibit admirable traits: idealism, courage, and integrity, for example.

Heroic Couplet: A rhyming couplet written in iambic pentameter (a verse with five iambic feet).

Heroic Line: The meter and length of a line of verse in epic or heroic poetry. This varies by language and time period.

Heroine: See *Hero/Heroine*

Hexameter: See *Meter*

Historical Criticism: The study of a work based on its impact on the world of the time period in which it was written.

Hokku: See *Haiku*

Holocaust: See *Holocaust Literature*

Holocaust Literature: Literature influenced by or written about the Holocaust of World War II. Such literature includes true stories of survival in concentration camps, escape, and life after the war, as well as fictional works and poetry.

Homeric Simile: An elaborate, detailed comparison written as a simile many lines in length.

Horatian Satire: See *Satire*

Humanism: A philosophy that places faith in the dignity of humankind and rejects the medieval perception of the individual as a weak, fallen creature. "Humanists" typically believe in the perfectibility of human nature and view reason and education as the means to that end.

Humors: Mentions of the humors refer to the ancient Greek theory that a person's health and personality were determined by the balance of four basic fluids in the body: blood, phlegm, yellow bile, and black bile. A dominance of any fluid would cause extremes in behavior. An excess of blood created a sanguine person who was joyful, aggressive, and passionate; a phlegmatic person was shy, fearful, and sluggish; too much yellow bile led to a choleric temperament characterized by impatience, anger, bitterness, and stubbornness; and excessive black bile created melancholy, a state of laziness, gluttony, and lack of motivation.

Humours: See *Humors*

Hyperbole: In literary criticism, deliberate exaggeration used to achieve an effect.

I

Iamb: See *Foot*

Idiom: A word construction or verbal expression closely associated with a given language.

Image: A concrete representation of an object or sensory experience. Typically, such a representation helps evoke the feelings associated with the object or experience itself. Images are either "literal" or "figurative." Literal images are especially concrete and involve little or no extension of the obvious meaning of the words used to express them. Figurative images do not follow the literal meaning of the words exactly. Images in literature are usually visual, but the term "image" can also refer to the representation of any sensory experience.

Imagery: The array of images in a literary work. Also, figurative language.

Imagism: An English and American poetry movement that flourished between 1908 and 1917. The Imagists used precise, clearly presented images in their works. They also used common, everyday speech and aimed for conciseness, concrete imagery, and the creation of new rhythms.

In medias res: A Latin term meaning "in the middle of things." It refers to the technique of beginning a story at its midpoint and then using various flashback devices to reveal previous action.

Induction: The process of reaching a conclusion by reasoning from specific premises to form a general premise. Also, an introductory portion of a work of literature, especially a play.

Intentional Fallacy: The belief that judgments of a literary work based solely on an author's stated or implied intentions are false and misleading. Critics who believe in the concept of the intentional fallacy typically argue that the work itself is sufficient matter for interpretation, even though they may concede that an author's statement of purpose can be useful.

Interior Monologue: A narrative technique in which characters' thoughts are revealed in a way that appears to be uncontrolled by the author. The interior monologue typically aims to reveal the inner self of a character. It portrays emotional experiences as they occur at both a conscious and unconscious level. Images are often used to represent sensations or emotions.

Internal Rhyme: Rhyme that occurs within a single line of verse.

Irish Literary Renaissance: A late nineteenth- and early twentieth-century movement in Irish literature. Members of the movement aimed to reduce the influence of British culture in Ireland and create an Irish national literature.

Irony: In literary criticism, the effect of language in which the intended meaning is the opposite of what is stated.

Italian Sonnet: See *Sonnet*

J

Jacobean Age: The period of the reign of James I of England (1603-1625). The early literature of this period reflected the worldview of the Elizabethan Age, but a darker, more cynical attitude steadily grew in the art and literature of the Jacobean Age. This was an important time for English drama and poetry.

Jargon: Language that is used or understood only by a select group of people. Jargon may refer to terminology used in a certain profession, such as computer jargon, or it may refer to any nonsensical language that is not understood by most people.

Journalism: Writing intended for publication in a newspaper or magazine, or for broadcast on a radio or television program featuring news, sports, entertainment, or other timely material.

K

Knickerbocker Group: A somewhat indistinct group of New York writers of the first half of the nineteenth century. Members of the group were linked only by location and a common theme: New York life.

Kunstlerroman: See *Bildungsroman*

L

Lais: See *Lay*

Lake Poets: See *Lake School*

Lake School: These poets all lived in the Lake District of England at the turn of the nineteenth century. As a group, they followed no single "school" of thought or literary practice, although their works were uniformly disparaged by the *Edinburgh Review*.

Lay: A song or simple narrative poem. The form originated in medieval France. Early French *lais* were often based on the Celtic legends and other tales sung by Breton minstrels—thus the name of the "Breton lay." In fourteenth-century England, the term "lay" was used to describe short narratives written in imitation of the Breton lays.

Leitmotiv: See *Motif*

Literal Language: An author uses literal language when he or she writes without exaggerating or embellishing the subject matter and without any tools of figurative language.

Literary Ballad: See *Ballad*

Literature: Literature is broadly defined as any written or spoken material, but the term most often refers to creative works.

Lost Generation: A term first used by Gertrude Stein to describe the post-World War I generation of American writers: men and women haunted by a sense of betrayal and emptiness brought about by the destructiveness of the war.

Lyric Poetry: A poem expressing the subjective feelings and personal emotions of the poet. Such poetry is melodic, since it was originally accompanied by a lyre in recitals. Most Western poetry in the twentieth century may be classified as lyrical.

M

Mannerism: Exaggerated, artificial adherence to a literary manner or style. Also, a popular style of the visual arts of late sixteenth-century Europe that was marked by elongation of the human form and by intentional spatial distortion. Literary works that are self-consciously high-toned and artistic are often said to be "mannered."

Masculine Rhyme: See *Rhyme*

Measure: The foot, verse, or time sequence used in a literary work, especially a poem. Measure is often used somewhat incorrectly as a synonym for meter.

Metaphor: A figure of speech that expresses an idea through the image of another object. Metaphors suggest the essence of the first object by identifying it with certain qualities of the second object.

Metaphysical Conceit: See *Conceit*

Metaphysical Poetry: The body of poetry produced by a group of seventeenth-century English writers called the "Metaphysical Poets." The group includes John Donne and Andrew Marvell. The Metaphysical Poets made use of everyday speech, intellectual analysis, and unique imagery. They aimed to portray the ordinary conflicts and contradictions of life. Their poems often took the form of an argument, and many of them emphasize physical and religious love as well as the fleeting nature of life. Elaborate conceits are typical in metaphysical poetry.

Metaphysical Poets: See *Metaphysical Poetry*

Meter: In literary criticism, the repetition of sound patterns that creates a rhythm in poetry. The patterns are based on the number of syllables and the presence and absence of accents. The unit of rhythm in a line is called a foot. Types of meter are classified according to the number of feet in a line. These are the standard English lines: Monometer, one foot; Dimeter, two feet; Trimeter, three feet; Tetrameter, four feet; Pentameter, five feet; Hexameter, six feet (also called the Alexandrine); Heptameter, seven feet (also called the "Fourteener" when the feet are iambic).

Modernism: Modern literary practices. Also, the principles of a literary school that lasted from roughly the beginning of the twentieth century until the end of World War II. Modernism is defined by its rejection of the literary conventions of the nineteenth century and by its opposition to conventional morality, taste, traditions, and economic values.

Monologue: A composition, written or oral, by a single individual. More specifically, a speech given by a single individual in a drama or other public entertainment. It has no set length, although it is usually several or more lines long.

Monometer: See *Meter*

Mood: The prevailing emotions of a work or of the author in his or her creation of the work. The mood of a work is not always what might be expected based on its subject matter.

Motif: A theme, character type, image, metaphor, or other verbal element that recurs throughout a single work of literature or occurs in a number of different works over a period of time.

Motiv: See *Motif*

Muckrakers: An early twentieth-century group of American writers. Typically, their works exposed the wrongdoings of big business and government in the United States.

Muses: Nine Greek mythological goddesses, the daughters of Zeus and Mnemosyne (Memory). Each muse patronized a specific area of the liberal arts and sciences. Calliope presided over epic poetry, Clio over history, Erato over love poetry, Euterpe over music or lyric poetry, Melpomene over tragedy, Polyhymnia over hymns to the gods, Terpsichore over dance, Thalia over comedy, and Urania over astronomy. Poets and writers traditionally made appeals to the Muses for inspiration in their work.

Myth: An anonymous tale emerging from the traditional beliefs of a culture or social unit. Myths use supernatural explanations for natural phenomena. They may also explain cosmic issues like creation and death. Collections of myths, known as mythologies, are common to all cultures and nations, but the best-known myths belong to the Norse, Roman, and Greek mythologies.

N

Narration: The telling of a series of events, real or invented. A narration may be either a simple narrative, in which the events are recounted chronologically, or a narrative with a plot, in which the account is given in a style reflecting the author's artistic concept of the story. Narration is sometimes used as a synonym for "storyline."

Narrative: A verse or prose accounting of an event or sequence of events, real or invented.

The term is also used as an adjective in the sense "method of narration." For example, in literary criticism, the expression "narrative technique" usually refers to the way the author structures and presents his or her story.

Narrative Poetry: A nondramatic poem in which the author tells a story. Such poems may be of any length or level of complexity.

Narrator: The teller of a story. The narrator may be the author or a character in the story through whom the author speaks.

Naturalism: A literary movement of the late nineteenth and early twentieth centuries. The movement's major theorist, French novelist Emile Zola, envisioned a type of fiction that would examine human life with the objectivity of scientific inquiry. The Naturalists typically viewed human beings as either the products of "biological determinism," ruled by hereditary instincts and engaged in an endless struggle for survival, or as the products of "socioeconomic determinism," ruled by social and economic forces beyond their control. In their works, the Naturalists generally ignored the highest levels of society and focused on degradation: poverty, alcoholism, prostitution, insanity, and disease.

Negritude: A literary movement based on the concept of a shared cultural bond on the part of black Africans, wherever they may be in the world. It traces its origins to the former French colonies of Africa and the Caribbean. Negritude poets, novelists, and essayists generally stress four points in their writings: One, black alienation from traditional African culture can lead to feelings of inferiority. Two, European colonialism and Western education should be resisted. Three, black Africans should seek to affirm and define their own identity. Four, African culture can and should be reclaimed. Many Negritude writers also claim that blacks can make unique contributions to the world, based on a heightened appreciation of nature, rhythm, and human emotions—aspects of life they say are not so highly valued in the materialistic and rationalistic West.

Negro Renaissance: See *Harlem Renaissance*

Neoclassical Period: See *Neoclassicism*

Neoclassicism: In literary criticism, this term refers to the revival of the attitudes and styles of expression of classical literature. It is generally used to describe a period in European history beginning in the late seventeenth century and lasting until about 1800. In its purest form, Neoclassicism marked a return to order, proportion, restraint, logic, accuracy, and decorum. In England, where Neoclassicism perhaps was most popular, it reflected the influence of seventeenth- century French writers, especially dramatists. Neoclassical writers typically reacted against the intensity and enthusiasm of the Renaissance period. They wrote works that appealed to the intellect, using elevated language and classical literary forms such as satire and the ode. Neoclassical works were often governed by the classical goal of instruction.

Neoclassicists: See *Neoclassicism*

New Criticism: A movement in literary criticism, dating from the late 1920s, that stressed close textual analysis in the interpretation of works of literature. The New Critics saw little merit in historical and biographical analysis. Rather, they aimed to examine the text alone, free from the question of how external events—biographical or otherwise—may have helped shape it.

New Journalism: A type of writing in which the journalist presents factual information in a form usually used in fiction. New journalism emphasizes description, narration, and character development to bring readers closer to the human element of the story, and is often used in personality profiles and in-depth feature articles. It is not compatible with "straight" or "hard" newswriting, which is generally composed in a brief, fact-based style.

New Journalists: See *New Journalism*

New Negro Movement: See *Harlem Renaissance*

Noble Savage: The idea that primitive man is noble and good but becomes evil and corrupted as he becomes civilized. The concept of the noble savage originated in the Renaissance period but is more closely identified with such later writers as Jean-Jacques Rousseau and Aphra Behn.

O

Objective Correlative: An outward set of objects, a situation, or a chain of events corresponding to an inward experience and evoking this experience in the reader. The term frequently appears in modern criticism in discussions of authors' intended effects on the emotional responses of readers.

Objectivity: A quality in writing characterized by the absence of the author's opinion or feeling about the subject matter. Objectivity is an important factor in criticism.

Occasional Verse: poetry written on the occasion of a significant historical or personal event. *Vers de societe* is sometimes called occasional verse although it is of a less serious nature.

Octave: A poem or stanza composed of eight lines. The term octave most often represents the first eight lines of a Petrarchan sonnet.

Ode: Name given to an extended lyric poem characterized by exalted emotion and dignified style. An ode usually concerns a single, serious theme. Most odes, but not all, are addressed to an object or individual. Odes are distinguished from other lyric poetic forms by their complex rhythmic and stanzaic patterns.

Oedipus Complex: A son's amorous obsession with his mother. The phrase is derived from the story of the ancient Theban hero Oedipus, who unknowingly killed his father and married his mother.

Omniscience: See *Point of View*

Onomatopoeia: The use of words whose sounds express or suggest their meaning. In its simplest sense, onomatopoeia may be represented by words that mimic the sounds they denote such as "hiss" or "meow." At a more subtle level, the pattern and rhythm of sounds and rhymes of a line or poem may be onomatopoeic.

Oral Tradition: See *Oral Transmission*

Oral Transmission: A process by which songs, ballads, folklore, and other material are transmitted by word of mouth. The tradition of oral transmission predates the written record systems of literate society. Oral transmission preserves material sometimes over generations, although often with variations. Memory plays a large part in the recitation and preservation of orally transmitted material.

Ottava Rima: An eight-line stanza of poetry composed in iambic pentameter (a five-foot line in which each foot consists of an unaccented syllable followed by an accented syllable), following the abababcc rhyme scheme.

Oxymoron: A phrase combining two contradictory terms. Oxymorons may be intentional or unintentional.

P

Pantheism: The idea that all things are both a manifestation or revelation of God and a part of God at the same time. Pantheism was a common attitude in the early societies of Egypt, India, and Greece—the term derives from the Greek *pan* meaning "all" and *theos* meaning "deity." It later became a significant part of the Christian faith.

Parable: A story intended to teach a moral lesson or answer an ethical question.

Paradox: A statement that appears illogical or contradictory at first, but may actually point to an underlying truth.

Parallelism: A method of comparison of two ideas in which each is developed in the same grammatical structure.

Parnassianism: A mid nineteenth-century movement in French literature. Followers of the movement stressed adherence to well-defined artistic forms as a reaction against the often chaotic expression of the artist's ego that dominated the work of the Romantics. The Parnassians also rejected the moral, ethical, and social themes exhibited in the works of French Romantics such as Victor Hugo. The aesthetic doctrines of the Parnassians strongly influenced the later symbolist and decadent movements.

Parody: In literary criticism, this term refers to an imitation of a serious literary work or the signature style of a particular author in a ridiculous manner. A typical parody adopts the style of the original and applies it to an inappropriate subject for humorous effect. Parody is a form of satire and could be considered the literary equivalent of a caricature or cartoon.

Pastoral: A term derived from the Latin word "pastor," meaning shepherd. A pastoral is a literary composition on a rural theme. The conventions of the pastoral were originated by the third-century Greek poet Theocritus, who wrote about the experiences, love affairs, and pastimes of Sicilian shepherds. In a pastoral, characters and language of a courtly nature are often placed in a simple setting. The term pastoral is also used to classify dramas, elegies, and lyrics that exhibit the use of country settings and shepherd characters.

Pathetic Fallacy: A term coined by English critic John Ruskin to identify writing that falsely endows nonhuman things with human intentions and feelings, such as "angry clouds" and "sad trees."

Pen Name: See *Pseudonym*

Pentameter: See *Meter*

Persona: A Latin term meaning "mask." *Personae* are the characters in a fictional work of literature. The *persona* generally functions as a mask through which the author tells a story in a voice other than his or her own. A *persona* is usually either a character in a story who acts as a narrator or an "implied author," a voice created by the author to act as the narrator for himself or herself.

Personae: See *Persona*

Personal Point of View: See *Point of View*

Personification: A figure of speech that gives human qualities to abstract ideas, animals, and inanimate objects.

Petrarchan Sonnet: See *Sonnet*

Phenomenology: A method of literary criticism based on the belief that things have no existence outside of human consciousness or awareness. Proponents of this theory believe that art is a process that takes place in the mind of the observer as he or she contemplates an object rather than a quality of the object itself.

Plagiarism: Claiming another person's written material as one's own. Plagiarism can take the form of direct, word-for-word copying or the theft of the substance or idea of the work.

Platonic Criticism: A form of criticism that stresses an artistic work's usefulness as an agent of social engineering rather than any quality or value of the work itself.

Platonism: The embracing of the doctrines of the philosopher Plato, popular among the poets of the Renaissance and the Romantic period. Platonism is more flexible than Aristotelian Criticism and places more emphasis on the supernatural and unknown aspects of life.

Plot: In literary criticism, this term refers to the pattern of events in a narrative or drama. In its simplest sense, the plot guides the author in composing the work and helps the reader follow the work. Typically, plots exhibit causality and unity and have a beginning, a middle, and an end. Sometimes, however, a plot may consist of a series of disconnected events, in which case it is known as an "episodic plot."

Poem: In its broadest sense, a composition utilizing rhyme, meter, concrete detail, and expressive language to create a literary experience with emotional and aesthetic appeal.

Poet: An author who writes poetry or verse. The term is also used to refer to an artist or writer who has an exceptional gift for expression, imagination, and energy in the making of art in any form.

Poete maudit: A term derived from Paul Verlaine's *Les poetes maudits* (*The Accursed Poets*), a collection of essays on the French symbolist writers Stephane Mallarme, Arthur Rimbaud, and Tristan Corbiere. In the sense intended by Verlaine, the poet is "accursed" for choosing to explore extremes of human experience outside of middle-class society.

Poetic Fallacy: See *Pathetic Fallacy*

Poetic Justice: An outcome in a literary work, not necessarily a poem, in which the good are rewarded and the evil are punished, especially in ways that particularly fit their virtues or crimes.

Poetic License: Distortions of fact and literary convention made by a writer—not always a poet—for the sake of the effect gained. Poetic license is closely related to the concept of "artistic freedom."

Poetics: This term has two closely related meanings. It denotes (1) an aesthetic theory in literary criticism about the essence of poetry or (2) rules prescribing the proper methods, content, style, or diction of poetry. The term poetics may also refer to theories about literature in general, not just poetry.

Poetry: In its broadest sense, writing that aims to present ideas and evoke an emotional experience in the reader through the use of meter, imagery, connotative and concrete words, and a carefully constructed structure based on rhythmic patterns. Poetry typically relies on words and expressions that have several layers of meaning. It also makes use of the effects of regular rhythm on the ear and may make a strong appeal to the senses through the use of imagery.

Point of View: The narrative perspective from which a literary work is presented to the reader. There are four traditional points of view. The "third person omniscient" gives the reader a "godlike" perspective, unrestricted by time or place, from which to see actions and look into the minds of characters. This allows the author to comment openly on characters and events in the work. The "third person" point of view presents the events of the story from outside of any single character's perception, much like the omniscient point of view, but the reader must understand the action as it takes place and without any special insight into characters' minds or motivations. The "first person" or "personal" point of view relates events as they are perceived by a single character. The main character "tells" the story and may offer opinions about the action and characters which differ from those of the author. Much less common than omniscient, third person, and first person is the "second person" point of view, wherein the author tells the story as if it is happening to the reader.

Polemic: A work in which the author takes a stand on a controversial subject, such as abortion or religion. Such works are often extremely argumentative or provocative.

Pornography: Writing intended to provoke feelings of lust in the reader. Such works are often condemned by critics and teachers, but those which can be shown to have literary value are viewed less harshly.

Post-Aesthetic Movement: An artistic response made by African Americans to the black aesthetic movement of the 1960s and early '70s. Writers since that time have adopted a somewhat different tone in their work, with less emphasis placed on the disparity between black and white in the United States. In the words of post-aesthetic authors such as Toni Morrison, John Edgar Wideman, and Kristin Hunter,

African Americans are portrayed as looking inward for answers to their own questions, rather than always looking to the outside world.

Postmodernism: Writing from the 1960s forward characterized by experimentation and continuing to apply some of the fundamentals of modernism, which included existentialism and alienation. Postmodernists have gone a step further in the rejection of tradition begun with the modernists by also rejecting traditional forms, preferring the anti-novel over the novel and the anti-hero over the hero.

Pre-Raphaelites: A circle of writers and artists in mid nineteenth-century England. Valuing the pre-Renaissance artistic qualities of religious symbolism, lavish pictorialism, and natural sensuousness, the Pre-Raphaelites cultivated a sense of mystery and melancholy that influenced later writers associated with the Symbolist and Decadent movements.

Primitivism: The belief that primitive peoples were nobler and less flawed than civilized peoples because they had not been subjected to the tainting influence of society.

Projective Verse: A form of free verse in which the poet's breathing pattern determines the lines of the poem. Poets who advocate projective verse are against all formal structures in writing, including meter and form.

Prologue: An introductory section of a literary work. It often contains information establishing the situation of the characters or presents information about the setting, time period, or action. In drama, the prologue is spoken by a chorus or by one of the principal characters.

Prose: A literary medium that attempts to mirror the language of everyday speech. It is distinguished from poetry by its use of unmetered, unrhymed language consisting of logically related sentences. Prose is usually grouped into paragraphs that form a cohesive whole such as an essay or a novel.

Prosopopoeia: See *Personification*

Protagonist: The central character of a story who serves as a focus for its themes and incidents and as the principal rationale for its development. The protagonist is sometimes referred to in discussions of modern literature as the hero or anti-hero.

Proverb: A brief, sage saying that expresses a truth about life in a striking manner.

Pseudonym: A name assumed by a writer, most often intended to prevent his or her identification as the author of a work. Two or more authors may work together under one pseudonym, or an author may use a different name for each genre he or she publishes in. Some publishing companies maintain "house pseudonyms," under which any number of authors may write installations in a series. Some authors also choose a pseudonym over their real names the way an actor may use a stage name.

Pun: A play on words that have similar sounds but different meanings.

Pure Poetry: poetry written without instructional intent or moral purpose that aims only to please a reader by its imagery or musical flow. The term pure poetry is used as the antonym of the term "didacticism."

Q

Quatrain: A four-line stanza of a poem or an entire poem consisting of four lines.

R

Realism: A nineteenth-century European literary movement that sought to portray familiar characters, situations, and settings in a realistic manner. This was done primarily by using an objective narrative point of view and through the buildup of accurate detail. The standard for success of any realistic work depends on how faithfully it transfers common experience into fictional forms. The realistic method may be altered or extended, as in stream of consciousness writing, to record highly subjective experience.

Refrain: A phrase repeated at intervals throughout a poem. A refrain may appear at the end of each stanza or at less regular intervals. It may be altered slightly at each appearance.

Renaissance: The period in European history that marked the end of the Middle Ages. It began in Italy in the late fourteenth century. In broad terms, it is usually seen as spanning the fourteenth, fifteenth, and sixteenth centuries, although it did not reach Great

Britain, for example, until the 1480s or so. The Renaissance saw an awakening in almost every sphere of human activity, especially science, philosophy, and the arts. The period is best defined by the emergence of a general philosophy that emphasized the importance of the intellect, the individual, and world affairs. It contrasts strongly with the medieval worldview, characterized by the dominant concerns of faith, the social collective, and spiritual salvation.

Repartee: Conversation featuring snappy retorts and witticisms.

Restoration: See *Restoration Age*

Restoration Age: A period in English literature beginning with the crowning of Charles II in 1660 and running to about 1700. The era, which was characterized by a reaction against Puritanism, was the first great age of the comedy of manners. The finest literature of the era is typically witty and urbane, and often lewd.

Rhetoric: In literary criticism, this term denotes the art of ethical persuasion. In its strictest sense, rhetoric adheres to various principles developed since classical times for arranging facts and ideas in a clear, persuasive, appealing manner. The term is also used to refer to effective prose in general and theories of or methods for composing effective prose.

Rhetorical Question: A question intended to provoke thought, but not an expressed answer, in the reader. It is most commonly used in oratory and other persuasive genres.

Rhyme: When used as a noun in literary criticism, this term generally refers to a poem in which words sound identical or very similar and appear in parallel positions in two or more lines. Rhymes are classified into different types according to where they fall in a line or stanza or according to the degree of similarity they exhibit in their spellings and sounds. Some major types of rhyme are "masculine" rhyme, "feminine" rhyme, and "triple" rhyme. In a masculine rhyme, the rhyming sound falls in a single accented syllable, as with "heat" and "eat." Feminine rhyme is a rhyme of two syllables, one stressed and one unstressed, as with "merry" and "tarry." Triple rhyme matches the sound of the accented syllable and the

two unaccented syllables that follow: "narrative" and "declarative."

Rhyme Royal: A stanza of seven lines composed in iambic pentameter and rhymed *ababbcc*. The name is said to be a tribute to King James I of Scotland, who made much use of the form in his poetry.

Rhyme Scheme: See *Rhyme*

Rhythm: A regular pattern of sound, time intervals, or events occurring in writing, most often and most discernably in poetry. Regular, reliable rhythm is known to be soothing to humans, while interrupted, unpredictable, or rapidly changing rhythm is disturbing. These effects are known to authors, who use them to produce a desired reaction in the reader.

Rococo: A style of European architecture that flourished in the eighteenth century, especially in France. The most notable features of *rococo* are its extensive use of ornamentation and its themes of lightness, gaiety, and intimacy. In literary criticism, the term is often used disparagingly to refer to a decadent or over-ornamental style.

Romance: A broad term, usually denoting a narrative with exotic, exaggerated, often idealized characters, scenes, and themes.

Romantic Age: See *Romanticism*

Romanticism: This term has two widely accepted meanings. In historical criticism, it refers to a European intellectual and artistic movement of the late eighteenth and early nineteenth centuries that sought greater freedom of personal expression than that allowed by the strict rules of literary form and logic of the eighteenth-century neoclassicists. The Romantics preferred emotional and imaginative expression to rational analysis. They considered the individual to be at the center of all experience and so placed him or her at the center of their art. The Romantics believed that the creative imagination reveals nobler truths—unique feelings and attitudes—than those that could be discovered by logic or by scientific examination. Both the natural world and the state of childhood were important sources for revelations of "eternal truths." "Romanticism" is also used as a general term to refer to a type of sensibility found in all periods of literary history and usually considered to be in opposition to the principles of classicism. In this sense, Romanticism signifies any work or philosophy in which the exotic or dreamlike figure strongly, or that is devoted to individualistic expression, self-analysis, or a pursuit of a higher realm of knowledge than can be discovered by human reason.

Romantics: See *Romanticism*

Russian Symbolism: A Russian poetic movement, derived from French symbolism, that flourished between 1894 and 1910. While some Russian Symbolists continued in the French tradition, stressing aestheticism and the importance of suggestion above didactic intent, others saw their craft as a form of mystical worship, and themselves as mediators between the supernatural and the mundane.

S

Satire: A work that uses ridicule, humor, and wit to criticize and provoke change in human nature and institutions. There are two major types of satire: "formal" or "direct" satire speaks directly to the reader or to a character in the work; "indirect" satire relies upon the ridiculous behavior of its characters to make its point. Formal satire is further divided into two manners: the "Horatian," which ridicules gently, and the "Juvenalian," which derides its subjects harshly and bitterly.

Scansion: The analysis or "scanning" of a poem to determine its meter and often its rhyme scheme. The most common system of scansion uses accents (slanted lines drawn above syllables) to show stressed syllables, breves (curved lines drawn above syllables) to show unstressed syllables, and vertical lines to separate each foot.

Second Person: See *Point of View*

Semiotics: The study of how literary forms and conventions affect the meaning of language.

Sestet: Any six-line poem or stanza.

Setting: The time, place, and culture in which the action of a narrative takes place. The elements of setting may include geographic location, characters' physical and mental environments, prevailing cultural attitudes, or the historical time in which the action takes place.

Shakespearean Sonnet: See *Sonnet*

Signifying Monkey: A popular trickster figure in black folklore, with hundreds of tales about this character documented since the 19th century.

Simile: A comparison, usually using "like" or "as," of two essentially dissimilar things, as in "coffee as cold as ice" or "He sounded like a broken record."

Slang: A type of informal verbal communication that is generally unacceptable for formal writing. Slang words and phrases are often colorful exaggerations used to emphasize the speaker's point; they may also be shortened versions of an often-used word or phrase.

Slant Rhyme: See *Consonance*

Slave Narrative: Autobiographical accounts of American slave life as told by escaped slaves. These works first appeared during the abolition movement of the 1830s through the 1850s.

Social Realism: See *Socialist Realism*

Socialist Realism: The Socialist Realism school of literary theory was proposed by Maxim Gorky and established as a dogma by the first Soviet Congress of Writers. It demanded adherence to a communist worldview in works of literature. Its doctrines required an objective viewpoint comprehensible to the working classes and themes of social struggle featuring strong proletarian heroes.

Soliloquy: A monologue in a drama used to give the audience information and to develop the speaker's character. It is typically a projection of the speaker's innermost thoughts. Usually delivered while the speaker is alone on stage, a soliloquy is intended to present an illusion of unspoken reflection.

Sonnet: A fourteen-line poem, usually composed in iambic pentameter, employing one of several rhyme schemes. There are three major types of sonnets, upon which all other variations of the form are based: the "Petrarchan" or "Italian" sonnet, the "Shakespearean" or "English" sonnet, and the "Spenserian" sonnet. A Petrarchan sonnet consists of an octave rhymed *abbaabba* and a "sestet" rhymed either *cdecde, cdccdc,* or *cdedce.* The octave poses a question or problem, relates a narrative, or puts forth a proposition; the sestet presents a solution to the problem, comments upon the narrative, or applies the proposition put forth in the octave. The Shakespearean sonnet is divided into three quatrains and a couplet rhymed *abab cdcd efef gg*. The couplet provides an epigrammatic comment on the narrative or problem put forth in the quatrains. The Spenserian sonnet uses three quatrains and a couplet like the Shakespearean, but links their three rhyme schemes in this way: *abab bcbc cdcd ee*. The Spenserian sonnet develops its theme in two parts like the Petrarchan, its final six lines resolving a problem, analyzing a narrative, or applying a proposition put forth in its first eight lines.

Spenserian Sonnet: See *Sonnet*

Spenserian Stanza: A nine-line stanza having eight verses in iambic pentameter, its ninth verse in iambic hexameter, and the rhyme scheme ababbcbcc.

Spondee: In poetry meter, a foot consisting of two long or stressed syllables occurring together. This form is quite rare in English verse, and is usually composed of two monosyllabic words.

Sprung Rhythm: Versification using a specific number of accented syllables per line but disregarding the number of unaccented syllables that fall in each line, producing an irregular rhythm in the poem.

Stanza: A subdivision of a poem consisting of lines grouped together, often in recurring patterns of rhyme, line length, and meter. Stanzas may also serve as units of thought in a poem much like paragraphs in prose.

Stereotype: A stereotype was originally the name for a duplication made during the printing process; this led to its modern definition as a person or thing that is (or is assumed to be) the same as all others of its type.

Stream of Consciousness: A narrative technique for rendering the inward experience of a character. This technique is designed to give the impression of an ever-changing series of thoughts, emotions, images, and memories in the spontaneous and seemingly illogical order that they occur in life.

Structuralism: A twentieth-century movement in literary criticism that examines how literary texts arrive at their meanings, rather than

the meanings themselves. There are two major types of structuralist analysis: one examines the way patterns of linguistic structures unify a specific text and emphasize certain elements of that text, and the other interprets the way literary forms and conventions affect the meaning of language itself.

Structure: The form taken by a piece of literature. The structure may be made obvious for ease of understanding, as in nonfiction works, or may obscured for artistic purposes, as in some poetry or seemingly "unstructured" prose.

Sturm und Drang: A German term meaning "storm and stress." It refers to a German literary movement of the 1770s and 1780s that reacted against the order and rationalism of the enlightenment, focusing instead on the intense experience of extraordinary individuals.

Style: A writer's distinctive manner of arranging words to suit his or her ideas and purpose in writing. The unique imprint of the author's personality upon his or her writing, style is the product of an author's way of arranging ideas and his or her use of diction, different sentence structures, rhythm, figures of speech, rhetorical principles, and other elements of composition.

Subject: The person, event, or theme at the center of a work of literature. A work may have one or more subjects of each type, with shorter works tending to have fewer and longer works tending to have more.

Subjectivity: Writing that expresses the author's personal feelings about his subject, and which may or may not include factual information about the subject.

Surrealism: A term introduced to criticism by Guillaume Apollinaire and later adopted by Andre Breton. It refers to a French literary and artistic movement founded in the 1920s. The Surrealists sought to express unconscious thoughts and feelings in their works. The best-known technique used for achieving this aim was automatic writing—transcriptions of spontaneous outpourings from the unconscious. The Surrealists proposed to unify the contrary levels of conscious and unconscious, dream and reality, objectivity and subjectivity into a new level of "super-realism."

Suspense: A literary device in which the author maintains the audience's attention through the buildup of events, the outcome of which will soon be revealed.

Syllogism: A method of presenting a logical argument. In its most basic form, the syllogism consists of a major premise, a minor premise, and a conclusion.

Symbol: Something that suggests or stands for something else without losing its original identity. In literature, symbols combine their literal meaning with the suggestion of an abstract concept. Literary symbols are of two types: those that carry complex associations of meaning no matter what their contexts, and those that derive their suggestive meaning from their functions in specific literary works.

Symbolism: This term has two widely accepted meanings. In historical criticism, it denotes an early modernist literary movement initiated in France during the nineteenth century that reacted against the prevailing standards of realism. Writers in this movement aimed to evoke, indirectly and symbolically, an order of being beyond the material world of the five senses. Poetic expression of personal emotion figured strongly in the movement, typically by means of a private set of symbols uniquely identifiable with the individual poet. The principal aim of the Symbolists was to express in words the highly complex feelings that grew out of everyday contact with the world. In a broader sense, the term "symbolism" refers to the use of one object to represent another.

Symbolist: See *Symbolism*

Symbolist Movement: See *Symbolism*

Sympathetic Fallacy: See *Affective Fallacy*

T

Tanka: A form of Japanese poetry similar to *haiku*. A *tanka* is five lines long, with the lines containing five, seven, five, seven, and seven syllables respectively.

Terza Rima: A three-line stanza form in poetry in which the rhymes are made on the last word of each line in the following manner: the first and third lines of the first stanza, then the second line of the first stanza and the first and third lines of the second stanza, and so on with the middle line of any stanza rhyming with the first and third lines of the following stanza.

Tetrameter: See *Meter*

Textual Criticism: A branch of literary criticism that seeks to establish the authoritative text of a literary work. Textual critics typically compare all known manuscripts or printings of a single work in order to assess the meanings of differences and revisions. This procedure allows them to arrive at a definitive version that (supposedly) corresponds to the author's original intention.

Theme: The main point of a work of literature. The term is used interchangeably with thesis.

Thesis: A thesis is both an essay and the point argued in the essay. Thesis novels and thesis plays share the quality of containing a thesis which is supported through the action of the story.

Third Person: See *Point of View*

Tone: The author's attitude toward his or her audience may be deduced from the tone of the work. A formal tone may create distance or convey politeness, while an informal tone may encourage a friendly, intimate, or intrusive feeling in the reader. The author's attitude toward his or her subject matter may also be deduced from the tone of the words he or she uses in discussing it.

Tragedy: A drama in prose or poetry about a noble, courageous hero of excellent character who, because of some tragic character flaw or *hamartia*, brings ruin upon him- or herself. Tragedy treats its subjects in a dignified and serious manner, using poetic language to help evoke pity and fear and bring about catharsis, a purging of these emotions. The tragic form was practiced extensively by the ancient Greeks. In the Middle Ages, when classical works were virtually unknown, tragedy came to denote any works about the fall of persons from exalted to low conditions due to any reason: fate, vice, weakness, etc. According to the classical definition of tragedy, such works present the "pathetic"—that which evokes pity—rather than the tragic. The classical form of tragedy was revived in the sixteenth century; it flourished especially on the Elizabethan stage. In modern times, dramatists have attempted to adapt the form to the needs of modern society by drawing their heroes from the ranks of ordinary men and women and defining the nobility of these heroes in terms of spirit rather than exalted social standing.

Tragic Flaw: In a tragedy, the quality within the hero or heroine which leads to his or her downfall.

Transcendentalism: An American philosophical and religious movement, based in New England from around 1835 until the Civil War. Transcendentalism was a form of American romanticism that had its roots abroad in the works of Thomas Carlyle, Samuel Coleridge, and Johann Wolfgang von Goethe. The Transcendentalists stressed the importance of intuition and subjective experience in communication with God. They rejected religious dogma and texts in favor of mysticism and scientific naturalism. They pursued truths that lie beyond the "colorless" realms perceived by reason and the senses and were active social reformers in public education, women's rights, and the abolition of slavery.

Trickster: A character or figure common in Native American and African literature who uses his ingenuity to defeat enemies and escape difficult situations. Tricksters are most often animals, such as the spider, hare, or coyote, although they may take the form of humans as well.

Trimeter: See *Meter*

Triple Rhyme: See *Rhyme*

Trochee: See *Foot*

U

Understatement: See *Irony*

Unities: Strict rules of dramatic structure, formulated by Italian and French critics of the Renaissance and based loosely on the principles of drama discussed by Aristotle in his *Poetics*. Foremost among these rules were the three unities of action, time, and place that compelled a dramatist to: (1) construct a single plot with a beginning, middle, and end that details the causal relationships of action and character; (2) restrict the action to the events of a single day; and (3) limit the scene to a single place or city. The unities were observed faithfully by continental European writers until the Romantic Age, but they were never regularly observed in English drama. Modern dramatists are typically more concerned with a unity of impression or emotional effect than with any of the classical unities.

Urban Realism: A branch of realist writing that attempts to accurately reflect the often harsh facts of modern urban existence.

Utopia: A fictional perfect place, such as "paradise" or "heaven."

Utopian: See *Utopia*

Utopianism: See *Utopia*

V

Verisimilitude: Literally, the appearance of truth. In literary criticism, the term refers to aspects of a work of literature that seem true to the reader.

Vers de societe: See *Occasional Verse*

Vers libre: See *Free Verse*

Verse: A line of metered language, a line of a poem, or any work written in verse.

Versification: The writing of verse. Versification may also refer to the meter, rhyme, and other mechanical components of a poem.

Victorian: Refers broadly to the reign of Queen Victoria of England (1837-1901) and to anything with qualities typical of that era. For example, the qualities of smug narrowmindedness, bourgeois materialism, faith in social progress, and priggish morality are often considered Victorian. This stereotype is contradicted by such dramatic intellectual developments as the theories of Charles Darwin, Karl Marx, and Sigmund Freud (which stirred strong debates in England) and the critical attitudes of serious Victorian writers like Charles Dickens and George Eliot. In literature, the Victorian Period was the great age of the English novel, and the latter part of the era saw the rise of movements such as decadence and symbolism.

Victorian Age: See *Victorian*

Victorian Period: See *Victorian*

W

Weltanschauung: A German term referring to a person's worldview or philosophy.

Weltschmerz: A German term meaning "world pain." It describes a sense of anguish about the nature of existence, usually associated with a melancholy, pessimistic attitude.

Z

Zarzuela: A type of Spanish operetta.

Zeitgeist: A German term meaning "spirit of the time." It refers to the moral and intellectual trends of a given era.

Cumulative Author/Title Index

Cumulative Nationality/Ethnicity Index

Cumulative Nationality/Ethnicity Index

Smith, Stevie
  Not Waving but Drowning: V3
Spender, Stephen
  *An Elementary School Classroom
    in a Slum:* V23
  What I Expected: V36
Spenser, Edmund
  Sonnet 75: V32
Swift, Jonathan
  A Description of the Morning: V37
  *A Satirical Elegy on the Death of a
    Late Famous General:* V27
Taylor, Edward
  Huswifery: V31
Taylor, Henry
  Landscape with Tractor: V10
Tennyson, Alfred, Lord
  The Charge of the Light Brigade: V1
  Crossing the Bar: V44
  The Eagle: V11
  The Lady of Shalott: V15
  Proem: V19
  Tears, Idle Tears: V4
  Ulysses: V2
Wordsworth, William
  I Wandered Lonely as a Cloud:
    V33
  *Lines Composed a Few Miles above
    Tintern Abbey:* V2
  The World Is Too Much with Us:
    V38
Wyatt, Thomas
  Whoso List to Hunt: V25

French

Apollinaire, Guillaume
  Always: V24
Baudelaire, Charles
  Hymn to Beauty: V21
  Invitation to the Voyage: V38
Chrétien de Troyes
  Perceval, the Story of the Grail:
    V44
Malroux, Claire
  Morning Walk: V21
Rimbaud, Arthur
  The Drunken Boat: V28

German

Amichai, Yehuda
  Not like a Cypress: V24
  Seven Laments for the War-Dead:
    V39
Blumenthal, Michael
  Inventors: V7
Erdrich, Louise
  Bidwell Ghost: V14
  *Indian Boarding School: The
    Runaways:* V43
Heine, Heinrich
  The Lorelei: V37

Mueller, Lisel
  Blood Oranges: V13
  The Exhibit: V9
Rilke, Rainer Maria
  Archaic Torso of Apollo: V27
  Childhood: V19
Roethke, Theodore
  My Papa's Waltz: V3
  Night Journey: V40
  The Waking: V34
Sachs, Nelly
  *But Perhaps God Needs the
    Longing:* V20
Sajé, Natasha
  The Art of the Novel: V23

Ghanaian

Du Bois, W. E. B.
  The Song of the Smoke: V13

Greek

Cavafy, C. P.
  Ithaka: V19
Sappho
  Fragment 2: V31
  Fragment 16: V38
  Fragment 34: V44
  Hymn to Aphrodite: V20

Hispanic American

Alvarez, Julia
  Exile: V39
  Woman's Work: V44
Baca, Jimmy Santiago
  Who Understands Me But Me:
    V40
Castillo, Ana
  While I Was Gone a War Began:
    V21
Cervantes, Lorna Dee
  Freeway 280: V30
Cruz, Victor Hernandez
  Business: V16
Espada, Martín
  Colibrí: V16
  My Father as a Guitar: V43
  We Live by What We See at Night:
    V13
Mora, Pat
  Elena: V33
  Legal Alien: V40
  Uncoiling: V35
Ortiz Cofer, Judith
  The Latin Deli: An Ars Poetica:
    V37
Sapia, Yvonne
  Defining the Grateful Gesture: V40
Walcott, Derek
  Sea Canes: V39

Indian

Divakaruni, Chitra Banerjee
  My Mother Combs My Hair: V34
Mirabai
  All I Was Doing Was Breathing:
    V24
Ramanujan, A. K.
  Waterfalls in a Bank: V27
Shahid Ali, Agha
  Country Without a Post Office:
    V18
Tagore, Rabindranath
  60: V18
Vazirani, Reetika
  Daughter-Mother-Maya-Seeta:
    V25

Indonesian

Lee, Li-Young
  Early in the Morning: V17
  *For a New Citizen of These United
    States:* V15
  The Gift: V37
  A Story: V45
  The Weight of Sweetness: V11

Iranian

Farrokhzaad, Faroogh
  A Rebirth: V21

Iraqi

Youssef, Saadi
  America, America: V29

Irish

Boland, Eavan
  Against Love Poetry: V45
  Anorexic: V12
  Domestic Violence: V39
  It's a Woman's World: V22
  Outside History: V31
Carson, Ciaran
  The War Correspondent: V26
Grennan, Eamon
  Station: V21
Hartnett, Michael
  A Farewell to English: V10
Heaney, Seamus
  Digging: V5
  A Drink of Water: V8
  Follower: V30
  The Forge: V41
  Midnight: V2
  The Singer's House: V17
Muldoon, Paul
  Meeting the British: V7
  Pineapples and Pomegranates: V22
Swift, Jonathan
  A Description of the Morning: V37

Subject/Theme Index

Bitterness
  Blandeur: 37
Bravery. *See* Courage
British culture
  Peace: 171
British history
  Peace: 167
  Sound and Sense: 206–207
Buddhism
  *The Esquimos Have No Word for
    "War":* 77–79
  A Story: 228
Bullying
  The Whipping: 284

C

Canadian culture
  Half-hanged Mary: 98–99
Child abuse
  The Whipping: 284, 286, 291
Childhood
  What Lips My Lips Have Kissed:
    279
  The Whipping: 291
Christianity
  Peace: 170–171, 173, 176
Civilization
  *The Esquimos Have No Word for
    "War":* 74, 75
Cold War
  Midcentury Love Letter: 155–159
Colonialism
  *The Esquimos Have No Word for
    "War":* 74
Compassion
  *The Esquimos Have No Word for
    "War":* 80
  A Story: 219
  The Whipping: 292, 293
Competition
  Defending Walt Whitman: 43
Complacency
  Blandeur: 37
Confidence
  Let America Be America Again:
    128
Confinement
  Against Love Poetry: 10
  What Lips My Lips Have Kissed:
    278–279
Conflict
  Against Love Poetry: 3, 4
Confucianism
  A Story: 226
Connectedness
  Against Love Poetry: 10
Consciousness
  A Story: 227
Contradiction
  Blandeur: 31
  Against Love Poetry: 1, 3, 4, 6

Control (Psychology)
  To the Ladies: 255
Courage
  Half-hanged Mary: 93
  What Lips My Lips Have Kissed:
    263
Courtship
  Meeting at Night: 141–142
Cruelty
  The Whipping: 291
Cultural identity
  Defending Walt Whitman: 54–56
  *The Esquimos Have No Word for
    "War":* 63, 75
  A Story: 231–234
Culture
  What Lips My Lips Have Kissed:
    274
Curiosity
  Question: 186, 194
Cynicism
  Half-hanged Mary: 98

D

Dark comedy
  Defending Walt Whitman: 51
Death
  Blandeur: 37
  Peace: 178
  Question: 184–186, 193, 195
  What Lips My Lips Have Kissed:
    265
Decay
  Blandeur: 37
Defiance
  Half-hanged Mary: 90, 93
  Against Love Poetry: 1, 10
  What Lips My Lips Have Kissed:
    277, 278
Desire
  What Lips My Lips Have Kissed:
    269, 270
Despair
  Half-hanged Mary: 87
  Against Love Poetry: 11
  A Story: 217
  What Lips My Lips Have Kissed:
    263
Desperation
  Midcentury Love Letter: 153
  A Story: 218
Detachment
  Blandeur: 29
  The Whipping: 291
Details
  *The Esquimos Have No Word for
    "War":* 75
Determination
  Meeting at Night: 145
Discrimination
  A Story: 232, 234

Disillusionment
  What Lips My Lips Have Kissed:
    278
Domesticity
  Against Love Poetry: 13
  Midcentury Love Letter: 151,
    163–164
  What Lips My Lips Have Kissed:
    278
Domination
  Meeting at Night: 148

E

Eastern philosophy
  *The Esquimos Have No Word for
    "War":* 77
Education
  To the Ladies: 253–255
  A Story: 219
Emotions
  Blandeur: 24
  *The Esquimos Have No Word for
    "War":* 74
  To the Ladies: 255
  Midcentury Love Letter: 160–161
  A Story: 217, 218, 221–222, 226
  What Lips My Lips Have Kissed:
    278
  The Whipping: 285, 289
Emptiness (Psychology)
  What Lips My Lips Have Kissed:
    261, 265
Enjambment
  Midcentury Love Letter: 161
  A Story: 221
Enthusiasm
  Defending Walt Whitman: 40, 44
Equality
  To the Ladies: 243–244
  Let America Be America Again:
    119, 121, 123
Essentialism
  A Story: 232
Ethics
  Blandeur: 37
  Half-hanged Mary: 100–101
  Sound and Sense: 212, 213
Ethnic identity
  A Story: 230, 232, 233–234
Excitement. *See* Enthusiasm
Exposure
  Question: 187, 188–189, 193

F

Faith
  *The Esquimos Have No Word for
    "War":* 81
  A Story: 227
Familial love
  A Story: 218, 219
Father-child relationships

Cumulative Index of First Lines

A

A brackish reach of shoal off
Madaket,— (The Quaker
Graveyard in Nantucket) V6:158
"A cold coming we had of it (Journey
of the Magi) V7:110
A few minutes ago, I stepped onto
the deck (The Cobweb) V17:50
A gentle spring evening arrives
(Spring-Watching Pavilion)
V18:198
A line in long array where they wind
betwixt green islands, (Cavalry
Crossing a Ford) V13:50
A narrow Fellow in the grass (A
Narrow Fellow in the Grass)
V11:127
A noiseless patient spider, (A
Noiseless Patient Spider)
V31:190–91
A pine box for me. I mean it. (Last
Request) V14: 231
A poem should be palpable and mute
(Ars Poetica) V5:2
A stone from the depths that has
witnessed the seas drying up
(Song of a Citizen) V16:125
A tourist came in from Orbitville,
(Southbound on the Freeway)
V16:158
A wind is ruffling the tawny pelt (A
Far Cry from Africa) V6:60
a woman precedes me up the long
rope, (Climbing) V14:113
Abortions will not let you forget.
(The Mother) V40:197

About me the night moonless
wimples the mountains
(Vancouver Lights) V8:245
About suffering they were never
wrong (Musée des Beaux Arts)
V1:148
According to our mother, (Defining
the Grateful Gesture) V40:34
Across Roblin Lake, two shores away,
(Wilderness Gothic) V12:241
After every war (The End and the
Beginning) V41:121
After the double party (Air for
Mercury) V20:2–3
After the party ends another party
begins (Social Life) V19:251
After you finish your work (Ballad of
Orange and Grape) V10:17
Again I've returned to this country
(The Country Without a Post
Office) V18:64
"Ah, are you digging on my grave
(Ah, Are You Digging on My
Grave?) V4:2
All Greece hates (Helen) V6:92
All I know is a door into the dark.
(The Forge) V41:158
All is fate (All) V38:17
All my existence is a dark sign a dark
(A Rebirth) V21:193–194
All night long the hockey pictures
(To a Sad Daughter) V8:230
All over Genoa (Trompe l'Oeil)
V22:216
All the world's a stage, And all the
men and women merely players
(Seven Ages of Man) V35:213

All winter your brute shoulders
strained against collars,
padding (Names of Horses)
V8:141
Also Ulysses once—that other war.
(Kilroy) V14:213
Always (Always) V24:15
Among the blossoms, a single jar of
wine. (Drinking Alone Beneath
the Moon) V20:59–60
Anasazi (Anasazi) V9:2
"And do we remember our living
lives?" (Memory) V21:156
And everyone crying out, (Perceval,
the Story of the Grail) V44:148
And God stepped out on space (The
Creation) V1:19
And what if I spoke of despair—who
doesn't (And What If I Spoke of
Despair) V19:2
Animal bones and some mossy tent
rings (Lament for the Dorsets)
V5:190
Announced by all the trumpets of the
sky, (The Snow-Storm)
V34:195
Any force— (All It Takes) V23:15
April is the cruellest month,
breeding (The Waste Land)
V20:248–252
As I perceive (The Gold Lily) V5:127
As I walked out one evening (As I
Walked Out One Evening)
V4:15
As I was going down impassive
Rivers, (The Drunken Boat)
V28:83

G

Gardener: Sir, I encountered Death (Incident in a Rose Garden) V14:190

Gather ye Rose-buds while ye may, (To the Virgins, to Make Much of Time) V13:226

Gazelle, I killed you (Ode to a Drum) V20:172–173

Get up, get up for shame, the Blooming Morne (Corinna's Going A-Maying) V39:2

Glory be to God for dappled things— (Pied Beauty) V26:161

Go, and catch a falling star, (Song) V35:237

Go down, Moses (Go Down, Moses) V11:42

God of our fathers, known of old, (Recessional) V42:183

God save America, (America, America) V29:2

Grandmothers who wring the necks (Classic Ballroom Dances) V33:3

Gray mist wolf (Four Mountain Wolves) V9:131

Grown too big for his skin, (Fable for When There's No Way Out) V38:42

H

"Had he and I but met (The Man He Killed) V3:167

Had we but world enough, and time (To His Coy Mistress) V5:276

Hail to thee, blithe Spirit! (To a Sky-Lark) V32:251

Half a league, half a league (The Charge of the Light Brigade) V1:2

Having a Coke with You (Having a Coke with You) V12:105

He clasps the crag with crooked hands (The Eagle) V11:30

He was found by the Bureau of Statistics to be (The Unknown Citizen) V3:302

He was seen, surrounded by rifles, (The Crime Was in Granada) V23:55–56

Hear the sledges with the bells— (The Bells) V3:46

Heard you that shriek? It rose (The Slave Mother) V44:212

Heart, you bully, you punk, I'm wrecked, I'm shocked (One Is One) V24:158

Her body is not so white as (Queen-Ann's-Lace) V6:179

Her eyes the glow-worm lend thee; (The Night Piece: To Julia) V29:206

Her eyes were coins of porter and her West (A Farewell to English) V10:126

Here, above, (The Man-Moth) V27:135

Here, she said, *put this on your head.* (Flounder) V39:58

Here they are. The soft eyes open (The Heaven of Animals) V6:75

His Grace! impossible! what dead! (A Satirical Elegy on the Death of a Late Famous General) V27:216

His speed and strength, which is the strength of ten (His Speed and Strength) V19:96

Hog Butcher for the World (Chicago) V3:61

Hold fast to dreams (Dream Variations) V15:42

Home's the place we head for in our sleep. (Indian Boarding School: The Runaways) V43:102

Hope is a tattered flag and a dream out of time. (Hope is a Tattered Flag) V12:120

"Hope" is the thing with feathers— ("Hope" Is the Thing with Feathers) V3:123

How do I love thee? Let me count the ways (Sonnet 43) V2:236

How is your life with the other one, (An Attempt at Jealousy) V29:23

How shall we adorn (Angle of Geese) V2:2

How soon hath Time, the subtle thief of youth, (On His Having Arrived at the Age of Twenty-Three) V17:159

How would it be if you took yourself off (Landscape with Tractor) V10:182

Hunger crawls into you (Hunger in New York City) V4:79

I

I am fourteen (Hanging Fire) V32:93

I am not a painter, I am a poet (Why I Am Not a Painter) V8:258

I am not with those who abandoned their land (I Am Not One of Those Who Left the Land) V36:91

I am silver and exact. I have no preconceptions (Mirror) V1:116

I am the Smoke King (The Song of the Smoke) V13:196

I am trying to pry open your casket (Dear Reader) V10:85

I became a creature of light (The Mystery) V15:137

I Built My Hut beside a Traveled Road (I Built My Hut beside a Traveled Road) V36:119

I cannot love the Brothers Wright (Reactionary Essay on Applied Science) V9:199

I caught a tremendous fish (The Fish) V31:44

I, being born a woman and distressed (I, being born a woman and distressed (Sonnet XVIII)) V41:203

I died for Beauty—but was scarce (I Died for Beauty) V28:174

I don't mean to make you cry. (Monologue for an Onion) V24:120–121

I don't want my daughter (Fear) V37:71

I do not know what it means that (The Lorelei) V37:145

I felt a Funeral, in my Brain, (I felt a Funeral in my Brain) V13:137

I gave birth to life. (Maternity) V21:142–143

I have been one acquainted with the night. (Acquainted with the Night) V35:3

I have eaten (This Is Just to Say) V34:240

I have just come down from my father (The Hospital Window) V11:58

I have met them at close of day (Easter 1916) V5:91

I have sown beside all waters in my day. (A Black Man Talks of Reaping) V32:20

I haven't the heart to say (To an Unknown Poet) V18:221

I hear America singing, the varied carols I hear (I Hear America Singing) V3:152

I heard a Fly buzz—when I died— (I Heard a Fly Buzz— When I Died—) V5:140

I know that I shall meet my fate (An Irish Airman Foresees His Death) V1:76

I know what the caged bird feels, alas! (Sympathy) V33:203

I leant upon a coppice gate (The Darkling Thrush) V18:74

I lie down on my side in the moist grass (Omen) v22:107

Q

Quinquireme of Nineveh from distant Ophir (Cargoes) V5:44

Quite difficult, belief. (Chorale) V25:51

R

Recognition in the body (In Particular) V20:125

Red men embraced my body's whiteness (Birch Canoe) V5:31

Remember me when I am gone away (Remember) V14:255

Remember the sky you were born under, (Remember) V32:185

Riches I hold in light esteem, (Old Stoic) V33:143

S

Sad is the man who is asked for a story (A Story) V45:216

Season of mists and mellow fruitfulness, (To Autumn) V36:295–296

Shall I compare thee to a Summer's day? (Sonnet 18) V2:222

She came every morning to draw water (A Drink of Water) V8:66

She reads, of course, what he's doing, shaking Nixon's hand, (The Women Who Loved Elvis All Their Lives) V28:273

She sang beyond the genius of the sea. (The Idea of Order at Key West) V13:164

She walks in beauty, like the night (She Walks in Beauty) V14:268

She was my grandfather's second wife. Coming late (My Grandmother's Plot in the Family Cemetery) V27:154

Side by side, their faces blurred, (An Arundel Tomb) V12:17

since feeling is first (since feeling is first) V34:172

Since the professional wars— (Midnight) V2:130

Since then, I work at night. (Ten Years after Your Deliberate Drowning) V21:240

S'io credesse che mia risposta fosse (The Love Song of J. Alfred Prufrock) V1:97

Sky black (Duration) V18:93

Sleepless as Prospero back in his bedroom (Darwin in 1881) V13:83

so much depends (The Red Wheelbarrow) V1:219

So the man spread his blanket on the field (A Tall Man Executes a Jig) V12:228

So the sky wounded you, jagged at the heart, (Daylights) V13:101

Softly, in the dark, a woman is singing to me (Piano) V6:145

Some say a host of cavalry, others of infantry, (Fragment 16) V38:62

Some say it's in the reptilian dance (The Greatest Grandeur) V18:119

Some say the world will end in fire (Fire and Ice) V7:57

Something there is that doesn't love a wall (Mending Wall) V5:231

Sometimes walking late at night (Butcher Shop) V7:43

Sometimes, a lion with a prophet's beard (For An Assyrian Frieze) V9:120

Sometimes, in the middle of the lesson (Music Lessons) V8:117

somewhere i have never travelled,gladly beyond (somewhere i have never travelled,gladly beyond) V19:265

South of the bridge on Seventeenth (Fifteen) V2:78

Stop all the clocks, cut off the telephone, (Funeral Blues) V10:139

Strong Men, riding horses. In the West (Strong Men, Riding Horses) V4:209

Such places are too still for history, (Deep Woods) V14:138

Sundays too my father got up early (Those Winter Sundays) V1:300

Sunset and evening star, (Crossing the Bar) V44:3

Sweet day, so cool, so calm, so bright, (Virtue) V25:263

Swing low sweet chariot (Swing Low Sweet Chariot) V1:283

T

Taped to the wall of my cell are 47 pictures: 47 black (The Idea of Ancestry) V36:138

Take heart, monsieur, four-fifths of this province (For Jean Vincent D'abbadie, Baron St.-Castin) V12:78

Take sheds and stalls from Billingsgate, (The War Correspondent) V26:235

Take this kiss upon the brow! (A Dream within a Dream) V42:80

Talent is what they say (For the Young Who Want To) V40:49

Tears, idle tears, I know not what they mean (Tears, Idle Tears) V4:220

Tell all the Truth but tell it slant— (Tell all the Truth but tell it slant) V42:240

Tell me not, in mournful numbers (A Psalm of Life) V7:165

Tell me not, Sweet, I am unkind, (To Lucasta, Going to the Wars) V32:291

Temple bells die out. (Temple Bells Die Out) V18:210

That is no country for old men. The young (Sailing to Byzantium) V2:207

That negligible bit of sand which slides (Variations on Nothing) V20:234

That time of drought the embered air (Drought Year) V8:78

That's my last Duchess painted on the wall (My Last Duchess) V1:165

The apparition of these faces in the crowd (In a Station of the Metro) V2:116

The Assyrian came down like the wolf on the fold (The Destruction of Sennacherib) V1:38

The bored child at the auction (The Wings) V28:242

The brief secrets are still here, (Words Are the Diminution of All Things) V35:316

The bright moon lifts from the Mountain of (The Moon at the Fortified Pass) V40:180

The broken pillar of the wing jags from the clotted shoulder (Hurt Hawks) V3:138

The bud (Saint Francis and the Sow) V9:222

The Bustle in a House (The Bustle in a House) V10:62

The buzz saw snarled and rattled in the yard (Out, Out—) V10:212

The couple on the left of me (Walk Your Body Down) V26:219

The courage that my mother had (The Courage that My Mother Had) V3:79

The Curfew tolls the knell of parting day (Elegy Written in a Country Churchyard) V9:73

The day? Memorial. (Grape Sherbet) V37:109

The fiddler crab fiddles, glides and dithers, (Fiddler Crab) V23:111–112

Cumulative
Index of Last Lines

A

. . . a capital T in the endless mass of the text. (Answers to Letters) V21:30–31

a fleck of foam. (Accounting) V21:2–3

A heart that will one day beat you to death. (Monologue for an Onion) V24:120–121

A heart whose love is innocent! (She Walks in Beauty) V14:268

A little while, that in me sings no more. (What Lips My Lips Have Kissed) V45:259

a man then suddenly stops running (Island of Three Marias) V11:80

A pattern of your love!" (The Canonization) V41:26

A perfect evening! (Temple Bells Die Out) V18:210

a space in the lives of their friends (Beware: Do Not Read This Poem) V6:3

A sudden blow: the great wings beating still (Leda and the Swan) V13:181

A terrible beauty is born (Easter 1916) V5:91

About him, and lies down to pleasant dreams. (Thanatopsis) V30:232–233

About my big, new, automatically defrosting refrigerator with the built-in electric eye (Reactionary Essay on Applied Science) V9:199

about the tall mounds of termites. (Song of a Citizen) V16:126

Across the expedient and wicked stones (Auto Wreck) V3:31

affirming its brilliant and dizzying love. (Lepidopterology) V23:171

Affliction shall advance the flight in me. (Easter Wings) V43:40

Ah, dear father, graybeard, lonely old courage-teacher, what America did you have when Charon quit poling his ferry and you got out on a smoking bank and stood watching the boat disappear on the black waters of Lethe? (A Supermarket in California) V5:261

All. (The Mother) V40:198

All deaths have a lingering echo (All) V38:17

All losses are restored and sorrows end (Sonnet 30) V4:192

Amen. (Recessional) V42:183

Amen. Amen (The Creation) V1:20

Anasazi (Anasazi) V9:3

and a father's love add up to silence. (A Story) V45:217

and a vase of wild flowers. (The War Correspondent) V26:239

and all beyond saving by children (Ethics) V8:88

and all the richer for it. (Mind) V17:146

And all we need of hell (My Life Closed Twice Before Its Close) V8:127

And, being heard, doesn't vanish in the dark. (Variations on Nothing) V20:234

And bid alternate passions fall and rise! (Sound and Sense) V45:201

and changed, back to the class ("Trouble with Math in a One-Room Country School") V9:238

and chant him a blessing, a sutra. (What For) V33:267

And consummation comes, and jars two hemispheres. (The Convergence of the Twain) V42:61

And covered up—our names— (I Died for Beauty) V28:174

And dances with the daffodils. (I Wandered Lonely as a Cloud) V33:71

And death i think is no parenthesis (since feeling is first) V34:172

And Death shall be no more: Death, thou shalt die (Holy Sonnet 10) V2:103

and destruction. (Allegory) V23:2–3

And drunk the milk of Paradise (Kubla Khan) V5:172

And each slow dusk a drawing-down of blinds. (Anthem for Doomed Youth) V37:3

and fear lit by the breadth of such calmly turns to praise. (The City Limits) V19:78

And Finished knowing—then— (I Felt a Funeral in My Brain) V13:137

before we're even able to name them. (Station) V21:226–227

behind us and all our shining ambivalent love airborne there before us. (Our Side) V24:177

Bi-laterally. (Legal Alien) V40:125

Black like me. (Dream Variations) V15:42

Bless me (Hunger in New York City) V4:79

bombs scandalizing the sanctity of night. (While I Was Gone a War Began) V21:253–254

But a dream within a dream? (A Dream within a Dream) V42:80

But, baby, where are you?" (Ballad of Birmingham) V5:17

But be (Ars Poetica) V5:3

But for centuries we have longed for it. (Everything Is Plundered) V32:34

but it works every time (Siren Song) V7:196

but the truth is, it is, lost to us now. (The Forest) V22:36–37

But there is no joy in Mudville— mighty Casey has "Struck Out." (Casey at the Bat) V5:58

But we hold our course, and the wind is with us. (On Freedom's Ground) V12:187

by a beeswax candle pooling beside their dinnerware. (Portrait of a Couple at Century's End) V24:214–215

by good fortune (The Horizons of Rooms) V15:80

C

Calls through the valleys of Hall. (Song of the Chattahoochee) V14:284

chickens (The Red Wheelbarrow) V1:219

clear water dashes (Onomatopoeia) V6:133

Columbia. (Kindness) V24:84–85

Come, my *Corinna*, come, let's goe a Maying. (Corinna's Going A-Maying) V39:6

come to life and burn? (Bidwell Ghost) V14:2

comfortless, so let evening come. (Let Evening Come) V39:116

Comin' for to carry me home (Swing Low Sweet Chariot) V1:284

cool as from underground springs and pure enough to drink. (The Man-Moth) V27:135

crossed the water. (All It Takes) V23:15

D

Dare frame thy fearful symmetry? (The Tyger) V2:263

"Dead," was all he answered (The Death of the Hired Man) V4:44

deep in the deepest one, tributaries burn. (For Jennifer, 6, on the Teton) V17:86

Delicate, delicate, delicate, delicate—now! (The Base Stealer) V12:30

delicate old injuries, the spines of names and leaves. (Indian Boarding School: The Runaways) V43:102

designed to make the enemy nod off. (The History Teacher) V42:101

Die soon (We Real Cool) V6:242

dispossessed people. We have seen it. (Grace) V44:68

Do what you are going to do, I will tell about it. (I go Back to May 1937) V17:113

down from the sky (Russian Letter) V26:181

Down in the flood of remembrance, I weep like a child for the past (Piano) V6:145

Downward to darkness, on extended wings. (Sunday Morning) V16:190

drinking all night in the kitchen. (The Dead) V35:69

Driving around, I will waste more time. (Driving to Town Late to Mail a Letter) V17:63

dry wells that fill so easily now (The Exhibit) V9:107

dust rises in many myriads of grains. (Not like a Cypress) V24:135

dusty as miners, into the restored volumes. (Bonnard's Garden) V25:33

E

endless worlds is the great meeting of children. (60) V18:3

Enjoy such liberty. (To Althea, From Prison) V34:255

Eternal, unchanging creator of earth. Amen (The Seafarer) V8:178

Eternity of your arms around my neck. (Death Sentences) V22:23

even as it vanishes—were not our life. (The Litany) V24:101–102

ever finds anything more of immortality. (Jade Flower Palace) V32:145

every branch traced with the ghost writing of snow. (The Afterlife) V18:39

F

fall upon us, the dwellers in shadow (In the Land of Shinar) V7:84

Fallen cold and dead (O Captain! My Captain!) V2:147

False, ere I come, to two, or three. (Song) V35:237

father. (Grape Sherbet) V37:110

filled, never. (The Greatest Grandeur) V18:119

Firewood, iron-ware, and cheap tin trays (Cargoes) V5:44

Fled is that music:—Do I wake or sleep? (Ode to a Nightingale) V3:229

For conversation when we meet again. (I, being born a woman and distressed (Sonnet XVIII)) V41:203

For I'm sick at the heart, and I fain wad lie down." (Lord Randal) V6:105

For nothing now can ever come to any good. (Funeral Blues) V10:139

For the coming winter (Winter) V35:297

For the love of God they buried his cold corpse. (The Bronze Horseman) V28:31

For the world's more full of weeping than he can understand. (The Stolen Child) V34:217

forget me as fast as you can. (Last Request) V14:231

4:25:9 (400—Meter Freestyle) V38:3

from one kiss (A Rebirth) V21:193–194

from your arm. (Inside Out) V43:121

full moon. (New World) V41:271

G

garish for a while and burned. (One of the Smallest) V26:142

gazing at the clouds (The End and the Beginning) V41:122

going where? Where? (Childhood) V19:29

guilty about possessing appetite. (Defining the Grateful Gesture) V40:34

H

Had anything been wrong, we should certainly have heard (The Unknown Citizen) V3:303

Had somewhere to get to and sailed calmly on (Mus,e des Beaux Arts) V1:148

half eaten by the moon. (Dear
    Reader) V10:85

hand over hungry hand. (Climbing)
    V14:113

Happen on a red tongue (Small
    Town with One Road) V7:207

hard as mine with another man? (An
    Attempt at Jealousy) V29:24

Has no more need of, and I have
    (The Courage that My Mother
    Had) V3:80

Has set me softly down beside you.
    The Poem is you (Paradoxes
    and Oxymorons) V11:162

Hath melted like snow in the glance
    of the Lord! (The Destruction
    of Sennacherib) V1:39

Have eyes to wonder, but lack
    tongues to praise. (Sonnet 106)
    V43:251

He rose the morrow morn (The Rime
    of the Ancient Mariner) V4:132

He says again, "Good fences make
    good neighbors." (Mending
    Wall) V5:232

He writes down something that he
    crosses out. (The Boy) V19:14

here; passion will save you. (Air for
    Mercury) V20:2–3

History theirs whose languages is the
    sun. (An Elementary School
    Classroom in a Slum) V23:88–89

home (in the inner city) V41:227

How at my sheet goes the same
    crooked worm (The Force That
    Through the Green Fuse Drives
    the Flower) V8:101

How can I turn from Africa and live?
    (A Far Cry from Africa) V6:61

How could I seek the empty world
    again? (Remembrance) V43:216

How sad then is even the marvelous!
    (An Africian Elegy) V13:4

I

I am a true Russian! (Babii Yar)
    V29:38

I am black. (The Song of the Smoke)
    V13:197

I am going to keep things like this
    (Hawk Roosting) V4:55

I am not brave at all (Strong Men,
    Riding Horses) V4:209

I am the captain of my soul (Invictus)
    V43:137

I could not see to see— (I Heard a
    Fly Buzz—When I Died—)
    V5:140

I cremated Sam McGee (The
    Cremation of Sam McGee)
    V10:76

I didn't want to put them down.
    (And What If I Spoke of
    Despair) V19:2

I have been one acquainted with the
    night. (Acquainted with the
    Night) V35:3

I have just come down from my
    father (The Hospital Window)
    V11:58

I hear it in the deep heart's core. (The
    Lake Isle of Innisfree) V15:121

I know why the caged bird sings!
    (Sympathy) V33:203

I lift my lamp beside the golden
    door!" (The New Colossus)
    V37:239

I never writ, nor no man ever loved
    (Sonnet 116) V3:288

I rest in the grace of the world, and
    am free. (The Peace of Wild
    Things) V30:159

I romp with joy in the bookish dark
    (Eating Poetry) V9:61

I see him properly buried" (Perceval,
    the Story of the Grail) V44:153

I see Mike's painting, called
    SARDINES (Why I Am Not a
    Painter) V8:259

I shall but love thee better after death
    (Sonnet 43) V2:236

I should be glad of another death
    (Journey of the Magi) V7:110

I stand up (Miss Rosie) V1:133

I stood there, fifteen (Fifteen) V2:78

I take it you are he? (Incident in a
    Rose Garden) V14:191

I, too, am America. (I, Too) V30:99

I turned aside and bowed my head
    and wept (The Tropics in New
    York) V4:255

I would like to tell, but lack the
    words. (I Built My Hut beside a
    Traveled Road) V36:119

If Winter comes, can Spring be far
    behind? (Ode to the West Wind)
    V2:163

I'll be gone from here. (The Cobweb)
    V17:51

I'll dig with it (Digging) V5:71

Imagine! (Autobiographia Literaria)
    V34:2

In a convulsive misery (The Milkfish
    Gatherers) V11:112

In an empty sky (Two Bodies)
    V38:251

In balance with this life, this death
    (An Irish Airman Foresees His
    Death) V1:76

in earth's gasp, ocean's yawn. (Lake)
    V23:158

In Flanders fields (In Flanders
    Fields) V5:155

In ghostlier demarcations, keener
    sounds. (The Idea of Order at
    Key West) V13:164

In hearts at peace, under an English
    heaven (The Soldier) V7:218

In her tomb by the side of the sea
    (Annabel Lee) V9:14

in the family of things. (Wild Geese)
    V15:208

in the grit gray light of day.
    (Daylights) V13:102

In the rear-view mirrors of the
    passing cars (The War Against
    the Trees) V11:216

In these Chicago avenues. (A Thirst
    Against) V20:205

in this bastion of culture. (To an
    Unknown Poet) V18:221

in your unsteady, opening hand.
    (What the Poets Could Have
    Been) V26:262

iness (l(a) V1:85

Into blossom (A Blessing) V7:24

Is breaking in despair. (The Slave
    Mother) V44:213

Is Come, my love is come to me. (A
    Birthday) V10:34

is love—that's all. (Two Poems for
    T.) V20:218

is safe is what you said. (Practice)
    V23:240

is going too fast; your hands sweat.
    (Another Feeling) V40:3

is still warm (Lament for the
    Dorsets) V5:191

It asked a crumb—of Me ("Hope" Is
    the Thing with Feathers) V3:123

It had no mirrors. I no longer needed
    mirrors. (I, I, I) V26:97

It hasn't let up all morning. (The
    Cucumber) V41:81

It is Margaret you mourn for.
    (Spring and Fall: To a Young
    Girl) V40:236

It is our god. (Fiddler Crab)
    V23:111–112

it is the bell to awaken God that
    we've heard ringing. (The
    Garden Shukkei-en) V18:107

it over my face and mouth. (An
    Anthem) V26:34

It rains as I write this. Mad heart, be
    brave. (The Country Without a
    Post Office) V18:64

It takes life to love life. (Lucinda
    Matlock) V37:172

It was your resting place." (Ah, Are
    You Digging on My Grave?)
    V4:2

it's always ourselves we find in the
    sea (maggie & milly & molly &
    may) V12:150

its bright, unequivocal eye. (Having it Out with Melancholy) V17:99

It's the fall through wind lifting white leaves. (Rapture) V21:181

its youth. The sea grows old in it. (The Fish) V14:172

J

Judge tenderly—of Me (This Is My Letter to the World) V4:233

Just imagine it (Inventors) V7:97

K

kisses you (Grandmother) V34:95

L

Laughing the stormy, husky, brawling laughter of Youth, half-naked, sweating, proud to be Hog Butcher, Tool Maker, Stacker of Wheat, Player with Railroads and Freight Handler to the Nation (Chicago) V3:61

Learn to labor and to wait (A Psalm of Life) V7:165

Leashed in my throat (Midnight) V2:131

Leaving thine outgrown shell by life's un-resting sea (The Chambered Nautilus) V24:52–53

Let my people go (Go Down, Moses) V11:43

Let the water come. (America, America) V29:4

life, our life and its forgetting. (For a New Citizen of These United States) V15:55

Life to Victory (Always) V24:15

like a bird in the sky ... (Ego-Tripping) V28:113

like a shadow or a friend. *Colombia.* (Kindness) V24:84–85

like it better than being loved. (For the Young Who Want To) V40:50

Like nothing else in Tennessee. (Anecdote of the Jar) V41:3

Like Stone— (The Soul Selects Her Own Society) V1:259

Little Lamb, God bless thee. (The Lamb) V12:135

Look'd up in perfect silence at the stars. (When I Heard the Learn'd Astronomer) V22:244

love (The Toni Morrison Dreams) V22:202–203

Love is best! (Love Among the Ruins) V41:248

Loved I not Honour more. (To Lucasta, Going to the Wars) V32:291

Luck was rid of its clover. (Yet we insist that life is full of happy chance) V27:292

M

'Make a wish, Tom, make a wish.' (Drifters) V10: 98

make it seem to change (The Moon Glows the Same) V7:152

May be refined, and join the angelic train. (On Being Brought from Africa to America) V29:223

may your mercy be near. (Two Eclipses) V33:221

midnight-oiled in the metric laws? (A Farewell to English) V10:126

Monkey business (Business) V16:2

More dear, both for themselves and for thy sake! (Tintern Abbey) V2:250

More simple and more full of pride. (I Am Not One of Those Who Left the Land) V36:91

must always think good thoughts. (Letter to My Wife) V38:115

My foe outstretchd beneath the tree. (A Poison Tree) V24:195–196

My love shall in my verse ever live young (Sonnet 19) V9:211

My soul has grown deep like the rivers. (The Negro Speaks of Rivers) V10:198

My soul I'll pour into thee. (The Night Piece: To Julia) V29:206

N

never to waken in that world again (Starlight) V8:213

newness comes into the world (Daughter-Mother-Maya-Seeta) V25:83

Nirvana is here, nine times out of ten. (Spring-Watching Pavilion) V18:198

No, she's brushing a boy's hair (Facing It) V5:110

no—tell them no— (The Hiding Place) V10:153

Noble six hundred! (The Charge of the Light Brigade) V1:3

nobody,not even the rain,has such small hands (somewhere i have never travelled,gladly beyond) V19:265

Nor swim under the terrible eyes of prison ships. (The Drunken Boat) V28:84

Not a roof but a field of stars. (Rent) V25:164

not be seeing you, for you have no insurance. (The River Mumma Wants Out) V25:191

Not even the blisters. Look. (What Belongs to Us) V15:196

Not of itself, but thee. (Song: To Celia) V23:270–271

Not to mention people. (Pride) V38:177

Nothing, and is nowhere, and is endless (High Windows) V3:108

Nothing gold can stay (Nothing Gold Can Stay) V3:203

Now! (Alabama Centennial) V10:2

nursing the tough skin of figs (This Life) V1:293

O

O Death in Life, the days that are no more! (Tears, Idle Tears) V4:220

O Lord our Lord, how excellent is thy name in all the earth! (Psalm 8) V9:182

O Roger, Mackerel, Riley, Ned, Nellie, Chester, Lady Ghost (Names of Horses) V8:142

o, walk your body down, don't let it go it alone. (Walk Your Body Down) V26:219

Of all our joys, this must be the deepest. (Drinking Alone Beneath the Moon) V20:59–60

of blackberry-eating in late September. (Blackberry Eating) V35:24

of blood and ignorance. (Art Thou the Thing I Wanted) V25:2–3

of existence (Constantly Risking Absurdity) V41:60

of gentleness (To a Sad Daughter) V8:231

of love's austere and lonely offices? (Those Winter Sundays) V1:300

of peaches (The Weight of Sweetness) V11:230

Of the camellia (Falling Upon Earth) V2:64

Of the Creator. And he waits for the world to begin (Leviathan) V5:204

of our festivities (Fragment 2) V31:63

Of what is past, or passing, or to come (Sailing to Byzantium) V2:207

Of which the chronicles make no mention. (In Music) V35:105

Oh that was the garden of abundance, seeing you. (Seeing You) V24:244–245

Old Ryan, not yours (The Constellation Orion) V8:53

On rainy Monday nights of an eternal November. (Classic Ballroom Dances) V33:3

On the dark distant flurry (Angle of Geese) V2:2

on the frosty autumn air. (The Cossacks) V25:70

On the look of Death— (There's a Certain Slant of Light) V6:212

On the reef of Norman's Woe! (The Wreck of the Hesperus) V31:317

On your head like a crown (Any Human to Another) V3:2

One could do worse that be a swinger of birches. (Birches) V13:15

"Only the Lonely," trying his best to sound like Elvis. (The Women Who Loved Elvis All Their Lives) V28:274

or a loose seed. (Freeway 280) V30:62

Or does it explode? (Harlem) V1:63

Or every man be blind— (Tell all the Truth but tell it slant) V42:240

Or hear old Triton blow his wreathed horn. (The World Is Too Much with Us) V38:301

Or help to half-a-crown." (The Man He Killed) V3:167

Or if I die. (The Fly) V34:70

Or just some human sleep. (After Apple Picking) V32:3

or last time, we look. (In Particular) V20:125

or last time, we look. (In Particular) V20:125

Or might not have lain dormant forever. (Mastectomy) V26:123

or nothing (Queen-Ann's-Lace) V6:179

Or pleasures, seldom reached, again pursued. (A Nocturnal Reverie) V30:119–120

Or the dazzling crystal. (What I Expected) V36:313–314

or the one red leaf the snow releases in March. (ThreeTimes My Life Has Opened) V16:213

ORANGE forever. (Ballad of Orange and Grape) V10:18

our every corpuscle become an elf. (Moreover, the Moon) V20:153

Our love shall live, and later life renew." (Sonnet 75) V32:215

outside. (it was New York and beautifully, snowing . . .

(i was sitting in mcsorley's) V13:152

owing old (old age sticks) V3:246

P

patient in mind remembers the time. (Fading Light) V21:49

Penelope, who really cried. (An Ancient Gesture) V31:3

Perhaps he will fall. (Wilderness Gothic) V12:242

Petals on a wet, black bough (In a Station of the Metro) V2:116

Plaiting a dark red love-knot into her long black hair (The Highwayman) V4:68

Powerless, I drown. (Maternity) V21:142–143

Práise him. (Pied Beauty) V26:161

Pro patria mori. (Dulce et Decorum Est) V10:110

Q

Quietly shining to the quiet Moon. (Frost at Midnight) V39:75

R

Rage, rage against the dying of the light (Do Not Go Gentle into that Good Night) V1:51

Raise it again, man. We still believe what we hear. (The Singer's House) V17:206

Remember. (Remember) V32:185

Remember the Giver fading off the lip (A Drink of Water) V8:66

Ride me. (Witness) V26:285

rise & walk away like a panther. (Ode to a Drum) V20:172–173

Rises toward her day after day, like a terrible fish (Mirror) V1:116

S

Sans teeth, sans eyes, sans taste, sans everything. (Seven Ages of Man) V35:213

Shall be lifted—nevermore! (The Raven) V1:202

shall be lost. (All Shall Be Restored) V36:2

Shall you be overcome. (Conscientious Objector) V34:46

Shantih shantih shantih (The Waste Land) V20:248–252

share my shivering bed. (Chorale) V25:51

she'd miss me. (In Response to Executive Order 9066: All Americans of Japanese Descent

Must Report to Relocation Centers) V32:129

Show an affirming flame. (September 1, 1939) V27:235

Shuddering with rain, coming down around me. (Omen) V22:107

Simply melted into the perfect light. (Perfect Light) V19:187

Singing of him what they could understand (Beowulf) V11:3

Singing with open mouths their strong melodious songs (I Hear America Singing) V3:152

Sister, one of those who never married. (My Grandmother's Plot in the Family Cemetery) V27:155

Sleep, fly, rest: even the sea dies! (Lament for Ignacio Sánchez Mejías) V31:128–30

slides by on grease (For the Union Dead) V7:67

Slouches towards Bethlehem to be born? (The Second Coming) V7:179

so like the smaller stars we rowed among. (The Lotus Flowers) V33:108

So long lives this, and this gives life to thee (Sonnet 18) V2:222

So prick my skin. (Pine) V23:223–224

so that everything can learn the reason for my song. (Sonnet LXXXIX) V35:260

Somebody loves us all. (Filling Station) V12:57

someone (The World Is Not a Pleasant Place to Be) V42:303

Speak through my words and my blood. (The Heights of Macchu Picchu) V28:141

spill darker kissmarks on that dark. (Ten Years after Your Deliberate Drowning) V21:240

Stand still, yet we will make him run (To His Coy Mistress) V5:277

startled into eternity (Four Mountain Wolves) V9:132

still be alive. (Hope) V43:81

Still clinging to your shirt (My Papa's Waltz) V3:192

Stood up, coiled above his head, transforming all. (A Tall Man Executes a Jig) V12:229

strangers ask. *Originally?* And I hesitate. (Originally) V25:146–147

Surely goodness and mercy shall follow me all the days of my life: and I will dwell in the house of

the Lord for ever (Psalm 23)
V4:103

switch sides with every jump.
(Flounder) V39:59

syllables of an old order. (A Grafted
Tongue) V12:93

T

Take any streetful of people buying
clothes and groceries, cheering
a hero or throwing confetti and
blowing tin horns ... tell me if
the lovers are losers ... tell me if
any get more than the lovers ...
in the dust ... in the cool tombs
(Cool Tombs) V6:46

Than from everything else life
promised that you could do?
(Paradiso) V20:190–191

Than that you should remember and
be sad. (Remember) V14:255

Than the two hearts beating each to
each! (Meeting at Night)
V45:137

that does not see you. You must
change your life. (Archaic
Torso of Apollo) V27:3

that floral apron. (The Floral Apron)
V41:141

that might have been sweet in
Grudnow. (Grudnow) V32:74

That story. (Cinderella) V41:43

That then I scorn to change my state
with Kings (Sonnet 29) V8:198

that there is more to know, that one
day you will know it.
(Knowledge) V25:113

That when we live no more, we may
live ever (To My Dear and
Loving Husband) V6:228

That's the word. (Black Zodiac)
V10:47

The benediction of the air. (Snow-
Bound) V36:248–254

the bigger it gets. (Smart and Final
Iris) V15:183

The bosom of his Father and his God
(Elegy Written in a Country
Churchyard) V9:74

the bow toward torrents of *veyz mir*.
(Three To's and an Oi) V24:264

The crime was in Granada, his
Granada. (The Crime Was in
Granada) V23:55–56

The dance is sure (Overture to a
Dance of Locomotives)
V11:143

The eyes turn topaz. (Hugh Selwyn
Mauberley) V16:30

the flames? (Another Night in the
Ruins) V26:13

The frolic architecture of the snow.
(The Snow-Storm) V34:196

The garland briefer than a girl's (To
an Athlete Dying Young)
V7:230

The Grasshopper's among some
grassy hills. (On the
Grasshopper and the Cricket)
V32:161

The guidon flags flutter gayly in the
wind. (Cavalry Crossing a
Ford) V13:50

The hands gripped hard on the desert
(At the Bomb Testing Site) V8:3

The holy melodies of love arise. (The
Arsenal at Springfield) V17:3

the knife at the throat, the death in
the metronome (Music
Lessons) V8:117

The Lady of Shalott." (The Lady of
Shalott) V15:97

The lightning and the gale! (Old
Ironsides) V9:172

The lone and level sands stretch far
away. (Ozymandias) V27:173

the long, perfect loveliness of sow
(Saint Francis and the Sow)
V9:222

The Lord survives the rainbow of
His will (The Quaker
Graveyard in Nantucket)
V6:159

The man I was when I was part of it
(Beware of Ruins) V8:43

the quilts sing on (My Mother Pieced
Quilts) V12:169

The red rose and the brier (Barbara
Allan) V7:11

The self-same Power that brought
me there brought you. (The
Rhodora) V17:191

The shaft we raise to them and thee
(Concord Hymn) V4:30

the skin of another, what I have made
is a curse. (Curse) V26:75

The sky became a still and woven
blue. (Merlin Enthralled)
V16:73

The song of the Lorelei. (The
Lorelei) V37:146

The spirit of this place (To a Child
Running With Outstretched
Arms in Canyon de Chelly)
V11:173

The town again, trailing your legs
and crying! (Wild Swans)
V17:221

the unremitting space of your
rebellion (Lost Sister) V5:217

The wide spaces between us. (Poem
about People) V44:175

The woman won (Oysters) V4:91

The world should listen then—as I
am listening now. (To a Sky-
Lark) V32:252

their dinnerware. (Portrait of a
Couple at Century's End)
V24:214–215

their guts or their brains?
(Southbound on the Freeway)
V16:158

Then chiefly lives. (Virtue) V25:263

There are blows in life, so hard ... I
just don't know! (The Black
Heralds) V26:47

There is the trap that catches noblest
spirits, that caught— they say—
God, when he walked on earth
(Shine, Perishing Republic)
V4:162

there was light (Vancouver Lights)
V8:246

They also serve who only stand and
wait." ([On His Blindness]
Sonnet 16) V3:262

They also serve who only stand and
wait." (When I Consider
(Sonnet XIX)) V37:302

They are going to some point true
and unproven. (Geometry)
V15:68

They have not sown, and feed on
bitter fruit. (A Black Man Talks
of Reaping) V32:21

They rise, they walk again (The
Heaven of Animals) V6:76

They say a child with two mouths is
no good. (Pantoun for Chinese
Women) V29:242

They think I lost. I think I won
(Harlem Hopscotch) V2:93

They'd eaten every one." (The
Walrus and the Carpenter)
V30:258–259

This is my page for English B (Theme
for English B) V6:194

This Love (In Memory of Radio)
V9:145

Tho' it were ten thousand mile! (A
Red, Red Rose) V8:152

Though I sang in my chains like the
sea (Fern Hill) V3:92

Till human voices wake us, and we
drown (The Love Song of J.
Alfred Prufrock) V1:99

Till Love and Fame to nothingness
do sink (When I Have Fears
that I May Cease to Be) V2:295

Till the gossamer thread you fling
catch somewhere, O my soul. (A
Noiseless Patient Spider)
V31:190–91

To an admiring Bog! (I'm Nobody!
Who Are You?) V35:83

Y

Ye know on earth, and all ye need to know (Ode on a Grecian Urn) V1:180

Yea, beds for all who come. (Up-Hill) V34:280

You live in this, and dwell in lovers' eyes (Sonnet 55) V5:246

You may for ever tarry. (To the Virgins, to Make Much of Time) V13:226

You must be proud, if you'll be wise. (To the Ladies) V45:239

you who raised me? (The Gold Lily) V5:127

You're all that I can call my own. (Woman Work) V33:289

you'll have understood by then what these Ithakas mean. (Ithaka) V19:114